Explore THE UNITED STATES

History

History is the study of events that happened in the past.

Colonial Williamsburg
Williamsburg, Virginia

You Are There You're on the streets of Colonial Williamsburg. You hear the ring of a blacksmith's hammer. A woman in a long dress and broad straw hat curtsies. "Good day to you!" Two oxen pull a cart down the road. As you look around, you can tell that important things happened in this place. Revolutionary patriots walked these streets in the 1700s. Colonial Williamsburg tells the story of those patriots. You can't wait to see more. What an exciting way to experience history!

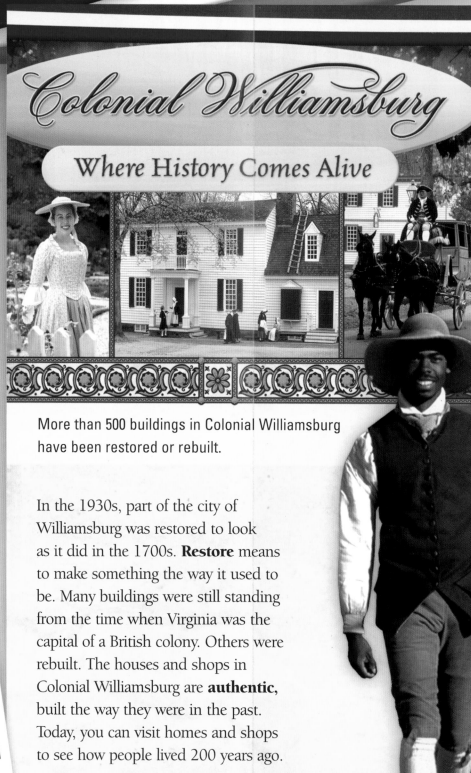

Colonial Williamsburg

Where History Comes Alive

More than 500 buildings in Colonial Williamsburg have been restored or rebuilt.

In the 1930s, part of the city of Williamsburg was restored to look as it did in the 1700s. **Restore** means to make something the way it used to be. Many buildings were still standing from the time when Virginia was the capital of a British colony. Others were rebuilt. The houses and shops in Colonial Williamsburg are **authentic**, built the way they were in the past. Today, you can visit homes and shops to see how people lived 200 years ago.

Williamsburg

Visitors can eat a colonial meal, ride in carriages, and experience what it was like to live in 1700s Williamsburg.

Fast Facts:

- On May 15, 1776, Virginia patriots meeting in Williamsburg were the first to call for the Declaration of Independence.

- Even the animals in Colonial Williamsburg are authentic! They are bred from the kinds of animals that were common in Virginia during colonial times.

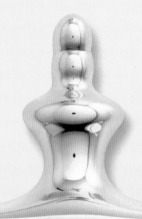

Link to You

What are some historic sites in your community that have been restored?

Economics

Economics is the study of how people produce, distribute, and use goods and services.

Pike Place Market
Seattle, Washington

You Are There You've never seen so much food or smelled so many different scents in your life. It's noisy and busy. People rush past you in a hurry, carrying bags of bread and flowers. You stop to look around. Restaurant chefs, local people, and tourists like you fill the streets of the enormous farmer's market in Seattle. "Heads up!" you hear, just in time. A giant fish whooshes by your head. Thirty feet away, a man behind a counter catches it and wraps it for a customer. The people selling fish shout and joke with one another. It's only Tuesday morning. The market is just getting started!

Economics at Work at the
Pike Place Market

Since it was built in 1907, many consumers have come to Pike Place Market. **Consumers** are people who buy and use products. **Products** are things that are made and sold. People like the products at Pike Place because they are usually fresher and more affordable. Producers, such as farmers or fishermen, can sell their goods directly to consumers at Pike Place. Supermarkets spend money to ship, display, and sell their products. This means they may have to charge more for the products in the stores. Foods at Pike Place are not shipped from far away or displayed in stores.

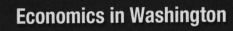

Seattle

The best stalls are given to shopkeepers who have been selling at the market for the longest time.

Fast Facts:

- During the 1960s, consumers began shopping more in supermarkets. The Pike Place Market was almost closed and demolished.

- More than 20,000 people visit the market on weekdays. More than 37,000 people visit on Saturdays.

Seattle is located between the fertile farmland of California and the fishing waters of Alaska. It has some of the world's best fresh food.

Link to You

What products do you buy directly from a producer?

Science and Technology

Science and technology change people's lives. These changes bring challenges and opportunities.

Edison Laboratory
Edison, New Jersey

You Are There You're in Edison, New Jersey. More than one hundred years ago, Thomas Edison's laboratory stood where you stand now. It did not look important. It was just a barn on a farm. But that barn was one birthplace of the light bulb and hundreds of other incredible inventions. Edison called it the "Invention Factory." The building is gone now. You can't help wondering: What would Edison invent today if he and his barn were still here?

An "Electric" Atmosphere! Thomas Edison's Menlo Park

The Menlo Park "Invention Factory" collapsed in 1913. The Thomas Alva Edison Memorial Tower was built on the same site in 1937, in honor of Edison's 91st birthday.

In 1876, Thomas Edison brought a team of workers to a neighborhood called Menlo Park. They planned to invent things. **Invent** means to make something for the first time. The team **researched**, or studied, subjects to find out new facts about them. When they had an idea, they would **experiment**, or test it, to see if it worked. The team worked in Menlo Park for fewer than 10 years. Edison and his team created more than 400 inventions in that time.

Edison

Fast Facts:

- Thomas Edison obtained 1,093 patents for inventions and improvements. That is more than any other person.

- In 1954, the Menlo Park area was named Edison, New Jersey, to honor Thomas Edison.

Edison said his Menlo Park team would "come up with a small thing every ten days and a big thing about every six months."

Link to You

What are some things you use every day that were invented by Thomas Edison?

Geography

Geography is the study of Earth's surface and climates, and the way they impact people in different regions.

The Kelso Dunes, The Mojave Desert
California

You Are There You're hiking up a giant sand hill. It's hard work since the sand gives way under every step. When you finally reach the top, you are exhausted. The sun reflects off the hot sand. Dunes spread out all around you. Then you hear a low groan, a deep rumble. Blowing sand is sliding across the dunes. It creates a sound you've never heard before. Suddenly, you understand why the Kelso Dunes in the Mojave Desert are called "The Booming Dunes."

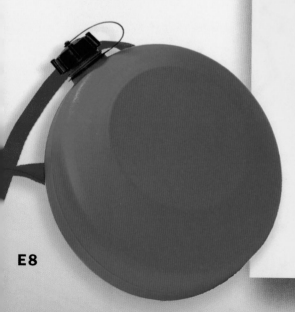

Geography's HOT SPOT

THE MOJAVE DESERT

The Mojave Desert is located primarily in California but stretches into portions of Nevada, Arizona, and Utah. The Mojave Desert has a very harsh climate. **Climate** is the kind of weather a place has, year after year. Animals and plants that live in the Mojave must tolerate big changes in temperature every day, and from season to season. Days can be very hot. Nights can be very cold. Summers are hot, dry, and windy. Winters are often freezing. Throughout the year, animals and plants must also survive with little water.

Mojave Desert

The Joshua Tree is a special kind of tree. The Mojave Desert is the only place in the world where it grows.

A desert is a dry, barren place that usually has sandy soil and very little water.

Fast Facts:

- The Mojave Desert covers more than 25,000 square miles. It is about five times larger than the state of Connecticut.

- The Mojave receives less than 5 inches of precipitation per year. **Precipitation** is water that falls in the form of rain or snow.

Link to You

How would you describe the climate in your region? How much precipitation do you receive?

Culture

Culture is the customs, traditions, habits, and values of a group of people.

Celebrating Culture on Cinco de Mayo

Cinco de Mayo
Nogales, Arizona

You Are There The Arizona sky is big and blue. It's a perfect day for the Cinco de Mayo parade. Nogales is on the border between Arizona and Mexico. Today, in Nogales, it feels almost like you are in Mexico. People wave Mexico's flag, eat tamales, and listen to mariachi bands. The members of mariachi bands wear colorful costumes as they walk among the audience singing traditional songs in Spanish. You watch the riders on horseback. The silver on the saddles sparkles as the sunlight hits them. Everywhere you turn there are bright colors and wonderful music. What a fun day!

Nogales

Cinco de Mayo means "Fifth of May." It is a celebration of Mexican heritage and pride. **Heritage** is the customs that are passed down from one generation to the next. On May 5, 1862, the French army attacked a puebla, or town, in Mexico. The small Mexican army surprised everyone by winning the battle! Many Mexicans and Americans of Mexican **descent**, or family origin, remember the victory on May 5. They celebrate Mexican culture by enjoying Mexican food, dance, and other traditions.

Nogales celebrates Cinco de Mayo with a parade of horse-riders, dancers, and performers.

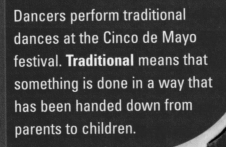

CINCO DE MAYO

USA 32

©1998, Cinco de Mayo, USPS.

Dancers perform traditional dances at the Cinco de Mayo festival. **Traditional** means that something is done in a way that has been handed down from parents to children.

Fast Facts:

- More than 120 cities in the United States have Cinco de Mayo festivals.

- Cinco do Mayo celebrations are especially large in Arizona, New Mexico, California, and Texas.

Link to You

Do you celebrate any holidays that honor a particular country or heritage?

E11

Citizenship

Citizenship is the rights, privileges, and duties of being a member of a community, state, or nation.

Naturalization Ceremony
in Chicago on Citizenship Day

You Are There The day is finally here! You're dressed in your best clothes, on the way to the citizenship ceremony. Today, your neighbor becomes a United States citizen. She worked hard to pass her test. She is ready, and you are excited for her. The room is filled with all kinds of families. Everyone looks happy. Your neighbor looks so proud when she says the oath. Some people have tears of joy in their eyes. Today, more people can say that they are proud to be Americans.

Celebrate the USA on CITIZENSHIP DAY!

Immigrants from around the world become citizens of the United States every day. **Immigrants** are people who move to a new country to live. A holiday called "Citizenship Day" is celebrated on September 17. The day honors citizens who came to the country as immigrants, as well as citizens who were born in the United States. Every year on Citizenship Day, cities such as Chicago hold special citizenship ceremonies. Each new citizen makes an **oath**, or promise, to accept the rights and responsibilities of being a citizen of the United States.

Immigrants must pass a test to become United States citizens. They need to understand the history and government of the country, and read, write, and speak English.

New citizens must promise their **allegiance**, or loyalty, to the United States.

Fast Facts:

- Chicago holds six citizenship ceremonies every week. About 30,000 people every year take part in these ceremonies.

- Immigrants must live in the United States for 5 years before they can become citizens.

Link to You

What does the United States mean to you? Why do you think so many people want to become United States citizens?

Government

A government is a system of rules and a group of people who make decisions about an area and its people.

Independence Hall
Philadelphia, Pennsylvania

You Are There You take a long deep breath. You scan the large, bright room and try to picture 56 men crowded into these wooden seats. Ben Franklin, Thomas Jefferson, and 54 others met here in the summer of 1776. You see the chairs where they sat and the table where they signed the Declaration of Independence. The room would have been hot like today, but the doors, windows, and curtains would have been closed. The men inside had a secret. They were putting their lives at risk to break away from British rule.

THE BIRTHPLACE OF OUR NATION

Independence Hall

Independence Hall is called the "birthplace of the United States." Two of the nation's most important documents, the Declaration of Independence and the United States Constitution, were signed here. **Documents** are papers that have official information written on them. The Declaration of Independence is the document in which the colonies declared themselves free from British rule. The **Constitution** is the document that explains the rules, rights, and responsibilities that the United States government and its people have to follow.

↑ Independence Hall is where the American **republic** began. A republic is a form of government in which people vote to choose their leaders.

Philadelphia

This painting, called *Declaration of Independence*, includes realistic portraits of 42 of the 56 men who signed the Declaration.

Fast Facts:

- The state of Pennsylvania saved money for 21 years to build Independence Hall.

- The Liberty Bell was last rung to celebrate the date of George Washington's 100th birthday.

In 1753, the Liberty Bell was hung in the building's steeple.

★ Link to You ★

What topics might you vote on in your classroom? Why does voting matter?

Vote Here

National Symbols

U.S. Capitol Building
Washington, D.C.

◀ The United States Capitol is a symbol of the American government. George Washington laid the cornerstone for this building in 1793. It has been the meeting place of the United States Congress for more than 200 years.

Lincoln Memorial
Washington, D.C.

The Constitution of the United States

▲ The Constitution of the United States is a written plan for our national government. It was written when the United States was a new nation. The Constitution is a symbol of our rights as citizens of the United States of America.

▲

Abraham Lincoln was the 16th President of the United States. He was President during the Civil War and is famous for issuing the Emancipation Proclamation, which declared slaves in some of the nation's states to be free. The Lincoln Memorial honors the memory of Lincoln and his belief that all people should be free.

SCOTT FORESMAN

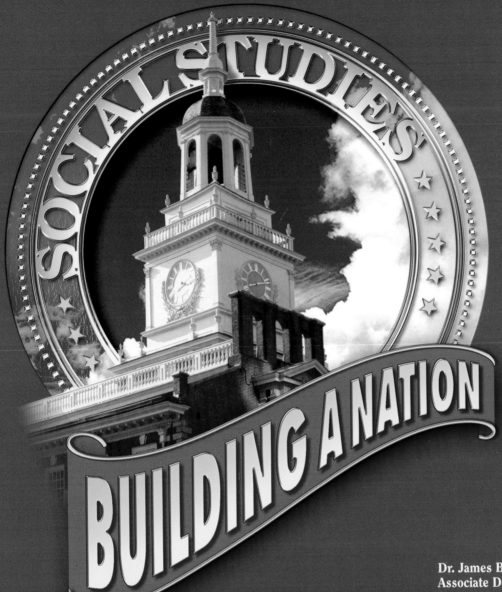

SOCIAL STUDIES

BUILDING A NATION

PROGRAM AUTHORS

Dr. Candy Dawson Boyd
Professor, School of Education
Director of Reading Programs
St. Mary's College
Moraga, California

Dr. Geneva Gay
Professor of Education
University of Washington
Seattle, Washington

Rita Geiger
Director of Social Studies and
Foreign Languages
Norman Public Schools
Norman, Oklahoma

Dr. James B. Kracht
Associate Dean for Undergraduate
Programs and Teacher Education
College of Education
Texas A&M University
College Station, Texas

Dr. Valerie Ooka Pang
Professor of Teacher Education
San Diego State University
San Diego, California

Dr. C. Frederick Risinger
Director, Professional Development
and Social Studies Education
Indiana University
Bloomington, Indiana

Sara Miranda Sanchez
Elementary and Early Childhood
Curriculum Coordinator
Albuquerque Public Schools
Albuquerque, New Mexico

CONTRIBUTING AUTHORS

Dr. Carol Berkin
Professor of History
Baruch College and the Graduate Center
The City University of New York
New York, New York

Lee A. Chase
Staff Development Specialist
Chesterfield County Public Schools
Chesterfield County, Virginia

Dr. Jim Cummins
Professor of Curriculum
Ontario Institute for Studies in Education
University of Toronto
Toronto, Canada

Dr. Allen D. Glenn
Professor and Dean Emeritus
Curriculum and Instruction
College of Education
University of Washington
Seattle, Washington

Dr. Carole L. Hahn
Professor, Educational Studies
Emory University
Atlanta, Georgia

Dr. M. Gail Hickey
Professor of Education
Indiana University-Purdue University
Fort Wayne, Indiana

Dr. Bonnie Meszaros
Associate Director
Center for Economic Education and
Entrepreneurship
University of Delaware
Newark, Delaware

CONTENT CONSULTANTS

Catherine Deans-Barrett
World History Specialist
Northbrook, Illinois

Dr. Michael Frassetto
Studies in Religions
Independent Scholar
Chicago, Illinois

Dr. Gerald Greenfield
Hispanic-Latino Studies
History Department
University of Wisconsin, Parkside
Kenosha, Wisconsin

Dr. Frederick Hoxie
Native American Studies
University of Illinois
Champaign, Illinois

Dr. Cheryl Johnson-Odim
Dean of Liberal Arts and Sciences and
Professor of History
African American History Specialist
Columbia College
Chicago, Illinois

Dr. Michael Khodarkovsky
Eastern European Studies
University of Chicago
Chicago, Illinois

Robert Moffet
U.S. History Specialist
Northbrook, Illinois

Dr. Ralph Nichols
East Asian History
University of Chicago
Chicago, Illinois

CLASSROOM REVIEWERS

Diana Vicknair Ard
Woodlake Elementary School
St. Tammany Parish
Mandeville, Louisiana

Sharon Berenson
Freehold Learning Center
Freehold, New Jersey

Betsy Blandford
Pocahontas Elementary School
Powhatan, Virginia

Nancy Neff Burgess
Upshur County Schools
Buckhannon-Upshur Middle School
Upshur County, West Virginia

Gloria Cantatore
Public School #5
West New York, New Jersey

Stephen Corsini
Content Specialist in Elementary Social Studies
School District 5 of Lexington
and Richland Counties
Ballentine, South Carolina

Deanna Crews
Millbrook Middle School
Elmore County
Millbrook, Alabama

Sally L. Costa
Hellen Caro Elementary School
Pensacola, Florida

LuAnn Curran
Westgate Elementary School
St. Petersburg, Florida

Kevin L. Curry
Social Studies Curriculum Chair
Hickory Flat Elementary School
Henry County, McDonough, Georgia

Sheila A. Czech
Sky Oaks Elementary School
Burnsville, Minnesota

Louis De Angelo
Office of Catholic Education
Archdiocese of Philadelphia
Philadelphia, Pennsylvania

Dr. Trish Dolasinski
Paradise Valley School District
Arrowhead Elementary School
Glendale, Arizona

Dr. John R. Doyle
Director of Social Studies Curriculum
Miami-Dade County Schools
Miami, Florida

Dr. Roceal Duke
District of Columbia Public Schools
Washington, D.C.

Peggy Flanagan
Roosevelt Elementary School
Community Consolidated School District #64
Park Ridge, Illinois

Sherill M. Farrell
Hillsborough County Schools
Valrico, Florida

Mary Flynn
Arrowhead Elementary School
Glendale, Arizona

Dr. Jacqueline Harrison
The Bob Bullock Texas State History Museum
Austin, Texas

Su Hickenbottom
Totem Falls Elementary School
Snohomish School District
Snohomish, Washington

Allan Jones
North Branch Public Schools
North Branch, Minnesota

Brandy Bowers Kerbow
Bettye Haun Elementary School
Plano ISD
Plano, Texas

Martha Sutton Maple
Shreve Island School
Shreveport, Louisiana

Lyn Metzger
Carpenter Elementary School
Community Consolidated School District #64
Park Ridge, Illinois

Marsha Munsey
Riverbend Elementary School
West Monroe, Louisiana

Christine Nixon
Warrington Elementary School
Escambia County School District
Pensacola, Florida

Cynthia K. Reneau
Muscogee County School District
Columbus, Georgia

Brandon Dale Rice
Secondary Education Social Science
Mobile County Public School System
Mobile, Alabama

Liz Salinas
Supervisor
Edgewood ISD
San Antonio, Texas

Beverly Scaling
Desert Hills Elementary
Las Cruces, New Mexico

Madeleine Schmitt
St. Louis Public Schools
St. Louis, Missouri

Barbara Schwartz
Central Square Intermediate School
Central Square, New York

Dr. Thad Sitton
St. Edward's University
Austin, Texas

Melody Stalker
Escambia County School District
Pensacola, Florida

Editorial Offices:
• Glenview, Illinois
• Parsippany, New Jersey
• New York, New York

Sales Offices:
• Parsippany, New Jersey
• Duluth, Georgia
• Glenview, Illinois
• Coppell, Texas
• Ontario, California
• Mesa, Arizona

www.sfsocialstudies.com

ISBN: 0-328-07573-6

Contents

UNIT 1

Early Life, East and West

UNIT 2

Connections Across Continents

UNIT 3

Colonial Life in North America

UNIT 5

Life in a New Nation

UNIT 6

A Growing Nation

UNIT 7

War Divides the Nation

Reference Guide

★ BIOGRAPHY ★

Maps

Skills

Reading Social Studies

Map and Globe Skills

raphic Organizers

Charts, Graphs, Tables & Diagrams

Time Lines

Citizenship Skills

There are six ways to show good citizenship: caring, respect, responsibility, fairness, honesty, and courage. In your textbook, you will learn about people who used these ways to help their community, state, and country.

Caring
Think about what someone else needs.

Respect
Treat others as you would want to be treated, and welcome differences among people.

Responsibility
Do what you are supposed to do and think before you act.

Fairness
Take turns and follow the rules. Listen to other people and treat them fairly.

Honesty
Tell the truth and do what you say you will do.

Courage
Do what is right even when the task might be hard.

★ Citizenship in Action ★

Good citizens make careful decisions. They solve problems in a logical way. How will the fifth-graders handle each situation as good citizens?

Decision Making

These students are voting in the school election. Before making a decision, each student follows these steps:

1. Tell what decision you need to make.
2. Gather information.
3. List your choices.
4. Tell what might happen with each choice.
5. Make your decision.
6. Act according to your decision.

Problem Solving

These students broke a window near the playground. They follow these steps to solve the problem.

1. Name the problem.
2. Find out more about the problem.
3. List ways to solve the problem.
4. Talk about the best way to solve the problem.
5. Solve the problem.
6. Figure out how well the problem was solved.

Living History from
Colonial Williamsburg
www.history.org

Think Like a Historian

Have you ever asked yourself "What was this building like long ago?"
At Colonial Williamsburg we ask ourselves that question all the time.

Wetherburn's Tavern before restoration

We dig in the ground.
Archaeologists carefully dig the
area around a building to search
for clues about the people who
used the building.

We search libraries to find documents. Letters, diaries, journals, and other records give us clues about the building and how it was used.

We carefully look at artifacts that are from the building.

Wetherburn's Tavern after restoration

From all this information we form a picture of how the building was used. We also learn about the people who used it. This building we are studying was known as Wetherburn's Tavern. Visitors came here for lodging and meals in the 1700s.

Collect information about an old building such as your house or your school. Look for old pictures, albums, news articles, and artifacts. Write a history of that building.

When gathering information for written reports and research projects, you will need to use resources in addition to your textbook. You can use **technology resources, print resources,** and **community resources.** These sources can be of two different kinds.

Primary sources are firsthand documents produced by people who were involved in the event. Primary sources include journals, diaries, letters, speeches, autobiographies, photographs, interviews, or eyewitness accounts.

Secondary sources are descriptions of an event written by people who did not participate in the event. Secondary sources include history books, encyclopedias, and biographies.

Print Resources

Libraries often have books, periodicals, and reference books such as atlases, almanacs, and encyclopedias.

An *encyclopedia* is a collection of articles, listed alphabetically, on various topics. Electronic encyclopedias often have sound and video clips in addition to words.

A *dictionary* is an alphabetical collection of words that includes the meanings of each word. A dictionary is the best source for checking the correct spelling of a word.

An *atlas* is a collection of maps. Some atlases have a variety of maps showing elevation, natural resources, historical events, and so on.

An *almanac* is a book or computer resource that contains facts about a variety of subjects. Almanacs are updated every year, so they usually have the latest statistics on populations, weather, and other number-based facts.

A *non-fiction book* is a factual book about a specific topic. In a library, you can search for books by subject, by title, or by author. Once you find a book that you want, the book's catalog number will guide you to the area of the library where you will find the book.

A *periodical,* such as a newspaper or magazine, has information that is usually more up-to-date than that found in an older book. Most libraries have a special periodical section.

Technology Resources

The Internet, CD-ROMs, and TV programs are some technology sources that you can use for research.

The Internet is a system of linked computers that store information to be accessed by others. There are online encyclopedias, dictionaries, almanacs, and Web sites for many different companies, individuals, projects, and museums.

Anyone can create a Web site and post information on the Internet. As a researcher, you must determine which information is accurate. It is important to know who put together the information. It is wise to check information by finding several different reliable sources that give the same facts.

Before you turn on your computer, you should plan your research. What do you need to find out? For example, to begin the research project that appears on H5, gather artifacts and primary sources from your home or school. List what they are and other information you can find out about them: Who might have owned them? Where do you think they were made? Then use a *search engine* to find more information. If you have not used the Internet before, you might want to ask a librarian, teacher, or parent for help.

Searching by Subject To find a search engine, click on SEARCH at the top of your screen. Type one of your subject words into the search engine field. Then click SEARCH or GO. Click on the site you are most interested in.

Searching by Address URLs, or Web addresses, are found in many places. Magazines, newspapers, TV programs, and books often give Web addresses. You will see URLs written in this form: *www.sfsocialstudies.com*.

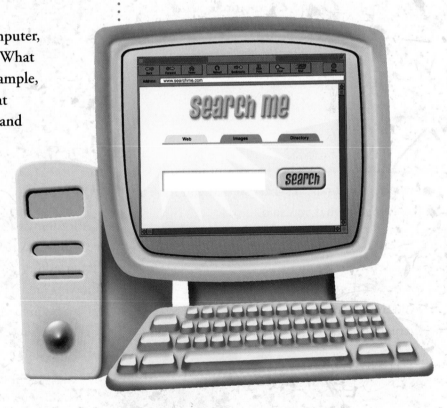

Community Resources

The people of your community are good sources of information.

Interviews

One way to find out what the people in your community know is to interview them. This means to ask them questions about the topic you are studying. If you want to conduct an interview, follow these steps.

Plan ahead

- List the people you want to interview.
- Call or write to ask permission. Let the person know who you are and why you need information.
- Agree on a time and place for the interview.
- Find out background information about your topic.
- Write down questions you want to ask.

Ask/Listen/Record

- Ask questions clearly.
- Listen carefully.
- Be polite.
- Take notes to remember important ideas. If possible, use a tape recorder so that you have a recording of what was said.

Wrap-up

- Thank the person for his or her time.
- Send a follow-up thank-you note.

Surveys

Another way to find information in your community is to conduct a survey. A survey is a list of questions that you ask people and a record of their answers. You can use either yes/no questions or short-answer questions. To record the information you find out, make a chart with a column for each question.

The following steps will help you plan a survey:
- Make a list of questions.
- Decide where you want to conduct the survey and how many people you want to ask.
- Use a tally sheet to record people's answers.
- After the survey, look through the responses and write down what you found out.

When did you go to school?	What was your favorite school lunch?	What subject did you like best?	What clubs did you belong to?
1965-1970	Roast Chicken	Social Studies	Student Council
1992-1997	Cheeseburgers	Math	Geography Club

Write for Information

Another way to use the people in your community as resources is to e-mail or write a letter asking for information. Use the following steps:
- Plan before you write.
- Tell who you are and why you are writing.
- Be neat and careful about spelling and punctuation.
- Thank the person.

Writing a Research Report

Prewrite

- Decide on a topic for your report. Your teacher may tell you what kind of report to write and how long it should be.
- Generate questions about your topic to help focus your report.
- Use a variety of sources to find information and answer your questions.
- Evaluate your sources to determine which will be the most helpful.
- Take notes from your sources.
- Review your notes and write down the main ideas related to the topic that you want to present in your report. Two or three main ideas are enough for most reports.
- Organize your notes into an outline, listing each main idea and the details that support it.

Write a First Draft

- Using your outline and your notes, write a draft report of what you have learned. You can correct mistakes at the revising step.
- Write in paragraph form. Each paragraph should be about a new idea.
- When you quote something directly from your sources, write down which source the quote came from.
- Your report should be organized with a strong introduction, a solid summary of information, a conclusion, and the list of sources you used.

Revise

- Read over your first draft. Does it make sense? Does it answer the questions you asked? Does it clearly explain facts and ideas? Do your ideas flow from one to the other in an organize way? Do you need more information about any main idea? Will the report hold a reader's interest?
- Change any sentences or paragraphs that do note make sense. Add anything that will make your ideas clear.
- Check your quotations to make sure you have used people's exact words and that you have noted the source.

Edit

- Proofread your report. Correct any errors in spelling, capitalization, or punctuation.

Publish

- Include illustrations, maps, time lines, or other graphics that will add to the report.
  - Write a table of contents.
  - Write or type a final copy of your report as neatly as possible.

My School

Geography Skills

Five Themes of Geography

Geography is the study of Earth. This study can be divided into five themes that help you understand why the Earth has such a wide variety of places. Each theme reveals something different about a spot, as the following example of Mt. Rushmore shows.

Place

How is this place different from others?
The place is in a wilderness of lakes and a national forest and park.

Human/Environment Interaction

How have people changed this place?
Mt. Rushmore has faces of four U.S. Presidents carved into its stone cliffs.

Location

Where can this place be found?
Mt. Rushmore is located in the Black Hills of South Dakota near 44°N, 103°W.

Movement

What idea should visitors carry away from this place?
Great people and deeds are the solid foundation of the United States.

Region

What is special about the Black Hills region in which this place is located?
The region mixes rugged mountains set among plains.

Geography Skills

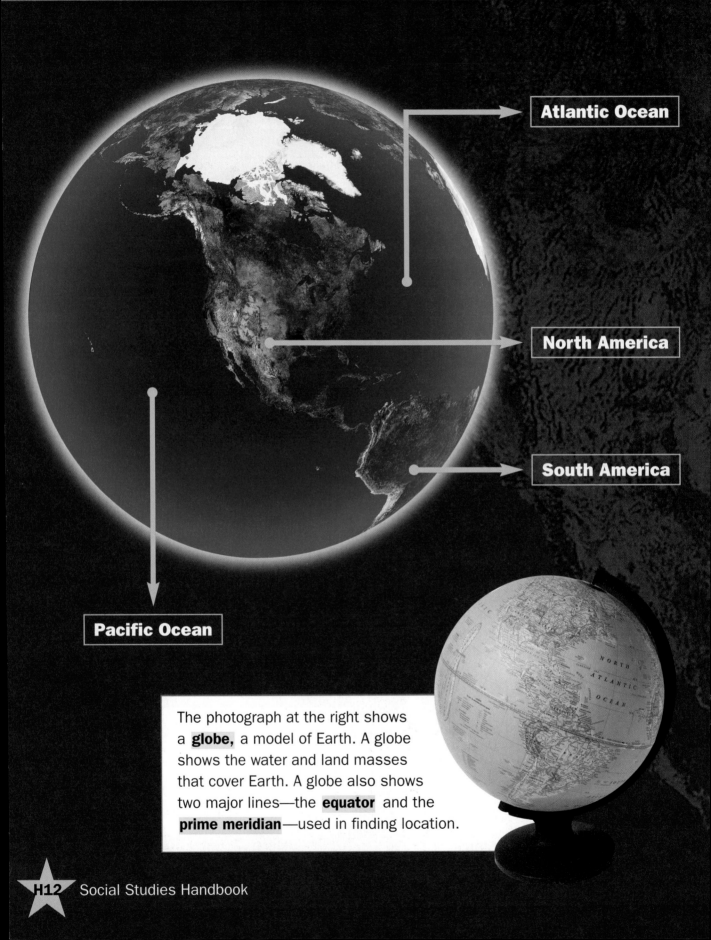

Atlantic Ocean

North America

South America

Pacific Ocean

The photograph at the right shows a **globe,** a model of Earth. A globe shows the water and land masses that cover Earth. A globe also shows two major lines—the **equator** and the **prime meridian**—used in finding location.

Vocabulary

globe
equator
prime meridian
hemisphere
Northern Hemisphere
Southern Hemisphere

Hemispheres: Northern and Southern

A globe, like Earth, is shaped like a sphere, or ball, so it can only show one half of Earth at a time. People commonly speak of Earth as being divided into half spheres called **hemispheres.** The **Northern Hemisphere** is the half north of the equator, an imaginary line that circles Earth at its widest point between the North and South poles. The **Southern Hemisphere** is the half south of the equator.

Complete views of these hemispheres are not possible when you are looking at a globe only from the side. For a complete view, you have to turn a globe until you are looking down directly at either the North or South Pole. The illustration below shows you these views.

Northern Hemisphere

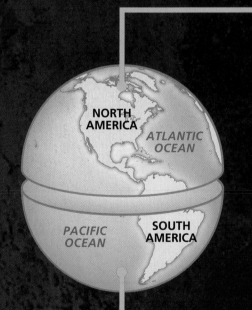

Southern Hemisphere

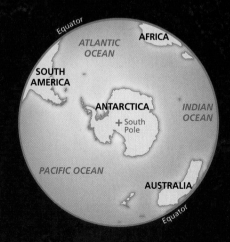

Hemispheres: Western and Eastern

Earth has two other hemispheres—the **Eastern Hemisphere** and the **Western Hemisphere.** These are formed by dividing the globe into halves along the prime meridian. The prime meridian is an imaginary line that extends from pole to pole and passes through Greenwich, England. To the east of the prime meridian, halfway around Earth, is the Eastern Hemisphere. To the west of the prime meridian is the Western Hemisphere. The illustration below shows you these views.

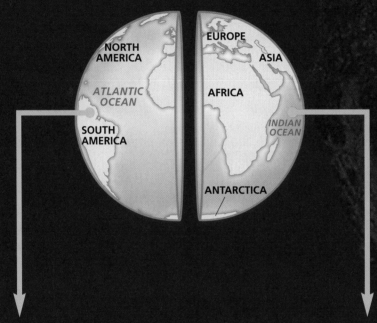

Western Hemisphere

Eastern Hemisphere

Vocabulary

Eastern Hemisphere
Western Hemisphere
latitude
longitude
parallel
degree
meridian

Latitude and Longitude on a Globe

Latitude and **longitude** are imaginary lines that help us find locations on Earth. The lines are found only on globes and maps.

Lines of latitude circle Earth in an east-west direction. They are also called **parallels** because they are parallel to the equator and to one another. These lines are measured in units called **degrees.** The equator is the latitude line of 0 degrees (0°) where measurements begin. Latitude lines tell how many degrees north or south of the equator a location is. A change of one degree of latitude in any direction on Earth is equal to about 69 miles.

Lines of longitude circle Earth in a north-south direction. They are also called **meridians**. The prime meridian is 0 degrees (0°) longitude. Longitude lines tell how many degrees east or west of the prime meridian a location is. Unlike latitude, longitude lines are not parallel. They are farthest apart at the middle of Earth but become closer together as they move toward the poles.

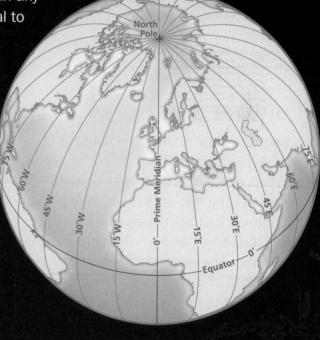

Longitude

Latitude

Geography Skills

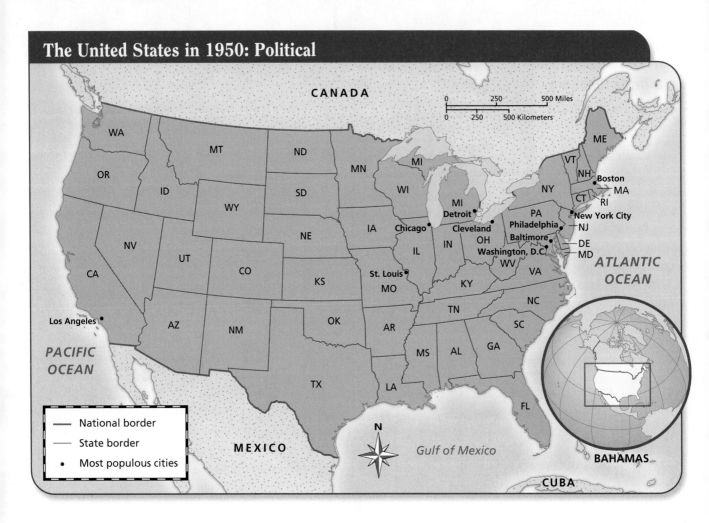

The United States in 1950: Political

CANADA

0 250 500 Miles
0 250 500 Kilometers

WA

MT

ND

MN

MI

ME

VT

NH •Boston

OR

ID

SD

WI

NY

MA

CT RI

WY

MI
Detroit•

PA

New York City

NE

IA   Chicago•

Cleveland•

Philadelphia•

NJ

NV

UT

IL   IN

OH
Baltimore•

DE

Washington, D.C.•

MD

CA

CO

KS

St. Louis•

WV   VA

ATLANTIC
OCEAN

MO

KY

Los Angeles•

AZ

NM

OK

AR

TN

NC

SC

PACIFIC
OCEAN

MS   AL   GA

TX

LA

FL

— National border
— State border
• Most populous cities

MEXICO

N

Gulf of Mexico

BAHAMAS

CUBA

Political Map

A **political map** shows how humans have divided the Earth's surface. This means that a political map can show borders that divide an area into countries, states, and counties. It can also show where cities, roads, buildings, and other human-made elements once were or still are today. Like other kinds of maps, political maps have many of the features, or parts, discussed below that help us read and use them.

A map's **title** tells what a map is about. What is the title of the historical map on this page?

A map's **symbols** are lines, small drawings, or fields of color that stand for something else. The map's **key,** or legend, is a small box that lists each symbol and tells what it stands for. What does the circled star stand for on the map? How is it labeled?

Sometimes inside a map there is a **locator,** a small map in a box or circle. It locates the subject of the main map in a larger area such as a state, country, continent, or hemisphere. In what larger area is the United States of 1950 shown?

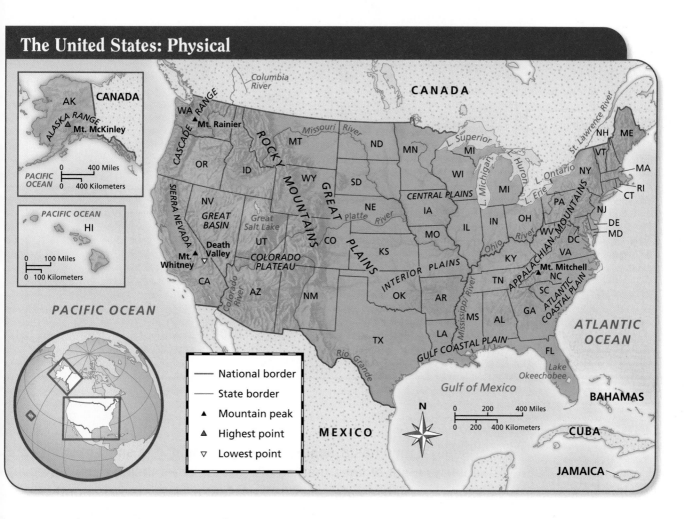

The United States: Physical

Key:
— National border
— State border
▲ Mountain peak
▲ Highest point
▽ Lowest point

Vocabulary

political map
title
symbol
key
locator
physical map
compass rose
cardinal direction
intermediate
direction

Physical Map

A **physical map** shows the major landforms and water on an area of Earth's surface. What are some examples of mountains, plains, rivers, gulfs, and oceans on this physical map? Notice that a physical map can have a few elements of a political map.

A **compass rose** is a design with four pointers that show the **cardinal directions.** The north pointer, which points toward the North Pole, is marked with an "N." East is to the right of north, south is opposite north, and west is to the left of north. The compass rose also shows **intermediate directions.** Intermediate directions are northeast, southeast, southwest, and northwest. They are named for the cardinal directions between which they fall. What direction is Lake Michigan from the Rocky Mountains?

Geography Skills

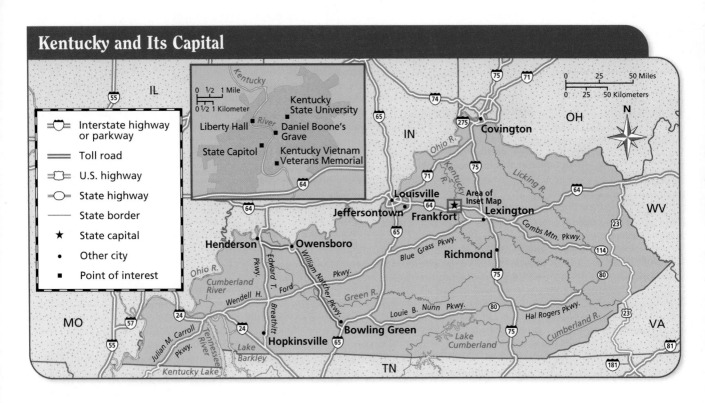

Kentucky and Its Capital

Legend:
- Interstate highway or parkway
- Toll road
- U.S. highway
- State highway
- State border
- ★ State capital
- • Other city
- ■ Point of interest

Inset map (Frankfort area): Kentucky River, Liberty Hall, State Capitol, Kentucky State University, Daniel Boone's Grave, Kentucky Vietnam Veterans Memorial

Main map labels: IL, IN, OH, WV, VA, TN, MO, Covington, Louisville, Jeffersontown, Frankfort, Lexington, Henderson, Owensboro, Richmond, Bowling Green, Hopkinsville, Ohio R., Licking R., Kentucky R., Combs Mtn. Pkwy., Blue Grass Pkwy., Green R., Cumberland River, William Natcher Pkwy., Edward T. Ford, Wendell H. Breathitt, Pkwy., Louie B. Nunn Pkwy., Hal Rogers Pkwy., Cumberland R., Julian M. Carroll Pkwy., Tennessee River, Lake Barkley, Kentucky Lake, Lake Cumberland, Area of Inset Map

Vocabulary

scale

inset map

Scale

Usually a map has a **scale.** A scale is a set of lines marked off in miles and kilometers. It allows you to estimate the actual distances between points on a map. It also tells you what a small distance on a map equals in actual miles on Earth. One way to use the scale is to hold the edge of a scrap of paper along two points on a map. Using a pencil, mark the points on the paper. Then hold the marked edge to the scale, lining up zero with the mark farthest left. Use the scale to mark off the distance between the two points. On the map above, use the scale to find out how far it is from Frankfort to Bowling Green.

Inset Map

An **inset** is a small map in a box that is set inside a main map. But an inset map is not the same as a locator map. It is not the purpose of an inset map to locate the main map in a larger area. Instead, an inset map shows either more of the main map or details about the main map. The map of the United States on page H17 has two inset maps, showing Alaska and Hawaii, which otherwise would not fit on the main map. Each inset map has its own scale, and this often lets you see something in greater detail. What do you see on the inset map of Frankfort above that you cannot see on the main map?

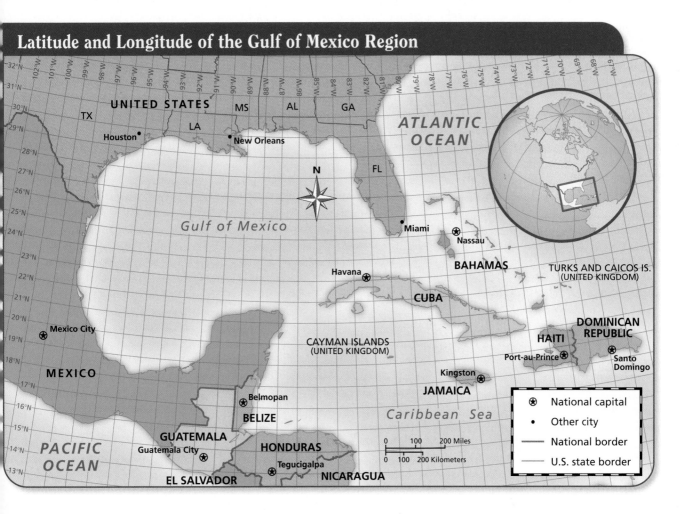

Latitude and Longitude of the Gulf of Mexico Region

Latitude and Longitude on a Map

Lines of latitude and longitude are imaginary lines on a map that help us find locations on Earth. They are usually drawn as thin, light-blue lines, with numbers at the edge of the map. The point where these horizontal and vertical lines cross shows the exact location of a place. We can find the locations of places just by knowing their latitude and longitude.

The lines on a map represent degrees (°) east and west (for longitude) and degrees north and south (for latitude). The map of the Gulf of Mexico area above has lines for each degree of latitude and longitude. However, mapmakers usually place the lines at intervals of every 5°, 10°, 15°, 20°, or 30°. On the map above, New Orleans is nearly exactly at the point where which lines cross? At about where 20°N and 100°W cross, what major city do you find?

Geography Skills

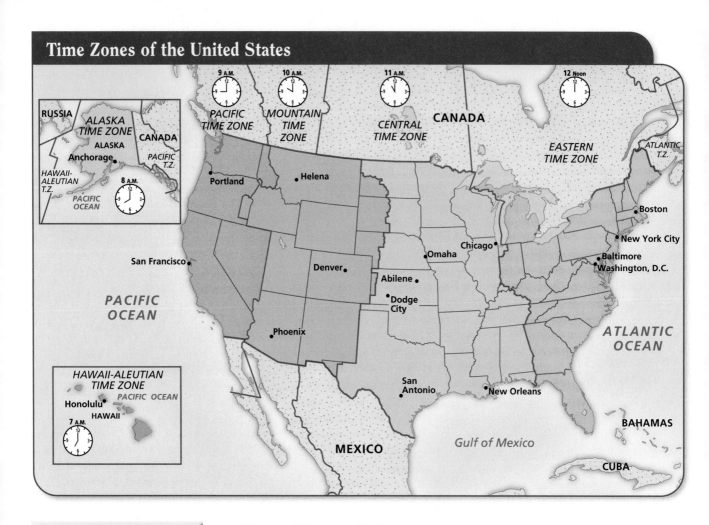

Time Zones of the United States

RUSSIA
ALASKA TIME ZONE
ALASKA
CANADA
Anchorage●
PACIFIC T.Z.
HAWAII-ALEUTIAN T.Z.
PACIFIC OCEAN
8 A.M.

9 A.M.
PACIFIC TIME ZONE

10 A.M.
MOUNTAIN TIME ZONE

11 A.M.
CENTRAL TIME ZONE
CANADA

12 Noon
EASTERN TIME ZONE
ATLANTIC T.Z.

Portland●
●Helena

●Boston
●New York City
●Baltimore
●Washington, D.C.

San Francisco●
Denver●
●Omaha
Chicago●

Abilene ●
●Dodge City

PACIFIC OCEAN

●Phoenix

ATLANTIC OCEAN

HAWAII-ALEUTIAN TIME ZONE
PACIFIC OCEAN
Honolulu●
HAWAII
7 A.M.

San Antonio●
●New Orleans

BAHAMAS

MEXICO
Gulf of Mexico
CUBA

Vocabulary

time zone map
elevation
climate

Time Zone Map

The world is divided into 24 time zones, one for each hour of the day. A **time zone map** shows the whole world's or any region's time zones. The United States has six times zones. Within a time zone almost every city has the same time. Look at the map above. What is the name of the time zone in which Anchorage is located? How many hours apart are New York City and San Francisco? If it is 11 A.M. in Chicago, what time is it in Denver?

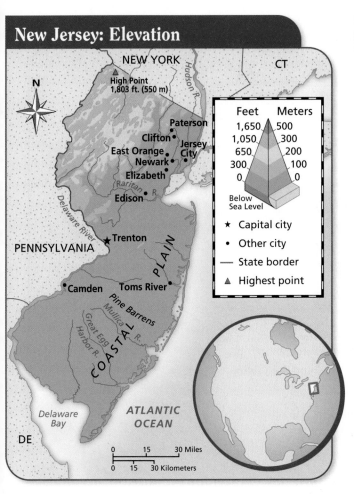

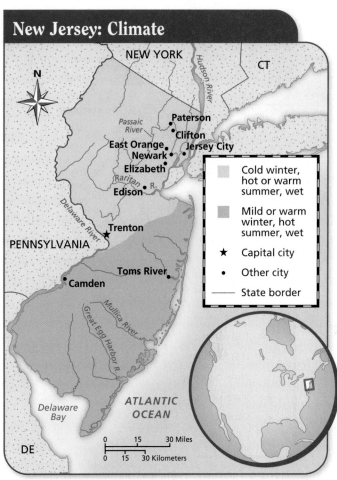

Elevation Map

Elevation is the height of land above sea level. The measurement is usually given in feet and meters. An elevation map often uses colors to show different elevations across a landscape. The key often contains a three-dimensional structure to emphasize height. Various colors are used to stand for certain ranges of elevation. On the map above, which color shows the highest elevation range? In what elevation range is New Jersey's capital city of Trenton? On average, is the land in New Jersey higher in the southeast or the northwest of the state?

Climate Map

Many people confuse climate with weather. The weather of a region is it precipitation (mostly rain or snow) and temperature recorded day to day. But the **climate** of a region is its weather over a long period of time and repeated year to year. Above is a climate map for New Jersey. What is the main climate for most of northern New Jersey? What large area of New Jersey can be described as having mild or warm winters, with hot and wet summers?

Geography Skills

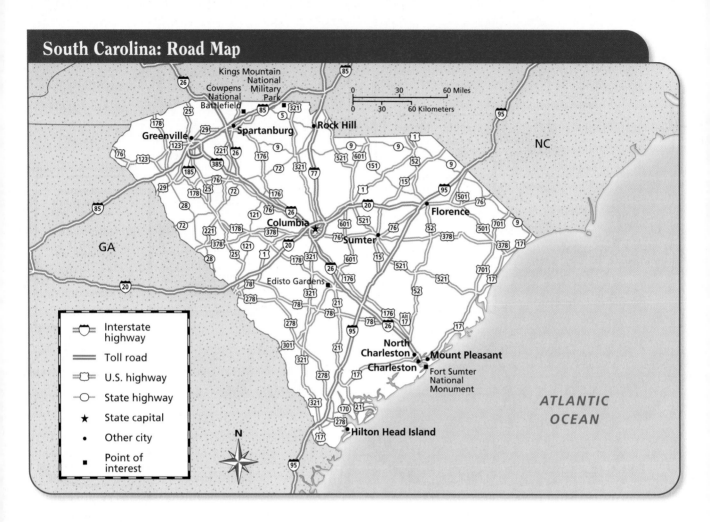

South Carolina: Road Map

Legend:
- Interstate highway
- Toll road
- U.S. highway
- State highway
- ★ State capital
- • Other city
- ■ Point of interest

Vocabulary

road map

Road Map

A **road map** is a special map that shows automobile routes between towns and cities for a region, county, state, or country. Different types of roads are usually shown through the use of thick and thin lines or by use of color. Most roads are numbered or lettered to make following them easier. Road maps may also show points of interest within a region.

Above is a road map of South Carolina. If you lived in Spartanburg and wanted to drive southeast to Columbia, which numbered highway would you take? What is the number of the road that is the most direct route from Charleston north to Florence? From Sumter, U.S. route 521, Interstate 95, and U.S. route 278 bring you to what popular vacation spot?

American People, American Land

What unites Americans as a people?

"We the People of the United States..."

—From the Preamble, or opening words, of the United States Constitution

America II, by Diana Ong, illustrates the diversity and unity of the American people.

American People, American Land

Main Idea and Details

Learning to find the main idea and details will help you understand most kinds of writing. Study the diagram below.

- A main idea is the most important idea about a topic.
- Details give information that tells more about the main idea.

Read the following paragraph. The **main idea** and **details** have been highlighted.

Because you live in the United States, you already know many things about it. The United States is a large and varied country. It has many different kinds of people who have different backgrounds and customs. The land differs greatly from place to place. The American people have many different ways of making a living. Yet some important beliefs and customs keep the country united.

Word Exercise

Compound Words A compound word is formed from two smaller words. The two words of a compound word may be combined into one word, separate, or connected by a hyphen. Breaking an unfamiliar compound word into its parts can help you determine its meaning. For example, the word *highland* is a compound word.

One Country, Varied Land and People

While the United States is a land of great differences, it is one country united in many ways. Americans are united by their beliefs in such things as freedom, representative democracy, and the free-enterprise system.

The people share important beliefs in freedom of speech, freedom of religion, and the freedom to live and work where they choose. They elect leaders to represent them and defend these freedoms in the government.

Yet, all Americans are not the same. They have backgrounds from different parts of the world and have variety in their ways of life. They live in large cities and small towns, on farms and ranches, on the seashores and far inland from the sea. They have many different ways of earning their living.

The land in the United States also has great variety. There are mountains and deserts, lowland and highland plains, river valleys and canyons. Some areas get plenty of rain and snow, while other areas are dry. Many kinds of natural resources provide for a great variety of jobs for people.

Although Americans are not all alike, Americans often work together. For example, businesses in one part of the country need to buy from and sell to businesses in other parts of the country. Our economic system allows people to start their own businesses and creates many opportunities for work.

A good way to describe the United States is in the words found on some of our coins and paper money: *"E Pluribus Unum."* These are Latin words meaning "Out of many, one."

Use the reading strategy of main idea and details to answer questions 1 and 2. Then answer the vocabulary question.

1 Which sentence tells the main idea of the reading?

2 What are three details that tell how Americans are different?

3 Another compound word in this passage is *representative democracy*. What do the two words that make up this compound word mean? What does *representative democracy* mean?

PREVIEW

Focus on the Main Idea
The United States has a varied population that shares many ideals.

VOCABULARY
culture
ideals
ethnic group
census
immigrants

▶ Benjamin Franklin

The American People

You Are There
July 4, 1776. It has been a long, hot day in Philadelphia, Pennsylvania. Earlier today, leaders here declared the United States of America to be an independent nation. Now three of these leaders—Benjamin Franklin, Thomas Jefferson, and John Adams—have taken on a new job. They will try to design a Great Seal for their new country. A Great Seal is an official symbol that can be used on money and documents. They want the seal to include a motto, or short saying, that says something important about the United States.

Franklin, Jefferson, and Adams each have ideas about what the Great Seal should look like. But will they be able to agree on one design that represents the entire country? That will be the hard part.

Main Idea and Details As you read, pay attention to the factors that unite our varied population.

Out of Many, One

Look below and you will see the Great Seal of the United States that was approved years later by Congress. On the seal you will see the motto Congress chose: *"E Pluribus Unum"*. You may have noticed this phrase on coins also. But what do these words mean? And what do they say about the United States?

E Pluribus Unum is Latin for "Out of many, one." Leaders thought this was a good motto for the United States because a variety of people from 13 different states were coming together to form one country.

It makes sense that our coins still display these words today. The population of the United States is tremendously varied. For example, Americans live everywhere from the mountains of Alaska to the beaches of Florida, from small farms in Iowa to huge cities like Los Angeles, Houston and New York. Across the 50 states, Americans of all ages spend their days at thousands of different jobs or schools. Our country also has a rich mix of cultures. A **culture** is the way of life of a group of people. Culture can include religion, customs, and language.

How can such a diverse population work together to form one country? One reason is that Americans share certain basic **ideals,** or important beliefs. These ideals include freedom of speech, freedom of religion, and the freedom to live and work where we choose. Americans also believe in equal rights and fairness for all people.

These shared ideals help strengthen our country, making it a special place to live. As the motto says: "Out of many, one."

REVIEW What does the motto *"E Pluribus Unum"* say about the United States?
 Main Idea and Details

The Great Seal of the United States

▶ **Many United States coins (*above*) include our country's motto.**

Star for each of the 13 original states

American bald eagle

Motto

Olive branch stands for the power of peace

13 arrows stand for the power of war

▶ People of many different ethnic groups are all Americans.

Our Varied Population

A tourist was visiting the city of Philadelphia, Pennsylvania. In his journal, he wrote about seeing busy shops and streets filled with people from many parts of the world. At dinner time, he ate in a restaurant with "a very mixed company of different nations and religions." This sounds like something a visitor to an American city might see today. But the visitor was in Philadelphia in 1744!

If you visit Philadelphia today, you will still see a mix of faces. This is true of cities and towns all across the country. This is because the United States is home to such a wide variety of ethnic groups. An **ethnic group** is a group of people who share the same customs and language. For example, Americans whose families originally came from Spanish-speaking Latin American countries are part of an ethnic group called Hispanics or Latinos. A graph in the Fact File gives you more information about different ethnic groups in the United States today.

REVIEW What is an ethnic group?
🔄 Main Idea and Details

United States Population

How would you like the job of counting all the people in the United States? This is exactly what the government does every ten years. This count is called a **census**. The most recent census was done in 2000. Here are some graphs showing information about the population of the United States and the world.

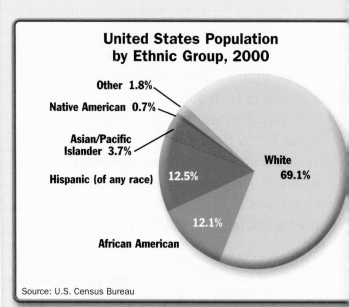

United States Population by Ethnic Group, 2000

Other 1.8%
Native American 0.7%
Asian/Pacific Islander 3.7%
Hispanic (of any race) 12.5%
White 69.1%
African American 12.1%

Source: U.S. Census Bureau

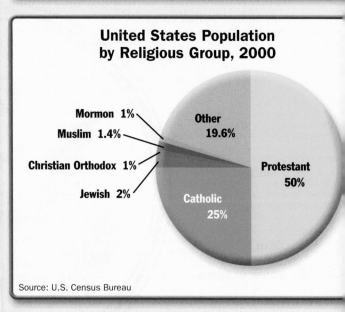

United States Population by Religious Group, 2000

Mormon 1%
Muslim 1.4%
Christian Orthodox 1%
Jewish 2%
Other 19.6%
Protestant 50%
Catholic 25%

Source: U.S. Census Bureau

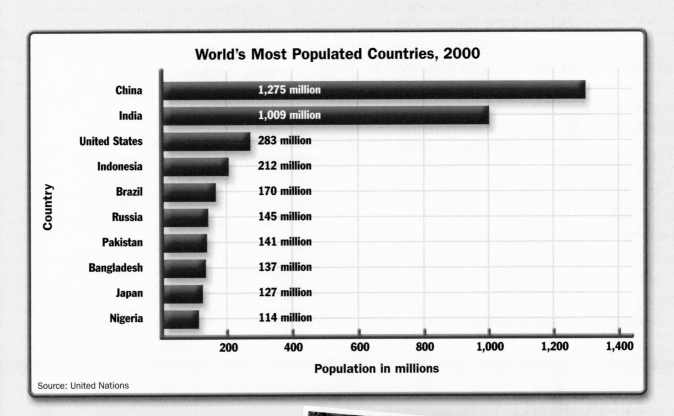

World's Most Populated Countries, 2000

Country	Population in millions
China	1,275 million
India	1,009 million
United States	283 million
Indonesia	212 million
Brazil	170 million
Russia	145 million
Pakistan	141 million
Bangladesh	137 million
Japan	127 million
Nigeria	114 million

Population in millions: 200 400 600 800 1,000 1,200 1,400

Source: United Nations

United States
Census 2000

This is the official form for a_____ ple at this addre___ easy, and your answers are pro_____ and in the help your community get what it ne_____

Start Here ✓
Please use a black or blue pen.

1. How many people were living or staying in this house, apartment, or mobile home on April 1, 2000?

☐ Number of people

4. What is Person 1's telephone n____ this person if we don't understand an a___ Area Code + Number

☐☐☐ - ☐☐☐ - ☐☐☐☐

5. What is Person 1's sex? Mark ☒ ONE box.
☐ Male   ☐ Female

___ what is Person 1's date of birth?

Where We Came From

One reason the United States is so diverse is that immigrants have come here from all over the world. **Immigrants** are people who leave one country to go live in another country.

Thousands of years before the United States was formed, there were people living on this land. These early people were the ancestors of today's Native Americans or American Indians.

About 500 years ago, Europeans began traveling here. Very early arrivals came as explorers. Some came in hopes of finding land of their own. Others sought the freedom to live and worship as they saw fit. Many people also arrived from Africa. Most Africans, however, did not choose to leave their homeland. They were captured and brought to the Americas as enslaved people. As you will read, slavery continued in the United States until after the Civil War.

Today, immigrants continue to arrive in the United States. Between 1990 and 2000 alone, people have moved here from nearly 200 different countries. The majority of these people have come from countries in Latin America and Asia. Why do people come? This question was answered by a recent immigrant named Ronnie Mervis who said, "I chose to come to America…because this is the land of opportunity and liberty."

REVIEW Identify the opportunities that have attracted immigrants to the United States. ↻ **Main Idea and Details**

Then and Now

Ellis Island and Angel Island

During the late 1800s and early 1900s, most immigrants from Europe passed through Ellis Island in New York Harbor. Here, immigrants had to pass a physical examination before entering the country. Located in San Francisco Bay, Angel Island was known as the "Ellis Island of the West." Thousands of Asian immigrants passed through here during the early 1900s. Many were held here for weeks while waiting for permission to enter the United States.

Today, both Ellis Island and Angel Island have immigration museums that you can visit.

▶ Immigrants from Asia (above) entered the United States at Angel Island. At Ellis Island, immigrants arrived mostly from Europe (right).

10

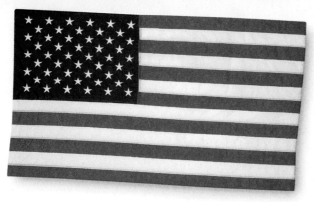

One Nation

You probably know the words to the Pledge of Allegiance from memory.

The Pledge of Allegiance

I pledge allegiance to the Flag of the United States of America and to the Republic for which it stands, one Nation under God, indivisible, with liberty and justice for all.

Why is this pledge important? There are over 283 million people living in the United States today. We have family roots in all parts of the world. But we are able to form one strong country because we share some basic ideals, such as the belief in "liberty and justice for all." Keep these ideals in mind as you read the story of American history.

REVIEW Why is the Pledge of Allegiance important? ⮑ Main Idea and Details

Summarize the Lesson

- **The population of the United States is diverse in many ways.**

- **Most Americans share certain basic ideals.**

- **One reason the United States is diverse is that immigrants have come here from all over the world.**

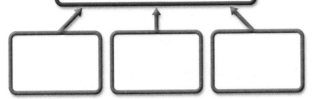

LESSON 1   REVIEW

Check Facts and Main Ideas

1. ⮑ **Main Idea and Details** On a separate sheet of paper, fill in some examples of the ideals most Americans share.

> While the population of the United States is diverse, we share important ideals, such as:

2. Why is *"E Pluribus Unum"* a good motto for the United States?

3. Why do **immigrants** continue to come to the United States?

4. What basic **ideals** unite most Americans?

5. **Critical Thinking:** *Point of View* How does the Pledge of Allegiance unite Americans?

Link to ⌒⌒ Writing

Write a Motto Suppose you were asked to think of a new motto for the United States. Write three ideas for a new motto. Put a star next to the one you think is the best.

Read Line and Circle Graphs

What? Graphs show information in a visual way. A **line graph** can be useful in showing change over time. The line graph below shows the growth of the U.S. population from 1790, when the government conducted the first census, to 2000. A **circle graph** shows how a whole is divided into parts. It can be useful to show how different groups compare to each other in size. The circle graph on the next page shows one way the American population can be divided into groups.

Why? As you read in Lesson 1, the government counts the people in the United States by taking a census every ten years. A line graph like the one on this page makes it possible for someone to see, at a glance, how the population of the United States has grown since the country began.

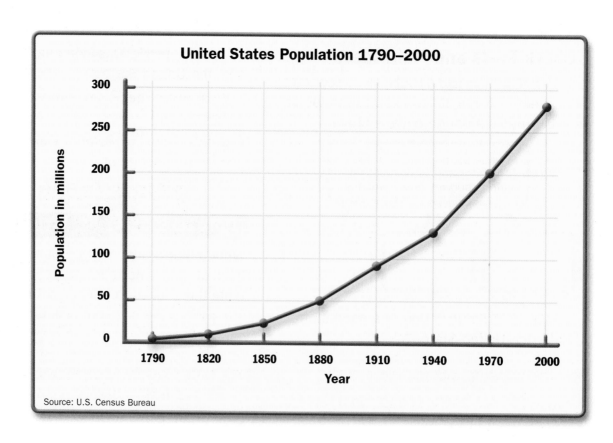

United States Population 1790–2000

Source: U.S. Census Bureau

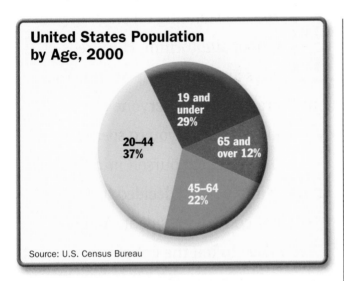

United States Population by Age, 2000

19 and under 29%

65 and over 12%

20–44 37%

45–64 22%

Source: U.S. Census Bureau

Unlike a line graph, a circle graph does not show change over time. Instead, it can give a certain view of the population at one moment in time. For example, when you look at the circle graph on this page, you get a picture of how large a part of the entire population is made up of each age group.

How? When you use a line graph, look first at the title. Notice that the title of the line graph on page 12 tells you what it is about. It shows you the changing United States population from 1790 to 2000. After you have read the title, look at the words along the axes, the lines at the edge of the graph, to see what the graph is showing. This line graph, for example, shows years along the bottom and population along the side. The dots in the middle of the graph show population in a certain year. When you connect those dots with a line, you have a line graph showing how the population has changed over time. The graph tells you that the country's population reached about 50 million in 1880. When did the population reach 130 million?

To use a circle graph, first look at the title. Then read the words in the graph to learn what each section represents. In this circle graph, each section represents an age group, and the numbers represent percentages. You can see that the smallest percentage of the population is 65 years and older. What age group represents the largest portion of the population?

Think and Apply

1. Does a **line graph** or **circle graph** show change over time? Which graph only shows information for a single year?

2. In which part of the circle graph would you be represented?

3. How many more people lived in the United States in 1970 than in 1940?

13

PREVIEW

Focus on the Main Idea
The United States is a republic in which citizens elect their leaders.

PEOPLE
Abraham Lincoln
John F. Kennedy

VOCABULARY
democracy
republic
constitution
citizen

Government by the People

 **You Are There**
You are standing on stage in your school auditorium. Hundreds of faces are looking up at you. Your friends are out there, and so is everyone else in the school. They are all waiting for you to speak.

How did you get yourself into this situation? Simple—you decided to run for student council president. And now you have to tell the entire school what you plan to do if they elect you. You want to let your fellow students know that you will help make sure that school rules are fair to everyone. You also want them to know that everyone has a responsibility to follow those rules. You step up to the microphone. You begin to speak.

 Main Idea and Details As you read, look for the important rights and responsibilities of United States citizenship.

14

Life in a Republic

No one likes to have to follow too many rules, but without rules it would be impossible to run a school, a city, or a country. What would happen in a school, city, or country that didn't have any rules or laws? Rules and laws protect us. It is the role of government to set rules and laws and to make sure that people follow them. In addition to making and enforcing laws, our government provides services, such as education and military defense. To pay for these services, the government must collect money in the form of taxes.

In a **democracy,** people have the power to make decisions about government. In our nation, we elect leaders to make decisions about the responsibilities of the government listed above.

In a direct democracy, all the voters in a community get together to make decisions about what their government should do. This type of democracy works well in a small community. But what if every voter in the United States had to get together every time we wanted the government to do something?

You can see that this would make it very difficult to get anything done.

For this reason, our government was designed as a representative democracy, or republic. In a **republic,** the people elect representatives to make laws and run the government. The President of the United States and members of Congress are examples of elected representatives. Our republic is based on the United States Constitution, which was written in 1787. A **constitution** is a written plan of government.

REVIEW What is the difference between a direct democracy and a republic?
🎯 **Main Idea and Details**

▶ Our government is divided into three levels: federal, state, and local. The federal, or national, government is centered in our nation's capital of Washington, D.C.

The Role of Citizens

Abraham Lincoln, President of the United States from 1861 to 1865, described the government as "of the people, by the people, and for the people...." In such a government, citizens play the most important role. A citizen is a member of a country. People born in the United States are United States citizens. People not born in the United States can also become citizens of this country.

United States citizenship comes with both rights and responsibilities. Many of our basic rights are protected by the Constitution. For example, the Constitution protects our freedom of speech and religion. People accused of a crime have the right to a fair trial. All citizens 18 years old and older have the right to vote in elections. Until 1971, citizens had to be 21 to vote. Many people felt this was unfair, however, and they worked to change the Constitution. As a result, the voting age was lowered to 18. This is an example of another right American citizens share—the right to try to change or improve a law they believe is wrong.

Along with these rights come certain responsibilities including paying taxes and serving on juries. One of the most important responsibilities is getting involved.

▶ Following the tradition of earlier Presidents, John F. Kennedy spoke to the nation on the day he took office in 1961.

Government "of the people" can work only if citizens participate in the process of choosing leaders and making laws. Obeying the law, respecting the rights of others, and going to school are also key responsibilities.

You may have heard a famous statement about citizens' responsibilities. On the day he became president in 1961, John F. Kennedy said,

> *"And so, my fellow Americans— ask not what your country can do for you—ask what you can do for your country."*

With these words, Kennedy was calling on Americans to meet the responsibilities we all share. The United States belongs to the people, so it is up to the people to make the country work.

REVIEW What are three basic rights of American citizens? ⟳ **Main Idea and Details**

▶ In the United States, people have the right—and responsibility—to vote, starting at the age of 18.

We the People

The first words of the United States Constitution are, "We the People of the United States. . . " This makes sense, because the Constitution sets up a government that is run by the people. Our

government is based on the ideals of freedom and representative democracy. These ideals have not changed in more than 200 years.

▶ The Constitution begins with the words "We the People."

As you will read, however, not all the people always enjoyed equal rights in this country. For example, women in most states were not able to vote until 1920. One of the most important parts of United States history is the changing of our government to include all Americans.

REVIEW Why are the words "We the People" a good beginning to the Constitution? ⟳ Main Idea and Details

Summarize the Lesson

- In the United States, people elect their leaders.
- Our government is based on the ideals of freedom and representative democracy.
- United States citizenship comes with important rights and responsibilities.

LESSON 2   REVIEW

Check Facts and Main Ideas

1. ⟳ **Main Idea and Details** On a separate sheet of paper, fill in examples of important responsibilities that United States **citizens** share.

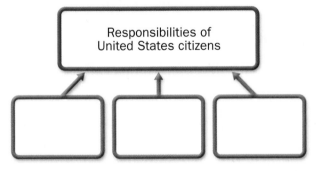

2. What is the difference between a direct **democracy** and a republic?

3. What are some important rights and responsibilities of United States citizens?

4. What are the ideals on which our government is based?

5. **Critical Thinking:** *Decision Making* Do you think lowering the voting age from 21 to 18 was a good idea? Do you think it should be lower than 18? Use the decision-making steps on page H3.

Link to ⌒⌒ Writing

Write a Speech Suppose you are running for class president. Write a one-page speech explaining why you would make a good president.

PREVIEW

Focus on the Main Idea
The free enterprise system gives Americans many economic freedoms.

PEOPLE
Madam C. J. Walker
Thomas Edison

VOCABULARY
private property
economy
free enterprise
profit
supply
demand
export
import
consumer
entrepreneur

Free Enterprise

 **You Are There** You and your sister Jane are sitting at the table. You are both waiting for the cookies you made to finish baking. They smell great! "I bet we could make a million dollars selling your cookies," you say. You start planning how to spend the money. "Maybe not a million dollars," Jane says, "but I could help you sell cookies to some of our friends and neighbors. The first thing you would need to do is make a budget." You learned in school that a budget helps you keep track of how much money you spend and how much you earn. You grab a piece of paper and ask Jane what you will need to sell the cookies. This will take some planning!

 Main Idea and Details As you read, look for examples of the benefits of free enterprise.

How Free Enterprise Works

You have already read about some of the many rights we have in the United States. These rights are important because they help our nation and community. Some of these rights are political, such as the right to vote. Now you will learn about economic rights, such as the freedom to start your own business and to own private property. **Private property** is something owned by individuals or groups, such as a house or a car.

We have these freedoms because the U.S. economy is based on a system called free enterprise. An **economy** is a system for producing and distributing goods and services. In an economy based on **free enterprise,** people are free to start their own businesses and own their own property. Individuals, groups, and governments use money to buy the goods and services they need.

Free enterprise has been an important part of life in North America for centuries. During the 1700s, for example, carpenters in Maine began building ships from the tall trees that grew in the area. They were able to sell these ships for a profit. **Profit** is the money a business has left after it has paid all its costs. The shipbuilders decided to charge enough for their ships to pay their costs and still make a profit. In the free enterprise system, prices are based on supply and demand. **Supply** is the amount of a good

or service that is available. **Demand** is the amount of a good or service that people are willing to buy. The rules of supply and demand can be complicated, but the basic idea is simple. When many people want to buy something, the price will usually go up. When only a few people want to buy, the price will usually go down.

In a free enterprise system, you must also consider opportunity costs when making a decision to produce or buy something. Opportunity cost is the value of the next best choice. If you buy a CD, you cannot spend that money on a game. U.S. history shows that the costs and benefits of alternative choices must be considered when making a decision. President John F. Kennedy thought the United States should spend money to be the first to land on the moon. Some people thought that the money should have been spent on schools instead.

REVIEW What are some important freedoms we have under the free enterprise system?
🔄 **Main Idea and Details**

▶ **Shipbuilding has been an important part of the American economy for nearly 300 years. What types of businesses are important in your area?**

Trading with the World

The United States trades a wide variety of goods with countries around the world. For example, the United States is the world's leading exporter of wheat and corn. An **export** is a good that one country sells to another country. The United States imports oil from Mexico, Saudi Arabia, and other countries. An **import** is a good that one country buys from another country. Different countries have different resources available to develop and sell. This allows them to specialize in certain goods or services. Specialization allows countries to produce greater amounts of a good or service at lower prices. Because nations specialize in certain goods, they trade with other countries for goods they need. This makes them interdependent.

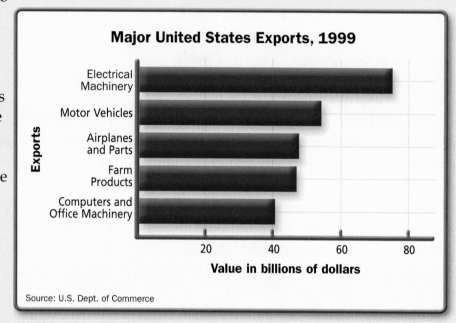

Major United States Exports, 1999

Exports

- Electrical Machinery
- Motor Vehicles
- Airplanes and Parts
- Farm Products
- Computers and Office Machinery

Value in billions of dollars

Source: U.S. Dept. of Commerce

Here is some more information about the goods the United States trades with other countries in the world today.

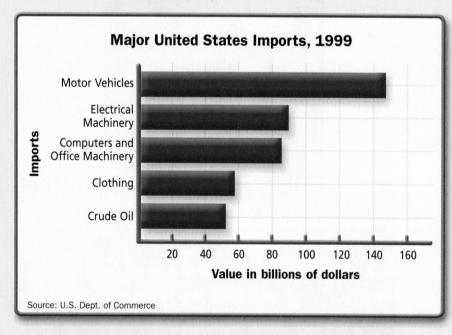

Major United States Imports, 1999

Imports

- Motor Vehicles
- Electrical Machinery
- Computers and Office Machinery
- Clothing
- Crude Oil

Value in billions of dollars

Source: U.S. Dept. of Commerce

Benefits of Free Enterprise

A writer named Anna Royall visited an outdoor market in Charleston, South Carolina, in 1830. She walked from stall to stall, surprised at what she saw. "I did not dream that such a variety of sweet potatoes, peas, and beans existed," she wrote. "There were a great variety of fruits, and all the nuts of the globe."

American consumers have an amazing variety from which to choose. A **consumer** is a person or group that buys or uses goods and services. This variety shows two major benefits of the free enterprise system for consumers. First, consumers can choose among a great many products. Second, consumers can make choices about how to spend their money.

In addition, the free enterprise system gives consumers certain rights. They have the right to expect producers to supply safe, quality goods. They also have the right to expect producers to be honest in their ads.

The free enterprise system also encourages inventors. Inventors know that if they

▶ **Thomas Edison worked hard on his inventions, such as the phonograph shown here.**

think of a good invention, they might be able to sell it. **Thomas Edison,** a famous inventor, always remembered the first time someone paid him for one of his inventions. After getting a check for $40,000, he said, "This caused me to come as near fainting as I ever got." This took place in 1870, when Edison was only 23 years old! He used the money to set up a laboratory where he could work on more inventions.

Another benefit of the free enterprise system is that people can become entrepreneurs (ahn truh preh NOORS). An **entrepreneur** is a person who starts a new business, hoping to make a profit. In 1906, **Madam C. J. Walker** started a beauty products business with only a few dollars. Ten years later, she had thousands of employees. Walker was the first African American woman to become a millionaire. She had some advice for young entrepreneurs: "Don't wait for opportunities to come. Get up and make them!"

REVIEW How can the free enterprise system help encourage inventors?
Draw Conclusions

▶ **Madam C. J. Walker advertised the many products made by her company.**

Scarcity

While the free enterprise system offers many opportunities, other things limit our economy. One of the most important is the scarcity of resources. Scarcity means that there are not enough resources to meet all of our wants and needs. Decisions have to be made because of this scarcity. For example, a river may seem to have plenty of water, but governments have to decide how it should be used. Some might want the water for livestock and crops, but others might want the river to be preserved for nature or for drinking water.

Even individuals must make economic decisions based on scarcity. Money is a limited resource, but you might have unlimited ideas on what you could buy. You have to make decisions on the best way to spend the limited amount of money you have.

REVIEW Give an example of an economic decision a family might make based on scarcity. **Predicting**

Summarize the Lesson

- **The United States economy is based on a system called free enterprise.**

- **In our free enterprise system, we have the right to own property and start businesses.**

- **Free enterprise gives us a wide variety of products to choose from and thousands of different career opportunities.**

LESSON 3 REVIEW

Check Facts and Main Ideas

1. ⬀ **Main Idea and Details** On a separate sheet of paper, fill in details of economic freedoms that Americans have.

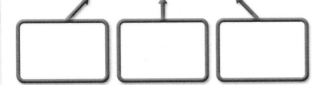

The free enterprise system gives Americans many economic freedoms.

2. How do **supply** and **demand** affect prices in a **free enterprise** system?

3. How did Thomas Edison benefit from the free enterprise system?

4. Name three goods that the United States both **imports** and **exports.**

5. **Critical Thinking:** *Decision Making* What decisions do you think Madam C. J. Walker had to make to start her business? Use the decision-making steps on page H3.

Link to ⌾⌾ Mathematics

Compare Exports and Imports The graphs on page 20 show the value of major United States imports and exports. What is the total value of these imports? What is the total value of these exports? Which value is greater?

Thomas Edison
1847–1931

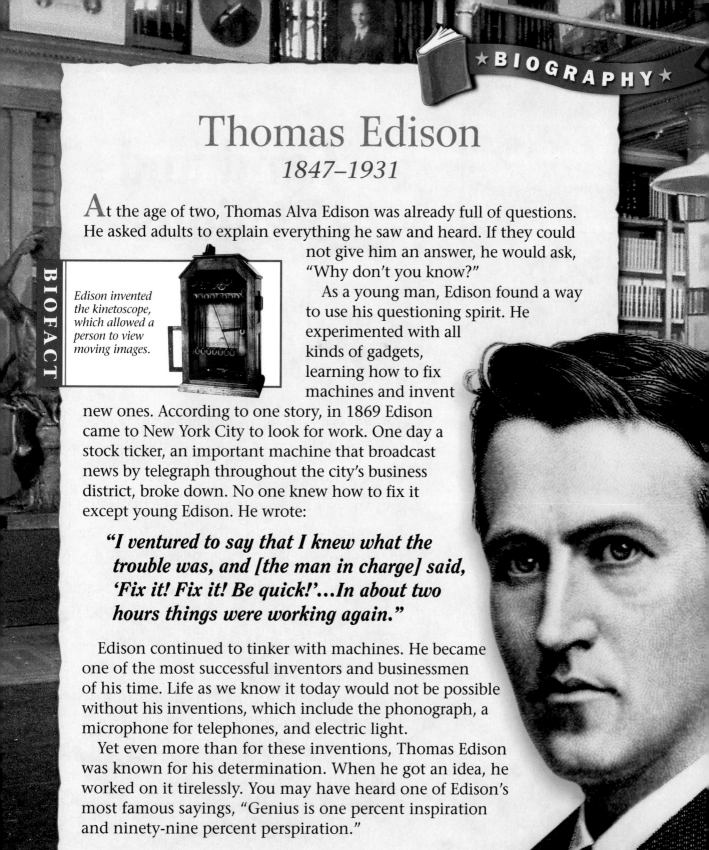

At the age of two, Thomas Alva Edison was already full of questions. He asked adults to explain everything he saw and heard. If they could not give him an answer, he would ask, "Why don't you know?"

Edison invented the kinetoscope, which allowed a person to view moving images.

As a young man, Edison found a way to use his questioning spirit. He experimented with all kinds of gadgets, learning how to fix machines and invent new ones. According to one story, in 1869 Edison came to New York City to look for work. One day a stock ticker, an important machine that broadcast news by telegraph throughout the city's business district, broke down. No one knew how to fix it except young Edison. He wrote:

> *"I ventured to say that I knew what the trouble was, and [the man in charge] said, 'Fix it! Fix it! Be quick!'...In about two hours things were working again."*

Edison continued to tinker with machines. He became one of the most successful inventors and businessmen of his time. Life as we know it today would not be possible without his inventions, which include the phonograph, a microphone for telephones, and electric light.

Yet even more than for these inventions, Thomas Edison was known for his determination. When he got an idea, he worked on it tirelessly. You may have heard one of Edison's most famous sayings, "Genius is one percent inspiration and ninety-nine percent perspiration."

Learn from Biographies

How did Edison's life reflect his belief that "Genius is one percent inspiration and ninety-nine percent perspiration?"

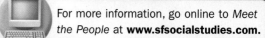

For more information, go online to *Meet the People* at **www.sfsocialstudies.com**.

LESSON 4

WEST   MIDWEST   NORTH-EAST
SOUTHWEST   SOUTHEAST

PREVIEW

Focus on the Main Idea
Dividing the United States into regions makes it easier to study our country's geography

PLACES
Northeast
Southeast
Midwest
Southwest
West

PEOPLE
George Washington Carver

VOCABULARY
region
geography
agriculture
irrigation
climate
precipitation
interdependent

Land and Regions

You Are There
Here are descriptions of five places in the United States. Read these clues and try to guess where you are in each of them.

1. You are standing at the foot of a giant volcano. It last erupted about 20 years ago, blowing off a part of the mountain.

2. You are walking along the shore of a lake that is so big you cannot see the other side. Storms can blow up suddenly, making it a dangerous place for ships.

3. You are on a mountain that rises more than a mile above sea level. The peak is one of the first places in the United States touched by the sun's rays each morning.

4. You are canoeing through a dark swamp, where trees grow right out of the shallow water. Be careful of the alligator that is gliding alongside your boat.

5. You are in a burning-hot desert near a narrow river. On the other side of the river is Mexico.

Main Idea and Details As you read, look for features that make each region different.

24

Regions of the United States

Look at the photographs below to find each of these five places. Each is located in a different region of the United States. A **region** is a large area that has common features that set it apart from other areas. The United States can be divided into five regions: the Northeast, Southeast, Midwest, Southwest, and West.

Why do we divide the country into regions? The United States is a huge country—the fourth-largest in the world. Dividing the land into regions makes it easier to study our country's geography. **Geography** is the study of Earth and how people use it. If you want to be a geographer, for instance, you might study the Mississippi River. You could study where the river begins, how long it is, and the kinds of land it flows through. You could also study how people use the river for things like farming and transportation.

REVIEW What are five regions of the United States? ⟳ **Main Idea and Details**

1. You are at Mount St. Helens in Washington.

2. You are on the shores of Lake Michigan.

5. You are in Big Bend National Park in Texas.

3. You are on Mt. Katahdin in Maine.

4. You are in the Okefenokee Swamp in Georgia.

AK

Regions of the United States

The regions of the United States vary in size and population. The Northeast has the smallest area. The Southeast has the largest population. The Southwest is made up of the fewest states. Here is information showing how each region is special.

The West

Area 1,576,336 square miles
Population 56,248,254

Key Facts The West is divided into two regions—the Pacific states and the Mountain states. Both regions include some of the country's highest mountains.

▶ Rocky Mountains

HI

The Southwest

Area 572,784 square miles
Population 31,252,152

Key Facts People come from all over to visit the Grand Canyon and other natural wonders of the Southwest. They also come to live here. The invention of air conditioning has made it possible for more people to live comfortably in this hot region.

▶ Grand Canyon

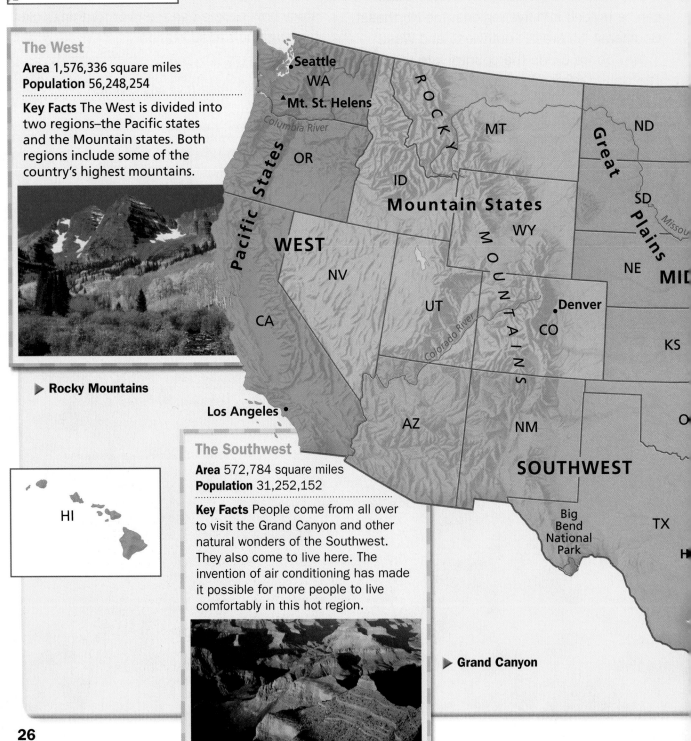

Map labels: Seattle, WA, Mt. St. Helens, Columbia River, OR, Pacific States, WEST, NV, CA, Los Angeles, AZ, Mountain States, ROCKY, MT, ID, WY, MOUNTAINS, UT, Colorado River, Denver, CO, NM, SOUTHWEST, Big Bend National Park, TX, Great Plains, ND, SD, Missouri, NE, MID, KS, O, H

26

The Midwest

Area 821,763 square miles
Population 64,392,776

Key Facts The Midwest is divided into two smaller regions—the Great Plains states and the Great Lakes states. Both regions have many large farms, helping the Midwest produce more wheat and corn than any other part of the country.

▶ **Wheat field in Wisconsin**

The Northeast

Area 191,678 square miles
Population 60,246,523

Key Facts The Northeast is divided into two smaller regions—New England and the Middle Atlantic states. Both regions take advantage of long coastlines and the sea's rich resources. The nation's largest city, New York City, is located in the Northeast.

▶ **New York City**

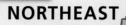

NORTHEAST

Mt. Katahdin

ME

New England States

VT

NY

NH

Middle **Atlantic States**

Boston

MA

CT

RI

Lake Michigan

WI

MI

Detroit

Great Lakes States

IA

Chicago

WEST

IL

IN

OH

PA

New York City

NJ

Philadelphia

DE

MD

Washington, D.C.

APPALACHIAN MOUNTAINS

Mississippi River

Ohio River

MO

WV

VA

KY

TN

NC

AR

SOUTHEAST

SC

MS

AL

Atlanta

GA

Okefenokee Swamp

LA

FL

Miami

The Southeast

Area 555,236 square miles
Population 69,282,201

Key Facts The Mississippi River flows though a large area of fertile farmland in the Southeast. At the southern end of the river, you will find two of the nation's busiest port cities: Baton Rouge and New Orleans, Louisiana.

▶ **New Orleans**

▶ **Irrigation makes it possible to grow crops like corn in the dry Southwest.**

People and the Land

As you have seen, our nation has a wide variety of landforms. Landforms are shapes on Earth's surface, such as mountains, canyons, and plains. But how do landforms affect how people can use the land?

One of the most important uses of land is agriculture. **Agriculture** is the business of growing crops and raising animals. Agriculture is important in all the regions of the United States. The best farmland is usually flat. So it makes sense that some of the nation's most productive farms are found in places like the flat land along the Mississippi River, the Great Plains of the Midwest, and the warm valleys of California.

People can help to make land even more productive. For example, many centuries ago, Native Americans in the Southwest began using irrigation to grow corn and beans. **Irrigation** is a method of bringing water to dry land. In the Biography on page 31 you will read about **George Washington Carver,** a scientist who discovered hundreds of new uses for crops such as peanuts and sweet potatoes. Since these crops grow well in the Southeast, Carver's discoveries helped farmers make better use of the land in this region. Other scientists have developed new types of fertilizers, substances that help plants grow.

Building cities is also a way of using the land. But how do people decide where to build cities? Look back at the map on pages 26–27 and find the nation's five biggest cities: New York City, Los Angeles, Chicago, Houston, and Philadelphia. These and many other cities are located along rivers, or on the shores of lakes or oceans. This did not happen by accident. People began building these cities long before there were cars and airplanes. Water made it easier for people to travel and to carry goods from place to place. Think about the land around your home and school. In what different ways are people using this land?

REVIEW How can irrigation help make land more productive? *Cause and Effect*

Check the Weather

What is the weather normally like where you live? Does it change from season to season? These are questions about your area's climate. **Climate** is the weather in an area over a long period of time.

Temperature is an important part of an area's climate. A region's climate also includes the amount of precipitation it gets. **Precipitation** is the moisture that falls to Earth in the form of rain, snow, or sleet.

Look at the map on this page. You will see that different parts of the country have very different climates. One thing that affects an area's climate is its distance from the equator. As the map shows, climates in the United States become cooler as you move north, or farther from the equator.

The amount of precipitation also varies from region to region. The eastern half of the United States usually gets more precipitation than the western half. In fact, the United States can be divided into two rainfall regions—one in the mostly arid west, and the other in the mostly humid east. Arid means dry. Humid means wet. Find the border between these regions on the map below.

REVIEW What is the main difference between the arid west and the humid east? **Compare and Contrast**

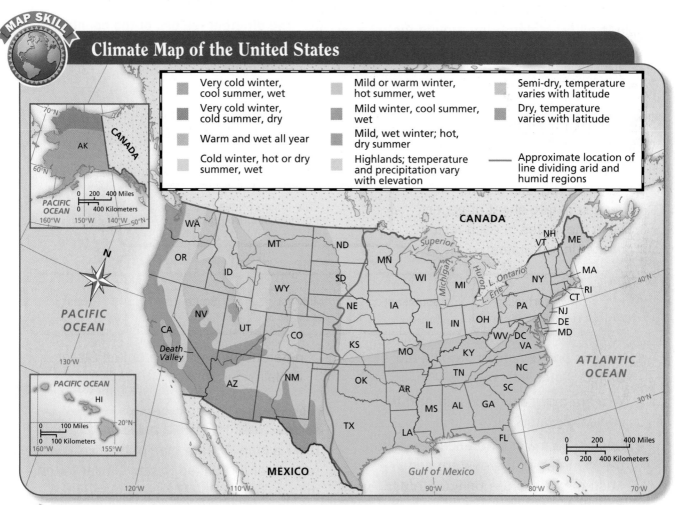

MAP SKILL

Climate Map of the United States

- Very cold winter, cool summer, wet
- Very cold winter, cold summer, dry
- Warm and wet all year
- Cold winter, hot or dry summer, wet
- Mild or warm winter, hot summer, wet
- Mild winter, cool summer, wet
- Mild, wet winter; hot, dry summer
- Highlands; temperature and precipitation vary with elevation
- Semi-dry, temperature varies with latitude
- Dry, temperature varies with latitude
- —— Approximate location of line dividing arid and humid regions

▶ This map shows 10 different climate types in the United States.

MAP SKILL Region *What is the main climate type of the Southeast region?*

Regions Work Together

One thing that makes the United States strong is the cooperation between different regions. The nation's largest airplane factory is located near Seattle, Washington, in the West region. But the factory relies on metal, engine parts, and computers made all around the country. This is an example of how the different regions are interdependent — meaning they need each other.

The connections between regions are growing stronger and stronger. For example, have you ever sent an e-mail to someone in another region? Or looked at a web site created by a person hundreds of miles away?

These things are possible because people in all 50 states—and around the world—are now connected by computers.

The regions of the United States have not always worked together so closely, however. In this book, you will read stories of both conflict and cooperation between the different regions of our country.

REVIEW Explain in your own words the statement: "The five regions of the United States are interdependent." **Summarize**

Summarize the Lesson

- **Geography is the study of Earth and how people use it.**
- **The United States is often divided into five regions: the Northeast, Southeast, Midwest, Southwest, and West.**
- **The different regions of the country are interdependent, meaning they need each other.**

LESSON 4 REVIEW

Check Facts and Main Ideas

1. **Main Idea and Details**
   On a separate sheet of paper, fill in the states in each region of the United States.

   The United States can be divided into five regions.

   | Northeast | Southeast | Midwest | Southwest | West |

2. What is one benefit of dividing the United States into regions?

3. Why are many cities located next to bodies of water?

4. Describe a major difference between the climates of the eastern and western parts of the United States.

5. Critical Thinking: *Draw Conclusions*
   Do you think the Internet has helped strengthen connections between the different regions of the United States? Explain your answer.

Link to ⚬⚬ Geography

Draw a Map Draw a map of the five regions of the United States similar to the map on pages 26–27. Use a different color for each region and make a map key. Identify and label regions, major rivers, mountain ranges, and states.

George Washington Carver *1861–1943*

When George Washington Carver was about ten, he walked eight miles to the nearest school that African American children were allowed to attend. Soon he had learned everything that this school could teach him, and had to move on again. Young George could not get enough of learning, especially about the science of living things. He later said:

BIOFACT

Carver promoted products such as peanut butter to increase the market for peanut products.

"My very soul thirsted for an education. I literally lived in the woods. I wanted to know every strange stone, flower, insect, bird, or beast."

Carver traveled from place to place, picking up odd jobs and learning whatever he could. He was accepted to a college, but after traveling all the way there he was turned away because of the color of his skin. But Carver was not easily stopped. He attended a different college, and then transferred to Iowa State College to study botany, the science of plants. He was the first African American to attend this school. After he graduated, he went on to earn his Master's Degree.

As an adult, Carver helped many poor farmers, both black and white, by teaching them modern farming practices. At that time, farmers were planting cotton year after year, using up the nutrients in the soil that help plants grow. Carver realized that farmers could alternate crops, growing such plants as peanuts, sweet potatoes, and soybeans to help renew the soil. When farmers complained that there would be no buyers for these plants, Carver responded by inventing about 300 new products using peanuts alone.

Learn from Biographies

As an adult, Carver became a noted teacher, scientist, and inventor. How do you think his early experiences with education affected his later work?

For more information, go online to *Meet the People* at **www.sfsocialstudies.com**.

Read an Elevation Map

What? An **elevation map** shows the **elevation**, or height, of land in different places. Elevation is measured in feet or meters above sea level. **Sea level** is the height of the surface of the ocean when it is halfway between high tide and low tide.

Why? As you read in Lesson 4, the United States has a wide variety of landforms. There are high mountains and low plains that meet the sea. Mapmakers use elevation maps to show how high or low different regions and places are. Elevation maps help you compare the elevations of different places on Earth.

How? To understand an elevation map, you first have to study the key. Look at the large elevation map key symbol below. Notice that the key symbol resembles a small mountain. The blue at the bottom shows sea level. The numbers at the left side of the key show the elevation in feet. At the right they show elevation in meters. The lowest number, 0, represents sea level. This is the height from which other elevations are measured.

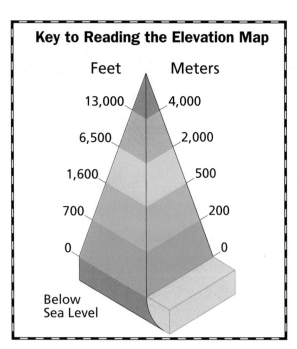

Key to Reading the Elevation Map

Feet	Meters
13,000	4,000
6,500	2,000
1,600	500
700	200
0	0

Below
Sea Level

The number at the bottom of each color in the key is the lowest elevation shown in that color. The number at the top of each elevation is the highest elevation shown in that color. For example, dark green represents all areas that are between sea level (0 feet) and 700 feet (200 meters) in elevation. What color is used to show elevations between 1,600 and 6,500 feet (500 and 2,000 meters)?

Now compare the map with the key. Each color on the map represents a band of elevation as shown by the key. The dark green areas, for example, are all between 0 and 700 feet (0 and 200 meters). Notice that the land along the oceans is always close to sea level. What is the elevation of most of the land in the western part of the country?

Elevation Map of the United States

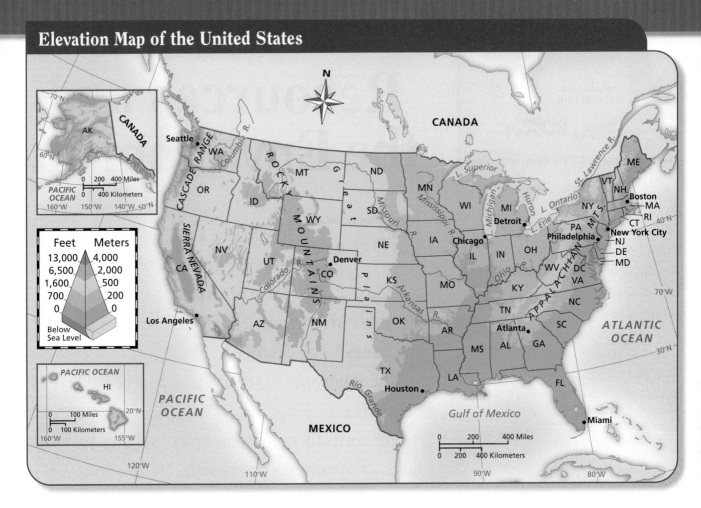

You can use an elevation map to see if mountains are higher in one place than in another. Find two major mountain ranges—the Appalachians in the east and the Rockies in the west. The map shows you that the Rockies are higher. Now find the Sierra Nevada range near the Pacific Ocean. Are the Sierra Nevada mountains higher or lower than the Appalachians?

Internet Activity

For more information, go online to the *Atlas* at **www.sfsocialstudies.com**.

Think and Apply

1. Use the map key to determine which state has higher land, Vermont or Colorado.

2. Which part of Texas is higher, the eastern or western?

3. Draw a conclusion about why **elevation maps** are useful.

4. According to the map, which state has an **elevation** below sea level?

Mount McKinley

Yellowstone National Park

Everglades National Park

PREVIEW

Focus on the Main Idea
Americans rely on natural resources for food, energy, and building materials.

PLACES
Yellowstone National Park
Mount McKinley
Everglades National Park

PEOPLE
Theodore Roosevelt
Marjory Stoneman Douglas

VOCABULARY
natural resource
mineral
fossil fuel
renewable resource
nonrenewable resource
conservation
environment
pollution

Resources and the Environment

You Are There
It has been a long day of studies and chores. But now you sit by a warm fire, reading a new pamphlet about life in a faraway land. As you read, you picture the things being described:

"The abundance of sea fish is almost beyond believing…"

"For beasts there are some bears, and they say some lions…also wolves, foxes, beavers, otters…great wild-cats, and a great beast called a molke [moose] as big as an ox."

"For wood there is no better in the world, I think, here being four sorts of oak…and other materials for building both of ships and houses."

You look at the cover of the pamphlet. It was written last year, 1629, by Francis Higginson. He is describing life in New England, a place in far-off North America. You like living in England. But you have to admit, North America sounds pretty interesting.

Main Idea and Details As you read, look for examples of important resources and think about why they are important.

A Land Rich in Resources

Francis Higginson's pamphlet described a land rich in natural resources. **Natural resources** are things found in nature that people can use. For example, water, soil, and trees are natural resources. Fish, deer, and other wild animals are also considered natural resources.

Today, the United States is still rich in a wide variety of natural resources. Like the people of New England in 1629, we rely on these resources for many things. We farm the land and catch fish in the rivers and oceans. We use wood from the forest to build homes and make other products such as paper. Many businesses are based on natural resources. Think about a company that sells bottled water, for example.

People also use another kind of natural resource called minerals. **Minerals** are substances found on Earth that are neither animal nor vegetable. Useful metals such as gold, copper, and aluminum are minerals. So are nonmetals like salt and granite, a type of stone used for buildings.

Another key type of mineral resource is fossil fuel. Fossils are the remains of animals or plants that lived long ago. **Fossil fuels** are fuels formed from the remains of plants and animals that lived thousands of years ago. Coal, oil, and natural gas are examples of fossil fuels. What makes these fuels so valuable? Fossil fuels are used for energy. Most car engines run on gasoline, which is made from oil. Fossil fuels are also used to heat homes and make electricity for our lights and computers.

REVIEW Why are natural resources important? ↩ **Main Idea and Details**

▶ The United States is rich in natural resources. What resources are shown here?

▶ Natural resources, such as trees and wildlife, are not unlimited. Today there are far fewer buffalo than there were in the middle 1800s.

Resources and People

Later in this book, you will read about two famous American explorers named Meriwether Lewis and William Clark. While exploring land west of the Mississippi River in the early 1800s, Lewis and Clark were amazed at the natural riches of the land. In their journals, they wrote about sparkling rivers, massive forests, and wildlife in incredible numbers. Lewis wrote: "The whole face of the country was covered with herds of buffalo, elk, and antelopes."

It might have seemed then that the country had enough natural resources to last forever. But today we know that there is a limited supply of most natural resources.

Some resources can be replaced, while others can not. Natural resources such as trees are renewable resources. **Renewable resources** are resources that can be renewed or replaced. Trees are renewable resources because we can plant new trees to replace the ones we cut down. Natural resources such as fossil fuels are nonrenewable resources. **Nonrenewable resources** are resources that cannot be easily replaced.

Both renewable and nonrenewable resources must be used carefully. Preserving and protecting resources is called **conservation.** Why is conservation important? You have seen how much we rely on natural resources. We need to make sure that there will be enough resources in the future.

Conserving natural resources is also important because resources are part of our environment. The **environment** is made up of all the things that surround us, such as land, water, air, and trees. All living things rely on their environment. We need clean air to breathe and clean water to drink. Can you think of some other ways that people, plants, and animals rely on their environment?

REVIEW Explain the difference between renewable and nonrenewable resources.
Compare and Contrast

Our National Parks

Have you ever hiked or camped in a park? Creating parks is one way to help protect the environment. National parks are parks that are protected by the federal government. Park rangers hired by the government provide services to visitors, such as informational talks. They also help protect the parkland.

The first national park in the United States was Yellowstone National Park, established in 1872. Congress created Yellowstone park "for the benefit and enjoyment of the people."

Since then, people of all ages have worked to create new parks around the country. Theodore Roosevelt, president from 1901 to 1909, helped create several national parks. Read what he said about protecting the Grand Canyon as a national park:

> *"Leave it as it is. You cannot improve on it.... What you can do is to keep it for your children, your children's children, and for all who come after you."*

Today, there are more than 50 national parks from Maine to Hawaii, covering more than 50 million acres. Each park has features that make it special. In Yellowstone National Park, you might see rare animals such as grizzly bears, mountain lions, and gray wolves. In Alaska's Denali National Park you can look up at Mount McKinley, the highest peak in North America. Explore the world's longest cave system at Mammoth Cave National Park in Kentucky. Or visit Florida's Everglades National Park to see alligators, manatees, and bottle-nosed dolphins. On page 39 you will read about Marjory Stoneman Douglas, a writer who dedicated many years of her life to protecting the Everglades.

REVIEW Why did Theodore Roosevelt want to protect the Grand Canyon?
Draw Conclusions

▶ **President Theodore Roosevelt** *(below, left)* **and naturalist John Muir** *(below, right)* **helped create many national parks. Shown below is Yellowstone, the nation's first national park.**

Protecting the Environment

One common environmental problem is pollution. **Pollution** is the addition of harmful substances to the air, water, or soil. Air pollution, for example, is a problem in some large cities. A major cause is the burning of fossil fuels in cars and power plants. Scientists and businesses are working to find cleaner ways to create the energy we need.

People can also help reduce pollution by doing simple things like recycling. Recycling is using something again. When we recycle paper, we can cut down fewer trees. We can also conserve valuable resources when we recycle plastic, glass, and metal.

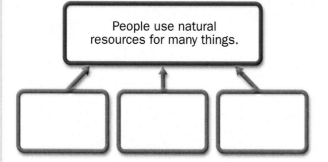

▶ **This symbol is used to mark items that can be recycled.**

Protecting the environment is important for many reasons. Businesses and people rely on natural resources for everything from food to electricity. We need clean air and clean water to live healthy lives. We also enjoy visiting beautiful places, and seeing all kinds of animals and plants.

REVIEW How can recycling help protect the environment? ↻ **Main Idea and Details**

Summarize the Lesson

- **The United States has always been rich in a wide variety of natural resources.**
- **Conservation is important because there is a limited supply of most natural resources.**
- **We rely on natural resources for food, energy, and building materials.**

LESSON 5 ▶ REVIEW

Check Facts and Main Ideas

1. ↻ **Main Idea and Details** On a separate sheet of paper, fill in the three details that support the main idea.

   People use natural resources for many things.

2. What are three examples of mineral resources?

3. How are **renewable** and **nonrenewable resources** the same? How are they different?

4. How do national parks help to protect the **environment?**

5. **Critical Thinking:** *Point of View* Do you think recycling is important in protecting the environment? Why or Why not?

Link to ⟨∞∞⟩ **Science**

Do Research One important environmental problem is acid rain. Do some research on this subject on the Internet or in an encyclopedia. What is acid rain? What are some of the major causes of acid rain? What are people doing to prevent acid rain?

Marjory Stoneman Douglas *1890–1998*

Marjory Stoneman Douglas was about four years old when she first saw Florida. She later remembered "being held up to pick an orange off of an orange tree..." She did not know then that she would spend many years fighting to protect the Florida Everglades. The Everglades is a large wetland area in southern Florida. Many rare animals and plants live there.

Douglas grew up with her mother and grandparents in Massachusetts. As a child, she loved being outdoors with her family. She wrote:

> *"We had three elm trees on our lot and all the way down the street there were elm trees....In the summer people would be sitting on their porches ...and the moonlight would be coming through the elm trees. ... It was so lovely in itself you could never forget it."*

Douglas went to college, which was unusual for women at that time. She moved to Florida and worked at her father's newspaper. There she learned about the Everglades. Some people wanted to drain parts of the Everglades in order to build on it. Douglas believed that the Everglades was an important part of the environment. In addition to being home to many plants and animals, it provided water for people. She fought to protect the Everglades. Her book *Everglades: River of Grass*, taught many people about the beauty and importance of the Everglades. She continued working to protect the Everglades until her death at age 108.

Learn from Biographies

Why did Marjory Stoneman Douglas feel it was important to protect the Florida Everglades?

BIOFACT

In 1993, President Clinton gave Douglas the Medal of Freedom for her years of work to protect the Everglades.

For more information, go online to *Meet the People* at **www.sfsocialstudies.com**.

39

Protecting the Land

Do you take pride in your neighborhood? Some people take the land they live on for granted, but not Mike Harris. His actions have had far-reaching effects.

Like most children growing up in Custer County, Oklahoma, Mike Harris loved being outdoors. By the time he was nine, Mike had roamed every inch of his family's ranch.

With his deep love of the land came a fierce urge to protect it. When Mike saw trash floating in a rain-filled ditch, he got angry. He knew he had to do something. While only in third grade, Mike started a group called Environmental CPR. The letters stood for Conserve, Preserve, Reserve. The group's goal was to clean up the countryside and teach other young people about pollution and its dangers.

But Mike faced a challenge. Because he was shy, he found it hard to speak out. However, with his mom's strong support, Mike was able to overcome his fears. He says:

"I took responsibility and did what needed to be done. When your heart's into it, nothing will stop you."

Mike worked hard to promote his cause. He spoke out at county speech contests. He passed out fliers, led recycling drives, and even appeared on radio and TV.

His efforts paid off. In its first few years, Environmental CPR collected and recycled more than 22,000 pounds of trash—about the weight of five sport utility vehicles. As you recall, by recycling things like paper and metal, we can use them again and reduce the amount of trash that damages the environment.

BUILDING
CITIZENSHIP
Caring
Respect
Responsibility
Fairness
Honesty
Courage

Of course, Mike could not do all this himself. Environmental CPR was a success because Mike Harris inspired the same sense of responsibility in several thousand people. In fact, the project continued for ten years under his leadership and spread out across the entire state. Today it continues its work on behalf of the environment.

Now a college student, Mike's goal remains the same.

"I want to create a better life for my kids and grandkids. It's beautiful country, where I'm from, and I want my kids to see it like I see it."

His words echo those of President Theodore Roosevelt and other famous Americans who have sought to conserve our nation's rich natural resources.

Responsibility in Action

"If everyone would take five minutes a day to do some single thing like pick up aluminum cans and put litter in its place, the land's going to benefit," says Mike Harris. What could you do in five minutes a day to improve *your* local environment?

Main Ideas and Vocabulary

TEST PREP

Read the passage below and use it to answer the questions that follow.

Most Americans are descended from families that immigrated from other parts of the world. Many immigrants came because they were attracted to American <u>ideals</u>, such as freedom and opportunity. American ideals have united our country and made it strong.

One American ideal is democratic government. Americans elect representatives to make laws and run the government. Americans have basic rights that are protected by the Constitution. They also have responsibilities, such as obeying the law.

Among the rights Americans have is the right to own property and to start businesses. Business owners can decide what to produce and how much to charge. Because of this freedom, American <u>consumers</u> have a great variety of products to buy.

The land of the United States is as varied as its people. It can be divided into five regions. The five regions are the Northeast, Southeast, Midwest, Southwest, and West.

Nature provides water, soil, and trees, animals and minerals that people can use. Many businesses use these natural resources. Americans are learning that they must use these resources wisely to be sure that we will have clean air and water and all the other resources we need in the future.

1 According to the passage, what unites the United States?
   A All people in the country have the same customs.
   B Business unites us.
   C Americans are united by basic ideals.
   D The transportation system unites us.

2 In the passage, the word <u>ideals</u> means—
   A government laws
   B customs
   C democracy
   D basic beliefs

3 In the passage, the word <u>consumers</u> means—
   A people who buy or use goods
   B people who start businesses
   C people who own private property
   D people who earn money

4 What is the main idea of this passage?
   A The American people are very much like one another.
   B Americans can start businesses.
   C Americans are different from one another but are united by certain ideals.
   D The United States has five geographic regions.

People

Match each person to his or her contributions.

1 **Marjory Stoneman Douglas** (p. 37)

2 **Abraham Lincoln** (p. 16)

3 **Theodore Roosevelt** (p. 37)

4 **Madam C. J. Walker** (p. 21)

5 **George Washington Carver** (p. 28)

6 **Thomas Edison** (p. 21)

a. set up a laboratory to work on inventions

b. started a beauty products business

c. discovered new uses for crops, such as peanuts

d. dedicated many years of her life to protecting the Everglades

e. helped create several national parks

f. described the U.S. government as, "of the people, by the people, and for the people"

Apply Skills

Prepare a Line Graph Get some graph paper or draw vertical lines on ruled paper. Use a state almanac or the Internet to find the population of your own community for every 10 years from 1950 to 2000. Prepare a line graph to show the change in population.

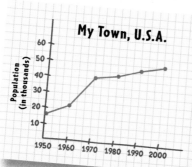

Write and Share

Explain the United States to a Stranger How would you tell somebody from another country about the United States? Select some students to act as Americans who describe their country. Let the rest of the class act as people from other countries. Have the "people from other countries" write questions about the American people, the land, the customs, the basic ideals. Have the "Americans" answer their questions, in writing. Then read your questions and answers as part of an information session for people considering immigrating to the United States.

Read on Your Own

Look for books like these in the library.

Discovery CHANNEL SCHOOL Project

As History Unfolds

Many of the events that make up social studies have been captured with pen and paper, often illustrated with pictures and drawings. Whatever the means, it is important to record the events as they unfold.

1 Form a group to create a record of what you learn this year in social studies.

2 Make a booklet with pages for each unit. Be as creative with your booklet as you want to be. Perhaps it could look like an accordion that when unfolded shows the information you entered for several units.

3 Add to your booklet each week by taking turns recording what you studied. Include such things as the main topics, vocabulary words, key places, or people. Add pictures and drawings. Share your booklet with the class.

The United States

Internet Activity

Find out more about the United States on the Internet. Go to **www.sfsocialstudies.com/ activities** and select your grade and unit.

Early Life, East and West

How does learning about past cultures help us understand the world today?

Begin with a Primary Source

5000 B.C.   A.D. 800   1000

about 7,000 years ago
First Americans grow food
in settled communities

about 700
Kingdom of
Ghana develops
in Africa

1000
Leif Ericsson
reaches North
America

**about
1050**
The Hopi village
of Oraibi is built

"I used to go to the ancient village…"

—Nampeyo, Pueblo potter, speaking about how she found the ancient designs to use in her pottery

Ceremonial Dance,
painted by Frank Reed Whiteside,
shows a Pueblo village
in the 1890s.

1200   1400   1600

about 1200
Aztec civilization
develops in Mexico

1405
Chinese fleets
under Zheng He
explore the seas

1498
Portuguese
explorer
da Gama
reaches India

about 1580
Five American
Indian tribes join
to form the
Iroquois League

47

Meet the People

Leif Ericsson

late 900s–early 1000s
Birthplace: Iceland
Sailor, explorer
- Son of Eric the Red, founder of Viking community of Greenland
- Led Viking exploration and settlement of Vinland, in North America
- Taught Christianity to the Vikings of Greenland

Marco Polo

about 1254–1324
Birthplace: Venice
Merchant, traveler
- Born to a family of successful merchants
- Traveled along Silk Road to China
- Wrote book, *Travels of Marco Polo*, which became a popular account of his travels

Mansa Musa

died about 1332
Birthplace: Mali
Emperor of Mali
- Controlled huge wealth of West African gold
- Took thousands of people with him on trip to Mecca
- Built the Great Mosque of Timbuktu

Zheng He

1371–1433
Birthplace: southern China
Admiral, explorer
- Commanded Chinese naval fleets
- Led seven major voyages of exploration
- Expanded Chinese trading in India and Africa

1000	1100	1200	1300	1400

late 900s–early 1000s
Leif Ericsson

about 1254–1324
Marco Polo

died about 1332
Mansa Musa

1371–1433
Zheng He

1394–1460
Prince Henry

Prince Henry

1394–1460

Birthplace: Portugal

Prince of Portugal

- Directed Portuguese efforts to improve sailing techniques
- Sent explorers to western coast of Africa
- Known as "Prince Henry the Navigator"

Deganawidah

1500s

Birthplace: Iroquois lands, probably New York State

Iroquois leader

- Preached peace and unity to the Iroquois
- With Hiawatha, helped form the Iroquois league
- Planted tree of peace to symbolize Iroquois unity

Hiawatha

1500s

Birthplace: Iroquois lands, probably New York State

Iroquois leader

- Preached peace and unity to the Iroquois
- Spoke for Deganawidah
- With Deganawidah, helped form the Iroquois league

Nampeyo

about 1860–1942

Birthplace: First Mesa, Arizona

Potter

- Studied ancient pottery to recreate designs
- Gained fame as potter
- Taught ancient styles to many others including her children and grandchildren

1500 1600 1700 1800 1900

1500s
Deganawidah

about 1860–1942
Nampeyo

1500s
Hiawatha

Reading Social Studies

Early Life, East and West

Summarize

Summarizing means telling the main idea of a paragraph, section, or story. Writers will use summarizing sentences to describe a main idea.

- A good **summary** is short. It tells the most important ideas. It should not include many words or details.

Sometimes a paragraph's **topic sentence** provides a summary. **Details** can be found in other parts of the paragraph.

> **People from other places have come to the Americas for thousands of years.** The first to arrive came from Asia more than 10,000 years ago. The earliest settlers probably traveled across a land bridge from Asia.

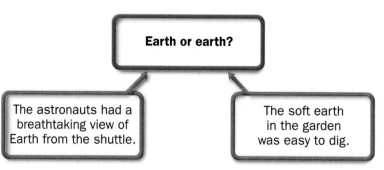

Word Exercise

Capitalization Knowing how capitalizing a word changes the meaning of that word helps you understand what you read. For example, the name *Earth* begins with a capital letter when it refers to a planet in our solar system. It begins with a lowercase letter, *earth*, when it is describing dirt or the ground.

Earth or earth?

The astronauts had a breathtaking view of Earth from the shuttle.

The soft earth in the garden was easy to dig.

Summarizing Early Life, East and West

People have moved around on Earth since early times. During the Ice Age people traveled from Asia to North America. At that time, the sea level dropped, and there was a bridge of land from Asia to America. After the sea level rose, the continents were separated by the Bering Sea.

People spread into new places throughout the Western Hemisphere. They went into North America and southward into Central America and South America.

Ideas and goods moved as well. The Mound Builders, people who lived near the Mississippi River, traded with people of the Rocky Mountains, the Gulf of Mexico, and the Great Lakes.

After the Spanish arrived with horses, the way of life of the Plains people changed greatly. The people rode swiftly on horseback to hunt buffalo.

Movements of people, goods, and ideas also occurred in the Eastern Hemisphere. Along the Silk Road, which led from China to Europe, people traded silk and other goods. The European merchant Marco Polo visited China in the 1200s and brought back tales of wonders.

In Africa, people were also moving. Camel caravans moved across the Sahara Desert. Arab traders from the north brought salt to exchange for gold. Mansa Musa, the powerful ruler of Mali, made a trip across northern Africa into Mecca in Arabia.

In the 1400s, explorers from China and Europe expanded their travels. Chinese ships reached the east coast of Africa. Shortly afterward, Portuguese ships sailed around the southern tip of Africa to India.

Use the reading strategy of summarizing to answer questions 1 and 2. Then answer the vocabulary question.

1 Which sentence gives a summary of the ideas in the reading?

2 What activity did both the Chinese and the Portuguese have in common?

3 Locate the term *Earth* in the passage. What meaning does the word *Earth* have here? Then write a sentence that uses the other meaning of *earth*.

Life in the Western Hemisphere

10,000–40,000 years ago

Bering Strait land bridge
People begin coming to the Americas from Asia.

Lesson 1

1

3,000 years ago

Serpent Mound
Mound Builders create huge mounds in present-day Ohio.

Lesson 2

2

1325

Tenochtitlan
Aztecs build a city in the Valley of Mexico.

Lesson 3

3

ASIA

Bering
Strait

PACIFIC
OCEAN

NORTH
AMERICA

ATLANTIC
OCEAN

Serpent
Mound

Tenochtitlan

Why We Remember

*Sharp, pointed stones pierced the hides of huge, hairy elephant-like mammals.
A twisting mound of earth, shaped like a snake, rose above the countryside.
Apartment-style dwellings clung to the face of a cliff.*

All these scenes took place many hundreds of years ago. They occurred in land that today is part of the United States, but they happened long before the United States was born. Each of them had something to do with the history of our country. As you will read, many more scenes are part of the story of the people who first settled this land.

40,000–10,000 years ago
Hunters from Asia cross into North America

10,000 years ago
Early people in the Americas live by hunting and gathering

7,000 years ago
People in the Americas develop agriculture

Migration to the Americas

PREVIEW

Focus on the Main Idea
People reached the Americas from Asia and began to settle throughout North and South America.

PLACES
Bering Strait

VOCABULARY
Ice Age
glacier
migrate
theory
artifact
archaeologist

You Are There

Though the cold air bites into your face and hands, you barely notice it. You are on your first big hunt. You're following a giant woolly mammoth—an elephant-like creature standing nine feet tall. Long tusks thrust forward from its face.

Silently, you and the other hunters creep up on the giant animal. Suddenly, you all stand up and hurl your spears. Sharp stone points pierce the mammoth. It staggers and you all rush toward it, jabbing it with your spears. Down goes the mammoth, soon to die.

You and your group will carve many pounds of meat from the slain animal, which will feed your people for weeks. Your first hunt has been a success.

Summarize As you read, look for details that summarize the ways of life of the first people to settle in the Americas.

▶ Woolly mammoth hunters used tools like this to throw spears.

Moving Into the Americas

The scene you just read could have occurred about 20,000 years ago, during the Ice Age. This was a long period of extreme cold. Low temperatures caused large areas of Earth's water to freeze, forming thick sheets of ice, or glaciers (GLAY shers). As the map on this page shows, much of Earth's water was frozen into glaciers. The level of the oceans dropped.

The Bering Strait is a narrow stretch of water that separates Asia from North America. During the Ice Age, the Bering Strait became shallower. Land that had been underwater was uncovered, forming a long land bridge that linked Asia and North America.

Many scholars believe that people first began to migrate, or move, to the Americas between 40,000 to 10,000 years ago. But how did they get here? The land bridge gave historians a theory, or a possible explanation. Perhaps large animals like mammoth and caribou began to cross the land bridge from Asia. Perhaps hunters began to follow these animals on foot. As the animals moved deeper into North America, so did the hunters.

Some scholars think that early people may have migrated to the Americas by boat. Perhaps both theories are right and different people arrived in different ways.

The first Americans migrated throughout North America and South America. You can trace their routes through the Americas on the map on this page. They lived in many different environments. They adapted, or changed, their ways of living to meet the challenges of these environments.

REVIEW What details explain how a land bridge might have made it possible for people to migrate to the Americas from Asia?
Summarize

MAP SKILL

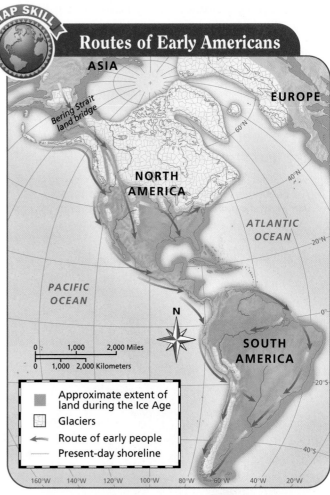

Routes of Early Americans

ASIA
EUROPE
Bering Strait land bridge
60°N
NORTH AMERICA
40°N
ATLANTIC OCEAN
20°N
PACIFIC OCEAN
N
0°
SOUTH AMERICA
20°S

0 — 1,000 — 2,000 Miles
0 — 1,000 — 2,000 Kilometers

Approximate extent of land during the Ice Age
Glaciers
Route of early people
Present-day shoreline

160°W 140°W 120°W 100°W 80°W 60°W 40°W 20°W
40°S

► Early people adapted to different environments throughout the Americas.

MAP SKILL Movement *In which direction were people moving as they traveled through the Americas?*

55

Ways of Life

Life was a struggle for the earliest people in the Americas. Getting enough food to eat for all was often a challenge. So they lived in small bands, or groups, of people. Their way of life centered on hunting. They depended on wandering herds of animals for food, so they moved often. The band you met earlier would have stayed near the mammoth they killed until its meat ran out. Then they would have moved on to begin a new hunt.

The early people used more than food from animals like the mammoth. They stripped the hides from the animals and made clothes from them. They also stretched hides over wood frames to make their temporary homes. They made tools like needles and scrapers from the animal's bones and tusks.

The early people also made tools from stone. Pressing one stone against another, they chipped spear points, knives, and hand axes. Look at the tools shown on this page to see how sharp and useful they could be.

▶ Archaeologists often find artifacts like these stone spear points buried deep in the ground.

How do you think the early people might have used them?

The earliest people left no written record of how they lived. So how do we know about their lives? Clues they left behind—called artifacts—tell us. An **artifact** is an object that someone made in the past. The stone tools on this page are artifacts that early Americans left behind.

Archaeologists (ahr key AHL uh jists) are scientists who interpret these clues. **Archaeologists** study the artifacts of people who lived long ago and draw conclusions from them. For example, sturdy bone needles reveal that people stitched strong hides together to make their clothing, blankets, and even shelter. What might the spear points on this page tell archaeologists? They tell that the early people hunted for their food.

REVIEW Summarize how the early Americans used the animals they killed.
↻ **Summarize**

Changing Way of Life

About 10,000 years ago, the Ice Age gradually came to an end. Earth's climate began to get warmer and glaciers melted. As time passed some of the large Ice Age animals became extinct, or died out. Perhaps they could not adapt to the new climate. Or perhaps the hunters had killed them off.

Whatever the cause, the first Americans had to find new food sources. They continued to hunt for smaller animals and to fish. They also gathered plants that grew wild, like grains, root vegetables, berries, and nuts. Hunters had become hunter-gatherers, but they were still on the move. They moved with the seasons to find whatever foods each season provided.

Then, about 7,000 years ago in present-day Mexico, people began to learn how to grow food themselves. Instead of gathering wild grain, they started planting its seeds. Agriculture made it possible for people to settle in one place. Now wandering bands of hunter-gatherers could become members of settled communities.

REVIEW How did the way of life change when the climate became warmer?
Summarize

Summarize the Lesson

- **40,000–10,000 years ago** During the Ice Age, hunters may have migrated across a land bridge from Asia to North America.

- **10,000 years ago** Early people lived by hunting and gathering.

- **7,000 years ago** The early people learned how to grow food and became members of settled communities.

LESSON 1 REVIEW

Check Facts and Main Ideas

1. **Summarize** On a separate sheet of paper, fill in the missing details from this lesson that support the summary.

```
┌──────────────┐   ┌──────────────┐   ┌──────────────┐
│ The first    │   │              │   │              │
│ Americans    │   │              │   │              │
│ hunted       │   │              │   │              │
│ mammoths.    │   │              │   │              │
└──────┬───────┘   └──────┬───────┘   └──────┬───────┘
       │                  │                  │
       └──────────────────┼──────────────────┘
              ┌────────────────────────────┐
              │  The way of life of the    │
              │  first Americans was       │
              │  centered on hunting until │
              │  the end of the Ice Age.   │
              └────────────────────────────┘
```

2. Why do some scholars think people migrated from Asia to North America during the **Ice Age?**

3. How did the first Americans live during the Ice Age?

4. Why did hunters have to find new ways to get food when Earth's climate began to get warmer?

5. **Critical Thinking:** *Draw Conclusions* How do you think the early people discovered how to grow food?

Link to ⚭ Art

Make a Diorama Work with several classmates to make a diorama showing how the early people lived. Be sure to show a hunt and how they used the animals they killed.

Chart and Graph Skills

Read Climographs

What? A <mark>climograph</mark> is a graph that shows two kinds of information about the climate of a place. It shows both the average temperature and the average precipitation—rain or snow—for a particular place over a period of time. You can see examples of climographs on these pages.

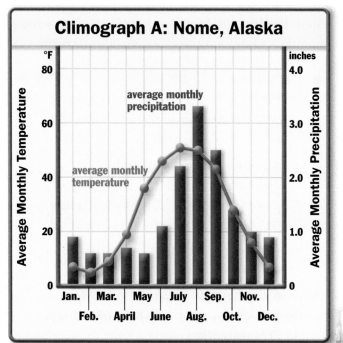

Why? Climographs help you understand the typical climate of a place. You have been reading about the land bridge that once connected Asia and North America during the Ice Age. That land bridge was where the Bering Strait is now. You learned that after the climate grew warmer, the sea levels rose and once again separated the land on the two continents. To study the climate today near the Bering Strait, you can use a climograph.

▶ **As the climographs show, Nome, Alaska, *(left)* has a very different climate than does the area around Holyoke, Colorado *(next page).***

How? Climograph A shows the average monthly temperature and precipitation today in Nome, Alaska, near the Bering Sea. Read each of the labels at the sides. The left side labels the average monthly temperatures in degrees Fahrenheit (F°). Temperature is shown on the line graph. You can see that the average January temperature for Nome is 7° Fahrenheit. You can see that the average temperature in May for Nome is 36°F.

The right side of the graph shows average monthly precipitation. Precipitation is shown on the bar graph. The average precipitation in January for Nome is 0.9 inches. What is the average monthly precipitation in May for Nome?

Climograph B shows the average monthly temperatures and precipitation for Holyoke, Colorado. In the next lesson, you will read about people who lived long ago in this area. Compare the average January temperatures for Nome, Alaska, and Holyoke, Colorado. Which is colder? How do you know? Which receives more precipitation in May? How do you know?

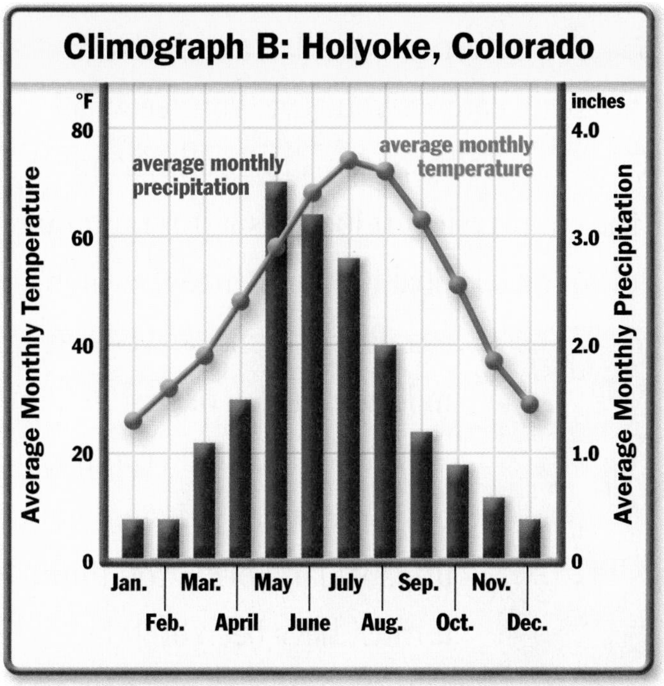

Climograph B: Holyoke, Colorado

(Bar and line graph showing average monthly temperature (°F, left axis 0–80) and average monthly precipitation (inches, right axis 0–4.0) by month from January to December. Labels: "average monthly precipitation", "average monthly temperature". X-axis months: Jan., Feb., Mar., April, May, June, July, Aug., Sep., Oct., Nov., Dec. Y-axis labels: "Average Monthly Temperature" and "Average Monthly Precipitation".)

Think and Apply

1. What two kinds of information are shown by a **climograph?**

2. During which months in Nome, Alaska is the average daily temperature below freezing—32°F or 0°C?

3. What month gets the most precipitation in Nome?

4. In Holyoke, Colorado, what is the warmest month? The wettest month?

3,000 years ago | 2,000 years ago

3,000 years ago
Mound Builders culture develops east of the Mississippi River

2,500 years ago
Inuit reach Alaska from Asia

2,000 years ago
The Anasazi culture develops in the Southwest

Early American Cultures

PREVIEW

Focus on the Main Idea
Early cultures developed in different parts of North America.

PLACES
Cahokia
Four Corners
Mesa Verde

VOCABULARY
ceremony
mesa
drought

PEOPLE
Nampeyo

 You Are There You're looking out the window of the plane as you fly over southwestern Ohio. All of a sudden something amazing catches your eye. You see what looks like a huge snake that seems to be slithering its way across the countryside. It looks as if it is built out of mounds of soil. It's probably about three feet high, as tall as you may have been in kindergarten or first grade.

What in the world can this be, you wonder. Is it an unusual landform? You think it must have been built by people. But who would have built it, and why? Was it built recently or long ago? What is this mysterious mound?

▶ **Great Serpent Mound in Ohio.**

Summarize As you read, look for details to help you summarize information about the different cultures that developed in North America.

The Mound Builders

The snake-like mound that you just read about is real. Called the Great Serpent Mound, it is near Hillsboro, Ohio. It was built more than 1,000 years ago by people often called the Mound Builders. They were one of several early American Indian groups that once flourished in North America, and then disappeared. Today we find signs of towns that no longer exist in many parts of our continent.

The Mound Builders culture began about 3,000 years ago and lasted about 2,500 years. Most Mound Builders lived east of the Mississippi River. The land there is rich in forests, fertile soil, lakes, and rivers. The Mound Builders were farmers who lived in settled communities. Their main crop was corn.

The Mound Builders were not a single group of people. The three main groups were the Adena, Hopewell, and Mississippians. They built thousands of mounds, in many different shapes. At **Cahokia** (kuh HO kee uh) in present-day Illinois, a mound rises 100 feet, as tall as a 10-story building.

Some mounds were burial places for important chiefs. Some, like the Great Serpent Mound, may have been built to honor animal spirits that were part of the Mound Builders' religion. Many of the mounds had platforms where religious or other ceremonies were held. A **ceremony** is an activity done for a special purpose or event, such as a birth, wedding, or death.

The Mound Builders left many clues about their way of life for archaeologists to study. Being able to build such enormous structures shows that they were well organized. Hundreds or even thousands of workers had to be directed to dig up tons of earth with the hand tools available. Then the earth had to be moved—often over long distances—to a mound location. Finally, workers had to create the shape the builder planned.

Artifacts also tell us that trade was important to their builders. Knives found in mounds were carved from a rock called obsidian that came from the Rocky Mountains, hundreds of miles to the west. Seashells used in jewelry came from the Gulf of Mexico, hundreds of miles to the south. Copper came hundreds of miles from near the Great Lakes, to the north. Mica, a glittering mineral the people of Cahokia prized, came from the Appalachian Mountains far to the east.

REVIEW What do the mounds tell us about the culture of the people who built them? **Summarize**

▶ **This mound can be seen today at Cahokia Mounds State Historic Site in Illinois.**

The Anasazi and Mound Builders

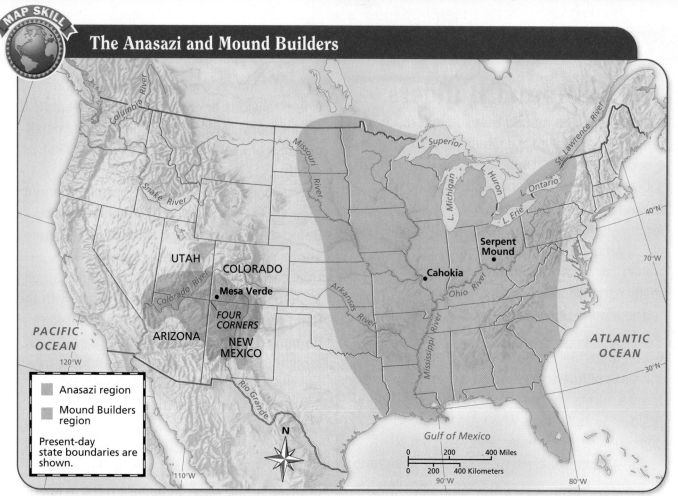

▶ The Anasazi and Mound Builders established early cultures in what today is the United States.

MAP SKILL Human-Environment Interaction *What major rivers could the Mound Builders have used for water and travel?*

The Anasazi

Another early farming group, called the Anasazi (ahn uh SAH zee), lived in what is today the Southwest of the United States. Their name is a Navajo Indian word for "the old ones." Anasazi communities were located in an area today called the **Four Corners.** Four present-day states come together here. Find this area on the map on this page. What are the four states? The Anasazi lived in this area from about the year 100 to about 1300.

The Anasazi grew corn, squash, beans, and pumpkins. Like the Mound Builders, they lived in permanent communities. Although the climate of the Four Corners region is dry, it did not limit the Anasazi's farming. They dug ditches to carry water from streams to the crops in their fields. The Anasazi were the first people to use irrigation in what would become the United States.

The Anasazi are also known as the "Cliff Dwellers" because they sometimes carved houses into the sides of cliffs. They also built apartment-style buildings several stories high on the top of mesas. A **mesa** is a high, flat landform that rises steeply from the land around it. *Mesa* means "table" in Spanish.

Let's visit the Anasazi community of **Mesa Verde,** in present-day Colorado. Here you can see a large village built into steep cliffs. If you look up, you see large overhanging rocks. These protect the people from bad weather as well as from attack by their enemies.

▶ **Today the Cliff Palace and other Anasazi cliff dwellings are protected as part of Mesa Verde National Park.**

The largest building is the Cliff Palace, which has about 150 rooms. It also has 23 kivas, which are large underground rooms. Kivas are important to Anasazi religion. They are where religious ceremonies are held. Only men are allowed to enter a kiva.

All around you, people are using beautiful woven baskets. They are so tightly and expertly woven that they can even hold water and be used for cooking. Hot coals are put into the baskets with corn that has been ground into flour, beans, and other foods to make a stew.

Anasazi culture reached its height in the 1100s. But then something mysterious happened. The Anasazi suddenly abandoned their villages in the Four Corners region. Why did they leave? Where did they go? No one knows for sure.

One theory is that a **drought,** or a long period without rain, forced them to leave. Streams dried up and irrigation became impossible. The Anasazi had to move to places where there was enough water for farming.

Historians believe that the Pueblo peoples of today's Southwest, including the Hopi, are descended from the Anasazi. In the Biography feature on page 65, you can read about a Pueblo woman named **Nampeyo** who found a way to re-create the ancient way of making pottery.

REVIEW What is a possible cause for the disappearance of the Anasazi from the Four Corners region? **Cause and Effect**

HERE AND THERE Cliff Dwellers in China

The Anasazi were not the only people to carve "apartments" into cliffs. In about the year 400, Buddhists were carving buildings into the cliffs at Bezeklik in northwestern China. The cliff structures shown here were monasteries, or places where Buddhists lived and studied the teachings of their religion. The monasteries also served as a resting place for traveling merchants.

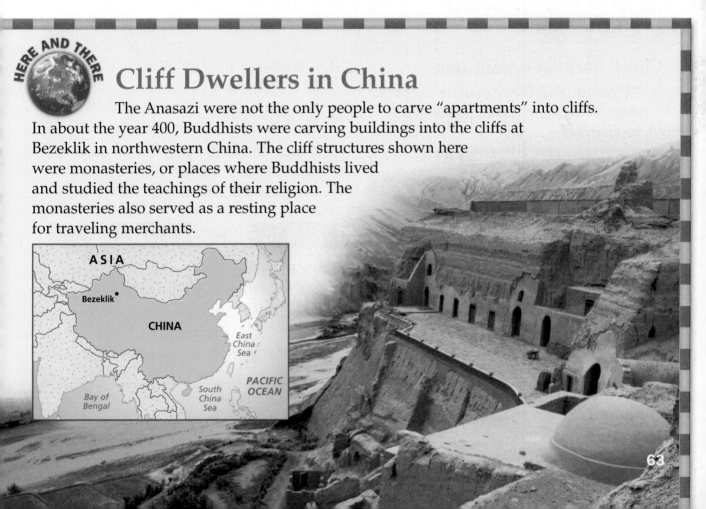

ASIA

Bezeklik

CHINA

East China Sea

Bay of Bengal

South China Sea

PACIFIC OCEAN

The Inuit

Far to the north, in what is today Canada, live people who call themselves Inuit (IN oo it), meaning "the people." Like the first Americans, the Inuit traveled from Asia to North America. But the Inuit came much later, probably about 2,500 years ago. Today they make their homes across the frozen lands near the Arctic Ocean, from Alaska through Canada and on to Greenland.

▶ The Inuit are known for their beautiful crafts, such as this sculpture of an owl.

The Inuit adapted to life in the cold climate. They hunted whales, walruses, and seals in the Arctic waters. They developed the kayak, a light, one-person boat that is used for hunting and transportation. In the winter some Inuit still build traditional houses called igloos from blocks of packed snow.

REVIEW What do the Inuit have in common with the first Americans?
Compare and Contrast

Summarize the Lesson

- **3,000 years ago** American Indian groups began building mounds in eastern North America.

- **2,500 years ago** Inuit reached Alaska from Asia.

- **2,000 years ago** The Anasazi culture developed in the Southwest.

LESSON 2 REVIEW

Check Facts and Main Ideas

1. ⟳ Summarize On a separate sheet of paper, fill in the missing details that support the summary.

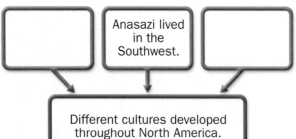

Anasazi lived in the Southwest.

Different cultures developed throughout North America.

2. Why did the people known as Mound Builders build mounds?

3. Explain how the Anasazi were able to farm in the desert.

4. How did the Inuit adapt to life in the cold climate near the Arctic Ocean?

5. **Critical Thinking: *Compare and Contrast*** Compare and contrast the cultures of the Mound Builders, Anasazi, and Inuit.

Link to ⟷ Writing

Write a Letter Write a letter to a government official encouraging the protection of an ancient site such as Great Serpent Mound. Use a vocabulary word in your letter.

Nampeyo
About 1860–1942

As a young Pueblo girl, Nampeyo helped her mother dig for clay to make the jars and bowls her family used. Nampeyo lived near the ruins of what was once a Hopi village. The ruins were covered with shards, pieces of broken pottery from long ago. These pots were decorated in ways that had been forgotten. By studying the shards and whole pots that were found, Nampeyo was able to teach herself the forgotten pottery art of the people who lived there long ago.

Nampeyo figured out where to find the clay and how to bake it to create the special sunshine-colored yellow of the ancient pottery. She mixed paints made from plants found in the area to create different colors. Then she decorated her pots with designs inspired by the ancient pottery. She told a visitor:

BIOFACT

Although she was a famous potter, Nampeyo never signed her pots.

"I used to go to the ancient village and pick up pieces of pottery and copy the designs. That is how I learned to paint. But now I just close my eyes and I see designs and I paint them."

By the early 1900s, Nampeyo had begun to lose her eyesight. She eventually went blind. She continued making pottery, along with her children and grandchildren. One grandchild, Tonita Hamilton Nampeyo, said:

"That's the most important thing, to keep tradition alive."

Learn from Biographies

How did Nampeyo's work keep tradition alive?

For more information, go online to *Meet the People* at **www.sfsocialstudies.com**.

3,000 years ago
Mayan civilization starts to develop

About A.D. 900
Mayan civilization declines

About 1200
Aztec and Incan civilizations develop

Tenochtitlan • Copán

Cuzco •

PREVIEW

Focus on the Main Idea
Powerful civilizations developed and spread in Mexico, Central America, and South America.

PLACES
Valley of Mexico
Tenochtitlan
Cuzco

VOCABULARY
civilization
surplus
specialize
pyramid
empire
tribute
slavery

The Rise of Empires

You Are There

This morning, you left your farm to journey to Copán. Built in the rain forest of Central America, it is just one of at least a hundred Mayan cities in Mexico and Central America. You have come today to attend a funeral ceremony for your ruler. As you walk along, you begin to see a tower in the city center where he will be buried.

Wall carvings celebrating his life will line the tomb. Precious goods will be buried with him—including jade jewelry, finely woven and decorated baskets, and exotic feathers. You step up your pace to get there in time to honor your dead king.

Summarize As you read, look for details to help you summarize the ways of life of the major empires in the Americas.

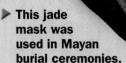

▶ This jade mask was used in Mayan burial ceremonies.

The Maya

The burial scene at Copán might have taken place around the year 400, as the Mayan civilization was reaching its peak. A **civilization** is a culture with organized systems of government, religion, and learning. The Maya settled in present-day Mexico about 3,000 years ago. They were farmers who cut down the thick forest to create open fields, where they grew corn and other crops.

The Maya were such successful farmers that they began to grow a **surplus,** or more food than they needed to feed their own families. People with extra food could trade it for things they needed. As a result, not everyone had to farm. Some Maya began to **specialize** (SPESH uh lize), or do only one kind of job. People began to develop skills such as basket weaving, jewelry making, and stone carving.

Specializing helped the Maya to develop a complex civilization with many achievements. Some Maya specialized in studying the world around them and developing new ideas. For example, some devoted themselves to studying the movements of the sun, moon, stars, and planets. What they learned helped them develop an extremely accurate calendar. Other Maya became skilled at mathematics. They were among the first people to use the number zero.

Other Maya specialized in building. They developed methods to build tall pyramids.

A **pyramid** is a building with three or more sides shaped like triangles that slant toward a point at the top. At the top of the Mayan pyramids were temples where religious ceremonies were held. As you have read, Mayan kings were buried in pyramids.

The Maya also developed a system of writing. They recorded their history and what they learned about mathematics and science. Though we cannot read all of their writing, what we can read adds to our knowledge of their civilization.

Mayan civilization began to decline as early as the year 750. By 900, the Maya had deserted most of their cities. Eventually, the forest grew back, completely covering them over. Today, however, descendants of the Maya continue to live in Mexico and Central America.

REVIEW What effect did specialization have on Mayan civilization? **Cause and Effect**

▶ **The Maya carved writing symbols into stone tablets like the one below. The larger photograph shows the pyramid at Chichen Itza, in today's Mexico.**

The Aztecs and the Inca

In about 1200, people called the Aztecs began to migrate south from northern Mexico. According to legend, they were following the instructions of one of their gods, who told them to travel until they saw an eagle with a snake in its beak sitting on a cactus. There, he said, they should settle. When the Aztecs reached an island in Lake Texcoco, they at last saw what they had been searching for. Here, in the Valley of Mexico, they built Tenochtitlan (te noch tee TLAHN), meaning "near the cactus." Today the eagle, cactus, and snake appear as the central symbols on the flag of the country of Mexico.

Tenochtitlan grew into a great city. Causeways, or low bridges, linked Tenochtitlan to the land around the lake. As many as 300,000 people lived there, making it one of the largest cities in the world.

In order to have more land for farming, Tenochtitlan farmers created "floating gardens" around their island city. Farmers on other Aztec lands developed irrigation systems and created more farmland by carving terraces, or wide, flattened steps, into hillsides.

From Tenochtitlan, the Aztecs sent out armies to conquer other peoples in the Valley of Mexico. Soon they had created an empire that stretched from the Atlantic to the Pacific oceans. An empire is a group of lands and peoples ruled by one leader.

The Aztecs forced the peoples they conquered to pay them tribute. Tribute is the payment demanded by rulers from the people they rule. Each year people in the Aztec Empire had to send gold, silver, and precious stones, as well as food, clothing, and weapons as tribute to Tenochtitlan.

The Aztecs also demanded to be given people as tribute. They enslaved people given to them as tribute as well as prisoners captured in war. Slavery is the practice of holding people against their will and taking away their freedom.

Like the Maya, the Aztecs worshipped many gods. Chief among them was Huitzilopochtli (we tsee loh POHCH tlee), the god of war. The Aztecs believed that they

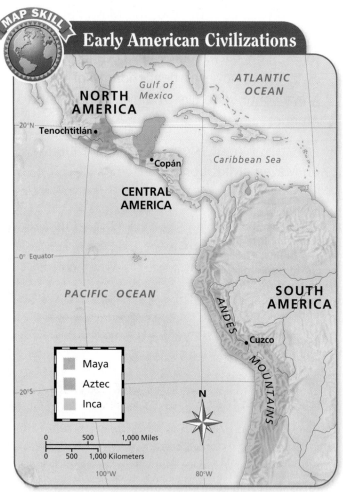

MAP SKILL

Early American Civilizations

ATLANTIC OCEAN

Gulf of Mexico

NORTH AMERICA

20°N · Tenochtitlán

· Copán

Caribbean Sea

CENTRAL AMERICA

0° Equator

PACIFIC OCEAN

SOUTH AMERICA

ANDES MOUNTAINS

· Cuzco

20°S

Maya
Aztec
Inca

N

| 0 | 500 | 1,000 Miles |
| 0 | 500 | 1,000 Kilometers |

100°W   80°W

▶ The Aztecs, Maya, and Inca were three powerful early cultures in the Americas.

MAP SKILL Place *Which mountain range was located in the Incan homeland?*

Painting by Diego Rivera

▶ **Tenochtitlan was one of the largest cities in the world.**

had to worship Huitzilopochtli by offering him human blood. Slaves and prisoners were sacrificed to the god. To sacrifice is to kill a person or an animal for a religious purpose.

At the same time as the Aztecs ruled central Mexico, the Incan Empire rose in South America. Like the Aztecs, the Inca created their empire through conquests.

The Inca built thousands of miles of roads to link all parts of the empire to their capital at **Cuzco** (KUH skoh) in present-day Peru. Government messengers could travel to the empire's far corners at a rate of 140 miles a day. That was probably the fastest communication system anywhere in the world at that time.

REVIEW What did the Inca and Aztecs have in common? *Compare and Contrast*

Summarize the Lesson

3000 years ago Mayan civilization began to develop.

about 900 Mayan civilization declined and the Maya began leaving their cities.

about 1200 Aztec civilization began in Mexico and the Incan civilization began in South America.

LESSON 3 REVIEW

Check Facts and Main Ideas

1. 🔄 **Summarize** On a separate sheet of paper, fill in the details to the summary about the Mayan, Aztec, and Incan **civilizations.**

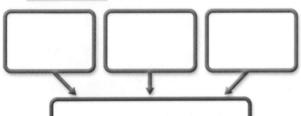

Early empires developed organized ways of life.

2. Name two achievements of the Mayan civilization.

3. What role did war play in the growth of the Aztec **Empire?**

4. How was the vast Incan Empire united?

5. **Critical Thinking:** *Compare and Contrast* How were the civilizations of the Maya, Aztecs, and Inca similar? How were they different?

Link to ⚭ Mathematics

Research the Zero Use the Internet to learn more about the development of the zero. Write a report telling why it was such an important discovery.

Aztecs, Maya, and Inca

Three great civilizations developed in Mexico, Central America, and South America. Their achievements included masterpieces of architecture, spectacular cities, and vast systems of trade. How were the civilizations alike? How did they differ?

Stone sculpture of
Aztec head

Incan Empire
clay portrait jar

The Aztecs

The Aztecs were a wandering people before they settled in the Valley of Mexico on swampy land in Lake Texcoco and founded Tenochtitlan. It grew in size and importance until it became the capital of the mighty Aztec Empire.

The Inca

The Incan Empire developed in the Andes Mountains when the Inca conquered the area around the city of Cuzco and made it their capital. Their roads and government system helped the Inca keep control over their vast empire.

Wooden cup, or kero, with
decoration of Incan man
holding spear and shield

Maya clay sculpture of powerful man

Large, heavy earplugs

Ornate necklace

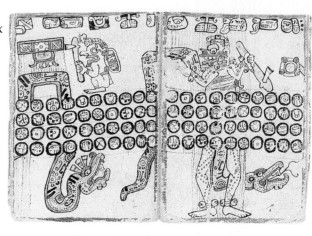

Mayan codex

Mayan Learning

The Maya made great advances in astronomy and mathematics. They also developed a system of writing. The Mayan codices, or books, that exist today, however, tell us little of their history. They focus on subjects such as religious ceremonies, astronomy, and calendars.

The Maya

The Maya shared a common culture and religion, but they did not have a single capital city or ruler. Each city governed itself and had its own ruler. Small Mayan sculptures, like this one, have been a great source of information on the life and customs of the Maya people.

The Founding of Tenochtitlan

This page of the *Codex Mendoza*, a book telling the history of the Aztecs, illustrates the founding of Tenochtitlan. Mexico City is built on the same site.

71

Chapter Summary

 Target Skill

Summarize

On a separate sheet of paper, complete the graphic organizer by writing a summary of the details from the chapter.

> The Anasazi developed a culture based on farming in the Southwest.

> Specialization helped the Maya develop a complex civilization in present-day Mexico.

> The Aztecs built a powerful empire in central Mexico.

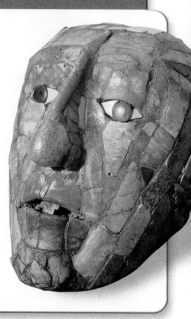

Vocabulary

Match each word with the correct definition.

1 migrate (p. 55)

2 artifact (p. 56)

3 civilization (p. 67)

4 drought (p. 63)

5 tribute (p. 68)

a. object made in the past

b. culture with organized systems of government, religion, and learning

c. payment demanded by rulers from their people

d. a long period without rain

e. to move to a different place

Terms and Places

Each number below has a vocabulary word and a place from the chapter. Use them together in a sentence to explain something about one of the cultures you read about.

1 empire, Tenochtitlan (p. 68)

2 mesa, Four Corners (p. 62)

3 Ice Age, Bering Strait (p. 55)

4 ceremony, Cahokia (p. 61)

5 specialize, Copán (p. 67)

3,000 years ago
Mayan civilization starts to develop

2,500 years ago
Inuit reach Alaska from Asia

2,000 years ago
Anasazi culture develops in the Southwest

About 1200
Aztec and Incan civilizations develop

Facts and Main Ideas

1 Why did hunters probably cross the land bridge from Asia into North America thousands of years ago?

2 How were the Anasazi able to grow crops in the dry lands of the Southwest?

3 How did the Aztec Empire grow and become powerful?

4 **Time Line** About how many years were there between the development of agriculture in North America and the beginning of the Anasazi culture?

5 **Main Idea** How did the first people in the Americas get food?

6 **Main Idea** Describe three early cultures that developed in North America.

7 **Main Idea** What three powerful civilizations grew up in the Americas south of the area that is now the United States?

8 **Critical Thinking:** *Draw Conclusions*
How did specialization play a part in the development of civilizations in the Americas?

Write About History

1 **Write a short story** about a person your age in one of the civilizations discussed in this chapter.

2 **Write a travel advertisement** encouraging people to visit Mayan or Aztec pyramids today.

3 **Write a mystery story** about the disappearance of the Mayan culture.

Apply Skills

Use Climographs
Study the climograph for Anchorage, Alaska, below. Then use the climograph to answer the questions that follow.

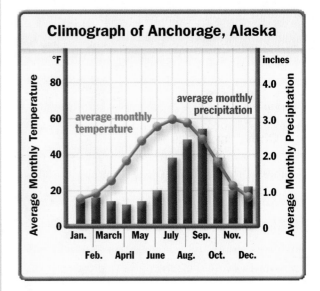

Climograph of Anchorage, Alaska

average monthly temperature

average monthly precipitation

°F / Average Monthly Temperature: 80, 60, 40, 20, 0
inches / Average Monthly Precipitation: 4.0, 3.0, 2.0, 1.0, 0

Jan. Feb. March April May June July Aug. Sep. Oct. Nov. Dec.

1 In which month is the average precipitation highest?

2 Which month is usually coldest?

3 Describe an average day in May in Anchorage.

Internet Activity

To get help with vocabulary, people, and terms, select dictionary or encyclopedia from *Social Studies Library* at **www.sfsocialstudies.com**.

Native Americans of North America

Late 1500s

Iroquois lands
Five tribes join to form the Iroquois League.

Lesson 1

1

Late 1700s

Cheyenne lands
The Cheyenne use of horses brings changes to their way of life.

Lesson 2

2

Today

Hopi lands
Hopi villages include Oraibi, probably the oldest town in the United States.

Lesson 3

3

Today

Kwakiutl lands
Potlatches are held among the Kwakiutl and other Northwest Coast Indians.

Lesson 4

4

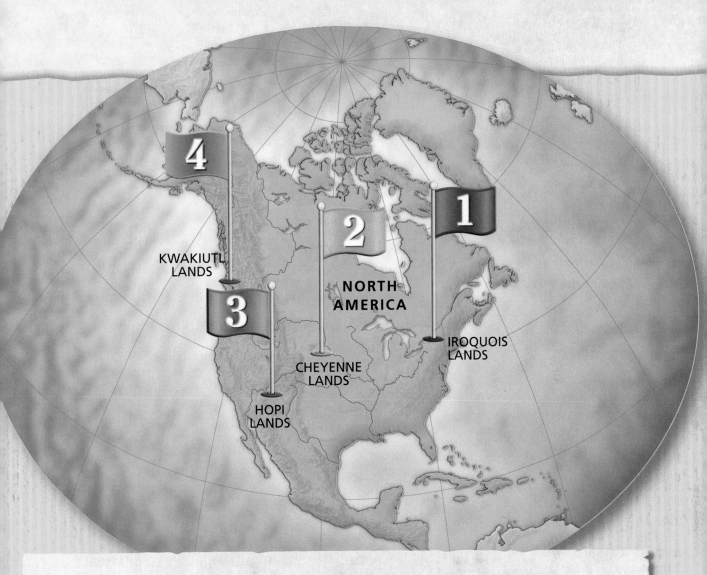

Why We Remember

Alabama, Illinois, Massachusetts, Mississippi.

What do these state names have in common? All are names of groups of Native Americans, the first people to live in what is now the United States. At one time all the rivers, mountains, valleys, and plains of this country had Native American names. Now our place names show many different heritages—English, Spanish, French, and others. But the Native American names live on, as do the Native American peoples themselves.

1000
2000

Late 1500s
Five tribes join to form the Iroquois League

Today
50,000 Iroquois live in Canada and the United States

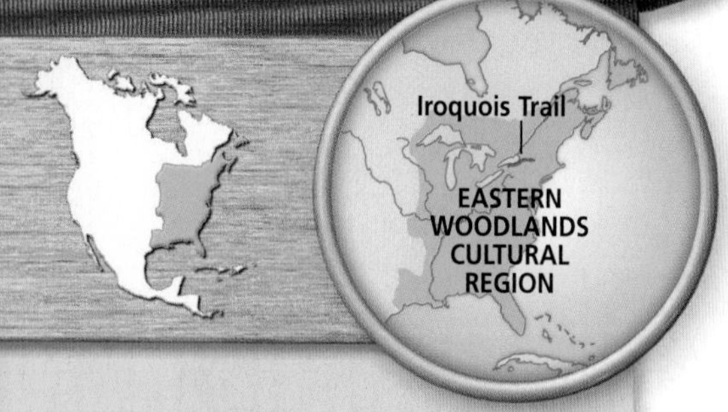

Iroquois Trail

EASTERN WOODLANDS CULTURAL REGION

The Eastern Woodlands

PREVIEW

Focus on the Main Idea
People of the Eastern Woodlands developed a variety of cultures based on hunting and farming.

PLACES
Iroquois Trail
Eastern Woodlands cultural region

PEOPLE
Deganawidah
Hiawatha

VOCABULARY
tribe
league
cultural region
longhouse
wampum
reservation

▶ Hiawatha

You Are There The campfire crackles and glows before you. An old man rises to tell a legend.

Long ago, he begins, your people often went to war. The battles were bloody and cost many lives. But then a man named Deganawidah (day gahn uh WEE duh) had a vision. He told the warring groups to stop their endless battling. They should agree to deal fairly with one another and establish a lasting peace.

The old man continues the legend by telling of Hiawatha (high uh WAH thuh), who convinced five warring groups to join together in a "Great Peace." People of the five groups buried their weapons. Over these weapons Deganawidah planted a magnificent white pine called the "Tree of Peace."

Summarize As you read, look for ways to summarize the ways of life of people who lived in the Eastern Woodlands.

The Iroquois

The legends about **Deganawidah** and **Hiawatha** are part of the early history told by the Iroquois (IR uh koy) people. The five groups were tribes of American Indians. A **tribe**—a group of families bound together under a single leadership—is a term often used to describe people who share a common culture.

The five tribes were the Seneca, Cayuga, Onondaga, Oneida, and Mohawk. Scholars think that in about 1580, these tribes came together to create the Iroquois League. A **league** is an organization that people form which unites them for a particular purpose. Later, a sixth tribe, the Tuscarora, joined the Iroquois league.

The five tribes sent 50 representatives—all men—to a Great Council. This council made decisions for the League as a whole. The older women of the tribes chose—and could remove—these representatives.

The **Iroquois Trail** linked the lands of the League. Find it on the map below. Today, the New York Thruway follows part of the route of the Iroquois Trail.

The Iroquois lived in the **Eastern Woodlands cultural region** of North America. It is just one of several regions that you will study in this chapter. Native American tribes within each of these regions developed similar cultures, using the resources of their environments. Each different one is a **cultural region**—an area in which people with similar cultures live.

REVIEW How did the tribes of the Iroquois League work together to govern themselves? **Main Idea and Details**

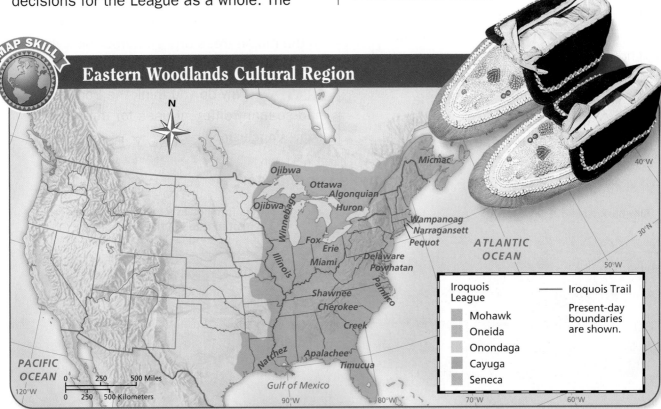

Eastern Woodlands Cultural Region

MAP SKILL

N

Ojibwa
Ottawa
Algonquian
Ojibwa
Huron
Winnebago
Micmac
Wampanoag
Narragansett
Pequot
Fox
Erie
Delaware
Miami
Powhatan
Illinois
Pamlico
Shawnee
Cherokee
Creek
Natchez
Apalachee
Timucua

ATLANTIC OCEAN

PACIFIC OCEAN

Gulf of Mexico

40°W
30°N
50°W
60°W
70°W
80°W
90°W
120°W

0   250   500 Miles
0   250   500 Kilometers

Iroquois League
- Mohawk
- Oneida
- Onondaga
- Cayuga
- Seneca

—— Iroquois Trail

Present-day boundaries are shown.

▶ The Iroquois, who created moccasins such as those above, lived in the Eastern Woodlands cultural region.

MAP SKILL Use Directions *In which directions did the Iroquois Trail lead?*

Living in the Woodlands

The Eastern Woodlands region provided rich resources for the Iroquois and other woodland people. Thick forests offered nearly endless supplies of wood. People hunted animals that were plentiful in the area—such as deer, bear, elk, and beaver—for food. They used the skins and furs of these animals for clothing. Thousands of lakes, rivers, and streams provided water and fish. Native Americans grew such crops as corn, beans, and squash in the fertile soil.

Look at the diagram on this page. It shows a **longhouse,** an Iroquois building used for shelter. Young trees provided poles for the frame, and slabs of elm bark served as walls. You may be wondering why it was called a longhouse. It could be as long as 150 feet, half of a football field. Each longhouse was divided into living areas for as many as 12 different families. Rows of shared cooking fires were placed in a center aisle of the longhouse. An Iroquois village or town could have as many as 150 longhouses.

The Iroquois called themselves the Haudenosaunee (hoo dee noh SHAW nee), which means "People of the Longhouse."

The name *Iroquois* originally came from other tribes, speakers of the Algonquian (al GONG kwee in) language. Algonquian speakers included the Wampanoag, Powhatan, and Pequot.

The Iroquois also used trees to make their swift birch-bark canoes. They bent birch saplings to make the frame. They then stretched wide strips of bark over the frame. First they used sharp, pointed tools called bone awls to punch holes in the bark. Then they used bone needles to sew the pieces together. Finally, they covered the seams with tree gum to make the canoes watertight.

The Iroquois used the woodlands for both food and clothing. For example, men hunted for deer. They used the animal hides for clothing and the meat for food. Women tanned the hides and sewed them into shirts and leggings. They also cleared parts of the woodlands of trees to make fields for crops. In spring, they attached birch-bark containers to the maple trees and gathered the sap for maple syrup.

REVIEW Why do you think the Iroquois had so many different uses for trees?
Draw Conclusions

An Iroquois Longhouse

Elm-bark covering

Cobs of corn drying on storage racks in roof rafters

All families in a longhouse were related through the women

Poles for the frame

▶ This model shows an eight-family Iroquois longhouse. There were four shared cooking fires along the central aisle.

DIAGRAM SKILL *Where were the drying cobs of corn kept?*

Iroquois Beliefs and Customs

Like other Native Americans, the Iroquois felt a deep connection to the animals, the trees, and other resources around them. When an Iroquois hunter killed a deer, he knelt beside it and spoke to it. He thanked it for the food and clothing it would provide for his family. Only then did the hunter take out his skinning knife.

At harvest time, the Iroquois gave thanks for their crops:

> *"Great Spirit in heaven, we salute you with our thanks, that you have preserved so many of us for another year, to participate in the ceremonies of this occasion."*

The photograph on this page shows **wampum,** polished seashells that were hung on strings or woven into belts. Wampum was highly valued by the Iroquois. A wampum belt might serve as a gift to honor a marriage. It might be given to comfort someone after the death of a loved one. Some belts were created to symbolize an important event. Wampum could even be used as an invitation to peaceful talks.

▶ Iroquois wampum belts could be many feet long.

REVIEW How did the Iroquois show appreciation for nature's resources?
🔄 Summarize

▶ Iroquois people sang and danced to the rhythms of rattles and drums. This rattle was made from a turtle shell.

Literature and Social Studies

The Rabbit Dance

This Mohawk story, *The Rabbit Dance*, shows the Iroquois respect for nature. It tells of a group of hunters who see a giant rabbit, but decide not to kill it. In return, the rabbit teaches them a dance. One Iroquois explains:

The Rabbit Chief has given us this special dance so that we can honor its people for all that they give to the human beings. If we play their song and do their dance, then they will know we are grateful for all they continue to give us. We must call this new song The Rabbit Dance and we must do it, men and women together, to honor the Rabbit People.

So it was that a new social dance was given to the Iroquois people. To this day the Rabbit Dance is done to thank the Rabbit People for all they have given, not only food and clothing, but also a fine dance that makes the people glad.

▶ A "high iron" Mohawk man works on a New York City skyscraper.

The Iroquois Today

There are about 50,000 Iroquois today. Many live on reservations —land set aside by the United States government for Native Americans—in northern New York state. Fifty members still form its Great Council. They meet a few miles south of Syracuse, New York, on the Onondaga reservation.

League members, mainly from the Mohawk tribe, have become skilled builders of city skyscrapers. They are known as "high iron" men, putting up girders as high as a thousand feet above the ground.

REVIEW What opportunities draw Iroquois to cities today? **Draw Conclusions**

Summarize the Lesson

- Five Iroquois tribes came together to form the Iroquois League.
- Iroquois people used their surrounding resources of the Eastern Woodlands to meet their needs.
- The Iroquois showed appreciation for nature in different ways.

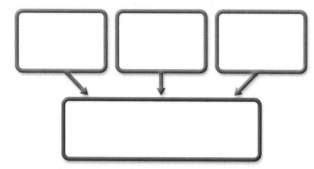

LESSON 1   REVIEW

Check Facts and Main Ideas

1. ↺ **Summarize** On a separate piece of paper, fill out the chart below. Choose the most important details from the lesson and organize them into a brief sentence.

```
┌──────────┐  ┌──────────┐  ┌──────────┐
│          │  │          │  │          │
│          │  │          │  │          │
└────┬─────┘  └────┬─────┘  └────┬─────┘
     │             │             │
     └─────────┐   │   ┌─────────┘
            ┌──▼───▼───▼──┐
            │             │
            │             │
            └─────────────┘
```

2. How did the Iroquois **League** make decisions?

3. How did the **tribes** of the Eastern Woodlands use natural resources to support themselves?

4. **Critical Thinking: *Point of View*** Explain the point of view of Deganawidah and Hiawatha about cooperation among the five tribes.

5. Where do the Iroquois live today?

Link to — ∞ — Writing

Solve Problems Suppose you are an Iroquois representative at the Great Council. Write about the different problems that might arise among the tribes. What are your ideas to solve the problems?

Theresa Hayward Bell *Born 1952*

When she was in the tenth grade Theresa Hayward lived with her grandmother, Elizabeth George, on the Mashantucket (mash in TUCK it) Pequot lands. In the early 1600s, members of the Mashantucket Pequot, an Algonquian-speaking tribe, lived on their traditional lands in what today is Connecticut. After the Europeans arrived, wars and diseases took the lives of many Pequots. Over the centuries, the Mashantucket Pequots struggled to keep their lands, even as many members left the reservation to find work. In the 1970s Elizabeth George was one of only two people living on the reservation. She encouraged other tribal members to move back, to "hold on to the land."

Theresa Hayward Bell was one of the first to answer her grandmother's call.

"As I got older something I wanted to do, always, from my heart, was to educate people and let them know that the Pequot were alive. We're right here."

Today there is again a thriving community on the Mashantucket Pequot lands. Hayward Bell helped to start businesses so the Pequots could afford to build housing and other things they needed. Later, she and others started a newspaper, *The Pequot Times*, and a museum. Today Hayward Bell is the Director of the Mashantucket Pequot Museum & Research Center. People from all around the world can visit and learn the continuing history of the Pequots and other Native American tribes.

BIOFACT

Native American artifacts, like this cornhusk doll, are on display in the Mashantucket Pequot Museum.

Learn from Biographies

How did Theresa Hayward Bell help fulfill her grandmother's vision?

For more information, go online to *Meet the People* at **www.sfsocialstudies.com**

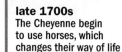

1500   2000

late 1700s
The Cheyenne begin to use horses, which changes their way of life

Today
About 12,000 Cheyenne live on the Great Plains

Lame Deer •

GREAT PLAINS CULTURAL REGION

The Great Plains

PREVIEW

Focus on the Main Idea
The culture of the Great Plains people changed after the horse was introduced.

PLACES
Great Plains cultural region
Lame Deer, Montana

VOCABULARY
lodge
tepee
travois
powwow

You Are There What could that strange creature have been? You've never seen anything like it. Was it a very big dog? Was it a deer without antlers? How powerfully it ran! And how fast!

"Go out onto the grassy plain," your mother had told you earlier. "Find some small game and bring them back to the village for me to cook." So you set out with your bow and a bag of arrows over your shoulder. Suddenly, this strange animal appears, then races off into the distance. You forget all about hunting game. Instead, you race back to your village to report your mysterious sighting.

The creature that startled you was a horse. It is the first one you and your people have ever seen. But it certainly will not be the last. Before long, the horse will change your people's way of life.

Cause and Effect As you read, determine the reasons Plains Native Americans chose to live in certain ways and why they sometimes changed these ways.

Life on the Plains

The scene described in "You Are There" might have taken place in the **Great Plains cultural region** of North America. The Great Plains was—and still is—a fairly flat region. Hundreds of years ago, much of it was covered with a sea of grass, waving in ever-blowing wind. Unlike the Eastern Woodlands, few trees grew on the dry Great Plains. But millions of buffalo grazed the huge area.

Tribes of the Great Plains include the Lakota, also known as the Sioux, as well as the Pawnee, and Osage. Among the later arrivals were the Cheyenne, an Algonquian-speaking people.

For a long time, most Plains people followed a farming and hunting life. Because much of the land was dry, they settled their villages along rivers. Here they could get water for their crops—corn, beans, squash, and pumpkins. They built **lodges** to live in. These were large, round huts built over a deep hole. The walls of a lodge were made of earth, packed over a wood frame.

The plentiful buffalo were central to the lives of the Plains Indians. People used these animals as a major source of meat. The people made buffalo hides into articles like clothing and blankets. They carved buffalo horns into bowls. They even used the stomachs of buffalos, hung from four poles, as cooking pots for stew.

In summer and fall, groups of Plains Indians traveled to hunt the massive beasts. A buffalo could weigh well over a ton and could run very fast. The hunters were on foot. It was difficult for them to get close enough to use their bows and arrows. Plains Indians could kill their prey by crouching near them in an animal disguise, or by getting the buffalo to stampede over a cliff.

While on the hunt, people lived in **tepees.** To make a tepee, women set up poles in a circle, their tops coming together at a point. Then they covered the frame with buffalo hides. People also used the poles to transport buffalo meat and other goods. They made a **travois** (truh VOY) by lashing the load to two poles. Dogs then pulled the travois. A travois's load could weigh about 75 pounds.

REVIEW How did village life differ from life during a hunt? **Compare and Contrast**

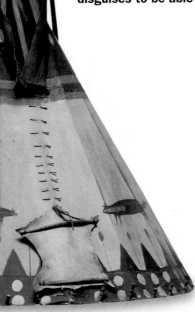

▶ Native Americans lived in tepees on the Great Plains. Hunters often used disguises to be able to approach buffalo herds without being seen.

Great Plains Cultural Region

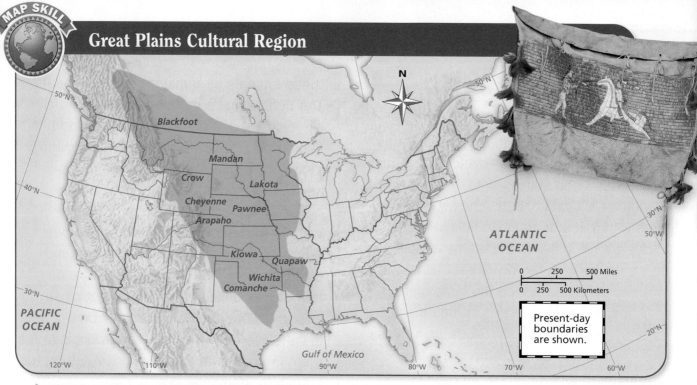

Blackfoot

Mandan

Crow

Lakota

Cheyenne

Pawnee

Arapaho

Kiowa

Quapaw

Wichita

Comanche

ATLANTIC OCEAN

PACIFIC OCEAN

Gulf of Mexico

0   250   500 Miles
0   250   500 Kilometers

Present-day boundaries are shown.

▶ **Women of the Great Plains cultural region often made saddlebags, like the one above, with porcupine quills.**

MAP SKILL Region *How would you describe the location of this region?*

The Cheyenne

In the 1500s, people from Spain brought the horse to the regions of the Aztec and Maya in Mexico. The tribes living near Spanish settlements were the first to learn of the horse. Some horses broke free and wandered north. In the late 1700s, the Cheyenne tamed some of the descendants of these horses which had become wild. The Cheyenne also got horses by raiding other tribes and by trading. Using the horse, the Cheyenne changed their way of life. Buffalo hunting became a major way to gain food.

The horse made buffalo hunting much easier. Mounted on a swift horse, a single Cheyenne hunter could ride close to a herd of buffalo. Then, he could use his bow and arrow to kill the animals. Later on, Plains hunters also used guns to hunt.

The horse also made the Cheyenne settlements much more mobile, or easy to move. A horse-drawn travois could move four times as much weight as a travois pulled by a dog. And horses could move twice as fast. Now Cheyenne women could more easily move tepees and set up new camps. The Cheyenne developed a way of life based on moving to different places in different seasons. They now referred to the past as the time "when we had only dogs for moving camp."

The horse became so important to the Cheyenne and other Plains people that they measured wealth in horses. Sometimes tribes raided other tribes to capture horses. Riders became skilled in war as well as in hunting.

REVIEW How did the Cheyenne change the way they hunted buffalo after the horse arrived? **Cause and Effect**

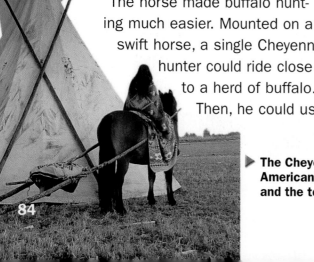

▶ **The Cheyenne and other Plains Native Americans used the horse-drawn travois and the tepee to move easily to hunt buffalo.**

▶ **Cheyenne wear traditional clothes for their annual powwow.**

Many Cheyenne follow their traditions, keeping their language and ceremonies alive. Every Fourth of July the Northern Cheyenne powwow is held in **Lame Deer, Montana.** Visitors to the **powwow** can see traditional dances and games of the Cheyenne. A Powwow is a gathering of American Indians.

REVIEW Why do you think many Cheyenne keep their traditions alive?
Draw Conclusions

The Cheyenne Today

Today, about 12,000 Cheyenne live on the Great Plains. Many live in present-day Montana on a reservation established by the government. You will read more about the conflict between the American Indians and the United States government in later chapters.

Summarize the Lesson

- **Some Plains Indians farmed and hunted buffalo.**
- **With the horse, the Cheyenne became more mobile.**
- **Today many Cheyenne live on the Great Plains and follow traditional customs.**

LESSON 2 REVIEW

Check Facts and Main Ideas

1. Cause and Effect On a separate piece of paper, fill in the missing causes.

Cause	Effect
	Plains Indians used horses to pull travois instead of dogs.
	Plains Indians built homes with earth or buffalo hides.
	Buffalo were used to make tepees, clothing, blankets, and bowls.
	Sometimes tribes raided other tribes for their horses.

2. How did the **travois** help move goods?

3. In what ways did the arrival of the horse change the way of life for the tribes of the Great Plains?

4. Critical Thinking: *Make Decisions* If you were a leader among the Cheyenne, how might you decide when it was time to move the settlement to a new area? Use the decision-making steps on page H3.

5. Where are Cheyenne reservations located today?

Link to ◦━◦ Science

Design Transportation Tools The travois is a tool that helped people move large, heavy things. Draw a diagram showing other transportation tools such as wheels or skis. Label your diagram.

85

Internet Research

What? You can find out more about a subject by doing research. Research is a way of gathering information to help solve a problem. Many people use books in the library for research. They may also use the Internet. The Internet is a worldwide network of computers linked together. On the Internet, information can be viewed and shared in on-screen pages called Web sites. A Web site can be set up by a company, school, government, or individual.

Why? Using the Internet to do research may let you find the most up-to-date information about a subject. Reference books and nonfiction books in the library may also hold useful information. The Internet, however, may have information that was found after a book was printed.

Another reason to use the Internet is that most libraries cannot keep books on every subject. You may need to research a topic for which your library has little information. The Internet lets you use a larger computer-based library. It also connects you to other students' projects and to homework help programs.

When using the Internet for research, you have to be careful that you are using reliable sources. Among the most reliable sources are Web sites sponsored by government and university groups. Some reliable reference sources, such as encyclopedias, also sponsor Web sites.

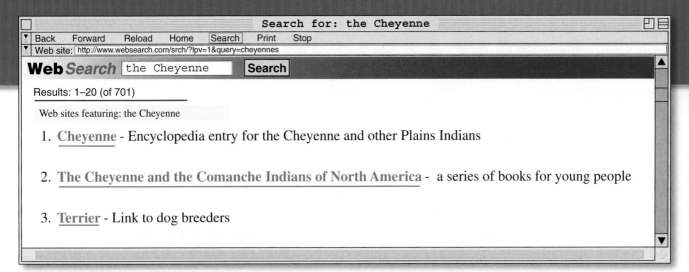

Back   Forward   Reload   Home   Search   Print   Stop

Web site: http://www.websearch.com/srch/?lpv=1&query=cheyennes

Web *Search* the Cheyenne   **Search**

Results: 1–20 (of 701)

Web sites featuring: the Cheyenne

1. **Cheyenne** - Encyclopedia entry for the Cheyenne and other Plains Indians

2. **The Cheyenne and the Comanche Indians of North America** - a series of books for young people

3. **Terrier** - Link to dog breeders

How? You can use search engines to find information on the Internet. A **search engine** is a computer site that searches for information. Search engines will lead you to other Web sites.

You do a search by typing in a word or phrase. Say you want information on the Cheyenne. You may know there is also a city named Cheyenne, but you want information on the Native American group. Type in "the Cheyenne" in quotation marks. The quotation marks tell that the topic you want is a complete phrase. Above is part of what appeared in a search for "the Cheyenne."

The search resulted in a list of 701 sites! That is a lot of information. You may want to start with an encyclopedia entry. Click on the underlined title. It will bring up even more information. Look also for study information and school sites. Do not bother with the site that leads you to dog breeders!

Underlined words in color are links to other sites. If you click on a link, you can get more information about a specific topic.

You can often print out information that you find on the Internet. Remember to keep the name of the Web site. It usually appears at the bottom of the page or in the rectangle at the top. Below is what one excerpt from a Web site about the Cheyenne might look like.

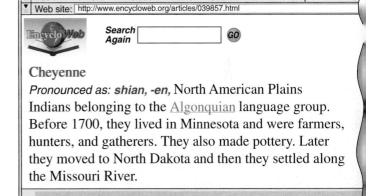

Web site: http://www.encycloweb.org/articles/039857.html

Encyclo *Web*   Search Again [   ] GO

Cheyenne
Pronounced as: shian, -en, North American Plains Indians belonging to the Algonquian language group. Before 1700, they lived in Minnesota and were farmers, hunters, and gatherers. They also made pottery. Later they moved to North Dakota and then they settled along the Missouri River.

Think and Apply

1. Look at the list of **Web sites** above resulting from a search. Which would take you to an Internet encyclopedia entry?

2. Look again at the Web site list. Why are some words shown in color and underlined?

3. How would you find information about the Iroquois?

1000   2000

About 1050
The Hopi village
of Oraibi is built.

Today
More than 7,000
Hopi live in
northern Arizona.

•Oraibi

SOUTHWEST
DESERT
CULTURAL
REGION

PREVIEW

Focus on the Main Idea
The need for water affected
the cultures developed by the
people of the Southwest.

PLACES
Southwest Desert
  cultural region
Oraibi

VOCABULARY
pueblo

The Southwest Desert

You Are There

Dum, dum, dum, dum, dum, dum, dum, dum, goes the beat of the drums. *Chika, chika, chika,* goes the beat of the rattles. Dancers appear, moving slowly to the beat. *Jangle, jangle, jangle,* go the bells tied around their knees. The dancers wear tall, pointed wooden masks, with slits for their eyes. Painted symbols and eagle feathers decorate the masks. The dancers' bodies are draped in white cloth. Red moccasins cover their feet as they stomp on the ground again and again and again. The dancers are performing an important ceremony. It is one which their people believe will help them survive in a hard and dry land.

Main Idea and Details As you read, describe ways American Indians of the Southwest survived in their harsh surroundings.

Living in a Dry Land

The dance you just read about has been occurring for hundreds of years among Pueblo people in the **Southwest Desert cultural region.** Find this region on the map. What present-day states does it include?

The Southwest Desert cultural region is mostly hot and arid. Several different tribes settled in this region long ago, including the Hopi and the Zuni. They developed a village way of life, based on farming. As a result, they later became known as Pueblo Indians. **Pueblo** is the Spanish word for *village*. The people of other tribes in the region were not farmers. They included the Apache, who were hunters, and the Navajo (NAH vuh ho), who raised sheep.

Pueblo Indians are thought to be descended from the Anasazi, the "Old Ones" of the land around Four Corners. Like the Anasazi, the Pueblo developed irrigation to grow corn, beans, squash, and cotton.

The Pueblo also followed Anasazi housing customs. Their villages looked like today's apartment buildings, rising several stories off the ground. The Hopi placed their villages on top of high mesas. Such sites helped them defend themselves against enemies.

Hopi men governed their villages. But women owned all the property and passed it down to their daughters. Men were the weavers of cloth and women were the weavers of baskets. In Hopi tradition, the groom's father wove the wedding robe for his son's bride. A woman from the bride's family wove a special basket for the groom.

REVIEW What Anasazi traditions were adopted by the Pueblo people? ↻ **Summarize**

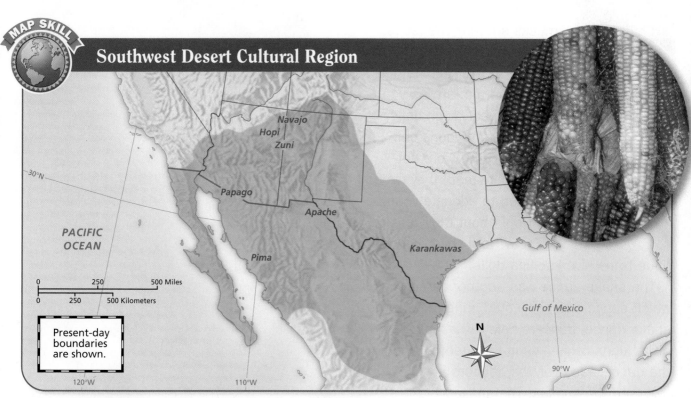

MAP SKILL

Southwest Desert Cultural Region

Navajo
Hopi
Zuni
Papago
Apache
PACIFIC OCEAN
Pima
Karankawas

0   250   500 Miles
0   250   500 Kilometers

Present-day boundaries are shown.

Gulf of Mexico

N

30°N
120°W   110°W   90°W

▶ The Hopi used irrigation to grow corn and other crops.

MAP SKILL Location *Which tribe lived in the most eastern part of this cultural region?*

The Need for Rain

Rain—that is what tribes like the Hopi needed most to survive in their harsh, dry region. They believed that beings called kachinas (kah CHEE nuhz) could bring them this rain and other kinds of help. Hopi dance ceremonies honored the kachinas and sought their aid.

The dance you read about in "You Are There" is one such ceremony. It traditionally began when a group of dancers emerged from a kiva (KEE vuh). This was an underground chamber where ceremonies were performed. A kiva symbolized the underworld, from which the Hopi people believed they came before entering this world. In the kiva, the dancers put on masks showing the faces of the kachinas.

Look at the kachina doll shown on the left. As you might expect, such dolls were given to young children. But they were not toys. Instead, they were used to educate young Hopi about their religion. Today Hopi children continue to receive kachina dolls.

The snake dance was another ceremony which dancers hoped would bring rain. In the snake dance, dancers held rattlesnakes and other kinds of snakes in their teeth. When the dance was over, the dancers released the snakes. The snakes then slithered away, looking like tiny streams of water.

Everyone in the community, young and old, came out to witness these ceremonies. To prepare, they washed their hair with suds made from the yucca plant. The men wore their hair hanging straight, under a knotted scarf or a broad-brimmed hat. The married women wore their hair in two long braids. Young unmarried women wore the hairstyle shown below. It was called the "squash blossom" because it looked like the blossoms on a squash plant. It announced to the world that the young woman was ready for marriage.

REVIEW What was the purpose of many Hopi ceremonies? **Main Idea and Details**

▶ **Kachina dolls (left) and squash blossom hair styles are important Hopi traditions.**

▶ Pueblo people, such as the Hopi and this group at San Ildefonso, New Mexico, help keep their customs alive by performing traditional dances.

The Hopi Today

Today Hopi continue to live on their traditional lands. More than 7,000 Hopi live on a reservation in northeast Arizona. Their reservation is completely surrounded by the much larger Navajo (NAH vuh ho) reservation. There have been tensions between the two tribes over land ownership.

The Hopi continue to live in villages. One of them is Oraibi, built on a mesa. Founded in about 1050, it is probably the oldest town in the United States. Many Hopi still follow their ancient traditions and customs, such as the kachina dances and the snake dance.

But they have adopted modern ways too. Some Hopi live in New Oraibi—a town built in the valley below the older Oraibi.

REVIEW How does life differ for the Hopi today compared to hundreds of years ago? **Compare and Contrast**

Summarize the Lesson

- People of the Southwest lived in villages and used irrigation to farm the land.
- Kachina dolls were used to educate Hopi children about their customs and traditions.
- Today about 7,000 Hopi live in Arizona.

LESSON 3 REVIEW

Check Facts and Main Ideas

1. **Main Idea and Details** On a separate sheet of paper, fill in the details that support the main idea from the lesson.

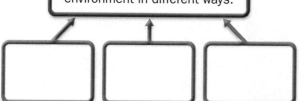

Pueblo Indians of the Southwest adapted to their dry environment in different ways.

2. How were Hopi villages governed?

3. How were kachinas honored in Hopi ceremonies?

4. What does the difference between Oraibi and New Oraibi tell you about the Hopi culture of today?

5. **Critical Thinking: *Draw Conclusions*** Why do you think **Pueblo** people adopted Anasazi building styles? Explain.

Link to 🔗 Geography

Analyze Regions Make a chart showing the advantages and disadvantages of the Southwest region's environment.

Saving Lives with Language

Have you ever used a secret language? During World War II a group of Navajo soldiers used their native language to create an unbreakable code—and helped the United States win the war.

In February 1945, United States Marine Thomas H. Begay jumped into the waves off the small Pacific island of Iwo Jima. Enemy fighter planes roared overhead. Bullets came from every direction. Begay carried a rifle, but his most important weapon was invisible. In his memory were several hundred words of a secret code based on his own Navajo language.

Thomas Begay was one of about 420 Navajo "Code Talkers" who helped the American effort against Japan in World War II. American troops needed to transmit messages to each other secretly so that the enemy could not find out their plans. These brave soldiers "talked" a complicated code to each other over a radio in the middle of heavy fighting. By performing this special service, they allowed commanders to communicate with soldiers on the battlefield without the enemy understanding. "Were it not for the Navajos," said Major Howard Connor, "the Marines would never have taken Iwo Jima." The Battle of Iwo Jima was a very important United States victory in the war.

▶ Code Talkers are shown above during World War II. At the left, Code Talker John Brown, Jr., receives the Congressional Gold Medal from President George W. Bush in 2001.

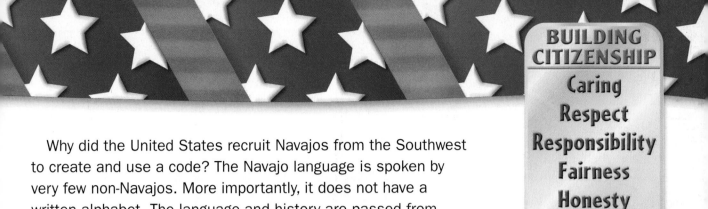

BUILDING CITIZENSHIP
Caring
Respect
Responsibility
Fairness
Honesty
★ Courage

Why did the United States recruit Navajos from the Southwest to create and use a code? The Navajo language is spoken by very few non-Navajos. More importantly, it does not have a written alphabet. The language and history are passed from person to person. Code Talker William McCabe explained:

> *"Well, in Navajo everything is in memory. From the songs, prayers, everything... That's the way we (were) raised up."*

The Navajos' memory allowed them to send and receive messages very quickly, which was very important for saving lives. When the code was first tested, two Navajo Code Talkers could relay a message in about 20 seconds. A code machine took about 30 minutes to send and decode a message. Soldiers under attack could not wait that long to tell their commanders what was going on.

For many years, few people knew of the Code Talkers' courage. The code was still top secret until 1968. In 1982, President Ronald Reagan named August 14 as National Navajo Code Talkers Day. In 2001, Congress honored the Code Talkers with the Congressional Gold Medal.

Courage in Action

Link to Current Events How can language be used to help others? Maybe you know of someone who has given a speech to create awareness about a problem in his or her community. Research newspaper reports or other sources to find other groups that have used language to fight for a cause.

1000   1500   2000

about 1700
The Kwakiutl number around 15,000.

Today
About 2,000 Kwakiutl live in the Northwest Coast region.

NORTHWEST COAST CULTURAL REGION

Vancouver Island

The Northwest Coast

PREVIEW

Focus on the Main Idea
People of the Northwest Coast developed cultures based on the region's rich natural resources.

PLACES
Northwest Coast cultural region
Vancouver Island

VOCABULARY
potlatch
totem pole
shaman

You Are There

The entire village is buzzing about the party being planned. The couple giving it is celebrating the completion of their new home. The party will go on for 12 days. At least 200 people will come to enjoy it.

Inside the house, you see different kinds of food—wild berries, meat, vegetables cooked in fish oil. Over the next several days, there will be much speechmaking as well as singing, dancing, and feasting. The floor is piled high with gifts. Are these housewarming gifts for the hosts? No, they are gifts the hosts will give to their guests. For this party, you don't bring presents. Instead, presents are given to you!

▶ At parties, people feasted on foods served in carved wooden bowls.

Draw Conclusions
As you read, form an opinion about why the people of the Northwest Coast used their resources the way they did.

94

Rich Resources

The party you just read about is called a **potlatch.** *Potlatch* comes from a Chinook (shuh NUK) word meaning "to give away." The tribes of the Northwest Coast, including the Kwakiutl (kwah kee OO tuhl), the Tlingit (TLIN git), the Haida, and the Nootka, gave such parties. Find them on the map on this page.

The **Northwest Coast cultural region** had plentiful natural resources. Its forests contained many tall, sturdy cedar trees. These forests were also rich in game for hunting. The coastal waters and rivers were filled with fish and seals. The people of the Northwest Coast did not have to grow crops for food. They got all they needed from hunting and gathering.

With such a wealth of resources, the Kwakiutl and other tribes were able to hold potlatches. The Kwakiutl lived on **Vancouver Island** and along the Pacific coast of what is now Canada. Displaying wealth and generosity was very important in Kwakiutl culture. Copper shields and stacks of blankets were common gifts. A single guest might be given as many as 20 blankets.

The **totem pole,** a carved post with animals or other images representing a person's ancestors, was another way to show wealth. Look at the one on the left. With so much wood available, some Kwakiutl became master wood carvers. People proudly displayed their totem poles, some as tall

as a four-story building, outside their door.

A master carver also used a single cedar log to make a dugout canoe. The Kwakiutl used such canoes to hunt at sea. They hunted not only seals, but also sea otters and even whales. Such prey provided meat for food, furs for clothing, and oil for lamps and heating.

REVIEW Compare ways the Kwakiutl used resources from the forest and oceans. **Compare and Contrast**

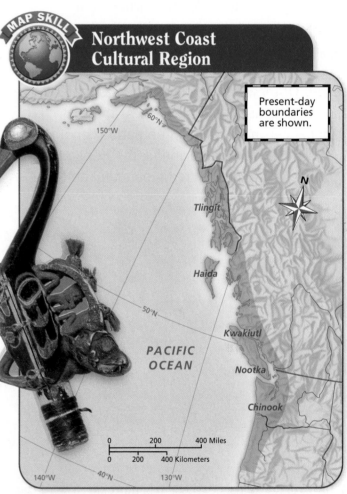

MAP SKILL

Northwest Coast Cultural Region

Present-day boundaries are shown.

150°W · 60°N · Tlingit · Haida · 50°N · Kwakiutl · PACIFIC OCEAN · Nootka · Chinook · N · 140°W · 40°N · 130°W

0   200   400 Miles
0   200   400 Kilometers

▶ **The people of the Northwest Coast cultural region carved beautiful objects like this wooden bird.**

MAP SKILL Place *In what type of environment would you expect skilled woodcarvers to live?*

Customs and Traditions

A shaman (SHAH men) was an important person in the Kwakiutl culture. A **shaman** was a person people came to when they were not feeling well. They believed that the shaman could cure them. Among the Kwakiutl, both men and women could become shamans.

Kwakiutl shamans sometimes performed dancing ceremonies. They wore carved masks, like the ones shown on this page. As they danced, they might change their appearance by opening or closing parts of the masks. Special effects often made the dances more exciting. Hidden performers made wooden birds swoop down on the audience. Or they made howling sounds that seemed to rise from the floor. At the end, the dancer might vanish in a puff of smoke!

Because food was plentiful, the Kwakiutl had plenty of time to create beautiful objects.

Many of them—masks, rattles, serving dishes—were carved from wood and decorated with paint. The objects reflected the Kwakiutls' respect for the spirits they felt around them.

Thanks to a mild coastal climate, the Kwakiutl could often wear light clothing. Kwakiutl women wove cedar bark into a fabric. Then they made it into skirts for themselves and long shirts for the men. The Kwakiutl also wore clothing made of buckskin, taken from the deer of the forests. In colder weather they put on animal furs.

The forests' cedar trees supplied the Kwakiutl with sturdy housing. Logs provided the upright posts for a house and its roof beams. Planks cut from logs formed the walls and roof.

REVIEW Why do you think shamans were so respected? **Draw Conclusions**

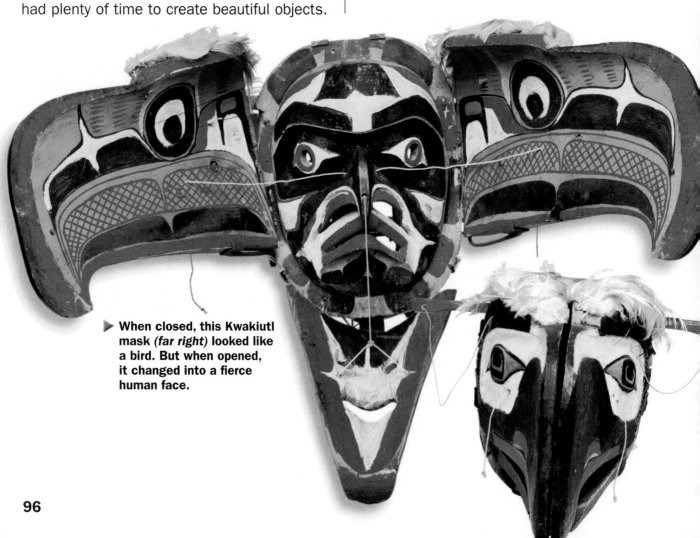

▶ When closed, this Kwakiutl mask *(far right)* looked like a bird. But when opened, it changed into a fierce human face.

▶ **Kwakiutl artists continue to paint traditional designs today.**

The Kwakiutl Today

Three hundred years ago, the Kwakiutl numbered about 15,000. Today, only about 4,000 survive. The forests and the sea remain important in their lives. Most of the men work in logging, construction, or fishing.

The Kwakiutl keep many aspects of their traditional culture. They have also added new customs. Foods such as sugar, flour, potatoes, and tea have joined berries, game, and fish. Powerboats have often replaced their cedar canoes. Newer building methods have replaced traditional cedar houses. Both medical doctors and shamans serve the people. The Kwakiutl still give potlatches today.

REVIEW Compare the resources the Kwakiutl used hundreds of years ago to those of today. **Compare and Contrast**

Summarize the Lesson

- **Indians of the Northwest Coast met their needs from hunting and gathering.**
- **Shamans were important people in Kwakiutl culture.**
- **Today many Kwakiutl work in logging, construction, and fishing.**

LESSON 4   REVIEW

Check Facts and Main Ideas

1. Draw Conclusions On a separate sheet of paper, fill in the boxes with the main facts from the lesson that support the conclusion about resources from the Northwest Coast.

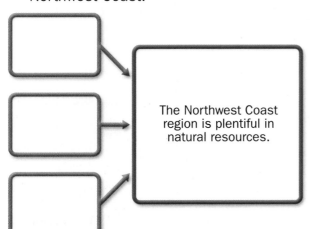

The Northwest Coast region is plentiful in natural resources.

2. Why did Northwest Coast people give **potlatches?**

3. What did **shamans** do to help people?

4. How much has the Kwakiutl population declined over the centuries?

5. Critical Thinking: *Predict* What changes might the Kwakiutl make in their culture if all the nearby trees were cut down?

Link to ⬤─⬤ Writing

Describe Details Suppose you are throwing a potlatch today. Write about what kinds of gifts you would give to your guests.

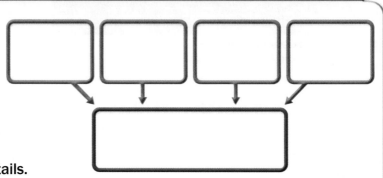

1000   1200

About 1050
Hopi village of
Oraibi founded

1300s
Plains Indians
begin moving
to Great Plains
region

Chapter Summary

Summarize

Read the paragraph below. Fill in the chart on a separate piece of paper by identifying the sentence that summarizes the paragraph and the sentences that present details.

The Indians of North America developed ways of living based on their environments and resources. Native Americans of the Eastern Woodlands used the resources of the forests. Native Americans who lived on the Great Plains adapted their cultures to take advantage of horses. In the Southwest Desert, Native Americans learned to live in a climate with little rain. And along the Northwest Coast, people depended on plentiful resources from forests and the sea.

Vocabulary

Match each word with the correct definition or description.

1 tribe (p. 77)

2 reservation (p. 80)

3 powwow (p. 85)

4 potlatch (p. 95)

5 lodge (p. 83)

a. gathering

b. group of families under one leadership

c. hut built over a deep hole

d. land set aside for Native Americans by the government

e. party at which the host gives guests gifts

Places and Vocabulary

Write a sentence explaining why each of the following places or terms was important to the Native Americans of North America. You may use two or more in a single sentence.

1 wampum (p. 79)

2 Iroquois Trail (p. 77)

3 longhouse (p. 78)

4 Great Plains cultural region (p. 83)

5 tepee (p. 83)

6 pueblo (p. 89)

7 Oraibi (p. 91)

8 Southwest Desert cultural region (p. 89)

9 shaman (p. 96)

10 totem pole (p. 95)

late 1500s
Five tribes joined to form the Iroquois League

about 1700
The Kwakiutl number about 15,000

late 1700s
The Cheyenne get horses

Facts and Main Ideas

1 What is a cultural region?

2 What kinds of dwellings did the various Native American groups live in?

3 **Time Line** How many years have passed since the Hopi village of Oraibi was founded?

4 **Main Idea** What did the Iroquois use their tree resources for?

5 **Main Idea** How did the Plains Indians live before the arrival of the horse?

6 **Main Idea** Compare the roles of men and women in Hopi villages.

7 **Main Idea** What kinds of natural resources were available to the Northwest Coast Indians?

8 **Critical Thinking:** *Cause and Effect* What effect did the formation of the Iroquois League have on its members?

Write About History

1 **Write a diary entry** for a Hopi person of your age who lived hundreds of years ago. Tell some of the things you did that day.

2 **Write a speech** that Hiawatha might have made to convince his people to unite.

3 **Write a menu** for a potlatch that a Kwakiutl might have given.

Apply Skills

Use the Internet for Research

Read the following paragraphs written in the style of an Internet encyclopedia Web site. Then answer the questions.

| | | | | | | | | Iroquois |
| Back | Forward | Reload | Home | Search | Print | Stop | | |

Web site: http://www.encycloweb.org/articles/080590.html

EncycloWeb   Search Again [   ] GO

Iroquois
A member of one of the six tribes belonging to the Iroquois League. The six tribes are the Cayuga, Mohawk, Oneida, Onondaga, Seneca, and Tuscarora. The Tuscarora joined the league after the original five tribes that were united by Deganawidah and Hiawatha.

The Iroquois language family includes the languages of other tribes who were not part of the league.

1 Why are some words and phrases shown in color and underlined?

2 What would happen if you clicked on the underlined words or phrases?

3 What other search words could you use to find more information about this topic?

Internet Activity

To get help with vocabulary, people, and terms, select the dictionary or encyclopedia from *Social Studies Library* at **www.sfsocialstudies.com.**

Life in the Eastern Hemisphere

1274

China
Kublai Khan welcomes Marco Polo, who has traveled the Silk Road to reach China.

Lesson 1

1

Early 1300s

Mali
Mansa Musa establishes Timbuktu as a center of art and learning.

Lesson 2

2

1420s

Portugal
Prince Henry sends ships to explore the coast of Africa.

Lesson 3

3

Why We Remember

In this chapter you will join in tales of great adventure. You will travel across the Silk Road with Marco Polo, and marvel as he sees fireworks for the first time. You will journey across the Sahara desert with the fabulously wealthy king Mansa Musa of Mali, whose slaves carried 2,000 pounds of gold. You will stand on the deck of wooden sailing ships, fighting waves and wind as sailors explore new lands.

All these adventures really happened—hundreds of years ago. Yet their effects are with us today. Explorers from the Eastern Hemisphere were the founders of new nations in the Western Hemisphere. One of these new countries would become the United States of America.

500   1000   1500

1274
Marco Polo
reaches China

1405
Chinese fleets,
led by Zheng He,
explore the seas

Venice • Silk Road • Shangdu

Traveling Asia's Silk Road

PREVIEW

Focus on the Main Idea
The desire for trade led people of Asia and Europe to travel and build stronger ties to people of other continents.

PLACES
Venice
Shangdu
Silk Road

PEOPLE
Marco Polo
Kublai Khan
Zheng He

VOCABULARY
emperor
magnetic compass

You Are There

The year is 1274 and Marco Polo has just reached China. It has taken him, his father, and his uncle three long years of hard traveling to get here. They traveled by ship, on foot, on horseback, and by wagon.

Young Marco is now thousands of miles from the land of his birth. How different and exciting everything must look to him! What is this money the people are using? It's made out of paper, not the gold and silver coins used at home. What are they burning for fuel? Instead of wood, they use black stones that burn like logs. And then there is that colorful display he sees in the night sky. What is the strange powder they lit to send spinning rockets skyward? Yes, he feels far, far from home.

▶ **Marco Polo arrived in China in 1274.**

Summarize As you read, look for the main idea of each section which explains why people traveled to new places.

The Silk Road

Paper money, coal, gunpowder—all of these were new to **Marco Polo.** They were completely unknown in Europe, where he came from. He was only 17 in 1271, when he set out on his great adventure with his father and uncle. They left their home in **Venice,** a trading city in what is today Italy.

The Polos were merchants. Their goal was to bring back valuable trade goods from China. When they reached **Shangdu,** they became guests of **Kublai Khan,** the emperor. An **emperor** is the ruler of an empire. The royal palace astounded the Polos with its riches. Marco Polo described it in his book, *The Travels of Marco Polo.*

> *"The hall is so vast and so wide that a meal might well be served there for more than 6,000 men."*

What caused such great wealth? Hundreds of years earlier, the Chinese had learned how to weave silk cloth. Over the years demand for silk grew, coming from people as far away as Europe and Africa. It was said that silk became worth its weight in gold. The Chinese also developed other valuable trade goods, including tea and spices. Europeans wanted spices to preserve food and to improve its flavor. The major trade route between China and other lands was a network of routes known as the **Silk Road.** Find the Silk Road on the map.

Traders and trade goods were not all that traveled the Silk Road. So did ideas, skills and customs. Marco Polo's journey made people in both Asia and Europe want to know more about each other.

REVIEW How did the Silk Road help people in different lands learn more about each other? ⟳ **Summarize**

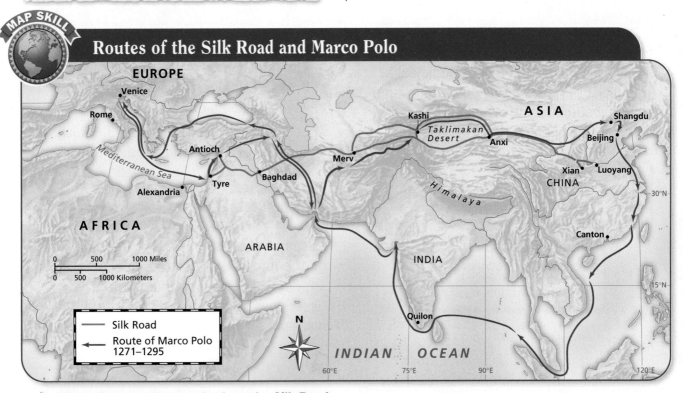

MAP SKILL

Routes of the Silk Road and Marco Polo

EUROPE
Venice
Rome
Antioch
Mediterranean Sea
Alexandria
Tyre
Baghdad
Merv
Kashi
Taklimakan Desert
Anxi
ASIA
Shangdu
Beijing
Xian
Luoyang
CHINA
Himalaya
30°N
Canton
AFRICA
ARABIA
INDIA
15°N
Quilon

	Silk Road
←	Route of Marco Polo 1271–1295

0   500   1000 Miles
0   500   1000 Kilometers

N

INDIAN OCEAN
60°E   75°E   90°E   120°E

▶ Marco Polo traveled partly along the Silk Road.

MAP SKILL Use Routes *At which city in Europe did Marco Polo begin his journey?*

Chinese Sailors

In about 1400, China began to build an enormous naval fleet. Its mission was to expand Chinese trade and to show Chinese power. With more than 300 ships, it was the largest fleet ever assembled up to that time. A Chinese invention, the magnetic compass, made it possible for the sailors to determine their direction far out at sea.

The fleet sailed under the command of Zheng He (JUNG HUH). A biography of Zheng He follows this lesson. He and his fleet set sail in 1405. Over the next 28 years, Chinese fleets made seven

▶ **This magnetic compass was used by Chinese sailors.**

voyages of trade and exploration. They reached such far-off lands as the spice-rich East Indies, India, the Persian Empire, Arabia and the Red Sea, and the east coast of Africa. Wherever Chinese ships stopped, demand grew for Chinese trade goods.

REVIEW Compare the journey of Marco Polo with the journeys of Zheng He. How were they similar? How were they different? **Compare and Contrast**

Summarize the Lesson

— **1274** Traveling from Venice, Marco Polo reached China.

— **1405** Chinese fleets began to explore the seas under Zheng He.

LESSON 1 ▷ REVIEW

Check Facts and Main Ideas

1. 🔊 **Summarize** On a separate sheet of paper, fill in the missing details or events of the summarizing statement. The first detail has been provided as an example.

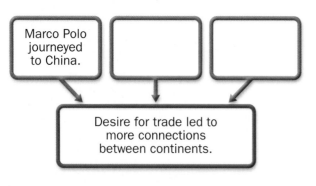

2. What effect did Marco Polo's journey have on people of Asia and Europe?

3. Name two goods that traveled along the Silk Road.

4. **Critical Thinking: *Cause and Effect*** What were the goals of Zheng He's journeys?

5. Look at the map on page 103. Which continents were connected by the Silk Road?

Link to 🔗 **Science**

Research the Compass In your library or on the Internet, investigate how a magnetic compass works. Write a descriptive paragraph and include a diagram.

Zheng He
1371–1433

Zheng He was born in southern China. His family opposed the rise to power of a new government supported by the Chinese army. Zheng He's father was killed in battle. Zheng He was captured and made the servant of a prince who was the emperor's uncle.

Zheng He impressed the prince with his intelligence and loyalty. The two became friends, and together they plotted to overthrow the emperor. They were successful and the prince became the emperor. He made Zheng He the commander of the army.

The new emperor wanted to show China's greatness to the world, so he sent out a huge fleet of ships to trade with other countries. He put the fleet under the command of Zheng He.

Zheng He led seven major voyages. He visited and traded with India and countries of Southeast Asia, the Persian Gulf, and the eastern coast of Africa. These words written by Zheng He are recorded on a monument in eastern China:

BIOFACT

Zheng He brought back to China many things from other lands. This giraffe, from the east coast of Africa, was drawn by a Chinese artist.

"We have traveled . . . immense waterspaces and have beheld waves like mountains rising sky high, and we have set eyes on (foreign) regions far away hidden in a blue (mist) of light vapors."

After Zheng He's death, a new emperor stopped all overseas voyages. China focused only on events at home. But a lasting knowledge of other lands was established and would not soon be forgotten.

Learn from Biographies

How was Zheng He able to go from being a prisoner to a great leader and world explorer?

 For more information, go online to *Meet the People* at **www.sfsocialstudies.com.**

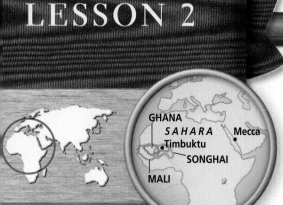

500	1000	1500

about 700
Kingdom of Ghana thrives

1324
Mansa Musa, King of Mali, goes to Mecca

Early 1500s
Kingdom of Songhai reaches its peak

GHANA
S A H A R A • Mecca
• Timbuktu
SONGHAI
MALI

PREVIEW

Focus on the Main Idea
Beginning more than one thousand years ago, rich trading kingdoms developed in West Africa.

PLACES
Sahara
Ghana
Timbuktu
Mali
Mecca
Songhai

PEOPLE
Mansa Musa

VOCABULARY
caravan
pilgrimage
astrolabe

Africa's Trading Empires

You Are There

For three long months, you have been on your way. For three long months, you have been sitting on a camel, swaying back and forth. Often it is a struggle just to stay on the camel's back. He's a mean-tempered beast, likely to bite and spit.

You are traveling across the huge Sahara. It is hot during the day and cold at night. The Sahara is like a great sea of sand. But instead of waves, you cross endlessly shifting sand dunes. No wonder they call the camel "the ship of the desert." It is the only kind of transportation that can carry you across the endless miles of sand.

Sequence As you read, look for clues that tell you the sequence of kingdoms that rose and fell in West Africa.

Ghana, Kingdom of Gold

You have just read the story of a caravan crossing Africa's huge **Sahara desert.** A **caravan** is a group of traders traveling together. For centuries, caravans on camelback traveled the Sahara, bringing goods to and from West Africa. This region became home to several powerful trading kingdoms.

The earliest kingdom, which was named **Ghana** (GAH nah), thrived around 700. Visitors called Ghana a "land of gold." Ghana received this name because its land was rich in the precious mineral. But Ghana lacked an important resource—salt.

Trading routes developed, bringing salt into Ghana in exchange for its plentiful gold. Arab traders from North Africa brought salt from the Sahara to cities on the southern edge of the desert, like **Timbuktu.** Trace the routes of these traders on the map. In Timbuktu, Arab traders bargained to get the best price for their salt in gold. Just as China's silk had become worth its weight in gold, so too did salt.

The Arab traders also brought their religion, Islam, with them to West Africa. The followers of Islam are known as Muslims. Islam began to spread throughout the region. The kings of Ghana hired Muslims as officials, to help them rule.

Ghana's rulers grew rich from trade. Its kings charged taxes on all imports and exports. The kingdom of Ghana weakened in the 1100s. But a new empire was emerging in the same area. It would become even larger and richer than Ghana.

REVIEW Explain why Ghana was known as a "land of gold." **Summarize**

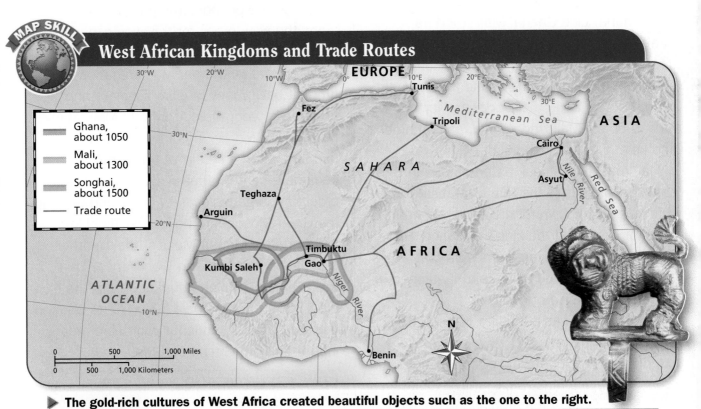

MAP SKILL

West African Kingdoms and Trade Routes

- Ghana, about 1050
- Mali, about 1300
- Songhai, about 1500
- Trade route

EUROPE

Tunis
Fez
Tripoli
Mediterranean Sea
ASIA
Cairo
SAHARA
Asyut
Nile River
Red Sea
Teghaza
Arguin
Timbuktu
AFRICA
Kumbi Saleh
Gao
Niger River
ATLANTIC OCEAN
N
Benin

0   500   1,000 Miles
0   500   1,000 Kilometers

▶ The gold-rich cultures of West Africa created beautiful objects such as the one to the right.

MAP SKILL Region *What desert did the trade routes cross to reach the cities of West Africa?*

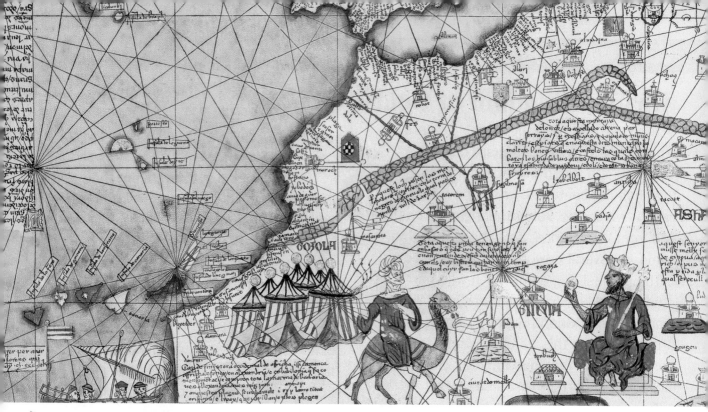

▶ The Catalan Atlas, created in the 1300s by Abraham Cresques of Spain, shows Mansa Musa wearing a crown.

Mali and Songhai

The kingdom of **Mali** controlled more land than Ghana. Like Ghana, Mali owed its wealth to trade. Caravans continued their trade of gold and salt. In addition, European ships from Spain, Portugal, and Italy brought cloth, horses, and other goods to North African ports. Mali traded gold, animal hides, and kola nuts for such goods.

Mali reached its peak as an empire in the early 1300s, during the rule of **Mansa Musa.** This king was known for his immense wealth. A visitor described the king's entrance. He was carried under a large umbrella that was "made of silk, (topped) by a bird fashioned in gold about the size of a falcon."

Mansa Musa was a Muslim who in 1324 went on a pilgrimage (PIL gruh mij). A **pilgrimage** is a journey taken for religious reasons. Mansa Musa's pilgrimage took him to **Mecca,** a city in the Arabian peninsula that is holy to Muslims. With him came thousands of people. Among them were about 500 slaves, each carrying a bar of gold weighing four pounds. The gold was used along the way to pay for traveling expenses.

The king's journey strengthened trade ties between Mali and other Muslim nations. He brought back many Muslim scholars and artists who contributed to life in Mali. Many of them settled in Timbuktu. This city, which had long been a center of trade, now also became a center of learning. Mansa Musa ordered a large building for study and worship, the Great Mosque, to be built in Timbuktu.

Soon after Mansa Musa's rule, another trading kingdom rose in West Africa. This was **Songhai,** which flourished from the middle 1300s through the 1500s. At its peak in the early 1500s, Songhai controlled more land than both Ghana and Mali.

REVIEW Name three powerful trading kingdoms of West Africa and the sequence in which they ruled. *Sequence*

Connecting Different Parts of the World

In this chapter you have been reading how people in different parts of the world reached out to one another. Zheng He's journeys showed that the Chinese were learning routes to India and Africa. Mansa Musa's pilgrimage showed how people from West Africa and the Arabian peninsula traveled between their two regions. The map on the previous page, created by a European in the 1300s, shows that the people of Europe were learning about the people and geography of Africa and Asia.

European map makers built on the knowledge of many travelers and geographers around the world. One tool in particular that helped them was developed by Arabs. It was the astrolabe (AS troh lab), an instrument that helped sailors use the sun and stars to find their location in latitude—their distance from the equator. With the astrolabe and other new tools and ideas, different parts of the world were becoming more closely connected.

▶ **Astrolabe**

REVIEW Give details that show how connections between different parts of the world were expanding. **Main Idea and Details**

Summarize the Lesson

- **About 700** The kingdom of Ghana thrived in West Africa.

- **1324** Mansa Musa, king of Mali, brought thousands of people on a pilgrimage to Mecca.

- **Early 1500s** The kingdom of Songhai reached its peak.

LESSON 2 REVIEW

Check Facts and Main Ideas

1. **Sequence** On a separate sheet of paper, fill in the missing events in this sequence chart showing the three major kingdoms of West Africa.

> The kingdom of Ghana developed in West Africa

↓

>

↓

>

2. Why did **caravans** cross the Sahara desert?

3. Why did Timbuktu develop into a center of Muslim learning?

4. What major resource did West African kingdoms control? Which important resource did they lack?

5. **Critical Thinking:** *Evaluate* Why did Mansa Musa travel with so many people and so much gold?

Link to ⚭ Geography

Make an Illustrated Map Look at the map on page 108 showing Mansa Musa of Mali. Create your own illustrated map on a subject you have read about in this chapter. Include symbols and a key.

Greenland
Vinland
Scandinavia
PORTUGAL
Cape of Good Hope

1000 — 1250 — 1500

1000
Leif Ericsson reaches North America

About 1350
The Renaissance begins

1420s
Prince Henry sends Portuguese ships to Africa

1498
Vasco da Gama reaches India

European Explorers

PREVIEW

Focus on the Main Idea
In the 1400s European explorers developed sea routes to Africa and Asia.

PLACES
Greenland
Vinland
Portugal
Cape of Good Hope

PEOPLE
Eric the Red
Leif Ericsson
Johann Gutenberg
Prince Henry
Bartolomeu Dias
Vasco da Gama

VOCABULARY
saga
Renaissance
navigation
slave trade

You Are There

Eric the Red had a lot of enemies. He was quick to anger and quick to use his sword. In about 965, the Viking people had had enough. They forced Eric to leave his homeland. But where would he go? Like many Vikings before him, he took to the sea. Eric the Red began a journey of exploration and settlement that would extend thousands of miles.

► The Vikings sailed great distances in longships such as this one.

Draw Conclusions As you read, draw conclusions about the reasons that European explorers sought to find new routes to Africa and Asia.

The Vikings

The Vikings were skilled sailors. Their homeland was Scandinavia in northern Europe. In their sleek wooden boats, powered only by sail and oars, they sailed as far east as Asia, as far south as North Africa, and as far west as North America.

Eric the Red sailed west to the island of Iceland. But Eric was soon thrown out of Iceland too. So he sailed west again, and in about 982, he came to a place he called Greenland. Despite the name, it was a very cold land. But Eric wanted the place to sound like a good land to settle. He called it Greenland to encourage Icelanders to come.

Eric's son, Leif Ericsson, was interested in rumors of a land still farther west. In 1000, he sailed to find it. When he and his crew set foot upon North America, they were probably the first Europeans to do so.

Ericsson had landed on Newfoundland on the east coast of what is today Canada. According to legend, his men found grapes growing there. So they called the place Vinland, or "Land of Wine." Soon groups of Vikings came to settle in Vinland. But conflict broke out with the American Indians living there. By about 1015, those Viking settlers who survived had returned home.

The Vikings did not have a written language. So how do we know about these adventures of a thousand years ago? They created long spoken tales called sagas, repeated from one generation to the next. Later, these sagas were written down. Archaeological evidence also tells us about these early explorers, as you will read below in the Then and Now feature.

REVIEW In one sentence, describe the most important information this page tells you about the Vikings. ⟳ Summarize

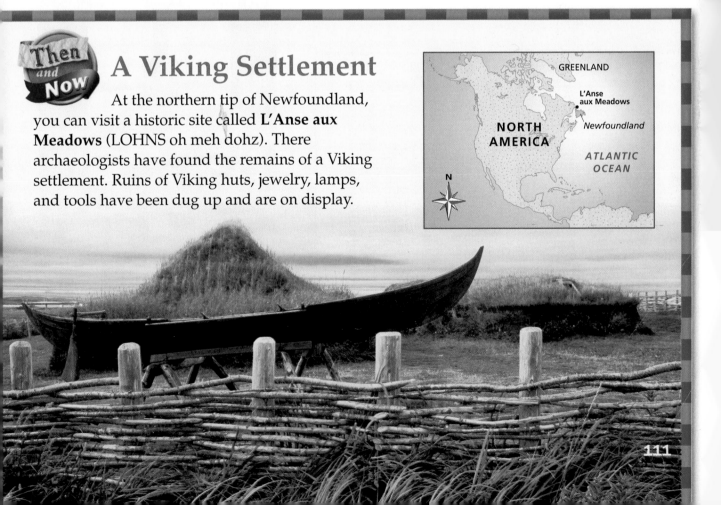

Then and Now
A Viking Settlement

At the northern tip of Newfoundland, you can visit a historic site called **L'Anse aux Meadows** (LOHNS oh meh dohz). There archaeologists have found the remains of a Viking settlement. Ruins of Viking huts, jewelry, lamps, and tools have been dug up and are on display.

GREENLAND

L'Anse aux Meadows

NORTH AMERICA

Newfoundland

ATLANTIC OCEAN

N

The Renaissance

For centuries, the Vikings had shown a spirit of adventure and curiosity about the rest of the world. By about 1350, a similar spirit was emerging far to the south of Scandinavia, in Italy. There, a new age was beginning that would last about another 250 years. It was known as the **Renaissance** (REN uh sahns) a word that means "rebirth."

Why was the Renaissance a "rebirth"? Because it marked a new beginning in arts and sciences and a desire to learn more about the world. Earlier in this chapter you read about Marco Polo. Italian cities like Polo's Venice had become centers of trade with places in other parts of the world. The wealth this trade created helped to support the arts and learning. Italians studied the learning of ancient European cultures, such as the Greeks and Romans, and of other cultures in the world, such as the Chinese and Arabs.

The Renaissance spread to other parts of Europe. In Germany, in about 1450, **Johann Gutenberg** developed a printing press, a machine that made it possible to print large numbers of books rapidly. Until this time in Europe, books had to be written and copied by hand, one copy at a time. This was a very slow process and made books scarce and expensive. Thanks to the inventions of Gutenberg and other early printers, books became available to many more readers. Now new ideas could spread more quickly.

Other advances came in ship design and ship building. Europeans adopted improvements from other cultures, such as the magnetic compass from the Chinese and the astrolabe from Muslims. Continuing to improve their ships, Europeans made them faster and safer to sail than ever before. As their ships improved, they were able to venture farther and farther from Europe.

REVIEW Where did the Renaissance begin, and what places did it spread to next?
Sequence

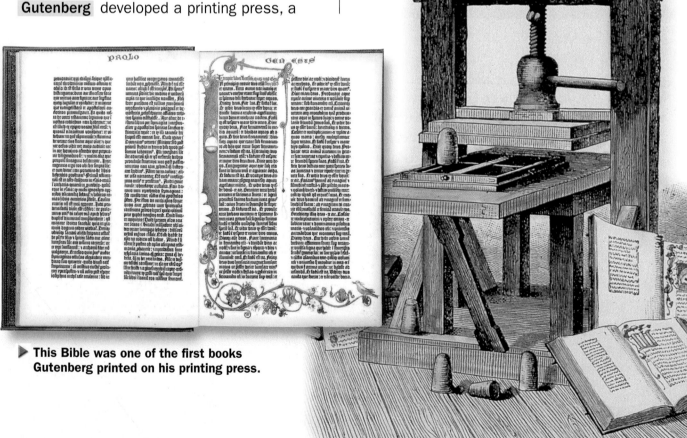

▶ **This Bible was one of the first books Gutenberg printed on his printing press.**

The Portuguese Explore the African Coast

By the early 1400s, the demand of Europeans for goods from Asia, especially spices, was stronger than ever. But Europeans could not get these goods easily. The Silk Road and other land routes were long and dangerous. They were often controlled by merchants who charged a high price for trade.

These problems sparked a drive to find new trade routes to Asia—sea routes. Beginning in the 1420s, the country of Portugal took the lead. The king's son, Prince Henry, gathered together the best and most experienced sea captains, mapmakers, ship designers, and other experts from many countries. They shared their knowledge to hire crews and design ships that could develop new sea routes. And to guide ships along the way, the experts improved methods of navigation. This is the science sailors use to plot their course and find their location far from land. Soon, Henry became known as "Prince Henry the Navigator."

Though Henry did not go himself, he began sending Portuguese ships south along the Atlantic coast of Africa. On each voyage, explorers traveled farther than the last, mapping the African shore and reporting sailing conditions. Portugal's ships began bringing home African gold.

The Portuguese also profited from the slave trade, the buying and selling of human beings. Slavery had existed throughout the world for thousands of years. For example, slavery had existed among the Aztecs and in the West African kingdom of Mali. Slave traders took captured people into and out of Africa along the Sahara trade routes. Many Arabs, Africans, and Europeans all participated in the slave trade by capturing people and forcing them into slavery.

In the 1400s, the slave trade grew. The Portuguese, and later other Europeans, began transporting African captives to Europe, where they became servants or slaves. A slave, unlike a servant, is owned by a person and has no freedom.

REVIEW Name two effects of Prince Henry's drive to explore the coast of Africa.
Cause and Effect

▶ **Under Prince Henry (above), Portugal took the lead in exploring the West coast of Africa. The Portuguese built forts along the coast to protect their trade in gold and slaves.**

113

A Sea Route to India

After Prince Henry died in 1460, Portuguese exploration continued. In 1488, Portuguese explorer **Bartolomeu Dias** (bahr too loo MAY oo DEE ush) and his three ships sailed within about 500 miles of Africa's southern tip. Then violent storms lashed the tiny fleet for many days. By the time the fierce winds let up, Dias made a startling discovery. His ships had been blown around the southern tip of Africa. They had reached the Indian Ocean. But his crew, far from home and frightened, refused to go on. So Dias turned back for Portugal.

Dias reported that he had found the tip of Africa, which he called the "Cape of Storms." But the king of Portugal renamed it the **Cape of Good Hope.** This name showed the Portuguese hope for sea routes to Asia.

Almost ten years later, in 1497, another Portuguese explorer left Portugal to sail around the Cape of Good Hope. **Vasco da Gama** and his four ships rounded Africa, sailed east across the Indian Ocean, and reached India in 1498. Before long, Portuguese merchants settled there in Calicut, India. There they bought spices at low prices and shipped them back to Europe. Portugal's sea routes made it a rich trading empire. Trace these sea routes in the Map Adventure on this page.

REVIEW Why did the king of Portugal name the southwestern tip of Africa the "Cape of Good Hope"? **Main Idea and Details**

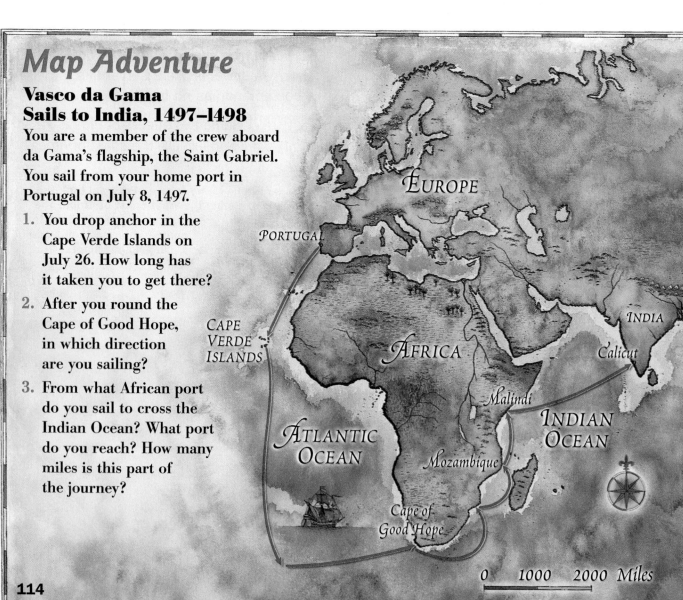

Map Adventure

Vasco da Gama Sails to India, 1497–1498

You are a member of the crew aboard da Gama's flagship, the Saint Gabriel. You sail from your home port in Portugal on July 8, 1497.

1. You drop anchor in the Cape Verde Islands on July 26. How long has it taken you to get there?

2. After you round the Cape of Good Hope, in which direction are you sailing?

3. From what African port do you sail to cross the Indian Ocean? What port do you reach? How many miles is this part of the journey?

EUROPE

PORTUGAL

CAPE VERDE ISLANDS

AFRICA

ATLANTIC OCEAN

Malindi

Mozambique

Cape of Good Hope

INDIA

Calicut

INDIAN OCEAN

0   1000   2000 Miles

▶ **A busy Portuguese harbor in the late 1400s.**

Asia. Soon they would be taking even longer sea journeys—journeys that brought them into contact with the peoples of the Americas. The Eastern Hemisphere and the Western Hemisphere were coming into lasting contact with each other.

REVIEW What was different about trade in the 1400s from trade in earlier periods? Compare and Contrast

Exploration Continues

You have read in this chapter how trade and exploration continued to increase among the peoples of Asia, Africa, and Europe. Of course, trade was nothing new. Caravans had traveled over land routes for centuries. Boats had always carried goods from place to place, often along coastal waters. Advances in sailing gradually increased how far and how fast ships could travel.

By the late 1400s, Europeans had established new ocean trade routes to Africa and

Summarize the Lesson

1000 Vikings under Leif Ericsson reached North America, but soon abandoned their settlement.

About 1350 The Renaissance, a rebirth of learning, began in Europe.

1498 Portuguese explorer Vasco da Gama established a sea route to India around the southern tip of Africa.

LESSON 3 REVIEW

Check Facts and Main Ideas

1. Draw Conclusions On a separate sheet of paper, list facts which lead to the conclusion shown.

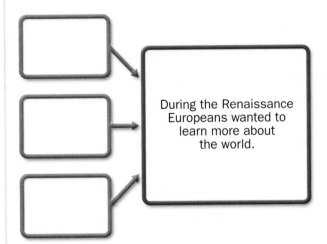

During the Renaissance Europeans wanted to learn more about the world.

2. What were some of the effects of the **Renaissance?**

3. What was the effect of Johann Gutenberg's new machine? What did it make possible?

4. Critical Thinking: *Cause and Effect* How did Prince Henry make Portugal the leading European country in the drive to explore other parts of the world?

5. What records of their attempt to settle North America did the Vikings leave behind?

Link to 🔗 **Reading**

Make Illustrated Manuscripts Before the printing press, people could only read manuscripts—books written, and often illustrated, by hand. Choose a passage from a book that you like and copy it. Use your most beautiful handwriting. Illustrate the passage.

115

Chart and Graph Skills

Use Parallel Time Lines

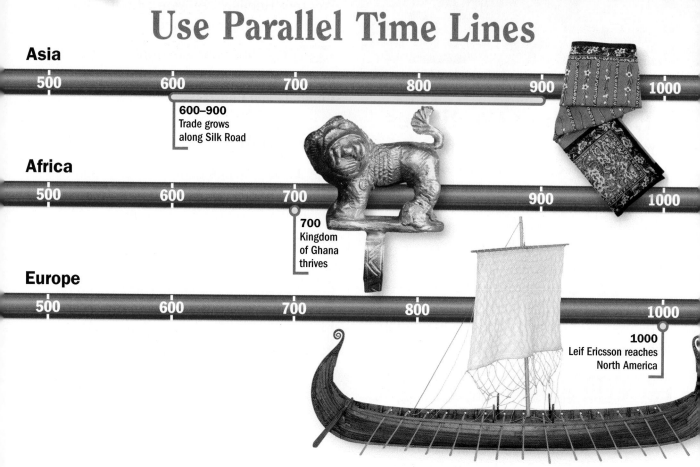

Asia

500   600   700   800   900   1000

600–900
Trade grows
along Silk Road

Africa

500   600   700   900   1000

700
Kingdom
of Ghana
thrives

Europe

500   600   700   800   1000

1000
Leif Ericsson reaches
North America

What? A time line, as you know, is a diagram showing the sequence of historical events. **Parallel time lines** are two or more time lines grouped together. Together, these parallel lines show major events in different places during the same period of time.

Why? You have been reading about events in Asia, Africa, and Europe. A parallel time line such as the one above shows events that took place on each continent. By comparing events that took place in different parts of the world, you can begin to recognize connections among the different continents. You can also discover what was taking place in one part of the world during the time something was happening in another.

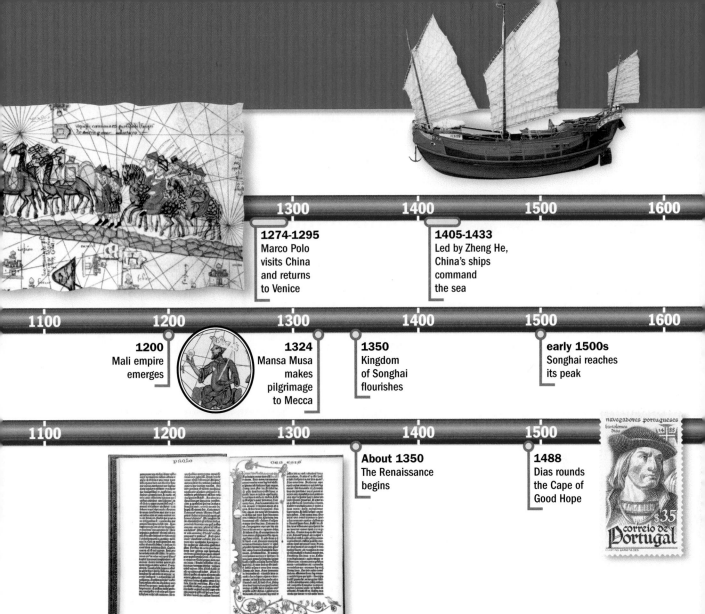

1300   **1400**   **1500**   **1600**

1274-1295
Marco Polo
visits China
and returns
to Venice

1405-1433
Led by Zheng He,
China's ships
command
the sea

1100   **1200**   **1300**   **1400**   **1500**   **1600**

1200
Mali empire
emerges

1324
Mansa Musa
makes
pilgrimage
to Mecca

1350
Kingdom
of Songhai
flourishes

early 1500s
Songhai reaches
its peak

1100   **1200**   **1300**   **1400**   **1500**

About 1350
The Renaissance
begins

1488
Dias rounds
the Cape of
Good Hope

How? Look at the three parallel time lines and compare them. They show events in Asia, Africa, and Europe between 600 and 1500. Although the time lines show the same period of time, different events were taking place on each of these continents. Sometimes events that began in one continent reached another continent.

To use the time lines, look at each one separately. Then compare what was taking place in two or three parts of the world during a particular time period. Then think about how these events may have been related or may have affected other places.

Think and Apply

1 What do **parallel time lines** show?

2 What was taking place in Africa as the Silk Road trade grew across Asia?

3 Did Zheng He command China's fleet of ships before or after Dias sailed around the tip of Africa?

4 What was taking place in Europe during the time the kingdom of Songhai arose?

117

CHAPTER 3
REVIEW

1000   1100   1200

about 700
Kingdom of Ghana
thrives

1000
Leif Ericsson
reaches North
America

Chapter Summary

 Summarize

Copy the graphic organizer on the right. Read the three sentences below and choose the one that best summarizes the chapter. Write that sentence in the correct place in the graphic organizer. Then fill in details from the chapter.

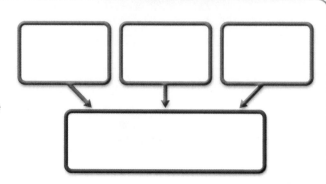

1 West Africa had a trading center and new empires.

2 Explorations took place on several continents between 1000 and 1500.

3 Ships became a very important way to travel during the period between 1000 and 1500.

Vocabulary

Match each word with the correct definition or description.

1 **saga** (p. 111)

2 **magnetic compass** (p. 104)

3 **pilgrimage** (p. 108)

4 **slave trade** (p. 113)

5 **navigation** (p. 113)

a. helps sailors determine direction at sea

b. the buying and selling of human beings

c. science of determining direction while traveling by sea

d. long spoken tale

e. journey taken for religious reasons

People and Places

For each of the people on the left, write a sentence connecting that person with one of the places on the right. You should have 5 sentences in all.

People

1 **Marco Polo** (p. 103)

2 **Kublai Khan** (p. 103)

3 **Mansa Musa** (p. 108)

4 **Leif Ericsson** (p. 111)

5 **Prince Henry** (p. 113)

Places

Timbuktu (p. 107)

Portugal (p. 113)

Shangdu (p. 103)

Venice (p. 103)

Vinland (p. 111)

74
lo
es
na

1324
Mansa Musa,
King of Mali,
goes to Mecca

about 1350
The Renaissance
begins in Europe

1405
Chinese fleets
explore the seas
under Zheng He

1420s
Prince Henry
sends Portuguese
ships to Africa

1498
Vasco da Gama
reaches India

early 1500s
Kingdom of
Songhai reaches
its peak

Apply Skills

Use Parallel Time Lines

Study the parallel time lines on pages 116–117.
Then answer the questions below.

1 What West African kingdom had already risen by the time Leif Ericsson sailed to North America?

2 Did Dias sail before or after the Renaissance began?

3 Did Mansa Musa make his pilgrimage before, during, or after the time Marco Polo visited China?

Facts and Main Ideas

1 In addition to goods, what else traveled along the Silk Road?

2 Name three powerful kingdoms of Africa.

3 What was the Renaissance and where did it begin?

4 **Time Line** How many years passed between the voyages of Leif Ericsson and Vasco da Gama?

5 **Main Idea** How did Zheng He's voyages help Chinese trade to grow?

6 **Main Idea** Which mineral resource contributed to the wealth of the kingdoms of West Africa?

7 **Main Idea** Why did Europeans desire new sea routes to Africa and Asia?

8 **Critical Thinking:** *Compare and Contrast* Choose any two of the following people and compare their travels: Leif Ericsson, Marco Polo, Mansa Musa, Zheng He, Vasco da Gama.

Write About History

1 **Write a travel diary entry** about experiences a merchant might have had along the Silk Road.

2 **Write a descriptive paragraph** about Mansa Musa and his pilgrimage to Mecca.

3 **Write an advertisement** for a book printed on the new Gutenberg press. Explain why the book is different from earlier kinds of books.

Internet Activity

To get help with vocabulary, people, and places, select dictionary or encyclopedia from *Social Studies Library* at **www.sfsocialstudies.com**.

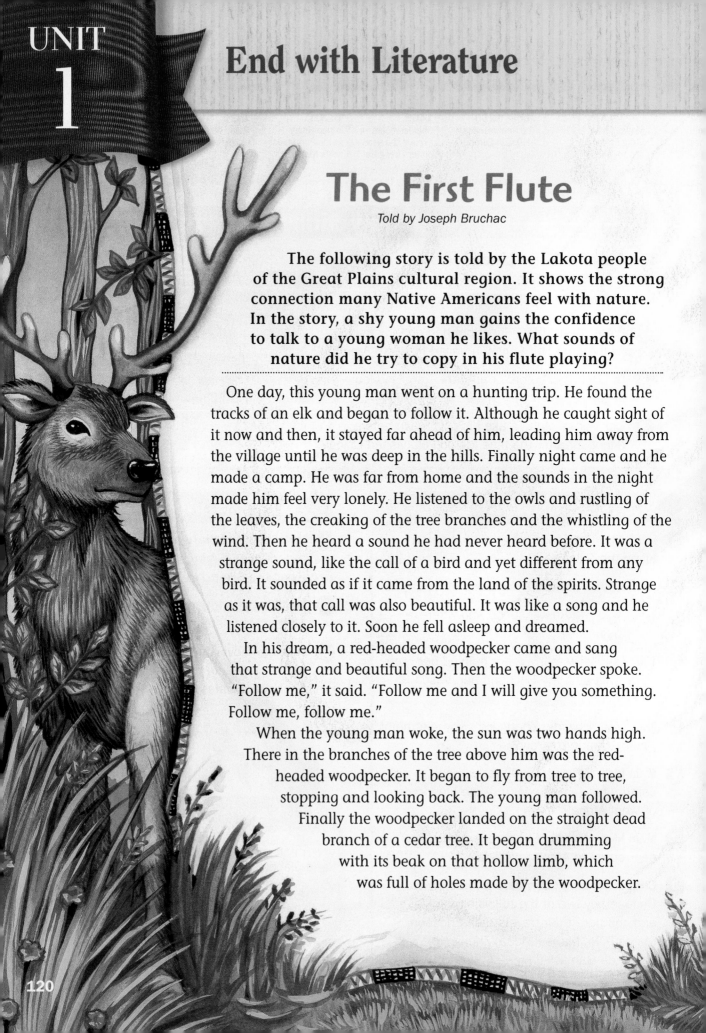

The First Flute

Told by Joseph Bruchac

The following story is told by the Lakota people of the Great Plains cultural region. It shows the strong connection many Native Americans feel with nature. In the story, a shy young man gains the confidence to talk to a young woman he likes. What sounds of nature did he try to copy in his flute playing?

One day, this young man went on a hunting trip. He found the tracks of an elk and began to follow it. Although he caught sight of it now and then, it stayed far ahead of him, leading him away from the village until he was deep in the hills. Finally night came and he made a camp. He was far from home and the sounds in the night made him feel very lonely. He listened to the owls and rustling of the leaves, the creaking of the tree branches and the whistling of the wind. Then he heard a sound he had never heard before. It was a strange sound, like the call of a bird and yet different from any bird. It sounded as if it came from the land of the spirits. Strange as it was, that call was also beautiful. It was like a song and he listened closely to it. Soon he fell asleep and dreamed.

In his dream, a red-headed woodpecker came and sang that strange and beautiful song. Then the woodpecker spoke. "Follow me," it said. "Follow me and I will give you something. Follow me, follow me."

When the young man woke, the sun was two hands high. There in the branches of the tree above him was the red-headed woodpecker. It began to fly from tree to tree, stopping and looking back. The young man followed. Finally the woodpecker landed on the straight dead branch of a cedar tree. It began drumming with its beak on that hollow limb, which was full of holes made by the woodpecker.

Just then a wind came up and blew through the hollow branch. It made the song that the hunter had heard!

Now the hunter saw what he should do. He climbed the tree and carefully broke off that branch. He thanked the red-headed woodpecker for giving him this gift and he took it home to his lodge. But he could not make it sing, no matter what he did. Finally he went to a hilltop and fasted for four days. On the fourth day a vision came to him. It was the woodpecker and it spoke again, telling him what to do. He must carve the likeness of the woodpecker and fasten it in a certain way near one end of the branch. He must shape the other end of the flute so it looked like the head and open mouth of a bird. Then when he blew into that end of the flute and covered the holes with his fingers, he would be able to play that song.

The man did as his vision told him. He carved the flute so that it looked like the head and open mouth of a bird. He tied on the bird reed near the other end and when he blew into the flute it made music. Then he began to practice long and hard, listening to the sounds of the wind and the trees, the rippling of the waters and the calls of the birds, making them all part of his playing. Soon he was able to play a beautiful song. Now when he hunted and camped far from the village he had his flute with him and could play it to keep himself company.

Finally, he knew that he was ready to visit that young woman he had liked so long from afar.

121

Review

Main Ideas and Vocabulary

Read the passage below and use it to answer the questions that follow.

People have long traveled for many reasons. Many early people moved from place to place in search of food. As they learned to farm, people settled in permanent communities. They began to trade with other people to get goods they needed or wanted. Traders traveled to exchange goods, and explorers looked for new trade routes. Some groups created large, powerful trading <u>empires</u>.

During the Ice Age, travelers included the first people to arrive in the Americas. They probably followed animals they hunted across a strip of land connecting Asia and North America. These first Americans lived by hunting and gathering. Later many Americans became farmers. They settled in communities and began trading with one another.

Trade became important around the world. In Africa, trading <u>caravans</u> crossed the Sahara. Rich trading empires grew as leaders ruled over many lands and people. The kingdom of Ghana traded gold for salt. Timbuktu became a great trading center. Mansa Musa, the king of Mali, made a great <u>pilgrimage</u> to Mecca. On this religious journey, he took gold and other riches.

In China, people made silk cloth. People from other lands wanted this silk and the spices and other goods that the Chinese had to trade. Traders traveled to and from China on routes known as the Silk Road. China's Zheng He commanded Chinese ships on exploration and trading trips west.

European explorers sailed down the coast of Africa as they searched for new trade routes east. In the late 1400s, Portugal's Vasco da Gama sailed around the tip of Africa and made his way to India.

1 According to the passage, why did people trade their goods?
  A to increase the value of their goods
  B to follow the orders of strong rulers who demanded their goods
  C to get rid of things they did not want or need
  D to get goods they needed or wanted

2 In the passage the word <u>caravans</u> means—
  A horse-drawn wagons
  B people traveling in groups
  C camels
  D wheeled vehicles

3 In the passage, the word <u>pilgrimage</u> means—
  A religious journey
  B trade route
  C exploration
  D exchange goods

4 What is the main idea of the passage?
  A People throughout the world moved from place to place and traded goods.
  B Sailing was the most important means of exploring the world.
  C Only China had silk to trade.
  D Agriculture changed the way people lived.

Vocabulary and Places

Match each place and term to its definition.

1 **glacier** (p. 55)

2 **travois** (p. 83)

3 **totem pole** (p. 95)

4 **Timbuktu** (p. 107)

5 **reservation** (p. 80)

a. a frame to transport goods

b. land set aside for Native Americans

c. trading city in Africa

d. carved tree trunk representing family history

e. thick sheet of ice

Write and Share

Stage a Quiz Show Use the format from a television quiz show to have a classroom quiz show. Divide the class into four teams. Have each team make up quiz questions and answers based on this unit. Each team will select contestants to answer one other team's questions. Set a timer for answers. After each team has had a chance to ask and answer questions, the team with the most points wins.

Read on Your Own

Look for books like these in the library.

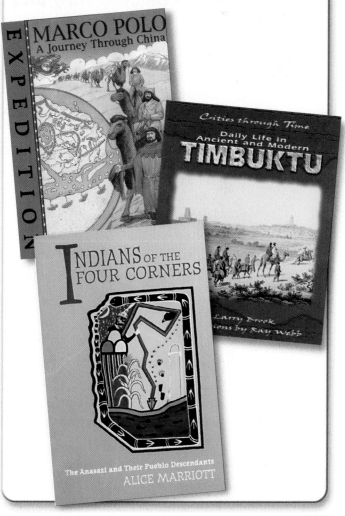

Apply Skills

Create a Summary Time Line Choose a chapter in this unit. For each lesson, create a time line and write a short summary describing significant events of each time period. Add illustrations to help remind you of information in your summary.

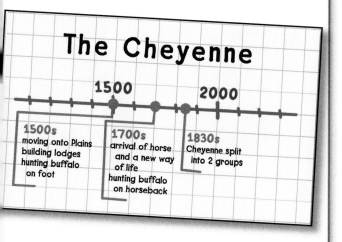

UNIT 1 Project

Early Cultures Documentary

Film makers often make documentaries showing people who lived in other times and places. They prepare a storyboard before they begin filming.

1 **Form** groups. In your group, choose an eastern or western culture from the unit to research and make a documentary.

2 **Make** a storyboard. Draw or find four pictures that illustrate details about the culture. Write a short paragraph describing each picture.

3 **Share** your storyboard with the class as the beginning of your documentary.

Internet Activity

Find out more about early cultures. Go to **www.sfsocialstudies.com/activities** and select your grade and unit.

Connections Across Continents

Why do we remember the feast now called Thanksgiving?

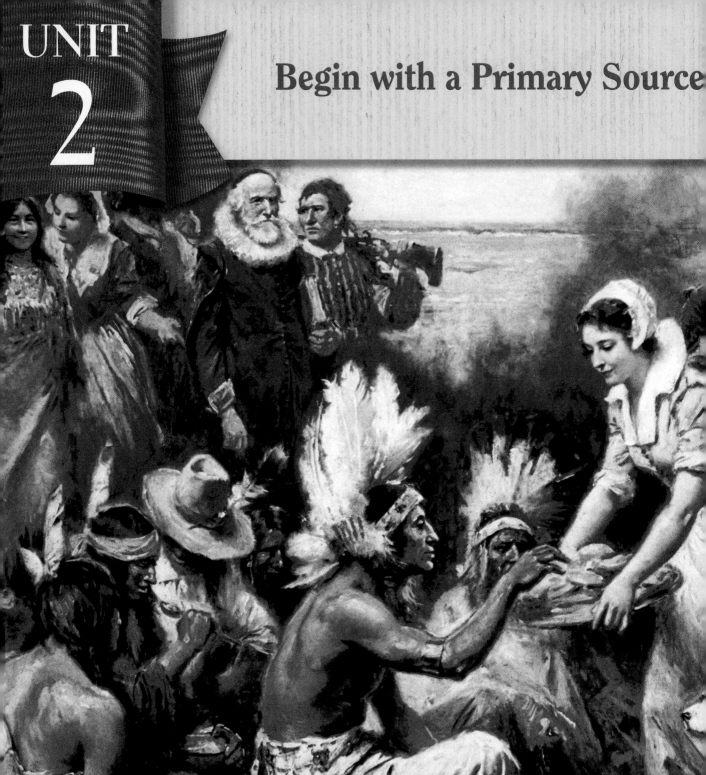

1450

1550

1492
Columbus reaches
the Americas

1521
Cortés defeats
the Aztecs

1527
Las Casas begins to defend
the native peoples

126

> ## "For three days we entertained and feasted."
> —Edward Winslow, English settler at Plymouth Plantation, 1621

The First Thanksgiving, a painting by J.L.G. Ferris, shows the Pilgrims and the Wampanoag celebrating the harvest in 1621.

1650 **1750**

1607
English
found
estown

1608
Champlain
founds
Quebec

1620
The Pilgrims
arrive at
Plymouth

1682
William Penn
establishes
Pennsylvania

1733
Georgia, 13th English
colony, is founded

Meet the People

Christopher Columbus

1451–1506
Birthplace: Genoa, Italy
Explorer

- Convinced Spanish king and queen to pay for an expedition to Asia
- Reached the Americas in 1492
- Opened the way for European colonization of the Americas

Bartolomé de Las Casas

1474–1566
Birthplace: Seville, Spain
Priest

- Traveled to the Americas to teach Indians about Christianity
- Criticized the treatment of American Indians
- Called for the end of Indian slavery

Samuel de Champlain

1567–1635
Birthplace: Brouage, France
Explorer

- Explored the St. Lawrence River for France
- Founder of the city of Quebec
- Defended Quebec against English attack

John Smith

1579?–1631
Birthplace: Willoughby, England
Soldier

- Helped establish the English colony of Jamestown, Virginia
- Led colonists through a difficult time with little food and few supplies
- Wrote several books to attract colonists to North America

1450	1500	1550	1600

1451 • Christopher Columbus   1506

1474 • Bartolomé de Las Casas   1566

1567 • Samuel de Champlain

1579? • John Smit

about 1585

1591

about 1

Squanto

about 1585–1622

Birthplace: Near present-day Plymouth, Massachusetts

Interpreter

- Learned English when kidnapped by English fishermen
- Sent by Wampanoag chief, Massasoit, to be interpreter during peace negotiations with Plymouth colonists
- Taught colonists key skills for survival

Anne Hutchinson

1591–1643

Birthplace: Alford, England

Religious leader

- Organized weekly religious meetings
- Banished from Massachusetts Bay Colony by Puritan leaders for holding opposing religious beliefs
- Cofounder of Portsmouth, Rhode Island

Pocahontas

about 1595–1617

Birthplace: Near present-day Jamestown, Virginia

Negotiator

- Daughter of Chief Powhatan
- Helped maintain peace between Powhatan Indians and English colonists at Jamestown
- Married English settler, John Rolfe, and moved to England

William Penn

1644–1718

Birthplace: London, England

Minister

- Imprisoned in England for publicly stating his Quaker beliefs
- Founder of Pennsylvania colony
- Established friendly relations with neighboring Lenni Lenape Indians

---

| 1650 | 1700 | 1750 |

1635

1631

• Squanto 1622

• Anne Hutchinson 1643

Pocahontas 1617

1644 • William Penn 1718

Reading Social Studies

Connections Across Continents

Sequence

Learning to find the sequence of events—the order things happen—will help you understand many kinds of writing. Learning to look for sequence is especially helpful when you are reading about history. Study the chart below.

- Sequence is the order in which events take place.
- Words such as first, then, after, once, afterwards, and later help signal the sequence of events. Dates also help establish sequence.

Word clue	Date	Event
First	1492	Columbus sails across the Atlantic Ocean.
Afterwards	1521	Cortés defeats the Aztecs.
Finally	1533	Pizarro conquers the Incas.

Read the following paragraph. **Words** that help signal sequence have been highlighted in blue. **Dates** are highlighted in yellow.

In Chapter 3, you read about European explorers who first sailed around Africa to find a sea route to Asia. Europeans became eager to find new territories. In 1492, Christopher Columbus sailed across the Atlantic Ocean. Afterwards, in 1521, Hernando Cortés led Spanish soldiers to defeat the Aztec empire. Finally, in 1533, Pizarro's army defeated the Incas in Peru. These events were the beginnings of a Spanish empire in the Americas.

Word Exercise

Inferring Meaning Use this process to figure out the meaning of an unfamiliar word in a sentence: 1) *Gather* clues by reading before and after the unfamiliar word; 2) *Connect* what you already know; 3) *Predict* a meaning for the word. Try it with this sentence: Settlers raised tobacco as a successful <u>cash crop</u>.

Context Clues		Connections		Prediction
• tobacco = a plant • crop = plants grown for food • cash = money	+	Farmers grow crops to sell so they can live.	=	Cash crop means "plants grown for the purpose of selling."

Connections Across Continents:
A Sequence of Events

After Europeans explored parts of Asia and Africa, they looked westward across the Atlantic Ocean. No maps existed to help sailors cross it.

First, Spain sent ships across the Atlantic. Christopher Columbus sailed in 1492. When he reached land, he thought he had reached the Indies in Asia. The people he met became known as Indians.

After Columbus's first voyage, Spain sent more explorers, soldiers, priests, and settlers. The Spanish conquered the Aztecs in 1521 and the Incas in 1533. By 1535, Spain had established the colony of New Spain in the Americas.

About one hundred years after Columbus's first voyage, English colonists attempted to set up a colony on Roanoke Island in 1587. The colony and its people disappeared by 1590.

Next, English colonists settled at Jamestown, Virginia, in 1607. After several difficult years, settlers raised tobacco as a successful cash crop. New people arrived, including Africans.

Farther north, the French established the city of Quebec in 1608, which later became the capital of the colony of New France. Sixteen years later, in 1624, the Dutch started New Amsterdam on Manhattan Island.

In 1620, a new group of English settlers landed at Plymouth. The Pilgrims wanted religious freedom. In 1630, a larger group of English settlers, the Puritans, arrived. They, too, wanted to practice their own religion. They founded the Massachusetts Bay Colony. Eventually there were 13 English colonies along the eastern coast of North America.

Apply it!

Use the strategy of sequence to answer questions 1 and 2. Then answer the vocabulary questions.

1. Which European country was the first to establish colonies in the Americas?

2. Who arrived first, the Puritans or the Pilgrims?

3. In your own words, describe how you would use the process of using context clues and connections to find out what *religious freedom* means in this passage.

CHAPTER 4

Spain Builds an Empire

1492

Bahama Islands
Columbus reaches the Americas.

Lesson 1

1

1521

Tenochtitlan
Cortés defeats the Aztec Empire.

Lesson 2

2

1574

Hispaniola
There are 12,000 enslaved Africans working the sugar plantations.

Lesson 3

3

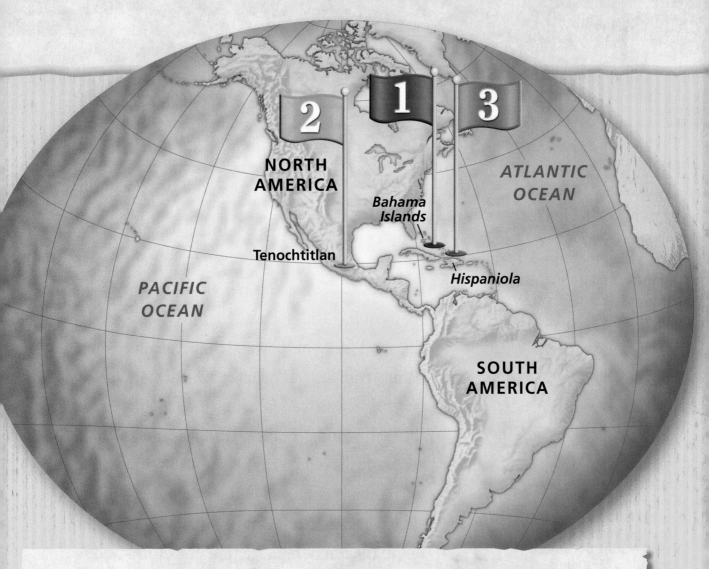

NORTH
AMERICA

ATLANTIC
OCEAN

Bahama
Islands

Tenochtitlan

Hispaniola

PACIFIC
OCEAN

SOUTH
AMERICA

Why We Remember

October 12, 1492. It may be one of the first historical dates you ever learned. It is recognized as a holiday—not only in the United States, but in many countries in North and South America. It is Columbus Day, of course, the day when Christopher Columbus and the sailors on three tiny Spanish ships first sighted land in the Americas. As you will read, Columbus met people he called Indians. He did not know then that he was far from India. He also could not have known that his journey would lead to powerful changes for the Americas, Europe, and the entire world.

1490   1500

1492
Columbus reaches the Americas

1501
Vespucci sails under the Portuguese flag

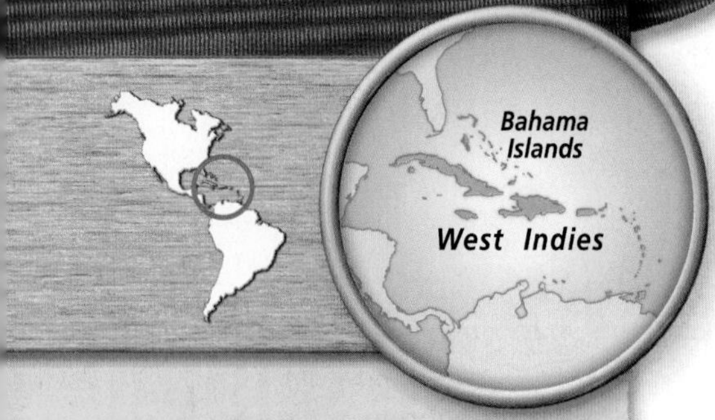

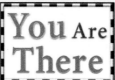

Bahama Islands

West Indies

PREVIEW

Focus on the Main Idea
Columbus's voyages led to European settlement of the Americas and an exchange of people, animals, goods, and ways of life between East and West.

PLACES
Bahama Islands
West Indies

PEOPLE
Christopher Columbus
King Ferdinand
Queen Isabella
Amerigo Vespucci
Vasco Núñez de Balboa
Ferdinand Magellan

VOCABULARY
expedition
colony
Columbian Exchange

The Voyages of Columbus

You Are There
They call their island Guanahaní. As the people prepare their meal over an open fire—which they call a "barbeque"—the chief watches his people. He strokes the short fur of his dog and thinks about tomorrow's fishing trip. Several men are hard at work on the beach. They are carving out the trunk of a large tree that will become a canoe. He hopes the canoe will be ready to take out on the water by tomorrow morning.

The chief's thoughts of the fishing trip are interrupted by a loud cry. One of the villagers is pointing out to the bright blue sea. The chief turns and squints in the same direction, and he sees what the villager sees. There, in the distance, is a large and strange ship. It looks nothing like a canoe. In fact, it looks like nothing he has ever seen before.

Sequence As you read, keep in mind the order in which events happened as Europeans explored the Americas.

Columbus and the Taino

The island you have just read about lies southeast of Florida. The village belonged to a group of people called the Taino (tah EE noh). The ship they saw that day in 1492 meant big changes were coming to their way of life.

On the other side of the Atlantic Ocean, Europeans were continuing their drive to explore the world. One of them, an Italian named **Christopher Columbus,** had a bold idea. He wanted to find a better way to reach the Indies, a part of Asia rich with gold, spices, and other goods. At the time, Europeans had only one way to reach the Indies—the difficult land journey over the Silk Road.

Columbus suggested sailing west, across the Atlantic Ocean. He needed money to pay for his expedition. An **expedition** is a journey made for a special purpose. Columbus took his plan to Spain's **King Ferdinand** and **Queen Isabella.** They did not agree right away, but finally he convinced them that he could find a cheaper and quicker way to the Indies.

On August 3, 1492, Columbus left Spain with three ships—the *Niña, Pinta,* and *Santa María.* After about one month at sea, the men feared they would never see their homes again. They had traveled farther west than they thought possible, and they wanted to turn back. Columbus pushed on.

Finally, on October 12, land was sighted from the *Pinta.* Columbus wrote: "At two hours after midnight, the *Pinta* fired a cannon, my prearranged signal for the sighting of land." He claimed the island for the Spanish king and queen. Soon after, some of the Taino came to greet the Europeans.

Historians believe that Columbus may have reached one of the **Bahama Islands.** Because he believed that he had reached the Indies, he called the Taino "Indians." This name later referred to the native people of the Americas. The Bahama Islands and other islands of the region became known as the **West Indies.**

REVIEW Which events happened to Columbus before October 12, 1492?

↻ **Sequence**

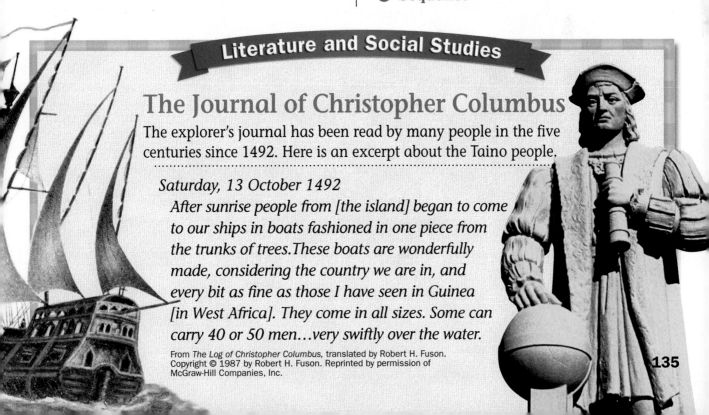

Literature and Social Studies

The Journal of Christopher Columbus

The explorer's journal has been read by many people in the five centuries since 1492. Here is an excerpt about the Taino people.

Saturday, 13 October 1492
After sunrise people from [the island] began to come to our ships in boats fashioned in one piece from the trunks of trees. These boats are wonderfully made, considering the country we are in, and every bit as fine as those I have seen in Guinea [in West Africa]. They come in all sizes. Some can carry 40 or 50 men...very swiftly over the water.

The Columbian Exchange

Columbus led three more expeditions to the Americas. On the second trip in 1493, he took 17 ships loaded with settlers, animals, and other supplies. In addition to finding riches, Spain had a new goal for this trip. This goal was to start a colony that would bring profits to Spain. A colony is a settlement far from the country that rules it. Before long, thousands of European settlers were living in colonies throughout the West Indies.

The Columbian Exchange had begun. This was a movement of people, animals, plants, diseases, and ways of life between the Eastern Hemisphere and Western Hemisphere. You can see examples of the Columbian Exchange in the chart on this page.

Europeans brought horses, cattle, sheep, and pigs with them to the Western Hemisphere. In the Eastern Hemisphere, people enjoyed new foods from the Americas, such as corn, potatoes, tomatoes, cocoa, and beans.

These changes helped the people of Europe, Africa, Asia, and the Americas. But not all of the effects of the Columbian Exchange were positive. Without knowing it, Europeans also brought disease germs to the Americas. Many Native Americans died because they had no defense against smallpox and measles.

As European colonies took hold in the West Indies, the native peoples' way of life changed. Many were forced to work on large farms growing sugarcane and other crops. Sugarcane is used to make sugar. Sugarcane growers made huge profits.

The Spanish also wanted to bring Christianity to the native peoples. They forced many to give up their own beliefs. As a result, the way of life of the Taino, and other native groups of the Caribbean, disappeared.

REVIEW Which events came before the Columbian Exchange? ↻ **Sequence**

▶ The Columbian Exchange brought change to both the Eastern and Western Hemispheres.

CHART SKILL *In which direction did sheep move?*

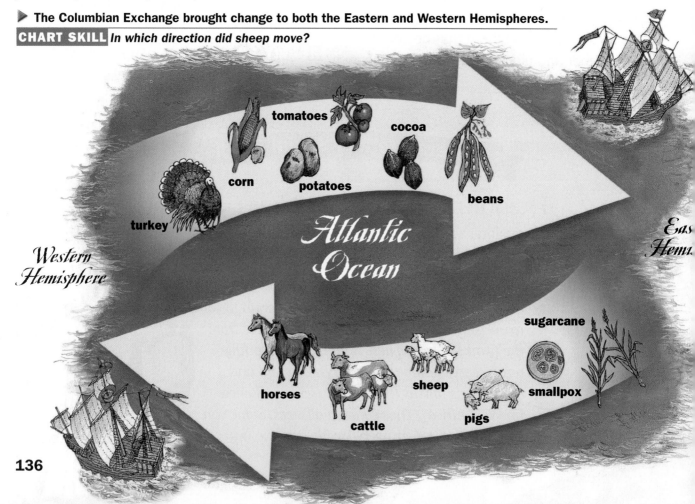

tomatoes

cocoa

corn

potatoes

beans

turkey

Atlantic Ocean

Western Hemisphere

Eas Hemi

sugarcane

horses

sheep

smallpox

cattle

pigs

Explorers for Spain

By the early 1500s, the Spanish realized that the islands of the Caribbean were not part of Asia, but the edge of a new continent. To them it was a "new world," one that was waiting to be explored and settled.

In fact, the Western Hemisphere was home to millions of people of many cultures. The map on this page shows the routes of some of the explorers sent by Spain. Who sailed first, Vespucci or Magellan?

Christopher Columbus (1451–1506)
- Born in Italy
- Led four voyages between 1492 and 1504. The map shows his first voyage.

Amerigo Vespucci (1454–1512)
- Born in Italy
- Sailed to the eastern coast of South America in 1501.

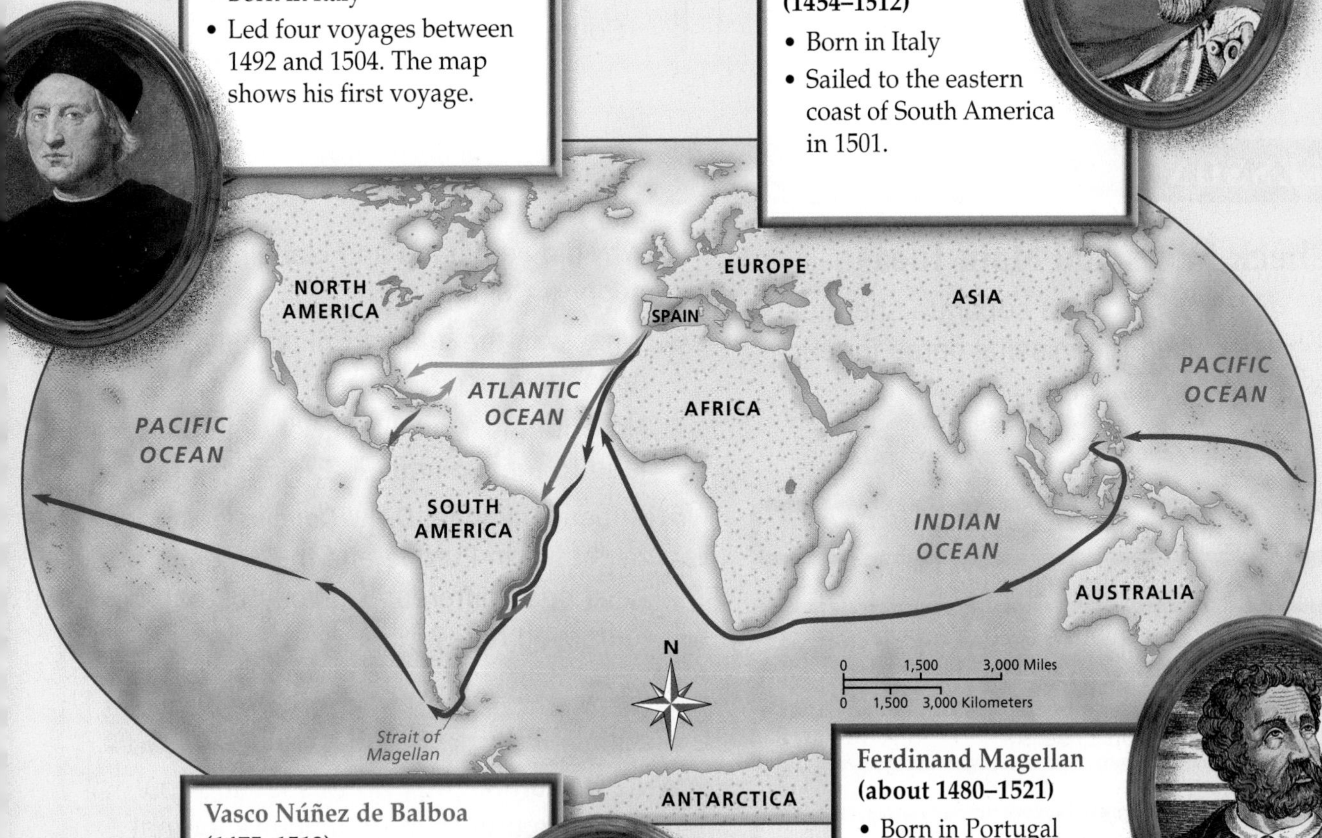

NORTH AMERICA

EUROPE

ASIA

SPAIN

ATLANTIC OCEAN

AFRICA

PACIFIC OCEAN

PACIFIC OCEAN

SOUTH AMERICA

INDIAN OCEAN

AUSTRALIA

N

| 0 | 1,500 | 3,000 Miles |
| 0 | 1,500 | 3,000 Kilometers |

Strait of Magellan

ANTARCTICA

Vasco Núñez de Balboa (1475–1519)
- Born in Spain
- In 1513 crossed the Isthmus of Panama and reached the Pacific Ocean.

Ferdinand Magellan (about 1480–1521)
- Born in Portugal
- Led the first expedition around the world, which began in 1519 and ended without him in 1522. He was killed during the voyage.

The Impact of Columbus

Christopher Columbus showed Europeans the way to the Americas. The name America itself comes from the explorer **Amerigo Vespucci,** who in 1502 became the first to call the Americas a "new world."

After Columbus and Vespucci, many more Europeans followed. Some came in search of land and riches and conquered mighty empires of native peoples to find them. By the early 1600s, explorers and settlers from Spain, Portugal, England, France, Sweden, and the Netherlands had come to the Americas. For hundreds of years, some of these countries fought among themselves, and against native peoples, for control of the lands in the Western Hemisphere. You will read of these events in upcoming lessons and chapters.

REVIEW Who was the first to call the Americas a "new world"? **Sequence**

Summarize the Lesson

1492 Columbus reached the Americas and claimed land in the West Indies for Spain.

1493 Columbus returned to start colonies, leading to the Columbian Exchange.

1501 Sailing under the Portuguese flag, Vespucci explored the eastern coast of South America.

LESSON 1 REVIEW

Check Facts and Main Ideas

1. **Sequence** On a separate sheet of paper, fill in the missing dates for each event on this chart.

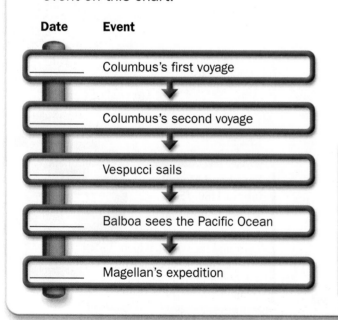

Date   Event

- Columbus's first voyage
- Columbus's second voyage
- Vespucci sails
- Balboa sees the Pacific Ocean
- Magellan's expedition

2. Why did Ferdinand and Isabella agree to support Columbus?

3. What was the goal of Columbus's second voyage?

4. How did the **expeditions** of Columbus lead to the **Columbian Exchange?**

5. **Critical Thinking: *Draw Conclusions*** How might life in Europe and the Americas have been different if Columbus had not journeyed here?

Link to ⬥⬥ Writing

Write a Journal Entry In this lesson you read an excerpt from Columbus's journal about meeting the Taino. Write a journal entry showing what a Taino might have written about meeting Columbus.

European Exploration

Even the most educated Europeans knew little about the world outside Europe in the late 1400s. They had no idea how wide the Atlantic Ocean was nor what lay on the other side. Then, in 1492, Christopher Columbus reached the Americas, where he thought the East Indies should be. This voyage changed the world forever.

An Astrolabe
Columbus used an astrolabe similar to this to measure his latitude on his voyage to the Americas.

Naming America
The Italian navigator Amerigo Vespucci was the first to realize that America was a separate continent—not part of China. The continents of North and South America are named for him.

Gold from the Americas
Columbus promised to return with gold and silver for King Ferdinand and Queen Isabella. The gold he found was used to make coins like this one, on which you can see the Spanish king and queen.

The *Santa María*
The *Santa María* was one of the three ships of Columbus's first voyage. He traveled on the *Santa María* until it was wrecked off the West Indies. For the voyage back to Spain, he transferred to the *Niña*.

Map and Globe Skills

Using Latitude and Longitude

MAP A: Latitude

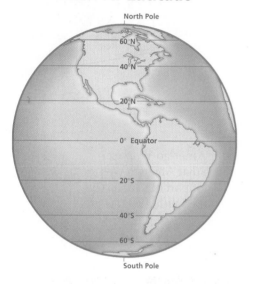

MAP B: Longitude

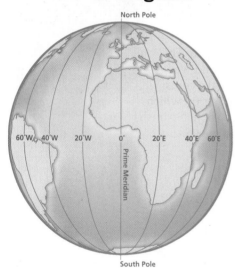

What? You have read that when Columbus sailed west, his sailors worried because they did not know where they were. At that time, Europeans did not have maps showing what lands were on the western side of the Atlantic Ocean. His sailors might have felt better if they had the maps we have today. They would also have been helped by a system of imaginary lines that geographers have created to help locate places on Earth. This system is called latitude and longitude.

Lines of **latitude** are imaginary lines that circle the globe in an east-west direction. They measure distances north and south of the equator. You can see lines of latitude on Map A. Lines of **longitude** are imaginary lines that run in a north-south direction. Look at Map B. Lines of longitude are also called **meridians.** They measure distances east and west of the prime meridian.

Why? The lines of latitude and longitude cross each other to form a **grid,** a set of crossing lines. We can describe every location on Earth by naming the latitude and longitude lines that cross there.

How? Find the equator on Map A. It is a line of latitude—the line at zero degrees, or 0°. The symbol ° means degree. A degree is a unit that measures latitude and longitude. Everything north of the equator is north latitude, which is labeled N. Everything south of the equator is south latitude, which is labeled S. Find the line of latitude 40° N (say "forty degrees north latitude"). Then find 40° S. Which line is closer to the North Pole?

The line of longitude marked 0° is also known as the **prime meridian.** Lines of longitude measure distances east and west of the prime meridian. All meridians west of the prime meridian are labeled W until they reach 180°W. Find the prime meridian on Map B.

Map C: The Four Voyages of Christopher Columbus

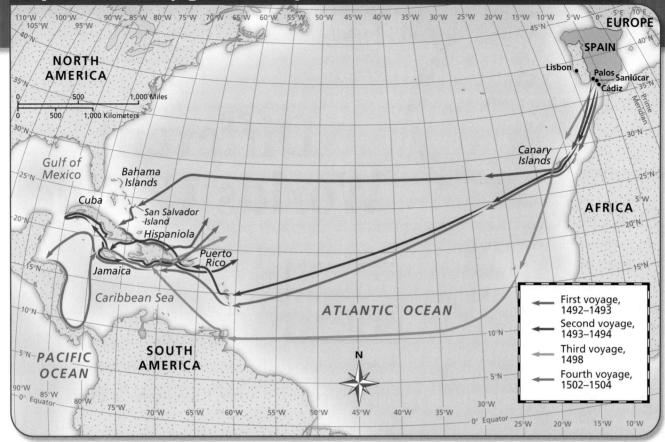

Unlike lines of latitude, lines of longitude are not always the same distance apart. Lines of longitude are farthest apart at the equator and meet at the North and South poles. Lines of latitude are also called parallels. They are always parallel, the same distance apart.

Now, look at Map C on this page, which shows Columbus's four voyages. He began his fourth expedition at about 35° N, 5° W.

To find the point (35° N, 5° W), find the line of latitude 35° N along the right side of the map. Then find the line of longitude 5° W along the top of the map. Trace your finger along each of these lines until they meet. That is the place you are looking for. Remember that you always state the latitude first, followed by the longitude. Maps do not show every line of latitude and longitude. Sometimes you have to describe a location by naming two lines that cross near it.

Think and Apply

1 Find the location 10° N, 60° W on Map C. During which voyage did Columbus sail here?

2 Locate the Canary Islands on Map C. Between which lines of **latitude** do they lie? Between which lines of **longitude**?

3 Locate San Salvador on Map C. Near which lines of latitude and longitude is San Salvador located?

Internet Activity

For more information, go online to the *Atlas* at **www.sfsocialstudies.com**.

141

Tenochtitlan
(Mexico City)
• NEW SPAIN

1520

1540

1521
Cortés defeats
the Aztecs

1533
Incan
Empire
falls to
Spain

1535
New Spain is
established

Different Worlds Collide

PREVIEW

Focus on the Main Idea
Spanish conquistadors
established new colonies in
North America and South
America.

PLACES
Tenochtitlan
New Spain
Mexico City
Cuzco
Lima

PEOPLE
Moctezuma
Hernando Cortés
Doña Marina
Francisco Pizarro
Atahualpa

VOCABULARY
conquistador
ally
conquest
convert
colonist

You Are There
The scene is Tenochtitlan, grand
capital city of the Aztec Empire. The
time is November 1519. On a wide
avenue leading to the center of the city, two powerful
men approach each other. Each leader is surrounded
by his soldiers.

One leader is Moctezuma (mahk teh ZOO mah),
the ruler of the Aztecs. He sits in a splendid carriage
decorated with gold, silver, jewels, and bright
green feathers. The other man is Hernando Cortés
(kor TEZ). He has come to conquer these lands
for Spain. His iron helmet shows that he is a soldier
ready to do battle for the Spanish king.

The mood is tense. The two men offer
each other gifts and talk peace. But
before long, the army of one will
conquer the other.

Sequence As you read, follow
the sequence of events as the
Spanish established
New Spain in the Americas.

Target Skill

The Aztecs Are Conquered

Even before the day they met in 1519, **Moctezuma** and **Hernando Cortés** knew of each other. Cortés had arrived in Mexico nine months earlier from Cuba. The Spanish had begun establishing colonies on the islands of the Caribbean Sea. Stories of great riches in Mexico encouraged Cortés and other Spaniards to gain some of the Aztecs' wealth.

Cortés was one of a group of Spanish soldiers who would later be called **conquistadors** (kon KEE stah dorz), or conquerors. But Cortés faced a major challenge in defeating the Aztecs. His force of about 500 men was greatly outnumbered.

However, Cortés did have a few advantages. Metal armor protected the Spanish from the Aztecs' stone weapons. Spanish soldiers had muskets, a kind of rifle. Spanish bullets could easily pierce the cloth suits the Aztecs wore. The conquistadors also had horses. The Aztecs had not seen horses before, and the animals frightened them. One native person said the horses "ran like deer and could catch anyone (the Spanish) told them to."

Biblioteca Nacional, Madrid

Cortés had allies too. An **ally** is a friend who will help in a fight. The people that Cortés met on his way to **Tenochtitlan** did not want to live under Aztec rule. Many of them decided to help Cortés defeat the Aztecs.

One ally of Cortés was an Aztec woman called **Doña Marina,** a name she took after becoming a Christian. Doña Marina spoke several Indian languages and spoke to the native peoples of Mexico for Cortés. Doña Marina helped Cortés persuade thousands to join him. One Spaniard described Doña Marina as "an excellent person, and a good interpreter."

An important ally that the Spanish did not know they had was the germ that causes smallpox. Some historians think thousands of Aztecs caught smallpox after Cortés arrived.

At their first meeting in 1519, Moctezuma agreed to let Cortés stay in Tenochtitlan. Almost a year later, the Aztecs rose up and threw the Spanish out of their city. Moctezuma was killed, perhaps by his own people. Cortés escaped. But he returned late in 1520 with many more native peoples as allies. In 1521, the mightiest empire of the Americas fell to the conquistadors.

REVIEW Describe the sequence of events that led to the fall of the Aztecs. 🌀 **Sequence**

▶ **This drawing, made in the 1500s, shows the battle for Tenochtitlan. The Spanish, on the left, carried muskets and wore metal armor.**

143

Mexico City

One of the oldest cities in the Western Hemisphere, Mexico City was built on the ruins of Tenochtitlan. Today, archaeologists find evidence of the ancient Aztec capital right in the center of the modern city. You can see artifacts like those on the right in museums in Mexico City.

Founding New Spain

After the conquest of the Aztecs, the Spanish destroyed Tenochtitlan. A **conquest** is the capture or taking of something by force. The conquistadors were helped once again by disease. Smallpox continued to take the lives of many throughout Mexico.

In 1535 Spain established the colony of **New Spain.** The capital of New Spain was **Mexico City.** Today, Mexico City is the capital of Mexico. Spanish officials came to set up a government, make laws, and build schools and universities. Roman Catholic priests came to **convert,** or change, native peoples from their own religion to Christianity.

Spanish leaders such as Cortés discouraged native peoples from continuing to sacrifice people to their gods. Colonists also came from Spain. A **colonist** is a person who lives in a colony. Spanish colonists hoped to gain wealth by starting farms, businesses, and gold and silver mines in New Spain.

REVIEW Summarize the goals of the colonists who came to New Spain.
Summarize

The Conquests Continue

One more powerful and wealthy native peoples' empire lay to the south. This was the empire of the Incas, who controlled a huge area of land in western South America. Ten years after the conquest of Mexico began, Spain sent **Francisco Pizarro** (pee ZAH roh) to South America to conquer the Incan empire.

Pizarro captured the Incan ruler **Atahualpa** (ah tah HWAHL pah) in 1532. The following year, Pizarro's forces captured **Cuzco,** the Incan capital city. By 1535 Pizarro had founded a new capital

▶ **This wooden cup shows Francisco Pizarro.**

called **Lima,** in a colony called Peru. Today, Lima is the capital of the country of Peru.

As you will read, conflict between the Spanish and native peoples continued. Like the Aztecs, some native peoples fought back. But most of them faced defeat. A new culture—part Indian, part Spanish—was born.

REVIEW Which came first, the conquest of the Aztecs or the Incas? ⟳ Sequence

Summarize the Lesson

- **1521** Hernando Cortés defeated the Aztec empire of Mexico and built Mexico City on the ruins of Tenochtitlan.

- **1533** Francisco Pizarro defeated the Incan empire and later founded the colony of Peru.

- **1535** Spain established the colony of New Spain, with its capital at Mexico City.

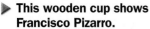

LESSON 2 ▸ REVIEW

Check Facts and Main Ideas

1. ⟳ **Sequence** On a separate sheet of paper, place these events in the correct sequence and fill in the missing dates.

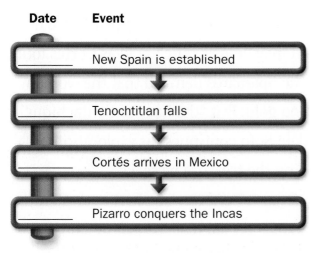

Date | Event

_____ New Spain is established

_____ Tenochtitlan falls

_____ Cortés arrives in Mexico

_____ Pizarro conquers the Incas

2. What were the key advantages of Hernando Cortés in defeating the Aztecs?

3. Why did Spain send priests to New Spain?

4. How long did it take Pizarro to conquer the Incan empire?

5. **Critical Thinking: *Problem Solving*** The Spanish set up a government to rule New Spain. Think about how you would rule this colony. Write a short description of one problem and a suggested solution. Use the problem-solving steps on page H3.

Link to ⟨⟩ Writing

Write a Dramatic Scene Suppose you are traveling with Hernando Cortés to meet Moctezuma. Describe the meeting between the **conquistador** and the Aztec ruler.

Hispaniola

1500			1550

1512
Africans are brought to Hispaniola

1527
Las Casas defends the native peoples

1540
Coronado explores the Southwest

Life in New Spain

PREVIEW

Focus on the Main Idea
Spain gained great wealth from the settlement and growth of New Spain.

PLACES
Hispaniola

PEOPLE
Hernando de Soto
Estéban
Álvar Núñez Cabeza de Vaca
Francisco Vásquez de Coronado
Juan Ponce de León
Bartolomé de Las Casas

VOCABULARY
society
plantation
encomienda
missionary
mission

You Are There

It is 1540. Spanish conquistador Hernando de Soto and about 700 men are traveling through what is now Georgia. They are searching for Cofitachiqui (koh FEE tah CHEE kee), a rich American Indian city they have heard about. De Soto and his soldiers meet a young Native American woman. They call her "the Lady of Cofitachiqui." De Soto asks her about the freshwater pearls she has with her. The young woman takes the men to a building that contains many more pearls.

De Soto is interested in more than pearls. He hopes that this land may hold as much gold as Cortés found in Mexico. The Spaniards demand that the woman help them find gold. But "the Lady of Cofitachiqui" escapes, and de Soto continues his explorations without finding the treasure he seeks.

Sequence As you read, sequence the major events in the Spanish attempt to build New Spain and explore North America.

The Search for Gold

The story you just read was told by a member of **Hernando de Soto's** expedition. It was one of many stories that the Spanish told about gold and other riches in the Americas.

One story was about a rich kingdom called Cíbola (SIH boh lah), located far to the north of Mexico. It was told by **Estéban,** an African sailor who had been enslaved. Estéban had survived a shipwreck off the coast of Texas with the conquistador **Álvar Núñez Cabeza de Vaca** (day BAH cah) in 1528. They traveled for eight years through what is now the Southwest region of the United States.

▶ **Gold nugget**

Three years later, Estéban joined another expedition to find Cíbola. But he did not find the kingdom. Estéban was killed by the Zuni people in what is now New Mexico.

The legend of Cíbola did not fade. The governor of New Spain decided to send **Francisco Vásquez de Coronado** (koh roh NAH doh) to find the cities. He did not find the cities of Cíbola either, because they did not exist. The Fact File on this page shows the routes of Coronado and other Spanish explorers of North America.

REVIEW Sequence these events: Estéban is killed, Estéban is shipwrecked, and Estéban travels in the Southwest. ⟳ **Sequence**

FACT FILE

The Spanish Explore to the North, 1513–1542

By the middle 1500s Spain had sent several expeditions to explore the lands that would one day become the United States.

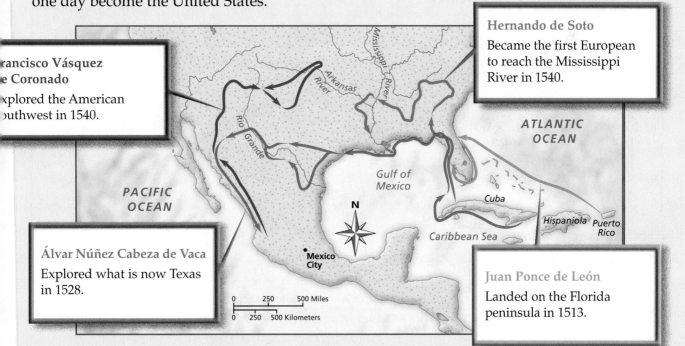

Francisco Vásquez de Coronado
Explored the American Southwest in 1540.

Hernando de Soto
Became the first European to reach the Mississippi River in 1540.

ATLANTIC OCEAN

PACIFIC OCEAN

Gulf of Mexico

Cuba

Hispaniola Puerto Rico

Caribbean Sea

Rio Grande

Arkansas River

Mississippi River

N

Mexico City

Álvar Núñez Cabeza de Vaca
Explored what is now Texas in 1528.

0   250   500 Miles
0   250   500 Kilometers

Juan Ponce de León
Landed on the Florida peninsula in 1513.

147

Society in New Spain

By the end of the 1500s, most of the fighting between native peoples and conquistadors north and south of Mexico City had ended. The Spanish gained enough control to move colonists into these lands. The map on this page shows New Spain in 1600.

A new way of life, and a new society, was developing in New Spain. A **society** is a group of people forming a community.

At the top of colonial society were the peninsulares (pay neen soo LAH rays). These were people born in Spain. The name was based on the geography of Spain, which is located on a peninsula. Next were creoles (kray OH lays), people of Spanish background who were born in the Americas. Under the creoles were the mestizos, the largest group in New Spain society. A mestizo is a person with Indian and Spanish background. People who had no Spanish ancestors, such as Indians and Africans, held the lowest position in this society.

The peninsulares were wealthy and powerful. Some owned **plantations,** or large farms with many workers who lived on the land they worked. Other peninsulares received grants called encomiendas. An **encomienda** (en koh mee EN dah) granted a peninsulare control of all of the native peoples who lived on an area of land. The encomienda owners could put the native peoples to work. They were supposed to care for the native peoples and convert them to Christianity. In return, the native peoples had to give the encomienda owners crops that they grew and other goods.

In the cities, colonists became merchants and shopkeepers or worked for the colonial government. Others had small businesses, such as making furniture or clothing.

REVIEW Describe the main idea of the paragraphs on this page about New Spain society. **Main Idea and Details**

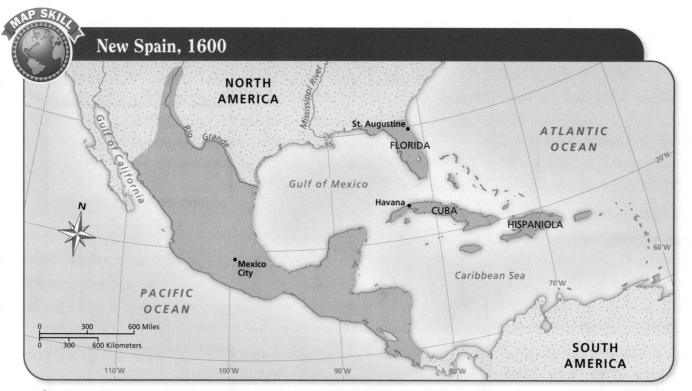

MAP SKILL

New Spain, 1600

NORTH AMERICA

Mississippi River

Gulf of California

Rio Grande

St. Augustine

FLORIDA

ATLANTIC OCEAN

Gulf of Mexico

Havana

CUBA

HISPANIOLA

N

Mexico City

Caribbean Sea

PACIFIC OCEAN

0   300   600 Miles
0   300   600 Kilometers

110°W   100°W   90°W   80°W   70°W   60°W   20°N

SOUTH AMERICA

▶ New Spain, shown in orange on this map, was established to rule lands claimed by Spain in North America.

MAP SKILL Use Latitude and Longitude *At about what latitude and longitude is Mexico City located?*

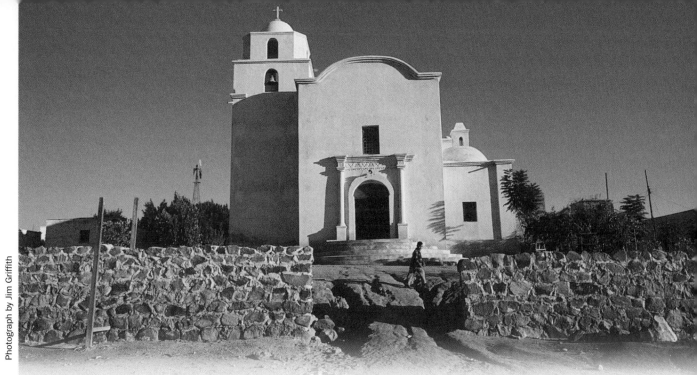

Photograph by Jim Griffith

▶ The Spanish built missions throughout Mexico to teach the native peoples about Christianity.

More Changes for Native Peoples

Many encomienda owners put native peoples to work as farm workers, miners, and servants. The native peoples had to work without pay and did not always have enough to eat. They could be beaten and forced to work long hours.

One type of encomienda was run by Roman Catholic missionaries. A **missionary** teaches his or her religion to others who have different beliefs. The priests built missions throughout New Spain. A **mission** is a religious settlement where missionaries live and work. The purpose of these missions was to teach native peoples about Christianity. Missionaries also taught them some European farming practices, such as raising cattle and sheep. The native peoples had to give up their traditional ways of life and become Christians. On some missions, they were treated cruelly.

A priest named **Bartolomé de Las Casas** (day las KAH sahs) spoke out against the mistreatment of native peoples under the care of the church. In 1527, Las Casas wrote angrily about what he had seen in the encomiendas.

> *"[The native peoples] die or lead lives harsher than death. They have been split into shares as if they were herds of cattle or sheep; that is, [divided] among the Spaniards and assigned by a specific number to each to become their slaves."*

The efforts of Las Casas had some success. He persuaded Spain to pass laws in 1542 saying that native peoples must be paid for their work. These laws were not enforced, however, and later were canceled. You will read more about Las Casas in the Biography feature on page 151.

REVIEW Compare the life of native peoples in the missions and other encomiendas.
Compare and Contrast

Slavery in the Americas

Despite the efforts of Las Casas, slavery did not end in the Americas. The Spanish first brought enslaved Africans to the Caribbean island of Hispaniola in 1512. The Spanish enslaved Africans to replace the native peoples who were dying in large numbers from disease and overwork.

At first, Las Casas supported bringing Africans to New Spain to work in place of native peoples. Later, he wrote that Africans should not be enslaved, either. But, gradually, the enslavement of captured Africans became an important part of the colonial economy. On Hispaniola alone, there were 12,000 enslaved Africans by 1574. Like the native peoples, African slaves on the encomiendas and plantations died from over-work and mistreatment. You will read more about slavery in later chapters.

The profits from colonial plantations and mines created great wealth for Spain. In the 1600s these riches helped make Spain one of the most powerful countries in the world. As you will read, the power of Spain would eventually come to an end.

REVIEW In what ways did native peoples and African workers create great wealth for Spain? **Cause and Effect**

Summarize the Lesson

1512 The Spanish took the first African slaves to Hispaniola.

1527 Roman Catholic priest Bartolomé de Las Casas defended the rights of native peoples.

1540 Francisco Vásquez de Coronado began a search for gold through the southwest part of what is today the United States.

LESSON 3   REVIEW

Check Facts and Main Ideas

1. 🔄 Sequence On a separate sheet of paper, fill in either the missing dates or the missing events from this time line.

Date   **Event**

| _____ | First Africans arrive in Hispaniola |

| _____ | de Leon's first expedition to Florida |

| 1527 | _____ |

| _____ | De Soto reaches the Mississippi River |

2. How did stories about Cíbola affect Spanish explorers?

3. How did the structure of society in New Spain benefit the Spanish?

4. How did conquest by the Spanish change life for native peoples?

5. **Critical Thinking:** *Point of View* Summarize the point of view of Las Casas about native peoples on the encomiendas.

Link to **Geography**

Interpret Maps Look at the map on page 147. Which explorer traveled along the shore of the Gulf of Mexico?

Bartolomé de Las Casas
1474–1566

One day in the spring of 1514, a Spanish priest named Bartolomé de Las Casas left the encomienda where he lived and paid a visit to the governor of Spanish Cuba. There was an important reason for this visit. Las Casas had come to announce that he wanted to free all of the native peoples enslaved on his encomienda. He added that he was going to preach against the enslavement and mistreatment of the native peoples.

The governor was shocked and tried to argue. Didn't Las Casas want to be rich? Didn't he want to be successful? Surely none of these things could happen if Las Casas did what he said he was going to do. But Las Casas had made his decision. He had already seen too much cruelty, and he did not want any part of it. Las Casas responded to the governor:

> *"If I repent of this purpose [change my mind]… and wish to possess Indians, and if you…want to entrust or give them to me anew [again]…may it be God who will severely punish you and not forgive you this sin."*

BIOFACT

Las Casas's writings, especially his book called History of the Indies, *are still important accounts of Spanish conquest in the Americas.*

Las Casas kept his word and freed the native peoples on his encomienda that day. He spent the rest of his life working to change the way the Spanish treated the native peoples in the Americas.

Learn from Biographies

When Las Casas chose to free the enslaved people on his encomienda, some thought he had given up his chance to be successful. Why do you think he was willing to take this action?

For more information, go online to *Meet the People* at **www.sfsocialstudies.com**.

151

1500   1525

1492
Columbus reaches the Americas

1501
Vespucci sails under the Portuguese flag

1521
Cortés defeats the Aztecs

1527
Las Casas defends native peoples

Chapter Summary

Sequence

On a separate sheet of paper, copy the chart and place the following events in the sequence in which they happened. Include the date for each one.

- Columbus reaches the Americas
- Cortés conquers the Aztecs
- Coronado explores the Southwest
- Pizarro conquers the Incas
- Vespucci calls the Americas a "new world"

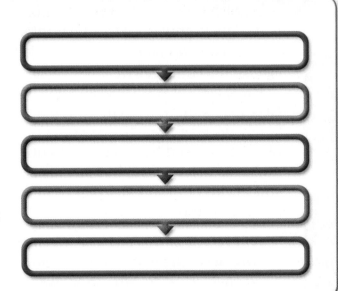

Vocabulary

Match each word with the correct definition or description.

❶ **expedition** (p. 135)

❷ **colony** (p. 136)

❸ **conquistador** (p. 143)

❹ **encomienda** (p. 148)

❺ **missionary** (p. 149)

a. granted someone control of Indians on an area of land

b. Spanish conqueror

c. settlement far from the country that rules it

d. journey made for a special purpose

e. person who teaches his or her religion to people of different beliefs

People and Places

Write a sentence explaining why each of the following people or places was important in the events involving the European exploration and settlement of the Americas.

❶ **Vasco Núñez de Balboa** (p. 137)

❷ **Tenochtitlan** (p. 143)

❸ **Doña Marina** (p. 143)

❹ **Moctezuma** (p. 143)

❺ **Cuzco** (p. 145)

❻ **Francisco Pizarro** (p. 145)

❼ **Atahualpa** (p. 145)

❽ **Hernando de Soto** (p. 147)

❾ **Francisco Vásquez de Coronado** (p. 147)

❿ **Bartolomé de Las Casas** (p. 149)

1533
Incan empire falls to Spain

1535
New Spain established

1540
Coronado explores the Southwest

1574
There are 12,000 enslaved Africans in Hispaniola

Facts and Main Ideas

1 What did Columbus think he would find by sailing west across the Atlantic Ocean?

2 How did diseases affect the conquest of the Americas?

3 What were the four levels of society in New Spain?

4 **Time Line** How many years were there between the conquest of the Aztecs and the conquest of the Incas?

5 **Main Idea** What was the Columbian Exchange?

6 **Main Idea** How did Cortés overcome being outnumbered and conquer the Aztecs?

7 **Main Idea** What were the goals of the colonists who came to New Spain?

8 **Critical Thinking:** *Fact and Opinion* Find an example of a fact and an opinion in the excerpt of Columbus's journal on page 135.

Write About History

1 **Write a "What If" story** in which you describe the world today if the peoples of the Eastern and Western Hemispheres had never had contact with one another.

2 **Write a story** telling about one of the sights that a conquistador saw in the Americas.

3 **Write a letter home** describing for people in Spain what it was like to live in New Spain in the 1500s.

Apply Skills

Use Latitude and Longitude

1 What do we call the parallel lines that circle the globe?

2 What is the name for the lines that meet at the north and south poles?

3 What is the name for the east-west line labeled 0°?

Internet Activity

To get help with vocabulary, people, and places, select the dictionary or encyclopedia from *Social Studies Library* at
www.sfsocialstudies.com.

CHAPTER 5

The Struggle to Found Colonies

1607
Jamestown
The first permanent English colony is started in North America.

Lesson 1

1

1609
Hudson River
Henry Hudson explores for the Dutch.

Lesson 2

2

1620
Plymouth
The Pilgrims arrive on the *Mayflower*.

Lesson 3

3

1682
Philadelphia
Pennsylvania colony is founded.

Lesson 4

4

NORTH AMERICA

PACIFIC OCEAN

ATLANTIC OCEAN

Plymouth

Hudson River

Philadelphia

Jamestown

Why We Remember

On a Thursday afternoon in late November, in homes across the country, one of the most popular and respected American traditions takes place. It is Thanksgiving dinner, and it helps us to remember an event that took place nearly 400 years ago. In the fall of 1621, a small group of English colonists and their Wampanoag neighbors celebrated a successful beginning to a new colony. The little colony of Plymouth, soon joined by other small settlements up and down the Atlantic coast, would grow into 13 thriving English colonies. Eventually, these colonies would become the United States of America.

1590 ——————————————————— 1620

1590
Lost Colony of
Roanoke founded

1607
Jamestown
founded

1619
House of Burgesses
formed

VIRGINIA
Jamestown •

Roanoke
Island

PREVIEW

Focus on the Main Idea
England founded Jamestown,
the first permanent English
settlement in North America,
in 1607.

PLACES
Roanoke Island
Virginia
Jamestown

PEOPLE
Queen Elizabeth I
Walter Raleigh
John White
Francis Drake
King James I
John Smith
Chief Powhatan
Pocahontas
John Rolfe

VOCABULARY
charter
stock
cash crop
indentured servant
House of Burgesses

Hard Times in Virginia

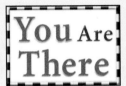

You Are There
How could 100 people just disappear? When John White left Roanoke Island three years ago, English colonists were beginning to build a settlement here. Among the colonists were his daughter Ellinor and baby granddaughter, Virginia. Now White is back on Roanoke Island with supplies for the new colony. But no one comes out to greet him.

White walks around the tiny colony. He hopes to find some clue that might tell him what happened. He finds a clue, but it only adds to the mystery. Carved into a tree is the word "CROATOAN." What does this word have to do with the disappearance of White's family and more than 100 other people? This is a question John White will never be able to answer. And today, we still have no answer.

Compare and Contrast As you read, compare the attempt to establish a colony at Roanoke Island with the attempt to found Jamestown.

The Lost Colony of Roanoke

England's rulers watched as their rival Spain established vast new colonies in the Americas. In the late 1500s, England began trying to establish colonies of its own. The colony at Roanoke Island was England's first attempt.

Queen Elizabeth I of England and other English leaders had many reasons for wanting colonies in North America. Like the Spanish, the English hoped to find gold in the Americas. And even if there was no gold, English leaders hoped that North America was rich in other natural resources.

But Queen Elizabeth knew that establishing a colony in North America would be difficult and expensive. It could also be dangerous. The powerful Spanish did not want other nations building colonies in the Americas.

A close advisor to Queen Elizabeth,

▶ Queen Elizabeth I ruled England from 1558 to 1603.

Walter Raleigh (RAH lee), offered to organize the first colony himself. Raleigh was a soldier who explored North America in the early 1580s. He knew of a place called Roanoke Island off the coast of what is now North Carolina.

The first group of colonists Raleigh sent to Roanoke Island landed in 1585. They faced a difficult winter during which they had trouble finding food. In 1586, the starving English returned home.

But Raleigh was not ready to give up the idea of starting a colony in North America. In 1587, John White led more than 100 men, women, and children to Roanoke Island. This colony also struggled. When supplies ran out, White sailed back to England for help. When he reached England, however, he found the country at war with Spain. England could not spare any ships to send supplies to the colony.

White was not able to return to Roanoke Island until August 1590. When he got there, everyone had disappeared. The only clue White found was the word "CROATOAN" carved into a tree. Croatoan was the name of an American Indian group that lived near Roanoke Island.

No one knows what happened to the Roanoke settlement. The colonists may have been captured by Spanish soldiers. They may have died in battles with Native Americans. Another possibility is that the starving colonists moved south to live with the Croatoan people. Because the mystery remains unsolved, the Roanoke Island settlement is known as "The Lost Colony."

REVIEW Which occurred first, Walter Raleigh's explorations in North America or the founding of the first settlement at Roanoke Island? ⟳ Sequence

The Battle of the Spanish Armada

Tensions were growing between England and Spain. England's attempt to build a colony in North America angered Spain's King Philip II. In addition, English sea captains had been raiding Spanish ships as they carried gold and silver from the Americas to Spain.

One of the most famous English captains was Francis Drake. In 1577, Drake began an historic voyage around the world. When he returned to England in 1580, Drake's ship was loaded with gold captured from Spanish ships. He became a hero in England. But the Spanish called Drake the "Master Thief."

In 1588, King Philip decided to attack England. He assembled the Spanish Armada, a huge fleet of war ships. Armada is a Spanish word for fleet. With 130 ships carrying about 30,000 soldiers and sailors, the Spanish Armada met the English fleet off the coast of England. The Spanish were confident of victory.

▶ **Sir Francis Drake** *(above)* **played a major role in the defeat of the Spanish Armada** *(below)*. **He was one of England's greatest heroes.**

But the English navy had some important advantages. The English ships were smaller and could move faster in the water. They also had more powerful guns. Lord Howard, commander of the English fleet, wrote of the Spanish:

> *"Their force is wonderful great and strong, yet we pluck their feathers by little and little."*

Many Spanish ships were sunk by English cannonballs. Others were caught in a storm and smashed against the rocky coast of Ireland. Of the Spanish Armada's 130 ships, only about 60 made it safely back to Spain.

The Battle of the Spanish Armada was a major victory for the English. The victory helped make England one of the world's most powerful nations. Now English leaders could turn their attention back to founding colonies in North America.

REVIEW What advantages did the English have over the Spanish in the battle of the Spanish Armada? **Compare and Contrast**

National Maritime Museum, London

Map Adventure

Where to Build a Colony?

John Smith and the other settlers from England have just reached Virginia. They sail up the James River and begin looking for a spot to build their colony.

1. Will they be the first people to live in this region? How can you tell?

2. What are some advantages and disadvantages of living on the James River?

3. The settlers stop at a peninsula on the north side of the James River. They begin building Jamestown here. Find this spot on the map.

4. Find two other places that might have been good locations for a colony.

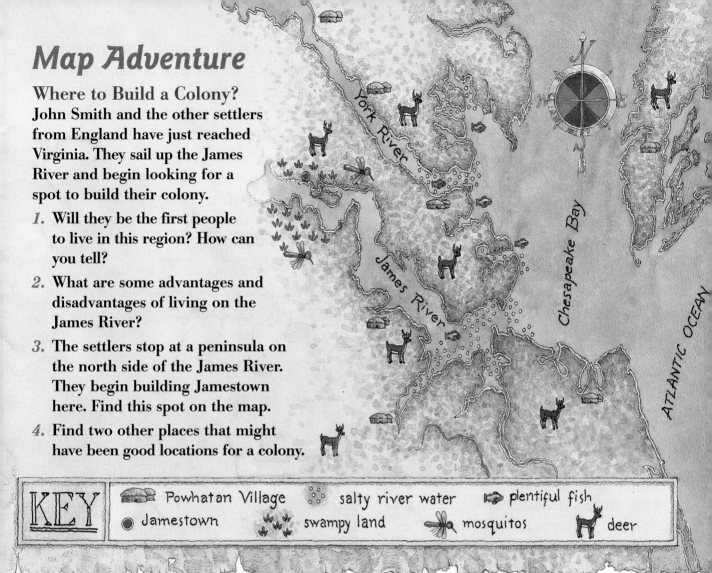

KEY

🏘️ Powhatan Village   ⚬⚬⚬ salty river water   🐟 plentiful fish

● Jamestown   🌿 swampy land   🦟 mosquitos   🦌 deer

The Jamestown Colony

In 1606, a group of merchants formed the Virginia Company of London. They asked King James I for a charter to set up a colony in Virginia. A **charter** was a document that permitted colonists to settle on land claimed by their ruler. The owners of the Virginia Company raised money by selling **stock,** or shares in the company. Each person who bought stock in the company would earn a profit if the colony was successful.

In 1607, three English ships carrying about 120 colonists reached the eastern coast of **Virginia.** They sailed up a river which they named the James River, in honor of King James. Looking for an area that would be easy to defend, they chose to unload their ships on a peninsula in the river. They called this spot **Jamestown.**

One of the settlers, **John Smith,** called Jamestown "a very fit place for erecting a great city." He was wrong. The land was low and swampy. The air was full of disease-carrying mosquitoes. The river water was not healthy to drink, and it made people sick. Almost as soon as they arrived in Jamestown, many settlers began to die.

REVIEW How did the owners of the Virginia Company raise money to build their new colony? **Main Idea and Details**

John Smith and the "Starving Time"

Some Jamestown colonists had expected to find gold in Virginia. Instead of planting crops and building houses, the men spent their days searching for gold. After some thought they had found gold, the colonists did nothing but dig for gold. But what they found was not gold.

Soon, men began dying of starvation and disease. By the end of their first year at Jamestown, only 38 of the settlers were still alive. A colonist wrote that what little wheat was left from the voyage from England "contained as many worms as grains." Then John Smith was elected leader of the colony. He issued an order to the surviving men based on the Bible:

> *"He that will not work, shall not eat."*

Under Smith's leadership, the colonists built houses and dug wells for fresh water. They planted crops and fished in the river. Smith also began trading with **Chief Powhatan,** leader of the Powhatan people. Corn from the Powhatan helped keep the colonists alive. For a brief period, relations between the English settlers and the Powhatan were peaceful. Chief Powhatan's young daughter, **Pocahontas,** often visited Jamestown.

John Smith later wrote that when he first met with Chief Powhatan he was taken prisoner. He was about to be executed when twelve-year-old Pocahontas saved his life. She then persuaded her father to let Smith go free. Historians are not sure if this story is true. Whether it is or not, Smith returned to England in 1609. You will read more about John Smith in his Biography on page 163.

The colony suffered without Smith's leadership. So many people died of hunger that this period became known as the "starving time." With the population dwindling, Jamestown was nearly abandoned. However, more settlers arrived including a new leader, Lord De La Warre. The Virginia Company gave him new powers, such as forcing colonists to work. The last survivors were saved and the colony was revived.

REVIEW What were the main causes of hardship at Jamestown before John Smith took over leadership of the colony? **Cause and Effect**

▶ **According to John Smith, his life was saved when Pocahontas convinced her father not to kill him.**

Tobacco Helps Jamestown Grow

Like corn and tomatoes, the tobacco plant is native to the Americas. Earlier European explorers and traders had learned from Native Americans how to grow tobacco. By the early 1600s, tobacco was becoming popular in England and other European nations.

In about 1612, a settler named **John Rolfe** raised a crop of tobacco in the rich Virginia soil. Tobacco soon became Virginia's first **cash crop**, or crop grown for profit. Tobacco was soon widely grown.

England's King James did not approve of tobacco. He called smoking "hateful to the nose, harmful to the brain, dangerous to the lungs." As we know today, King James was right about the harmful effects of smoking. But the king's opposition to smoking did not stop people in Virginia from raising tobacco. As the graph below shows, tobacco exports to England rose rapidly. Farms were growing so quickly that farmers needed more

▶ Tobacco *(right)* helped Jamestown to succeed. In 1614 Pocahontas and John Rolfe were married.

The Granger Collection, New York

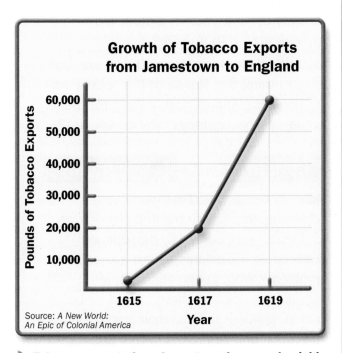

Growth of Tobacco Exports from Jamestown to England

Source: *A New World: An Epic of Colonial America*

▶ Tobacco exports from Jamestown increased quickly.

GRAPH SKILL *Between which two years did exports grow the most?*

workers. Thousands of English indentured servants began arriving in Jamestown.

Indentured servants agreed to work for someone for a certain amount of time in exchange for the cost of the ocean voyage to North America. Most indentured servants hoped to buy land of their own when they gained their freedom. Many never lived that long. Between 1619 and 1622, many of the newly arrived indentured servants died from disease, overwork, and mistreatment by their masters.

In 1619, another group of newcomers came to Jamestown. A Dutch ship arrived with 20 Africans who were sold as indentured servants and later released. Some of them established their own tobacco plantations. Later, Africans brought to Virginia would be enslaved.

In spite of the hardships of life in Jamestown, the colony continued to grow steadily. The marriage of John Rolfe and Pocahontas in 1614 helped maintain peace between the English and the Powhatan people.

REVIEW In three sentences, summarize the important information on this page. *Summarize*

Self-Government in Virginia

The Virginia Company of London continued to try to attract more settlers to their colony. With this goal in mind, leaders of the company declared that settlers in Virginia should have "such a form of government…as may be to the greatest benefit and comfort of the people."

On July 30, 1619, the Virginia House of Burgesses met for the first time. The House of Burgesses was the first law-making assembly in an English colony. Members were chosen to represent each district. The House of Burgesses helped establish the tradition of self-government in the English colonies.

REVIEW Why do you think the formation of the House of Burgesses would help attract settlers to Virginia? **Draw Conclusions**

Summarize the Lesson

- **1588** England defeated the Spanish Armada.
- **1607** Jamestown was founded, becoming England's first permanent colony in North America.
- **1612** John Rolfe grew a successful crop of tobacco in Virginia.
- **1619** The House of Burgesses met for the first time.

LESSON 1 REVIEW

Check Facts and Main Ideas

1. **Compare and Contrast** On a separate piece of paper fill in the diagram below comparing and contrasting these details about Roanoke and Jamestown:
   - Why did some English leaders want to build colonies in North America?
   - How did John Smith help the Jamestown colony?
   - How did tobacco help Jamestown grow?

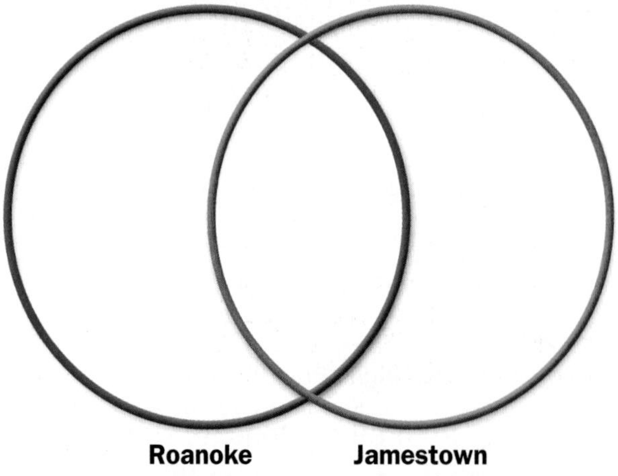

Roanoke   Jamestown

2. Why did England want to begin a colony on North America's eastern shore?

3. How did England defeat the Spanish Armada in 1588?

4. Why did Jamestown almost fail? How was it able to survive?

5. **Critical Thinking:** *Make Decisions* Do you think the House of Burgesses was the best type of government for the Jamestown colony? Why or why not?

Link to ⚭ Geography

Identify Geographic Features Some diseases that struck the first Jamestown colonists were carried by mosquitoes. How could the colonists have avoided this problem? What geographic features should the colonists have looked for before deciding where to build their colony? Include elevation and landforms in your answer.

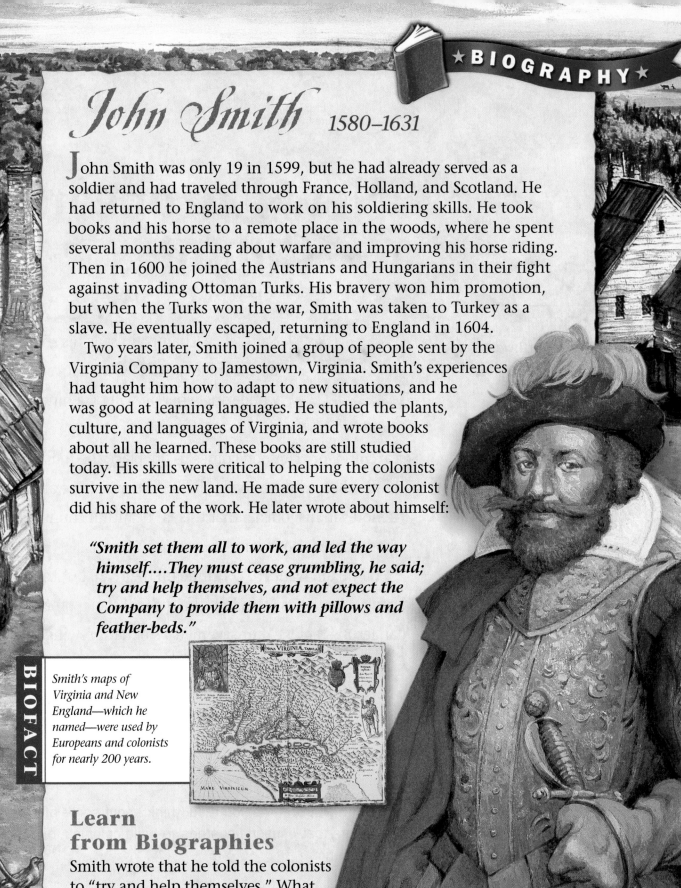

John Smith 1580–1631

John Smith was only 19 in 1599, but he had already served as a soldier and had traveled through France, Holland, and Scotland. He had returned to England to work on his soldiering skills. He took books and his horse to a remote place in the woods, where he spent several months reading about warfare and improving his horse riding. Then in 1600 he joined the Austrians and Hungarians in their fight against invading Ottoman Turks. His bravery won him promotion, but when the Turks won the war, Smith was taken to Turkey as a slave. He eventually escaped, returning to England in 1604.

Two years later, Smith joined a group of people sent by the Virginia Company to Jamestown, Virginia. Smith's experiences had taught him how to adapt to new situations, and he was good at learning languages. He studied the plants, culture, and languages of Virginia, and wrote books about all he learned. These books are still studied today. His skills were critical to helping the colonists survive in the new land. He made sure every colonist did his share of the work. He later wrote about himself:

"Smith set them all to work, and led the way himself....They must cease grumbling, he said; try and help themselves, and not expect the Company to provide them with pillows and feather-beds."

BIOFACT

Smith's maps of Virginia and New England—which he named—were used by Europeans and colonists for nearly 200 years.

Learn from Biographies

Smith wrote that he told the colonists to "try and help themselves." What did he mean by this, and how did this statement relate to his own early experiences as a young man in England?

For more information, go online to *Meet the People* **www.sfsocialstudies.com.**

1600

1608
Champlain
founds Quebec

1609
Hudson seeks a
Northwest Passage

1620

1624
New Netherland
is founded

Quebec
St. Lawrence R.
NEW FRANCE
Hudson R.
NEW NETHERLAND
New Amsterdam

New European Colonies

PREVIEW

Focus on the Main Idea
The search for a Northwest Passage led to the founding of French and Dutch colonies in North America.

PLACES
Quebec
St. Lawrence River
New France
Hudson River
New Netherland
New Amsterdam

PEOPLE
Samuel de Champlain
Henry Hudson

VOCABULARY
Northwest Passage

You Are There
Samuel de Champlain sails his ship up the mighty St. Lawrence River, wondering where it will take him. Could this be the river so many explorers have been searching for? He soon comes to the place the Indians call Quebec, where a rocky cliff towers over the water. He notes in his journal that this is "beautiful country, where there is good land covered with trees."

Champlain wants to continue up the river, but the Native Americans warn him that he will soon come to dangerous rapids. After several days of hard rowing, Champlain and his fellow French sailors reach a place where whitewater rapids crash over rocks and dark whirlpools spin. They can travel no farther. This is not the river that explorers have been hoping to find.

Cause and Effect As you read, think about some of the factors that caused countries to build colonies in North America.

French and Dutch Settlements

Who was Samuel de Champlain and what was he hoping to find? **Samuel de Champlain** was a French explorer. In 1603, he was part of an expedition that explored the St. Lawrence River in present-day Canada. The expedition was hoping to find the **Northwest Passage,** a waterway connecting the Atlantic and Pacific Oceans.

Explorers had been searching for a Northwest Passage for over 100 years. Such a waterway would make it easier for trading ships to sail from Europe to Asia. Many European countries, including France, England, and the Netherlands, hoped to be the first to find the Northwest Passage. No one ever found the Northwest Passage— because one does not exist. But the search did lead to the founding of new European colonies in North America.

In 1608, Champlain founded the French colony of **Quebec** on the **St. Lawrence River.** This proved to be a good location for a colony, because millions of beavers lived in the forests of this region. Beaver fur could be sold for huge profits in Europe. Quebec quickly developed into a thriving trading center. Huron Indians trapped the beavers and brought the furs to Quebec. Here, they traded the furs for European goods. The French started other colonies in North America, including the town of Montreal. These French colonies were called **New France.**

In 1609, Dutch leaders sent an English sea captain named **Henry Hudson** to search for

▶ Henry Hudson went ashore to meet the Lenni Lenape Indians while exploring the river that was later named for him.

new water routes to Asia. Like Champlain, Hudson sailed up a wide river, hoping it would prove to be the Northwest Passage. After sailing about 150 miles, however, the river became too shallow for his ship. But before turning back, Hudson claimed the land he explored for the Dutch. In honor of Henry Hudson, this river was later named the **Hudson River.**

The Dutch colonies in North America became known as **New Netherland.** The Netherlands is another name for Holland, the country of the Dutch.

In 1624, Dutch settlers began building the town of **New Amsterdam** on Manhattan Island. From this spot, the Dutch could control trade on the Hudson River. This ideal location helped New Amsterdam become the biggest and most important Dutch settlement in North America.

REVIEW Which town was founded first, Quebec or New Amsterdam? ⟳ Sequence

▶ Beaver hats became very popular in Europe.

165

Explorers and Early Settlements of North America

The search for a Northwest Passage led to the founding of several European colonies in North America. Find the name of each colony and the country that began it.

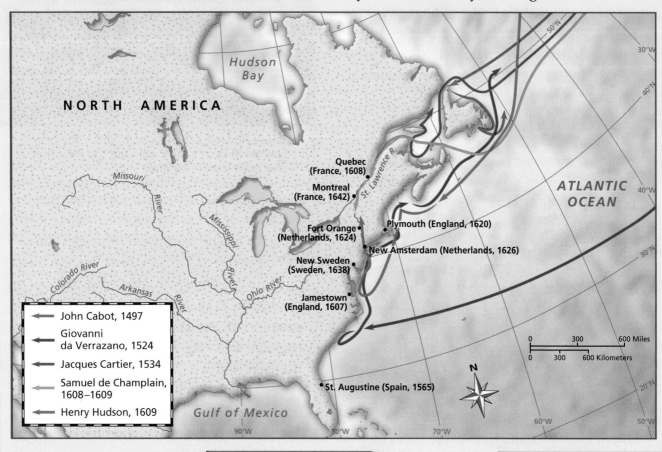

Map labels:
- Hudson Bay
- NORTH AMERICA
- Missouri River
- Mississippi River
- Colorado River
- Arkansas River
- Ohio River
- St. Lawrence R.
- ATLANTIC OCEAN
- Gulf of Mexico
- Quebec (France, 1608)
- Montreal (France, 1642)
- Fort Orange (Netherlands, 1624)
- Plymouth (England, 1620)
- New Amsterdam (Netherlands, 1626)
- New Sweden (Sweden, 1638)
- Jamestown (England, 1607)
- St. Augustine (Spain, 1565)

Legend:
- John Cabot, 1497
- Giovanni da Verrazano, 1524
- Jacques Cartier, 1534
- Samuel de Champlain, 1608–1609
- Henry Hudson, 1609

Scale: 0 300 600 Miles / 0 300 600 Kilometers

John Cabot
- Born in Italy
- Sailing under the flag of England, he reached the mainland of North America in 1497.

Giovanni da Verrazano
- Born in Italy
- Sailing under the flag of France, he became the first European to reach the mouth of what became known as the Hudson River in 1524.

Jacques Cartier
- Born in France
- Sailing under the flag of France, he reached the present-day country of Canada in 1534.

Samuel de Champlain
- Born in France
- He explored the St. Lawrence River for France in 1603. In 1608 he reached Lake Champlain, which is named for him.

Henry Hudson
- Born in England
- Sailing under the flag of the Netherlands in 1609, he explored the Atlantic coast of what is now the United States.

166

New Amsterdam Grows

To help their colony grow, the Dutch encouraged people from many countries to settle in New Netherland. Settlers arrived from Belgium, France, Germany, Finland, Norway, and many other countries. New Amsterdam became a thriving town with a diverse population. While in New Amsterdam in 1644, a French visitor named Isaac Jogues wrote that "there were persons there of eighteen different languages."

Later you will read the story of how New Amsterdam was taken over by the English and given a new name. The town continued to grow, and today it is the largest city in the United States. You probably know this city by its English name—New York City.

REVIEW Why did the Dutch encourage settlers from many countries to come to New Netherland? **Main Idea and Details**

Summarize the Lesson

— **1608** Samuel de Champlain founded Quebec and helped build the colony of New France.

— **1609** Henry Hudson sailed up the Hudson River and claimed the land for the Dutch.

— **1624** New Netherland was founded.

LESSON 2 REVIEW

Check Facts and Main Ideas

1. Cause and Effect On a separate sheet of paper, fill in the chart below by listing one important effect of each cause.

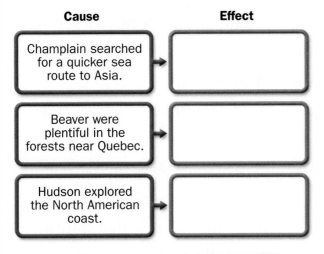

Cause	Effect
Champlain searched for a quicker sea route to Asia.	
Beaver were plentiful in the forests near Quebec.	
Hudson explored the North American coast.	

2. How did the search for a **Northwest Passage** lead to the founding of New France and New Netherland?

3. What kind of benefits did France gain from its colony of New France?

4. Why was New Amsterdam a good location for a city?

5. Critical Thinking: *Draw Conclusions* Do you think Native Americans played an important role in the growth of French and Dutch settlements? Explain.

Link to 🔗 Writing

Write a Letter Suppose that you are a French or Dutch explorer in the 1500s. Write a letter to your ruler explaining why he or she should pay for your expedition. Explain what you hope to find and why it will be valuable to your country.

1620

1630

1620
The Pilgrims
arrive in
Plymouth

1621
A thanksgiving feast is
celebrated at Plymouth

1630
The Puritans
establish Boston

NEW ENGLAND

MASSACHUSETTS
BAY COLONY
Boston
Plymouth

PREVIEW

Focus on the Main Idea
In search of religious freedom,
English settlers established
colonies in New England.

PLACES
New England
Plymouth
Massachusetts Bay Colony
Boston

PEOPLE
William Bradford
Samoset
Squanto
Massasoit
John Winthrop

VOCABULARY
Pilgrim
Separatist
persecution
Mayflower Compact
Puritan

The First Colonies

You Are There

In 1621, Pilgrims and Native
Americans celebrated a feast of
thanksgiving together. You know
about today's Thanksgiving holiday, which is based on
this 1621 celebration. But see if you can guess the
answers to these questions about the event that is
often called "the first Thanksgiving."

1. In what season was the 1621 Thanksgiving celebration held—summer, fall, winter, or spring?

2. Which food was not served at the celebration—
   duck, steak, deer, or corn?

3. How many days did the celebration last—one,
   two, three, or four?

    You may also have some questions of your own.
   Who held this celebration? And why were
   they thankful? You will read that story in this
   lesson, and you will find the answers to the
   questions above.

Compare and Contrast As you read, compare the early
experiences of the Pilgrims and the Puritans. How were
they similar? How were they different?

The Pilgrims

As you have read in the stories of Jamestown, Quebec, and New Amsterdam, colonists came for many reasons. They came to explore, to gain wealth, to spread their religion, and to live on land of their own. Some of the early settlers, however, had another. They came in search of religious freedom.

The story of the **Pilgrims** begins in England during the early 1500s. At this time, England broke away from the Roman Catholic Church. England's King Henry VIII created a new Christian church called the Church of England. Everyone in England had to belong to this church. As time passed, some people felt that the Church of England was too much like the Roman Catholic Church. One group was called **Separatists** because they wanted to separate from the Church of England. Separatists often faced **persecution,** or unjust treatment because of their beliefs.

A man named **William Bradford** was a leader of a group of Separatists. Bradford's group decided to leave England and start a settlement of their own, where they could worship as they pleased. These colonists became known as the Pilgrims. A pilgrim is a person who journeys for religious reasons.

William Bradford went to the Virginia Company and asked for permission to begin a new settlement in Virginia. He said that the Pilgrims would live "by themselves, under the general government of Virginia." Leaders of the Virginia Company agreed. The Pilgrims began preparing for their journey, knowing there were hard times ahead. "The dangers were great," Bradford wrote. "The difficulties were many."

REVIEW Name one important event that led to the Pilgrims' decision to leave England. **Cause and Effect**

▶ William Bradford led the Pilgrim colony for 30 years. This statue of him stands in the Pilgrim Hall Museum in Plymouth, Massachusetts.

▶ After the long journey across the Atlantic Ocean in the *Mayflower (left),* the Pilgrims wrote the Mayflower Compact to establish "just and equal laws" for their new colony.

The *Mayflower*

In September 1620, about 100 Pilgrims crowded into a small ship called the *Mayflower.* Storms battered the *Mayflower* during its long journey across the Atlantic Ocean. The ship was pushed off course. Instead of arriving in Virginia, the Pilgrims landed much farther north at Cape Cod. John Smith had named this region of North America **New England**—the name we still use today. The Pilgrims decided to find a place to settle in New England. They chose a rocky harbor the English called **Plymouth.**

Before landing their ship, Pilgrim leaders decided to write a plan of government for their colony. They called the plan the **Mayflower Compact.** It said that the Pilgrims' government would make "just and equal laws...for the general good of the colony." All adult males aboard the *Mayflower* signed the Mayflower Compact. Women were not allowed to participate. Like Virginia's House of Burgesses, the Mayflower Compact was an important step toward self-government in the English colonies.

In November of 1620, the Pilgrims finally set foot on solid land. Bradford wrote that they "fell upon their knees and blessed the God of heaven, who had brought them over the vast and furious ocean."

It was not the best time of year to start a colony in New England. As William Bradford wrote: "They that know the winters of that country know them to be sharp and violent." Many Pilgrims were already weak from the long voyage. Now they faced freezing weather, hunger, and disease. In their first three months at Plymouth, nearly half of the settlers died.

When spring finally arrived, something unexpected happened. While the Pilgrims were at work planting seeds they had brought from England, a Native American named **Samoset** walked into their settlement and called out, "Welcome, Englishmen!" Samoset explained that he had learned English from fishermen and traders. This meeting began a period of friendly relations between the Pilgrims and the Wampanoag people.

REVIEW What effect did weather have on the Pilgrims when they first reached New England? **Cause and Effect**

A Thanksgiving Celebration

Samoset told the Pilgrims of another Native American named **Squanto.** Squanto had been captured by European traders and sold into slavery in Spain. Later freed, he went to England, where he learned English. Now he lived with the Wampanoag people.

Acting as translator, Squanto helped the Pilgrims make a peace treaty with **Massasoit** (MAS us soyt), the leader of the Wampanoag. Squanto also showed the Pilgrims where the best hunting and fishing areas were located. And he taught them how to grow corn in the rocky New England soil.

That fall, the Pilgrims gathered their first harvest in Plymouth. "Our corn did prove well, and God be praised," wrote a Pilgrim named Edward Winslow. The Pilgrims decided to hold a celebration of thanksgiving. They invited the Wampanoag, who had helped them survive a very difficult year. Edward Winslow described the celebration:

> *"Many of the Indians coming amongst us, and among the rest their greatest King Massasoit, with some ninety men, whom for three days we entertained and feasted."*

The Pilgrims and the Wampanoag feasted on deer, wild duck, lobster, fish, cornbread, pumpkin, squash, berries, and wild plums. The three-day celebration also included parades, games, and races.

REVIEW Why do you think the Pilgrims invited the Wampanoag to their thanksgiving celebration? **Draw Conclusions**

HERE AND THERE Where Was the First Thanksgiving?

The celebration of the Pilgrims and the Wampanoag in 1621 is often called "the first Thanksgiving." But at about the same time, there were thanksgiving celebrations in several different parts of North America. Settlers in Virginia, for example, declared "a day of thanksgiving to Almighty God." Look at the map to see some other places where early European colonists held thanksgiving celebrations.

Map:
- Location of early European thanksgiving celebrations
- Present-day boundaries are shown.
- Plymouth (1621)
- Berkeley Plantation (1619)
- Palo Duro Canyon (1541)
- El Paso (1598)
- St. Augustine (1565)

The Puritans Arrive

In 1630, another group sailed from England to North America in search of religious freedom. This group was called the **Puritans,** because they wanted to "purify," or reform the Church of England. Like the Pilgrims, the Puritans faced persecution in England. Many were put in jail for their beliefs.

The Puritans were led by a lawyer named **John Winthrop.** Winthrop believed that the Puritans should build their own colony in New England. There, they could worship as they pleased, and set an example for how other people should live. John Winthrop described this idea when referring to the Bible, he said:

> *"For we must consider that we shall be as a City upon a hill, the eyes of all people are on us."*

The Puritans had learned important lessons from the hardships faced by early settlers in Jamestown and Plymouth. In 1628 a small group of Puritans sailed to New England to get the colony started. Then, in 1630, Winthrop sailed for New England with about 1,000 colonists and about 15 ships loaded with food, tools, horses, and cows. When the colonists arrived, some small buildings and farms had already been built. Thanks to this good planning, the Puritans did not face a time of starvation.

The Puritans called their colony the **Massachusetts Bay Colony.** They began looking for a location on which to build their main settlement. They chose a peninsula in Massachusetts Bay. They named this place **Boston.**

The Massachusetts Bay Colony grew very rapidly. The colony's economy thrived on fishing, fur trading, and shipbuilding. By 1634, about 1,000 people had come to Boston. This would remain the largest city in the English colonies for over 100 years.

REVIEW Explain how the Puritans were able to avoid starvation upon their arrival in New England. **Summarize**

▶ Today Boston is the capital and largest city of Massachusetts.

The Puritan Way of Life

Puritan towns were carefully planned. Each family had its own land on which to build a home and a farm. At the center of each town was a building called a meetinghouse, where religious services and town meetings were held. The Puritans also believed in education. They especially wanted children to learn how to read, so they could read the Bible for themselves and understand the laws of the community. In 1635, Puritans built the first public school in the English colonies.

The Puritans had found a place where they could live according to their religious beliefs. But what happened when someone disagreed with their beliefs? You will read about these conflicts in the next lesson.

REVIEW Why did the Puritans want their children to learn how to read?
Main Idea and Details

Summarize the Lesson

1620 The Pilgrims sailed to Plymouth on their ship, the *Mayflower*.

1621 Pilgrims and Wampanoag held a thanksgiving celebration together.

1630 Led by John Winthrop, the Puritans founded the Massachusetts Bay Colony.

LESSON 3 | REVIEW

Check Facts and Main Ideas

1. **Compare and Contrast** On a separate sheet of paper, fill in the chart comparing and contrasting these details:

   · Name of group and year founded
   · Group's leader
   · Reason people came to colony

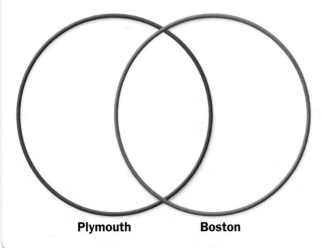

Plymouth   Boston

2. What was the main reason that the **Pilgrims** came to New England?

3. What was the purpose of the **Mayflower Compact?**

4. How did the Native Americans help the Pilgrims?

5. **Critical Thinking:** *Point of View* John Winthrop wrote that the **Puritan** colony would be like "a City upon a hill, the eyes of all people are on us." Explain how this statement reflects the Puritan view about the colony.

Link to ⬥⬥ Citizenship

Write Rules Suppose you were one of the Pilgrims on the *Mayflower*. Write three rules that you think all the people of Plymouth should agree to obey.

"That which was most sad and lamentable [unfortunate] was that in two or three months' time half of their [the Pilgrims'] company died, especially in January and February, being the depth of winter, and wanting [lacking] houses and other comforts....So as there died sometimes two or three of a day in the aforesaid [already mentioned] time, that of one hundred and odd persons, scarce fifty remained."

Excerpt A

"About the 16th day of March, a certain Indian came boldly among them [the Pilgrims] and spoke to them in broken English, which they could well understand but marveled at....His name was Samoset."

Excerpt B

Fact and Opinion

What? One of our most important records of the past is the words of the people who participated in events. But words can be tricky, because they can express both facts and opinions. A **fact** is a statement that can be checked. It can be proved to be true. An **opinion** is a personal view. It cannot be proved to be true or false.

Why? One of the most important accounts of the beginning of the Plymouth Colony is William Bradford's book, *Of Plymouth Plantation*, below. Over the years historians have recognized Bradford's books as a fairly reliable account of Plymouth's early years. One way that historians make this judgment is by deciding what is fact and what is opinion. Facts can be checked by looking at other sources. Opinions need to be identified so that they are not accepted as facts.

▶ **The Pilgrims walked to church as a group for protection.**

How? To separate fact from opinion, first read the passage, then determine the subject matter, and then look for clue words.

Read Excerpt A from Bradford's book, on page 174. The subject matter is about the Pilgrims' difficult first winter. Certain clues can help you tell fact from opinion. For example, facts are often supported by dates, numbers, and specific information. The passage tells you the time of year and the number of people who died. These numbers indicate statements that are facts.

Word clues that indicate opinion include descriptive adjectives such as *sad* and *lamentable*. Other word clues for opinions include *believe* and *think*.

It is not always easy to identify facts and opinions. Sometimes a writer may express an opinion with such confidence that it will sound like a fact. Other times a writer may state a fact as if it were an opinion. Still, learning to think about fact and opinion as you read will

help you understand many different types of writings. Study Excerpt B, also from Bradford's book. Then answer these questions.

Think and Apply

1 What is the topic of this excerpt?

2 Give one clue that indicates a **fact.**

3 Give one clue that indicates an **opinion.**

4 Why do you think historians find Bradford to be a good source for understanding the history of Plymouth?

▶ **According to legend, Plymouth Rock is the place where the Pilgrims first stepped on land at Plymouth.**

1630 ── 1730

1636
Rhode Island
is founded

1664
The English take over
New Netherland

1733
Georgia becomes
the 13th colony

Middle
Colonies

New
England
Colonies

THE 13
COLONIES

Southern
Colonies

PREVIEW

Focus on the Main Idea
By 1733 the English had
established 13 colonies along
the east coast of North
America.

PLACES
New England Colonies
Middle Colonies
Southern Colonies

PEOPLE
Roger Williams
Anne Hutchinson
Thomas Hooker
William Penn
James Oglethorpe
Tomochichi

VOCABULARY
dissenter
proprietor
debtor

The 13 English Colonies

You Are There

You have been waiting seven years
for this day. Seven years of working
14 hours a day as an indentured
servant for a carpenter in Philadelphia. And now you
are finally on your own. So what next?

You go for a walk and think things over. You are
twenty-one years old. You have a little bit of money
saved. Besides that, you own a new suit and a set of
carpentry tools—and not much else.

You know some carpenters who moved north to
Massachusetts to work in the busy shipbuilding yards
there. The pay is good, but you have always dreamed
of owning a piece of land. Maybe you could try moving
south, where the sun is warm and the land is fertile.
Then again, there is lots of good land right here in
Pennsylvania.

This is going to be a hard decision. You have your
whole life ahead of you—and 13 different colonies
from which to choose.

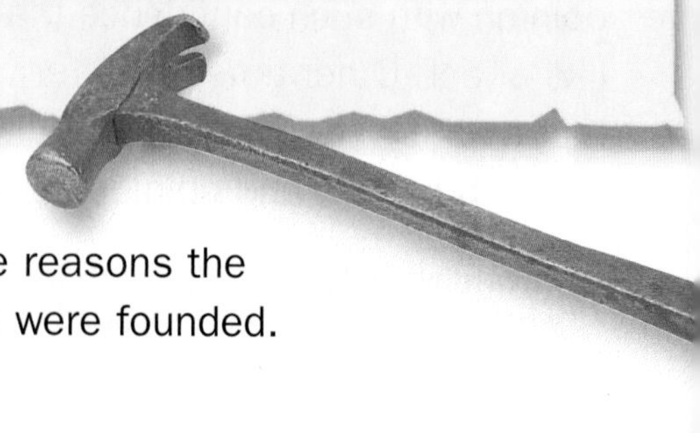

Compare and Contrast
As you read, compare the reasons the
different English colonies were founded.

Geography of the 13 Colonies

The 13 English Colonies were located in the eastern region of the present-day United States. All 13 Colonies lay between the Atlantic Ocean in the east and the Appalachian Mountains in the west. The colonies can be divided into three regions— the New England Colonies, the Middle Colonies and the Southern Colonies. Find each region on the map.

The New England Colonies had thin and rocky soil, making them a difficult place to farm. People found that the region was rich in other valuable resources, however. The thick woods provided excellent timber for homes and ships. The coastal waters were rich in fish and whales.

With a warmer climate and more fertile soil, the Middle Colonies were better for farming than New England. Because farmers in the Middle Colonies grew so much wheat, the region was called "the breadbasket of the colonies." Long, wide rivers like the Delaware and the Hudson made it easier for colonists to travel and transport goods.

Farmers in the Southern Colonies enjoyed the warmest climate and the longest growing season. The rich soil produced valuable crops such as tobacco and rice. Many rivers connected inland farms with ports along the region's coast.

REVIEW Which of the three regions had the coldest climate? Which had the warmest? How did these different climates affect the way land was used in each region?
Compare and Contrast

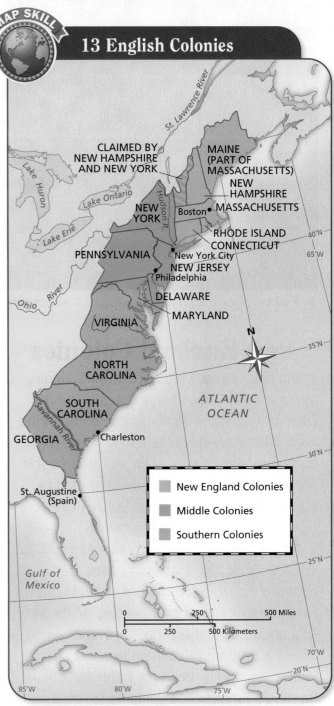

MAP SKILL

13 English Colonies

▶ The 13 English Colonies were all on the Atlantic coast.

MAP SKILL Location *What colonies were in New England?*

▶ **Thomas Hooker started the colony of Connecticut in 1636.**

New England Colonies

You have already read about the founding of the Massachusetts Bay Colony in 1630. During the 1630s, many Puritan settlements were built in Massachusetts. In these towns, Puritan leaders made strict laws that people were required to follow. All citizens had to attend church, for example. But not everyone agreed with all of the Puritan laws.

Roger Williams was an outspoken young minister in Salem, Massachusetts. He believed that the government should not punish citizens for what they believe. Williams was known as a **dissenter,** a person whose views differ from those held by most people in the community. Because of his beliefs, Puritan leaders forced Williams to leave Massachusetts. He traveled south in the snowy winter of 1636, founding a settlement he named Providence. This was the start of a new colony that would be called Rhode Island. Under Williams's leadership, Rhode Island became the first English colony in North America to offer complete religious freedom to its settlers.

Anne Hutchinson was another dissenter who angered Puritan leaders in Massachusetts. She believed that a person's own faith in God was more important than the church's rules and laws. She often held religious discussions in her Boston home. Like Roger Williams, Hutchinson was forced to leave Massachusetts because of her beliefs. She moved to Rhode Island. You will read more about Williams and Hutchinson in Citizen Heroes on page 184.

In 1636, a Puritan minister named Thomas Hooker left Massachusetts with about 100 followers. They founded the colony of Connecticut. Hooker and his followers came to this new land in search of greater religious and political freedom. They also wanted to build farms on the fertile land along the Connecticut River. English settlers were also moving to New Hampshire during this time. The earliest settlements in this colony were small fishing villages.

REVIEW Describe the important achievements of Roger Williams.
Main Idea and Details

178

The Middle Colonies

By the mid 1600s, there were about 5,000 European settlers living in the Dutch colony of New Netherland. Religious freedom, rich farmland, and the fur trade attracted people from many different nations to this region.

England's King Charles II decided to expand the English colonies by taking over New Netherland. He gave his brother James, the Duke of York, the task of capturing the colony. In 1664, English warships sailed into New Amsterdam harbor. Dutch leader Peter Stuyvesant saw that he could not defend the settlement. The English captured New Netherland without firing a shot. In honor of the Duke of York, New Netherland was renamed New York. New Amsterdam became New York City. The Duke gave a part of New York to his friends George Carteret and John Berkeley so they could establish their own colony. This new English colony was named New Jersey.

In 1681, King Charles II gave a huge section of land in North America to a young man named **William Penn.** The king had borrowed money from Penn's wealthy father. Now Penn asked for land as repayment. Penn wanted to build a colony based on his religious beliefs.

Penn was a Quaker. Quakers opposed war and believed that people could worship God without going to church or following religious leaders. You will read more about Penn and the Quaker beliefs in the Biography on page 183.

The English king named this new colony Pennsylvania, meaning "Penn's Woods" in honor of William Penn's father. William Penn said that this new colony would be a "holy experiment," where people from different nations and of all religions could live together in peace. He also promised to pay Native Americans a fair price for land. In a letter to the Lenni Lenape (LEN ah pee) Indians, Penn wrote: "I desire…that we may always live together as neighbors and friends."

For the site of Pennsylvania's main settlement, Penn chose land between the Schuylkill and Delaware Rivers. He named this new town Philadelphia, which means "city of brotherly love." A section of Pennsylvania to the south of Philadelphia later became a separate colony called Delaware.

REVIEW In one sentence, explain William Penn's goals for the colony of Pennsylvania. Summarize

▶ **Today Philadelphia is the largest city in Pennsylvania.**

The Southern Colonies

You have already read about colonies that were founded by Pilgrims, Puritans, and Quakers seeking religious freedom. Like these groups, Catholics also had faced persecution in England. They wanted a colony of their own. In 1632, King Charles I gave a large section of land north of Virginia to a Catholic landowner named Lord Baltimore. Baltimore named his colony Maryland. Maryland became a refuge, or safe place, both for Catholics and Protestants. Maryland was a proprietary (proh PREYE uh tehr ree) colony, meaning a colony where the land was controlled by an individual or a group of **proprietors,** or owners.

The next southern colony to be formed was Carolina. This happened in 1663, when King Charles II gave eight proprietors a charter to the large section of land between Virginia and the Spanish colony of Florida. Over the next few decades, this region's fertile land and good harbors attracted many new settlers. In 1729, Carolina was divided into two separate colonies—North Carolina and South Carolina.

An English leader named **James Oglethorpe** helped found the last of the English colonies in North America. Oglethorpe saw that English jails were crowded with **debtors,** or people who owed money. He came up with a plan to help them. He would start a new English colony in North America where debtors could go to start new lives on their own land. In 1732, King George II gave Oglethorpe a charter to land south of the Carolinas. Oglethorpe named the new colony Georgia.

Georgia's location helped the other English colonies. Look back at the map on page 177. You will see that Georgia lay between the Carolinas and Spanish Florida. Because of this location, Georgia helped protect the other English colonies from possible Spanish attacks.

Like William Penn, James Oglethorpe wanted his colony to have peaceful relations with the Native Americans of the region. As soon as he arrived in Georgia, Oglethorpe met with **Tomochichi** (toh moh CHEE chee), chief of the Yamacraw tribe. The Yamacraw agreed to give land to Oglethorpe and his settlers. With about 100 released debtors, Oglethorpe founded his first settlement in Georgia, which he named Savannah.

REVIEW How did persecution of Catholics in England help lead to the founding of Maryland? **Cause and Effect**

▶ Chief Tomochichi and James Oglethorpe met to trade goods.

FACT FILE

The 13 English Colonies

More than 100 years passed from the settlement of Jamestown, Virginia, to the founding of Georgia, the 13th English colony. This chart summarizes the reasons the colonies were started.

Colony	Year	Early Leaders	Reasons for Founding
New England Colonies			
Massachusetts Bay	1630	William Bradford, John Winthrop	Escape religious persecution in England
Connecticut	1636	Thomas Hooker	Farming, trade, political freedom
Rhode Island	1636	Roger Williams	Establish colony for people of all religions
New Hampshire	1679	John Wheelwright	Trade, fishing
Middle Colonies			
New York	1664	Duke of York	Build colony on land captured from Dutch
New Jersey (under English rule)	1664	John Berkeley, George Carteret	Build colony on land captured from Dutch
Pennsylvania	1682	William Penn	Establish Quaker colony in North America
Delaware	1704	William Penn	Trade, farming
Southern Colonies			
Virginia	1607	John Smith	Establish English colony in North America, search for gold
Maryland	1634	Lord Baltimore	Establish refuge for Catholics in North America
North Carolina	1729	William Berkeley	Farming
South Carolina	1729	Anthony Ashley-Cooper	Farming
Georgia	1733	James Oglethorpe	Refuge for debtors, colony between Carolinas & Florida

Growing Colonies

The English colonies grew very quickly during their early years. From 1650 to 1700, the population of the colonies increased from 50,000 to over 250,000. Fifty years later, the population had topped one million. People moved to the colonies' three largest cities—Boston, Philadelphia, and New York. They also moved away from the cities and towns, clearing forests and building farms. In a letter written in 1711, a farmer named John Urmstone described farm life in North Carolina:

> *"I am forced to work hard with axe, hoe, and spade. I have not a stick to burn for any use but what I cut down with my own hands."*

In the next chapter, you will read more about what life was like in the 13 English colonies.

REVIEW Do you think John Urmstone considered his life difficult? How can you tell? **Draw Conclusions**

Summarize the Lesson

1636 Roger Williams founded Rhode Island as a place of religious freedom.

1664 The English captured New Netherland and renamed it New York.

1733 James Oglethorpe founded Georgia as a new home for debtors.

LESSON 4   REVIEW

Check Facts and Main Ideas

1. **Compare and Contrast** On a separate piece of paper, fill in the chart below for two of the three regions—New England, Middle, and Southern Colonies. Compare and contrast based on such topics as geography and reason for founding.

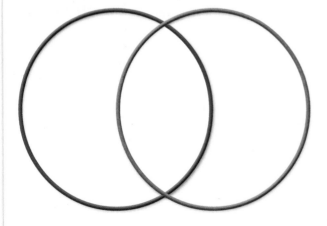

2. Why were the Middle Colonies known as "the breadbasket of the colonies"?

3. Explain how one New England colony was founded by a **dissenter.**

4. What attracted settlers to Georgia?

5. **Critical Thinking: *Decision-Making*** In which of the Middle Colonies would you have most liked to live? Explain your thinking. Use the decision-making steps on page H3.

Link to ⚭ Geography

Make a Map Using the map in this lesson as a guide, create your own map of the 13 Colonies. Label the colonies, important cities, the Atlantic Ocean, the Appalachian Mountains, and other information that might make the map better.

William Penn
1644–1718

At the age of 22, William Penn, the son of a high-ranking English naval officer, found himself locked in a cell. Earlier that day—September 3, 1667—Penn had been sitting in a quiet room, praying with a group known as the Religious Society of Friends, or "Quakers." The law of England at that time did not allow for a group of Quakers to worship together. Penn and his fellow Quakers believed that they should have the right to pray in the way that felt right to them.

Just after the start of the meeting, an English soldier entered the room. Soon more soldiers arrived and arrested everyone present.

From his cell, William wrote a letter asking that all the imprisoned Quakers be released. He wrote:

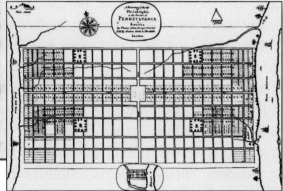

Philadelphia was the first colonial city to be planned on paper before it was built. Penn wanted the city to have wide streets with lots of trees and green spaces.

"Religion, which is at once my crime and my innocence, makes me a prisoner . . . but mine own free man."

Penn and the other Quakers were set free, but Penn would spend much more time in prison because of his religious beliefs. Years later, in 1682, William established Pennsylvania as a new colony in North America. His belief in religious freedom was one of the ideals that guided the new colony. The city of Philadelphia welcomed people of many different backgrounds and religious faiths.

Learn from Biographies

As a young man, Penn believed in religious freedom. How did he put these beliefs into action later in life?

For more information, go online to *Meet the People* at **www.sfsocialstudies.com.**

Respecting Religious Freedom

Roger Williams and Anne Hutchinson insisted that Puritan leaders respect their right to worship God in their own way. Instead of being granted that right, Williams and Hutchinson were sent away from the Massachusetts Bay Colony.

It was a bitterly cold January evening in 1636 when Roger Williams and a few friends walked into the woods of New England. The Salem minister had been banished, or sent away, from the Massachusetts Bay Colony. Even though he had been put on trial many times, Williams had continued to express beliefs that the leaders of Massachusetts saw as "new and dangerous."

The Puritan leaders were angry with Roger Williams because he preached that government leaders should not interfere with religious practices or tell people what to believe. These were threatening ideas to the officials of Massachusetts, who were both government and religious leaders. Finally, Williams's statements that the Native Americans had not been treated fairly by the colonists also angered the Massachusetts leaders.

Williams's friendships with the Wampanoag and Narragansett (na rah GAN set) peoples saved his life that bitter winter of 1636. With their help, he founded the first settlement in what is now Rhode Island. He called it Providence, meaning "the care of God," and said people with different religious beliefs would be treated fairly there. He wrote:

> *"I desired it [Providence] might be a shelter for persons distressed for conscience [persecuted for their beliefs]."*

BUILDING
CITIZENSHIP
Caring
Respect
Responsibility
Fairness
Honesty
Courage

In 1638, Anne Hutchinson, her husband William, and their fifteen children found safety in Williams's new colony. Like Williams, Hutchinson had been tried for disagreeing with Massachusetts leaders. As a woman, however, her views were greeted with even more alarm. Some leaders believed religious questions should be decided only by men.

Hutchinson often held prayer meetings at her home. She taught that faith alone, not membership in the organized church, was enough to be considered a good Christian. Her teachings angered colony leaders, who demanded that she give up her beliefs. During her trial, she was questioned about holding her prayer meetings. She said,

> ### *"Can you find a warrant [permission] for yourself and condemn me for the same thing?"*

When she did not give up her beliefs, the leaders declared her "a woman not fit for our society." Like Roger Williams, she was banished from the colony.

In the United States today, people cannot be punished because of their religious beliefs. Americans have the right to worship freely. This freedom has been established because of people like Roger Williams, Anne Hutchinson, and many others, who insisted on respecting religious differences, even though their own lives were in danger.

Respect in Action

Link to Current Events Religious conflict and persecution continue today in many parts of the world. Research the story of people who are working to build respect for religious differences.

1600 **1625** **1650**

1607 Jamestown is founded

1608 Champlain founds Quebec

1620 Pilgrims arrive at Plymouth

1624 New Netherland is founded by Dutch

1630 Puritans found Massachusetts Bay Colony

1636 Rhode Island is founded by Roger Willia▶

Chapter Summary

 Sequence

On a separate sheet of paper, copy the chart and place the following events in the sequence in which they happened.

- Georgia is founded
- House of Burgesses is formed
- Jamestown is founded
- Pilgrims arrive
- Puritans arrive

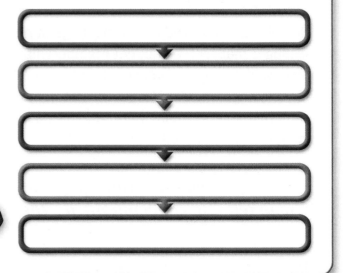

Vocabulary

Match each word with the correct definition or description.

❶ **cash crop** (p. 161)

❷ **charter** (p. 159)

❸ **Northwest Passage** (p. 165)

❹ **Separatist** (p. 169)

❺ **dissenter** (p. 178)

a. permitted colonists to settle on land

b. waterway thought to connect Atlantic and Pacific Oceans

c. person who didn't want to belong to the Church of England

d. person whose views differ from those of most people in the community

e. farm product grown to sell for profit

People and Places

Write a sentence explaining why each of the following people or places was important in the European settlement of the Americas.

❶ **John Smith** (p. 159)

❷ **Jamestown** (p. 159)

❸ **Chief Powhatan** (p. 160)

❹ **Samuel de Champlain** (p. 165)

❺ **William Bradford** (p. 169)

❻ **New Amsterdam** (p. 165)

❼ **Squanto** (p. 171)

❽ **Massachusetts Bay Colony** (p. 172)

❾ **Middle Colonies** (p. 177)

❿ **Anne Hutchinson** (p. 178)

1664
English take over
New Netherland

1682
William Penn establishes
Pennsylvania

1733
Georgia becomes
13th colony

Facts and Main Ideas

1 Why did European explorers hope to find a Northwest Passage?

2 **Time Line** How many years passed between the founding of Jamestown and the founding of Massachusetts Bay Colony?

3 **Main Idea** Why did the English want to establish colonies in North America?

4 **Main Idea** Explain how the search for the Northwest Passage led to the founding of new colonies in North America.

5 **Main Idea** Why did the Pilgrims and Puritans come to New England?

6 **Main Idea** Name three English colonies and the reasons each was founded.

7 **Critical Thinking:** *Fact and Opinion* Find an example of a fact and an opinion in the words of Samuel de Champlain on page 164.

Apply Skills

Read the passage below about the building of the Jamestown colony. Decide what information is fact and what is opinion. Then answer the questions.

> *By the 15th of June, we had built and finished our fort, which was triangle-shaped, having three bulwarks [defensive walls] at every corner like a half moon and four or five pieces of artillery mounted in them. We had made ourselves sufficiently strong for these Indians. We had also sown [planted] most of our corn.*

1 Which of the descriptions of the fort is fact?

2 Which of the statements is opinion?

3 Is the statement about the corn fact or opinion?

Write About History

1 **Write a descriptive paragraph** as if you were a settler at Plymouth or a Wampanoag who lived nearby. Describe the land, the climate, plants and animals.

2 **Write an adventure story** in which you describe the search for a Northwest Passage.

3 **Write a newspaper article** in which you describe the feast later known as the first Thanksgiving.

Internet Activity

To get help with vocabulary, people, and terms, select the dictionary or encyclopedia from *Social Studies Library* at **www.sfsocialstudies.com.**

UNIT 2

End with a Poem

New England's Annoyances

Early New England colonists had to deal with harsh conditions, such as scarce food and severe winters. With few luxuries and countless challenges, colonists had plenty of complaints. Read these excerpts from a poem, written by an unknown author about 1642, telling some of the difficulties of early New England. Did the author find anything rewarding about colonial life?

New England's annoyances you that would know them,
Pray ponder these verses which briefly do show them.
The place where we live is a wilderness wood,
Where grass is much **wanting** that's fruitful and good.

From the end of November till three months are gone,
The ground is all frozen as hard as a stone,
Our mountains and hills and valleys below,
Being commonly covered with ice and with snow.

And when the **north-wester** with violence blows,
Then every man pulls his cap over his nose;
But if any's so hardy and will it withstand,
He **forfeits** a finger, a foot, or a hand.

When the ground opens we then take the hoe,
And make the ground ready to plant and to sow;
Our corn being planted and seed being sown,
The worms destroy much before it is grown.

Instead of **pottage** and puddings and custards and pies,
Our pumpkins and parsnips are common supplies;
We have pumpkin at morning and pumpkin at noon;
If it was not for pumpkins, we should be undone.

But you who the Lord intends **hither** to bring,
Forsake not the honey for fear of the sting;
But bring both a quiet and contented mind,
And all needful blessing you surely shall find.

—Anonymous

Glossary of terms:
Pray please
wanting lacking
north-wester storm
forfeits loses
pottage soup
hither to this place
Forsake abandon

189

Main Ideas and Vocabulary

TEST PREP

Read the passage below and use it to answer the questions that follow.

After Europeans arrived in the Americas, a great variety of plants and animals, foods, and customs traveled in both directions across the Atlantic Ocean. This movement is known as the Columbian Exchange. It is a process that began with Columbus's first voyage and continues to this day.

Unfortunately, germs that cause diseases also made the ocean crossing in both directions. Many native peoples and settlers died from diseases that were new to them.

Spain was the first European country to set up colonies in the Americas. Spanish explorers and soldiers claimed some islands in the Caribbean Sea for their country. Then they defeated the Aztecs in Mexico and established the colony of New Spain, with a capital at Mexico City. Later, they conquered the Inca Empire in what is now Peru.

Despite Spain's power at sea, England challenged Spain's powerful armada and defeated it in 1588. After that, England sent its explorers and settlers to form a <u>colony</u> in the Americas.

Roanoke, the first of the English colonies, disappeared mysteriously. The colony established at Jamestown in 1607 faced many difficulties but managed to survive. The Pilgrims and the Puritans came seeking freedom from religious <u>persecution</u>. They established colonies in New England.

Meanwhile, French and Dutch settlers were establishing colonies near the English. The French colonies were in what is now Canada. The English eventually captured the Dutch colonies.

By the early 1700s there were thirteen English colonies in North America.

1 According to this passage, what is the Columbian Exchange?
   A the goods Columbus gave to native peoples to buy land
   B the Spanish conquest of the empires of native peoples in the Americas
   C the establishment of European colonies in the Americas
   D the movement of plants, animals, and customs between Europe and the Americas

2 In the passage, the word <u>colony</u> means—
   A a settlement
   B a company
   C a fort
   D a trade agreement

3 In the passage, the word <u>persecution</u> means—
   A trial in court
   B unjust treatment because of beliefs
   C a fair process of investigation
   D religious freedom

4 What is the main idea of this passage?
   A European countries established colonies for various reasons.
   B England established thirteen colonies in North America to challenge other European powers.
   C The English colonies were generally better than colonies of other countries.
   D Native peoples got sick and many died of European diseases.

People and Terms

Match each person and term to its definition.

1. **Amerigo Vespucci** (p. 138)
2. **Hernando Cortés** (p. 143)
3. **ally** (p. 143)
4. **indentured servant** (p. 161)
5. **Moctezuma** (p. 143)
6. **Pocahontas** (p. 160)

a. helped achieve peace between English and Powhatan

b. Aztec leader

c. friend who will help in a fight

d. first to use the term "New World"

e. worked for a certain period of time to pay for the cost of passage

f. conquistador

Write and Share

Prepare a Spotlight Exhibit Work in small groups to select important people and places from the unit and create drawings or make copies of illustrations. Each group should choose one person or place and write a paragraph describing why each was important in American history. Then your group can present its person or place to the class by having someone read the paragraph aloud while shining a flashlight "spotlight" on the drawing.

Read on Your Own

Look for books like these in the library.

Apply Skills

Locate Latitude and Longitude Make a list of five places named in your text. Then use the United States map (page R10 in the Reference Section) to locate the latitude and longitude lines that are nearest to each place. Remember to indicate north or south for latitude and east or west for longitude. Explain why it is important to use these lines to locate places.

Locating Places

	Place	Latitude	Longitude
1.			
2.			
3.			
4.			
5.			

It is important to use latitude and longitude lines to locate places because

UNIT 2 Project

Breaking News

News reporters go wherever news is breaking. Describe being at the first meeting of a Native American and a European.

1 **Form** groups. In your group, choose a Native American culture studied in this unit and a European country that sent explorers or settlers to the Americas.

2 **Brainstorm** the first impressions the Native Americans and the Europeans may have had of each other.

3 **Write** several questions they may have asked each other.

4 **Choose** one person to be the news reporter, one to be a Native American, and one to be a European. The reporter will describe the meeting between the two for the class.

Where are you from?

Where do you live?

What do you eat?

 Internet Activity

Explore life in the "New World." Go to **www.sfsocialstudies.com/activities** and select your grade and unit.

Colonial Life in North America

Why do people live in cities?

1600

1650

1630
Puritans begin building small
towns in New England

1647
Massachusetts law requires
towns to build public schools

"The streets are crowded with people, and the river with vessels."

—Said by Andrew Burnaby, visitor to Philadelphia, about 1760

This print, called *Philadelphia in the Olden Time*, shows the city in the late 1700s.

1750   1800

1730s
Great Awakening begins

1739
Enslaved people organize Stono Rebellion

1744
Eliza Lucas Pinckney grows first indigo crop

1789
Olaudah Equiano publishes an autobiography

Meet the People

John Peter Zenger

1697–1746
Birthplace: Germany
Printer, journalist
- Started New York's first independent newspaper
- Arrested for articles critical of New York's governor
- Found not guilty in a victory for freedom of the press in the colonies

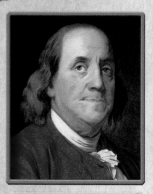

Ben Franklin

1706–1790
Birthplace: Boston, Massachusetts
Diplomat, inventor, publisher
- Founded Philadelphia's first library and hospital and published its first newspaper
- Helped write the Declaration of Independence
- Invented a stove, the lightning rod, and bifocal eyeglasses

Jacques Marquette

1637–1675
Birthplace: Laon, France
Missionary, explorer
- Explored the Mississippi River for France
- Realized the river was not the Northwest Passage as the French hoped
- First to record the correct course of the Mississippi River

Robert La Salle

1643–1687
Birthplace: Rouen, France
Explorer
- Traveled to the mouth of the Mississippi River by canoe
- Claimed all the territory surrounding the river for France
- Named the territory Louisiana in honor of King Louis XIV of France

1630	1650	1670	1690	1710

1637 • Jacques Marquette 1675

1643 • Robert La Salle 1687

1697 • John Peter Zenger

1706

1713

Junípero Serra

1713–1784
Birthplace: Majorca, Spain
Missionary

- Founded San Diego, the first mission in what is today California
- Established several other missions in the area
- Helped Spain maintain its control over California

Pontiac

about 1720–1769
Birthplace: present-day Ohio
Leader of the Ottawa people

- Led an American Indian revolt against British settlers
- Fought to save Native American lands from being taken by the British
- Won key battles during Pontiac's Rebellion

Eliza Lucas Pinckney

about 1722–1793
Birthplace: Antigua, West Indies
Planter

- Ran her family's plantation
- Cultivated the first successful indigo crop in the United States
- Her introduction of indigo helped South Carolina's economy thrive

Olaudah Equiano

about 1750–1797
Birthplace: Benin, West Africa
Writer

- Enslaved as a child, but was later freed
- Wrote a book about his life
- Became an abolitionist in Britain, speaking about the evils of slavery

1730   **1750**   **1770**   **1790**

	1746	
• Ben Franklin		**1790**
• Junípero Serra		**1784**
about 1720 • Pontiac	**1769**	
about 1722 • Eliza Lucas Pinckney		**1793**
about 1750 • Olaudah Equiano		**1797**

Reading Social Studies

Colonial Life in North America
Compare and Contrast

The two charts below show different ways to compare and contrast information. The chart at left helps you to see differences. The chart at right helps you see differences and similarities.

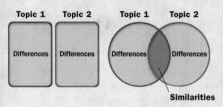

- Writers may use clue words, such as *similar to* or *like* to compare things or events. They may use words such as *different from* or *but* to contrast two or more things or events.

- Often there are no clue words. Then you compare and contrast by asking, "How are these events or things similar? How are they different?"

Read the following paragraph. **Similarities** and **differences** have been highlighted.

In Unit 2 you learned about the founding of the 13 Colonies. By the middle 1700s, all the colonies had thriving economies. But each region was developing a different type of economy. There were cities in each region. But the population of cities in the New England and Middle Colonies was much larger than in the Southern Colonies.

Word Exercise

Synonyms A **synonym** is a word that means the same thing or nearly the same thing as another word. When you are learning a new word, it may help you to look up synonyms for it. If the word's synonyms are words that are familiar to you, they will help you remember what the new word means. The passage reads, "**Rival** claims by Britain and France led to the French and Indian war." A thesaurus shows that *competing* is a synonym for *rival* in this case. Remembering that synonym will remind you that *rival* can describe someone or something competing with something else.

Compare and Contrast Colonial Life in North America

As the 13 Colonies grew, they were similar in many ways. All the colonies were ruled by England. All had cities, towns, and farms.

But the 13 Colonies also had many differences. The ways of life differed in the three regions. In the New England Colonies, people depended on the sea and the forests. Farms in the region were small. New England had many small towns and some large cities. The Middle Colonies also had small towns and large cities. These colonies produced large amounts of wheat and flour. The Southern Colonies had towns, small farms, and large plantations. Slavery provided the main workforce for these plantations.

The Spanish and the French were also building colonies in North America. Spain founded St. Augustine in Florida in 1565 and Santa Fe in New Mexico in 1610. French explorers reached the Mississippi River and claimed it and the land near it for France. In 1718, France founded New Orleans, which became a thriving port city.

As the British colonies grew, many colonists wanted to move west. But France claimed land west of the colonies. Rival claims by Britain and France led to the French and Indian War. During this war, Algonquian Indians sided with the French. Eventually the Iroquois helped the British. The war ended with a British victory.

Apply it!

Use the reading strategy of compare and contrast to answer questions 1 and 2. Then answer the vocabulary question.

1 How were the 13 Colonies similar?

2 How were the 13 Colonies different?

3 The passage reads, "In the New England colonies, people *depended* on the sea and the forests." What is a synonym for *depend* that would help you remember what it means?

CHAPTER 6

Life in the English Colonies

1700s

West Africa
The slave trade continues to grow.

Lesson 1

1

1723

Philadelphia
Benjamin Franklin moves to Philadelphia and works as a printer.

Lesson 2

2

1735

New York
The trial of John Peter Zenger wins the first victory for freedom of the press.

Lesson 3

3

1739

South Carolina
Enslaved people clash with slave owners in the Stono Rebellion.

Lesson 4

4

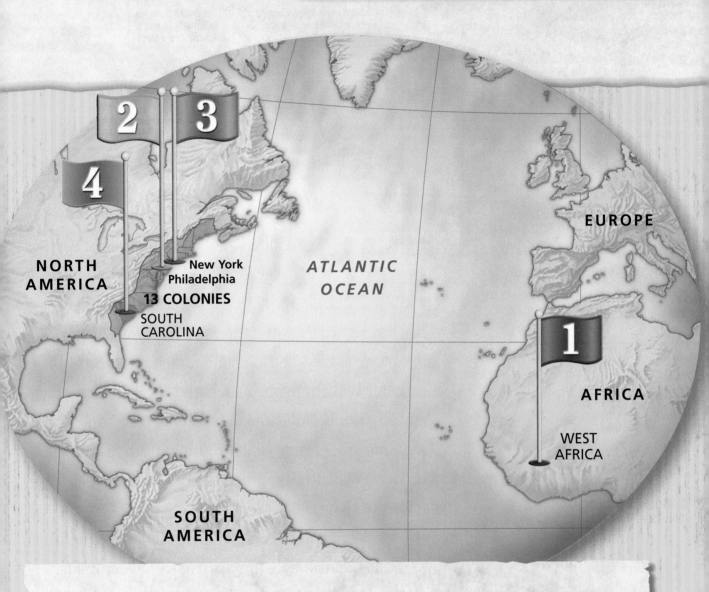

Why We Remember

"Haste makes waste."
"No gains without pains."

You've often heard advice like this. But did you know these sayings were first written in the 13 Colonies? As you will read, work was important in the colonies. But the colonists had other interests as well. Religion was an important part of life. There were free public schools. The colonies were developing many of the ideals that remain important to Americans today.

1710   1760

1718
William Mathews begins
work as an apprentice

1756
Olaudah Equiano
brought to North
America as a slave

Charleston

West Indies   **WEST
AFRICA**

PREVIEW

Focus on the Main Idea
People in the 13 colonies
produced a wide variety of
goods and developed thriving
trade routes.

PLACES
Charleston
West Africa
West Indies

VOCABULARY
apprentice
artisan
triangular trade routes
Middle Passage

Working and Trading

You Are There
William Mathews will probably never forget today's date—August 15, 1718. At 11 years old, William has just signed a contract to work for a rope maker in New York City. The agreement includes plenty of rules for William to obey, such as: "At cards, dice, or any other unlawful game, he shall not play." And: "He shall not absent himself day or night from his master's service." William has agreed to work for the rope maker until he is 21.

Over the next ten years, William will learn a useful trade that will help him earn a living later in life. He will get food and a place to live, and will be taught to read and write. And when William turns 21, his master has promised to give him a new suit and four new shirts.

Compare and Contrast As you read, think about how life was different for colonists who did different types of work.

Life for Young Workers

As an apprentice (uh PREN tis) rope maker in the early 1700s, William Mathews had ten years of hard work ahead of him. An **apprentice** is a young person who learns a skill from a more experienced person. Apprentices could expect to work long hours—often more than twelve hours a day. They had very little free time and rarely got a day off.

In spite of the hardships, becoming an apprentice could be a great opportunity. For many young people in the colonies, this was the only way to become an artisan. An **artisan** is a skilled worker—such as a rope maker, blacksmith, or carpenter—who makes things by hand. Young surgeons also learned their job by working as apprentices. As a surgeon's apprentice, you would help carry medical instruments and observe the doctor at work. You also had the important responsibility of holding patients down during painful operations.

As the colonial economy grew during the early and mid-1700s, there was a growing need for artisans. This created opportunities for thousands of young apprentices. Most were boys, but girls also worked as apprentices. Young girls learned trades like cooking and sewing.

Not all young people in colonial times worked as apprentices. Most children grew up on farms, where they had just as much work to do as apprentices in towns and cities. From a very young age, children were given jobs like gathering wood for fires, serving food, and helping in the garden. As they grew older, boys hunted, chopped firewood, and joined their fathers at work in the fields.

Girls helped their mothers make household products such as soap, candles, clothing, and food for the family.

These were hard jobs. Candles, for example, were made from the fat of sheep or cows. First the candle maker melted the chunks of fat in an iron kettle. Then she dipped a candle wick into the fat and let it harden. She did this over and over until she had a thick candle. These candles gave off plenty of light, but they gave off something else too—a bad smell. Colonists were very happy when they discovered that they could make candles out of pleasant-smelling wax from wild berries.

REVIEW Do you think it was more difficult to work as an apprentice or on a farm? Why?
↻ Compare and Contrast

▶ A woman displays candle-making skills at Colonial Williamsburg in Virginia, a living museum recreating the colonial way of life. Candlestick holders (*above*) were often made from pewter, a kind of metal.

203

Colonists at Work

As you have read, most colonists lived on farms. As the colonies grew, however, there were a wider variety of ways that people could make a living. This chart shows you some of the different types of work that colonists did. Which of these jobs would you have wanted to try?

Colonial Jobs

	Job	What They Did
	**Shoemaker**	Made shoes from leather and wood
	Blacksmith	Made and repaired iron goods, such as horseshoes, axes, gun parts, and nails
	Fisherman	Caught cod and other fish in the Atlantic Ocean
	Cooper	Made barrels from wood and iron
	Printer	Printed posters, newspapers, and books
	Surveyor	Made maps and marked boundary lines
	Miller	Ran mills where colonists could grind corn and wheat into flour
	Merchant	Traded goods with England and other countries
	**Dressmaker**	Made clothes from woven material

Colonial Economies

You have already read that different parts of the 13 Colonies were rich in different natural resources. So it makes sense that the New England, Middle, and Southern Colonies each developed a different type of economy.

The New England economy was based on products from the forests and the sea. Timber was a valuable export—especially to England, where most of the forests had already been cut down. Trees from the New England forests were also used to build houses, ships, and barrels. Barrels were needed to store everything from wine to wheat to dried fish. Once colonists had their own ships, they could fish in the rich waters off the New England coast. Fishing and whaling quickly became important industries.

The economy of the Middle Colonies was based on farm products and valuable minerals such as iron. As you have read, Middle Colony farmers grew so much wheat, the region became known as "the breadbasket of the colonies." Mills were built to grind grain into flour. The mills were powered by running water or wind. From the mills, flour was shipped to other colonies and exported to other countries.

The Southern Colonies had rich soil, warm weather, and plenty of rain, and they developed an economy based on farming. Farms ranged in size from small family farms to large plantations powered by the work of slaves. Cash crops included tobacco, rice, and indigo, a plant used to make a blue dye.

Look at the map to see where indigo and other key colonial products were produced.

REVIEW Compare the important products of the New England, Middle, and Southern Colonies. 🔄 Compare and Contrast

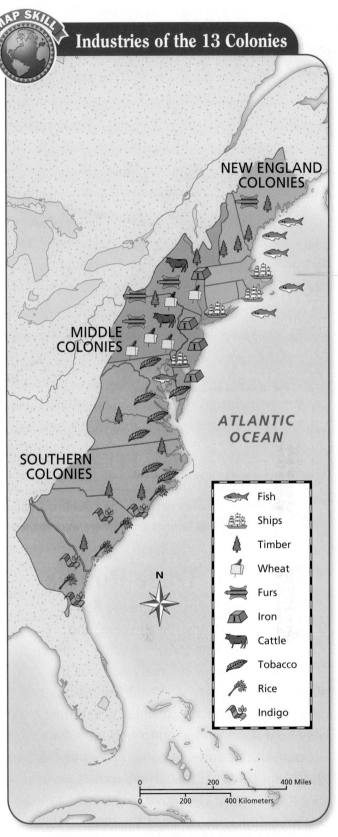

MAP SKILL Industries of the 13 Colonies

NEW ENGLAND COLONIES

MIDDLE COLONIES

SOUTHERN COLONIES

ATLANTIC OCEAN

N

🐟	Fish
⛵	Ships
🌲	Timber
	Wheat
	Furs
	Iron
🐄	Cattle
	Tobacco
	Rice
	Indigo

0	200	400 Miles
0	200	400 Kilometers

▶ The three colonial regions developed different economies.

MAP SKILL Use a Map Key *In which region did fishing play an important role?*

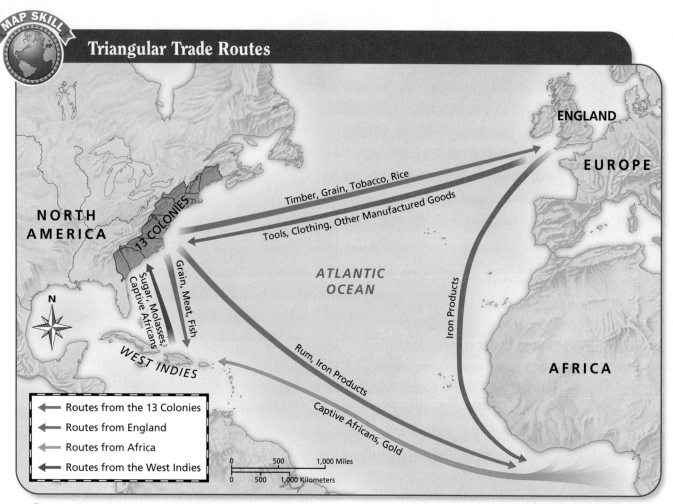

ENGLAND
EUROPE
NORTH AMERICA
Timber, Grain, Tobacco, Rice
Tools, Clothing, Other Manufactured Goods
13 COLONIES
ATLANTIC OCEAN
Sugar, Molasses, Captive Africans
Grain, Meat, Fish
Iron Products
AFRICA
N
WEST INDIES
Rum, Iron Products
Captive Africans, Gold

Routes from the 13 Colonies
Routes from England
Routes from Africa
Routes from the West Indies

0   500   1,000 Miles
0   500   1,000 Kilometers

The shipping routes between the colonies, England, and Africa were known as triangular trade routes.

MAP SKILL Use Routes *From where were tobacco and rice shipped? To where were these products shipped?*

Colonial Trade Routes

As the colonial economy grew, cities like Boston, New York, Philadelphia, and Charleston became thriving trading centers. An important part of colonial trade was the slave trade. In this type of trade, ships brought captive Africans to the colonies, where they were sold and then forced to work as slaves.

Some trade routes became known as triangular trade routes. These routes were called "triangular" because they were shaped like giant triangles. Look at the map on this page and you will see examples of the slave trade and triangular trade routes.

On one common triangular trade route, ships began in New England. They carried guns and other goods to ports on the coast

of West Africa. Here, they traded these goods for gold and captive Africans.

The ship then sailed for the West Indies. Because it was the second leg of the voyage, this was known as the Middle Passage. Captive Africans suffered terribly during the Middle Passage. Many died as a result of hunger, thirst, disease, or cruel treatment. A West African boy named Olaudah Equiano (OL uh dah eh kwee AH noh) was probably brought to North America on a trading ship in about 1756. He later wrote a book about the Middle Passage, writing that people were

"so crowded that each had scarcely room to turn himself...many died."

In the West Indies, the ships exchanged captive Africans and gold for sugar and molasses, a syrup made from sugarcane. The ships completed the triangle by carrying the sugar and molasses back to colonial ports. The molasses was used to make rum. And with this rum, trading ships set sail for Africa, beginning the triangular route over again.

▶ **Millions of enslaved Africans were held in this building on Goree Island, off the coast of Senegal in West Africa. The stairs led down to the ships that carried them to the Americas.**

Many Africans were enslaved in the West Indies, where they were forced to work on sugar plantations. Others were brought north to the 13 Colonies.

REVIEW How were the first and second legs of a triangular trade route different?
↻ **Compare and Contrast**

Summarize the Lesson

- In the 1700s, many young people in the colonies gained skills by working as apprentices.

- While many colonists were farmers, some men and women worked at a wide variety of other jobs.

- Triangular trade routes developed with Europe, Africa, and the West Indies.

LESSON 1   REVIEW

Check Facts and Main Ideas

1. ↻ **Compare and Contrast** On a separate sheet of paper, complete this diagram by comparing and contrasting the economies of two different colonial regions.

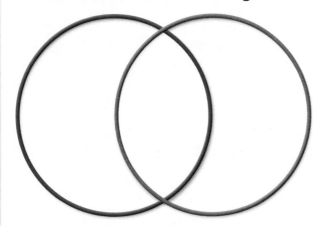

2. Explain the hardships and benefits of working as an **apprentice.**

3. Which region was known as "the breadbasket of the colonies"? Why?

4. Describe a common **triangular trade route.** Where did the ships sail? What did they carry from each port?

5. **Critical Thinking:** *Make Decisions* Think about all the types of work described in this lesson. If you were a colonist, which would you most like to do? Explain.

Link to ⎯∞⎯ Mathematics

Use a Map Scale Look at the map on page 206. Suppose a trading ship sailed from the 13 Colonies to England to West Africa to the West Indies and back to the colonies. Using the map scale, determine about how many miles this ship would have traveled.

Read Newspapers

What? Newspapers are sources of news and events that are taking place now. They are usually printed daily or weekly. As you will discover in Lesson 3, the first regularly published newspaper in the colonies first appeared in 1704 in Boston, Massachusetts. Newspapers have several parts. **News articles** are news stories based on facts about recent events. **Feature articles** have information about places, people, or events that would interest readers. For example, a story about a snowstorm that came yesterday is a news article. A story about the five major blizzards in the last 50 years is a feature article.

Students Find Old Kitchen Utensils at Leeville

LEEVILLE, APRIL 15—Students digging last week near the ruins of a kitchen in Leeville found items that were once used in a colonial kitchen. Among the items found were remains of old wooden spoons, iron cooking pots, and broken pottery bowls. The students from nearby Bridgetown were on a class field trip. They were taking part in activities the historic site offers as part of its educational program.

Why? Newspaper articles can tell what happened at a particular time. They can also give you an idea of what people thought about events at the time they happened.

How? To read a news article, you should know what its main parts are. Look at the example of the news article on the previous page. First look at the **headline,** the large type that is the title of the article. The headline tells you the subject of the article.

Then look at the **dateline,** which tells you where and when a story was written. Notice that the dateline gives the city name, but not the state or country. The state or country name is given only if the reader might not know where the city is. The dateline gives the month and date, but not the year. That is because the paper itself has a date that includes the year.

The first paragraph of a news story tries to make the reader interested enough to continue reading. The news story itself usually answers the 5 Ws—*who?, what?, where?, when?,* and *why?* Who tells the people involved. *What* tells what happened. *Where* tells where the events took place. *When* tells when they happened. *Why* tells why the people involved in the event did what they did.

Read the news article again and then answer the questions.

Think and Apply

1. What is the event reported in the **news article?**

2. What does the dateline tell you?

3. Why were the students digging at the site?

Philadelphia

1600 **1700**

1630
Puritans begin
building small towns
in New England

1723
Benjamin Franklin
moves to Philadelphia

1744
Eliza Lucas
Pinckney grows
first indigo crop

PREVIEW

Focus on the Main Idea
The 13 Colonies had big cities, small towns, and farms of all sizes.

PLACES
Philadelphia

PEOPLE
Benjamin Franklin
Eliza Lucas Pinckney

VOCABULARY
self-sufficient
town common

Cities, Towns, and Farms

You Are There This is Ben Franklin's first day in Philadelphia. He is 17 years old. His clothes are dirty from traveling. He is tired and hungry, and he has very little money in his pocket. He knows no one in this city. What do you think he should do?

First, he finds a bakery and asks for three pennies worth of bread. He comes out with three large rolls—he is chewing on one and has one under each arm. He wanders through the busy streets, looking at the buildings and the people. Out of curiosity, he steps into a Quaker meeting house, where a meeting is going on. He sits down and rests. Later, back out on the street, he starts looking for a place to stay for the night. And tomorrow he will try to find a job.

Compare and Contrast As you read, think about what life was like for colonists in cities, towns, and on farms. How were their lives similar? How were they different?

210

City Life

Benjamin Franklin needed to live in a city. He wanted to be a printer, and printing businesses were only found in cities. When he could not find work in his hometown of Boston, he looked elsewhere.

Franklin arrived in Philadelphia, Pennsylvania in 1723. He found a growing city, with a diverse population. There were people of different ethnic backgrounds and religions. There was a busy port on the Delaware River. And most importantly for Franklin, there was a printer who gave him a job.

The graph on this page shows the population of the largest colonial cities. You can see that by the middle 1700s, Philadelphia was the largest city in the 13 Colonies. Benjamin Franklin had a lot to do with the success of the city. He founded the city's first newspaper. He established the city's first public library and first hospital. To help fight dangerous fires, he started the first volunteer fire department in the 13 Colonies. Fires were a very serious problem in colonial cities, where most buildings were made of wood.

In about 1760, a traveler named Andrew Burnaby visited Philadelphia. He wrote that the city was thriving. "The streets are crowded with people, and the river with vessels [boats]."

REVIEW Contrast the populations of New York and Charleston in 1760. How many more people lived in New York?

🔄 **Compare and Contrast**

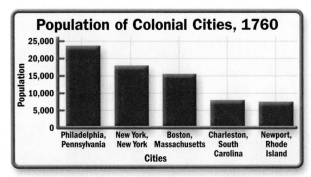

Population of Colonial Cities, 1760

(bar graph showing population by city)

- Philadelphia, Pennsylvania: nearly 25,000
- New York, New York: ~18,000
- Boston, Massachusetts: ~15,500
- Charleston, South Carolina: ~8,000
- Newport, Rhode Island: ~7,500

▶ Philadelphia had nearly 25,000 people by 1760.

GRAPH SKILL *What was the population of Charleston?*

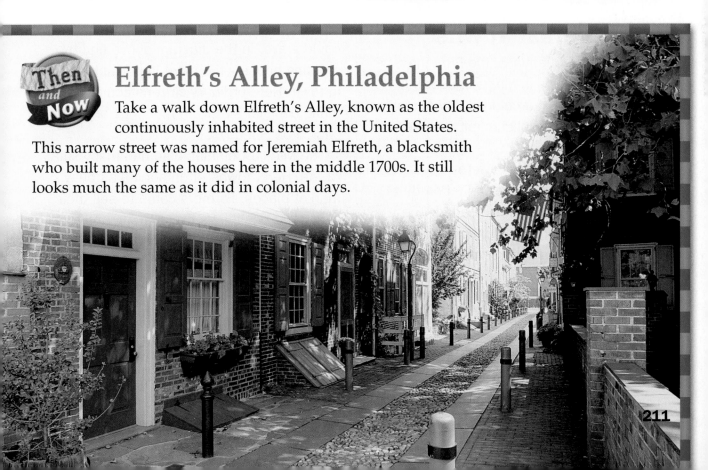

Then and Now

Elfreth's Alley, Philadelphia

Take a walk down Elfreth's Alley, known as the oldest continuously inhabited street in the United States. This narrow street was named for Jeremiah Elfreth, a blacksmith who built many of the houses here in the middle 1700s. It still looks much the same as it did in colonial days.

Fields House Meeting house Fields Minister's house Houses Garden Inn General Store School Stocks Cooper Well Town Common Shoemaker Blacksmith Mill River

▶ **Many New England towns grew around the common, a central open area.**

DIAGRAM SKILL *Where was the Mill located in this town?*

Colonial Towns

As you read in Chapter 5, the Puritans began building towns in Massachusetts in the 1630s. Throughout colonial times, similar small towns were established all over New England.

Many New England towns were **self-sufficient,** meaning they relied on themselves for most of what they needed. The food came from fields surrounding the town. Families who lived in town owned small plots of land, where they grew crops and raised animals. Other work was done in town. Workshops belonging to the blacksmith, cooper, and shoemaker were often found around the town common. The **town common** was an open space where cattle and sheep could graze. In the diagram above find the meeting house—the most important building in town. Here ordinary citizens could help make decisions at town meetings and attend church on Sundays.

The Middle Colonies also had many small towns. Here, towns often served as busy market places. Farmers came to sell their crops and buy things like clothing and tools. The town's general store might also have imported goods, such as tea and sugar. Like New England towns, many Middle Colony towns had workshops and a mill where grain could be turned into flour.

REVIEW What was the purpose of the town common? **Main Idea and Details**

Southern Plantations

While there were many small farms in the Southern Colonies, this region was also home to a different kind of farm—the plantation. Southern plantations were large farms where cash crops such as tobacco, rice, and indigo were grown. Most of the work on plantations was done by enslaved Africans. As the diagram on this page shows, plantations were similar to small towns. Like small towns, plantations were largely self-sufficient.

Plantations were owned by wealthy landowners known as planters. Planters were usually men, though women also ran plantations. One example was **Eliza Lucas Pinckney.** Pinckney began managing plantations in South Carolina when she was still a teenager.

In 1744, she became the first person in the 13 colonies to raise a successful crop of indigo. You will read more about her in the Biography following this lesson.

The day-to-day work on a plantation was directed by the plantation manager, known as the overseer. The overseer gave the slaves orders. Slaves could be beaten as punishment for not doing what they were told. Many slaves had to work from morning to night planting and harvesting crops. Others, often women and children, cooked and cleaned in the planter's house. Enslaved people also worked in blacksmith and carpentry workshops, smokehouses, bakeries, laundry buildings, and stables.

REVIEW What was the role of the overseer on a plantation? **Main Idea and Details**

▶ **Many different jobs were done on plantations.**

DIAGRAM SKILL *What is the largest building on this plantation?*

A Southern Plantation

Carpentry workshop · Fields · Stable · Fields · Slave quarters · Blacksmith workshop · Overseer's house · Barn · Ice house · Garden · Laundry house · Planter's house · Smoke house · Kitchen · Well

Farming Families

From New Hampshire to Georgia, most colonists, free and slave, lived on small family farms. No matter where they lived, all farming families had one thing in common—hard work. Read these lines from a poem by a woman named Ruth Belknap.

> *Up in the morning I must rise*
> *Before I've time to rub my eyes...*
> *But, Oh! It makes my heart to ache,*
> *I have no bread till I can bake,*
> *And then, alas! it makes me sputter,*
> *For I must churn or have no butter.*

Ruth Belknap lived and worked on a small farm in New Hampshire in the 1700s. As her poem illustrates, farming families had to make or grow most of what they needed.

REVIEW Do you think Ruth Belknap enjoyed her life on a small farm? Explain your opinion. **Draw Conclusions**

Summarize the Lesson

- Benjamin Franklin helped the city of Philadelphia become the largest in the colonies.
- Many small towns developed in both the New England and Middle Colonies.
- The work of enslaved Africans helped plantations in the Southern Colonies produce valuable crops.

LESSON 2 REVIEW

Check Facts and Main Ideas

1. ⟳ **Compare and Contrast** On a separate sheet of paper, complete this diagram comparing and contrasting a Middle Colony town and a Southern plantation.

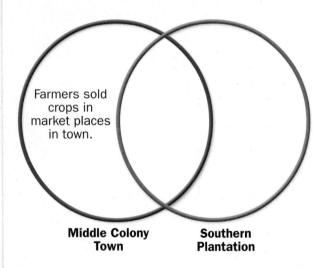

Farmers sold crops in market places in town.

Middle Colony Town   **Southern Plantation**

2. What are some ways that Benjamin Franklin helped improve life for people in Philadelphia?

3. **Critical Thinking:** *Evaluate* You know that New England towns were often built according to a careful design. Do you think this design helped the towns become self-sufficient? Explain.

4. What types of crops were grown on plantations in the Southern Colonies?

5. Suppose you lived during colonial times. What are four different kinds of places you could live? Which would you choose?

Link to ⟨◦◦⟩ Geography

Draw a Diagram Using the diagram on page 212 as a model, draw your own diagram of a New England town. Include important buildings and make any changes that you think would improve the town.

Elizabeth Lucas Pinckney 1722–1793

At age 16, Elizabeth Lucas Pinckney, called Eliza, had already lived in England and the West Indies. Now she had just arrived in South Carolina. Eliza's mother was sick, and her father hoped that a new life on a plantation would help her get better. Soon after the family arrived, Eliza's father, an officer in England's army, was called away. He left his daughter in charge of the family's plantation.

Eliza loved the challenge of her new role. On a typical day, she would get up at 5 A.M., read until 7 A.M., then go through the fields to look over the plantation, all before breakfast. The rest of her busy day included teaching her sister and two girls who were enslaved on the plantation how to read. Eliza even studied law and helped her neighbors write their wills. She wrote to a friend that running a plantation "requires much writing and more business and fatigue [tiredness]...than you can imagine."

BIOFACT

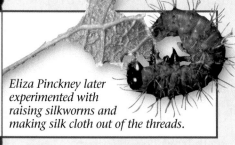

Eliza Pinckney later experimented with raising silkworms and making silk cloth out of the threads.

Eliza Pinckney believed that she could make the plantation—and all of South Carolina—richer by experimenting with new crops. She was especially interested in indigo, a plant that makes a blue dye that was very valuable in Europe. Eliza wrote:

"I had greater hopes from the Indigo...than any of the rest of the things I had tried."

After several years of hard work, Pinckney successfully grew indigo on her plantation. Soon she gave indigo seeds to her neighbors. Indigo became a major export of South Carolina for many years. By 1754 South Carolina was exporting more than 1 million pounds of indigo every year.

Learn from Biographies

Eliza Pinckney added to her many responsibilities on the plantation by experimenting with new crops. How did the demand for indigo help South Carolina?

▶ This Eliza Lucas Pinckney doll is clothed in an indigo-blue dress similar to the kind worn in the 1700s.

For more information, go online to *Meet the People* at **www.sfsocialstudies.com**.

1650

1750

1647
Massachusetts law requires towns to build public schools

1704
First edition of *Boston News-Letter* published

1730s
Great Awakening begins

PREVIEW

Focus on the Main Idea
Going to school, attending religious services, and reading for news and entertainment were important parts of everyday life in the colonies.

PLACES
Boston
Williamsburg
Newport

PEOPLE
George Washington
George Whitefield
John Peter Zenger

VOCABULARY
Great Awakening
almanac

▶ Colonial students learned to read using a hornbook, a page covered with a clear horn for protection.

216

Everyday Life in the Colonies

You Are There

It is winter, 1757. You are sitting in a dark, one-room schoolhouse. A fire has just been lit in the fireplace, but the room is still freezing. Luckily you remembered to bring some firewood today. Students who forget to bring wood have to sit at the desks farthest from the fireplace. You watch the small orange flames, wondering when the room will start to warm up.

Now you notice that the teacher is looking at you. Did he ask you a question? If so, you did not hear it. This could be a problem. Your teacher always punishes students for daydreaming in class. You might have to put on a giant painted cap and wear a sign saying something embarrassing like "Baby good-for-nothing." Or maybe he will make you sit on the unipod, a stool with only one leg. Five minutes on this stool and you will be exhausted from the effort of trying to keep your balance. Your teacher is still looking at you. Yes, this could be a problem.

 Compare and Contrast As you read, compare and contrast life in the colonies with life today.

Studying and Playing

Education was very important to early settlers in New England. In 1647, the leaders of Massachusetts passed a law requiring towns to establish free public schools. For most colonists this was a new idea. Free schools did not exist in Europe at this time.

In the years that followed, small public schools were built throughout the colonies. As you can tell from the story on the previous page, schools in colonial times were very different from schools today. Most schools had just one room. Students of different ages sat together. They learned the basics—reading, writing, and arithmetic.

Students also learned rules of polite behavior. When **George Washington** was a young student in Virginia, he copied lists of rules into his notebook. He wrote down rules such as:

> *"Every action done in company, ought to be with some sign of respect, to those that are present."*
> *"Be careful to keep your promise."*

Most students did not stay in school for as many years as children do today. When they reached their early teens, many boys and girls started working full time on family farms. Others began apprenticeships. Only a small percentage of students went to college. Harvard, established near **Boston,** Massachusetts, in 1636, is the oldest college in the United States. The next was the College of William and Mary, which opened in **Williamsburg,** Virginia, in 1693.

When children were not at school, they spent a lot of time doing chores around their family's house or farm. Most young people had less free time than they do today. But children still found time for games and sports. They danced, played hide-and-seek, and invented a wide variety of games of tag. They climbed trees, went swimming, and flew kites. In winter, children enjoyed ice-skating and sledding.

Museum of the City of New York

REVIEW How were colonial schools different from schools today? How were they the same? **Compare and Contrast**

▶ This drawing shows Harvard College in 1720.

▶ **Touro Synagogue is the oldest standing synagogue in the United States.**

Religion in the Colonies

Religion was an important part of life in all regions of the English Colonies. You know that several of the colonies were founded as places where people could enjoy religious freedom. Some colonies continued to be refuges for religious groups that faced persecution in Europe. For example, many Jews came to the 13 Colonies. They settled in Rhode Island, New York, and South Carolina. In 1763, Jews in **Newport,** Rhode Island built what today is the oldest synagogue in the United States.

Among Christians, an important religious movement known as the **Great Awakening** began in the 1730s. This movement "awakened" or revived many colonists' interest in religion. The Great Awakening was led by Protestants. Protestant preachers traveled from town to town, giving sermons that were fiery and emotional. Services were often held outside, because churches could not hold all the people who wanted to attend.

Many new churches were built during the Great Awakening. New colleges were established to train ministers. The Great Awakening also inspired people to help others. One of the leaders of the Great Awakening, **George Whitefield,** traveled throughout the colonies collecting money to build an orphanage in Georgia. When Whitefield was in Philadelphia in 1739, Benjamin Franklin went to hear him preach. Franklin was so impressed with Whitefield's sermon, he decided to contribute all the money he had with him to the orphanage. "I emptied my pocket wholly into the collector's dish, gold and all," Franklin later wrote.

REVIEW What was one effect of the Great Awakening? **Cause and Effect**

▶ **George Whitefield (center) was a powerful preacher and leader of the Great Awakening.**

Reading

A colonist walking down the streets of Boston on April 24, 1704, could have bought the first edition of the *Boston News-Letter*. This became the first newspaper in the 13 Colonies to be published on a regular basis. By the 1770s, there were dozens of newspapers in the colonies. Sometimes, however, printing a newspaper could be a dangerous job. In Issues and Viewpoints on pages 222–223, you will read the story of a printer named John Peter Zenger. In 1734, Zenger was thrown in a New York City jail for printing his political opinions in *The New-York Weekly Journal*.

Reading was an important form of entertainment in the colonies. When the day's work was done, families often sat together and listened as one family member read aloud from a book. Benjamin Franklin's *Poor Richard's Almanack* was one of the most popular books in the 13 Colonies. Only the Bible sold more copies during this time. An almanac is a reference book with facts and figures. In the Biography following this lesson, you will read how Franklin got started as a writer while he was still a teenager.

Letter writing was another important activity for colonists. Letters were folded and sealed with melted wax. Envelopes were not used because they were considered a waste of paper, which was expensive and hard to make. Letters helped colonists living far apart to stay in touch.

REVIEW Summarize the role of reading in the colonies. **Summarize**

▶ John Peter Zenger faced trial for printing criticism of New York's royal governor.

Poor Richard, 1733.
AN
Almanack
For the Year of Christ
1 7 3 3,

Literature and Social Studies

Each year, *Poor Richard's Almanack (Almanac)* included many of Benjamin Franklin's clever sayings. Have you ever heard any of these famous pieces of advice?

- *An egg today is better than a hen tomorrow.*
- *Early to bed, early to rise, makes a man healthy, wealthy, and wise.*
- *Haste makes waste.*
- *He that speaks much, is much mistaken.*
- *The sleeping fox catches no poultry. Up! Up!*
- *No gains without pains.*

Colonial Meals

As you know, early colonists learned to grow corn from Native Americans. Colonists used corn to make breads, puddings, and pancakes that were served with maple syrup. Colonists also cooked stews in large iron pots. Stews were made of fish or meat with vegetables, and seasoned with salt and pepper.

Many desserts were common in the colonies, including ice cream, donuts, and a variety of fruit pies. Desserts were not always tasty, though. In 1758, a Swedish traveler wrote home about an apple pie he ate in

Delaware. The pie was "made of apples neither peeled nor freed from their cores, and its crust is not broken if a wagon wheel goes over it."

REVIEW Do you think you would have liked the food in colonial times? Why or why not? **Draw Conclusions**

Summarize the Lesson

1647 Massachusetts passed a law requiring towns to establish free public schools.

1704 The *Boston News-Letter* became the first regularly published colonial newspaper.

1730s The Great Awakening revived many people's interest in religion.

LESSON 3   REVIEW

Check Facts and Main Ideas

1. **Compare and Contrast** On a separate sheet of paper, fill in this diagram comparing and contrasting school in colonial times with school today.

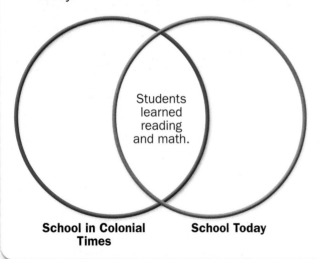

Students learned reading and math.

School in Colonial Times   **School Today**

2. How were schools in colonial times different from schools today?

3. **Critical Thinking: *Cause and Effect*** Why were some of the English colonies home to people of many different religions?

4. What was the only book in the colonies that sold more copies than *Poor Richard's Almanac* during the mid-1700s?

5. Describe some common meals that a colonial family might enjoy.

Link to   Science

Do Research Benjamin Franklin was also a scientist. Do some research in books or on the Internet. Write a one-page report about Franklin's work as a scientist.

Benjamin Franklin *1706–1790*

Benjamin Franklin was 12 years old when he became an apprentice to his older brother James, a printer. Until he turned 21, Ben was to obey James in exchange for learning about printing. James Franklin started the second newspaper in the 13 Colonies. Although Ben had not attended much school, he was interested in being a writer. Sometimes he would write an article, sign it "Silence Dogood," and slip it under the printing shop door. James printed the articles, not suspecting that Ben was the author!

But Ben was not completely happy. He did not like having to obey his brother, and wanted more say in running the newspaper. He later wrote,

BIOFACT

One of Franklin's most famous experiments used a key and a kite to prove that it was possible to attract and use the electricity from lightning.

"Thinking my apprenticeship very tedious [boring], I was continually wishing for some opportunity of shortening it,..."

When Ben was 16, James was arrested for printing articles critical of colonial leaders. Ben had to run the paper by himself. While this helped Ben gain independence and confidence in his writing, he believed that it was wrong for a government to jail people because of their opinions.

Soon after James was freed, Ben left his brother's shop in Boston to start a new life in Philadelphia. He became a successful printer. As an adult, Ben Franklin was a famous writer, scientist, and inventor, as well as one of the founders of our nation's government. He helped write the Declaration of Independence and the Constitution. Franklin hoped every person would take advantage of the liberties provided by the new country. He said,

"The declaration only guarantees the American people the right to pursue happiness. You have to catch it yourself."

Learn from Biographies

Ben Franklin was very upset when his brother was sent to jail for things he had written in the newspaper. How do you think this experience later affected Ben Franklin as a leader in Philadelphia?

For more information, go online to *Meet the People* at **www.sfsocialstudies.com**.

Printing the Truth

Writers throughout history have believed printing the truth was a necessary freedom, even if it meant criticizing the government.

In colonial times, loyalty to the British government was considered more important than the truth. It was well known that New York's Governor William Cosby was greedy and dishonest. Yet, not a single newspaper in the entire colony dared to publish articles that criticized him.

Then, in 1733, John Peter Zenger started New York's first independent newspaper, *The New-York Weekly Journal*. The paper published many articles describing Governor Cosby's misdeeds. Cosby was furious. In 1734 Zenger was arrested for "seditious libel," writing untrue and harmful things about a government or government official.

Andrew Hamilton, a lawyer from Philadelphia, defended Zenger at his trial in 1735. When Hamilton admitted that Zenger had printed all of the offending articles, the judge was shocked. Was he admitting Zenger's guilt? No, said Hamilton. He argued that since Zenger had written the truth, he could not be found guilty of libel. Hamilton gave a powerful speech about the importance of truth in the press.

The courtroom spectators cheered when the jury gave its verdict, "Not Guilty!" John Peter Zenger's determination to print the truth was the first colonial victory for freedom of the press.

"Every man of common sense will judge that he is an enemy to his king and country who pleads for any restraint [limit] upon the press."

—from an anonymous essay published in John Peter Zenger's New-York Weekly Journal, 1733.

"Give me the liberty to know, to utter, and to argue freely according to conscience, above all liberties."

John Milton, England, 1644

"The constitution grants citizens the right to criticize their leaders, because these leaders are human beings and not gods. It is only through the people's criticism and supervision that those leaders will make fewer mistakes . . . Then, and only then, will the people be able to breathe freely."

Wei Jingsheng, opponent of communist government of China, 1979

"Censorship [restrictions on speech or the press] is never over for those who have experienced it. It . . . affects the individual who has suffered it, forever."

Nadine Gordimer, South Africa, 1990

Issues and You

In many countries in the world, people still do not have the right to freedom of the press. Do research on the Internet to learn more about the issue of freedom of the press. Why do you think some countries do not allow this freedom?

1730   1780

1739
Enslaved people
organize Stono
Rebellion

1765
Venture Smith
gains his freedom

1789
Olaudah Equiano
publishes an
autobiography

Slavery in the Colonies

PREVIEW

Focus on the Main Idea
Slavery expanded rapidly in
the English Colonies during
the 1700s, especially in the
Southern Colonies.

PEOPLE
Venture Smith
Olaudah Equiano

VOCABULARY
Stono Rebellion

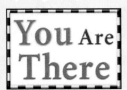 **You Are There** "I am now sixty-nine years old," says Venture Smith. "Though once straight and tall, measuring without shoes six feet one inch and a half…I am now bowed down with age and hardship."

Venture Smith is telling the story of his long and incredible life. He thinks back to his early childhood in West Africa, where he was born in 1729. He explains that he was captured when he was six years old, and was eventually put aboard a slave ship bound for North America. For about the next 30 years, he lived and worked as a slave in New England. In 1765, at the age of 36, Smith purchased his own freedom. Then, working almost nonstop, he saved enough money to purchase the freedom of his wife and children, and many other enslaved Africans.

Smith ends his story by talking about the things that make him happy today. "Meg, the wife of my youth," he says. "My freedom," he adds, "which nothing else can equal."

 Compare and Contrast As you read, pay attention to the similarities and differences between slavery in different regions of the colonies.

Slavery, North and South

Venture Smith told the story of his life in a book that was published in 1798. Smith was one of thousands of Africans who were enslaved in the 13 Colonies during the 1700s. The graph on this page shows you how slavery grew in the different regions of the colonies.

Some of the Africans enslaved in the north—the New England and Middle Colonies—worked on farms. Most, however, worked in towns and cities. They worked in stores, inns, and as skilled artisans. They worked in people's homes, as cooks or personal servants.

In the north, slaves usually had more opportunities to improve their lives than did slaves in the south. For example, some enslaved people in the north were able to earn money by taking on extra jobs at night and on weekends. Venture Smith wrote that he earned money "by catching muskrats and minks, raising potatoes and carrots...and by fishing in the night." Some enslaved people saved enough money to purchase their freedom. This was a long and difficult process, though. It took Venture Smith many years to save the money needed to buy his freedom.

Strict laws limited the rights of enslaved people in most northern colonies. Slaves could not travel or go onto a ship without written permission. Colonies passed these laws to make it more difficult for enslaved people to escape.

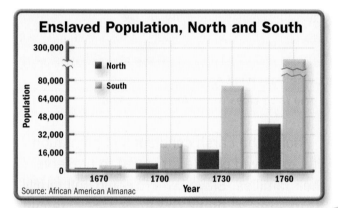

Enslaved Population, North and South

■ North
■ South

Population (y-axis): 0, 16,000, 32,000, 48,000, 64,000, 80,000, 300,000

Year (x-axis): 1670, 1700, 1730, 1760

Source: African American Almanac

GRAPH SKILL *About how many slaves were there in the South in 1730?*

▶ Enslaved people were sold at slave auctions such as the one shown below.

REVIEW What is one way that slavery in the North was different from slavery in the South? ↻ **Compare and Contrast**

225

Peoples of West Africa

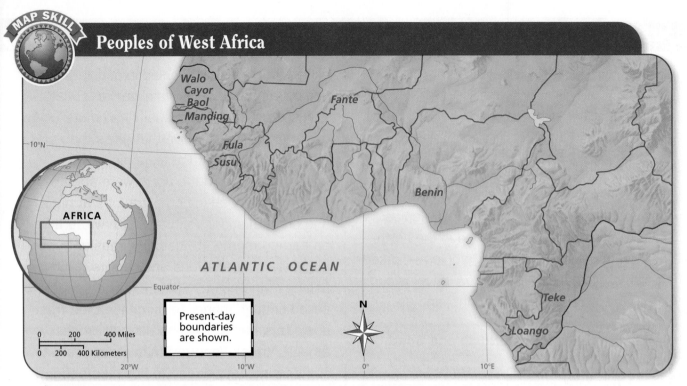

Walo
Cayor
Baol
Manding
Fula
Susu
Fante
Benin
Teke
Loango

AFRICA

ATLANTIC OCEAN

Equator

Present-day boundaries are shown.

N

0   200   400 Miles
0   200   400 Kilometers

20°W   10°W   0°   10°E

10°N

► Most of the enslaved people brought to the colonies came from West Africa.

MAP SKILL Region *Name three West African peoples who lived close to the Atlantic Ocean.*

Slavery in the South

As the graph on page 225 shows, the enslaved population of the Southern Colonies grew quickly during the 1700s. Some enslaved people were held on small farms or in cities. But most were forced to work on large plantations. Sometimes hundreds of slaves worked on a single huge plantation.

The map above shows you some of the places from which groups of African people were captured. Enslaved people brought a variety of skills to Southern plantations. Some West Africans, for example, had experience growing rice. In the Carolinas, they showed planters how to raise this valuable crop. Other enslaved people were expert carpenters, blacksmiths, or tailors. No matter what types of skills enslaved people had, their work lasted all day, and sometimes the night. A Virginia planter wrote that he forced slaves to work at night, "by moon or candlelight."

Facing the harsh conditions of plantation life, enslaved people struggled to preserve their families. Slave owners could sell family members and break up families. Still, family members tried to get together whenever they could.

Enslaved people kept African culture alive. They made drums, banjos, and other instruments similar to the ones they knew from Africa. Some of the Southern Colonies banned the use of these instruments. Plantation owners were afraid that enslaved people were using instruments to send secret messages to each other.

REVIEW What were some of the skills enslaved Africans used on Carolina plantations?
Main Idea and Details

► This drum, found in Virginia, was made in a West African style.

Resisting Slavery

In Lesson 1 of this chapter, you read about **Olaudah Equiano,** who was enslaved as a young boy. Equiano later gained his freedom and wrote a book about his life. Published in 1789, his book demanded that readers think about the evils of slavery:

> *"Surely this...violates [breaks] that first natural right of mankind, equality and independency."*

Enslaved people found many ways to resist slavery. They tried to trick owners and overseers by working slowly, breaking tools, or pretending to be sick. Many attempted to escape. Free African men and women, as well as whites, often helped escaping slaves by hiding them or giving them money. Armed rebellions also occurred. In the bloody **Stono Rebellion,** a group of enslaved people fought with slave owners near the Stono River in South Carolina in 1739. About 25 white colonists were killed before the slaves were captured and executed.

REVIEW What are some ways that enslaved people resisted slavery?
Summarize

Summarize the Lesson

- Slavery in the colonies expanded rapidly during the 1700s.
- Slaves in the north had more opportunities to improve their lives than slaves in the south.
- Enslaved people found a variety of ways to resist slavery.

LESSON 4   REVIEW

Check Facts and Main Ideas

1. ◎ **Compare and Contrast** On a separate sheet of paper, complete this diagram comparing and contrasting slavery in the different regions of the colonies.

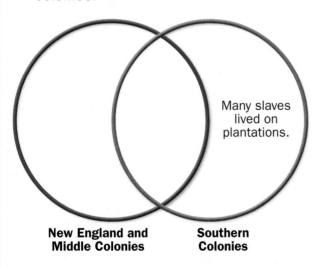

New England and Middle Colonies | Many slaves lived on plantations. | Southern Colonies

2. In which region of the 13 Colonies did slavery expand most rapidly during the 1700s?

3. How were enslaved Africans able to keep their traditions alive on plantations?

4. What happened during the **Stono Rebellion?**

5. **Critical Thinking: *Analyze Primary Sources*** Based on the quote on this page, how would you describe Olaudah Equiano's opinion of slavery?

Link to 🔗 Writing

Write Questions Suppose you had a chance to interview a person who had been enslaved in the colonies. Write five questions that you would like to ask the person.

1625   1650   1675   1700

1630
Puritans begin building small towns in New England

1647
Massachusetts law requires towns to build public schools

1704
First edition of *Boston News-Letter* published

Chapter Summary

Compare and Contrast

On a separate sheet of paper, copy the graphic organizer and complete it to compare and contrast farming in the New England and Southern Colonies.

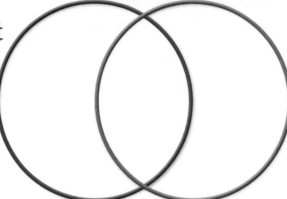

New England Colonies   Southern Colonies

Vocabulary

Choose a word or term to complete the sentences that follow.

almanac (p. 219)
apprentice (p. 203)
town common (p. 212)

Great Awakening (p. 218)
Middle Passage (p. 206)

1 At the center of a colonial town was a _____, an open space where animals could graze.

2 A young person had to become an _____ before becoming an artisan.

3 An _____ is a source of facts and figures.

4 The _____ revived many colonists' interest in religion.

5 The journey from West Africa to the West Indies was known as the _____.

People and Places

Write a sentence explaining the significance of each of the following people or places in colonial North America. You may use two or more in a single sentence.

1 **West Indies** (p. 206)

2 **Charleston** (p. 206)

3 **Eliza Lucas Pinckney** (p. 213)

4 **Benjamin Franklin** (p. 211)

5 **George Whitefield** (p. 218)

6 **John Peter Zenger** (p. 219)

7 **Boston** (p. 217)

8 **Venture Smith** (p. 225)

9 **Newport** (p. 218)

10 **Olaudah Equiano** (p. 227)

1723
Ben Franklin moves to Philadelphia

1730s
Great Awakening begins

1739
Enslaved people organize Stono Rebellion

1744
Eliza Lucas Pinckney grows the first indigo crop in the 13 colonies

1756
Olaudah Equiano brought to North America as a slave

1765
Venture Smith gains his freedom

1789
Olaudah Equiano publishes autobiography

Facts and Main Ideas

1. Describe one of the triangular trade routes.

2. What were some of the skills Africans brought with them to the colonies?

3. **Time Line** How many years passed between the year Olaudah Equiano was brought to North America as a slave and the year he published his autobiography?

4. **Main Idea** What were some of the main goods and products produced in the New England, Middle, and Southern Colonies?

5. **Main Idea** How were colonial towns similar to and different from colonial cities?

6. **Main Idea** How did people spend their time in the 13 Colonies?

7. **Main Idea** Compare and contrast slavery in the northern and southern colonies.

8. **Critical Thinking:** *Cause and Effect* What was the effect on the 13 Colonies of diverse populations?

Write About History

1. **Write a diary entry** that an apprentice might have written about a day in his or her life.

2. **Write a short story** about a captured West African's experience in the Middle Passage.

3. **Write an advertisement** identifying the different kinds of goods that can be purchased in the Southern Colonies.

Apply Skills

Using Newspaper Articles

Read the newspaper article below. Then answer the questions.

Sailing Ship Reaches Boston

Boston, May 6—After crossing the Atlantic in a colonial-style sailing ship, a group of students and sailors arrived in Boston yesterday. The crossing took 25 days and relied on sailing techniques used by immigrants in colonial times. The ship, however, carried modern communication equipment in case of emergency and to report on its position.

The voyage was planned so that people of the twenty-first century could try to experience what it was like for people to sail to America in the eighteenth century. Food and other necessities were as close to colonial conditions as possible. After the ship reached Boston, one of the passengers commented, "It's amazing how all of us fit into such small quarters!"

1. What is the event reported in the article? When was the article written?

2. Why was the voyage made?

3. What modern equipment was used and why?

Internet Activity

To get help with vocabulary, people, and terms, select dictionary or encyclopedia from *Social Studies Library* at **www.sfsocialstudies.com.**

The Fight for a Continent

1680

New Mexico
The Pueblo leader Popé leads a revolt against the Spanish.

Lesson 1

1

1718

New Orleans
The French establish a port city near the mouth of the Mississippi River.

Lesson 2

2

1754

Fort Necessity
George Washington's troops lose a battle to French soldiers.

Lesson 3

3

NORTH
AMERICA

Mississippi River

Fort
Necessity

ATLANTIC
OCEAN

NEW
MEXICO

New Orleans

PACIFIC
OCEAN

SOUTH
AMERICA

Why We Remember

Take a look at a map of North America. You will see three large countries—
Canada, the United States, and Mexico—and smaller countries as well. Not
one of these nations existed before 1776, the year the United States was born.
In this chapter you will travel back in time to the 1700s, when three
European countries—France, Great Britain, and Spain—along with many
Native Americans, were struggling for control over this huge continent. This
struggle led to a British victory over France. It also set the stage for the later
struggles that established the United States and other independent nations.

1550   1650   1750

1565
Spanish establish
St. Augustine,
Florida

1610
Spanish establish
Santa Fe, New Mexico

1680
Pueblo
Revolt
begins

1718
Spanish
establish San
Antonio, Texas

PREVIEW

Focus on the Main Idea
During the 1500s and 1600s,
New Spain expanded by
establishing colonies in Florida
and New Mexico.

PLACES
Florida
St. Augustine
New Mexico
Santa Fe
San Antonio

PEOPLE
Pedro Menendez de Avilés
Popé
Junípero Serra

VOCABULARY
hacienda
presidio
El Camino Real
Pueblo Revolt

The Spanish Move North

You Are There It is a warm summer evening in
1565. Five Spanish warships sail
along the coast of Florida. The sun
has set and the sky is growing dark when Pedro
Menendez de Avilés (meh NEN dehs day ah vee
LAYS), commander of this Spanish fleet, sees what he
has been looking for—French ships anchored near
the mouth of the St. Johns River. Menendez sails close
to the French.

"What are you doing here?" Menendez demands.

"We are from France," comes the reply.

"I am Pedro Menendez, General of the fleet of the
King of Spain," shouts the Spanish commander. "At
daybreak I shall board your ships!"

"If you are a brave man, don't wait till day!" the
French yell back. "Come on now, and see what you
will get!"

Menendez does not wait until day. The battle begins
in darkness.

Compare and Contrast As you read, compare
the Spanish attempts to establish colonies in
different parts of North America.

Fighting for Florida

As you read in Chapter 4, the Spanish established the vast colony of New Spain in 1535. New Spain stretched from South America to Mexico, with its capital in Mexico City. In the middle 1500s, Spanish leaders decided to extend their colony into **Florida.** The Spanish explorer Juan Ponce de León had traveled through this region in the early 1500s. Now the Spanish hoped that a settlement in Florida would prevent the French or English from gaining a foothold in this part of North America.

In 1565, **Pedro Menendez de Avilés** led a small fleet of Spanish warships to Florida. Menendez knew that the French had already started building a settlement in Florida. His mission was to find the French, defeat them, and take control of Florida for Spain. In a series of bloody battles, Menendez and his soldiers defeated the French. Florida became part of New Spain. The Spanish founded **St. Augustine** on the east coast of Florida. This was the first permanent European settlement in what is now the United States.

REVIEW Why did Spanish leaders want to establish a colony in Florida?
Main Idea and Details

▶ Pedro Menendez de Avilés *(left)* led the Spanish effort to conquer Florida. He helped establish the colony of St. Augustine *(above)* in 1565.

233

New Mexico

Soon after moving into Florida, the Spanish began expanding into what is now the Southwest region of the United States. In 1598, Don Juan de Oñate (oh NYAH tay) led a small Spanish army north across the Rio Grande. The Spanish called this region **New Mexico.** The town of **Santa Fe** was founded in 1610 and named the capital of New Mexico. The Pueblo, Apache, and Navajo peoples had been living on this land for centuries. Now the Spanish were claiming it.

The Spanish hoped to find gold and silver in New Mexico. They soon realized, however, that the region was not rich in these minerals. Settlers also learned that New Mexico was too hot and dry for many kinds of farming. The open grasslands, however, were good for sheep and cattle ranching. Some wealthy ranchers built **haciendas** (hah see EN dahs) or large estates. Haciendas were often self-sufficient communities, with vegetable gardens, workshops, and mills. Workers, many of them Native Americans, lived on the haciendas.

Spanish religious leaders began building missions in New Mexico to try to convert Native Americans to Christianity. To protect the missions, the Spanish built **presidios** (pray SEE dee ohs), or military forts.

To connect New Mexico to Mexico City, the Spanish built a road called **El Camino Real** (ray AHL), "the Royal Road." It was used to carry goods between Mexico City and Santa Fe. Find it on the map below.

REVIEW What was the purpose of El Camino Real? **Main Idea and Details**

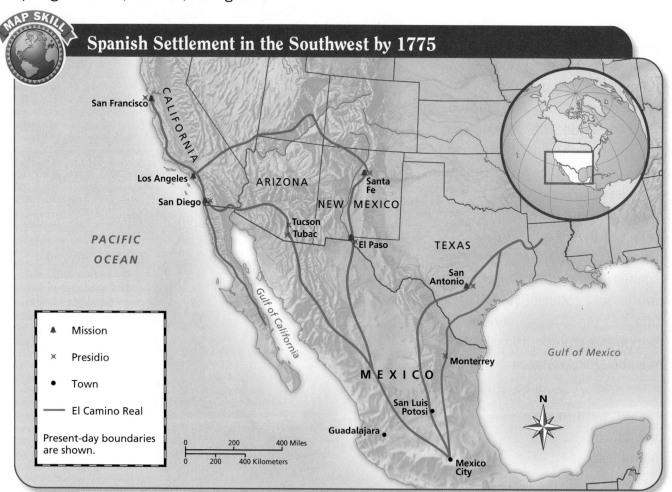

MAP SKILL

Spanish Settlement in the Southwest by 1775

San Francisco

CALIFORNIA

Los Angeles

San Diego

ARIZONA

Tucson
Tubac

Santa
Fe

NEW MEXICO

El Paso

TEXAS

San
Antonio

PACIFIC
OCEAN

Gulf of California

Gulf of Mexico

Monterrey

MEXICO

San Luis
Potosi

Guadalajara

Mexico
City

N

▲ Mission
× Presidio
• Town
— El Camino Real

Present-day boundaries are shown.

0   200   400 Miles
0   200   400 Kilometers

▶ The Spanish moved north from Mexico to establish settlements in what is today the United States.

MAP SKILL Movement *What settlements were connected by El Camino Real?*

The Pueblo Revolt

In 1680, a Pueblo leader named **Popé** (poh PAY) led a revolt against the Spanish in New Mexico. For several reasons, many Pueblo people were ready to join in this fight. The Spanish were enslaving Pueblo people, sending some to Mexico and forcing others to work on ranches and missions in New Mexico. Spanish settlers were taking over Pueblo land and villages. And Spanish leaders were trying to force the Pueblo to give up their traditional ways of worshiping and living.

The Pueblo attacked settlements all over New Mexico, killing hundreds of Spanish settlers. Joined by Apache and Navajo fighters, Popé and his men surrounded Santa Fe. A Pueblo leader named Juan rode into the city carrying two crosses, one white and one red.

The Spanish governor asked Juan to explain the meaning of the two crosses. Juan declared:

> *"If you choose the white there will be no war but you must all leave the country. If you choose the red, you must all die, for we are many and you are few."*

The Spanish refused to leave New Mexico. The Pueblo continued their attacks. In fierce fighting that became known as the **Pueblo Revolt,** the Spanish were driven out of New Mexico.

REVIEW What was one effect of the Pueblo Revolt? **Cause and Effect**

HERE AND THERE

The Taj Mahal

At the Same Time that Spain was building colonies throughout the Americas, one of the most famous buildings in the world was being built in India. Construction of the Taj Mahal began in 1632 under the orders of Shah Jahan, the Muslim emperor of India. It took 20,000 workers 22 years to complete the Taj Mahal. Expert workers from all over Asia came to work on this beautiful building.

The Spanish Return

By the early 1690s, Popé had died. The Pueblo and other peoples of the region were not as united as they had been. The Spanish recaptured New Mexico from the Pueblo in 1692. Spanish settlers and missionaries began moving back to New Mexico. They also moved into land that is now Texas and Arizona. The town of San Antonio, Texas, was founded in 1718. Spanish leaders hoped that these new settlements and missions would help Spain keep control of the Southwest. They did not want to be driven out again by Native American forces. And they were also concerned that the French might try to take over this region.

New Spain continued to expand throughout the 1700s. In the Biography following this lesson, you will read about Father Junípero Serra, who founded the first Spanish missions in another part of New Spain—California.

REVIEW Why did the Spanish build new settlements in the Southwest in the 1700s? *Summarize*

Summarize the Lesson

1565 The Spanish founded St. Augustine, the first permanent European settlement in what is now the United States.

1610 The Spanish founded Santa Fe and made it the capital of New Mexico.

1680 In the Pueblo Revolt, the Spanish were temporarily driven out of New Mexico.

LESSON 1 REVIEW

Check Facts and Main Ideas

1. ⟳ **Compare and Contrast** On a separate sheet of paper, complete this chart by comparing Spanish attempts to begin colonies in different regions of North America.

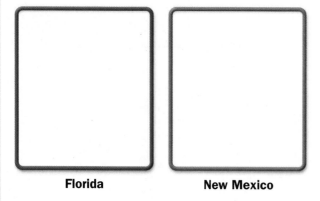

Florida   New Mexico

2. Why did the Spanish want to build a colony in Florida?

3. **Critical Thinking:** *Make Inferences* Did the geography of New Mexico influence the economic activities of Spanish settlers in this region? Explain.

4. Explain the purpose of missions in New Spain.

5. Describe three causes of the Pueblo Revolt.

Link to 🔗 Writing

Write a Letter Suppose you are a settler in New Mexico during the 1600s. Write a letter to a family member in Spain, describing life in New Mexico. Mention Native Americans, the climate, haciendas, missions, presidios, and El Camino Real.

Junípero Serra
1713–1784

Miguel Serra, a 17-year-old living in Spain, was about to make a very serious decision. He had chosen to become a Franciscan priest, which meant that he would devote his life to the Catholic Church. Miguel had read many books about famous Catholics. The stories that interested him most were those about missionaries who traveled to distant lands to try to spread their religion. He had a strong feeling that he, too, would like to be a missionary. He would even choose a new name, Junípero, to show that he was ready to begin a new way of living.

At the age of 35, Father Serra decided to travel to the Americas. His family did not want him to go, thinking they would never see him again. In a goodbye letter, he wrote:

Although he had an injured leg, Father Serra followed the Franciscan tradition by walking nearly everywhere he went.

"Let them not be concerned about me now, but rather let them commend me to [put me in the care of] God that I may be a good priest and a holy minister."

When Father Serra reached the Americas, his goal was to establish missions in New Spain. He traveled from Mexico to the present-day state of California in 1769. On July 16 he set up the first mission in California—San Diego de Alcalá. This was the beginning of the city of San Diego.

Father Serra remained in California for the rest of his life. He set up a chain of nine missions. Eventually, there were 21 missions in California.

Learn from Biographies

How did Junípero Serra contribute to the beginning of what we now know as California?

For more information, go online to *Meet the People* at **www.sfsocialstudies.com**.

The Spanish in the Southwest

Searching for the legendary cities of gold during the 1500s, Spanish explorers journeyed thousands of miles through what is today the Southwest of the United States. They returned without success to Mexico, but their explorations opened the region to Spanish settlement. Missionaries came to try to convert the Native Americans to Christianity. Ranchers built haciendas and raised cattle and sheep.

Searching for Golden Cities

In 1540, Francisco Vásquez de Coronado headed an expedition from Mexico into the Southwest. Looking for the legendary cities of gold, he led 300 soldiers and many Native Americans. He found no riches, but opened the region to further exploration and settlement.

Elegant Shade

Broadbrimmed felt hats are called sombreros, from the Spanish *sombra*, meaning "shade."

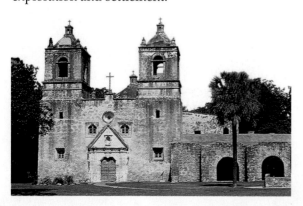

An Early Mission

Spanish missionaries built Mission Concepción on the San Antonio River in Texas in the middle 1700s. The mission was built near a Native American community so that the people could be taught the Roman Catholic religion.

Pride of the Hacienda
The Spanish love of fine horses is seen in the splendid saddle and blanket on the horse outside this hacienda.

New Mexican Box
Carvings decorate this wooden box made in northern New Mexico in about 1800. It was used to store clothing, tools, and valuables.

Cuera

A Leather-Jacket Soldier
During Colonial times, Spanish soldiers wore thick leather jackets called "*cueras*." They were known as *Soldados de Cueras*, meaning "soldiers in leather jackets."

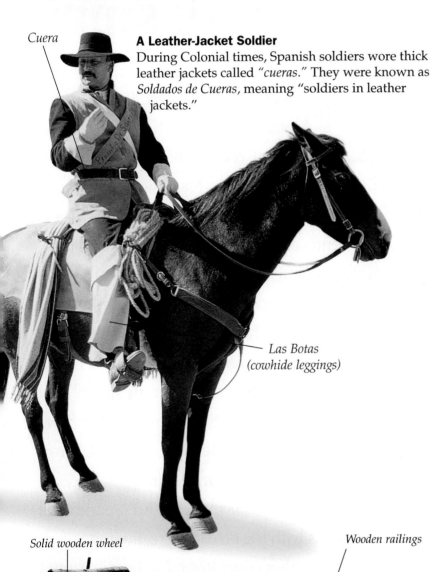

Las Botas
(cowhide leggings)

Patterns combine Spanish and Native American styles.

Colorful Serape
This woolen serape, or shawl, was worn as a coat in Spanish America.

Solid wooden wheel

Wooden railings

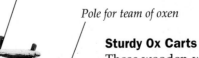

Pole for team of oxen

Sturdy Ox Carts
These wooden-wheeled carts, the most common vehicles in the Spanish Southwest, were pulled by oxen.

1670   1720

1673
Marquette and Jolliet explore the Mississippi River

1682
La Salle claims Louisiana for France

1718
New Orleans is established near mouth of Mississippi River

Mississippi River

LOUISIANA   New Orleans

PREVIEW

Focus on the Main Idea
French exploration of the Mississippi River led to new French colonies in North America.

PLACES
Mississippi River
Louisiana
New Orleans

PEOPLE
Jacques Marquette
Louis Jolliet
Robert La Salle

VOCABULARY
trading post
tributary

French Explore the Mississippi

You Are There

A French missionary, Jacques Marquette (ZHAHK mar KET), makes a note of the date in his journal: June 17, 1673. He has just seen the Mississippi River for the first time. Traveling in two birch-bark canoes, he and six other French explorers begin paddling down the river. And Marquette begins filling his journal with descriptions of one incredible sight after another.

He is amazed by the herds of massive buffalo, which he calls "wild cattle." He and his men hunt the buffalo, and quickly learn that this is a dangerous animal. "If a person fires at them from a distance with either bow or gun, he must, immediately after the shot, throw himself down and hide in the grass."

Marquette also visits many Native American villages. He speaks with the people there, finding out all he can about the Mississippi River. But he still cannot answer the most important question—where does this river end?

Sequence As you read, pay attention to the sequence of events that led to French control of the Mississippi River.

Exploring the Mississippi

As you read in Chapter 5, the French established New France in 1534. The major settlements of New France were Quebec and Montreal, in present-day Canada. The French moved west slowly, building trading posts and missions along the St. Lawrence River and Great Lakes. **Trading posts** were places where the French and Native Americans met to trade goods.

French traders and missionaries learned important skills from the Native Americans of this region. They learned how to build canoes from birch bark, and how to make snowshoes for walking in deep snow. Native Americans also told the French about a big river to the west. Algonquian-speaking Indians called this river *Mississippi*, which means "big water."

The leaders of New France were eager to explore the **Mississippi River.** Control of this river would help them reach new lands where they could build trading posts. And the French were still hoping to find a river that flowed west to the Pacific Ocean—the Northwest Passage. Could the Mississippi be this river?

▶ **Marquette and Jolliet explored the Mississippi River by canoe, meeting many Native Americans along the way.**

In the summer of 1673, the French missionary **Jacques Marquette** set out to explore the Mississippi. He was accompanied by a fur trader named **Louis Jolliet** (JOH lee et) and five other French adventurers. As they traveled, Marquette drew maps of the Mississippi. He also spoke with many Native Americans who lived along the river. In his journal, Marquette wrote about entering one Native American village and introducing himself.

> *"They replied that they were Illinois, and, as a token of peace, they offered us their pipes to smoke."*

After sharing a meal with the Illinois, the explorers resumed their journey. Since the river continued to flow south, however, Marquette realized that this was not the Northwest Passage.

The explorers had paddled almost 1,000 miles south on the Mississippi. Now they had to turn around and head back north.

REVIEW Why did the leaders of New France want control of the Mississippi River?
Main Idea and Details

Founding Louisiana

Nine years later, a French explorer named **Robert La Salle** continued the French exploration of the Mississippi River. La Salle's goal was to travel all the way to the mouth of the Mississippi. He set out from the St. Lawrence River in the winter of 1681. To reach the Mississippi, La Salle and his French and Native American companions put their canoes on sleds and dragged them over snow and frozen streams. They began rowing down the Mississippi River in February 1682. Follow La Salle's route on the map.

La Salle reached the Gulf of Mexico in April. While French soldiers fired muskets in the air and shouted "Long live the king!" La Salle claimed the entire Mississippi River valley for France. He also claimed all of the river's tributaries. A **tributary** is a stream or river that flows into a larger river. La Salle named this territory **Louisiana,** for King Louis XIV of France. Louisiana became a part of New France. New France was now a vast empire.

REVIEW Describe the sequence of La Salle's expeditions. Sequence

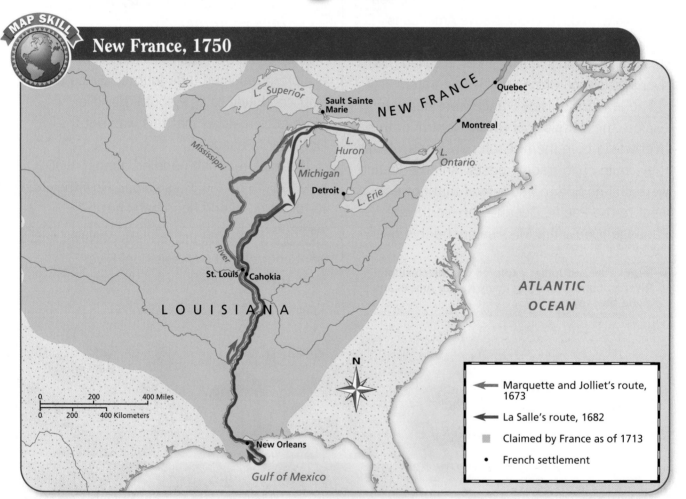

▶ French explorer Robert La Salle (*above*) traveled the Mississippi River nine years after Marquette and Jolliet.

MAP SKILL Use a Map Scale *About how far from the Gulf of Mexico were Marquette and Jolliet when they turned around?*

New French Settlements

During the late 1600s and early 1700s, the French built trading posts, forts, and missions in New France. Many French settlements, such as Detroit and New Orleans, later grew into major American cities. **New Orleans,** founded in 1718, was Louisiana's territorial and later state capital from 1722 to 1849.

▶ Today New Orleans is a major port city.

With an ideal location near the mouth of the Mississippi River, New Orleans became a busy trading center. Today, nearly 300 years later, New Orleans is one of the busiest ports in the United States.

REVIEW Name two French settlements that are now major American cities.
Main Idea and Details

Summarize the Lesson

1673 Marquette and Jolliet explored the Mississippi River for France.

1682 La Salle reached the mouth of the Mississippi and claimed Louisiana for France.

1718 New Orleans was founded and quickly became a busy port.

LESSON 2 ▷ REVIEW

Check Facts and Main Ideas

1. Sequence On a separate sheet of paper, fill in the sequencing chart by putting the lesson's events in correct order:

> New France is established.

↓

>

↓

>

↓

>

2. How did French settlers first learn about the Mississippi River?

3. Critical Thinking: *Point of View* Give two reasons the French were interested in exploring the Mississippi and its **tributaries.**

4. What did La Salle do when he reached the mouth of the Mississippi?

5. How did New Orleans' location help the city grow?

Link to ◦◦◦ Science

Research Birch-Bark Canoes Using the library or Internet, research the birch-bark canoes used by Native Americans. Write a one-page report about these canoes. How were they made? What advantages did canoes have over other kinds of boats? What did they look like? Include a small diagram of a birch-bark canoe.

Compare Maps at Different Scales

What? You know that a map scale uses a unit of measurement, such as one inch, to represent an actual larger distance on Earth, such as one mile. On a **small-scale map** an inch on the map represents a very large distance on Earth. Therefore, a small-scale map shows a big area of Earth, such as a state or a country. Map A is a small-scale map.

On a **large-scale map** an inch represents a shorter distance on Earth. Therefore, this kind of map can show more details than a small-scale map. Map B is a large-scale map.

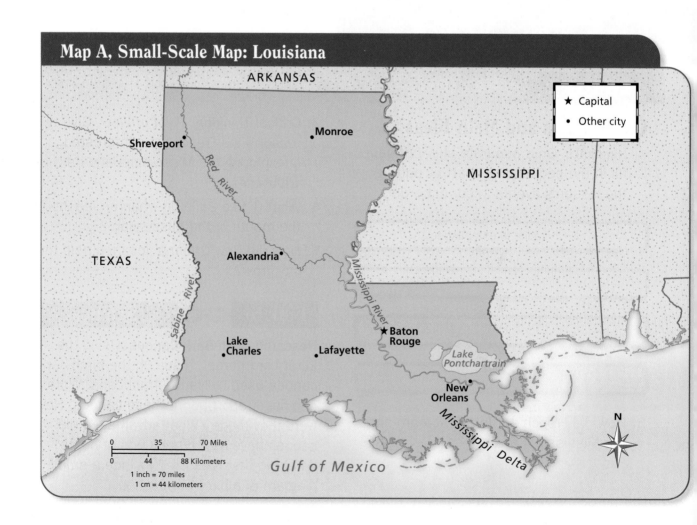

Map A, Small-Scale Map: Louisiana

ARKANSAS

★ Capital
• Other city

Monroe

Shreveport

Red River

MISSISSIPPI

TEXAS

Alexandria

Sabine River

Mississippi River

Lake
Charles

Lafayette

★ Baton
Rouge

Lake
Pontchartrain

New
Orleans

Mississippi Delta

N

0   35   70 Miles
0   44   88 Kilometers
1 inch = 70 miles
1 cm = 44 kilometers

Gulf of Mexico

Map B, Large-Scale Map: New Orleans

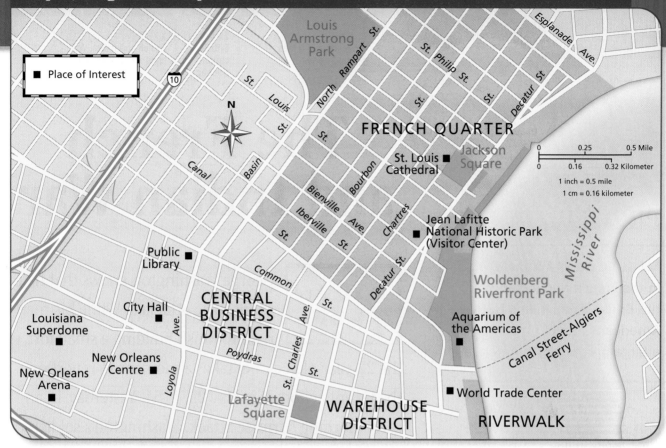

Why? In Lesson 2 you read about the founding of New Orleans. To locate New Orleans in relation to other cities in present-day Louisiana, you need a small-scale map. To see places in New Orleans and other details of the city, you need a large-scale map.

How? You can compare Map A and Map B to see the difference between a large-scale map and a small-scale map. Look at the scale on Map A. How many miles does one inch represent? Measure the distance between New Orleans and Shreveport. New Orleans is about 275 miles southeast of Shreveport. Now measure the distance between New Orleans and Lafayette. How far apart are these cities?

Look at the scale on Map B. On this map, one inch represents 0.5 miles—69.5 less miles than on Map A. The area shown is smaller, so details of New Orleans can be shown. Find the French Quarter on this map.

Think and Apply

1. Which map would you use to locate Baton Rouge?

2. Which map would you use to locate Lafayette Square?

3. Turn to the map of New France on page 242 in Lesson 2. Is this a **large-scale** or **small-scale map?**

Internet Activity

For more information, go online to the *Atlas* at **www.sfsocialstudies.com.**

1750   1770

1754
French and Indian
War begins

1759
British
capture
Quebec

1763
French and Indian War
ends with British victory

PREVIEW

Focus on the Main Idea
In the French and Indian War,
the British, French, and Native
Americans fought for control of
a large part of North America.

PLACES
Fort Necessity
Ohio River valley
Fort Duquesne
Quebec

PEOPLE
George Washington
Metacom
Hendrick
Pontiac
George III

VOCABULARY
King Philip's War
backcountry
French and Indian War
Pontiac's Rebellion
Proclamation of 1763

The French and Indian War

You Are There George Washington knows that he is about to be attacked. While his men rush to finish building a small fort, the 22-year-old colonel takes a moment to report on the recent action. It is May 29, 1754. Yesterday, in an early morning surprise attack, Washington's soldiers defeated a small French force. "The battle lasted about 10 or 15 minutes, sharp firing on both sides," Washington writes.

But Washington knows he is in greater danger than ever. There are hundreds of French soldiers nearby, and it will not be long until they find him. He hopes his men have time to finish their fort—a small shelter with log walls. It is not much of a fort, but it is all they have time to build. They call it Fort Necessity. "We expect every hour to be attacked by a superior force," Washington writes. "Let them come, what hour they will."

Cause and Effect As you read, pay attention to the causes and effects of the French and Indian War.

Conflicts Over Land

George Washington was a young military leader from Virginia. Washington and his soldiers built **Fort Necessity** on a meadow in what is now southwestern Pennsylvania. What was Washington doing here in 1754? And why was he fighting the French? This story begins many years earlier.

As you have read, the first English colonists in North America built small settlements along the Atlantic coast. Throughout the 1600s, the population of the colonies grew quickly. Settlers wanted more land to build towns and farms and they began moving west. Native Americans, who had been living on this land for thousands of years, resisted English settlement.

In New England, the conflict led to war in 1675. A Wampanoag leader named **Metacom,** son of Chief Massasoit, led several Native American groups into battle against the English settlers. Metacom's goal was to force the English out of New England. The English called Metacom "King Philip," and this war became known as **King Philip's War.** After a year of bitter fighting, Metacom was killed. The English settlers won King Philip's War. They now controlled most of New England.

During the 1700s, settlers continued moving west. As colonial cities, towns, and plantations grew, land along the Atlantic coast became more and more expensive. In search of land of their own, some families

began moving to an area called the **backcountry.** This was a rugged stretch of land near the Appalachian Mountains. Families built log cabins, hunted, and carved small farms from the rocky soil.

By the middle 1700s, settlers were moving even farther west. They crossed the Appalachian Mountains and entered the **Ohio River valley**—a region of fertile land and thick forests along the Ohio River. But other groups also claimed these lands. Powerful Native American tribes lived there. And the French claimed it was part of New France. Who would control this region? As George Washington discovered in May 1754, this question would be decided by war.

REVIEW What was one effect of King Philip's War? *Cause and Effect*

▶ **Metacom led the Wampanoag and other Native Americans in King Philip's War. This club (above) was probably used by Metacom.**

The Ohio River Valley

France's claim on the Ohio River valley was based on the explorations of Robert La Salle. Do you remember what La Salle did when he reached the mouth of the Mississippi River? He claimed the river and all its tributaries for France. One of these tributaries is the Ohio River. Therefore, the French claimed the Ohio River valley as part of New France. The French began building forts to defend this region.

England, now known as Great Britain, also claimed the Ohio River valley. In 1753, British leaders wrote a stern letter to the French, stating that the land along the Ohio River was "known to be the property of the Crown of Great Britain." The British demanded that the French leave the area immediately. George Washington was sent to deliver the letter.

Four months later, Washington returned with the French response. The French refused to leave. In March 1754, Washington marched west again. This time he commanded about 150 soldiers. His mission was to help build a British fort at the strategic spot where the Allegheny and Monongahela rivers join to form the Ohio River. But he soon learned that the French were already there, building **Fort Duquesne** (doo KAYN). Washington decided to try to capture this French fort.

REVIEW On what did France base its claim of the Ohio River valley?
Summarize

▶ **This painting shows George Washington around the time he was a British army officer.**

Map Adventure

Washington's First Battle

George Washington fought his first battle in the woods south of Fort Duquesne.

1. Do you think Fort Duquesne was built on an important spot? Why or why not?

2. Did Washington accomplish his goal of capturing Fort Duquesne? How can you tell?

3. What did Washington do after the battle?

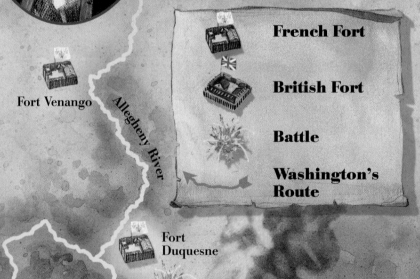

French Fort

British Fort

Battle

Washington's Route

Fort Venango

Allegheny River

Fort Duquesne

Fort Cumberland

Fort Necessity

Monongahela River

Ohio River

Potomac River

► **George Washington led British soldiers in the French and Indian War.**

The French and Indian War

Washington and his soldiers did not reach Fort Duquesne. In the woods near the French fort, Washington attacked and defeated a group of French soldiers. After the battle, Washington and his men returned to Fort Necessity—a small log fort they had begun building a few days before. The French attacked on a rainy day in early July 1754. After many of his men were killed or wounded, Washington was forced to surrender. Soaked and exhausted, the soldiers returned to Virginia.

These small battles were the start of a long war between Britain and France. In the 13 Colonies, the war was called the French and Indian War, because British forces fought against the French and their American Indian allies.

The British tried to gain Native American allies of their own. At a meeting in Albany, New York in 1754, leaders of the British colonies asked the powerful Iroquois League to join in the fight against the French. Iroquois leaders resisted, however. An Iroquois leader named Hendrick said that the British and French were "quarrelling about lands which belong to us, and their quarrel may end in our destruction."

In 1755, the British made another attempt to capture Fort Duquesne. Led by General Edward Braddock, 2,100 soldiers chopped their way through the Pennsylvania forests. George Washington was with this army. On July 9, just eight miles from Fort Duquesne, the British were attacked by French and Indian forces. Washington later wrote that many British soldiers panicked and "ran as sheep before the hounds." General Braddock was killed, and the British were defeated. Washington wrote to his family that,

> *"...I had four bullets through my coat and two horses shot under me, and yet escaped unhurt."*

This was the first in a series of French victories over the British. It looked like Britain would lose the war. Then, in 1758, things began to change.

REVIEW According to Hendrick, why did the Iroquois resist joining the British? **Draw Conclusions**

British Victory

In London, British leaders were worried about the way the war was going. They decided to send more soldiers to fight in North America. In 1758, British forces began winning battles against the French. The British were also helped by the Iroquois, who agreed to join the British side in 1759. Iroquois leaders hoped that victory in battle would help the Iroquois increase their power and maintain control of their lands.

The key battle of the war was fought at **Quebec,** the capital of New France. Led by British General James Wolfe, British forces captured Quebec in September 1759. This victory helped Great Britain win the French and Indian War. The war officially ended when Britain and France signed the Treaty of Paris in 1763. As the maps below show, Britain took over most of New France. Spain gained control of French lands west of the Mississippi.

The French and Indian War also had a major impact on the Native Americans of North America. The traditional lands of many American Indian peoples were now part of the British empire. And British settlers were eager to move onto this land.

REVIEW Where was the key battle of the French and Indian War fought?
Main Idea and Details

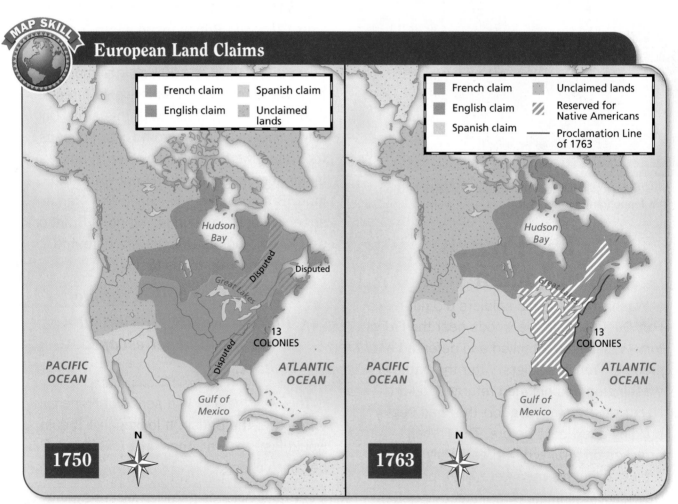

European Land Claims

French claim   Spanish claim
English claim   Unclaimed lands

Hudson Bay
Disputed
Great Lakes
Disputed
Disputed
13 COLONIES
PACIFIC OCEAN
ATLANTIC OCEAN
Gulf of Mexico
N
1750

French claim   Unclaimed lands
English claim   Reserved for Native Americans
Spanish claim   Proclamation Line of 1763

Hudson Bay
Great Lakes
13 COLONIES
PACIFIC OCEAN
ATLANTIC OCEAN
Gulf of Mexico
N
1763

▶ As a result of the French and Indian War, Britain gained a huge amount of land from France.

MAP SKILL Region *Which country claimed land in the northern part of North America?*

Pontiac's Rebellion

Many Native Americans resisted the new British settlers. In 1763, an Ottawa leader named **Pontiac** called on his warriors to revolt against the British. Britain, he declared, "seeks only to destroy us." Native Americans from many tribes attacked British forts and settlements in the Ohio River valley and along the Great Lakes. This fighting was known as **Pontiac's Rebellion.** Pontiac won several victories before the British put down the rebellion.

British leaders were alarmed by Pontiac's Rebellion. They did not want to continue fighting Native Americans on lands won from France. Britain's King **George III** issued the **Proclamation of 1763.** This proclamation, or official announcement, said that colonists were no longer allowed to settle on land west of the Appalachian Mountains.

The king hoped this would prevent future Native American rebellions. The proclamation was not popular among many colonists who wanted new lands to settle. Tensions between the colonists and the British government began to grow.

REVIEW What was a cause of the Proclamation of 1763?
Cause and Effect

▶ Pontiac led a revolt of several tribes against the British.

Summarize the Lesson

— **1754** George Washington fought in the first battles of the French and Indian War.

— **1759** British forces captured Quebec, helping Britain win the French and Indian War.

— **1763** The Treaty of Paris gives Britain control of most of New France.

LESSON 3 ▸ REVIEW

Check Facts and Main Ideas

1. **Cause and Effect** On a separate sheet of paper, complete this diagram showing causes and effects of the French and Indian War.

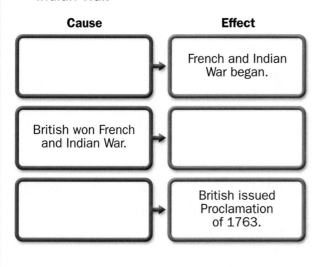

Cause	Effect
	French and Indian War began.
British won French and Indian War.	
	British issued Proclamation of 1763.

2. What factors led to conflicts between the British and the Native Americans?

3. Where and when did the **French and Indian War** begin?

4. What factors helped the British begin winning battles in the late 1750s?

5. **Critical Thinking:** *Evaluate* Why did the outcome of the French and Indian War lead to new conflicts between British settlers and Native Americans?

Link to ⟷ Geography

Use an Atlas Look back at the map on page 248 and find Fort Duquesne. An important American city now stands on this spot. Using an atlas, find the name of this city.

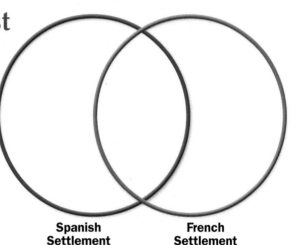

| 1600 | 1620 | 1640 | 1660 |

1565
Spanish establish
St. Augustine, Florida

1610
Spanish establish
Santa Fe, New Mexico

Chapter Summary

Target Skill

Compare and Contrast

On a separate sheet of paper, fill in the diagram to compare and contrast information about Spanish and French settlement in North America. Similarities should be written in the space where the circles overlap. Differences should be written in the outer areas.

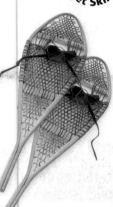

Spanish
Settlement

French
Settlement

Vocabulary

Use each word or term in a sentence that explains the definition.

1 **hacienda** (p. 234)

2 **presidio** (p. 234)

3 **Pueblo Revolt** (p. 235)

4 **trading post** (p. 241)

5 **tributary** (p. 242)

6 **backcountry** (p. 247)

7 **Pontiac's Rebellion** (p. 251)

8 **Proclamation of 1763** (p. 251)

People and Places

Fill in the blanks with the person or place from this chapter that best completes the sentence.

1 _____ and his fleet chased the French out of Florida in 1565. (p. 233)

2 _____ founded the first Spanish missions in California. (p. 236)

3 _____ was the first French explorer to map the Mississippi River. (p. 241)

4 _____ and the British army could not capture France's Fort Duquesne in the French and Indian War. (p. 248)

5 The French lost a key battle to the British in _____. (p. 250)

1680	1700	1720	1740	1760	1780

.673
Marquette and olliet explore Mississippi iver

1680
Pueblo Revolt begins

1682
La Salle claims Louisiana for France

1692
Spanish recapture New Mexico from the Pueblo

1718
New Orleans is founded

1754
French and Indian War begins

1759
British capture Quebec

1763
British win French and Indian War

Facts and Main Ideas

1 What European country founded St. Augustine?

2 Explain why New Orleans was a good location for a trading center.

3 Why were the Iroquois unwilling to join the British in the French and Indian War?

4 **Time Line** How many years did the French and Indian War last?

5 **Main Idea** Why did Spain want to establish a colony in Florida?

6 **Main Idea** How did La Salle's explorations lead to the expansion of France?

7 **Main Idea** What were the effects of the French and Indian War?

8 **Critical Thinking:** *Compare and Contrast* Compare and contrast the Pueblo Revolt and Pontiac's Rebellion.

Write About History

1 **Write a poem** about what it would be like to see the Mississippi River or another impressive natural feature for the first time.

2 **Write a conversation** between a European colonist and a Native American in which each person explains why his or her group seeks to live on a piece of land.

3 **Write a newspaper article** announcing the beginning of the French and Indian War. Describe its causes and the outcome of the first attack.

Apply Skills

Use Maps at Different Scales
Look at Map A and Map B on pages 244–245. Then answer the questions.

1 Which map would you use to locate the French Quarter?

2 What is the distance in miles between New Orleans and Lake Charles?

3 On which map can you locate the Mississippi River?

▶ **Iron balconies at night in the French Quarter**

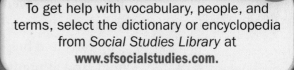

Internet Activity

To get help with vocabulary, people, and terms, select the dictionary or encyclopedia from *Social Studies Library* at **www.sfsocialstudies.com.**

End with Literature

In many ways, children during colonial times lived much like children today. They did chores, played games, and celebrated holidays. Read the following excerpts from a question and answer book about life in the 13 Colonies. How is your life similar to the lives of the children it describes? How is it different?

... if you lived in Colonial Times

By Ann McGovern

Did people work hard in colonial days?

People *had* to work hard in colonial days. They had to, because almost everything they used they made themselves.

Think of the clothes the people wore. There was spinning and weaving and knitting to be done. The spinning wheels and looms were homemade, too.

Think of the food they ate. There were gardens to weed, rows and rows of corn to hoe, food to cook, bread to bake, butter to churn—no end to work!

Think of the dishes they used. There were trenchers (a wooden board on which to carve or serve meat) and bowls and spoons and mugs to make.

Think of the houses they lived in. There were beds and tables and chairs and brooms and buckets and barrels to make. And when these things got broken, they had to be fixed.

Making soap and making candles took more than a day. Sometimes neighbors came to help and the job went faster.

When did boys and girls work?

Boys and girls were taught that work was good for them. In colonial days, people thought it was a sin to be lazy. So every morning the children got up early and helped with the work. Boys worked before school, after school, and at night. Girls worked just as hard.

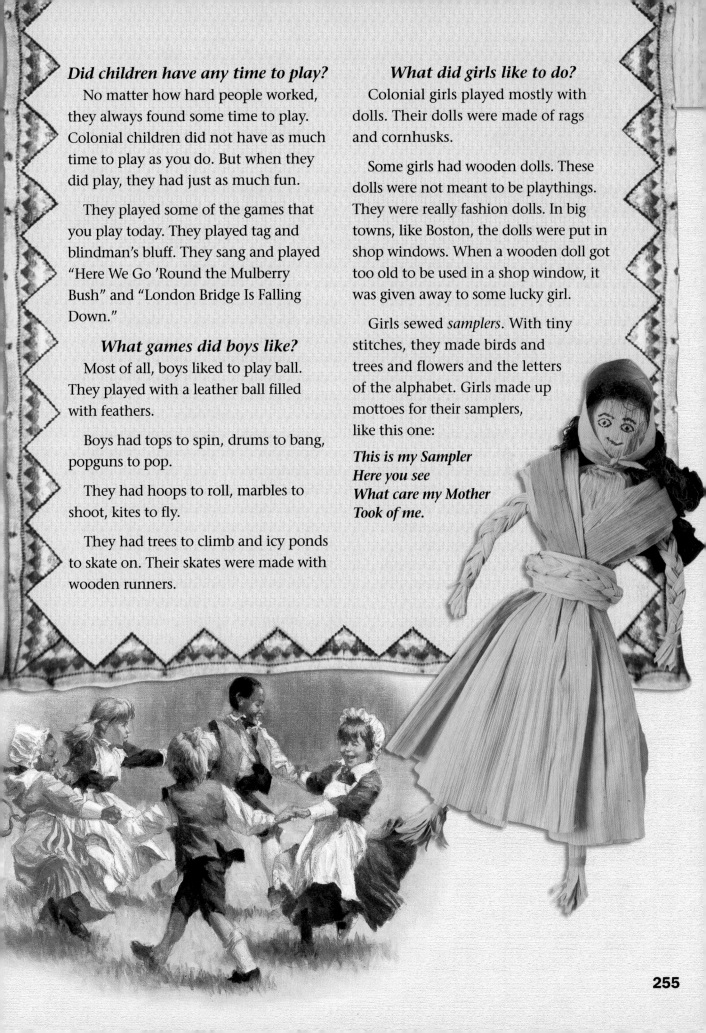

Did children have any time to play?

No matter how hard people worked, they always found some time to play. Colonial children did not have as much time to play as you do. But when they did play, they had just as much fun.

They played some of the games that you play today. They played tag and blindman's bluff. They sang and played "Here We Go 'Round the Mulberry Bush" and "London Bridge Is Falling Down."

What games did boys like?

Most of all, boys liked to play ball. They played with a leather ball filled with feathers.

Boys had tops to spin, drums to bang, popguns to pop.

They had hoops to roll, marbles to shoot, kites to fly.

They had trees to climb and icy ponds to skate on. Their skates were made with wooden runners.

What did girls like to do?

Colonial girls played mostly with dolls. Their dolls were made of rags and cornhusks.

Some girls had wooden dolls. These dolls were not meant to be playthings. They were really fashion dolls. In big towns, like Boston, the dolls were put in shop windows. When a wooden doll got too old to be used in a shop window, it was given away to some lucky girl.

Girls sewed *samplers*. With tiny stitches, they made birds and trees and flowers and the letters of the alphabet. Girls made up mottoes for their samplers, like this one:

This is my Sampler
Here you see
What care my Mother
Took of me.

Review

Test Talk

Narrow the answer choices. Rule out answers you know are wrong.

Main Ideas and Vocabulary

Read the passage below and use it to answer the questions that follow.

Daily life in the English colonies was filled with lots of hard work. Children spent much of their time working on their parents' farms when they were not in school. Young people served as apprentices so that they could become blacksmiths, shoemakers, or other <u>artisans</u>. Most colonists lived on farms, so many adults spent long hours tending to farms.

The New England, Middle, and Southern Colonies differed in the types of crops they grew and the sizes of their towns. Although some New England towns were largely <u>self-sufficient</u>, all the colonies traded with other nations. Some colonies participated in the slave trade. In the South, many slaves worked on plantations. Slaves in the North often worked in businesses or as servants in people's homes.

Spain began establishing colonies in North America in the 1500s. The Spanish settled in Central America, Mexico, Florida, and the Southwest. Pueblo people who were natives of New Mexico drove the Spanish out during the Pueblo Revolt in 1680. In 1692 Spain recaptured New Mexico.

The French expanded their colony of New France, which began in what is today's Canada. French explorers traveled down the Mississippi River and claimed it and the surrounding land for France. Explorer Robert La Salle named the territory Louisiana.

When English settlers wanted more land and started moving west, they came into conflict with the French, who also claimed the land. Britain and France fought the French and Indian War to settle the dispute. Britain won the war, gaining the Louisiana territory. Native Americans continued to fight the colonists who were moving onto their land. George III's Proclamation of 1763 stated that colonists could not settle west of the Appalachian Mountains.

1 According to the passage, why was the French and Indian War fought?
  A The Indians kept attacking the French.
  B The French and British wanted to settle the same land.
  C Colonists were enslaving Africans.
  D Colonists worked too hard.

2 In the passage the word <u>artisans</u> means—
  A children
  B farmers
  C skilled workers
  D colonies

3 In the passage the word <u>self-sufficient</u> means—
  A farming
  B trading with others
  C depending on others
  D depending on themselves

4 All of the English colonies
  A had plantations.
  B grew cotton.
  C warred with Spain.
  D participated in trade.

People and Places

Match each person and place to its definition.

1 **Olaudah Equiano** (p. 227)

2 **St. Augustine** (p. 233)

3 **George Whitefield** (p. 218)

4 **Newport** (p. 218)

5 **Fort Necessity** (p. 247)

6 **Hendrick** (p. 249)

a. first permanent European settlement in the present-day United States

b. leader of the Great Awakening

c. writer of an autobiography

d. Iroquois leader

e. British base during the French and Indian War

f. site of the oldest Jewish synagogue in the United States

Apply Skills

Analyze a Newspaper Article Clip an interesting article from a newspaper. Paste the article onto a piece of construction paper and circle and label the *who, what, where, when,* and *why* of the article.

Historical documents going online

Researchers Find Journals, Letters, And Other Documents on the Internet

DRY CREEK, May 18—

Write and Share

Present a Play Work with a group of students to write a script reenacting an event you learned about in Unit 3. Present the play to your class. Each student should have a character to represent in the play. Be creative. Use drawings, costumes, and other props to add to your play.

Read on Your Own

Look for books like these in the library.

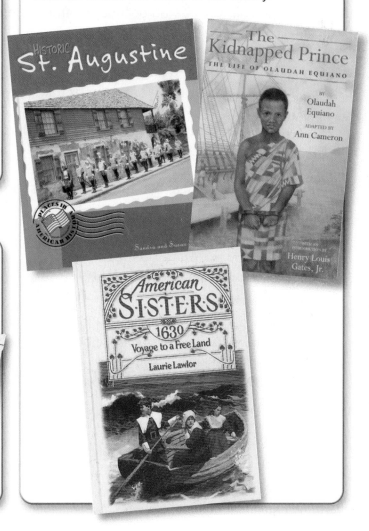

Discovery CHANNEL SCHOOL

UNIT 3 Project

Colonial Living

In this game show, you have all the answers.

1 Choose an occupation from colonial times.

2 Research at least five facts that can be used as clues about the occupation. Write them on an index card.

3 Have the class ask you questions to try to guess your occupation.

4 Share a clue after each question until someone guesses your occupation.

Internet Activity

Explore American colonial life on the Internet. Go to **www.sfsocialstudies.com/activities** and select your grade and unit.

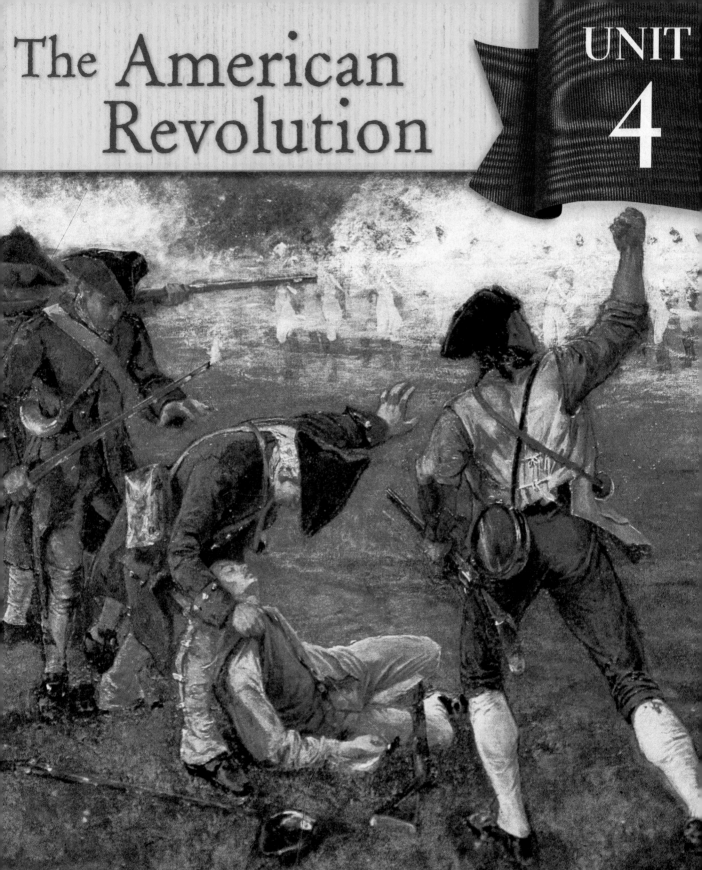

The American Revolution

What do people believe is worth fighting for?

1760

1763
French and Indian
War ends

1765
Colonists protest
British laws

1770

1770
First colonists die in
struggle against British

> "*Stand your ground. Don't fire unless fired upon, but if they mean to have a war, let it begin here.*"
>
> —Said by Captain John Parker to the Lexington minutemen, April 19, 1775

J. Henry Sandham's 1886 painting, **The Dawn of Liberty**, illustrates the Battle of Lexington.

1780   1790

1776
Colonies declare independence

1783
United States wins the war and its independence

1765   1770

1765
Stamp Act
passed

1766
Stamp Act
repealed

1767
Townshend
Acts

Trouble over Taxes

PREVIEW

Focus on the Main Idea
British taxes led to greater cooperation among colonies.

PLACES
Williamsburg, Virginia
New York City, New York
Boston, Massachusetts

PEOPLE
King George III
Patrick Henry
Samuel Adams
Mercy Otis Warren

VOCABULARY
Parliament
Stamp Act
repeal
Sons of Liberty
Townshend Acts
tariff
boycott
Daughters of Liberty

You Are There

George Grenville has a hard job. As prime minister of Great Britain in 1765, Grenville knows that his country needs money. Britain faces huge debts as a result of the French and Indian War. The high cost of keeping thousands of British soldiers in North America to protect the colonies is making things worse. How, Grenville wonders, can Britain raise more money? His solution will set off years of bitter protest and help spark the American Revolution.

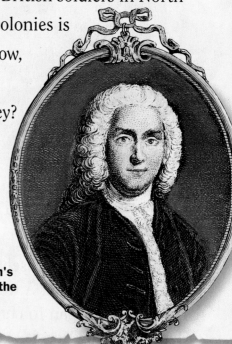

▶ George Grenville was Britain's prime minister, or leader of the government.

Cause and Effect As you read, look for the causes for British taxes and the effects they had on the colonies.

Britain Taxes the Colonies

George Grenville's solution seemed simple—tax the American colonists. According to Grenville's plan, money raised from taxing the colonists would be used to help pay the costs of defending the colonies.

Britain's **King George III** supported the idea of taxing the colonists. So did many members of **Parliament** [PAHR luh ment], Britain's law-making assembly. To them the tax seemed fair. The American colonists benefited from the protection of British soldiers. So, the British thought the colonists should help pay the army's costs.

To achieve this goal, Parliament passed the **Stamp Act** in 1765. This law placed a tax on printed materials in the colonies, such as legal documents, newspapers, and even playing cards. When the colonists bought these items, they had to buy a stamp and put it on the item to show they had paid the tax.

When news of the Stamp Act reached the colonies, many colonists reacted with anger. By 1765 the American colonies already had a long tradition of self-government. Since they never voted for Parliament, colonists complained, Parliament had no right to tax them. This idea led to a popular protest cry:

> **"No taxation without representation!"**

More and more people throughout the colonies decided that they did not want to pay British taxes.

REVIEW Why did British leaders decide to tax the colonists? ⟳ **Cause and Effect**

▶ King George III *(left)* and members of Parliament *(below)* supported new laws to tax the colonists.

Colonists Protest

A young Virginia lawyer named **Patrick Henry** was one of the first to speak out against the Stamp Act. In **Williamsburg,** Virginia, Henry made a fiery speech before the House of Burgesses, the colony's legislature. Henry warned King George III that Britain had no right to tax the people of Virginia. As you will read in Citizen Heroes, Henry became famous for his brave speeches in defense of colonists' rights.

Henry's words inspired other colonists to protest the new tax. In October 1765 leaders from nine colonies held a meeting in **New York City** called the Stamp Act Congress. Here, colonial leaders urged Parliament to **repeal** or cancel, the Stamp Act. Christopher Gadsden of South Carolina summed up the feeling of cooperation that was growing in the colonies:

> *"There ought to be no more New England men, no New Yorkers...but all of us Americans."*

The colonies were beginning to unite against British taxes. **Samuel Adams** of Massachusetts soon became an important leader. Adams had failed at several businesses, but there was one thing he did very well—inspire other people to take action. A friend once said of Adams that "he eats little, drinks little, sleeps little, thinks much." In 1765 Samuel Adams was thinking about how to protest the Stamp Act.

REVIEW How did the colonists respond to the Stamp Act? ⟳ **Cause and Effect**

▶ A cartoon by Benjamin Franklin *(above)* urged colonies to unite during the French and Indian War, but it also expressed colonial feelings about the Stamp Act. An engraving *(right)* showed protesters punishing tax stamp agents.

JOIN, or DIE.

Sons of Liberty

Adams organized the **Sons of Liberty**, a group that led protests against the new tax. Soon Sons of Liberty groups were started in towns throughout the colonies. Their members burned stamps and threatened stamp agents—the people who were hired to collect the stamp taxes. In some towns stamp agents were attacked or had their homes destroyed. In

▶ **The Stamp Act required that stamps like this be placed on all printed materials.**

Boston, Samuel Adams and other Sons of Liberty members created a life-sized puppet of the local stamp agent and hung it from a tree.

They pinned a sign on the puppet: "What greater joy did New England see, than a stamp man hanging on a tree."

The goal was to scare stamp agents, and it worked. By the time the Stamp Act officially went into effect, there was not an agent in the colonies who dared try to sell the stamps.

REVIEW What effect did the Sons of Liberty have on the Stamp Act? ↺ **Cause and Effect**

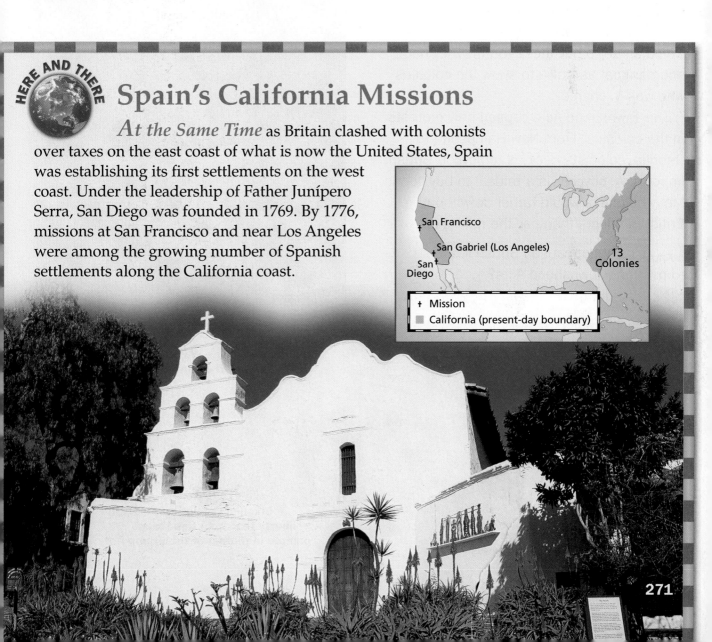

HERE AND THERE

Spain's California Missions

At the Same Time as Britain clashed with colonists over taxes on the east coast of what is now the United States, Spain was establishing its first settlements on the west coast. Under the leadership of Father Junípero Serra, San Diego was founded in 1769. By 1776, missions at San Francisco and near Los Angeles were among the growing number of Spanish settlements along the California coast.

San Francisco

San Gabriel (Los Angeles)

San Diego

13 Colonies

✝ Mission

California (present-day boundary)

The Townshend Acts

Leaders in Britain saw that it would be nearly impossible to collect any money from the stamp tax. Parliament voted to repeal the Stamp Act in 1766. This news was celebrated with parades and fireworks in the colonies. But Britain still needed money. And King George III insisted that Britain had the right to tax the colonies, no matter what Patrick Henry and Samuel Adams said.

Charles Townshend (TOUN zend) agreed with the king. As treasurer of the British government, Townshend called for a new tax. In 1767 Parliament passed the **Townshend Acts.** These laws placed a **tariff**—a tax on imported goods—on paper, wool, tea, and other goods that the colonies imported from Britain. British leaders hoped that colonists would agree to pay these tariffs. They had another goal as well—to show the colonies who was in charge.

The Townshend Acts caused new protests in the colonies. From New Hampshire to Georgia, colonists decided to boycott British imports. A **boycott** is a refusal to buy goods. Many colonists would rather do without British products than pay the new taxes.

REVIEW What caused British leaders to pass the Townshend Acts?
🔁 Cause and Effect

Women Join the Boycott

In Boston, writer **Mercy Otis Warren** encouraged people to stop buying imported goods such as tea and wool. "We'll quit the useless vanities [expensive items] of life," she wrote. Rather than buying British tea, colonial women began making their own "liberty tea" out of berries and herbs. New groups called the **Daughters of Liberty** formed in the colonies. To help the boycott, Daughters of Liberty began weaving cloth that could be used instead of British wool.

▶ Mercy Otis Warren urged a boycott of British goods.

▶ Stamps were sometimes kept in a leather box, like the one above.

▶ Colonists might have served "liberty tea" from this teapot, painted in protest of the Stamp Act.

▶ **British warships landed troops in Boston in 1768.**

Engraving detail by Paul Revere

The boycott was hurting British businesses. The British government decided to take stronger action. In 1768 British warships arrived in Boston Harbor. British leaders hoped this show of force would convince colonists to stop protesting. Benjamin Franklin was in London at this time. He warned the British government that British

soldiers and warships would only increase tensions in the colonies and lead to more violence. He was right.

REVIEW What caused the British to send warships to Boston? ⟳ **Cause and Effect**

Summarize the Lesson

1765 After the French and Indian War, Parliament passed the Stamp Act to help raise money.

1766 Parliament repealed the Stamp Act after bitter protest in the colonies.

1767 Parliament passed the Townshend Acts, causing colonists to boycott British products.

LESSON 1   REVIEW

Check Facts and Main Ideas

1. ⟳ **Cause and Effect** On a separate sheet of paper, fill in the missing causes of the major events from this lesson.

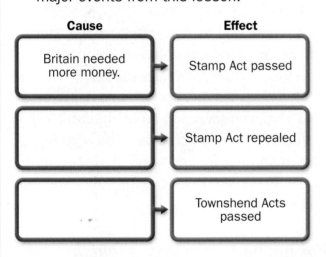

Cause		Effect
Britain needed more money.	→	Stamp Act passed
	→	Stamp Act repealed
	→	Townshend Acts passed

2. What was the **Stamp Act?**

3. Who were the **Sons of Liberty** and **Daughters of Liberty?**

4. How did the British taxes lead to greater cooperation among the colonies?

5. **Critical Thinking:** *Evaluate* Were the colonists' protests successful? Explain your answer.

Link to ⟨∞⟩ Writing

Write a Speech Suppose you are a member of the Virginia House of Burgesses in 1765. Write a speech persuading people to oppose or support the Stamp Act.

Facing the Truth

Is the truth sometimes hard to hear? Is it always easy to be honest? Patrick Henry understood that sometimes facing the truth is difficult, but honesty is still the best policy.

Patrick Henry started working when he was 15. However, business did not suit him. His real love was the law, and in his early 20s, he began studying to become a lawyer. He immediately became a success, and soon was famous not only as a lawyer but also as an orator, or person who speaks very well in public.

Henry valued duty, honesty, and doing the right thing. Because he could speak well and could be relied upon to tell the truth, Henry became widely respected. In 1765 the 28-year-old Henry was elected to the Virginia House of Burgesses. He soon became known as a patriot and as a man who valued liberty.

Henry became an influential leader. He was a delegate to the Continental congresses of 1774 and 1775. But his most famous speech was delivered at the second Virginia Convention on March 23, 1775. He knew that people might choose to do what was easy, rather than what was right. He also knew that many people do not like to face facts. Henry wanted to set a good example. He said,

> *"For my part, whatever anguish [pain] of spirit it may cost, I am willing to know the whole truth; to know the worst, and to provide for it."*

BUILDING CITIZENSHIP

Caring
Respect
Responsibility
Fairness
★ Honesty
Courage

Henry understood that the only way to be prepared for the future was to honestly look at the facts. He knew that not everyone would like the truth, but he felt that it was his duty to speak the truth.

The truth that Patrick Henry wanted to express in this speech was that people need to act in order to make things better. He also wanted people to understand that liberty has a price. Because he realized that most people will turn away from an unpleasant truth, Henry also said,

> *"We are apt [likely] to shut our eyes against a painful truth. Is this the part [role] of wise men, engaged in a great...struggle for liberty?"*

Liberty was Henry's goal. After the American Revolution, Henry was determined to protect the liberty that had just been gained. He said that "The Constitution is not an instrument for the government to restrain [limit] the people, it is an instrument for the people to restrain the government, lest [unless] it come to dominate our lives." Henry was largely responsible for the passage of the Bill of Rights, which he hoped would guarantee liberty for all Americans.

Patrick Henry realized that truth and honesty were important in both private life and public life. Because he was also brave and willing to work to protect liberty, we are able to continue the work he began, including making things better by facing the truth.

Honesty in Action

Link to Current Events Research the story of a person who has tried to make things better by facing the facts and telling the truth, even when it was difficult. What are the facts that needed to be faced? What situation was improved or might be improved? How did being honest contribute to people understanding the situation?

1770   1775

1770
Boston
Massacre

1773
Boston
Tea Party

1774
First Continental
Congress

• Boston

• Philadelphia

• Richmond

The Colonists Rebel

PREVIEW

Focus on the Main Idea
Events in Boston brought Britain and the colonies closer to war.

PLACES
Boston, Massachusetts
Philadelphia, Pennsylvania
Richmond, Virginia

PEOPLE
Crispus Attucks
John Adams
Paul Revere
Thomas Gage
George Washington

VOCABULARY
Boston Massacre
Committee of Correspondence
Tea Act
Boston Tea Party
Intolerable Acts
Patriots
Loyalists
First Continental Congress
militia
minutemen

You Are There It is the night of March 5, 1770. The streets of Boston are covered with newly-fallen snow. Despite the cold, many people are out walking. Edward Garrick is among the Bostonians yelling insults at Hugh White, a British soldier on duty.

White loses his temper and hits Garrick in the head with the butt of his musket. Garrick's friends run over and begin shouting at White, calling him "bloodyback!" and "lobster!"—insults based on the red uniforms worn by British soldiers. The crowd of colonists surrounding White grows quickly. White calls for help and a group of soldiers, their muskets loaded, join White in the street. Colonists pelt the soldiers with snowballs, icicles, and oyster shells. Tempers rise. And then the unexpected happens. The British fire their weapons into the angry crowd.

Cause and Effect As you read, look for events in Boston and their effects on the relationship between the colonies and Britain.

The Boston Massacre

Tensions had been rising in Boston since the British soldiers first arrived in 1768. Fist fights between soldiers and colonists were a common sight in the streets. So on the night of March 5, 1770, the city was ready to explode. When angry colonists surrounded Hugh White and his fellow soldiers, the soldiers panicked. They fired into the crowd, killing five people.

The event became known as the Boston Massacre. A massacre is the killing of many people who cannot defend themselves.

▶ **Crispus Attucks (above) was one of the victims of the Boston Massacre.**

One of the victims was Crispus Attucks. Born into slavery, Attucks escaped slavery at age 27 and began working as a sailor. On the night of the shooting, he had led a group of sailors to the scene of the protest.

The British soldiers were put on trial for murder in Boston. They were defended in court by John Adams, a cousin of Samuel Adams. Like Samuel, John Adams opposed British taxes and did not like having British soldiers in Boston. Still, he felt the soldiers deserved a fair trial. The court ruled that the soldiers were not guilty of murder.

REVIEW What caused British soldiers to fire at the colonists? ↻ **Cause and Effect**

Then and Now

The Boston Massacre

In the center of Boston, you can find a patch of cobblestones near the Old State House. They have been preserved in memory of Crispus Attucks and the other protesters who were killed at this spot—the site of the Boston Massacre.

▶ **An engraving (left) shows the Boston Massacre with the Old State House in the background. The building (above) still stands today.**

The Committees of Correspondence

On the same day as the Boston Massacre, Parliament voted to repeal the Townshend Acts. The colonial boycott was hurting British businesses. So Parliament cancelled all the taxes but one. They kept the tax on tea.

British leaders knew they would not collect much money from the tea tax. Their goal was to show the colonists that they still had the right to tax the colonies.

Samuel Adams kept busy working on a new problem. He felt it took too long for news to travel from one colony to another. If the colonies were going to work together in the future, they would need a faster way to share news.

Adams formed a **Committee of Correspondence** in Boston in 1772. Soon Committees of Correspondence were formed in towns all over the colonies. Members of these committees corresponded, or wrote to each other, about local events. The letters were delivered by "express riders" on fast horses. One rider was a silversmith named **Paul Revere.** He could make the trip from Boston to New York and back in about a week. Look at the map below to see the time it took for the express riders to deliver messages.

REVIEW What problem led Samuel Adams to create a Committee of Correspondence? **Main Idea and Details**

Map Adventure

Express Riders, 1770s

You are an express rider delivering messages from Sam Adams in Boston.

1. Adams asks you to leave today to get a message to Charleston. He wants to know by what date you can get it there. It is now May 2. What do you tell him?

2. When you reach Baltimore, the local Committee of Correspondence gives you a message for the committee in Williamsburg. By what date do you deliver this message?

3. After reaching Charleston, you rest for 2 days before beginning the return trip to Boston. By what date do you return home?

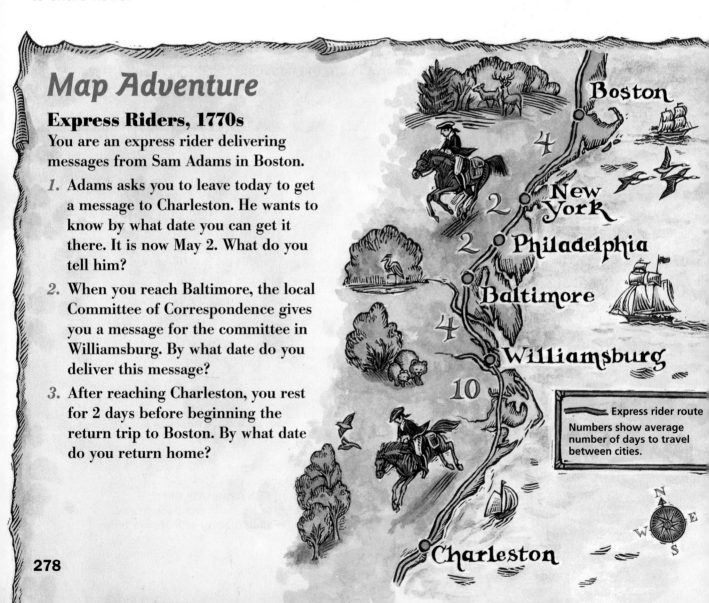

Boston

4

New York

2

Philadelphia

2

Baltimore

4

Williamsburg

10

Charleston

Express rider route
Numbers show average number of days to travel between cities.

► **This painting shows disguised Sons of Liberty dumping tea into Boston Harbor. This event came to be known as the Boston Tea Party.**

The Library of Congress

The Boston Tea Party

In 1773, Committees of Correspondence began writing about the **Tea Act,** a new law passed by Parliament. The Tea Act said that one British company—the East India Company—would be the only company allowed to sell tea to the colonies. If you owned a store in the colonies, you would have to buy your tea from the East India Company. And you would still have to pay the tea tax.

The Tea Act had two goals. The first goal was to help the struggling East India Company. The second goal was to get the colonists to pay taxes to Britain. So far the colonists had refused to pay British taxes. They were not about to start. They also did not like the idea of being forced to buy tea from one company. Colonists declared that ships bringing British tea to the colonies would not be allowed to unload in any colonial port.

In late 1773, three ships carrying British tea sailed into Boston Harbor. On the night of December 16, members of the Sons of Liberty disguised themselves as Mohawks. They rowed out to the British ships shouting "Boston Harbor a teapot tonight!" They boarded the ships, chopped open the chests of tea with axes, and dumped the tea into the harbor. This became known as the **Boston Tea Party.**

Soon colonists were singing a new song:

> *"Rally Mohawks! Bring out your axes and tell King George, we'll pay no taxes!"*

When news of the Boston Tea Party reached London, British leaders were furious. King George III and Parliament believed that Boston must be punished.

REVIEW Why did Parliament pass the Tea Act? **Main Idea and Details**

A VIEW OF THE TOWN OF BOSTON WITH SEVERAL SHIPS OF WAR IN THE HARBOUR.

Engraving by Paul Revere

▶ **After the Boston Tea Party, British ships closed the port of Boston.**

Britain Punishes Boston

Britain punished the people of Boston severely for the Boston Tea Party. The punishment included the following actions:

- The British soldiers who had been removed from Boston after the Boston Massacre were now sent back. Colonists were ordered to feed and house the soldiers.
- The colony of Massachusetts was put under the control of a British general named **Thomas Gage.**
- The port of Boston was closed. No ships would be allowed to come or go until the people of Boston paid for the tea they had destroyed.

Colonists began calling these new laws the **Intolerable Acts.** The closing of Boston's port hurt the city badly. Boston's economy depended on trade, and soon many people were out of work. Other colonies began helping Boston by sending food, supplies, and money.

The Intolerable Acts had another effect. They forced many colonists to take sides in the conflict between Boston and Britain. Colonists who opposed British rule were known as **Patriots.** Colonists who remained loyal to King George and the British government were known as **Loyalists.**

At the same time, Committees of Correspondence began spreading the idea of a meeting. Leaders from 12 colonies agreed to meet in **Philadelphia,** the largest city in the colonies. They would discuss how to oppose the Intolerable Acts.

REVIEW What happened as a result of the Boston Tea Party?
ᯤ **Cause and Effect**

▶ **Patriots used lanterns like this one to send messages.**

The Continental Congress

In September 1774 representatives from every colony except Georgia met at the **First Continental Congress** in Philadelphia. One man who represented Virginia at the meeting was **George Washington.** Washington was a wealthy farmer and a member of the Virginia House of Burgesses. As you read in Chapter 7, he had fought with the British during the French and Indian War. Now he was ready to fight against the British, if necessary. He made a promise:

> *"I will raise one thousand men...and march myself at their head for the relief of Boston."*

At the First Continental Congress, Washington and his fellow Patriots voted to stop all trade with Britain until the Intolerable Acts were repealed. They also agreed that each colony should begin training **militias,** or volunteer armies. The colonial leaders agreed to meet again in one year if the situation had not improved. At this point, however, most colonists hoped that their dispute with Britain could be settled peacefully.

Patriot leaders went home and began organizing militias. Some militia groups called themselves **minutemen** because they could be ready at a minute's notice to fight for their colony.

REVIEW What decisions did Patriot leaders make at the First Continental Congress?
Main Idea and Details

▶ **Patriots formed militia groups to defend the colonies against the British.**

Liberty or Death

In March 1775 Patrick Henry made the most famous speech of his career. Speaking in a church in Richmond, Virginia, Henry warned Virginia's militias to prepare for battle. War with Britain was coming, he said, and he was ready for it. He ended with these bold words:

> *"I know not what course others may take; but as for me, give me liberty or give me death!"*

British leaders were not about to back down. Like Patrick Henry, King George was ready to fight. He told Parliament that "blows must decide" how the conflict between Britain and the colonies would be settled.

Patrick Henry and King George could agree on one thing—a war was about to begin.

REVIEW Why did Patrick Henry believe Virginia's militias should be prepared?
Draw Conclusions

Summarize the Lesson

1770 In the Boston Massacre, British soldiers fired at a group of colonists, killing five.

1773 Disguised as Mohawks, colonists dumped British tea into Boston Harbor to protest the Tea Act.

1774 Colonial leaders met at the First Continental Congress in Philadelphia to decide how to oppose the Intolerable Acts.

LESSON 2   REVIEW

Check Facts and Main Ideas

1. ⟳ **Cause and Effect** On a separate sheet of paper, fill in the missing effects.

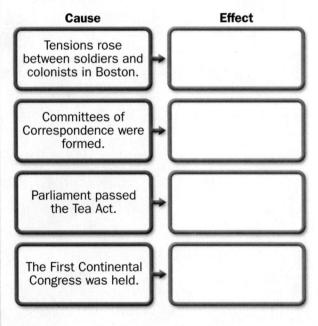

Cause	Effect
Tensions rose between soldiers and colonists in Boston.	
Committees of Correspondence were formed.	
Parliament passed the Tea Act.	
The First Continental Congress was held.	

2. What was the goal of the Committees of Correspondence?

3. What were the Intolerable Acts?

4. What events in Boston helped bring Britain and the colonies closer to war?

5. **Critical Thinking:** *Decision-Making* If you had been a colonist in 1773, would you have been a Patriot or a Loyalist ? Explain your choice. Use the decision-making steps on page H3.

Link to ◦━◦ Mathematics

Determine Number of Days Paul Revere once impressed his friends by riding from Boston to Philadelphia and back in 11 days. Look at the map on page 278. What is the number of days that trip took, on average? How many fewer days did the trip take Revere?

282

George Washington
1732–1799

George Washington was chosen to command the Continental Army during the Revolutionary War. As a young man, he learned the skills that later helped him to become a strong military leader. When he was 16 he began working as a surveyor, mapping the mountains of western Virginia. His first night in the woods was memorable. He wrote in his journal:

"I...went into the bed, as they called it, when to my surprise I found it to be nothing but a little straw matted together...with double its weight of vermin such as lice, fleas, etc."

Surveying was difficult and tiring, but Washington seemed made for it. At 16 he was ❶ already an expert horseman. And he was very strong, standing well over six feet tall, with broad shoulders and powerful arms. According to friends he was nearly impossible to beat in wrestling.

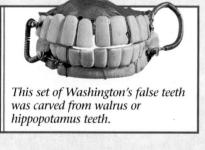

BIOFACT

This set of Washington's false teeth was carved from walrus or hippopotamus teeth.

Washington worked as a surveyor for three years. The experience was valuable for the lessons it taught him about hard work, commitment, and leadership under challenging conditions. Thirty years later General George Washington would draw on these lessons while leading his fellow colonists to victory in the American Revolution.

Learn from Biographies

In 1789, George Washington was elected our nation's first President. How do you think his work as a surveyor helped prepare him for this job?

For more information, go online to *Meet the People* at **www.sfsocialstudies.com**.

Use Primary Sources

What? Primary sources are eyewitness accounts, or observations, of history. They are made by people who participated in the events being described. Primary sources can be letters, diaries, documents, speeches, interviews, and even photographs, paintings, and newspapers.

The primary source, published in 1770, shows an original etching and an account from the *Boston Gazette and Country Journal*. It is an article about the Boston Massacre and the funeral of four of the Patriots who died in it.

Last Thursday, **agreeable to** a general request of the inhabitants, and by the consent of parents and friends, were carried to their grave **in succession,** the bodies of Samuel Gray, Samuel Maverick, James Caldwell, and Crispus Attucks, the unhappy victims who fell in the bloody massacre of **Monday evening preceding!**

agreeable to: due to

in succession: one after the other

Monday evening preceding: the Monday evening before last Thursday

▶ **Pictures can also be primary sources. This primary source is a famous engraving made by Paul Revere shortly after the Boston Massacre. It is in the newspaper article from the *Gazette and Country Journal*.**

Why? Primary sources can give you a firsthand idea about how people lived and how they felt about important events of their time. This newspaper article will help you understand how some people of Boston, in 1770, viewed a major historical event.

How? To use primary sources you study the source, determine the subject matter, and consider the viewpoint.

To study this source, read the excerpt enlarged at the far right of page 284. Notice that sometimes a letter very similar to an *f* occurs in place of a regular *s*. In the first line, for example, the word *Laft* is actually *Last* and *Thurfday* is *Thursday*. This was the style of writing in the British colonies in the 1770s.

To determine the subject matter, figure out the main idea of the primary source. If you had trouble reading the paragraph, read the version in modern spelling at the bottom of the page. Some of the terms are shown in bold and defined for you.

Consider the language in a primary source to give you clues about the writer's point of view. In this excerpt, the writer uses phrases such as "unhappy victims" and "bloody massacre." These terms tell you that the author feels sympathy for the men who were killed and is angry at the British. A pro-British writer would probably describe this event very differently.

Think and Apply

❶ Who were the four victims named in this **primary source?**

❷ Do you think the writer was a Patriot or a Loyalist? How can you tell?

❸ Why do you think the drawings of coffins were included in the article?

1775   1780

April 18
Paul Revere's
ride

April 19
Battles of
Lexington
and Concord

June 17
Battle of
Bunker Hill

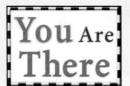

Concord
• Lexington

• Charlestown

PREVIEW

Focus on the Main Idea
The American Revolution
began with the battles at
Lexington and Concord.

PLACES
Concord, Massachusetts
Lexington, Massachusetts
Charlestown, Massachusetts

PEOPLE
John Hancock
William Dawes
Samuel Prescott
John Parker
William Prescott

VOCABULARY
American Revolution
Battle of Bunker Hill

The Revolution Begins

You Are There

It is late at night, April 18, 1775. The streets of Boston are quiet.

Most people are at home. You are outside gathering wood for the fire. Suddenly you hear the pounding feet of a young man as he races past you. He looks upset and seems intent on getting somewhere quickly.

You wonder, "Where is he going?" You don't know it at the time, but he carries important information. He is bringing it to Paul Revere. The young man has learned the British soldiers are on the move. Where are they going? What do they plan to do? How will all of this affect the colonists?

▶ **Paul Revere warned colonists that the British were advancing.**

 Cause and Effect As you read, note the causes of the first battles of the American Revolution.

Paul Revere's Ride

On the night of April 18, 1775, 700 British soldiers began to march from Boston. They were on their way to Concord, a town about 20 miles northwest of Boston. Over the past year, Patriot militias had been storing weapons in Concord. Now the British soldiers had orders to "seize and destroy" these military supplies.

There were rumors that the British had another goal as well—to arrest Samuel Adams and John Hancock. Like Adams, Hancock was an important Patriot leader in Boston. Both men were staying in Lexington, a town located between Boston and Concord.

The British wanted their march to be a secret. They did not want the militias in Lexington or Concord to know they were coming. So General Gage put extra guards on duty and gave them strict orders not to let any colonists leave Boston that night.

However, Paul Revere had learned of their secret plans. He set out to warn the militias in Lexington and Concord. "Two friends rowed me across Charles River," he later wrote. They passed dangerously close to a British warship. Then Revere rode west "upon a very good horse" shouting the news that the British were coming. "I alarmed almost every house, till I got to Lexington," he wrote. At the same time, a shoemaker named William Dawes talked his way past British guards at Boston Neck. Dawes also rode toward Lexington, spreading the warning.

Revere reached Lexington first. He warned Adams and Hancock, who prepared their escape. When Dawes arrived, he and Revere set out for Concord together. They were joined by a young doctor named Samuel Prescott.

British soldiers spotted the three riders on the road and ordered them to stop. Revere was captured. Dawes jumped from his horse and escaped into the woods. Prescott got away and rode on to Concord, where he warned the Concord militia to get ready.

REVIEW What was the effect of the ride of Revere, Dawes, and Prescott?
Cause and Effect

Literature and Social Studies

Paul Revere's Ride

In 1863 Henry Wadsworth Longfellow wrote about Paul Revere's midnight ride. Below are the first two stanzas from this famous poem.

Listen my children and you shall hear
Of the midnight ride of Paul Revere,
On the eighteenth of April, in Seventy-five;
Hardly a man is now alive
Who remembers that famous day and year.

He said to his friend, "If the British march
By land or sea from the town to-night,
Hang a lantern aloft in the belfry arch
Of the North Church tower as a signal light,—
One if by land, and two if by sea;
And I on the opposite shore will be,
Ready to ride and spread the alarm
Through every Middlesex village and farm,
For the country folk to be up and to arm."

The Shot Heard Round the World

At 5 A.M. on April 19, sixteen-year-old William Diamond began to beat his drum. This was the signal for the Lexington minutemen to come running. About 70 men gathered, including 12 teenagers and 3 men over age 60. Prince Estabrook was one of several African Americans to answer the call to arms.

▶ Patriots carried drums like this one into battle.

John Parker, captain of the Lexington minutemen, gave his men their orders:

> *"Stand your ground. Don't fire unless fired upon, but if they mean to have a war, let it begin here."*

British soldiers soon marched into Lexington and surrounded Captain Parker's men. British Major John Pitcairn shouted at the minutemen: "Ye villains, ye rebels! Lay down your arms!" Then someone fired—no one is sure who. British soldiers quickly opened fire on the minutemen, killing eight

MAP SKILL

The Battles of Lexington and Concord, April 1775

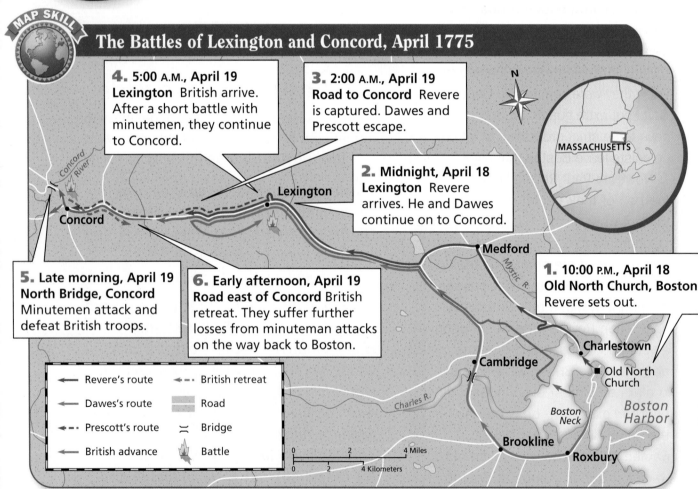

4. 5:00 A.M., April 19 **Lexington** British arrive. After a short battle with minutemen, they continue to Concord.

3. 2:00 A.M., April 19 **Road to Concord** Revere is captured. Dawes and Prescott escape.

2. Midnight, April 18 **Lexington** Revere arrives. He and Dawes continue on to Concord.

MASSACHUSETTS

1. 10:00 P.M., April 18 **Old North Church, Boston** Revere sets out.

5. Late morning, April 19 **North Bridge, Concord** Minutemen attack and defeat British troops.

6. Early afternoon, April 19 **Road east of Concord** British retreat. They suffer further losses from minuteman attacks on the way back to Boston.

Legend:
- ← Revere's route
- ← Dawes's route
- ←-- Prescott's route
- ← British advance
- ←-- British retreat
- ▬ Road
- ⋈ Bridge
- ✦ Battle

0 2 4 Miles
0 2 4 Kilometers

Concord River, Concord, Lexington, Medford, Mystic R., Charlestown, Old North Church, Cambridge, Charles R., Boston Neck, Boston Harbor, Brookline, Roxbury

▶ Paul Revere moved by boat and then horseback to get his warning to Lexington.

MAP SKILL Use Map Scale *About how far did Revere travel from the Old North Church to Lexington?*

▶ Minutemen clashed with British troops at the Battle of Lexington.

and wounding nine more. Only one British soldier was wounded during the short Battle of Lexington. The British cheered their victory and marched on to Concord.

The first shot at Lexington came to be known as "the shot heard round the world." But the day's fighting had just begun. When the British soldiers reached Concord, they searched for weapons. But they could not find any. The women of Concord had helped hide the town's military supplies in fields and barns all over town.

Meanwhile, militia men from nearby towns began pouring into Concord. Suddenly the Patriots had an advantage in numbers. After a brief battle at North Bridge in Concord, the British began the long 20-mile retreat to Boston. Find their route on the map on page 288. Thousands of Patriots now lined the road, firing at the British as they marched. "We were fired on from houses and behind trees . . . . We were fired on

from all sides," said British Lieutenant John Barker.

By the time they reached the safety of Boston, the British had suffered heavy losses. About 250 soldiers had been either killed or wounded. By the end of the day, about 50 Patriots had been killed and about 40 had been wounded. The **American Revolution,** a war Americans fought for independence, had begun.

REVIEW List the sequence of events of April 19, 1775. Begin with John Parker's order to the minutemen and end with the British retreat to Boston. **Sequence**

▶ Minutemen carried this flag at the Battle of Concord.

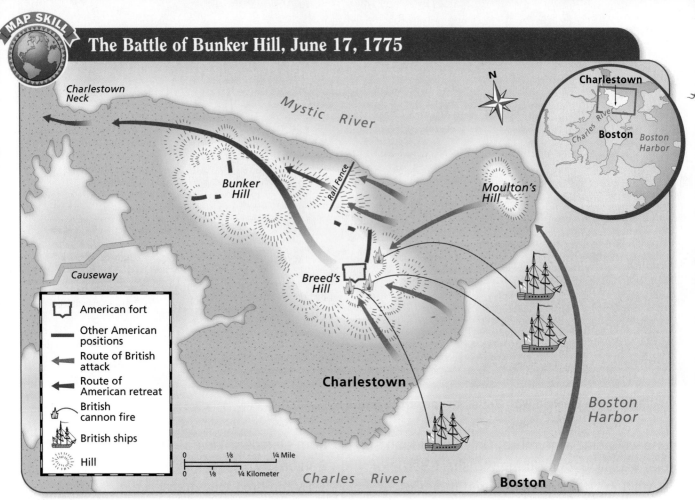

The Battle of Bunker Hill, June 17, 1775

American fort

Other American positions

Route of British attack

Route of American retreat

British cannon fire

British ships

Hill

0 1/8 1/4 Mile
0 1/8 1/4 Kilometer

▶ The Charlestown Peninsula was the scene of the Battle of Bunker Hill.

MAP SKILL Follow Routes *What direction did the Americans travel in their retreat from Breed's Hill?*

The Battle of Bunker Hill

On the night of June 16, a Patriot colonel named **William Prescott** led about 1,200 men up the hills of **Charlestown.** Find Charlestown on the map on this page. Notice how close Bunker Hill and Breed's Hill are to Boston. Patriot leaders knew that if they could control these hills, they could bring up cannons and fire them down on the British in Boston. Their goal was to force the British to leave Boston.

Prescott's men worked all night, building a fort out of earth and logs on Breed's Hill. When the British woke the next morning, they were shocked to see the fort. British generals decided to take the hill back before it was too late. More than 2,000 British soldiers prepared to attack.

Tired and hungry after a long night's work, the Patriots prepared to face the British attack. Colonel Prescott gave his men some last-second advice:

> ***"Don't fire until you see the whites of their eyes."***

After British ships fired on the fort, British soldiers marched up Breed's Hill. "The enemy advanced and fired very hotly on the fort," Prescott said. But the Patriots just waited. When the British got within a hundred feet of the fort, the Patriot guns exploded with a blast of deadly fire, driving the British back. British soldiers attacked again and were driven back again.

Now Prescott's men were nearly out of ammunition. Yelling "Push on!" the British attacked a third time and captured the hill. The battle was over. Though the fighting took place on Breed's Hill, this battle is known as the **Battle of Bunker Hill** for a nearby hill.

The British won the Battle of Bunker Hill, but it was a costly victory. More than 1,000 British soldiers were killed or wounded. About 400 Patriots were killed or wounded. Although they lost the battle, the Patriots were proud of the way they had fought. Patriot farmers and craftsmen had stood up to the mighty British army. "I wish we could sell them another hill at the same price," said Nathanael Greene, a Patriot general.

REVIEW Compare the results of the Battle of Bunker Hill from both a Patriot and British point-of-view. **Compare and Contrast**

Summarize the Lesson

April 18, 1775 Paul Revere warned colonists that the British were coming to Lexington and Concord.

April 19, 1775 The American Revolution began with the Battles of Lexington and Concord.

June 17, 1775 Patriots and British troops fought at the Battle of Bunker Hill.

LESSON 3 REVIEW

Check Facts and Main Ideas

1. **Cause and Effect** On a separate sheet of paper, fill in the two missing effects of the first battles of the **American Revolution.**

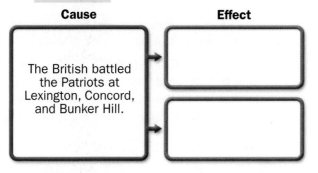

| Cause | Effect |

The British battled the Patriots at Lexington, Concord, and Bunker Hill.

2. How did Paul Revere warn the colonists that the British were coming?

3. What happened at the Battle of Lexington?

4. What events marked the beginning of the American Revolution?

5. **Critical Thinking:** *Fact or Opinion* Before the Revolution began, one British leader said, "the very sound of cannons" would cause Patriots to run away "as fast as their feet will carry them." Was this a fact or an opinion? How can you tell?

Link to Geography

Draw a Map of the **Battle of Bunker Hill.** Label Boston, Charlestown, Bunker Hill, Breed's Hill, and Boston Harbor. Draw and label the Patriot fort on Breed's Hill and the line of British attack up the hill. Include any illustrations you think are important, such as British ships in the harbor, soldiers, or flags.

1765

1765	1766	1767
Stamp Act passed	Stamp Act repealed	Townshend Acts passed

Chapter Summary

Target Skill

Cause and Effect

On a separate sheet of paper, fill in the three effects that followed from Britain's attempts to tax the colonies.

Cause

Britain begins to tax the colonies.

Effect

Vocabulary

Match each word with the correct definition or description.

1. **parliament** (p. 269)
2. **repeal** (p. 270)
3. **tariff** (p. 272)
4. **boycott** (p. 272)
5. **militias** (p. 281)

a. volunteer armies

b. refusal to buy goods

c. tax on imported goods

d. cancel

e. Britain's law-making assembly

People and Terms

Write a sentence explaining why each of the following people or terms was important in the events that led to the start of the American Revolution. You may use two or more in a single sentence.

1. **King George III** (p. 269)
2. **Stamp Act** (p. 269)
3. **Patrick Henry** (p. 270)
4. **Samuel Adams** (p. 270)
5. **Crispus Attucks** (p. 277)
6. **John Adams** (p. 277)
7. **Paul Revere** (p. 278)
8. **Intolerable Acts** (p. 280)
9. **Patriots** (p. 280)
10. **Loyalists** (p. 280)

1770   **1775**

1770
Boston
Massacre

1773
Boston
Tea Party

1774
First
Continental
Congress

1775
Fighting
begins

Facts and Main Ideas

1 Why did the British government want to tax the American colonists?

2 What was the British response to the Boston Tea Party?

3 What events led to the Battle of Lexington?

4 **Time Line** How many years were there between the passing of the Stamp Act and the First Continental Congress?

5 **Main Idea** How did taxation lead to trouble between Britain and the colonies?

6 **Main Idea** What events in Boston led the colonists closer to war?

7 **Main Idea** What were the results of the first three battles of the American Revolution?

8 **Critical Thinking:** *Draw Conclusions* What do you think was the biggest mistake that Britain made in the colonies before 1776? Explain.

Write About History

1 **Write a journal entry** as an American who has just fought in the Battle of Bunker Hill. Did the outcome lead you to believe that the Patriots would win or lose the war? Include any other thoughts you may have had.

2 **Write a "What If" story** describing what life might be like today if the colonists had never gained independence from Britain.

3 **Write an advertisement** urging colonists to join the American Army. Make a poster using slogans, drawings, and other attention-grabbing advertising techniques.

Apply Skills

Using Primary Resources

Read the primary source below. Then answer the questions.

Alarm sent by Committee of Watertown, Massachusetts April 19, 1775

Wednesday Morning near 11 O'clock

To all friends of American liberty, be it known that this morning before break of day, a brigade, consisting of about 1,000 or 1,200 men, landed at Phipp's farm at Cambridge and marched to Lexington, where they found a company of our militia in arms, upon whom they fired without any provocation . . . . I have spoken with several who have seen the dead and wounded.

J. Palmer, one of the Committee of Safety

1 How do you know that this is a primary source?

2 What is the purpose of this writing?

3 What is the point of view of the writer? How do you know?

Internet Activity

To get help with vocabulary, people, and terms, select dictionary or encyclopedia from *Social Studies Library* at
www.sfsocialstudies.com.

Winning the Revolution

1776

Philadelphia, Pennsylvania
The Declaration of Independence is signed.

Lesson 1

1

1778

Monmouth, New Jersey
Mary Ludwig Hays fights for the Patriot cause in the Battle of Monmouth in New Jersey.

Lesson 2

2

1781

Yorktown, Virginia
The British surrender to the Americans.

Lesson 3

3

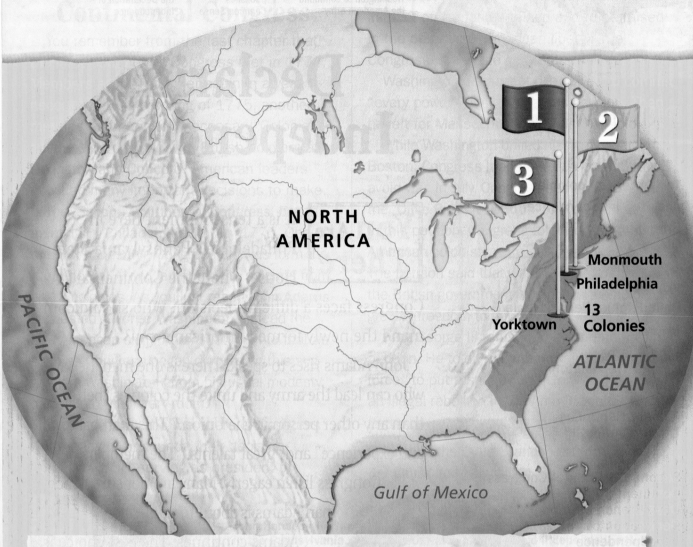

NORTH AMERICA

1

2

3

Monmouth

Philadelphia

Yorktown

13 Colonies

PACIFIC OCEAN

ATLANTIC OCEAN

Gulf of Mexico

Why We Remember

The Fourth of July is the day we celebrate our nation's birth. On this day in 1776, colonial leaders approved the Declaration of Independence, which announced the separation of the 13 Colonies from Great Britain. But, as you will read, several more years of fighting against Britain followed for independence to be achieved. Colonists were fighting the world's most powerful country. American soldiers often faced shortages in food, clothing, and ammunition. Help came, though, from other nations, and civilians at home. Many people risked their lives for the cause of independence. Thanks to their efforts, the United States was born.

"Time to Part"

Was it time for the American colonies to declare independence from Britain? A recent immigrant from Britain named **Thomas Paine** insisted that it was. Paine had settled in Pennsylvania in 1774. In January 1776, he published a pamphlet called *Common Sense*. Using language that was easy for most people to understand, Paine argued that it was "time to part" with Britain. "A government of our own is our natural right," he wrote. Paine's powerful words convinced many Americans that it was time to declare independence.

In June, Congress took a bold step. A member of Congress from Virginia named **Richard Henry Lee** rose and asked Congress to vote for independence. He declared that "these United Colonies are, and of right ought to be, free and independent states." Many members agreed with Lee, but Congress decided to delay the vote on independence until early July. Before voting, leaders wanted to make sure that every colony supported the break with Britain. In the meantime, Congress decided to prepare a document explaining why the colonies wanted independence. A committee was formed to draft the **Declaration of Independence.**

The committee members were Benjamin Franklin, John Adams, Roger Sherman from Connecticut, Robert Livingston from New York, and a 33-year-old lawyer from Virginia named **Thomas Jefferson.** Jefferson had served in the Virginia House of Burgesses before joining the Continental Congress in 1775. He had a reputation for being quiet, very intelligent, and an excellent writer. You will read more about Jefferson in the Biography following this lesson.

Adams believed that Jefferson should write the Declaration of Independence. Jefferson felt the task should go to a more experienced political leader. But Adams insisted that Jefferson was perfect for the job. "You can write ten times better than I can," Adams explained. Jefferson said, "Well, if you are decided, I will do as well as I can." He spent the next two weeks working in his rented room. By the end of June, he was finished.

REVIEW What was the purpose of the Declaration of Independence?
Main Idea and Details

▶ The pamphlet *Common Sense* sold over 500,000 copies. Thomas Paine (*right*) donated his profits to Congress to support the Revolution.

The Declaration of Independence

In the Declaration of Independence, Jefferson explained why the American colonies must declare independence from Britain. The argument in the Declaration was fairly simple. Jefferson stated that people are born with certain "unalienable rights," meaning rights that cannot be taken away.

> *"We hold these truths to be self-evident, that all men are created equal; that they are endowed [given] by their Creator with certain unalienable rights, that among these are life, liberty, and the pursuit of happiness."*

Next, the Declaration said that if a government abuses these rights, people should be free to create a new government. Had the British government abused the rights of the American colonists? Yes, the Declaration said.

> *"The history of the present King of Great Britain is a history of repeated injuries."*

The Declaration listed the "injuries," which include many of the things you read about in Chapter 8. For example, one of the charges against the king was: "imposing taxes on us without our consent."

The Declaration then said that because the king had abused his power, the American colonists had decided to declare independence. And they had a right to form a government of their own.

> *"We, therefore, the representatives of the United States of America...declare that these United Colonies are, and of right ought to be, free and independent states."*

Finally, the Declaration ended with a brave vow. The signers of the document agreed to defend their new nation with "our lives, our fortunes, and our sacred honor."

REVIEW According to the Declaration of Independence, what are three "unalienable rights"? **Summarize**

▶ **Thomas Jefferson (left) worked with John Adams (middle) and Benjamin Franklin (right) on the Declaration of Independence. A draft of the Declaration is shown below.**

A Dangerous Decision

Congress approved the Declaration of Independence on July 4, 1776. There were celebrations from New England to Georgia. In New York, Patriots pulled down a statue of King George III and melted the metal into bullets for the Continental Army.

In August, members of Congress gathered to sign the Declaration of Independence. They knew it would be dangerous to sign this document. They would be considered traitors by King George III. A **traitor** is a person who works against his or her country. During the Revolution, traitors were put to death by hanging.

John Hancock signed the document first. Then he cautioned his fellow signers. "There must be no pulling different ways. We must all hang together." Benjamin Franklin agreed and added a warning of his own. "We must indeed all hang together, or most assuredly [surely] we shall all hang separately." Now everything depended upon the outcome of the war.

REVIEW Why was signing the Declaration of Independence a dangerous act?
Main Idea and Details

Summarize the Lesson

— **June 1775** George Washington took command of the Continental Army.

— **January 1776** Thomas Paine's pamphlet, *Common Sense,* urged separation from Great Britain.

— **July 4, 1776** The Continental Congress approved the Declaration of Independence.

LESSON 1 REVIEW

Check Facts and Main Ideas

1. **Cause and Effect** On a separate sheet of paper, fill in the missing effects of the major events from this lesson.

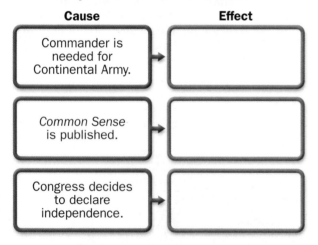

Cause	Effect
Commander is needed for Continental Army.	
Common Sense is published.	
Congress decides to declare independence.	

2. Describe two important decisions made by the **Second Continental Congress.**

3. How did Thomas Paine's *Common Sense* help lead to the **Declaration of Independence?**

4. Describe Thomas Jefferson's role in creating the Declaration of Independence.

5. **Critical Thinking:** *Point of View* Do you think it took courage to sign the Declaration of Independence? Why or why not?

Link to Writing

Write a Declaration Suppose you were helping to write the Declaration of Independence. What rights would you list as "unalienable rights"? Write a paragraph listing these rights and explaining why they are important. Remember to begin your paragraph with a topic sentence.

Thomas Jefferson
1743–1826

Thomas Jefferson was tall and skinny, with red hair and freckles. He was moody and quiet. He liked to be called Tom. And he was facing the hardest time of his young life. He later wrote:

"...the whole care and direction of myself was thrown on myself entirely, without a relation or friend qualified to advise or guide me...."

Tom's father had just died. Tom and his father had been very close and now, though he still had a large family, he felt alone in the world. As his father had wished, Tom left home to attend school.

Tom had always been very bright, but now it seemed as if he wanted to learn everything there was to know. He often spent 14 hours a day studying. His classmates remembered that Tom always had schoolbooks in his pockets, even when he played games.

BIOFACT

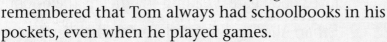

Jefferson wrote a draft of the Declaration of Independence on this portable desk.

As an adult, Jefferson looked back on his years at school as an important time. He recovered from his grief and developed a love of learning that was to reward him throughout his entire life. When he was just 33, Thomas Jefferson was chosen to write our nation's Declaration of Independence.

Learn from Biographies

What role did learning play in young Tom Jefferson's life?

For more information, go online to *Meet the People* at **www.sfsocialstudies.com**.

December 1776
Washington captures Trenton

October 1777
Americans defeat British at Saratoga

Winter 1777–1778
Continental army suffers through winter at Valley Forge

PREVIEW

Focus on the Main Idea
The contributions of a wide variety of people helped the Continental Army win important battles.

PLACES
Fort Ticonderoga
Trenton, New Jersey
Saratoga, New York
Valley Forge, Pennsylvania

PEOPLE
Ethan Allen
Henry Knox
Nathan Hale
John Burgoyne
Thaddeus Kosciusko
Benedict Arnold
Peter Salem
James Armistead
Prince Hall
Martha Washington
Mary Ludwig Hays
Deborah Sampson
Phillis Wheatley

VOCABULARY
Green Mountain Boys
mercenary
Battle of Saratoga

Patriots at War

You Are There
It is just before dawn, May 10, 1775. Another quiet morning at Fort Ticonderoga, a British fort on Lake Champlain. A single guard sits outside the fort, dozing.

Suddenly, the guard opens his eyes to see about 80 men charging toward him. He stands, fires his musket, then runs into the fort.

The men are shouting now as they rush through the fort's open gate. Leading the men is the 6-foot 6-inch Ethan Allen, yelling and waving his sword.

Allen and his men bolt up to the British commander's headquarters. Allen pounds on the door and is reported to demand, "Come out of there, you old rat!" The British officer steps out and sees that he is surrounded. He surrenders the fort to Allen.

▶ Ethan Allen demanded that the British surrender Fort Ticonderoga.

Sequence As you read, pay attention to the sequence of important events in the American Revolution.

Washington Takes Command

Ethan Allen was known for his bravery and strength. In Vermont, where Allen lived, people told stories about his wrestling matches with bears and mountain lions. Allen was also an outspoken Patriot. He commanded a group of Vermont soldiers who called themselves the Green Mountain Boys. Their capture of Fort Ticonderoga in May 1775 was an important early victory for the Americans. They did not just seize a fort—they also captured badly needed British cannons.

George Washington wanted those cannons. Washington's army had surrounded the British army in Boston. With cannons, he might be able to force the British out of this important city. So Washington sent a young colonel named Henry Knox to get the captured cannons. This would not be easy. Some of the guns weighed over 5,000 pounds. Knox and his men built sleds and used horses and oxen to drag the cannons 250 miles over the winter snow. People came out and cheered as the men passed through towns.

Washington put the cannons on hills above Boston. When the British saw the guns pointing down at them, they decided to leave the city. A Patriot newspaper reported: "This morning the British army in Boston...fled from before the army of the United Colonies."

Washington reported his victory to Congress "with the greatest pleasure." But he knew that the Americans were a long way from winning the war. The British had the best navy in the world. They had well-trained and well-equipped soldiers. And they had the money to hire thousands of German mercenaries. Mercenaries are soldiers from one country who are paid to fight for another country. It was clear that King George III was determined to defeat the Americans.

REVIEW How did the capture of Fort Ticonderoga lead to the American victory in Boston?
🔁 Cause and Effect

▶ Henry Knox and his men dragged more than 50 cannons from Fort Ticonderoga to Boston.

▶ Washington and his army crossed the Delaware River for a surprise attack on Trenton, New Jersey.

Defeat and Victory

After the victory at Boston, things began to go badly for the American army. Washington suffered several defeats in New York City in the summer of 1776. He decided to send spies into the British camp to find out about the enemy's military plans. He asked for volunteers for this dangerous job. One person who stepped forward was a 21-year-old teacher named Nathan Hale. Hale slipped behind enemy lines and began gathering information. But he was captured and condemned to death. It was reported that right before he was hanged, he told his British captors:

> *"I only regret that I have but one life to lose for my country."*

Washington's army retreated into New Jersey. After marching across New Jersey, the army crossed the Delaware River and camped in Pennsylvania in December 1776. This was a low point for the Americans. Short on food and clothing, the soldiers were often sick, cold, and hungry. A 17-year-old soldier named Joseph Plumb Martin wrote that the men baked tasteless wheat cakes that were "hard enough to break the teeth of a rat."

Washington decided that it was time to make a move. He made plans for an attack on Trenton, New Jersey. Trenton was held by an army of German mercenaries. These soldiers were known as Hessians because many of them came from the region of Hesse in Germany. Washington hoped to take the Hessians by surprise. He wrote a letter to a fellow officer describing his plan. "Christmas Day at night…is the time fixed for our attempt on Trenton. For Heaven's sake, keep this to yourself."

Washington's soldiers began crossing the Delaware River after dark on December 25th. "The night was cold and stormy; it hailed with great violence," wrote Henry Knox. "The floating ice in the river made the labor almost incredible."

The Americans attacked Trenton early the next morning. They succeeded in surprising the Hessians. Washington's men captured the town and took nearly 1,000 Hessian prisoners. The victory gave new hope to many Americans. "This is a glorious day for our country," Washington said.

REVIEW Why was Washington's victory at Trenton important for the Americans? Summarize

The Turning Point

When winter ended, the British went on the offensive again. British General **John Burgoyne** sailed south on Lake Champlain with an army of over 7,000 soldiers. His goal was to capture Albany, New York, and then continue south on the Hudson River. Look at the map below and you will understand the British strategy. By controlling Lake Champlain and the Hudson River, the British could cut the United States in two. Burgoyne predicted that this would end the American Revolution. His orders to his soldiers were simple: "This army must not retreat."

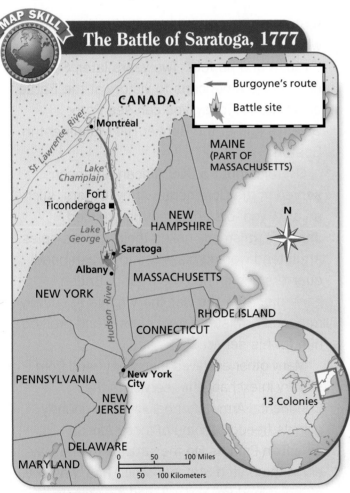

The Battle of Saratoga, 1777

Burgoyne's route
Battle site

CANADA
Montréal
St. Lawrence River
Lake Champlain
MAINE (PART OF MASSACHUSETTS)
Fort Ticonderoga
NEW HAMPSHIRE
N
Lake George
Saratoga
Albany
Hudson River
MASSACHUSETTS
NEW YORK
RHODE ISLAND
CONNECTICUT
PENNSYLVANIA
New York City
NEW JERSEY
13 Colonies
DELAWARE
MARYLAND

0   50   100 Miles
0   50   100 Kilometers

▶ **The British advance was stopped near Saratoga, New York.**

MAP SKILL Use Map Scale *How many miles was Burgoyne's route from Montréal to Saratoga?*

But a large American army was standing in Burgoyne's way. **Thaddeus Kosciusko** (kahs ee US koh), a Polish engineer who had joined the Americans, designed a fort near the town of **Saratoga.** Here, the Americans planned to stop the British advance.

The two armies clashed in late September and early October. This fighting is known as the **Battle of Saratoga.** One of the key American leaders at Saratoga was General **Benedict Arnold.** Arnold led charge after charge against the British, yelling "Come on, brave boys, come on!"

Burgoyne's army suffered heavy losses. He was running out of food. And the American army was growing in size every day, as volunteers from nearby towns poured into the Patriot camp. On October 17, 1777, Burgoyne surrendered his entire army to the Americans.

The Battle of Saratoga is often called the turning point of the American Revolution. The defeat of a strong British army showed the world that the Continental Army could win the war. In France, Benjamin Franklin had been trying to convince the French government to assist the Americans. But French leaders were not convinced the Americans could really defeat the British. After Saratoga, France agreed to join the fight against their old enemy, Britain.

The Battle of Saratoga was a turning point for Benedict Arnold as well. He was wounded in the fighting and never led American troops in battle again. In 1780, Arnold shocked the country by joining the British army in exchange for money. To this day, Benedict Arnold is one of the most famous traitors in American history.

REVIEW Why did the British want to control Lake Champlain and the Hudson River? **Draw Conclusions**

▶ Peter Salem (*at left, shooting musket*) was one of the American heroes at the Battle of Bunker Hill.

African Americans and the Revolution

Both sides encouraged African Americans to fight in their armies. Early in the war, the royal governor of Virginia, Lord Dunmore, offered freedom to all slaves who could escape their owners and fight for the British. Dunmore put together a force of more than 500 African American soldiers. A newspaper reported that their uniforms included the words "Liberty to Slaves." By the end of the war, thousands of African Americans had gained their freedom by serving in the British army. Thousands more joined the Loyalists who had fled to British-controlled Canada.

Many African Americans fought on the side of the Patriots. They believed that a war for freedom should mean freedom for all Americans—including those who were held in slavery. African American soldiers fought in almost every battle of the war. Peter Salem gained fame at Bunker Hill, where he stood his ground in the face of a charge led by British officer John Pitcairn. Pitcairn leapt onto the wall of the American fort shouting, "The day is ours!" Accounts of the battle state that Pitcairn had hardly finished this cry when "Salem, a black soldier...shot him through and he fell." Two years later, Salem helped the Americans to victory at the Battle of Saratoga. Today, you can see Peter Salem's gun at the Bunker Hill Monument in Boston.

Overall, about 5,000 African Americans served in the Continental Army. Others, such as a 21-year-old enslaved man named James Armistead, risked their lives as spies. Armistead worked his way into British head-quarters and gained the trust of British generals. After the war, the Virginia Assembly released Armistead from slavery and praised him for his service.

Many other enslaved men were freed from slavery in exchange for service in the Continental Army. After helping their country gain its freedom, some of these African American Patriots led the struggle to end slavery in the United States. Prince Hall was one of these leaders. You will read his story in Issues and Viewpoints on pages 310–311.

REVIEW How did Peter Salem contribute to the American Revolution? Summarize

Women in the Revolution

Finding soldiers was just one problem Washington faced. His army never seemed to have enough equipment, warm clothing, or food. "No army was ever worse supplied than ours," Washington wrote. This explains why Washington's men stood and cheered one freezing day in 1778 when women drove 10 carts into camp. The carts were filled with food.

Throughout the war, Patriot women helped keep the Revolution alive by collecting food, raising money, and making clothing for the soldiers. One of the most active female Patriots was Martha Washington, George Washington's wife. Martha Washington often traveled with the army. She spent the mornings cooking, delivering food, and visiting wounded soldiers. In the afternoons, she joined other women in knitting socks and mending uniforms.

A young woman named Mary Ludwig Hays contributed to the struggle for independence in a different way. Putting herself in the line of enemy fire, she carried pitchers of water to soldiers on the battlefield. The soldiers nicknamed her Molly Pitcher. When her husband collapsed from the heat at the Battle of Monmouth in New Jersey, she took his place and helped fire cannons at the British.

Another woman who joined the fight was 21-year-old Deborah Sampson. In May 1782, Sampson put on men's clothes and entered the Continental Army as Robert Shurtleff. No one knew she was a woman. Sampson fought in several battles and was wounded twice before her secret was discovered. Her commanding officer, Colonel Henry Jackson, remembered Sampson as "a faithful and good soldier."

Other women helped the struggle for independence with their pens. Mercy Otis Warren, who had helped lead the boycotts against British tea, wrote plays in support of the Revolution. Abigail Adams, the wife of John Adams, wrote bold letters supporting American independence. She also spoke out for women's rights, urging John Adams to "remember the ladies" when making laws for the new country. A young African American woman named Phillis Wheatley published poems supporting the Revolution and opposing slavery. You will read more about Wheatley's remarkable life in the Biography on page 309.

REVIEW In what ways did women contribute to the war effort?
Summarize

► **Many women were active Patriots, including Martha Washington (above) and Mary Ludwig Hays (left).**

Winter at Valley Forge

The victory at Saratoga may have been the turning point of the Revolution, but the war was far from over. In late 1777, the British captured Philadelphia. Washington's army marched to **Valley Forge**, Pennsylvania, and set up camp for the winter.

Washington knew it was going to be a difficult winter. The army was dangerously short of food and warm clothing. Many of the soldiers did not even have shoes. When they marched, they left a trail of blood from their feet. While serving guard duty, men stood on their hats to keep their bare feet from freezing in the snow.

During that winter at Valley Forge, more than 2,500 men died of hunger, cold, and disease. Washington worked endlessly to find food and clothing for his men. "I pity their miseries," he wrote. Washington was struggling to hold his army together.

REVIEW What caused the death of thousands of American soldiers at Valley Forge? ⟳ **Cause and Effect**

Summarize the Lesson

December 1776 General Washington surprised the Hessian mercenaries at Trenton, New Jersey, and captured the town.

October 1777 The American victory at Saratoga, New York, was a turning point of the war.

1777–1778 Short of supplies, the Continental Army suffered through winter at Valley Forge, Pennsylvania.

LESSON 2 · REVIEW

Check Facts and Main Ideas

1. **Sequence** On a separate sheet of paper, fill in this diagram by listing four major events from this lesson in the correct order.

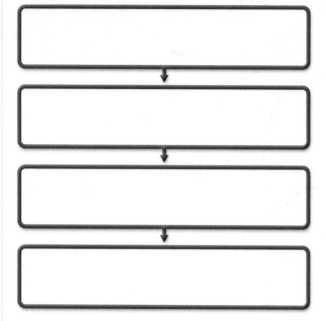

2. How was Washington able to force the British to leave Boston?

3. Describe one important effect of the **Battle of Saratoga.**

4. **Critical Thinking:** *Fact or Opinion* When the Revolution began, some American leaders did not think African Americans would make good soldiers in the Continental Army. Was this a fact or an opinion? How can you tell?

5. Describe three different ways in which women helped support the American Revolution.

Link to ⟳ **Reading**

Read about the Revolution In the library or on the Internet, read more about one of the Patriot heroes described in this lesson. Write a one-page report about this person. How did he or she help win the American Revolution?

Phillis Wheatley
about 1753–1784

Phillis Wheatley was seven years old when she was kidnapped from her home in West Africa. She was shipped to Boston and sold as a slave to the wealthy Wheatley family.

The Wheatley family realized that Phillis was extremely intelligent. They encouraged her to study, which very few slaves were allowed to do. In 1773 she became the first African American to have a book of poetry published. That same year, Phillis was released from slavery. Now famous throughout New England, she became a strong supporter of the colonists' struggle for freedom from Britain.

In 1775, she wrote a poem about General George Washington. He liked the poem so much that he invited Phillis Wheatley to come visit him.

Phillis Wheatley also spoke out against slavery. She wrote:

"In every human…God has implanted a principle, which we call love of freedom."

POEMS

ON

VARIOUS SUBJECTS,

RELIGIOUS AND MORAL.

BY

PHILLIS WHEATLEY,

NEGRO SERVANT to Mr. JOHN WHEATLEY, of BOSTON, in NEW ENGLAND.

LONDON:
Printed for A. BELL, Bookseller, Aldgate; and sold by Mess. COX and BERRY, King-street, BOSTON.

MDCCLXXIII.

BIOFACT

Wheatley's book contained a letter that declared she was the actual author of the poems. It was signed by 18 important Boston citizens.

Learn from Biographies

How do you think Phillis Wheatley's personal experiences influenced her view of freedom?

For more information, go online to *Meet the People* at **www.sfsocialstudies.com**.

Seeking Freedom

Struggles for freedom and independence have taken place throughout history and in all parts of the world.

During the American Revolution, thousands of African American Patriots risked their lives in the fight for freedom. But at the same time, slavery was still legal in all 13 Colonies. To Prince Hall this did not make sense. How could slavery be allowed in a country that was fighting for freedom?

Prince Hall was a well-known Boston minister and an outspoken supporter of American independence. When the fighting began, Hall grabbed a gun and joined his fellow Patriots at the fierce Battle of Bunker Hill. Hall was fighting for more than freedom from Britain, however. To Hall the American Revolution was a war about freedom for all colonists, black and white.

Hall took his fight for freedom from the battlefield to the legislature. In 1777, he sent a petition, or official written request, to the Massachusetts House of Representatives. His request was simple and bold—to end slavery now. Hall's brave stand for freedom gained results in the 1780s, when Massachusetts banned slavery in the state.

"[African Americans] have in common with all other men a natural . . . right to that freedom which the Great Parent of the Universe hath bestowed equally on all mankind."

Prince Hall *Massachusetts, 1777*

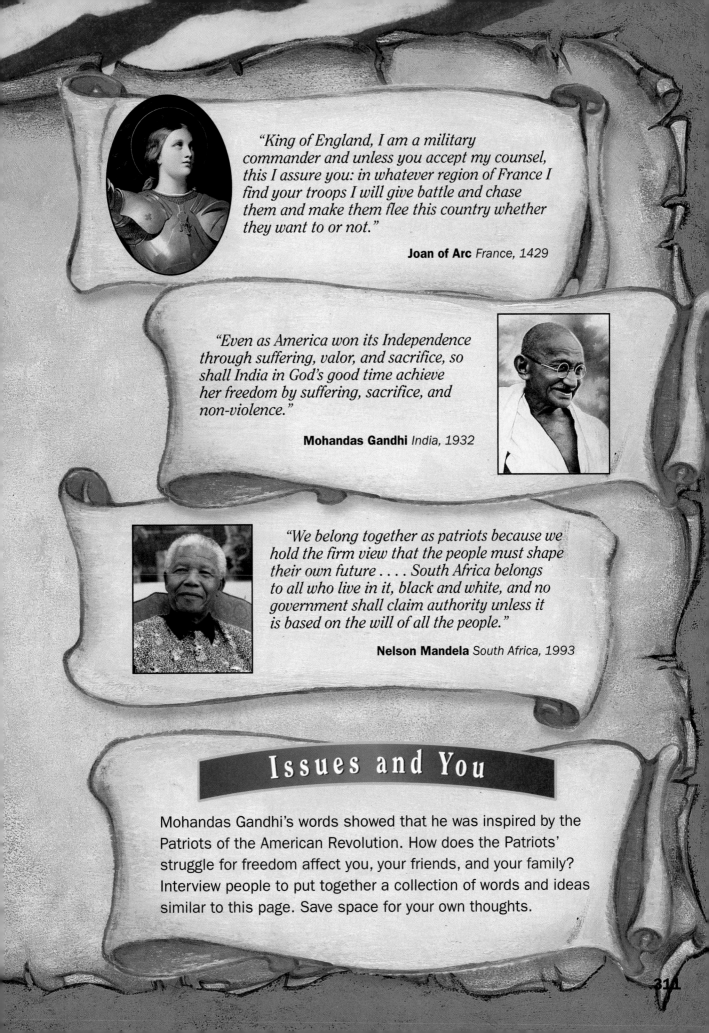

"King of England, I am a military commander and unless you accept my counsel, this I assure you: in whatever region of France I find your troops I will give battle and chase them and make them flee this country whether they want to or not."

Joan of Arc *France, 1429*

"Even as America won its Independence through suffering, valor, and sacrifice, so shall India in God's good time achieve her freedom by suffering, sacrifice, and non-violence."

Mohandas Gandhi *India, 1932*

"We belong together as patriots because we hold the firm view that the people must shape their own future . . . . South Africa belongs to all who live in it, black and white, and no government shall claim authority unless it is based on the will of all the people."

Nelson Mandela *South Africa, 1993*

Issues and You

Mohandas Gandhi's words showed that he was inspired by the Patriots of the American Revolution. How does the Patriots' struggle for freedom affect you, your friends, and your family? Interview people to put together a collection of words and ideas similar to this page. Save space for your own thoughts.

Uniforms of the American Revolution

The uniforms shown are all infantry, or soldiers who moved and fought on foot. What are the major differences you see among the three uniforms?

British Infantry

Braid

Horsehair cockade

Button

Cocked hat

Shirt

Horsehair stock

Goatskin knapsack

Crossbelt

Knapsack strap

Coat

Lapel

Bayonet

Waistcoat

Musket

Braid

Picker for musket lock

Brush for musket lock

Turnback

Cartridge box

Breeches

Sling

Button

Lock

Stocking

Spatterdash

Butt

Shoe

Bearskin

Officer's Coat, British Infantry

Collar

Lapel

Tassel

Cap plate

Bearskin Cap, British Infantry

Piping

Facing

Pocket flap

Turnback

Turnback ornament

Horsehair

Chain

Varnished leather

Pleated cloth

Death's head badge

Officer's "Tarleton" Helmet, British Cavalry

French Infantry

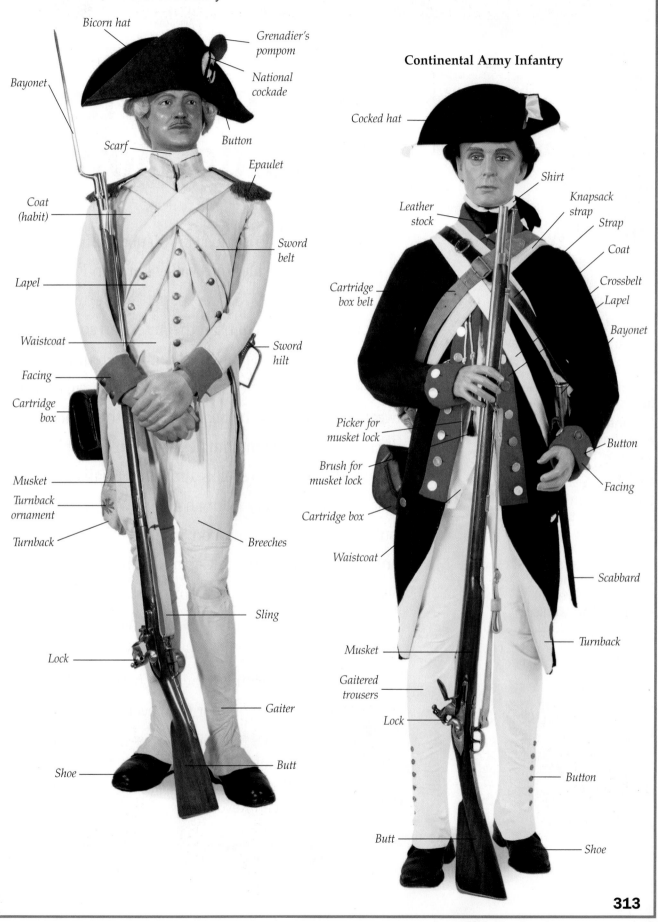

Bicorn hat

Grenadier's pompom

National cockade

Bayonet

Scarf

Button

Epaulet

Coat (habit)

Sword belt

Lapel

Waistcoat

Sword hilt

Facing

Cartridge box

Musket

Turnback ornament

Turnback

Breeches

Sling

Lock

Gaiter

Shoe

Butt

Continental Army Infantry

Cocked hat

Shirt

Knapsack strap

Leather stock

Strap

Coat

Crossbelt

Cartridge box belt

Lapel

Bayonet

Picker for musket lock

Brush for musket lock

Cartridge box

Button

Facing

Waistcoat

Scabbard

Musket

Turnback

Gaitered trousers

Lock

Button

Butt

Shoe

1775   1785

1778
France joins
the war against
Britain

1781
Americans
defeat British
at Yorktown

1783
Treaty of Paris
ends American
Revolution

The World Turned Upside Down

Fort
Vincennes
Yorktown
Savannah

PREVIEW

Focus on the Main Idea
With help from France and
Spain, the Continental Army
won the American Revolution.

PLACES
Savannah, Georgia
Fort Vincennes
Yorktown, Virginia

PEOPLE
Friedrich von Steuben
Marquis de Lafayette
Bernardo de Gálvez
Francis Marion
George Rogers Clark
John Paul Jones
Nathanael Greene
Charles Cornwallis

VOCABULARY
Treaty of Paris

You Are There

Friedrich von Steuben (SHTOI ben)
rides into Valley Forge in February
1778. An experienced German sol-
dier, he is here to help train the American soldiers.

When he calls the men together, von Steuben is
shocked by the sight of starving soldiers in rags, their
weapons rusting. As he begins to train them, however,
he is shocked by something else—the men's spirit.

Von Steuben, who speaks almost no English, shouts
out orders in a heavy German accent. When the young
soldiers make a mistake, von Steuben calls to his
interpreter and shouts in German, "These fellows
won't do what I tell them! Come swear for me!"

The drilling continues. This army has survived battles with the British and a terrible winter. And now
they are learning to be even better soldiers.
They will be tougher than ever.

Draw Conclusions As you read, think about the
factors that enabled the Continental Army to win
the American Revolution.

▶ **Friedrich von Steuben helped
American soldiers train for battle.**

Help from Other Nations

By the spring of 1778, things were improving for George Washington at Valley Forge. The supply of food and clothing was finally increasing. New soldiers were arriving in camp. And, as you have just read, a German officer named **Friedrich von Steuben** was helping turn the American soldiers into a professional army. "The army grows stronger every day," reported a newspaper called the *New Jersey Gazette.* The soldiers knew that George Washington was beginning to relax when he agreed to join them in a game of cricket, a sport similar to baseball.

More good news arrived in April. Washington learned that in February, France had agreed to join the war against Britain. The French were sending ships, soldiers, and money to aid the American war effort.

The aid from France was just one way in which other countries helped the Patriots. You have read about the contributions of Thaddeus Kosciusko and Friedrich von Steuben. Another valuable European volunteer was the **Marquis de Lafayette** (mahr KEE de laf ay ET),

a young soldier from France. At the age of 19, Lafayette joined Washington's staff at Valley Forge. Lafayette soon became one of Washington's favorite officers. "I love him as my own son," Washington said of Lafayette.

Valuable help also came from Spain. In 1779, Spain joined the war against Britain. As governor of Spanish Louisiana, **Bernardo de Gálvez** (GAHL ves) led Spanish troops against the British. Gálvez captured key British forts along the Mississippi River and Gulf of Mexico. These Spanish victories severely weakened British power in what is now the Southeast region of the United States.

USA
15c

Gen. Bernardo de Gálvez
Battle of Mobile 1780

©1980 USPS

REVIEW What was one effect of Spain's entry into the war against Britain?
◑ **Cause and Effect**

▶ **Bernardo de Gálvez (above) captured British forts in the Southeast. The Marquis de Lafayette (below) joined Washington at Valley Forge.**

The Fighting Continues

In December 1778, the British army captured **Savannah,** Georgia. This was the start of a new strategy for the British. They had been unable to defeat the Continental Army in the north. British leaders hoped to have better success in the south. They believed that many people in this region were still loyal to King George III.

But southern Patriots rose up to oppose the British. A daring militia leader from South Carolina named **Francis Marion** became famous for his surprise attacks on the British army. With bands as small as 20 men, Marion would attack suddenly and then disappear into the forests and swamps. These attacks frustrated the British and earned Marion the nickname the "Swamp Fox."

Fighting also continued in the west. Look at the map on the next page and find **Fort Vincennes** (vihn SENZ). The British controlled this fort in early 1779. But a small American force led by **George Rogers Clark** was determined to take Vincennes. It was a freezing, rainy February, and Clark knew the British would not expect an attack in such weather. Clark and his 170-man army marched 180 miles through flooded swamplands. They spent entire days wading through icy water that often came up to their shoulders. Clark surprised the British and captured Vincennes in February 1779. This victory strengthened American control of the Ohio River valley.

The Patriots also battled the British on the ocean. One of the first men to join this fight was **John Paul Jones.** He volunteered for the Continental navy in 1775—a time when the navy had just four ships. In 1779, Jones was captain of a ship he named *Bonhomme Richard*. On a calm September evening off the coast of Britain, Jones attacked a British ship named *Serapis*. Under a bright full moon, the ships pounded each other with cannonballs and grenades for over two hours. Jones' ship was blasted full of holes and leaking badly. But when the British captain asked Jones if he was ready to surrender, Jones shouted back:

> ### *"I have not yet begun to fight!"*

Jones and his sailors continued to battle until the British ship surrendered. This was a proud moment for the young American navy.

REVIEW Why was victory of the *Bonhomme Richard* so important? **Draw Conclusions**

▶ John Paul Jones *(above)* refused to surrender his ship. George Rogers Clark *(below)* led his troops through freezing swamps and surprised the British.

Battles of the American Revolution

The first battle of the American Revolution was fought in Massachusetts. The last was fought in Virginia. What was the name of this last battle? Which side won?

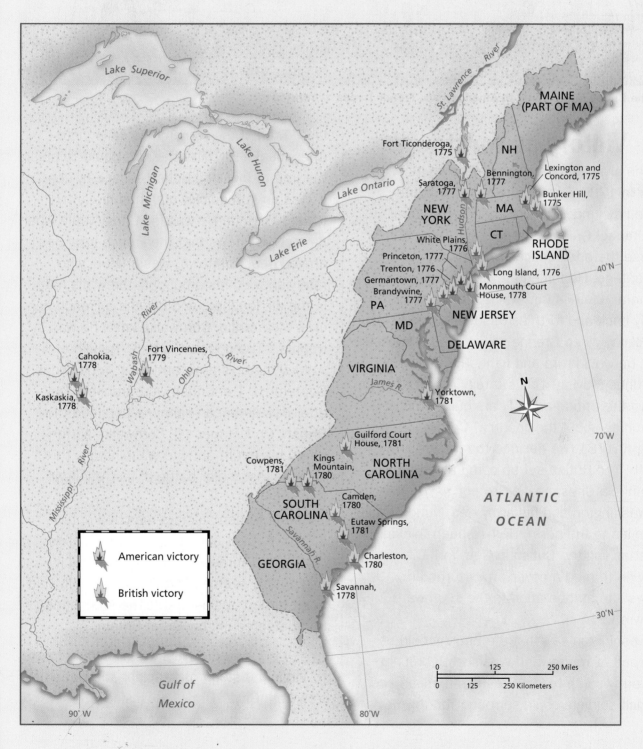

▶ **The British surrendered to American and French forces at Yorktown.**

Victory at Yorktown

The American Revolution entered its sixth year in 1780. Patriot forces in the south were now under the command of General Nathanael Greene. Greene's strategy was to use the open spaces of the south to his advantage. He forced the British, under General Charles Cornwallis, to chase his army back and forth across North and South Carolina. When Greene saw a good opportunity, he would turn and fight. Then he would continue moving. This strategy began to wear down the British army. "I am quite tired of marching about the country," Cornwallis wrote in April 1781. He decided to take his army north. The British set up camp at Yorktown, Virginia, a Chesapeake Bay port.

Washington and his army were hundreds of miles to the north. He had been thinking of attacking the British in New York City. But now he formed a new plan. "I turned my views...to an operation to the southward," he wrote.

Washington saw that the British could be trapped at Yorktown. If Washington brought his army south to join Greene, American and French soldiers could surround Yorktown by land. Then, if the French navy sailed into Chesapeake Bay, French ships could complete the trap by blocking British escape by sea.

Washington quickly marched his army toward Virginia. He was in Pennsylvania when he received news that the French navy had arrived near Yorktown. Washington, who rarely showed his emotions, threw his hat in the air, laughed, and hugged a French general. Meanwhile, Cornwallis knew he was in trouble. "The position is bad," he wrote.

Washington's army arrived at Yorktown in September. The British were trapped. Day after day, American cannons pounded the British. On October 19, Cornwallis surrendered his entire army to Washington. This was the last major battle of the American Revolution.

As the British soldiers marched out of Yorktown, their band played a tune called "The World Turned Upside Down." And it might have seemed like the world really had been turned upside down. The Americans had defeated mighty Great Britain.

REVIEW Why did Washington decide to go to Virginia instead of attacking the British in New York City? *Draw Conclusions*

The Treaty of Paris

News of Washington's victory spread quickly. Americans celebrated by ringing bells, firing cannons, feasting, and dancing. The reaction was very different in London. When Lord North, the Prime Minister of Britain, heard of Cornwallis's defeat he cried, "It is over! It is all over!" The American Revolution was officially ended by the **Treaty of Paris,** signed in 1783 by Americans Benjamin Franklin, John Adams, and John Jay. In this treaty, Great Britain recognized the United States of America as an independent nation.

"We now stand an independent people," wrote Washington in 1783. One struggle was over, but a new one was beginning. Americans faced new questions. What kind of government would the country have? How long would slavery continue in the United States? What would happen to Native Americans who lived on lands now controlled by the United States? You will read these stories in the coming chapters.

REVIEW Summarize the effects of the Treaty of Paris. **Summarize**

Summarize the Lesson

1778 France joined the war against Britain.

1781 The Americans' defeat of the British at Yorktown was the last major battle of the Revolution.

1783 The Treaty of Paris ended the American Revolution.

LESSON 3 ▶ REVIEW

Check Facts and Main Ideas

1. **Draw Conclusions** On a separate sheet of paper, complete this diagram by filling in three factors that helped the United States win the American Revolution.

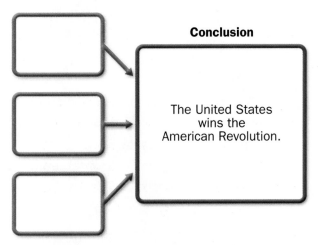

Conclusion

The United States wins the American Revolution.

2. Did other nations help the United States win the American Revolution? Explain.

3. What achievements made John Paul Jones a famous Patriot?

4. Explain Washington's strategy for trapping the British at Yorktown.

5. **Critical Thinking:** *Make Predictions* What effect do you think the outcome of the **Treaty of Paris** will have on Native Americans? Explain.

Link to ⦿⦿ Art

Design a Flag In 1777, Congress approved the first official flag of the United States of America. Find a picture of this flag in a book or on the Internet. Draw a picture of this original flag. Then suppose you were in charge of designing the original flag for the United States. Draw your own design. Explain the symbols on your flag.

Make Generalizations

What? A generalization is a broad statement or idea about a subject. It explains the way different facts might have some important idea in common. For example, in Lesson 3, you learned that other countries helped the United States win the American Revolution. This is a generalization. It is based on the specific examples of how German, French, and Spanish soldiers aided the American cause.

▶ George Washington once told his soldiers, "You have done all I have asked you to do and more."

Robert Morris was born in England in 1734. He moved to the American colonies in 1747. In 1776, he signed the Declaration of Independence. During the American Revolution, Morris was in charge of raising money to pay the expenses of the war. His fundraising made it possible for George Washington to move the Continental Army to Yorktown, where the British surrendered.

A man named Haym Salomon helped Morris in his support of the Revolution. Salomon was born in Poland in 1740. He came to New York City in 1772, where he became a successful businessman. During the Revolution, the British arrested Salomon twice. The second time he escaped to Philadelphia. He served without pay to help raise money for the French forces in the United States. He also loaned his own money to supply military units and support colonial governments. From 1781 through 1784, Salomon lent more than $200,000 to the government.

The money the two men raised was essential to the success of the Continental Army.

Why? Generalizations are useful because they help explain the big picture and make it easier to remember many facts. They can also help you understand new information about a topic you have already studied. Knowing that the United States received essential help from other countries in the American Revolution will help you better understand what you will be reading about the new nation in future chapters.

How? To make a generalization, you need to identify the topic and gather facts about the topic. Then, figure out what all the different information has in common. Finally, come up with one statement that is true for all the information.

To practice making generalizations, read the passage above. It is about two men who helped raise money for the United States during the Revolutionary War.

To gather facts, make a list of everything Robert Morris and Haym Salomon did to help the Americans.

Compare all the information you have gathered. How were Morris's and Salomon's actions similar?

Finally, write a one-sentence statement describing what all the examples have in common.

Think and Apply

1. How did Morris and Salomon help the Continental Army?

2. What sentence in this story is a **generalization?**

3. Why are generalizations helpful in learning about history?

1775

July 4, 1776
Congress approves
the Declaration of
Independence

**September–October
1777**
Americans defeat
British at Saratoga

**December 1777–
June 1778**
Continental Army suffers
during winter at Valley Forge

Chapter Summary

Cause and Effect

On a separate sheet of paper, fill in three effects that followed from the cause.

Cause

Britain refuses to grant the colonists greater self-government.

Effect

Vocabulary

Match each word with the correct definition or description.

1 Olive Branch Petition (p. 297)

2 traitor (p. 300)

3 mercenary (p. 303)

4 Battle of Saratoga (p. 305)

5 Treaty of Paris (p. 319)

a. soldier who is paid to fight for another country

b. document that ended the American Revolution

c. person who acts against his or her country

d. letter Congress sent to Britain to try to avoid war

e. turning point of the American Revolution

People and Groups

Write a sentence explaining why each of the following people or groups was important in winning the American Revolution. You may use two or more in a single sentence.

1 Continental Army (p. 297)

2 Thomas Paine (p. 298)

3 Richard Henry Lee (p. 298)

4 Green Mountain Boys (p. 303)

5 Thaddeus Kosciusko (p. 305)

6 James Armistead (p. 306)

7 Mary Ludwig Hays (p. 307)

8 Marquis de Lafayette (p. 315)

9 Bernardo de Gálvez (p. 315)

10 John Paul Jones (p. 316)

October 1781
British surrender
at Yorktown

September 1783
Treaty of Paris ends
American Revolution

Facts and Main Ideas

1. Why was it dangerous for the colonists to declare independence from Britain?

2. What were some difficulties the Continental Army faced during the fight for independence?

3. Why did George Washington attack Trenton, New Jersey, and what was the result of the attack?

4. **Time Line** How many years were there between the Declaration of Independence and the Treaty of Paris?

5. **Main Idea** What key events led the American colonists to declare their independence from Britain?

6. **Main Idea** How did women and African Americans contribute to the success of the United States in the war?

7. **Main Idea** How did other countries help the Americans in their victory over the British?

8. **Critical Thinking: *Draw Conclusions*** Why do you think people from other countries helped the Americans in their battle for independence?

Apply Skills

Making Generalizations
Read the paragraph below. Then answer the questions.

During the American Revolution, Benjamin Franklin of Pennsylvania went to France to gain French support against Britain for the cause of American independence. John Jay of New York represented the colonies in Spain to try to gain support and recognition for the Americans in their fight against Britain. John Adams of Massachusetts went to Holland to gain Dutch support, and Francis Dana of Massachusetts served the United States in Russia.

1. What common theme can you find in the information in this paragraph?

2. Why did each of these men go to the various countries?

3. What generalization can you make about the paragraph?

Write About History

1. **Write a journal** that an American soldier might have written during the American Revolution. Describe what you see and the dangers you face.

2. **Write a story** about George Rogers Clark's army marching through icy swamplands to launch an attack at Fort Vincennes. Describe how the soldiers survived to go on to defeat the British.

3. **Write a letter** that Martha Washington might have written to American soldiers at Valley Forge to raise their spirits.

Internet Activity

To get help with vocabulary, people, and terms, select dictionary or encyclopedia from *Social Studies Library* at **www.sfsocialstudies.com.**

End with a Song

Yankee Doodle

There is a lot of mystery about when "Yankee Doodle" was written and who wrote it. One story of the song's origin tells that new words were written by a British officer in 1755 to make fun of the colonial soldiers in America. The colonial soldiers, instead of being offended by the words, liked them. "Yankee Doodle" is the most famous song to come out of the American Revolution.

Words by Dr. Richard Shuckburgh

Traditional

VERSE

1. ⅄ Fath'r and I went down to camp, A - long with Cap - tain Good-in',
2. And there we saw a thou-sand men, As rich as Squire __ Da - vid;

And there we saw the men and boys As thick as hast - y pud - din'.
And what they wast-ed ev - 'ry day, I wish it could be sav - ed.

REFRAIN

Yan - kee Doo - dle, keep it up, Yan - kee Doo - dle dan - dy,

Mind the mu - sic and the step And with the girls be hand - y.

3. And there was Captain Washington
Upon a slapping stallion,
A-giving orders to his men;
I guess there was a million. *Refrain*

Main Ideas and Vocabulary

Read the passage below and use it to answer the questions that follow.

At the end of the French and Indian War, Americans were proud to be British colonists. Even after Britain began to tax the colonists, they remained loyal to Britain. They wrote to King George III protesting the taxes.

Britain ended the stamp tax, but ordered new taxes. Many colonists decided to <u>boycott</u> British goods. They hoped this would make Britain stop taxing the colonies.

British soldiers arrived in Boston in 1768 and often clashed with colonists. In 1770, soldiers killed five colonists in the Boston Massacre.

Britain repealed most taxes except for a tax on tea. Colonists responded by dumping tea in Boston Harbor. This led to harsh treatment of Boston. The British closed Boston's port and placed the city under the control of their army.

The First Continental Congress met in 1774. The Congress agreed to stop all trade with Britain. It also decided to train local <u>militias</u> in order to prepare colonists to defend themselves.

When British soldiers went to search for weapons the militias stored near Boston, colonists were ready. Shots rang out at Lexington and Concord. The Second Continental Congress then declared independence from Britain.

Now the colonists were at war with Britain. Each side won some battles, but the Americans finally won their independence.

1 According to the passage, why did soldiers search near Boston?

　A They were looking for homemade tea.

　B They were searching for arms.

　C British soldiers wanted to start a fight.

　D They heard that members of the Continental Congress were hiding there.

2 In the passage, the word <u>boycott</u> means—

　A gladly buy

　B refuse to buy

　C throw out

　D hide

3 In the passage, the word <u>militias</u> means—

　A government officials

　B tax agents

　C young people

　D citizen armies

4 What is the main idea of the passage?

　A Americans did not like taxes.

　B The British needed money.

　C The colonies started out under British rule and became an independent nation.

　D The British decided to punish Americans for the French and Indian War.

People and Vocabulary

Match each person and term to its definition.

1 **American Revolution** (p. 289)

a. war fought for independence

2 **Phillis Wheatley** (p. 307)

b. the first African American to publish a book

3 **Townshend Acts** (p. 272)

c. put tax on imported goods

4 **Boston Tea Party** (p. 279)

d. ended the war

5 **Marquis de Lafayette** (p. 315)

e. led to the Intolerable Acts

6 **Treaty of Paris** (p. 319)

f. French supporter of the revolution

Apply Skills

Prepare a Primary Source Poster Create a poster about an event in your life, such as a birthday, a trip, or a special occasion. Gather photos, letters, or diary entries from the event. Explain how each object is a primary source and what it tells about the event.

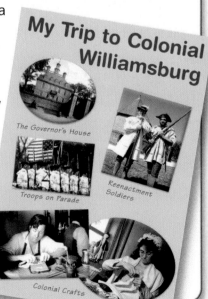

My Trip to Colonial Williamsburg

The Governor's House

Troops on Parade

Reenactment Soldiers

Colonial Crafts

Write and Share

Present a Talk Show Choose students to represent the points of view of the British, the Patriots, and the Loyalists. Form a talk show panel with a host. Have the remaining classmates write questions that will be asked of the guests appearing on the show. The guests should have an opportunity to write their answers before the show is presented. Perform your show for another class in your school.

Read on Your Own

Look for books like these in the library.

PHOEBE The Spy
by JUDITH BERRY GRIFFIN

...IF YOU LIVED AT THE TIME OF THE American Revolution
by Kay Moore
illustrated by Daniel O'Leary

A YOUNG PATRIOT
The American Revolution as Experienced by One Boy
by JIM MURPHY

UNIT 4 Project

News Then

Present a special news program about an event during the 1760s or an event during the American Revolution.

1 Form a group to create a news program about an event described in the unit.

2 Assign jobs, including news anchors, reporters, and residents who were eyewitnesses to the events.

3 Report events that were interesting and significant to people living during the time period.

4 Make a banner or scenic backdrop for your news program. Bring in or make props, or dress in clothing that illustrates the time period and the event.

5 Present your program to the class.

Internet Activity

Explore the American Revolution. Go to **www.sfsocialstudies.com/activities** and select your grade and unit.

Life in a New Nation

Why do people form governments?

Begin with a Primary Source

1780

1781
Articles of
Confederation
approved by states

1787
Constitutional
Convention
begins

1790

1788
Constitution
is ratified

1789
George Washington
becomes the first president

1791
Bill of Rights
ratified

> ## "...in order to form a more perfect Union..."
> —From the Preamble to the United States Constitution

This painting of George Washington taking office as the first President of the United States was painted in 1899.

1800 Federal government moves to Washington, D.C.

1803 Louisiana Purchase expands the size of the country

1810

1812 War of 1812 begins

1815 War of 1812 ends

1820

Benjamin Banneker

1731–1806

Birthplace: Ellicott's Mills, Maryland

Inventor, mathematician, astronomer

- Served on the committee to plan the United States capital
- Helped survey the land that became Washington, D.C.
- Built a working clock entirely out of wood

Abigail Adams

1744–1818

Birthplace: Weymouth, Massachusetts

First Lady

- Wrote letters that have helped historians learn about United States history
- Strong supporter of independence from England
- Advocated women's rights and the abolition of slavery

Benjamin Rush

1746–1813

Birthplace: Byberry, Pennsylvania

Doctor, political leader

- Signer of the Declaration of Independence
- Led Pennsylvania in ratifying the United States Constitution
- Helped write the Pennsylvania State Constitution

James Madison

1751–1836

Birthplace: Port Conway, Virginia

Political leader

- Kept a written record of the Constitutional Convention
- A leader of the drive to approve the Constitution
- Elected fourth President of the United States in 1808

1730	1740	1750	1760	1770	1780

1731 • Benjamin Banneker

1744 • Abigail Adams

1746 • Benjamin Rush

1751 • James Madison

1755? • Alexander Hamilton

1768 • Tecumseh

1774

Alexander Hamilton

1755?–1804

Birthplace: Nevis, British West Indies

Lawyer

- Appointed by George Washington to serve as his aide in the American Revolution
- A leader of the drive to ratify the Constitution
- First secretary of the treasury of the United States

Tecumseh

1768–1813

Birthplace: Present-day Clark County, Ohio

Shawnee leader

- Persuasive speaker and leader
- Unified many Native Americans to resist American settlement
- Joined forces with British during the War of 1812

Meriwether Lewis

1774–1809

Birthplace: near Charlottesville, Virginia

Army captain, explorer

- Teamed with William Clark to explore the Louisiana Territory
- Kept detailed records of his explorations
- Named governor of the Louisiana Territory

Sacagawea

about 1786–1812?

Birthplace: near present-day Lemhi, Idaho

Interpreter, guide

- Shoshone who accompanied Lewis and Clark on their expedition
- Helped the explorers communicate with Native Americans
- Saved important journals and other valuable items when an expedition boat tipped over

| 1790 | 1800 | 1810 | 1820 | 1830 |

1806

1818

1813

1836

1804

1813

• Meriwether Lewis   1809

about 1786 • Sacagawea   1812?

Reading Social Studies

Life in a New Nation
Draw Conclusions

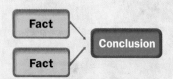

Drawing conclusions about what you have read can help you better understand history. Sometimes a writer presents facts from which you can form an opinion, or conclusion. Writers may also present you with their own conclusions.

Identify **facts** and then **draw a conclusion** based on the facts.

- To draw conclusions, think logically. You can also use clues from what you have read and from your own knowledge and experience.

- Make sure you check your conclusion. Ask yourself if your conclusion makes sense or if there are any other possible conclusions.

In this paragraph, the **facts** and the **conclusion** that was drawn from them are highlighted.

In Chapters 8 and 9, you read about the conflict between the colonies and Britain. Britain taxed the colonists without their consent. The colonists insisted that the British were violating their right to have a voice in government. The colonies declared independence from Britain and defended their right to govern themselves.

Word Exercise

Suffixes A **suffix** is a syllable or syllables put at the end of a word to change its meaning or to make another word. Knowing what a suffix means can help you figure out the meaning of an unfamiliar word. Sometimes a suffix can have multiple meanings. For example, the suffix *-ion* can mean "act of" and also "result of."

word	word parts	Meaning of *-ion*	Meaning of word
revolution	revolt + -ion	"act of"	"the act of revolting"
constitution	constitute (legally form) + -ion	"result of"	"the result of legally forming"

Draw Conclusions About Life in a New Nation

During the American Revolution, the states had to determine a plan to govern themselves. In 1781, the 13 states approved the Articles of Confederation, which established a weak central government. Events such as the revolt of farmers in Shays' Rebellion made some people worry that the government was too weak.

In 1787, representatives of most of the states met to make the central government stronger. They ended up getting rid of the Articles of Confederation and writing the Constitution.

Not everyone liked the new document. Both those who wanted it adopted and those who did not, worked hard to convince others. Eventually, the Constitution was approved.

The country chose its first President, George Washington, in 1789. Washington established the practice of choosing a Cabinet, or group of advisors. He also directed the plan to move the site of the capital to what is now called Washington, D.C., and chose key members of the planning team.

The government would soon have a larger area to govern. Americans began moving west in greater numbers. They crossed the Appalachian Mountains in search of new hunting grounds, fresh farmlands, and a new home. In 1803, the United States purchased even more land—the Louisiana Territory. The country's territory now expanded all the way to the Rocky Mountains.

The United States went to war again with Britain in the War of 1812. The official song of the United States, "The Star-Spangled Banner," was written to celebrate an American victory during this war.

Use the reading strategy of drawing conclusions to answer questions 1 and 2. Then answer the vocabulary question.

1 What can you conclude about George Washington's role in early United States history?

2 What facts support the following conclusion: Americans moved west to look for new opportunities?

3 Look at the word *rebellion* in the passage. Which meaning does the suffix *-ion* have in *rebellion*? What does *rebellion* mean?

Forming a New Government

1786

Springfield, Massachusetts
Rebellion of farmers shows the weakness of the central government.

Lesson 1

1

1787

Philadelphia, Pennsylvania
Delegates meet to write the Constitution.

Lesson 2

2

1787

New York City, New York
Writings of *The Federalist* encourage the acceptance of the Constitution.

Lesson 3

3

THE

FEDERALIST:

A COLLECTION

OF

ESSAYS,

WRITTEN IN FAVOUR OF THE

NEW CONSTITUTION,

3 **1** **2**

Springfield

New York City
Philadelphia

UNITED STATES
1783

ATLANTIC
OCEAN

Why We Remember

In the summer of 1787, fifty-five people met in Philadelphia to write the Constitution. This document is the plan for a government that has lasted for more than 200 years. The Constitution created a lasting structure to govern the United States. The Constitution not only set up the plans for our representative democracy, it also protects our freedoms. Later changes, such as those giving greater numbers of people the right to vote, show that the Constitution continues to change through time.

NORTHWEST TERRITORY Springfield

1780   1790

1781
Articles of Confederation ratified by states

1786-1787
Shays' Rebellion is fought in western Massachusetts

1787
Northwest Ordinance organizes the Northwest Territory

A Weak Government

PREVIEW

Focus on the Main Idea
The new nation struggled to govern itself under the Articles of Confederation.

PLACES
Springfield, Massachusetts
Northwest Territory

PEOPLE
Daniel Shays

VOCABULARY
Articles of Confederation
ratify
legislative branch
executive branch
judicial branch
inflation
Shays' Rebellion
Northwest Ordinance of 1787

You Are There

You are tucked in bed, but voices coming from downstairs keep you awake. The Declaration of Independence has just been proclaimed. The adults in your family are excitedly discussing it and what it means.

"At last," says one, "we will be free of tyranny from the British government."

"But," says another, "what kind of government will we create to take its place? Will we simply replace British tyranny with American tyranny?"

Like many other Americans, members of your family have a deep distrust of government. They don't want a repeat of powerful governors and unfair laws. What they want is a government that is strong enough to protect citizens' rights. But they fear that government can just as easily threaten citizens' freedoms. How can a balance be found?

Draw Conclusions As you read, decide how successful the Articles of Confederation were in setting up a strong government.

The Articles of Confederation

With British rule removed, Americans had to create new plans of government for themselves. Leaders knew that they wanted their new nation to be a republic. But they did not want this government to have too much power over the people. Shortly after the members of the Continental Congress adopted the Declaration of Independence in 1776, they began debating a new plan for a national government. The plan was called the Articles of Confederation. A confederation is a group or league.

The Articles of Confederation stated that the states would keep their "freedom and independence." States would be joined in "a firm league of friendship," not a strong central government. The plan could not take effect until all 13 states ratified it. To ratify is to approve something. The Articles of Confederation were ratified in 1781.

Under the Articles of Confederation, Congress was the main governing body. It would make the laws for the new nation. But it could not pass laws to collect taxes to run the government. Congress could only ask each state to give taxes to pay for the expenses of Congress. However, it was difficult for Congress to collect enough money this way. Each state had one vote in Congress. To pass a law, at least 9 of the 13 states had to vote for it.

The Articles set up a central government with only one branch—a legislature, called Congress. A legislative branch is the part of government that passes laws. There was no executive branch to carry out the laws. An executive branch of government is headed by a leader such as a President. There was also no judicial branch, or court system, to interpret the laws.

REVIEW Why did the writers of the Articles of Confederation purposely create a weak central government? ⊙ Draw Conclusions

▶ **Robert Livingston helped write the Declaration of Independence and the Articles of Confederation.**

Painting by John Trumbull

A Government in Trouble

The weaknesses of the Articles of Confederation meant trouble for the new nation. Think about how difficult it would be for a government to operate without being able to pass laws to collect taxes. For example, Congress had to borrow large amounts of money to fight the American Revolution. It borrowed from both private people and foreign countries. Without the ability to collect taxes, it could not repay these debts. It also could not pay its soldiers.

The new nation also had other money problems. Today, we have coins and paper money that have the same value across the country. But then, both the Congress and the different states could make their own money. And each kind of money might have a different value. If you were alive then, you would have carried a jumble of money—paper bills printed by Congress, called "continentals," and perhaps some paper money printed by Vermont or by Pennsylvania. You might even have had a few foreign coins.

People had a hard time figuring out the value of these different kinds of money. Congress's paper money became almost worthless. This happened because of inflation that took place during the American Revolution. **Inflation** happens when prices rise very quickly. When this happens, money does not buy as much as it used to. The saying "not worth a continental" came to describe something of little or no value. How could businesses run well with such a jumble of money?

Under the Articles of Confederation, the national government was not only weak at home. It was also powerless in dealings with other countries. The new nation needed to develop strong trade with the nations of Europe. But because Congress could not pass laws making rules for such trade, some governments had little respect for the United States. Many of them hoped the new nation would fail.

By the middle 1780s, some Americans became alarmed about the nation's weakness. A group called the nationalists began arguing for a newer, stronger form of national government. The nationalists included leaders of the Revolution, such as George Washington and Ben Franklin. George Washington made this plea for change: "If the powers of Congress are inadequate [not strong enough], amend or alter [change] them."

REVIEW What conclusions did the nationalists draw about the Articles of Confederation? ↻ **Draw Conclusions**

▶ Congress and the states printed paper money during and after the Revolution.

Shays' Rebellion

An uprising of farmers in western Massachusetts in 1786 alarmed the nationalists even more than the nation's weakness. Like the other states, Massachusetts had borrowed money to fight the Revolutionary War. And like other states, it had the power to tax its citizens. One way to pay off its debt was to tax property. These taxes hit the farmers of the state especially hard.

Farmers found it harder and harder to pay property taxes and other debts. When they could not pay, state courts seized their farms. The courts also threw farmers who owed money into jail. The anger of the farmers grew. **Daniel Shays** was one of the angry farmers. A Revolutionary War veteran, he had fought at the battles of Bunker Hill, Ticonderoga, and Saratoga, rising to the rank of captain. The Marquis de Lafayette had presented Shays with a ceremonial sword to honor his service. But debts had forced Shays to sell this prized sword.

Shays became a leader in a movement that demanded lower taxes and the closing of courts that punished debtors. A debtor is a person who owes money. In September 1786, Captain Shays led a ragtag "army" of about 700 to close the court at **Springfield, Massachusetts.** Fewer than a quarter of them were armed with anything more than clubs. To keep **Shays' Rebellion** going, the farmers needed better weapons. So in January 1787, Shays led an attack on the federal arsenal at Springfield, where rifles and ammunition were stored.

Shays' attack was unsuccessful, and he fled to Vermont. But his rebellion gave the nationalists more ammunition in their battle to strengthen the national government.

REVIEW Why did Shays' Rebellion frighten the nationalists and other Americans?
 Draw Conclusions

HERE AND THERE Revolution in France

At the Same Time as the United States was struggling to create a government, France was having a revolution of its own. On July 14, 1789 in Paris, an angry crowd rose up against the king of France. Like the American Revolution, the French Revolution aimed at creating a representative government. France soon declared itself a republic. But it too faced many challenges before it could make a stable, representative government a reality.

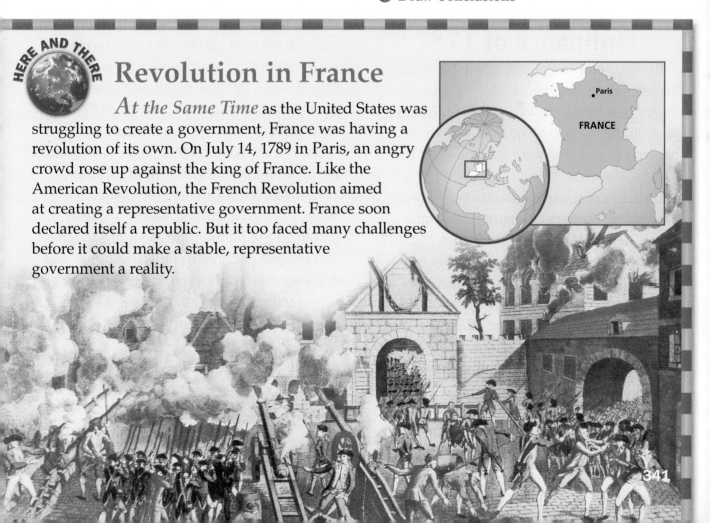

Paris

FRANCE

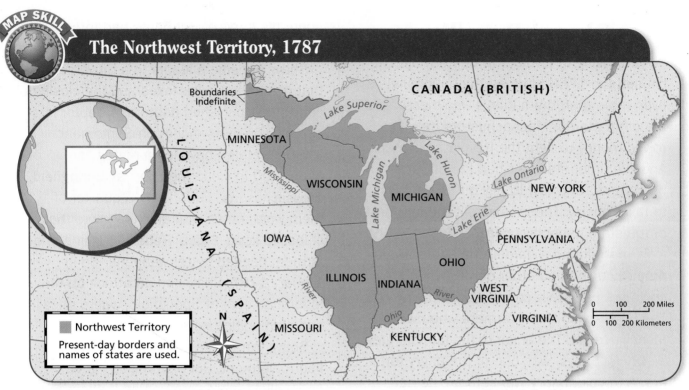

The Northwest Territory, 1787

CANADA (BRITISH)

Boundaries Indefinite

MINNESOTA

Lake Superior

LOUISIANA (SPAIN)

Mississippi River

WISCONSIN

Lake Michigan

MICHIGAN

Lake Huron

Lake Ontario

NEW YORK

Lake Erie

IOWA

PENNSYLVANIA

ILLINOIS

INDIANA

OHIO

River

Ohio River

WEST VIRGINIA

VIRGINIA

Northwest Territory

Present-day borders and names of states are used.

N

MISSOURI

KENTUCKY

0   100   200 Miles
0 100 200 Kilometers

► The Northwest Territory was divided into smaller territories that later became states or parts of states.

MAP SKILL **Location** *What rivers bordered the Northwest Territory on the west and the south?*

The Northwest Ordinance of 1787

By the Treaty of Paris of 1783, the United States gained vast lands from the British. These new lands stretched to the Mississippi River in the west. How could these lands become states that were the equals of the original 13?

One part of these lands was called the Northwest Territory. Congress drew up a plan called the Northwest Ordinance of 1787. An ordinance is an official order. This ordinance commanded that the Northwest Territory be divided into smaller territories. The ordinance described the steps that all territories would follow to become states.

First, Congress would name a governor and three judges to govern the territory. Next, when the population of the territory reached 5,000 free adult males, the territory could elect a legislature. Then, when the population reached 60,000 adult males, the territory could petition, or ask, to become a state. Finally, when Congress ratified the territory's petition, the new state would stand "on an equal footing with the original states."

Look at the map on this page. What states were formed from the Northwest Territory?

The Northwest Ordinance prohibited slavery in the Northwest Territory. It also promised the rights of freedom of speech and religion and trial by jury to settlers. And it stated that public schools would be established throughout the territory.

REVIEW Why can the Northwest Ordinance be considered a successful action by Congress under the Articles of Confederation? ↻ **Draw Conclusions**

Growing Concerns

Despite the success of the Northwest Ordinance, nationalists were still alarmed by the weakness of the central government. Disorders like Shays' Rebellion increased their fears. Once again, George Washington expressed their concern:

> *"What stronger evidence can be given of the want of energy in our government than these disorders?...Thirteen [states] pulling against each other and all tugging at the...head [central government] will soon bring ruin on the whole."*

Congress called on the states to send representatives to a meeting in Philadelphia in May 1787. This meeting was to be held for "the sole and express purpose of revising the Articles of Confederation."

REVIEW Why did George Washington conclude that greater unity among the states was necessary? ⟳ **Draw Conclusions**

Summarize the Lesson

1781 All 13 states ratified the Articles of Confederation, making it the framework for the national government.

1786 Western Massachusetts farmers led by Daniel Shays rebelled against taxes.

1787 Congress passed the Northwest Ordinance, which provided a model for how territories could be turned into new states.

LESSON 1 REVIEW

Check Facts and Main Ideas

1. ⟳ **Draw Conclusions** On a separate sheet of paper, fill in the missing facts that lead to the given conclusion.

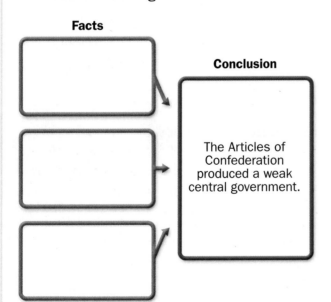

Facts

Conclusion

The Articles of Confederation produced a weak central government.

2. What were the goals of the **Articles of Confederation?**

3. What caused **Shays' Rebellion?**

4. **Critical Thinking:** *Cause and Effect* Identify the events that led to the **Northwest Ordinance** of 1787.

5. What led George Washington to say: "What stronger evidence can be given of the want of energy in our government?"

Link to ⬤—⬤ Writing

Write a Letter to the Editor Suppose that you have just read about Shays' Rebellion in your local newspaper. Write a letter to the editor of your local newspaper in which you explain why you support or oppose the rebellion.

343

1785   1790

May 1787
Constitutional
Convention
begins

September 1787
Delegates to Constitutional
Convention approve Constitution

Philadelphia

PREVIEW

Focus on the Main Idea
At the Constitutional Convention, a group of leaders wrote the Constitution, a new plan for a stronger national government.

PLACES
Philadelphia, Pennsylvania

PEOPLE
James Madison
Alexander Hamilton

VOCABULARY
delegate
Constitutional Convention
Virginia Plan
New Jersey Plan
compromise
Great Compromise
Three-Fifths Compromise
Preamble
reserved powers
separation of powers
checks and balances
veto

Debate in Philadelphia

You Are There
You are a reporter for a Philadelphia newspaper in 1787. You are about to cover your first big story.

Representatives from around the country are meeting in your city. The goal of the representatives? To strengthen the shaky national government.

Among the representatives is the beloved George Washington. On his arrival, he is greeted with an artillery salute and chiming bells. Hosting the convention is Pennsylvania's Benjamin Franklin. At 81, he is the oldest to take part.

Will the assembly succeed in its goal? You wonder what plan they can work out that will strengthen the nation's representative democracy.

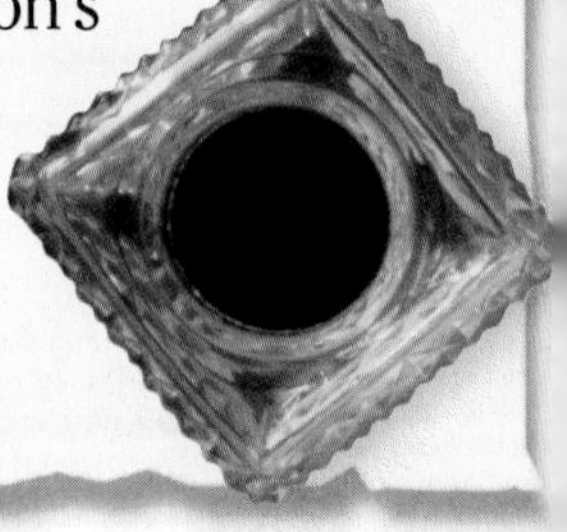

Draw Conclusions As you read, see what conclusions you can draw about why the writers of the Constitution made the decisions they did.

The Constitutional Convention

In late May 1787, 55 representatives, or **delegates,** began filing into the State House in **Philadelphia, Pennsylvania.** Some of them had been here many times before, as members of the Second Continental Congress. In this same hall, some had heard the Declaration of Independence proclaimed. Here some had faced the challenge of fighting the Revolution. Now they faced the challenge of strengthening the government in the new republic. The original goal of the delegates was to revise the Articles of Confederation. However, they would end up replacing the Articles with a new Constitution. Their meeting would become known as the **Constitutional Convention.**

One of the first delegates to arrive was **James Madison** of Virginia. Madison had been one of the youngest members of the Continental Congress. A leading nationalist, his day-to-day notes are the most complete record of the Constitutional Convention. The effort, he later admitted, "nearly killed me."

You will read more about Madison in the Biography on page 351.

From New York came **Alexander Hamilton.** He was barely out of his teens when he had become military aide to General Washington during the Revolutionary War. By now, he was a well-known lawyer and he had strong opinions of how government can and should work.

Like these men, the other delegates were among the smartest leaders in the country. More than half of them had fought in the Revolutionary War, and many had helped write their state constitutions.

To no one's surprise, the delegates unanimously elected George Washington to be the leader of the convention. They also decided that they must work in secret. In his writings, Madison explained why. The delegates had to be able to speak freely and to change their minds. So guards were placed at the doors. Windows were nailed shut. Gravel was spread on the street outside to quiet street noises.

REVIEW Why did the delegates maintain secrecy about their work?
Draw Conclusions

▶ James Madison (*right*) was one of the leaders of the Constitutional Convention. Today the State House where the delegates met is called Independence Hall.

James Madison

Alexander Hamilton

George Washington

Ben Franklin

The Granger Collection

▶ The 55 delegates to the Constitutional Convention included many of the country's most important men. They elected George Washington as leader of the convention.

Competing Plans

Delegate George Mason of Virginia set the tone for the Constitutional Convention:

> *"The eyes of the United States are turned upon this assembly... God grant that we may be able to satisfy them by establishing a wise and just government."*

Just about all the delegates agreed that the national government must be made stronger. Many believed that with a few changes the Articles of Confederation could do this. But James Madison and some other delegates thought differently. They wanted to throw out the Articles entirely and write a new constitution. So they made up their own plan. Virginia delegate Edmund Randolph presented it to the Convention.

The Virginia Plan proposed that Congress be given much greater power over the states. It also stated that the national government should have an executive branch to carry out laws created by Congress. In addition, the Virginia Plan stated that the national government should have a judicial branch to interpret the laws passed by Congress. This plan also said that states with larger populations, like Virginia, should have more representatives in Congress than should smaller states.

Smaller states had one major objection to the Virginia Plan. They did not believe that larger states should have more power than smaller states. So New Jersey delegate William Paterson proposed the New Jersey Plan. It stated that each state, large or small, would have the same number of representatives in Congress. In this way, all the states would have equal power.

Paterson argued for his plan this way: "There is no more reason that a great individual state, contributing much, should have more votes than a small one, contributing little, than a rich individual citizen should have more votes than a [poor] one."

Debate over the two competing plans continued into the hot summer.

REVIEW How would you compare and contrast the Virginia Plan and the New Jersey Plan? **Compare and Contrast**

A Compromise Plan

The only thing that could save the Convention from failure was compromise. In a **compromise,** each side gives up something to reach an agreement. Roger Sherman of Connecticut suggested that Congress should be made up of not just one part but of two parts, called houses. One of the houses would be a Senate and the other a House of Representatives. In the Senate, each and every state would be represented by two senators. The states would be equal in power in the Senate. But in the House of Representatives, population would determine the number of representatives each state had. Large states would have more representatives than small states.

After a month's discussion, the Convention finally agreed to Sherman's compromise. It came to be known as the **Great Compromise.**

At the same time, the delegates faced another difficult problem. States where slavery was practiced widely—Southern states— wanted enslaved people counted as part of their populations. This would give them more representation in Congress. But they did not want slaves counted when it came to being taxed. States without widespread slavery— Northern states—objected.

Finally the **Three-Fifths Compromise** was worked out. Enslaved people would be counted as part of a state's population for both representation in Congress and for taxes. However, only three-fifths of their number would count. This meant that only three out of every five slaves would be counted. If a state had 50,000 slaves, only 30,000 people would be added to the count of its population.

Northern and Southern states also compromised about the slave trade. Northern delegates agreed that Congress would take no action against importing slaves for 20 years. Twenty years later, in 1808, Congress did outlaw the importing of enslaved people into the United States.

By September, the long, hot summer of debate finally ended in Philadelphia. Little did the delegates know that this Constitution would one day make the United States the world's oldest continuous republic.

REVIEW Explain how Roger Sherman helped the Constitutional Convention succeed. *Summarize*

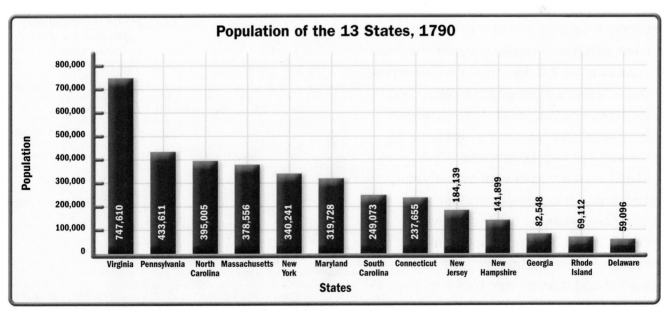

Population of the 13 States, 1790

State	Population
Virginia	747,610
Pennsylvania	433,611
North Carolina	395,005
Massachusetts	378,556
New York	340,241
Maryland	319,728
South Carolina	249,073
Connecticut	237,655
New Jersey	184,139
New Hampshire	141,899
Georgia	82,548
Rhode Island	69,112
Delaware	59,096

▶ The population of the states varied greatly in 1790.

GRAPH SKILL *Which states had the largest and smallest populations in 1790?*

Our Constitution

The Constitution begins with a **Preamble,** or introduction. It includes these ringing words:

> *"We the People of the United States, in Order to form a more perfect Union, establish Justice, insure domestic Tranquility, provide for the common defense, promote the general Welfare, and secure the Blessings of Liberty to ourselves and our Posterity, do ordain and establish this Constitution for the United States of America."*

The Preamble clearly set out the Constitution's major goals: to establish justice, to ensure peace, to defend the nation, and to protect the people's well-being and liberty.

The Constitution then spelled out those powers that only the national government will have. For example, only the national government can make laws about trade with other countries. Only the national government may produce coins and paper money. The Constitution leaves many other powers strictly to state governments. These are called **reserved powers,** because they are "reserved," or left, for the states. Reserved powers include managing education and elections. The two levels of government share certain other powers, like passing tax laws and managing roads.

The Constitution divides the national government into three branches. Congress makes up the Legislative Branch, which is charged with making laws. The job of putting the laws into practice and making sure they are obeyed falls to the Executive Branch,

headed by the President. The Judicial Branch, headed by the Supreme Court, sees that the laws are interpreted according to the Constitution. Look at the chart on the next page to study the powers of the three branches. This three-part government provides a **separation of powers.** In other words, each branch has different and separate powers.

To guard against any one branch becoming too powerful, the Constitution provides a system of **checks and balances.** As the chart shows, Congress has the right to pass laws. But the President can **veto,** or refuse to sign into law, an act that Congress wants. This is a check, or limit, that the President has on Congress. But Congress can overturn this veto if two-thirds of its members still want the law. This is a check Congress has on the President. Finally, the courts, or the Judicial Branch, can overturn what the Legislative or Executive Branch does if the courts find the actions to be against the Constitution.

One branch can check the power of another. So all branches can maintain a balance of power among them. Find more examples of checks and balances on the chart.

REVIEW Identify the role of each of the three branches of government.
Main Idea and Details

▶ **The Preamble states the goals of the Constitution.**

FACT FILE

The Three Branches of Government

The writers of the Constitution believed that government's powers should be limited. They created three separate branches with a system of checks and balances to limit the power of each branch. The people provide the final check over all three branches.

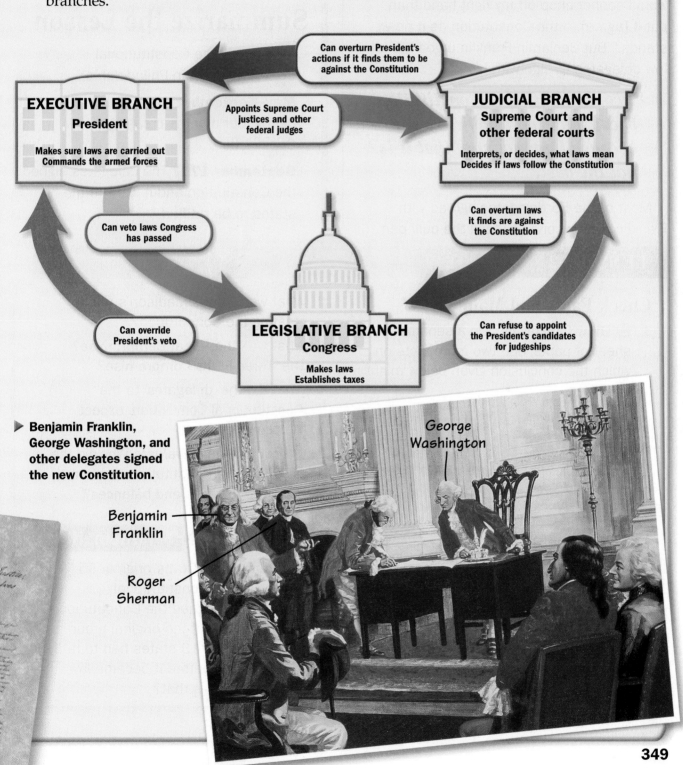

Can overturn President's actions if it finds them to be against the Constitution

EXECUTIVE BRANCH
President

Makes sure laws are carried out
Commands the armed forces

Appoints Supreme Court justices and other federal judges

JUDICIAL BRANCH
Supreme Court and other federal courts

Interprets, or decides, what laws mean
Decides if laws follow the Constitution

Can veto laws Congress has passed

Can overturn laws it finds are against the Constitution

LEGISLATIVE BRANCH
Congress

Makes laws
Establishes taxes

Can override President's veto

Can refuse to appoint the President's candidates for judgeships

▶ Benjamin Franklin, George Washington, and other delegates signed the new Constitution.

George Washington

Benjamin Franklin

Roger Sherman

The Work Still Ahead

September 17, 1787, dawned as a cool, clear Monday. The time had come for the delegates to the Constitutional Convention to vote on the document they had created.

Weary of four months of disagreement and compromise, many had doubts about what they had created. One had even said, "I would sooner chop off my right hand than put it [agree] to the Constitution as it now stands." But Benjamin Franklin urged his fellow delegates to sign with him:

> *"I consent...to this Constitution because I expect no better and because I am not sure that it is not the best."*

Most of the 55 delegates agreed with Franklin. One by one, 39 took the quill pen and signed. But the work had just begun. Nine of the states had to ratify the Constitution before it could become the supreme law of the land. And convincing them would not be easy.

REVIEW What was the sequence of events that had to take place for the Constitution to become the supreme law of the land? Sequence

Summarize the Lesson

— **May 1787** The Constitutional Convention met in Philadelphia.

— **May–September 1787** Delegates spent nearly four months creating a new Constitution.

— **September 1787** The delegates signed the Constitution and it went to the states to be ratified.

LESSON 2 REVIEW

Check Facts and Main Ideas

1. ⟳ **Draw Conclusions** On a separate sheet of paper, add two more facts on which the conclusion given below might be based.

Facts

A legislative branch can concentrate on the work of making laws.

Conclusion

A separation of powers is a good way to divide the work of governing.

2. What was James Madison's role in creating the Constitution?

3. What was the **Great Compromise?** The **Three-Fifths Compromise?**

4. What did the **delegates** to the **Constitutional Convention** expect to accomplish?

5. **Critical Thinking:** *Evaluate* Why did the writers of the Constitution create a system of **checks and balances?**

Link to ⟨⟩ Mathematics

Figure Percentage Of the original 55 delegates to the Constitutional Convention, 39 signed the Constitution. What percentage of the original group signed it? Nine of 13 states had to ratify the Constitution before it became law. What percentage is that?

James Madison

1751–1836

As a child James Madison was small, shy, soft-spoken, and often sick. He did not have all of the obvious qualities of a leader. But he grew up to become the fourth President of the United States. He may have had a quiet voice, but he used it to speak out for what he believed.

One of the things he strongly believed in was religious freedom. In 1776, Madison attended the convention that met to create a constitution for the state of Virginia. He made sure the state's constitution guaranteed a person's "free exercise of religion." About ten years later Madison worked to pass the Virginia Statute of Religious Freedom, which was written by his lifelong friend, Thomas Jefferson. The statute prevented the state government from interfering with religion. This idea had also been supported in many other states and later became the law for all of the United States under an addition to the Constitution called the First Amendment.

Madison and Jefferson wrote to each other in a code to make sure their letters would be secret.

Madison also believed a strong central government was important to the success of the nation. He was an important leader at the Constitutional Convention in 1787 and many of his ideas became part of the Constitution. Later, his writings published in *The Federalist* papers helped convince people to ratify the Constitution. Madison became president in 1809. Under his leadership, the country fought another war with Britain. Shortly before his death, Madison expressed the importance of a country united under one central government:

> *"The advice nearest my heart and deepest in my convictions [belief] is that the Union of the States be cherished and perpetuated [made to last]."*

Learn from Biographies

Madison had a very quiet voice, but his ideas were heard and had great influence. How do you think Madison made himself heard?

For more information, go online to *Meet the People* at **www.sfsocialstudies.com.**

New York City

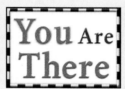

1785

1787
Delaware is first
state to ratify
the Constitution

1788
Constitution
is ratified

1790

1791
Bill of
is rati

PREVIEW

Focus on the Main Idea
After a long debate, the states ratified the United States Constitution.

PLACES
New York City, New York

PEOPLE
Benjamin Rush

VOCABULARY
Federalists
federal
Antifederalists
The Federalist
amendment
Bill of Rights

Ratifying the Constitution

You Are There

It is June 4, 1788. You have just taken your seat as a delegate to the Virginia Constitutional Convention. George Mason rises to speak. He is the same man who expressed great hope for the Constitutional Convention in Philadelphia a year ago. But now he speaks out against the Constitution:

"The very idea of converting what was once a confederation to a consolidated [central] government is totally [against] every principle which…governed us….Will the people…submit to be individually taxed by two different and distinct powers? [the states and the national government]…These two…powers cannot exist long together. The one will destroy the other…"

Debates like this one have been raging across the 13 states. In each one, citizens of the state have met to decide whether or not that state will ratify the Constitution. It will be a close fight.

Draw Conclusions As you read, see what conclusions you can draw about why the Constitution was so hotly debated in the state conventions.

The Federalists and Antifederalists

The Constitution gave the nationalists the strong national government they had wanted. Now they became known as the **Federalists.** The word **federal** refers to the national government. But many people, like George Mason, were not happy with the Constitution. These people came to be known as the **Antifederalists.**

Many famous and powerful Americans were Antifederalists. In Virginia, along with Mason, there was Patrick Henry. In Massachusetts, Samuel Adams and John Hancock voiced opposition to the Constitution.

The Antifederalists strongly expressed their fears. One fear was that the Constitution would reduce the powers of the states. Patrick Henry expressed a second fear: "Your President may easily become king." The Antifederalists worried that the federal government would pass laws that were not suitable for one part of the country or another. It was "impossible," said some Antifederalists, to please all parts of the country with the same laws.

Antifederalists also argued that the Constitution did not truly protect important rights of Americans from the government. These rights included freedom of religion, freedom of the press, trial by jury, and others. Though not an Antifederalist, Thomas Jefferson, who was still in France, supported this argument. Jefferson believed that the people should be guaranteed certain rights. He said that these rights could not be taken away by the government. Jefferson said: "A bill of rights is what the people are entitled to against every government on earth."

James Madison, Alexander Hamilton, and John Jay led the Federalist fight for the Constitution. They organized actions to educate the people about it. Madison, Hamilton, and John Jay of New York wrote a series of essays called *The Federalist.* The essays appeared at first in New York City, New York newspapers in 1787 and were read by many people. Each essay explained the weaknesses of an Antifederalist argument.

In *The Federalist: Number 51,* Madison defended the national government that the Constitution had created. Madison wrote:

> *"If men were angels, no government would be necessary. If angels were to govern men, [no]… controls on government would be necessary."*

REVIEW How would you summarize arguments made against and for the Constitution? **Summarize**

▶ **Alexander Hamilton wrote many of the essays that were printed in *The Federalist.***

THE

FEDERALIST:

A COLLECTION

OF

ESSAYS,

WRITTEN IN FAVOUR OF THE

NEW CONSTITUTION,

Bill of Rights

Amendment	Subject
First	Protects freedom of religion, freedom of speech, freedom of the press, the right to assemble peacefully, and the right to voice complaints to the government.
Second	Protects the right to own and bear firearms.
Third	States that the government cannot force people to house soldiers during peacetime.
Fourth	Protects people from unfair searches and seizures of property.
Fifth	Guarantees that no one can be deprived of life, liberty, or property without the decision of a court of law.
Sixth	Guarantees the right to a trial by a jury and a lawyer in criminal cases.
Seventh	Guarantees the right to a trial by a jury in most civil cases.
Eighth	Prohibits very high bail, fines, and extreme punishments.
Ninth	Declares that the rights of the people are not limited to those in the Constitution.
Tenth	States that powers not granted to the federal government are left to the states or to the people.

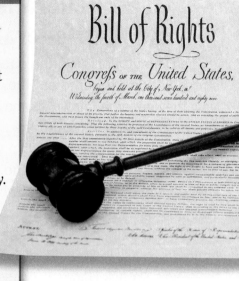

▶ **The first 10 amendments to the Constitution are known as the Bill of Rights.**

CHART SKILL *What does the Ninth Amendment state?*

The Bill of Rights

A few states ratified the Constitution quickly. Delaware was the first, on December 7, 1787. Pennsylvania was the second state to ratify the Constitution, thanks in part to the efforts of **Benjamin Rush.** Rush was a prominent doctor and writer who had signed the Declaration of Independence. He wrote articles in Philadelphia newspapers urging Pennsylvania to accept the new Constitution. By January 1788, five of the necessary nine states had ratified the Constitution.

In Massachusetts, the Constitution's lack of a bill of rights helped Antifederalists. But the Federalists pledged that Congress would add a Bill of Rights to the Constitution. An addition, or change, to the constitution is called an **amendment** . The Bill of Rights amendments would guarantee freedoms by placing specific limits on government. Because of the Federalists' pledge, in February 1788, a constitutional convention in Massachusetts voted for ratification.

This pledge of a Bill of Rights won over other states as well. In June 1788, New Hampshire became the ninth state to ratify the Constitution. Congress set March 4, 1789, as the date for the new government to begin work. By 1790, all 13 states had accepted the Constitution as the supreme law of the land.

When the first Congress under the Constitution met, one of its first acts was to pass the 10 amendments that would come to be called the **Bill of Rights.** The chart on this page summarizes the Bill of Rights. You can find the entire text of the Constitution and its amendments on pages R30–R60.

REVIEW Why was the Bill of Rights added to the Constitution? **Main Idea and Details**

A New Government

It had been about five years since the nationalists began pushing for a stronger central government. Now at last, the Constitution provided a framework for that government. George Washington called the Constitution "that precious depository [safe place] of American happiness."

Benjamin Franklin knew that the battle to create a fair and strong government was not over. According to Maryland delegate James McHenry, Franklin was approached at the end of the Convention and asked what type of government the country had. He replied,

"A republic, if you can keep it."

The American people would have much work ahead of them to keep the republic strong.

REVIEW What do you think Washington meant when he called the Constitution "that precious depository of American happiness? ⏱ **Draw Conclusions**

Summarize the Lesson

1787 Delaware was the first state to ratify the Constitution.

1788 The Constitution was ratified.

1791 The Bill of Rights was ratified.

LESSON 3 REVIEW

Check Facts and Main Ideas

1. ⏱ **Draw Conclusions** On a separate sheet of paper, fill in the diagram with two more facts that support the conclusion.

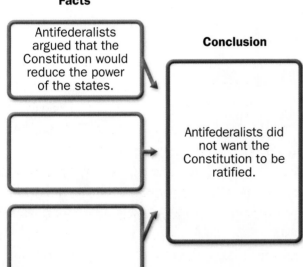

Facts

Antifederalists argued that the Constitution would reduce the power of the states.

Conclusion

Antifederalists did not want the Constitution to be ratified.

2. Who were the **Federalists?** The **Antifederalists?**

3. What was *The Federalists?*

4. Why is the **Bill of Rights** so important in American government?

5. **Critical Thinking:** *Express Ideas* Why do you think the Constitution is called a "living document"?

Link to 🔗 Art

Create a Poster Using photographs cut out of newspapers or magazines, illustrate several of the first 10 amendments— the Bill of Rights—to the Constitution. Paste or tape the photographs on posterboard to make a poster. Label each photograph, telling which amendment it represents. Give your poster a title.

Research and Writing Skills

Gather and Report Information

What? To write a report, you will often have to find information beyond what is available in your textbook. Where can you find facts on topics you want to learn more about? The library and the Internet hold a vast amount of resources that provide information on almost any topic. But gathering a lot of information does not guarantee a good report. You must also know how to organize your report, including the most important information, and how to write it clearly.

Why? In the previous lesson, you learned that the Federalists worked for the ratification of the Constitution and the Antifederalists worked against it. Suppose you want to gather more information on the Federalists to write a report. First, you have to collect facts about the key Federalists and what they did to encourage the ratification of the Constitution. You can use various reference sources, such as their own writings, encyclopedias, nonfiction books, and the Internet. Then you need to organize the information, and finally, write the report.

Federalists
I. What they believed

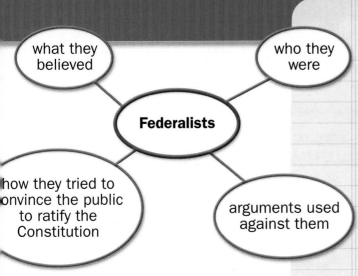

Federalists

I. **What they believed**
   A. A strong central government was needed in the United States.
   B. The Constitution provided a good plan for this type of government.

How? Before you begin your research, you should ask yourself: What do I want to know about the Federalists? You can use a graphic organizer like the one shown above to help you organize your thoughts. Notice how the subject of the report is in the middle and the branches are key subtopics. As you begin your research, you will be able to add branches to the subtopics that give more specific information on the subtopics. This will help you organize your report later on.

Once you have created a basic graphic organizer, you can begin your research. In the library, you will find the writings of many of the Federalists as well as encyclopedias that have information on almost any subject. These sources are organized alphabetically by topic. To find information on the Federalists, you might look up Federalists, the Constitution, or United States history. You can use the library's catalogue to find nonfiction books on the Federalists. A historical atlas, which contains maps and information about the past, might be a helpful resource as well. The Internet contains online encyclopedias and many Web

sites with historical information. Remember to write down your sources for each piece of information you find.

Once you have gathered information on your topic and subtopics, it is time to organize and write the report. You can use your graphic organizer to help you make an outline for your report. Make sure you place your information in the correct order. Then write a rough draft. Read your rough draft to check for errors in spelling and grammar. Check to make sure you have expressed your ideas clearly. Have a classmate or teacher read your rough draft as well. Finally, write or type the final version of your report.

Think and Apply

1. Write the steps for gathering and reporting information in order.

2. What subjects might you look up in an encyclopedia if you needed to write a report on the Bill of Rights?

3. Why is it important to write a rough draft?

CHAPTER 10
REVIEW

1780

1781
Articles of
Confederation
ratified by states

Chapter Summary

 Draw Conclusions

On a separate sheet of paper, fill in the diagram to supply three facts upon which the given conclusion could be based.

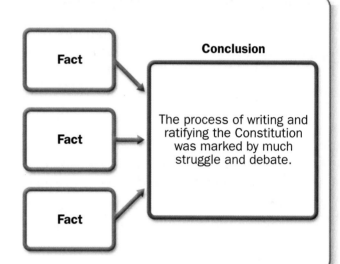

Fact	
Fact	**Conclusion**
Fact	The process of writing and ratifying the Constitution was marked by much struggle and debate.

Vocabulary

Write a sentence that explains the meaning of each vocabulary word. You may use two or more vocabulary words in a sentence.

1 **ratify** (p. 339)

2 **amendment** (p. 354)

3 **delegate** (p. 345)

4 **New Jersey Plan** (p. 346)

5 **reserved powers** (p. 348)

6 **checks and balances** (p. 348)

7 **Antifederalists** (p. 353)

8 **Bill of Rights** (p. 354)

People and Places

Fill in the blanks with the person or place that best completes the sentence.

1 _____ organized Massachusetts farmers in a rebellion against the state's government. (p. 341)

2 The Constitutional Convention took place in _____. (p. 345)

3 A record of the debates at the Constitutional Convention was kept by _____. (p. 345)

4 One contributor to *The Federalist* papers was _____ of New York. (p. 353)

5 In 1787, Congress decided how areas in the _____ could become states. (p. 342)

1786
Shays' Rebellion
begins

1787
Constitutional
Convention begins

1788
Constitution is
ratified

1791
Bill of Rights
is ratified

Facts and Main Ideas

1. According to the Northwest Ordinance of 1787, how could a territory become a state?

2. Explain the purpose of each branch of government set up by the Constitution.

3. What rights does the First Amendment guarantee?

4. **Time Line** How many years were there between the Constitutional Convention and the ratification of the Constitution?

5. **Main Idea** Why was the national government so weak under the Articles of Confederation?

6. **Main Idea** Why was compromise important to the making of the Constitution? Give an example to support your answer.

7. **Main Idea** What two important things did the Federalists do to help get the Constitution passed in the states?

8. **Critical Thinking:** *Compare and Contrast* Compare and contrast the government set up by the Articles of Confederation and the government set up by the Constitution.

Apply Skills

Gather and Report Information

Use the graphic organizer below and the information on pages 356–357 to answer the questions below.

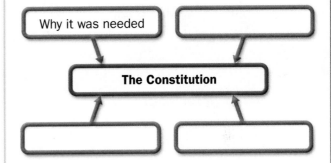

1. What steps would you follow to gather information for a report on the Constitution?

2. Complete the graphic organizer above with three more subtopics on the Constitution.

3. Using what you learned in Chapter 10, begin writing an outline using two of the subtopics from the Constitution graphic organizer.

Write About History

1. **Write a pamphlet** as Daniel Shays, explaining the issues that farmers have about actions of the Massachusetts government. Use words and slogans to attract the legislature's attention.

2. **Write an editorial** for a newspaper explaining why you think states should or should not ratify the Constitution.

3. **Write a biography** on Alexander Hamilton. Use information from the text and from library resources to write a one-page biography. Include an illustration or photograph in your biography.

Internet Activity

To get help with vocabulary, people, and terms, select dictionary or encyclopedia from *Social Studies Library* at **www.sfsocialstudies.com.**

The Young United States

1800

Washington, D.C.
The federal government moves to the new capital city.

Lesson 1

1

1805

Near Present-Day Astoria, Oregon
Lewis and Clark reach the Pacific Ocean in their exploration of the West.

Lesson 2

2

1814

Baltimore, Maryland
Francis Scott Key writes The "Star-Spangled Banner" while watching the battle at Fort McHenry.

Lesson 3

3

Astoria

NORTH

AMERICA

Baltimore

Washington, D.C.

UNITED STATES

ATLANTIC
OCEAN

PACIFIC OCEAN

Gulf of Mexico

Why We Remember

"...our flag was still there..."

As Francis Scott Key wrote down these words, which would become part of our national anthem, the United States was facing a serious threat. The year was 1814. British troops had invaded the nation's capital, burning the President's House and the Capitol Building. Key must have been wondering that day if the young republic could survive. But it did. In its early years the country faced many challenges. But after each, its flag was still waving. The young country was establishing itself as a strong nation filled with expanding opportunity.

1785   1800

1789
George Washington is elected first President of the United States

1796
John Adams is elected second President of the United States

1800
Federal government moves to Washington, D.C.

PREVIEW

Focus on the Main Idea
George Washington became the nation's first President and organized the new government.

PLACES
New York City, New York
Washington, D.C.

PEOPLE
Pierre L'Enfant
Benjamin Banneker
Abigail Adams

VOCABULARY
electoral college
inauguration
Cabinet
political party

▶ This button was made in honor of George Washington becoming the first President of the United States. His swearing in was originally scheduled for "March the Fourth," as shown on the button.

Washington as President

You Are There It has been the most exciting time in your young life. You are part of the group accompanying George Washington on a 235-mile journey from Mount Vernon, his plantation in Virginia, to New York City, the nation's temporary capital. There, he is going to be sworn in as the first President of the United States.

All along the way, Americans pour out of their homes to cheer him. In Philadelphia, crowds pack the streets. Church bells ring. Fireworks streak across the sky.

Then, after you reach the New Jersey shore of the Hudson River, a satin-trimmed barge carries Washington on the final part of the trip. Colorfully decorated boats come out to welcome him. And the entire New York shoreline is packed with people. You can't wait to tell your friends back home all you have seen.

Draw Conclusions As you read, see what conclusions you can draw about why George Washington was popular with the American people.

President Washington Takes Office

George Washington had said that he did not want to become President. At 56, he thought he was too old, and his health was not good. But Thomas Jefferson and Alexander Hamilton finally changed his mind. Hamilton convinced Washington that he was "indispensable"—absolutely needed—for the process of setting up the new government.

On February 4, 1789, Washington was elected President by the electoral college. The **electoral college** is made up of people chosen by each state who vote for President and Vice-President. The number of electors from each state equals the number of its senators plus the number of its representatives to the House of Representatives.

The vote for Washington was unanimous. In other words, all the members of the electoral college voted for him. No President since Washington has been elected unani-

▶ **George Washington placed his hand on a Bible when he was inaugurated as President.**

mously. He was later described by one of his generals as "First in war, first in peace, and first in the hearts of his countrymen." John Adams, a signer of the Declaration of Independence, was elected Vice-President.

April 30 was the date set for Washington's inauguration. An **inauguration** is the ceremony in which a newly elected President swears loyalty to the Constitution and takes office. At about noon, Washington stepped out on the balcony of the Federal Hall in **New York City, New York.** As the crowd below watched, he placed one hand on a Bible and raised his other hand in the air to take his oath as President of the United States. A cheer went up from the crowd: "Long live George Washington, President of the United States!"

Washington began dividing the work of the Executive Branch into different departments and choosing people to head them. Conducting foreign affairs, or relationships with other countries, became the job of the Department of State. Washington appointed Thomas Jefferson to become Secretary of State, the head of the Department of State. The Department of the Treasury would handle money matters. Alexander Hamilton was named its Secretary.

The heads of these and other departments became part of the President's **Cabinet.** Their job was to advise the President and help him to govern. The Constitution did not set up the Cabinet and its departments. That was Washington's idea. Washington made his decisions with great care. He was deeply aware that his actions would set examples for future leaders.

REVIEW Why did Washington's general say that Washington was first in war *and* peace?
🔄 Draw Conclusions

George Washington *Henry Knox* *Alexander Hamilton* *Thomas Jefferson* *Edmund Randolph*

▶ **President Washing[ton] chose well-known leaders to serve in his Cabinet.**

Lithograph by Currier and Ives

Political Parties Are Born

Major decisions faced the new government, and key officials had very different ideas on how to make them. On one side stood Alexander Hamilton, the secretary of the treasury. His belief in a strong national government had not weakened. He believed that this strong government should be active in encouraging the growth of cities, trade, and factories. On the other side stood Thomas Jefferson, the secretary of state. He did not believe in a strong national government. He wanted the nation to remain a land of small farmers and skilled crafts workers. He believed that such a country would not need the strong government that Hamilton wanted.

Time and again, the two clashed in Cabinet meetings. When Hamilton announced plans to set up a national bank, Jefferson objected. He argued that the Constitution did not give the national government that power.

Hamilton and Jefferson each had a large following among Americans. Eventually, the two sides organized themselves into two political parties. A **political party** is an organized group of people who share a view of what government should be and do. The political parties work to elect their members to government offices.

Hamilton's party continued under the name of Federalists. Federalists were generally in favor of a strong, active federal government. Jefferson's party came to be known as the Democratic-Republicans. This political party favored a weaker, less active federal government.

In 1796, in his Farewell Address as President, Washington warned against "the baneful [destructive] effects of the spirit of party." You can read more about the beginning of political parties in Issues and Viewpoints on pages 368–369.

REVIEW How would you compare and contrast Hamilton's and Jefferson's ideas of government? **Compare and Contrast**

A New City

For 10 years, Congress had argued about a permanent site for the nation's capital. In 1790, a decision settled the matter.

The District of Columbia was selected as the nation's capital. It was a 10-square-mile area along the Potomac River not far from Washington's Virginia home. After Washington's death in 1799, it was renamed **Washington, D.C.** The D.C. stands for District of Columbia.

To design the city, Washington chose **Pierre L'Enfant** (lahn FAHNT), a French artist and engineer who had come to fight in the Revolution. An astronomer was needed to use latitude and longitude to survey the land. **Benjamin Banneker,** an inventor, mathematician, as well as astronomer, and the son of a freed slave, was asked to help with this task. You can read more about Banneker on page 367. The Map Adventure below gives you a chance to investigate the work of L'Enfant and Banneker.

REVIEW Why was an astronomer needed to help build the new capital city? **Summarize**

Map Adventure

Designing Washington, D.C.

You are looking at a present-day map of Washington, D.C. Can you identify the location of some of the capital city's major landmarks?

1. L'Enfant wanted the Capitol Building, where Congress meets, to go on a hill. Broad diagonal streets fan out from it. It faces toward the west. What letter marks this site?

2. They wanted to place a 12,000-foot-long grassy area in front of the Capitol Building. It is now called the Mall. What letter marks this site?

3. They placed the President's House, now known as the White House, at the end of a street that runs northwest from the Capitol. This street is now known as Pennsylvania Avenue. What letter marks the White House?

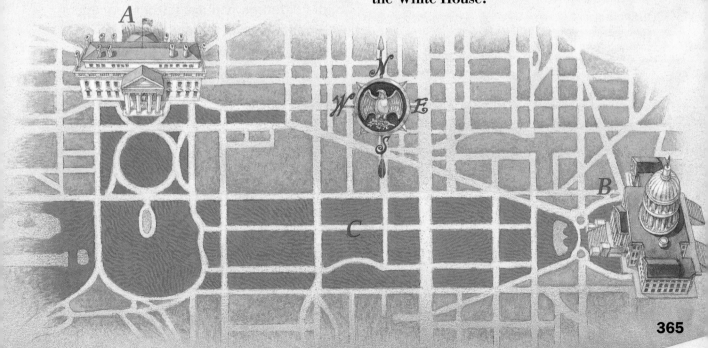

Living in the President's House

In 1800, when John Adams was President, the federal government moved to Washington, D.C., but few of its buildings were finished and its few streets were muddy paths. Congress met there for the first time in November. Its members had to crowd into the limited housing available. President John Adams, who had become the second President of the United States in 1796, and his wife Abigail moved into the President's House. Later, the building would be called the White House. The President's House was so new that the plaster on

Painting by Gilbert Stuart

▶ **Abigail Adams was the first "first lady" to live in the White House.**

its walls was still wet. **Abigail Adams** described it in a letter to a friend:

> *"There is not a single apartment [room] in it finished...We have not the least fence, yard, or other convenience."*

Even worse, the house was built in what was then a marshy area full of mosquitoes.

REVIEW What can you conclude about conditions in and around the President's House when John and Abigail Adams moved into it? ⟳ **Draw Conclusions**

Summarize the Lesson

1789 George Washington became the first President and organized the Executive Branch around a Cabinet.

1796 John Adams was elected second President of the United States.

1800 The federal government moved to Washington, D.C.

LESSON 1 ▶ REVIEW

Check Facts and Main Ideas

1. ⟳ **Draw Conclusions** On a separate sheet of paper, fill in the missing facts.

Facts

Conclusion

> George Washington was extremely popular with the American people.

2. Explain Washington's purpose in naming people to his **Cabinet.**

3. **Critical Thinking:** *Draw Conclusions* Why did different **political parties** emerge in American government?

4. Who were the leaders of the Federalist and Democratic-Republican parties?

5. Why was Benjamin Banneker asked to help design the new capital?

Link to 🔗 Geography

Draw a Map Look back at the map of Washington, D.C., on page 365. How might you have laid out the area differently from L'Enfant? Draw a map showing how you might have designed the nation's capital.

Benjamin Banneker

1731–1806

When Benjamin Banneker was about 21, he saw a pocket watch that belonged to a man named Josef Levi. Banneker was fascinated by the watch. Levi gave it to him, and Banneker took it apart to see how it worked. He studied the pieces and used them as a model to create a clock made entirely out of wood.

Years later Banneker's attention to detail helped save the plan for the nation's new capital city. In 1790, Banneker was placed on the surveying team for the capital at Thomas Jefferson's request. When Pierre L'Enfant, the head designer, suddenly quit, he took the city plans with him. Banneker was able to re-create the work from memory in a few days, saving the project from a serious setback.

Banneker made use of his growing fame to speak out against slavery. Although Banneker grew up free on his family's farm in Maryland, his father had been a slave and he knew the effects of slavery. When Banneker completed his first book, he sent it to Secretary of State Thomas Jefferson and included a note asking Jefferson to help improve the treatment of African Americans. He wrote:

BIOFACT

Banneker's clock was recognized as the first to be made in colonial America and was said to strike every hour for over 40 years.

"However variable [different] we may be in society or religion, however diversified in situation or color, we are all in the same family and stand in the same relation to [God]."

Learn from Biographies

In what ways did Banneker's desire to understand the world around him influence his own life and that of others?

For more information, go online to *Meet the People* at **www.sfsocialstudies.com**.

367

Forming Political Parties

Different ideas about government continue to exist in the United States today, just as they did more than 200 years ago.

"… Mr. Jefferson is at the head of a faction [group] decidedly hostile [unfriendly] to me…" Alexander Hamilton wrote these words to a friend in May 1792. Hamilton and Thomas Jefferson were two of President George Washington's most valued advisors. Yet, they had very different views, and the groups that formed around them became the nation's first political parties.

Political parties formed when George Washington was President because people had different ideas about government. Alexander Hamilton and his followers became known as the "Federalists." They favored a strong national government. Thomas Jefferson and his followers became known as the "Democratic-Republicans." They opposed a strong national government.

President Washington wanted members of his government to work together. As you have read, in his Farewell Address, he warned against "the baneful [destructive] effects of the spirit of party."

> *"[The spirit of party] serves always to distract the public councils and enfeeble [weaken] the public administration. It agitates the community with ill-founded jealousies and false alarms; kindles [starts up] the animosity [dislike] of one part against another; foments [stirs up] occasionally riot and insurrection [revolt]."*
>
> —**George Washington**, *1796*

Yet Washington realized that parties reflected "the strongest passions of the human mind." After he left office, political parties became even stronger. Today, more than 200 years later, political parties continue to debate different visions of government.

► **George Washington (left) meets with two members of his Cabinet—Thomas Jefferson (center) and Alexander Hamilton (right).**

"It is true, there has been some agitation of spirits [disturbance] between existing parties; but doubtless the prudence [caution] of the inhabitants of the United States will suffer this to evaporate [cause this to go away]."

—**Mercy Otis Warren,**
1728–1814

"I do not admire the contentions [battles] of parties…tho' on my own… I am anxious to know all the maneuverings [plans] of both, the one and the other…."

—**Dolley Madison**
1768–1849

"Men…are naturally divided into two parties: 1. Those who fear and distrust the people, and wish to draw all powers from them into the hands of the higher classes. 2. Those who identify themselves with the people, [and] have confidence in them….

In every country these two parties exist.

—**Thomas Jefferson,**
1743–1826

Issues and You

In the late 1700s and early 1800s many people feared that political parties would destroy the new republic. Do you think that rivalry between political parties is good or bad for the United States? Write an argument either for or against political parties. Find examples from newspapers, magazines, or the Internet to support your position.

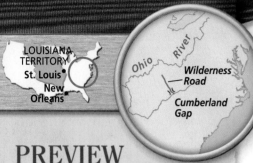

1800   1805

1800
Thomas Jefferson is elected third President of the United States

1803
Louisiana Purchase expands the size of the country

1804
Lewis and Clark set out to explore the Louisiana Territory

Jefferson Looks West

PREVIEW

Focus on the Main Idea
The new nation doubled its size and expanded settlement westward.

PLACES
Wilderness Road
Cumberland Gap
Mississippi River
New Orleans
Louisiana Territory
St. Louis, Missouri
Missouri River

PEOPLE
Daniel Boone
James Monroe
Meriwether Lewis
William Clark
York
Sacagawea

VOCABULARY
pioneer
frontier
Louisiana Purchase

The Presidential election campaign of 1800 is in full swing. It is a bitter and nasty campaign. The Democratic-Republicans and their candidate, Thomas Jefferson, hurl charge after charge at the Federalists and their candidate, President John Adams. The Federalists hurl charges right back. You don't know which charges to believe.

The Federalists are the party of the rich, say the Democratic-Republicans. *Federalist officials have put banks first and the people second.*

The Federalists reply, *The Democratic-Republicans are troublemakers. They are trying to turn the nation's citizens against one another.*

Which side is right? Americans are going to cast votes soon. They have a lot to think about before they do.

Summarize As you read, note ideas that will help you summarize how federal government actions helped the new nation grow and develop.

Jefferson Wins Election of 1800

On the morning of March 4, 1801, Thomas Jefferson left his rooming house and walked up the hill to the Capitol Building, to be inaugurated as the third President of the United States. He had won a bitter election. However, he hoped that he and those who had opposed him could work together. In his inaugural speech, he said, "Every difference of opinion is not a difference of principle….We are all Republicans, we are all Federalists."

The new President had a wide range of interests and talents. He was a good writer, as the Declaration of Independence shows. He was a skilled violinist, a lifelong student of nature and science, and a talented architect. Among the buildings he designed was his own beautiful house called Monticello.

▶ Today visitors can tour Monticello to see how Jefferson lived. A man of many interests, he used a machine *(top right)* to write a letter and make a copy at the same time, and a tool *(bottom right)* for surveying.

As President, Jefferson wanted to "give government back to the people." He believed that the only way to guarantee the liberties of all citizens was to keep power in their hands. He got Congress to lower taxes it had passed under the Federalists. He reduced the size of the government and of the armed forces. "I am not among those that fear the people," he said. "They, and not the rich, are our dependence for continued freedom."

After Jefferson left office, he summed up his philosophy of government:

> *"The care of human life and happiness, not their destruction, is the first and only legitimate [true] object of good government."*

REVIEW According to Jefferson, who should have the power of government?
🔁 Draw Conclusions

Lewis and Clark

Long before the Louisiana Purchase, Thomas Jefferson had been fascinated by lands in the West. Who lived there, he wondered? What was the land like? Could the Missouri River possibly lead to a water route to the Pacific Ocean? Jefferson wanted to know the answers to these questions.

To find the answers, Jefferson sent an expedition to the newly acquired land, now called the **Louisiana Territory.** Jefferson chose **Meriwether Lewis,** who was an army captain, to lead the expedition. Lewis chose a fellow army captain, his friend **William Clark,** to share command.

Jefferson told the two captains they had three goals. One was to search for a water route to the Pacific Ocean. The second was to establish relationships with the Native Americans they met. Jefferson wanted the Indians to know his "wish to be neighborly, friendly, and useful to them." The third goal was to pay close attention to "the soil and face of the country," to its plants, animals, minerals, climate, and to keep careful, written records of their findings. Today, the journals of Lewis and Clark are the main source of information about their expedition.

In May 1804, Lewis and Clark and other members of the expedition set out westward from **St. Louis, Missouri,** along the **Missouri River.** Follow their route on the map on the next page. The expedition included soldiers, river boatmen, hunters, and **York,** Clark's slave and childhood friend. During the expedition, York worked at Clark's side much of the time, and had shown he was ready to sacrifice his life to save Clark's. Nevertheless, when York later asked to be freed as a reward for his contributions to the expedition, Clark refused.

Three boats carried expedition members, equipment, and supplies. They did not know it then, but they would not return for another 28 months.

During their first winter, they hired a French Canadian fur trapper and his Shoshone wife, **Sacagawea** (sah KAH gah way ah), to act as

Literature and Social Studies

In his journal, Captain Meriwether Lewis wrote the following account of a sandstorm.

April 24th, 1805
The wind blew so hard during the whole of this day, that we were unable to move.... Sore eyes is a common complaint among the [people]. I believe it [comes] from the immense quantities of sand which is driven by the wind from the sandbars of the river in such clouds that you are unable to discover the opposite bank of the river...."

▶ **Sacagawea was a guide for Lewis and Clark.**

The Louisiana Purchase

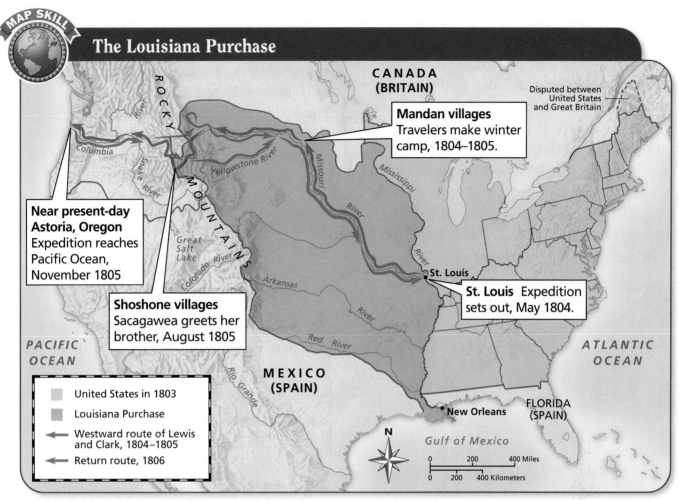

CANADA (BRITAIN)

Disputed between United States and Great Britain

Mandan villages
Travelers make winter camp, 1804–1805.

Near present-day Astoria, Oregon
Expedition reaches Pacific Ocean, November 1805

Shoshone villages
Sacagawea greets her brother, August 1805

St. Louis Expedition sets out, May 1804.

St. Louis

PACIFIC OCEAN

ATLANTIC OCEAN

MEXICO (SPAIN)

FLORIDA (SPAIN)

New Orleans

Legend:
- United States in 1803
- Louisiana Purchase
- Westward route of Lewis and Clark, 1804–1805
- Return route, 1806

N

Gulf of Mexico

0   200   400 Miles
0   200   400 Kilometers

▶ The Lewis and Clark Expedition explored the Louisiana Territory and traveled on to the Pacific Ocean.

MAP SKILL Use Map Scale *About how many miles did the expedition travel from the Shoshone villages to the Pacific Ocean?*

interpreters and guides. Sacagawea helped Lewis and Clark establish good relations with Native Americans along the way. She helped translate Indian languages for the expedition. The baby she carried on her back signaled the peaceful purposes of the expedition.

Throughout the expedition, its members faced many hardships. They had to paddle their boats against strong river currents. Every now and then, a boat would turn over, sending equipment splashing into the water. And there was always the danger of being attacked by dangerous animals, like 900-pound grizzly bears.

But Lewis and Clark were rewarded with some fabulous views. They saw a herd of 20,000 bison stretching across the plain and fast deerlike animals called pronghorns racing by. They crossed the tall, spectacular Rocky Mountains. Finally their eyes were filled with the sight of the great Pacific Ocean—"Ocean in view! O! the joy!" wrote Clark.

The explorers finally returned to St. Louis in September 1806. They had not found a water route to the Pacific. But they had recorded and described thousands of varieties of plants and animals, and even brought some back for Jefferson to examine. They had also mapped a vast area, opening it to future exploration and new settlers from the United States.

REVIEW Compare what the people of the United States knew about the Louisiana Territory before and after the Lewis and Clark Expedition. **Compare and Contrast**

A Growing Nation

From the time that Daniel Boone started marking the Wilderness Road to the end of Jefferson's second term as President in 1809, the American population almost tripled. It grew from about two and a half million to about seven million. New states joined the Union. Vermont became the fourteenth state in 1791. Kentucky, whose settlement had been led by Daniel Boone, followed in 1792. Then came Tennessee, in 1796.

Some states carved out of the Northwest Territory—Ohio, Indiana, and Illinois—would soon follow. So would the southern states of Louisiana, Mississippi, and Alabama. The nation was on the move, with pioneers venturing even beyond the Mississippi River. As the frontier moved farther west, new states continued to join the nation.

REVIEW What details can you supply to support the main idea that the nation was expanding to the west? **Main Idea and Details**

Summarize the Lesson

1800 Thomas Jefferson became the third President of the United States.

1803 The Louisiana Purchase doubled the size of the country.

1804 Lewis and Clark set out to explore the Louisiana Territory.

▶ **Pioneers began moving into the Northwest Territory in the late 1700s.**

LESSON 2 REVIEW

Check Facts and Main Ideas

1. **Summarize** On a separate sheet of paper, fill in the events that are summarized.

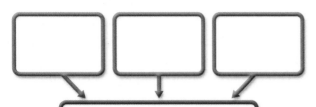

These events opened up new lands, allowing the United States to expand.

2. In your own words, summarize Jefferson's ideas about government.

3. How did Daniel Boone help the pioneers move westward?

4. **Critical Thinking: Evaluate** Was the Louisiana Purchase a good deal for the United States? Explain your answer.

5. In what ways did the Lewis and Clark Expedition fulfill its mission?

Link to ⚬⚬ Mathematics

Calculate a Price You read that the Louisiana Territory covered 828,000 square miles and that the United States paid $15 million for it. Calculate the price per square mile.

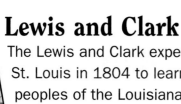

Lewis and Clark

The Lewis and Clark expedition set out from St. Louis in 1804 to learn about the lands and peoples of the Louisiana Territory. Meriwether Lewis organized the expedition and chose William Clark to help lead it. Clark was responsible for mapping the landforms and bodies of water.

Detailed Diary
Lewis and Clark kept careful notes in the journal above of everything they saw.

Buffalo Robe
This robe, collected by Lewis and Clark during their expedition, is painted with a scene of Mandan and Minnetaree Native Americans fighting the Sioux and Arikara.

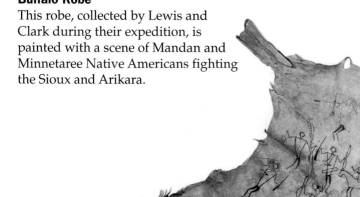

Where the Buffalo Roam
Early explorers of North America were amazed to see millions of buffalo roaming the plains. This painting is by John Audubon.

Measuring Tape
Surveyors in the 1800s used linen measuring tapes like this one, which was stored in a leather case.

Compare Population Density Maps

What? Distribution Maps show the pattern of how things such as population and natural resources are spread out over an area. One type of map that shows the distribution of population is called a **population density map.** An area where a lot of people live is densely populated. If the area has few people living in it, it is lightly populated.

Why? In Lesson 2 you learned about the westward movement of people from the original 13 states after the Revolution. Later, more and more people continued moving west. Comparing population density maps from different time periods can show how population in an area has changed.

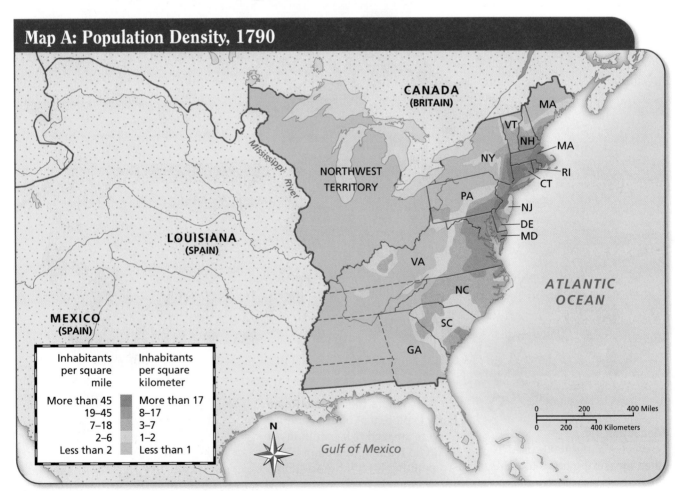

Map A: Population Density, 1790

Inhabitants per square mile	Inhabitants per square kilometer
More than 45	More than 17
19–45	8–17
7–18	3–7
2–6	1–2
Less than 2	Less than 1

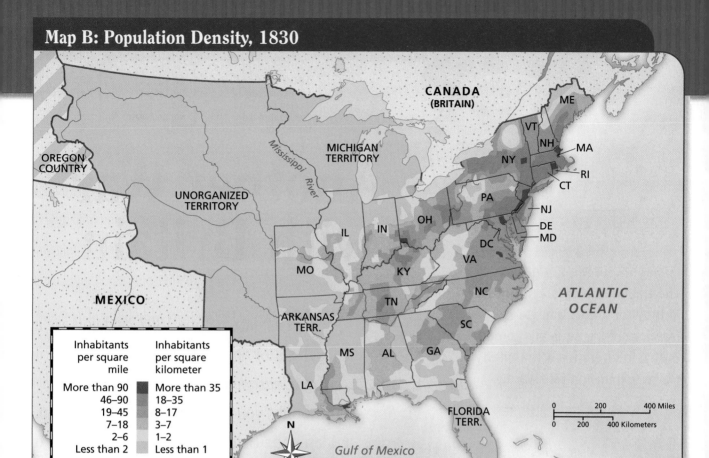

Map B: Population Density, 1830

CANADA (BRITAIN)

ME

VT

NH

MA

NY

RI

CT

PA

NJ

DE

MD

OREGON COUNTRY

MICHIGAN TERRITORY

Mississippi River

UNORGANIZED TERRITORY

IL

IN

OH

DC

VA

MO

KY

NC

ATLANTIC OCEAN

MEXICO

ARKANSAS TERR.

TN

SC

MS

AL

GA

LA

FLORIDA TERR.

Gulf of Mexico

N

Inhabitants per square mile	Inhabitants per square kilometer
More than 90	More than 35
46–90	18–35
19–45	8–17
7–18	3–7
2–6	1–2
Less than 2	Less than 1

0   200   400 Miles
0   200   400 Kilometers

How? Map A shows the population density of the United States in 1790, based on the nation's first census. The census did not count Native Americans, so these maps do not show Native American population density. Each color on the map represents a number of people living in one square mile. To understand a square mile, picture a large square drawn on land in which each side measures one mile. According to Map A, the most densely populated areas are those in which more than 45 people lived within one square mile of land. What color represents these areas on the map? Notice that the population is most dense along the coast in the 13 original states. Few Americans lived outside these areas in 1790.

Map B shows United States population density in 1830. You can see that areas such as Kentucky had become more populated by

this time, about 50 years after Daniel Boone settled there. Lands that were part of the Louisiana Purchase, such as Missouri and Louisiana, were becoming more populated as well.

Think and Apply

1. What is a **distribution map?** What is a **population density map?**

2. How did the population of Virginia change from 1790 to 1830?

3. Which part of the Mississippi was most densely populated in 1830? Why was this area densely populated?

Internet Activity

For more information, go online to the *Atlas* at **www.sfsocialstudies.com**.

379

1808
James Madison is
elected the fourth
President of the
United States

1812
The United
States declares
war on Britain

1815
The War of
1812 ends

Another War with Britain

PREVIEW

Focus on the Main Idea
The United States fought Britain
in the War of 1812 to gain
freedom of the seas and to end
British interference with United
States expansion westward.

PLACES
Baltimore, Maryland
Fort McHenry
New Orleans, Louisiana

PEOPLE
Tecumseh
James Madison
Henry Clay
Oliver Hazard Perry
Francis Scott Key
Dolley Madison
Andrew Jackson

VOCABULARY
neutral
Battle of Tippecanoe
War Hawks
War of 1812
national anthem
Battle of New Orleans

You Are There

The date is June 1807, and you are a
sailor aboard the American Navy ship
Chesapeake. When you sailed from
Virginia, you thought you were on a peaceful mission.
But now suddenly the British frigate *Leopard* looms up
and its crew demands to board your ship. "We're looking
for deserters from the British Navy," the British captain
shouts.

Your captain refuses to let the British board the
Chesapeake. The British respond with thundering cannon fire, killing three of your fellow sailors. To avoid
further bloodshed, your captain allows the British to
board. The British sailors pick out four of your crew,
claim they are British deserters, and take them aboard
the *Leopard*.

You don't know it at the time, but you have been part
of an event that will help push the United States
back into war with Britain.

Cause and Effect As you read, identify the
causes and effects of major events described
in the lesson.

Moving Toward War

In the early 1800s, events like the one you just read about happened again and again to ships of the United States. American ships were stopped not only by the British, but also by the French. During that time, Britain and France were at war. Neither country wanted the other to receive any supplies from the United States. So both interfered with United States shipping.

The actions by the British particularly angered the United States. The British often seized United States' sailors, claiming they were deserters from the British Navy. The British forced these sailors to work on British ships. Often, the men they seized were not British deserters at all but citizens of the United States. In addition, the British seized the cargoes, or goods, carried by the ships. Because of these actions by the British, trade between the United States and countries across the seas had nearly stopped by 1808.

This situation caused great tension between the United States and Britain. But President Jefferson did not want the United States to take the side of either the French or the British in their war. He wanted the nation to remain **neutral,** or to not take sides. "Peace is our passion," he wrote.

In the Northwest Territory, there was another major source of tension with the British. The Shawnee leader **Tecumseh** (tih KUHM suh) was uniting Native Americans to resist pioneer settlement. Speaking of the tribes that had once lived in the territory, he said: "They have vanished before the [greed] and oppression of the white man as snow before a summer sun." The United States suspected, correctly, that the British were supporting Tecumseh.

In 1811, United States forces and Tecumseh's soldiers fought each other in what is now Indiana. Known as the **Battle of Tippecanoe** (tip ee kuh NEW), this fight was seen as a victory for the United States. This weakened Tecumseh's standing among the Native Americans, who had expected a great victory. You will read more about Tecumseh on page 385.

REVIEW What can you conclude about Britain's attitude toward the United States during the early 1800s?  Draw Conclusions

▶ Although neither side won the Battle of Tippecanoe, it was seen as a United States victory.

▶ **The USS *Constitution*, also called "Old Ironsides," defeated the British *Guerrière*.**

The War of 1812

In 1809, James Madison became President. Like Jefferson, he wanted to keep the nation out of war with Britain. But British actions on the seas caused a wave of anger to sweep the country. In Congress, a group called the War Hawks pressed for war against Britain. These members of Congress protested Britain's attacks on American shipping. One of their leaders, Henry Clay of Kentucky, said that the United States had to go to war or "you had better abandon the ocean."

The War Hawks also wanted war for other reasons. First, they hoped to end British-supported attacks against settlers on the Northwestern frontier. Second, they wanted to drive the British out of Canada. Finally, in June 1812, President Madison asked Congress to declare war on Britain.

The War of 1812 is remembered for dramatic battles at sea. In the waters of the Atlantic Ocean east of Canada, the American warship *Constitution* defeated the British war-

ship *Guerrière* (gair YAIR). British cannonballs just seemed to bounce off the *Constitution*. "Her sides are made of iron!" shouted an American sailor. Actually, the sides of the *Constitution* were built of oak. Today, you can visit that ship, nicknamed "Old Ironsides," in Boston harbor. It is still part of the United States Navy and is the navy's oldest ship.

In 1813, the *Chesapeake*, which you read about in "You Are There," battled the British ship *Shannon* off Boston harbor. The *Chesapeake's* captain, James Lawrence, was badly wounded. His last words were, "Don't give up the ship!" Unfortunately, his crew had to give up. But his words became the navy's rallying cry.

That same year, Americans fought another famous naval battle, this time in the Great Lakes, on Lake Erie. For more than three hours, a United States fleet commanded by Oliver Hazard Perry fought a British fleet in one of the war's fiercest battles. After winning the battle, Perry sent the following

North Wind Picture Archives

message: "We have met the enemy and they are ours."

Probably the lowest point for the United States in the war came in August 1814. A British force marched into Washington, D.C. and took control of the city. President Madison and other government officials barely got out in time. Important historical documents, like the Declaration of Independence, were hastily bundled up and carried off to safety. British troops set fire to the Capitol. They also broke into the President's House, which they burned.

The same British force then moved on to invade **Baltimore, Maryland.** But this time United States defenders were better prepared. **Fort McHenry,** defended by 1,000 United States troops, stood in the harbor. The British fleet had to sail past its guns to reach Baltimore. On the morning of September 13, 1814, the British ships began bombarding the fort with cannon fire.

A young Washington lawyer, **Francis Scott Key,** watched as the bombardment continued into the night. He wondered how long the fort could hold out. As dawn broke on September 14, he had his answer. The United States flag still flew over the fort!

The British invaders finally gave up their attempt to capture Baltimore. Key scribbled a few verses on the back of an envelope describing what he had seen. His poem was later set to music and became known as "The Star-Spangled Banner." In 1931, this became the official song of the United States, its **national anthem.** You can read its words and music on pages 388–389.

REVIEW How would you sequence the important events in the British invasion of the United States? *Sequence*

Dolley Madison Saves a Painting

As British forces neared Washington, D.C., *Dolley Madison,* wife of the President, was told she had to leave the President's House quickly. She refused, saying that she must first make sure that Gilbert Stuart's "precious portrait" of George Washington was removed to safety. But the painting's frame was firmly screwed to the wall. "I have ordered the frame to be broken," she later wrote, "and the canvas taken out" and brought to safety. Only then did Dolley Madison leave the President's House. Today, you can visit the White House and see that famous painting on a wall in the East Room.

383

Battle of New Orleans

Another British fighting force set its sights on the port city of New Orleans, Louisiana. There the American general Andrew Jackson waited with an army of Kentucky and Tennessee militiamen.

On January 8, 1815, the British marched through the morning mist to attack Jackson's men. Jackson's forces killed thousands of British soldiers. Said one Kentucky soldier, "The field, it looked…like a sea of blood."

The victory turned Jackson into a national hero. However, the Battle of New Orleans would not have happened if a certain bit of news had arrived in New Orleans before January 8, 1815. A treaty ending the war had been signed in Europe two weeks earlier. But by January 8, news of the treaty had not yet crossed the Atlantic.

The War of 1812 turned out to have fewer effects than those who fought it had expected. Since Britain and France had stopped fighting each other in 1814, they no longer interfered with United States ships. The United States never gained control of Canada. But the United States did show the world that it intended to defend itself at sea or on land.

REVIEW Identify a detail that supports the main idea that the War of 1812 had fewer effects than those who fought it expected. **Main Idea and Details**

Summarize the Lesson

- **1808** James Madison was elected the fourth President of the United States.
- **1812** The War of 1812 between the United States and Britain began.
- **1815** The War of 1812 ended.

LESSON 3   REVIEW

Check Facts and Main Ideas

1. **Cause and Effect** On a separate sheet of paper, fill in each missing cause or effect.

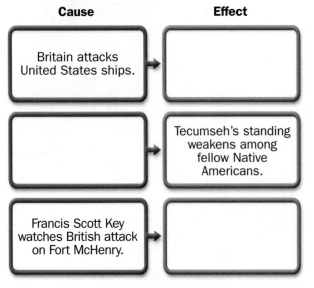

Cause	Effect
Britain attacks United States ships.	
	Tecumseh's standing weakens among fellow Native Americans.
Francis Scott Key watches British attack on Fort McHenry.	

2. In what ways did Britain interfere with American shipping on the high seas?

3. **Critical Thinking:** *Make Decisions* If you had been President, would you have gone to war with Britain in 1812? Use the decision-making steps on page H3 to explain why or why not.

4. What was produced during the battle of Fort McHenry other than a United States victory?

5. If known, what fact would have prevented the Battle of New Orleans?

Link to ⚭ Writing

Write a Song Suppose that you had witnessed a battle in the War of 1812. Write the words to a song about the battle as Francis Scott Key did after the battle of Fort McHenry.

Tecumseh 1768–1813

Tecumseh grew up during a time of struggle. The Shawnee people were beginning a long struggle to defend their land in the Ohio River valley from the new American settlers. Fierce battles took place all around the young boy, resulting in the deaths of many Shawnee, including Tecumseh's father. As an adult, Tecumseh would lead the Shawnee in their efforts to keep their land.

Tecumseh fought his first battle at the side of his older brother when he was only 14 years old. Tecumseh earned respect for his bravery and also came to be known as a powerful speaker. After some Native American leaders signed a treaty giving up some Indian lands in Ohio, Tecumseh explained to a United States governor why the land should be returned:

BIOFACT

British General Isaac Brock gave this compass to Tecumseh before the Battle of Detroit in the War of 1812.

"The white people have no right to take the land from the Indians, because they had it first; it is theirs."

The Native Americans did not get their land back, but Tecumseh did not get discouraged. He believed that all Indian groups needed to unite. He traveled for miles and miles, urging members of other groups to unite to protect Native American lands. His fiery speeches won over hundreds of followers.

Tecumseh decided to make his force an ally of the British army during the War of 1812. His soldiers helped the British win the Battle of Detroit. He was determined to keep fighting for the American Indians. In one powerful speech, Tecumseh said:

"Our lives are in the hands of the Great Spirit. We are determined to defend our lands, and if it is His will, we wish to leave our bones upon them."

Tecumseh's speech turned out to be a prediction of his own future. He was killed at the Battle of the Thames in 1813.

Learn from Biographies

How did Tecumseh use his ability to speak clearly and passionately to help him achieve his goals?

For more information, go online to *Meet the People* at **www.sfsocialstudies.com.**

CHAPTER 11
REVIEW

1789
George Washington
elected first President
of the United States

Chapter Summary

 Draw Conclusions

On a separate sheet of paper, fill in the three facts upon which the given conclusion could be based.

| Fact |
| Fact |
| Fact |

Conclusion

The War of 1812 did not affect the United States as the country had expected, but it did benefit the country in other ways.

Vocabulary

Fill in the blanks with the vocabulary word that best completes the sentence.

1. The _____ is chosen by the President to advise the President and help govern. (p. 363)

2. The _____ mistakenly took place after a treaty ending the War of 1812 had already been signed. (p. 384)

3. Thomas Jefferson chose James Monroe to help complete the _____ in 1803. (p. 373)

4. Tecumseh's soldiers fought the Americans in the _____. (p. 381)

5. Members of the _____ are chosen by people in each state to elect the President. (p. 363)

People and Places

Match each person or place with the correct description.

1. **New York City** (p. 363)

2. **Benjamin Banneker** (p. 365)

3. **William Clark** (p. 374)

4. **Cumberland Gap** (p. 372)

5. **Oliver Hazard Perry** (p. 382)

6. **Baltimore** (p. 383)

a. United States fleet commander

b. explored Louisiana Territory

c. temporary capital where George Washington was inaugurated

d. surveyed the site of the nation's new capital

e. British failed to capture this city in the War of 1812

f. part of the Wilderness Road

1800				1815	

1800
Federal
government moves
to Washington, D.C.

1803
Louisiana Purchase
expands the size
of the country

1804
Lewis and Clark
begin to explore the
Louisiana Territory

1812
The United
States declares
war on Britain

1815
The War of
1812 ends

Facts and Main Ideas

1 How did Sacagawea help Lewis and Clark on their expedition?

2 Describe the battle Francis Scott Key witnessed as he wrote the words for "The Star-Spangled Banner."

3 **Time Line** How many years were there between the Louisiana Purchase and its exploration?

4 **Main Idea** What changes in government took place under President George Washington?

5 **Main Idea** How did the efforts of Daniel Boone and the Louisiana Purchase encourage people to move westward?

6 **Main Idea** Why did the United States declare war on Britain in 1812?

7 **Critical Thinking:** *Evaluate* Do you think Washington, D.C., was a good location for the capital in 1800? Is it a good location today? Explain your answer.

Apply Skills

Compare Population Density Maps

The map below shows population density for each county of Virginia. Use the map to answer the questions that follow.

1 What color represents the counties with the lowest population density?

2 What is the population density of the county in which Roanoke is located?

3 How many counties have the highest level of population density? How do you know?

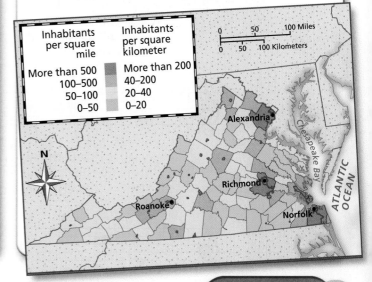

Write About History

1 **Write a letter** to the United States government as a person living in 1812 explaining why you think the country should or should not enter into a war with Britain.

2 **Write an advertisement** encouraging Americans to settle in the new western lands of the United States. Include catchy phrases and photographs or illustrations.

3 **Write a journal entry** as Tecumseh. Explain why you think Native American groups should unite and how you plan to encourage them to do so.

Internet Activity

To get help with vocabulary, people, and terms, select dictionary or encyclopedia from *Social Studies Library* at **www.sfsocialstudies.com.**

The Star-Spangled Banner

By Francis Scott Key

As you read on page 383, Francis Scott Key wrote the words of what would become our national anthem during a key battle of the War of 1812. It quickly became popular across the nation. Read the verses of "The Star-Spangled Banner" below. What emotion did the sight of the American flag inspire in Key? Why do you think the song was chosen as our national anthem?

Oh, __ say! can you see, by the dawn's ear - ly light,
On the shore, dim - ly seen through the mists of the deep,
Oh, __ thus be it ever when __ free men shall stand

What so proud - ly we hailed at the twi - light's last gleam-ing,
Where the foe's haugh-ty host in dread si - lence re - pos - es,
Be - tween their loved homes and the war's des - o - la-tion!

Whose broad stripes and bright stars, through the per - il - ous fight,
What is that which the breeze, o'er the tow - er - ing steep,
Blest with vict - 'ry and peace, may the heav'n-res - cued land

O'er the ram - parts we watched were so gal - lant - ly stream-ing?
As it fit - ful - ly blows, half con - ceals, half dis - clos - es?
Praise the Pow'r that hath made and pre - served us a na - tion!

And the rock - ets' red glare, the bombs burst - ing in air,
Now it catch - es the gleam of the morn - ing's first beam,
Then __ con - quer we must, for our cause it is just,

Gave proof through the night that our flag was still there.
In full glo - ry re - flected now __ shines on the stream;
And this be our motto: "In __ God is our trust!"

Oh, say, does that __ Star - Span - gled Ban - ner __ yet __ wave __
'Tis the Star - Span - gled __ Ban - ner, oh, long may __ it ___ wave __
And the Star - Span - gled __ Ban - ner in tri - umph __ shall __ wave __

O'er the land ___ of the free and the home of the brave?
O'er the land ___ of the free and the home of the brave!
O'er the land ___ of the free and the home of the brave!

Main Ideas and Vocabulary

TEST PREP

Read the passage below and use it to answer the questions that follow.

In 1781, the states adopted the Articles of Confederation. This plan established a weak central government, but the individual state governments were very strong. Rebellions and widespread inflation throughout the 13 states led many people to believe that a new plan of government was needed.

In 1787 delegates from many of the states met in Philadelphia to rewrite the Articles of Confederation. Instead, they created a new Constitution, which outlined a plan for a strong central government but also gave individual states the ability to govern themselves.

The backers of the Constitution faced a challenge in convincing the states to <u>ratify</u> it. Some people approved of the new plan for government, but others did not. In 1788 the Constitution was approved. The following year

George Washington was elected as the country's first President.

During this time, Americans had begun moving west across the Appalachian Mountains. These <u>pioneers</u> wanted to build new homes and farm the land. In 1803 the United States purchased the Louisiana Territory from France, which expanded the country's territory all the way to the Rocky Mountains. President Thomas Jefferson sent Meriwether Lewis and William Clark to explore this land.

As the country expanded westward, conflicts broke out with Native Americans and the British. In June 1812, the United States declared war on Britain. Neither the British nor the Americans won the War of 1812, but the Americans proved they would fight to defend their country.

1 According to the passage, what was the main problem with the plan of government created by the Articles of Confederation?
  A It created a strong central government and weak state governments.
  B It caused wars between the states.
  C It created a weak central government and strong state governments.
  D It made the leaders of the country too powerful.

2 In the passage, the word <u>ratify</u> means—
  A approve
  B disapprove
  C help
  D allow

3 In the passage, the word <u>pioneers</u> means—
  A explorers
  B settlers
  C business people
  D politicians

4 What is the main idea of the passage?
  A George Washington was the country's first President.
  B The United States fought another war with Britain in 1812.
  C The United States created a new plan for government and expanded its territory after the Revolution.
  D The Articles of Confederation were not an effective plan of government for the United States.

Test Talk

Use the diagram to help you find the answer.

People and Vocabulary

Match each person and vocabulary word to its definition.

1 **Northwest Ordinance** (p. 342)

2 **Great Compromise** (p. 347)

3 *The Federalist* (p. 353)

4 **Pierre L'Enfant** (p. 365)

5 **York** (p. 374)

6 **Tecumseh** (p. 381)

a. Shawnee leader

b. described how new states would be created

c. said Congress would be made up of two houses

d. essays that appeared in New York newspapers in support of the Constitution

e. took part in the Lewis and Clark expedition

f. helped design Washington, D.C.

Apply Skills

Create a Distribution Map Create a population density map of your school cafeteria. First record the number of people sitting at each table. Then draw a map showing the population of each table in the room. Be sure to create a key to show the number of people each color represents. Which table has the highest population density?

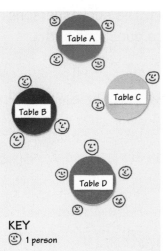

Write and Share

Have a Debate Think back to 1787, when the Constitution was first written. Not everyone was in favor of it. Divide into two groups. One group will represent the Federalists, the other will represent the Antifederalists. The groups will debate whether or not the 13 states should ratify the Constitution. Each member of each group should write an argument for or against ratification, and then present it in a formal debate in your classroom.

Read On Your Own

Look for books like these in the library.

Discovery CHANNEL SCHOOL

UNIT 5 Project

Virginia

New Jersey

Two Sides

Tune in to the past for a special town meeting.

1 **Prepare** to hold a town meeting to present arguments for and against the Virginia Plan and the New Jersey Plan.

2 **Assign** roles. Include roles for reporters, spokespersons for each plan, and audience members to ask questions.

3 **Research** the arguments for and against each plan. Write questions to ask each spokesperson. The spokespersons of each plan will respond to audience questions and comments.

4 **Stage** the town meeting. Take turns asking questions and giving responses.

Internet Activity

Learn more about the United States and its growth as a nation. Go to **www.sfsocialstudies.com/activities** and select your grade and unit.

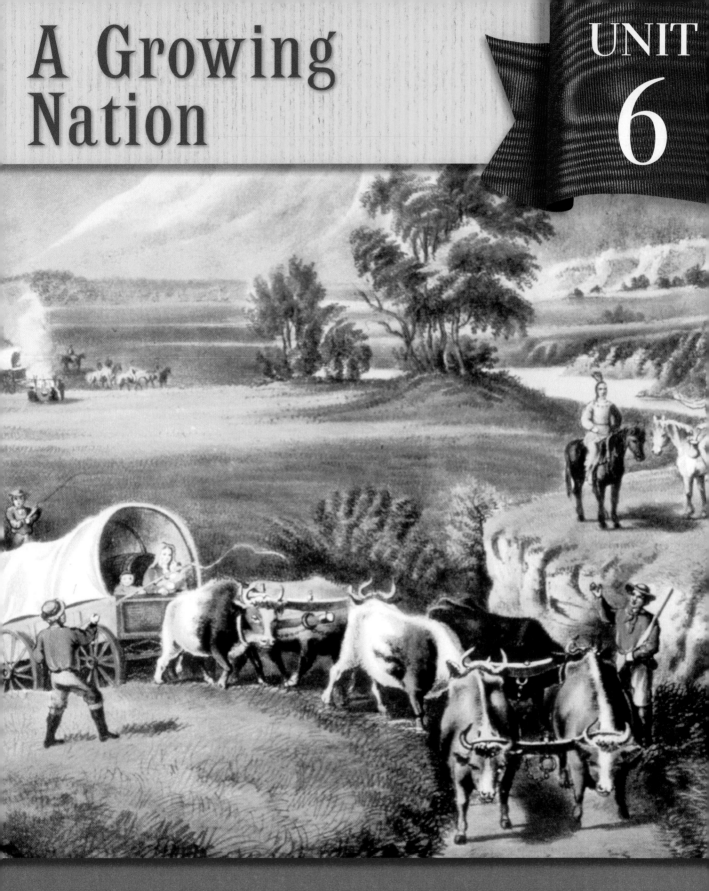

A Growing Nation

Why do people move in search of new homes?

1820

1830

1823
Monroe Doctrine
is issued

1825
The Erie Canal
is completed

1828
Andrew Jackson is elected
seventh President of the
United States

> *"I could hardly believe that the long journey was accomplished and I had found a home."*
>
> —Sarah Smith, settler in Oregon Country, 1838

This 1886 print by Currier and Ives shows pioneers crossing the Rocky Mountains.

1840

1850

1836
Texas becomes an independent country

1838
Frederick Douglass escapes slavery and becomes a leader in the movement to abolish it

1846
Mexican War begins

1847
Mormons settle in Utah

1848
Gold is discovered in California

Meet the People

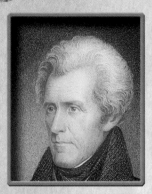

Andrew Jackson

1767–1845

Birthplace: Waxhaw, South Carolina

Soldier, political leader

- Led the American army to victory in the Battle of New Orleans, 1815
- Served as a senator in Congress
- Elected President of the United States in 1828

John Ross

1790–1866

Birthplace: Near Lookout Mountain, Tennessee

Cherokee leader

- Tried to stop American settlers from taking Cherokee lands
- Was forced to lead the Cherokee on the "Trail of Tears"
- Helped write a constitution for the Cherokee

Stephen F. Austin

1793–1836

Birthplace: Wythe County, Virginia

Pioneer, political leader

- Led early settlers from the United States to Texas
- Helped Texans win independence from Mexico
- Served as Secretary of State of the Republic of Texas

James K. Polk

1795–1849

Birthplace: Mecklenburg County, North Carolina

Political leader

- Elected President of the United States in 1844
- Wanted United States to expand
- Achieved goals of gaining much of Oregon country, all of California, and other western lands

---

| 1760 | 1780 | 1800 | 1820 | 1840 |

1767 • Andrew Jackson

1790 • John Ross

1793 • Stephen F. Austin   1836

1795 • James K. Polk

about 1797 • Sojourner Truth

1815 • Elizabeth Cady Stanton

1817 • Frederick Douglass

1829 • Levi Strauss

Sojourner Truth

about 1797–1883

Birthplace: Ulster County, New York

Abolitionist

- Traveled to preach for an end to slavery
- Made many speeches for women's rights
- Visited President Abraham Lincoln in the White House in 1864

Elizabeth Cady Stanton

1815–1902

Birthplace: Johnstown, New York

Abolitionist, women's rights leader

- Helped organize the first women's rights convention
- Called for equal rights for women
- Leader of movement to give women the right to vote

Frederick Douglass

1817–1895

Birthplace: Tuckahoe, Maryland

Abolitionist

- A leader of the movement against slavery
- Started the anti-slavery newspaper, the *North Star*
- Published his autobiography, *Narrative of the Life of Frederick Douglass*, in 1845

Levi Strauss

1829–1902

Birthplace: Bavaria, Germany

Salesperson, clothing manufacturer

- Opened a dry goods store in San Francisco
- Made sturdy work pants for miners
- Founded a company to manufacture denim jeans

1860   1880   1900   1920

1845

1866

1849

1883

1902

1895

1902

Reading Social Studies

Target Skill

A Growing Nation
Compare and Contrast

You can use graphic organizers to help you compare and contrast as you read. A Venn diagram, shown below at left, helps you show how two things or events are similar or different. The other graphic organizer shows just differences.

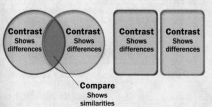

- To compare, writers may use clue words or phrases such as <u>both, as,</u> or <u>like.</u> To contrast, writers may use clue words or phrases such as <u>unlike, in contrast, different</u>.

Read the following paragraph. **Comparisons** and **contrasts** have been highlighted.

In Chapter 11, you read about how the Louisiana Purchase helped the United States gain territory to the west. Several years later, the United States began gaining territory from Spain and Mexico. Wars in Florida and Texas resulted in land gains for the United States. The country gained Florida from Spain and Texas and California from Mexico.

Word Exercise

Antonyms This passage compares and contrasts changes in the growing United States. When writers contrast two things, they often use **antonyms**, which are words that are opposite in meaning. Below is a chart that shows some antonyms from the passage.

farms	cities
factory made	made by hand
men	women

Compare and Contrast Events in a Growing Nation

After the War of 1812, the United States began changing greatly. Significant changes occurred in the ways that goods were produced and shipped.

Water power ran factories to make thread and cloth. People once made these goods by hand. Young people moved from farms to cities to work in factories. New inventions, such as the steel plow and mechanical reaper, speeded farm work.

The transportation system also grew. The country built canals, a national road, and railroads. These cut travel time for people and goods.

More people gained the right to vote. Before, in most places, only white male property holders could vote. By 1828 almost all white men could vote. But most non-white men and all women were denied the right to vote.

The United States grew in land and in power. In 1819, after a series of battles between United States and American Indian forces in Florida, Spain agreed to sell Florida to the United States. At about the same time, Mexico began allowing United States citizens to settle in Texas. In the 1840s, Mexico and the United States fought a war over Texas. Mexico lost that war and in 1848 sold much of its land to the United States. This land included California as well as part of the Southwest region.

Use the reading strategy of compare and contrast to answer questions 1 and 2. Then answer the vocabulary question.

1 Who gained the right to vote during this time and who did not?

2 Compare and contrast the ways that Florida and California became part of the United States. How were they similar? How were they different?

3 The passage talks about people who were denied the right to vote. What is another word in the passage that acts as an antonym for *denied*?

Times of Change

1829

Washington, D.C.
Andrew Jackson becomes the seventh President of the United States.

Lesson 1

1

1830

Baltimore, Maryland
Tom Thumb, a steam-powered locomotive, races a horse.

Lesson 2

2

1848

Seneca Falls, New York
The Seneca Falls Convention issues a call for women's rights.

Lesson 3

3

Locating Time and Place

UNITED STATES in 1829

Seneca Falls

Baltimore

Washington, D.C.

PACIFIC OCEAN

ATLANTIC OCEAN

Gulf of Mexico

Why We Remember

Today the majority of people in the United States live in cities and suburbs. In the early 1800s, the majority of Americans were farmers living in rural areas. It was the Industrial Revolution that began this huge change. People began leaving farms and moving to cities to work in the new factories. Inventions in transportation also came about during the Industrial Revolution. The steam engine, the steamboat, and the digging of canals meant that people and goods could travel farther and faster. The United States was growing, and very quickly. With that growth would also come conflict and struggles for change.

1820   1830   1840

1823
Monroe Doctrine
is issued

1828
Andrew Jackson
is elected seventh
President of the
United States

1838
Trail of Tears
begins

INDIAN
TERRITORY

FLORIDA

The United States Turns Fifty

PREVIEW

Focus on the Main Idea
In the 1820s and 1830s, the United States expanded its territory in North America and its power in the Western Hemisphere.

PLACES
Florida
Indian Territory

PEOPLE
James Monroe
Andrew Jackson
Sequoyah
John Ross

VOCABULARY
nationalism
Era of Good Feelings
Monroe Doctrine
suffrage
Indian Removal Act
Trail of Tears

▶ In 1776, the Liberty Bell rang to celebrate the Declaration of Independence. Fifty years later, it rang in memory of Jefferson and Adams.

You Are There

It is July 4, 1826—50 years from the day the Declaration of Independence was approved in Philadelphia. Americans hope that two founding fathers, although they are old and ill, can witness this celebration. Then something extraordinary happens! Thomas Jefferson, lying near death in Virginia, asks, "This is the Fourth?" Many miles to the north in Massachusetts—and a few hours later—John Adams murmurs his last words, "Thomas Jefferson survives." But Jefferson has already died. These two men have died on their nation's fiftieth birthday. But they lived to see the country they helped create grow strong and confident.

Compare and Contrast As you read, compare and contrast the United States during President Monroe's presidency and after the presidency of Andrew Jackson.

The Monroe Doctrine

In 1817, a new President, James Monroe, took office. He was a believer in nationalism, the idea that all the people should pull together with a sense of strong pride in their country. At his inauguration speech, Monroe urged the American people to act as "one great family with a common interest."

Many Americans seemed to agree with Monroe. For a brief time, disagreements about national issues grew quiet. One Boston newspaper called the period an "Era of Good Feelings."

However, Monroe faced major challenges from outside the country. Spain ruled Florida and a vast region from Texas to California. For years, slaves escaping from the southern United States had found safety in Florida. Some of the escaped people had found homes with the Seminole, a Florida American Indian tribe. The Seminole sometimes attacked American settlers in Georgia who had taken over American Indian lands. The Spanish did little to stop these attacks.

In 1817, Monroe sent General Andrew Jackson, the popular hero of the War of 1812, to stop the raids. Jackson attacked the Spanish in Florida and seized two of their forts. Troubled by uprisings in its other colonies, Spain found it hard to defend Florida. In a treaty in 1819, Spain agreed to sell Florida to the United States for $5 million.

Monroe was still concerned about other European nations. Both Russia and Britain were interested in taking over parts of Spain's weakened empire in the Americas. In 1823, Monroe issued a daring statement called the Monroe Doctrine. It warned European nations against interfering in the Western Hemisphere. "The American continents," Monroe said, "are…not to be considered as subject for future colonization by any European powers."

REVIEW How would you contrast the "Era of Good Feelings" with the period that came before it? ↩ Compare and Contrast

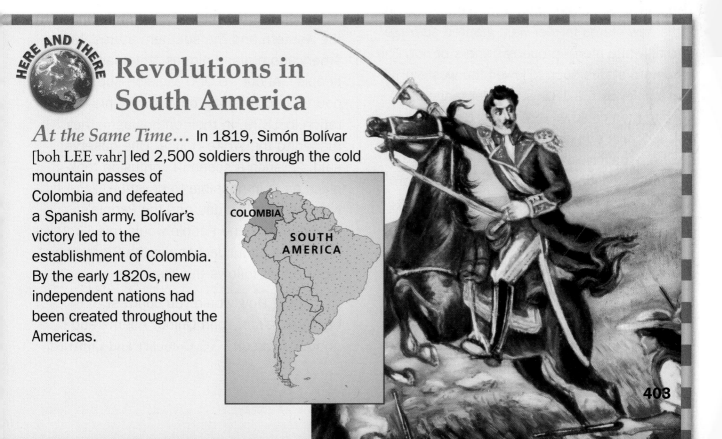

HERE AND THERE

Revolutions in South America

At the Same Time… In 1819, Simón Bolívar [boh LEE vahr] led 2,500 soldiers through the cold mountain passes of Colombia and defeated a Spanish army. Bolívar's victory led to the establishment of Colombia. By the early 1820s, new independent nations had been created throughout the Americas.

COLOMBIA

SOUTH AMERICA

403

► Thousands of people went to the White House to celebrate Andrew Jackson's inauguration in 1829.

"The People's President"

Every one of the first six Presidents came from a wealthy Virginia or Massachusetts family. But the seventh was the son of poor pioneers. This was a sure sign that the country was changing.

In the early 1800s more people had moved west than ever before. With this movement came new ideas, some of which would spread back to the east. For example, the eastern states granted **suffrage**—the right to vote—mainly to white men who owned property. But the new states farther west granted suffrage to all white men—property owners or not. The eastern states soon followed the western example. By the 1820s, a wider range of white men could vote. Women, Native Americans, and most African Americans still were not allowed to vote.

In the election of 1828, Andrew Jackson ran against President John Quincy Adams. President Adams was the highly educated and wealthy son of the second President, John Adams. In contrast, Jackson had not gone to college, and he had taught himself law. He was also the military leader who won the Battle of New Orleans in the War of 1812. One of Jackson's election slogans declared that, "Adams…can write [but] Jackson…can fight."

Jackson headed a new political party, the Democrats. Adams's party was called the National Republicans. Both parties claimed they were following the ideas of Thomas Jefferson. Democrats urged everyone to vote, especially the "common people"—those with little property or wealth. Jackson's campaign promised "Equal rights for all; special privilege for none."

Jackson won a huge victory, sweeping both the western and the southern states. Many Americans praised him as "the man of the people." About 20,000 Jackson supporters poured into Washington, D.C., for his inauguration in 1829. In their enthusiasm, they rushed to the White House. One observer said, "…such a scene of confusion took place as is impossible to describe….But it was the People's day, and the People's President and the People would rule." You will read more about Jackson in the Biography feature that follows this lesson.

REVIEW How would you contrast the backgrounds of John Quincy Adams and Andrew Jackson? ◑ **Compare and Contrast**

American Indian Removal

In the 1820s and 1830s, many people were moving west. In the Southeast, settlers began moving into lands that belonged to five major American Indian groups—the Cherokee, Creek, Chickasaw, Choctaw, and Seminole.

The people of these Native American groups lived much as white settlers did—by farming, herding, hunting, and trading. A Cherokee named **Sequoyah** developed an alphabet for the Cherokee language. Using Sequoyah's alphabet, the Cherokee produced written materials, such as a newspaper called the *Phoenix*.

Life would soon change for the five Native American groups of the Southeast. In search of good farmland and gold, settlers continued moving onto the land of the five groups.

President Jackson supported the settlers. In 1830, Jackson encouraged Congress to pass the **Indian Removal Act.** This act gave the President the power to move Native Americans to land west of the Mississippi River. They would be moved to **Indian Territory,** land in what is now Oklahoma.

The five groups resisted. The Seminole fought for their land. After several years of battles, they were defeated by the United States army and forced to move west. Follow their route on the map below.

The Cherokee tried to keep their land by going to court. When the state of Georgia tried to take control of Cherokee land, Cherokee leader **John Ross** took his people's case to the Supreme Court. Chief Justice John Marshall agreed with Ross. The Court ruled that the Cherokee had the right to keep control of their traditional land.

When he heard of this ruling, President Jackson was reported to say, "John Marshall has made his decision, now let him enforce it." Without Jackson's support, the Supreme Court could not enforce its ruling.

REVIEW Contrast the views of John Marshall and Andrew Jackson on the rights of the Cherokee. 🔄 **Compare and Contrast**

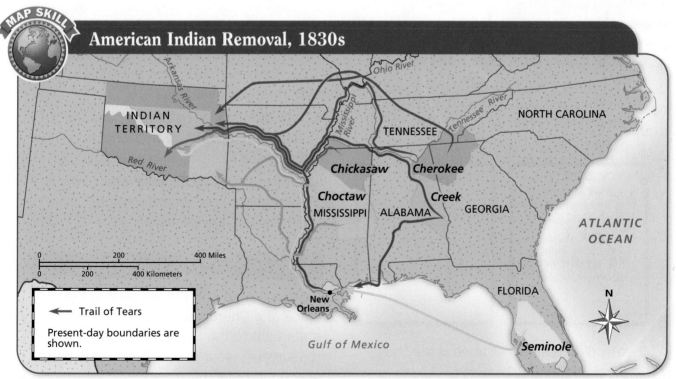

MAP SKILL

American Indian Removal, 1830s

Arkansas River

Ohio River

INDIAN TERRITORY

Red River

Mississippi River

Tennessee River

NORTH CAROLINA

TENNESSEE

Chickasaw

Cherokee

Choctaw

Creek

MISSISSIPPI   ALABAMA

GEORGIA

ATLANTIC OCEAN

| 0 | 200 | 400 Miles |
| 0 | 200 | 400 Kilometers |

New Orleans

FLORIDA

N

⟵ Trail of Tears

Present-day boundaries are shown.

Gulf of Mexico

Seminole

▶ **This map shows the routes different groups traveled to reach Indian Territory.**

MAP SKILL Movement *Which Native American group crossed the Gulf of Mexico?*

405

The Trail of Tears

In 1838, President Martin Van Buren ordered United States soldiers to force the Cherokee to leave their land. The 800-mile journey to Indian Territory was so terrible that it became known as the Trail of Tears.

A soldier named John Burnett never forgot what he saw on the Trail of Tears:

> *"I saw the helpless Cherokees arrested and dragged from their homes... I saw them loaded like cattle or sheep into six hundred and forty-five wagons and started toward the west."*

By 1839, the Trail of Tears had ended. Of the 15,000 Cherokee who began the journey as many as one-fourth did not survive the trip. Many died from disease and bad weather.

REVIEW Compare the way the Cherokee people lived before the Trail of Tears with

▶ **The route of the Cherokee became known as the Trail of Tears.**

their experiences during the journey.

⊙ Compare and Contrast

Summarize the Lesson

1823 President James Monroe issued the Monroe Doctrine.

1828 Andrew Jackson was elected the seventh President of the United States.

1838 The long journey of the Cherokee on the Trail of Tears began.

LESSON 1 REVIEW

Check Facts and Main Ideas

1. ⊙ **Compare and Contrast** On a separate sheet of paper, fill in the "1830" box to show how conditions in the United States changed from 1817 to 1830.

1817	1830
• James Monroe is President. • Florida belongs to Spain. • American Indians live on land in the southern states.	

2. Why did President Monroe issue the **Monroe Doctrine?**

3. How did the election of Andrew Jackson as President show that the United States was changing?

4. Why did the United States pass the **Indian Removal Act,** and what was the result?

5. **Critical Thinking:** *Express Ideas* Why is the right to vote important in a democratic government?

Link to ⟶ Writing

Write a Statement Put yourself in the place of a Cherokee leader. Write a statement to the Supreme Court giving reasons why your people have the right to stay on their land.

Andrew Jackson
1767–1845

Andrew Jackson was nine years old when the Declaration of Independence was signed in 1776. His mother and two brothers listened as he read it aloud. Andrew, like the rest of his family, was a strong supporter of the American Revolution.

When he was 13, he joined the militia, or volunteer army, of South Carolina. After a difficult battle, Andrew and his brother Robert went to a relative's home to rest and heal. But British troops soon found the brothers. A British officer ordered Andrew to clean his boots. When Andrew refused, the officer hit him with his sword.

Andrew and Robert were then taken to a prison camp, where both became ill with smallpox. During a prisoner exchange in 1781, Andrew and Robert were allowed to go home, but Robert had become too ill and soon died. Just after Andrew became healthy again, his mother died of illness while taking care of sick and wounded American soldiers. Andrew was alone.

BIOFACT

The soldiers who served under Jackson nicknamed him "Old Hickory," after a very strong type of wood.

The sacrifices of Andrew Jackson and his family during the American Revolution made him determined to protect people who, like him, grew up poor. He later said:

"In general, the great can protect themselves, but the poor and humble require the arm and shield [protection] of the law."

Andrew Jackson became a teacher, lawyer, soldier, senator, and finally President of the United States.

Learn From Biographies

How did Jackson's experiences during the American Revolution affect his views about government?

For more information, go online to *Meet the People* at **www.sfsocialstudies.com**.

Erie Canal
National Road
• Lowell

1790 ———————————————————————————— 1830

1790
Samuel Slater builds the nation's first cotton-spinning factory

1811
Construction begins on the National Road

1825
The Erie Canal is completed

1830
Peter Cooper develops the first United States locomotive

A New Kind of Revolution

PREVIEW

Focus on the Main Idea
The Industrial Revolution dramatically changed the way Americans lived and worked.

PLACES
Lowell
National Road
Erie Canal

PEOPLE
Samuel Slater
Francis Cabot Lowell
Eli Whitney
Robert Fulton

VOCABULARY
Industrial Revolution
manufacture
technology
cotton gin
mechanical reaper
canal

You Are There

Bells startle you out of your sleep at 5:40 in the morning. It's time to get up. The seven other young women who share your room in the boardinghouse are getting up too. Just like you, they are from farm families and have recently moved to town.

You all go into the street to join the crowds of workers heading for the mills. At 6:00, the bells ring again. Hurry! The mills will start running in just 10 minutes.

The year is 1845 and you are a "mill girl" in the town of Lowell, Massachusetts. You earn 40 cents a day for a long day of hard work!

Compare and Contrast
As you read, contrast ways of making and moving goods before the Industrial Revolution and after.

The Industrial Revolution

A time of change known as the Industrial Revolution caused the young women you just read about to leave their farm homes and move to town. The Industrial Revolution was a change in the way goods were produced, from handmade goods to goods made by machines. And businesses needed workers, like young farm women, to run the machines.

The invention of machines helped businesses manufacture goods much faster and more cheaply than before. To manufacture is to make goods, like cloth, from raw materials, like cotton fiber. The Industrial Revolution began in Britain in the middle 1700s. By the late 1700s, it had arrived in the United States. Samuel Slater, who began his career as a skilled worker in a cloth factory in Britain, helped bring the Industrial Revolution to the United States.

▶ Like Slater's cotton-spinning factory, this flour mill was powered by a rushing river.

Slater wanted to start a cloth factory in the United States. However, the British government wanted to keep its technology a secret. Technology is the way people use new ideas to make tools that improve people's lives. Britain had passed laws that made it illegal to take plans for the new technology out of the country.

Slater knew it was dangerous for him to try to take written plans with him. So he memorized the plans and then sailed for the United States. When Slater got to the United States, he used the plans he had memorized to build the first cotton-spinning mill, or factory, in the country. The mill was built in 1790 in Pawtucket, Rhode Island.

Slater used the flow of river waters to power his mill. The currents of river water turned giant water wheels, which were attached to belts and gears that set the machines in motion.

In 1812, Francis Cabot Lowell, a Boston merchant, decided to bring all the stages in cloth-making together. Spinning thread, weaving cloth, and dyeing it would all be done in one place. He put this idea into practice by building a large factory in Lowell, Massachusetts. Why in Lowell? There were two reasons: A river flowed through it, and there was a source of cheap and plentiful labor nearby.

The labor came from young women who lived on farms in the countryside. Because few of these young women had skills outside of farming and household tasks, they could not earn much money at home. In the 1830s and 1840s, thousands of these "mill girls," as they were called, came to work and live in Lowell and other New England factory towns.

REVIEW Explain why mill owners chose to build their factories near farms.
Cause and Effect

Inventions Change Factories and Farms

The new mills of New England made cloth from cotton plants. The cotton was grown in the South on huge plantations, where most of the workers were enslaved people. Cotton was known as "King Cotton," because it ruled the South's economy.

The harvesting of cotton had been given a huge boost by the invention of a young New Englander, **Eli Whitney.** While visiting Georgia in 1792, he heard planters complain about how hard it was to clean the seeds out of cotton. This step was necessary before the cotton could be sold. Whitney learned that a worker could clean only about one pound of cotton a day. He later wrote:

> *"I... struck on a plan, a machine with which one man will clean ten times as much cotton...."*

Whitney's machine was called a **cotton gin.** The machine could clean 50 times as much cotton a day as could be done by hand. Mills needed the cotton, and plantations expanded to supply it. The increased demand for cotton led to the demand for more slaves to grow and pick it. The graph on this page shows how quickly cotton production increased.

Machines were helping with other kinds of farm work. Before the 1830s, farm workers harvested wheat by swinging a long blade. In 1831, Cyrus McCormick developed a horse-drawn **mechanical reaper** that could do the job more easily. Soon after, John Deere developed a plow made of steel rather than of iron. It could plow through thick soil more easily than older plows.

The new machines Americans were inventing meant that factories could produce more goods, often more cheaply. Farmers could grow more foods, and planters more cotton. More goods and more food meant more products for the people at home and for trade.

REVIEW Compare and contrast the cleaning of cotton before and after the invention of the cotton gin.
🔄 **Compare and Contrast**

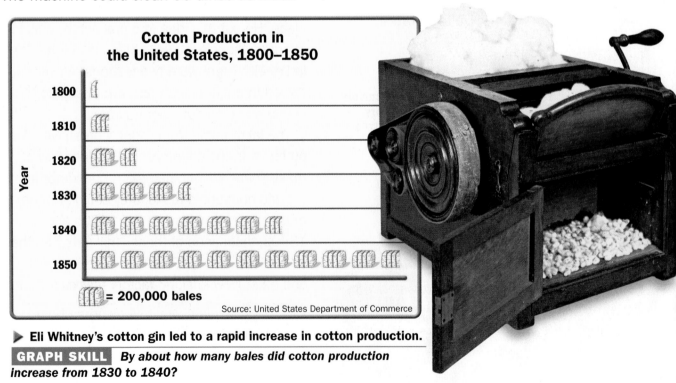

Cotton Production in the United States, 1800–1850

Year	
1800	▯
1810	▯▯▯
1820	▯▯▯ ▯▯▯
1830	▯▯▯ ▯▯▯ ▯▯▯ ▯
1840	▯▯▯ ▯▯▯ ▯▯▯ ▯▯▯ ▯▯▯ ▯▯▯ ▯▯▯ ▯▯▯
1850	▯▯▯ ▯▯▯ ▯▯▯ ▯▯▯ ▯▯▯ ▯▯▯ ▯▯▯ ▯▯▯ ▯▯▯ ▯▯▯ ▯▯▯ ▯▯▯ ▯▯▯

▯▯▯ = 200,000 bales

Source: United States Department of Commerce

▶ Eli Whitney's cotton gin led to a rapid increase in cotton production.

GRAPH SKILL *By about how many bales did cotton production increase from 1830 to 1840?*

▶ Robert Fulton's *Clermont* could travel between New York City and Albany in 32 hours.

Moving Goods and People

Americans were producing more manufactured and farm goods than ever before. But people needed better ways to get their products to market. Settlers heading west also needed better methods of transportation. These needs led to major changes in transportation in the early 1800s.

In 1811, the federal government began building the **National Road.** Eventually it stretched from Cumberland, Maryland to Vandalia, Illinois. Settlers traveled west on the National Road while sheep, cattle, and hogs bound for eastern markets were sent along the road in the opposite direction.

Traveling the National Road—and all roads at the time—could be rough. Wagons got stuck in mud and in deep ruts left by other wagons. Rivers could provide smoother travel than roads. But boats powered by sails or oars had difficulty traveling upstream against a river's current.

Robert Fulton, an American engineer, set out to solve this problem. He developed a riverboat powered by a steam engine. On an early afternoon in August 1807, a crowd gathered to watch his boat, the *Clermont,* set off from New York City. An observer said, "Cheer after cheer went up from the vast throng." The *Clermont's*

destination was Albany, New York—150 miles upstream on the Hudson River. Thirty-two hours later, the *Clermont* arrived at Albany. It took four days for sailing ships to make the same trip. River travel took a giant leap forward.

Water transportation could carry both people and goods and was much cheaper than land transportation. But rivers did not flow in all parts of the country. Canals were one solution. A **canal** is a ditch dug through the land and filled with water. It is a narrow waterway that usually connects other bodies of water such as rivers, lakes, and seas.

One of the longest canals built in the early 1800s was the **Erie Canal.** In 1817, thousands of workers began digging a ditch that extended from Albany on the Hudson River to Buffalo on Lake Erie. In 1825, the Erie Canal opened. It linked the Great Lakes and the Atlantic Ocean. Thousands of people used the Erie Canal to travel from New York City to the Midwest. Manufactured goods could be shipped from eastern factories to the western frontier. Farm goods could be shipped in the opposite direction.

REVIEW How did Americans change their environment in order to improve transportation? **Main Idea and Details**

Early Railroads

Railroads began simply as rails laid down in a road. The rails were made of wood topped with iron. Horses pulled carts running along the rails. Since the rails were smoother than the roads, the horses could pull the carts faster than they could pull wagons over roads.

Then Peter Cooper, one of the directors of the Baltimore & Ohio Railroad, got a better idea. Why not develop a steam engine, or locomotive, to pull the carts? He believed a locomotive would be able to pull heavier loads faster than horses could.

In 1830, Cooper built a steam-powered locomotive. Because of its small size—weighing barely a ton—it became known as the Tom Thumb, after a tiny hero of old English stories. To let people know about his new

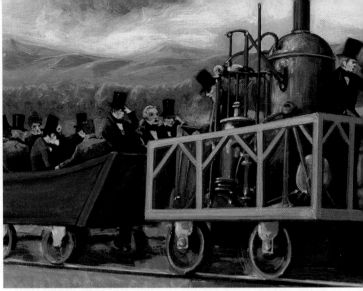

▶ **The Tom Thumb lost its race against a horse, but soon locomotives were pulling many more goods than horses.**

machine, Cooper advertised "a race between a gray horse and the Tom Thumb." Which would win? A race horse or the "Iron Horse"?

On an August day that year, the locomotive and the gray horse lined up side by side.

Map Adventure

Getting Around a Growing Nation

You are in charge of arranging shipping and travel for a manufacturing company.

1. You have three tons of goods that you want to ship along the National Road from Baltimore to Wheeling, Virginia. A freight wagon will carry the goods 260 miles in about 13 days. If the wagon travels the same number of miles each day, how many miles per day will it travel? At $125 a ton, how much will the trip cost?

2. One of your clerks has to travel from Buffalo to Albany, a distance of about 360 miles. You decide to send him by boat over the Erie Canal. He will travel at 6 miles an hour and the cost will be 2 cents a mile. How many hours will the trip take? How much will it cost?

3. A few years later, you are able to send him on the same trip by railroad. The train travels at 40 miles per hour. How many hours shorter will the trip be by railroad than it was by boat?

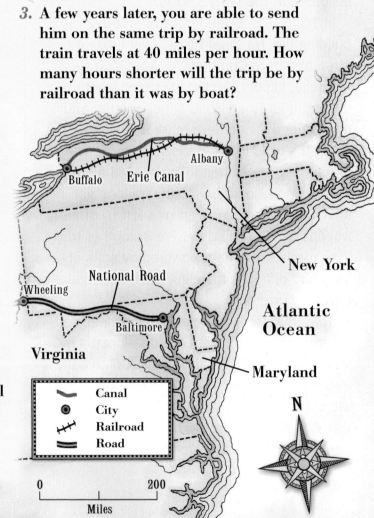

Buffalo
Erie Canal
Albany
New York
National Road
Wheeling
Baltimore
Atlantic Ocean
Virginia
Maryland

Canal
City
Railroad
Road

N

0   200
Miles

Cooper stood at the controls of the Tom Thumb. The race began. At first, the horse pulled ahead. But then the train picked up speed. Soon it was neck and neck with the horse, and then the Tom Thumb pulled ahead. A great cheer went up.

But suddenly, a safety valve broke in the engine. The locomotive slowed, and then fell behind the horse. The Tom Thumb lost this race. But locomotives would soon take over from horses.

Over the next 20 years, railroads replaced canals as the easiest and cheapest way to travel. By 1840, the United States had about 3,000 miles of railroad tracks, almost twice as much as Europe. A person could travel about 90 miles from New York City to Philadelphia by railroad in just a few hours instead of the day and a half the trip took by horse-drawn wagon.

REVIEW What effects did changes in transportation have on travel? *Cause and Effect*

Summarize the Lesson

1790 Samuel Slater built the nation's first cotton-spinning factory.

1811 Construction began on the National Road.

1825 The Erie Canal was completed.

1830 Peter Cooper developed a steam-powered locomotive.

LESSON 2 — REVIEW

Check Facts and Main Ideas

1. **Compare and Contrast** On a separate sheet of paper, fill in the box to compare the way goods were produced and transported before and after the Industrial Revolution.

Before the Industrial Revolution	After the Industrial Revolution
• Goods were made by hand. • Cotton plants were cleaned by hand. • Wheat was harvested with a long blade. • Goods were moved by horse over rough road.	

2. How did the **Industrial Revolution** change the way Americans produced goods?

3. Why were New England factory towns built near rivers?

4. **Critical Thinking:** *Problem Solving* Suppose you were an inventor in the early 1830s. What problem would you have wanted to solve? Use the problem-solving steps on page H3.

5. What advantages did the locomotive have over carts pulled along rails by horses?

Link to 🔗 Mathematics

Figure Hourly Wage In 1845, many mill girls earned 40 cents a day for working 12 hours. In 2001, the minimum, or lowest allowed, wage in the United States was $5.15 hour. About how much did mill girls earn an hour?

Read a Cross-Section Diagram

What? A cross-section diagram is a drawing that shows a view of something as if you could slice through it. Cross-section diagrams can be used to show you how something works.

Why? It is difficult to understand how a device works if you cannot see inside it. In a cross-section diagram, the artist "removes" part of the outside so that you can see how the inside

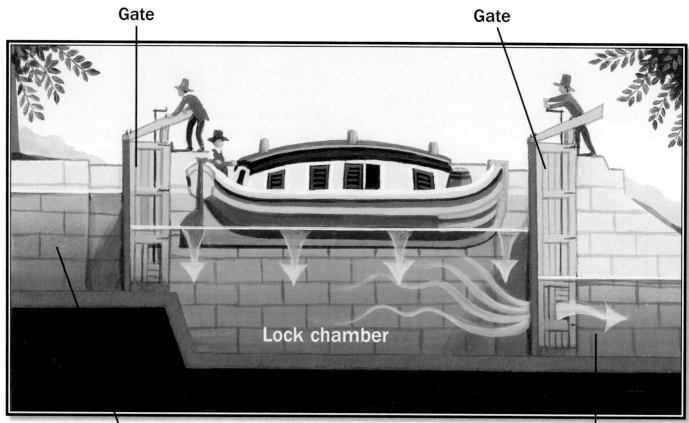

Gate   Gate

Lock chamber

Upstream
water level

Downstream
water level

works. A cross-section diagram helps you see how canals like the Erie Canal work.

How? To use a cross-section diagram, you have to study the drawing carefully. Read the labels to identify each part of the diagram.

The diagram on this page shows how a boat moves from higher to lower water in the lock of a canal. A lock is a section of a canal that is closed off so that water can be removed or added. The water coming in or going out changes the level of the water in the lock so that a boat can be moved higher or lower.

Look at the cross-section diagram. Notice that the boat has to be moved to a lower water level. Locate the gates that will keep the boat in the lock while the water level is being changed. Notice where the boat will go after the water level has been changed.

Think and Apply

1. What is the purpose of a canal lock?

2. What do the lock gates do?

3. This **cross-section diagram** shows how a boat is moved from a higher water level to a lower water level. How do you think a lock could be used to move a boat from a lower water level to a higher water level?

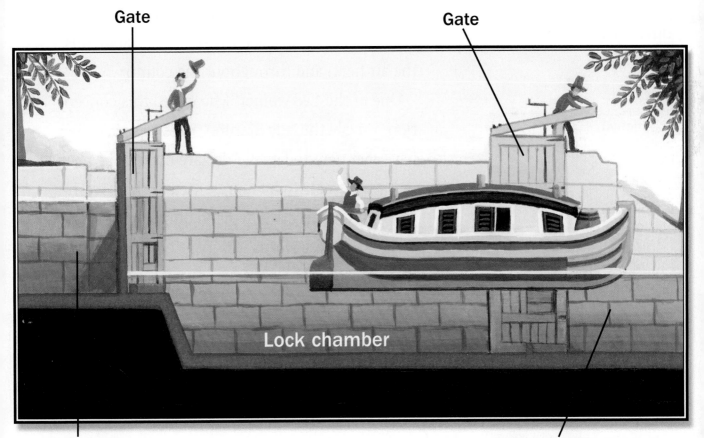

Gate

Gate

Lock chamber

Upstream
water level

Downstream
water level

Seneca Falls

1830   1850

Early 1830s
Second Great Awakening sweeps the country

1838
Frederick Douglass escapes slavery and leads movement to abolish it

1848
Seneca Falls Convention issues call for women's rights

The Struggle for Reforms

PREVIEW

Focus on the Main Idea
Beginning in the 1830s, a spirit of reform changed life in the United States.

PLACES
Seneca Falls

PEOPLE
Frederick Douglass
William Lloyd Garrison
Sojourner Truth
Lucretia Mott
Elizabeth Cady Stanton

VOCABULARY
reform
revival
temperance
abolitionist
Seneca Falls Convention

You Are There
It is the summer morning of Wednesday, July 19, 1848. You are part of a crowd heading for Wesleyan Chapel in Seneca Falls, New York. There you will witness the first women's rights convention ever held in the United States.

More than a hundred people—women and men—file into the rows of seats. A spirit of change fills the air here, and throughout the country.

One of the two women who called this convention, Elizabeth Cady Stanton, rises to speak. "We have met here today to…declare our right to be free…to be represented in the government…[to] demand our right to vote." These words will inspire people throughout the country.

 Compare and Contrast As you read, contrast conditions in the United States with the ways people wanted to change these conditions.

▶ **Elizabeth Cady Stanton spoke at the first women's rights convention.**

The Second Great Awakening

A spirit of **reform,** or change, began sweeping the country in the early 1800s. This movement grew out of a new awakening of religious feeling. The movement was called the Second Great Awakening. Like the first Great Awakening of a century earlier, this one stirred Americans to examine religion in their lives.

Camp meetings, like the one shown on this page, drew hundreds of people. The meetings were called **revivals,** because they revived, or brought back and strengthened, people's religious feelings. In the 1830s, Christian preachers like Charles G. Finney spoke to these gatherings for many hours. Finney demanded that his listeners accept "a new life of the spirit." His sermons were so fiery that the area where he preached, in central and western New York State, came to be called the "Burned-Over District."

Many became convinced that religion could make them better people. Once they became better people, they hoped to make life better for others too. In this way, they believed, they could create a better country.

The Second Great Awakening brought in the nation's first great era of reform. Some reformers attacked what they considered bad behavior, like gambling and drinking alcohol. Wives especially opposed alcohol, since husbands who drank heavily often treated their families badly. A major crusade to stop the drinking of alcohol began. It was called the **temperance** movement. Temperance means moderation. People in the temperance movement urged others to drink only small amounts of alcohol or none at all.

Reformers also had other causes. As you will see, bringing an end to slavery and gaining rights for women were important reform goals.

REVIEW How did the Second Great Awakening lead to the temperance movement? **Cause and Effect**

▶ **Outdoor revivals often drew large crowds.**

417

Fighting Against Slavery

In the North, anti-slavery groups had formed as early as the Revolution. Colonial leaders such as Benjamin Franklin, Abigail Adams, and Benjamin Rush were members of such groups. Delegates to the Constitutional Convention had argued about ending slavery. Years later, John Quincy Adams, sixth President of the United States, wrote a poem that included these words: "nature's God commands the slave to rise…till not a slave shall on this earth be found."

In the 1830s, the movement to end slavery took on new life. Reformers attacked slavery as an evil that had to be erased, or abolished. Called abolitionists, these reformers made speeches and printed newspapers to spread their message.

Frederick Douglass was a powerful and eloquent voice for the abolitionists. Born into slavery in Maryland, Douglass had escaped to New York City in 1838 by posing as a free sailor. Soon, he was traveling around the North on speaking trips for the Massachusetts Anti-Slavery Society. In one speech he said:

> *"I appear before [you] this evening as a thief and a robber. I stole this head, these limbs, this body from my master and ran off with them."*

Douglass's stories of his own experiences as a slave—of merciless beatings and near starvation—won many supporters for the abolitionist movement. You will read more about Douglass in the Citizen Heroes feature on page 422.

In 1831 in Boston, William Lloyd Garrison started an abolitionist newspaper, *The*

► Abolitionist William Lloyd Garrison declared that his newspaper, *The Liberator*, would never stop fighting against slavery in the United States.

Liberator. Garrison condemned slavery loudly and clearly, writing: "I will be as harsh as truth and as uncompromising as justice. On this subject, I do not wish to think, or speak, or write, with moderation….and I will be heard!"

Another tireless abolitionist, Sojourner Truth, was born into slavery in New York State in the late 1700s. She escaped and became a preacher. She adopted the name Sojourner Truth to make clear her mission—to sojourn, or travel, spreading the truth. Though she could not read or write, Sojourner Truth could quote the Bible to convince listeners of the evils of slavery. She also preached in support of women's rights. You will read more about Sojourner Truth in the Biography feature following this lesson.

REVIEW How did abolitionists raise support for their movement? Cause and Effect

Women's Rights

Women in the early 1800s had few rights. For example, married women could not own property. Anything they owned when single immediately became the property of their husbands after marriage. Women were not allowed to vote, and most colleges did not accept women.

Many women of the time were active in reform movements. For example, **Lucretia Mott** and her friend **Elizabeth Cady Stanton** worked hard for both temperance and abolition. But when they went to London to attend an anti-slavery convention in 1840, they were forbidden to speak or to take any part in it. As women, all they could do was sit in the balcony and watch.

In 1848, Mott and Stanton decided to take a stand for women's rights by calling a convention in **Seneca Falls,** New York, which you read about in You Are There. At the **Seneca Falls Convention,** Stanton presented a Declaration of Sentiments based on the Declaration of Independence. In it she stated:

> *"We hold these truths to be self-evident: that all men and women are created equal..."*

Both women and men at the convention went on to debate a series of resolutions, or statements, of the rights women should have. You can read some of these below. At the end, 68 women and 32 men signed the Declaration. Frederick Douglass was among the signers. Though Sojourner Truth did not attend, she soon began traveling to support women's rights.

Much of the press attacked the convention. One newspaper said, "A woman is a nobody." Many others claimed women were unfit for citizenship. But Stanton was pleased that the press at least reported on the convention. "Imagine the publicity given to our ideas," she said. "It will start women thinking, and men too."

REVIEW How would you summarize the rights that women lacked in the 1800s? **Summarize**

▶ Elizabeth Cady Stanton *(left)* and Lucretia Mott *(right)* helped lead the struggle for women's rights.

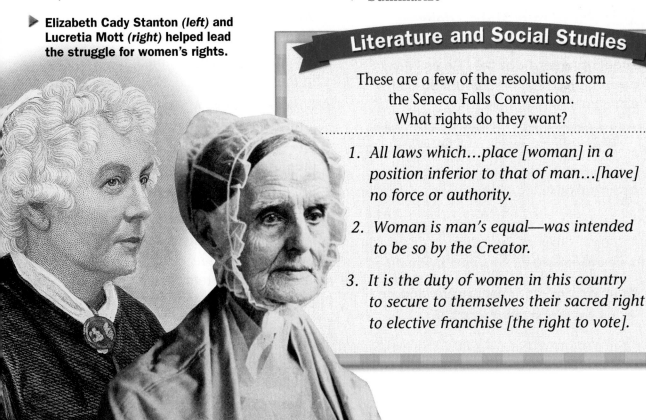

Literature and Social Studies

These are a few of the resolutions from the Seneca Falls Convention. What rights do they want?

1. All laws which...place [woman] in a position inferior to that of man...[have] no force or authority.

2. Woman is man's equal—was intended to be so by the Creator.

3. It is the duty of women in this country to secure to themselves their sacred right to elective franchise [the right to vote].

The Spirit of Reform

In the first half of the 1800s, reformers identified a number of conditions in the United States that needed changing. In addition to slavery and the unequal treatment of women, these included a poor educational system, very bad living conditions in prisons, and the terrible treatment of mentally ill people.

In Massachusetts, Horace Mann believed that education was a way to fight poverty. Education, he said, could produce "intelligent and practical men" who would not remain poor. So Mann led the way in expanding public education. He got the school year in Massachusetts extended to at least six months. He also established more high schools and improved teacher training.

Also in Massachusetts, Dorothea Dix investigated the prisons and insane asylums of the state. Her findings exposed horrible conditions that needed reform. The mentally ill, Dix found, were "beaten with rods" and "lashed into obedience."

Few reforms came quickly. Many would take decades to accomplish. But the reformers carried on their work.

REVIEW What conclusions do you think readers of Dorothea Dix's reports drew from them? **Draw Conclusions**

Summarize the Lesson

- **1830s** The Second Great Awakening stirred a spirit of reform.
- **1838** The fight to end slavery gained a powerful speaker when Frederick Douglass escaped slavery and became a leader of the abolition movement.
- **1848** The movement for women's rights was launched at a convention in Seneca Falls, New York.

LESSON 3   REVIEW

Check Facts and Main Ideas

1. **Compare and Contrast** On a separate sheet of paper, fill in the "Goals" box to compare problems in the United States with goals of reformers.

Problems	Goals
• Slavery • Women did not have equal rights with men.	

2. What **reform** movements were produced by the Second Great Awakening?

3. What did Frederick Douglass and Sojourner Truth have in common?

4. Compare the rights of men and women in the early 1800s.

5. **Critical Thinking: Make Inferences** Why might many reformers have worked for—or at least supported—several different reforms?

Link to   Art

Draw a Poster You are a supporter of one of the reforms you read about in this lesson. Choose a reform and draw a poster that you use to tell others about your cause.

Sojourner Truth
about 1797–1883

Sojourner Truth was born into slavery in New York State with the name Isabella. When she was nine years old she was taken from her parents and sold to a new slaveowner. Later she said of this time, "Now the war began." (She meant that without her family, her life became even more difficult.)

She became hopeful when a new law in New York in 1817 said that enslaved people older than twenty-eight would be freed. Her owner, John Dumont, promised that if she worked especially hard, she would be freed in 1826, one year early. Sojourner Truth worked long hours, even when she cut her hand badly and it did not heal well. However, at the end of 1826 her owner broke his promise and refused to free her.

This was more than Sojourner Truth could take. At dawn, she left the farm where she had been enslaved and escaped to freedom.

In 1843, she changed her name to Sojourner Truth, because "sojourn" means "travel," and she believed that her

BIOFACT

The Narrative of Sojourner Truth: A Northern Slave *was published in 1850. Because she could not write, Truth told her story aloud, and someone else wrote it down for her.*

purpose was to travel the country preaching about God and the injustices of slavery. To begin one of her most famous speeches, she sang a hymn that she had created. One of the verses said:

"I am pleading that my people
May have their rights restored;
For they have long been toiling,
And yet have no reward."

Learn from Biographies

Reread the hymn verse that Sojourner Truth sang. In your own words, what do you think she was trying to say?

For more information, go online to *Meet the People* at **www.sfsocialstudies.com.**

Exposing Slavery's Evils

He lived the first twenty years of his life in slavery. But Frederick Douglass escaped to tell his own story and to fight for fair treatment for all people and an end to slavery.

The speaker was a tall African American. His voice boomed out over the crowd as he held up his hands. "These hands—are they not mine?" he asked. "This body—is it not mine?" But, he said, "I'm still a slave and the bloodhound may chase me down." The hundreds of people attending the American Anti-Slavery Convention listened closely to his every word.

The speaker was Frederick Douglass. Three years before, in 1838, he had escaped slavery in Maryland and fled to the North. Like many abolitionists, Frederick Douglass believed deeply that slavery was wrong. Yet, unlike the white abolitionists, Douglass could speak about slavery from firsthand experience—and he spoke powerfully.

In fact, Frederick Douglass spoke so well that some people began to accuse him of being a fake. "How could such an expressive man actually have been a slave?" some asked. Both to prove doubters wrong and expose the horrors of slavery, Frederick Douglass wrote his own story. His book, *Narrative of the Life of Frederick Douglass: An American Slave,* was published in 1845 and became an immediate success.

People were shocked to read about how slaves were treated. As a boy, Douglass said, he

BUILDING CITIZENSHIP

Caring
Respect
Responsibility
★ Fairness
Honesty
Courage

only had one shirt to wear throughout the cold winters and often did not have enough to eat. He saw his aunt beaten severely. When he was older, a cruel owner whipped him with tree branches until his back was bloody.

Some owners treated him better. A woman in Baltimore began to teach him how to read. But Douglass always hated being someone else's property. He told of looking at boats on the Chesapeake River and thinking:

> *"You move merrily before the gentle gale [wind], and I sadly before the bloody whip... O that I were free!... Why am I a slave?... I will not stand it.... God helping me...It cannot be that I shall live and die a slave."*

NARRATIVE

OF THE

LIFE

OF

FREDERICK DOUGLASS,

AN

AMERICAN SLAVE.

WRITTEN BY HIMSELF.

THE NORTH STAR.

When he was twenty, Douglass escaped to New York. He gave thousands of speeches and wrote articles and three autobiographies. In 1847, he started his own anti-slavery newspaper, called *The North Star*. Frederick Douglass's fight against the unfairness of slavery inspired many people to join the fight to abolish it. Today his powerful words continue to inspire people seeking freedom and fairness around the world.

Fairness in Action

Research a situation in a part of the world today where people are treated unfairly because of their color or ethnic background. Write a short speech about the situation, making the speech as powerful as you can. Give facts to support your position.

Ideals of the 19th-Century Reformers

The Declaration of Independence promised liberty and equality for all Americans. However, many people still were not treated equally after it was signed. Women did not have the same rights as men. Many African Americans were slaves. Most children did not go to school, and many worked in fields and shops. People of the nineteenth century reform movements worked to change these conditions.

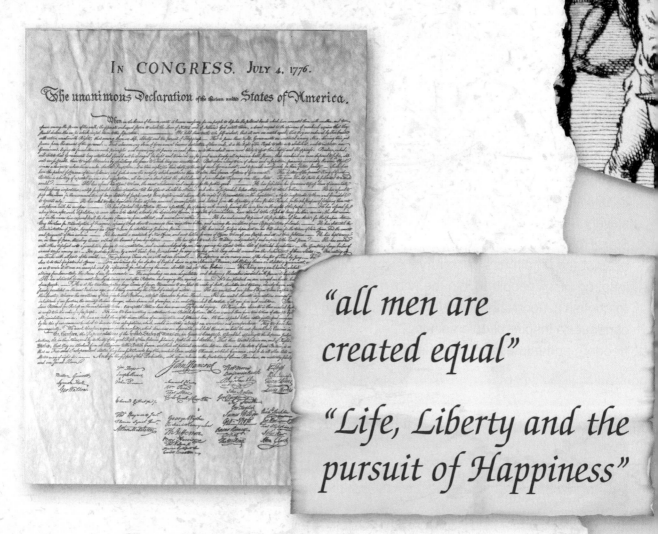

"all men are created equal"

"Life, Liberty and the pursuit of Happiness"

Children who were not from wealthy families often did not get a formal education. Reformers worked to give all Americans the right to an education. The changes these reformers started grew into our modern public-school system. The first law requiring children to attend school was passed in Massachusetts in 1852. That was 76 years after the Declaration of Independence. ▶

It was legal for African Americans to be enslaved from the time they first arrived in North America in the 1600s. The Declaration of Independence did not change this. African American reformers made speeches and printed newspapers to protest slavery and unfair treatment. In 1865, the Thirteenth Amendment to the Constitution ended slavery in the United States. That was 89 years after the Declaration of Independence. ▼

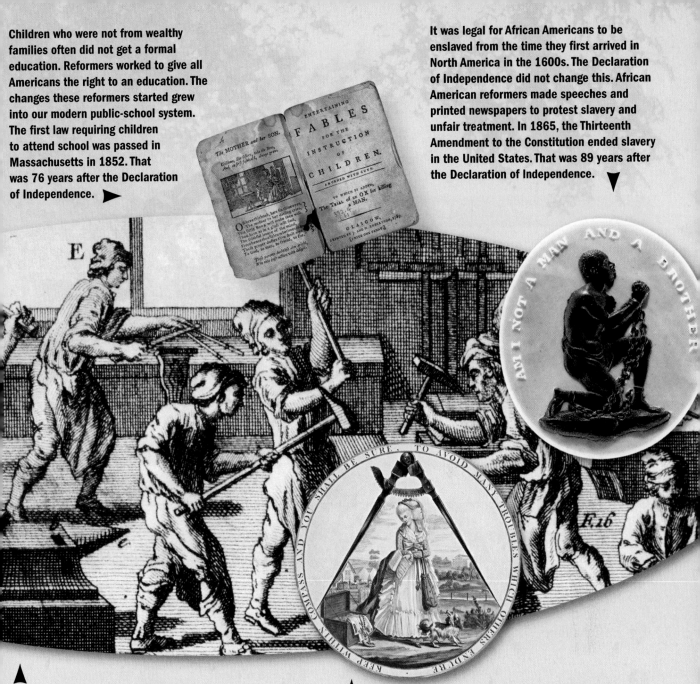

▲
Children as young as seven had to work in early America. They worked on farms and in factories. Reformers worked throughout the nineteenth century to stop child labor. Finally, in 1938 Congress passed the Fair Labor Standards Act. It set eighteen as the youngest age for factory workers. That was 162 years after the Declaration of Independence.

▲
Women's rights were not the same as men's. They could not vote. Married women could not own property. Women became more active in politics as the reform movement began. They helped create groups against slavery. They acted in support of the temperance movement. Women also wanted to vote, but their right to vote was not granted until 1920. That was 144 years after the Declaration of Independence.

The Declaration of Independence promised liberty and equality for all Americans. We still work today to make sure this promise is kept. Think of a group that you feel is not treated equally today. In a well-organized paragraph, identify the problem and the things you or others could do to change it.

425

1790

1800

1810

1790
Samuel Slater builds nation's
first cotton-spinning factory

1811
Construction
begins on
National Road

Chapter Summary

Compare and Contrast

On a separate sheet of
paper, copy the graphic
organizer to compare and
contrast the United States
before and after the
1820s. Include
information about these
two topics: suffrage and
technology.

Before 1820s	After 1820s

Vocabulary

Match each word with the correct definition or
description.

1 nationalism
(p. 403)

2 suffrage
(p. 404)

3 cotton gin
(p. 410)

4 mechanical
reaper (p. 410)

5 abolitionist
(p. 418)

a. reformer who
fought against
slavery

b. people pulling
together with a
sense of pride in
their country

c. machine to
harvest grain

d. the right to vote

e. machine to clean
cotton

People and Events

Write a sentence explaining why each of the
following people or events was important in the
development of a growing nation. You may use
two or more in a single sentence.

1 Era of Good
Feelings
(p. 403)

2 Monroe
Doctrine
(p. 403)

3 Sequoyah
(p. 405)

4 Indian Removal
Act (p. 405)

5 Industrial
Revolution
(p. 409)

6 Eli Whitney
(p. 410)

7 Robert Fulton
(p. 411)

8 Erie Canal
(p. 411)

9 Lucretia Mott
(p. 419)

10 Seneca Falls
Convention
(p. 419)

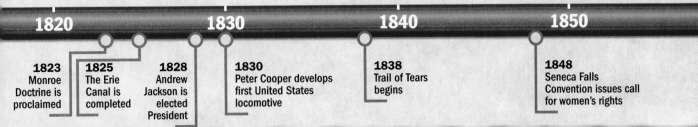

1820   1830   1840   1850

1823
Monroe Doctrine is proclaimed

1825
The Erie Canal is completed

1828
Andrew Jackson is elected President

1830
Peter Cooper develops first United States locomotive

1838
Trail of Tears begins

1848
Seneca Falls Convention issues call for women's rights

Apply Skills

Read a Cross-Section Diagram

Study the cross-section diagram of a modern locomotive. Then answer the questions.

1 How do you know this is a cross-section diagram?

2 What information does it give you?

3 What is the generator connected to?

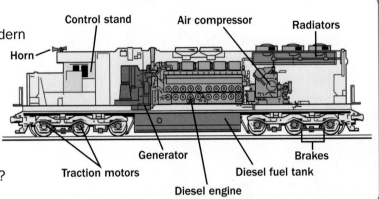

Control stand   Air compressor   Radiators

Horn

Generator   Brakes

Traction motors   Diesel fuel tank

Diesel engine

Facts and Main Ideas

1 Why did the United States send Andrew Jackson to Florida in 1817?

2 What invention led to the increase in cotton production?

3 **Time Line** How many years were there between the beginning of the National Road and the completion of the Erie Canal?

4 **Main Idea** In what ways did the United States expand its territory and power during the 1820s and 1830s?

5 **Main Idea** What important changes in the ways Americans lived and worked occurred as a result of the Industrial Revolution?

6 **Main Idea** Name three important movements started by reformers in the 1800s and describe their goals.

7 **Critical Thinking:** *Draw Conclusions* Why do you think Jackson was called "the People's President"?

Write About History

1 **Write a letter** that a soldier witnessing the Trail of Tears might have written to his family.

2 **Write a journal entry** of a young factory worker describing the activities of the day.

3 **Write a newspaper article** reporting on the events that took place at the Seneca Falls Convention.

Internet Activity

To get help with vocabulary, people, and terms, select dictionary or encyclopedia from *Social Studies Library* at **www.sfsocialstudies.com**.

CHAPTER 13

People Moving South and West

1836

San Antonio, Texas
Texans fall at the Battle of the Alamo.

Lesson 1

1

1846

Oregon Country
The United States and Britain sign a treaty agreeing on the border between Oregon and Canada.

Lesson 2

2

1848

American River, California
Gold is discovered in California.

Lesson 3

3

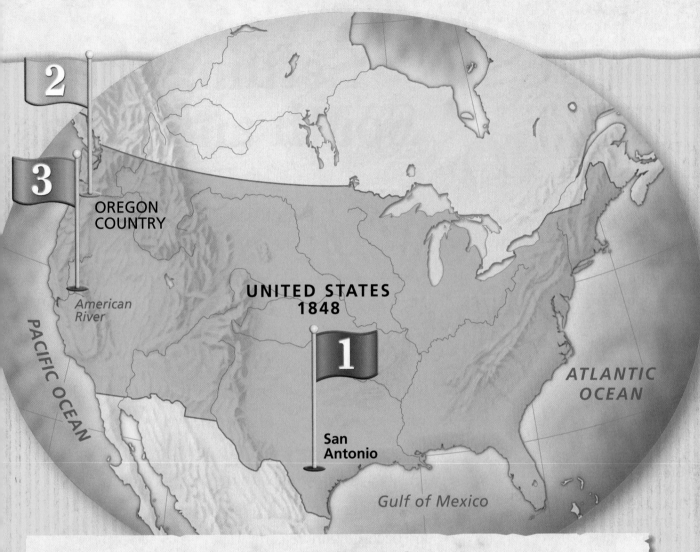

2

3

OREGON
COUNTRY

American
River

PACIFIC OCEAN

UNITED STATES
1848

1

San
Antonio

ATLANTIC
OCEAN

Gulf of Mexico

Why We Remember

Think about the place where you live. Was it part of the United States when our country began? If you live west of the Mississippi River, the answer to that question is no. From 1819 to 1848—just less than 30 years—the United States expanded west to the Pacific Ocean. American settlers poured into these places and established homes and communities. Other people, such as Native Americans and Mexican Americans, lost their homes as the newcomers arrived. The story of how these areas—perhaps your own area—became part of this country is the story of Chapter 13.

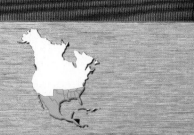

1820

1820s
United States settlers
begin moving to Texas
and continue settling
the South

1840

1836
Republic of
Texas is formed

1845
Texas and Florida
become states

Settling the South and Texas

You Are There

It's 1835 in Texas. Your family was one of the first 300 families from the United States to move to this Mexican-ruled territory. Your parents decided to leave your home in New Orleans in 1822 for the chance to buy cheap land for cattle ranching. Stephen F. Austin, who started a settlement along the Brazos River, led you and the other families to the area.

Your settlement has grown and thrived. But now tensions are growing with the Mexican government. The settlers from the United States are becoming increasingly unhappy being ruled by Mexico. Your family and others want Texas to be independent. Will there be a war between Texas and Mexico?

▶ **Stephen F. Austin**

Compare and Contrast

As you read, compare how the borders of the United States and Mexico changed over time.

PREVIEW

Focus on the Main Idea
The United States expanded as Americans settled the South, revolted in Texas, and fought a war with Mexico.

PLACES
Florida
Texas
Mexico
San Antonio

PEOPLE
Osceola
Stephen F. Austin
Antonio López de Santa Anna
Juan Seguín
Sam Houston
James K. Polk

VOCABULARY
Texas Revolution
annex
manifest destiny
Mexican War
Bear Flag Revolt
Treaty of Guadalupe Hidalgo

Moving South

Texas was not the only region attracting settlers in the early 1800s. (You will read about Texas on the next page). Treaties with Britain and Spain gave America control of the South. However, settlers did not come in great numbers until after 1814, when Andrew Jackson defeated the Native Americans at the Battle of Horseshoe Bend in present-day Alabama. You have read how Jackson's military role helped cause Spain to sell Florida in 1819, and he became the first military governor of this new American territory.

The great Seminole leader Osceola was captured in 1837, and Florida's Seminoles were finally defeated in 1842.

▶ Osceola fought to keep Seminole lands in Florida.

Settlers from Kentucky, Tennessee, and even New England began to move into the new southern frontier. But most settlers were farmers and planters from Georgia and the Carolinas, who brought enslaved people with them. The rich soil and warm climate of central Alabama and Mississippi were perfect for growing cotton, and the invention of the cotton gin made growing cotton even more profitable. In northern Alabama, settlers found rich deposits of iron. By 1817, enough people had moved to Mississippi for it to become a state. Alabama became a state in 1819. Florida had enough people for statehood by 1840, but was not admitted as a slave state until 1845 when the free state of Iowa could be admitted to keep a balance.

REVIEW What brought settlers into the new southern frontier? **Cause and effect**

MAP SKILL

Agriculture Expands in the South

Key:
- Tobacco
- Wheat
- Corn
- Cotton
- Rice
- Sheep
- Cattle
- Hogs

UNORGANIZED TERRITORY
INDIAN TERRITORY
MO
IL
KY
VA
TN
NC
AR
SC
MS
LA
AL
GA
TX
FL
ATLANTIC OCEAN
Gulf of Mexico

N

0   100   200 Miles
0   100   200 Kilometers

▶ This map shows animals and crops raised by settlers in the new southern frontier.

MAP SKILL Use a Key *What crop is not shown in any of the five states bordering the Gulf of Mexico?*

The Story of Texas

A project to settle people from the United States in **Texas** was pursued by **Stephen F. Austin** in the 1820s. Texas was then part of **Mexico,** and Mexico needed more settlers to build towns, farms, and ranches. By 1832 there were about 20,000 settlers from the United States in Texas. In some areas they outnumbered Mexican settlers—called *Tejanos* (tay HAH nohs)—ten to one.

Tensions grew between the Mexican government and the new settlers. Slavery was illegal in Mexico, but many settlers brought enslaved people with them from the United States. The Americans also refused to convert to the Catholic religion. They wanted more say in the government and resented being ruled from distant Mexico City. Fearing a rebellion, Mexico passed a law in 1830 forbidding additional American settlers.

By 1835, large numbers of Texas settlers, including Tejanos, decided to fight for their independence from Mexico. They began to

▶ David Crockett fought in the Creek Indian War, served as a congressman from Tennessee, and died at the Alamo.

organize an army and a new government. The **Texas Revolution** began. In December 1835 the Mexican president **Antonio lopez de Santa Anna** led an army from Mexico City to put down the rebellion. The Texans declared independence and formed the Republic of Texas on March 2, 1836.

Santa Anna's forces had reached **San Antonio** in February, where he found Texans in a fortified Spanish mission called the Alamo. There were only 184 men in the Alamo facing thousands of Mexican soldiers. After a 13-day siege, the Mexicans attacked the walls on March 6. Almost all of the defenders were killed, including their leader, William Travis, and two famous frontiersmen, David Crockett and James Bowie. Tejano soldiers serving under **Juan Seguín** (say GEEN) also died defending the Alamo, but Seguín survived because he was sent to get help before the Alamo fell.

The Texans had been defeated, but they delayed the Mexican advance long enough for Texas to sign up more soldiers. **Sam Houston,** leader of the Texas army, decided to attack the Mexican army near the San Jacinto (hah SIN toh) River. Before the battle Houston encouraged the Texans,

> *"Some of us may be killed. . . . But soldiers, remember the Alamo! the Alamo! the Alamo! Victory is certain!"*

On April 21, Houston's forces surprised Santa Anna's army. Shouting "Remember the Alamo," they defeated the Mexican army and captured Santa Anna. In exchange for his freedom, Santa Anna agreed to withdraw his troops south of the Rio Grande.

The Republic of Texas was now an independent country with Sam Houston as its elected president. It had its own flag with a single star, which is why Texas became known as the "Lone Star State." But it faced many problems. It needed to defend against raids from Mexico, and it was nearly broke. Many Texans wanted the United States to **annex,** or add, Texas as a state.

Sam Houston wrote a letter to President Andrew Jackson in 1836, asking him to "save us." Jackson refused, knowing that people in the United States disagreed about whether to annex Texas and make it a state. Many people in the United States believed in the idea of **manifest destiny,** or the belief that the United States should expand west to the Pacific Ocean. However, people opposed to slavery did not want Texas admitted because it would expand slavery in the United States.

Also, many feared that annexing Texas could lead to war with Mexico. The debate over Texas continued for almost ten years.

James K. Polk, who supported manifest destiny and annexing Texas, was elected President in 1844. The next year Congress voted to annex Texas and make it a state. You will read more about Polk in the Biography on page 437.

Tensions increased quickly between Mexico and the United States after Texas became a state. Although Mexico had signed a treaty granting Texas independence, it still thought of the area as part of Mexico. In addition, the United States and Mexico disagreed on the location of the Texas border.

REVIEW Why were people in the United States divided on the issue of Texas becoming a state? **Summarize**

The Alamo

Then and Now

In 1905, the Alamo was made a historic monument. Today the Alamo still stands in downtown San Antonio. You can visit the place that played such an important role in the history of Texas and the United States.

War With Mexico

Attempts to find a peaceful solution to the conflict between the United States and Mexico broke down. To prepare for a possible war, President Polk sent troops led by General Zachary Taylor into the area between the Rio Grande and the Nueces River in January 1846. Fighting began when Mexican troops crossed the Rio Grande in April. Polk told the American people that Mexico "has invaded our territory, and shed American blood upon American soil." Congress declared war on May 13, 1846—The **Mexican War** had begun.

Not all Americans supported the war. Abraham Lincoln, then a congressman from Illinois, believed that the United States had unfairly started the war to gain more land from Mexico. Mexico, he said, claimed the land where fighting began, just as the United States did. The writer, Henry David Thoreau, agreed and was put in jail when he refused to pay taxes to support the war.

▶ **The Bear Flag Revolt got its name from the California flag. General Zachary Taylor led his troops to victory in Mexico.**

CALIFORNIA REPUBLIC

Despite opposition to the war at home, United States troops were winning victories, especially in Mexico's northern territory. In June 1846 American settlers in California revolted, or rebelled, against the Mexican government. They captured the town of Sonoma and declared themselves independent. This became known as the **Bear Flag Revolt** because of the grizzly bear on the settlers' flag. The settlers joined with United States troops to drive the Mexican army south. By 1847, United States forces controlled all of New Mexico and California.

General Zachary Taylor had a more difficult time south of the Rio Grande. In the Battle of Buena Vista in February 1847, his troops were greatly outnumbered by those of Santa Anna. Before the battle began, Santa Anna sent a message to Taylor. "I wish to save you from a catastrophe," Santa Anna said. "You may surrender."

Taylor refused to give up. By the second day of fighting, the situation looked grim for the United States army. An American officer told Taylor, "General, we are whipped." But Taylor replied, "That is for me to determine." His troops went on to force Santa Anna to retreat. The victory made him a national hero.

REVIEW Why were some people opposed to the war with Mexico? **Main Idea and Details**

Expansion of the United States, 1783–1898

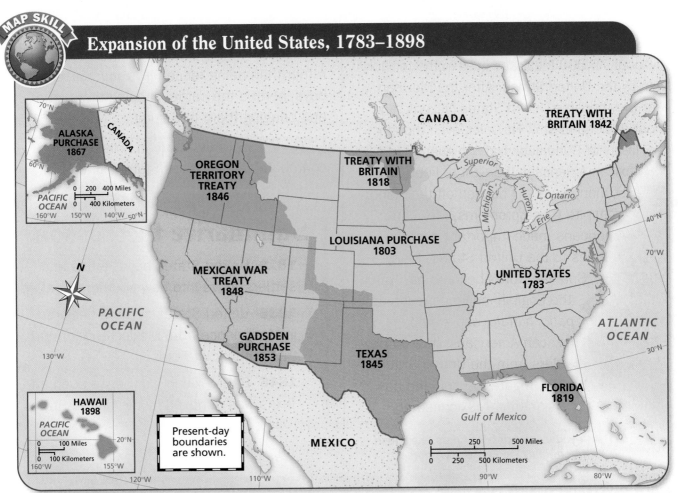

ALASKA PURCHASE 1867

CANADA

PACIFIC OCEAN

OREGON TERRITORY TREATY 1846

TREATY WITH BRITAIN 1818

CANADA

TREATY WITH BRITAIN 1842

L. Superior

L. Michigan

L. Huron

L. Ontario

L. Erie

LOUISIANA PURCHASE 1803

MEXICAN WAR TREATY 1848

PACIFIC OCEAN

GADSDEN PURCHASE 1853

TEXAS 1845

UNITED STATES 1783

ATLANTIC OCEAN

FLORIDA 1819

HAWAII 1898

PACIFIC OCEAN

Present-day boundaries are shown.

MEXICO

Gulf of Mexico

► As a result of the Mexican War, the territory of the United States extended to the Pacific Ocean.

MAP SKILL Place *What was the last state to become part of the United States?*

New Borders

President Polk ordered General Winfield Scott to invade Mexico by sea. Scott, like Taylor, was a veteran of the War of 1812. Scott's army captured the city of Veracruz on the eastern coast of Mexico and then marched to Mexico City. Scott captured Mexico City on September 14, 1847.

The **Treaty of Guadalupe Hidalgo** officially ended the Mexican War in February 1848. Mexico had to give up most of its northern territory to the United States. In return, the United States paid Mexico $15 million dollars. Look at the map to see the land that became part of the United States after the Mexican War. The states of California, Nevada, Utah, New Mexico, and parts of Arizona, Colorado, and Wyoming were later created out of the territory gained from Mexico.

Five years later, the United States paid Mexico $10 million for more land in present-day southern Arizona and southwestern New Mexico. This was called the Gadsden Purchase.

The United States now stretched across the continent, from the Atlantic to the Pacific oceans. But, as you will read, the question of slavery in the new territories would soon begin to split the nation.

REVIEW How did the United States benefit from the Mexican War? **Cause and Effect**

Mexican Americans

About 75,000 Mexicans lived in the territory won by the United States. After the Mexican War they became United States citizens, and most decided to stay. However, even though the Treaty of Guadalupe Hidalgo guaranteed Mexican Americans the right to keep property, many were still pushed off their land. Despite these problems, Mexican Americans made important contributions to the United States. Many Spanish words became part of the English language, such as *patio, buffalo,* and *stampede.* Mexican Americans showed new settlers from the United States how to irrigate the soil and how to raise cattle. Mexicans had

created the open-range system where cattle were allowed to roam freely over the land, rather than being fenced in. *Vaqueros,* or cowboys, herded the cattle, keeping them safe and bringing them to market.

REVIEW How did Mexican Americans contribute to the United States culture? **Main Idea and Details**

▶ A *vaquero* wore boot spurs like these when riding, to control the horse.

Summarize the Lesson

1819 United States buys Florida and settlers move into new southern frontier.

1836 United States settlers declared independence from Mexico and formed the Republic of Texas.

1846 The Mexican War began soon after Texas was annexed by the United States.

LESSON 1 ❯ REVIEW

Check Facts and Main Ideas

1. ↺ **Compare and Contrast** On a separate sheet of paper, fill in the diagram comparing and contrasting United States boundaries in 1844 and 1854.

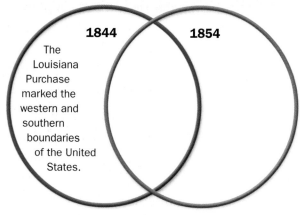

1844 The Louisiana Purchase marked the western and southern boundaries of the United States.

1854

2. What factors attracted settlers to the new southern frontier?

3. **Critical Thinking: *Summarize*** How did Texas gain its independence from Mexico?

4. Why did President Andrew Jackson refuse Sam Houston's request for the United States to **annex** Texas?

5. How did Generals Winfield Scott and Zachary Taylor contribute to the United States victory in the **Mexican War**?

Link to ⚭⚭ **Geography**

Make Tables of New States Look again at the map on page 435 that shows the land gained from Mexico. Make a table listing each new state created from this new United States territory and the year it became a state. Use the library or Internet for your research.

James K. Polk
1795–1849

Many historians believe that James K. Polk is one of the most underrated presidents. That means they think he should be more famous because he accomplished so much. During his one term in office, 1.2 million square miles were added to our country.

Polk was born in North Carolina, but his family later moved to Tennessee. He became a Congressman, then Speaker of the House of Representatives, and later, governor of Tennessee. Several more famous men were trying to be the Democratic presidential candidate in 1844, but no one could get a majority of votes, so Polk was chosen to break the deadlock.

The big issue was whether the United States should annex Texas and expand further west. Polk made it clear he favored both ideas so his election encouraged Congress to vote to annex Texas. In 1846 Polk stood firm on American claims to the Oregon country. The resulting treaty avoided war with Britain and gave the United States an area including the present-day states of Washington, Oregon, and Idaho. You have already read how Polk led the nation into war with Mexico. Although the war had opponents, the victory assured Texas would stay American and added a vast area to the United States, including California. The idea of manifest destiny seemed fulfilled.

Polk was one of our hardest working presidents. He once said:

> *"No president who performs his duties faithfully and conscientiously [with care] can have any leisure"*

BIOFACT

Polk graduated with honors from the University of North Carolina in 1818.

Learn from Biographies

What did Polk do that makes some historians think he is underrated?

For more information, go online to *Meet the People* at **www.sfsocialstudies.com.**

OREGON COUNTRY
Mormon Trail
Salt Lake City
Oregon Trail

1840   1850

1840s
Families begin moving west along the Oregon Trail

1846
Border is established between Oregon Country and Canada

1847
Mormons settle in Salt Lake City

PREVIEW

Focus on the Main Idea
Using a network of trails, people moved west to make better lives for themselves.

PLACES
Oregon Country
Oregon Trail
Mormon Trail
Salt Lake City

PEOPLE
Marcus Whitman
Narcissa Whitman
Joseph Smith
Brigham Young

VOCABULARY
mountain men
wagon train

Trails to the West

You Are There Teenager Mary Ellen Todd is learning to use a whip so that she can drive the team of oxen that is pulling her family's wagon west to Oregon. Since her parents decided to sell their farm in the east in 1852 and start over in Oregon, Mary Ellen says her life has been busy with "many things to be thought about and done."

Now they are finally on the westward trail with a group of other families and life has been very different from the routine on the farm. Just yesterday they had to cross a river, where one of the wagons was swept away in the fast-moving current.

Despite the dangers of the trail, Mary Ellen looks forward to a new life in Oregon. From the news she has heard, she expects her new home to be a beautiful place where she can make a better life.

Summarize As you read, consider what opportunities moving west offered settlers.

"Oregon Fever"

Mary Ellen Todd was just one of the more than 350,000 people who moved to Oregon Country between 1840 and 1860. **Oregon Country** was the name given to the region that makes up the present-day northwestern United States. Before 1846, both the United States and Great Britain claimed it.

The first settlers to Oregon Country from the United States were fur trappers and missionaries. The fur trappers in the West were known as **mountain men.** They explored the area, often using survival skills taught to them by Native Americans.

Missionaries traveled to Oregon Country to teach the Christian religion to Native Americans. **Marcus Whitman** and his wife, **Narcissa,** left New York to live and work among the Cayuse Indians in 1836. Like other missionaries, they sent letters back east praising their new home.

The large movement of people to Oregon Country began in the 1840s. The 2,000-mile route they traveled became known as the **Oregon Trail.** In 1846, the United States and Great Britain signed a treaty agreeing on the border between Oregon and Canada. Settlement of the border question encouraged even more settlers to head for Oregon. People eagerly seeking a new life in Oregon were said to have "Oregon fever."

This long and difficult journey was taken in covered wagons pulled by oxen or horses. People traveled in large groups, creating a long line of wagons called a **wagon train.** Life was hard and tiring for everyone. Rebecca Ketcham wrote in her journal:

> *"We can all, as soon as we stop, lie down on the grass or anywhere and be asleep in less than no time at all."*

There were many dangers on the trail. A fast-running river current could easily carry away a wagon trying to cross. Bad weather slowed the wagon trains. Many people died along the way from sickness and accidents.

Despite all the problems faced by the new settlers, they continued to pour into Oregon Country. One settler, Sarah Smith, wrote, "I could hardly believe that the long journey was accomplished and I had found a home."

REVIEW What kinds of difficulties did people on wagon trains face on the Oregon Trail? **Main Idea and Details**

▶ **Long wagon trains moved west on the Oregon Trail.**

FACT FILE

On the Western Trails, 1840s

As you can see from this map, there were many trails westward. Notice that many of these trails followed the path of rivers, which provided travelers with water for drinking, cooking, and cleaning.

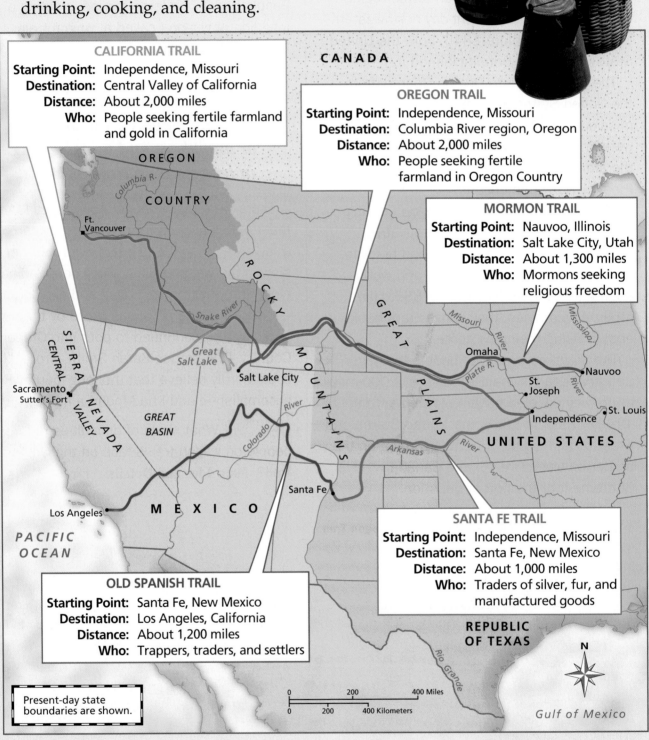

CALIFORNIA TRAIL
Starting Point: Independence, Missouri
Destination: Central Valley of California
Distance: About 2,000 miles
Who: People seeking fertile farmland and gold in California

OREGON TRAIL
Starting Point: Independence, Missouri
Destination: Columbia River region, Oregon
Distance: About 2,000 miles
Who: People seeking fertile farmland in Oregon Country

MORMON TRAIL
Starting Point: Nauvoo, Illinois
Destination: Salt Lake City, Utah
Distance: About 1,300 miles
Who: Mormons seeking religious freedom

SANTA FE TRAIL
Starting Point: Independence, Missouri
Destination: Santa Fe, New Mexico
Distance: About 1,000 miles
Who: Traders of silver, fur, and manufactured goods

OLD SPANISH TRAIL
Starting Point: Santa Fe, New Mexico
Destination: Los Angeles, California
Distance: About 1,200 miles
Who: Trappers, traders, and settlers

Present-day state boundaries are shown.

200   400 Miles
200   400 Kilometers

The Mormon Trail

Some people moved west for religious freedom. **Joseph Smith** founded the Church of Jesus Christ of Latter-day Saints in Fayette, New York, in 1830. He and his followers, known as Mormons, were often treated badly because of their religious beliefs. After an angry anti-Mormon crowd in Illinois killed Smith, the new leader, **Brigham Young**, decided that church members should build their own community farther west to be able to live and worship as they chose.

Starting in 1846, Young led a large group of Mormons from Illinois across the Great Plains, and over the Rocky Mountains. Many others followed, and the path Young took came to be known as the **Mormon Trail**. In

▶ **Joseph Smith (above) was 25 when he founded the Church of Jesus Christ of Latter-day Saints.**

1847, Young and his followers reached the Great Salt Lake area, which then belonged to Mexico. The Mormons founded **Salt Lake City** in the present-day state of Utah. Their well-planned community grew rapidly.

As you will read in the next lesson, the possibility of finding gold also attracted many people to the West.

REVIEW What events led to the founding of Salt Lake City? **Sequence**

Summarize the Lesson

- **1840s** Families began to travel in wagon trains along the Oregon Trail.

- **1846** The United States and Great Britain agreed on a border in Oregon Country, encouraging more settlers to move to the area.

- **1847** Mormons settled in Salt Lake City after moving west in search of religious freedom.

LESSON 2   REVIEW

Check Facts and Main Ideas

1. **Summarize** On a separate sheet of paper, fill in the missing detail and summary of the lesson.

```
┌─────────────┐  ┌─────────────┐  ┌─────────────┐
│ People moved│  │ Missionaries│  │             │
│ to Oregon   │  │ moved west  │  │             │
│ Country for │  │ to teach the│  │             │
│ fertile land│  │ Christian   │  │             │
│             │  │ religion.   │  │             │
└─────────────┘  └─────────────┘  └─────────────┘
        │              │                │
        ▼              ▼                ▼
      ┌──────────────────────────────────┐
      │                                  │
      │                                  │
      └──────────────────────────────────┘
```

2. What were the advantages and disadvantages of traveling west by **wagon train?**

3. Write a one-sentence summary describing each of the main trails leading west.

4. Explain the reasons different groups of people moved west.

5. **Critical Thinking: *Draw Conclusions*** Why do you think the 1846 treaty between the United States and Great Britain encouraged more settlement in Oregon Country?

Link to ⬥⬥ Writing

Write a Short Story Suppose you are a settler moving west in the 1840s. Which of the trails would you take and why? Write a short story describing your journey by wagon train.

1840   1850

1848
Gold is discovered in California

1849
Miners rush to California from all over the world

1850
The new state of California has a fast-growing, varied population

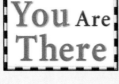
California Trail

San Francisco

American River

PREVIEW

Focus on the Main Idea
The discovery of gold in California led to rapid settlement of the region.

PLACES
American River
California Trail
San Francisco

PEOPLE
James Marshall
John Sutter
Luzena Stanley Wilson
Levi Strauss

VOCABULARY
gold rush
forty-niners
discrimination

The Golden State

You Are There James Marshall is in charge of the construction of a sawmill near the banks of the American River in California. On January 24, 1848, Marshall is inspecting the water-filled ditch that leads back to the river.

Suddenly he sees something shiny. He picks up the shiny speck and examines it. "It made my heart thump," he later says, "for I was certain it was gold."

James Marshall has discovered gold at Sutter's Mill. Soon the whole world will hear about the discovery and many people will head to California in search of riches.

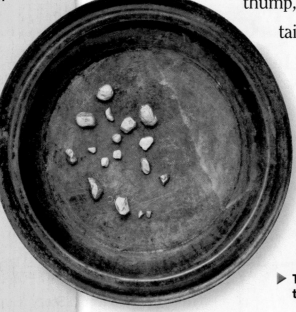

▶ The dream of finding gold nuggets like these drew thousands to California.

Compare and Contrast As you read, think about how California changed after the discovery of gold.

The California Gold Rush

In 1848, carpenter James Marshall discovered gold while building a sawmill near California's American River. His employer was John Sutter, a pioneer and owner of the land where the gold was found. Sutter reported that his workers "got the gold fever like everybody else," and left to search for gold. Miners set up camps all over his land.

This was the gold rush—a time when people were leaving their jobs, farms, and homes to come to California in search of riches. Reports of the discovery of gold traveled by word of mouth and in newspapers and letters sent back east and all over the world. In 1849, more than 80,000 people arrived in California. People coming to California during the gold rush became known as forty-niners, after the year in which so many of them arrived there. Signs reading "Off to the Mines" went up in businesses around the United States.

Thousands of forty-niners came by wagon and horseback over the California Trail, which climbed over the dangerous high slopes of the Sierra Nevada range. Pioneers followed trails established by guides such as James Beckwourth. Beckwourth Pass, high in the Sierra Nevada, is named after this guide, who made a trail through a gap in the high peaks.

Thousands of forty-niners also traveled by ship to San Francisco, which was near the gold fields. Some of the sea travelers sailed from the east coast of the United States, around the southern tip of South America and then north to California. This difficult 17,000-mile journey took from five to seven months to complete. Some forty-niners sailed to the east coast of Central America, made their way through thick forests to the Pacific Ocean, and there boarded ships bound for San Francisco. Still other forty-niners crossed the Pacific Ocean from China. As the table on this page shows, the small port village of San Francisco quickly grew into one of the major cities of the West.

REVIEW What caused the population of San Francisco to grow rapidly from 1848 to 1850? **Cause and Effect**

▶ The gold rush caused San Francisco to grow quickly from a small town to a busy city.

CHART SKILL *Between which two years on the chart did the population of San Francisco grow the most?*

Population of San Francisco, 1847-1860	
Year	Population
1847	800
1848	6,000
1850	25,000
1852	35,000
1856	50,000
1860	57,000

Source: U.S. Bureau of the Census

443

▶ **Hard-working gold miners (above) liked the tough denim pants made by Levi Strauss (below).**

Mining for Gold

For some, the dangers and hardships of the journey across land or sea were worth the goal of reaching California. For most, only disappointments waited for them. Most forty-niners found only small amounts of gold—if they found any at all. Searching for gold in streams and digging in gravel pits was hard work. When miners became sick, one wrote, they often had "no medicine, no bed but the ground."

Life was not easy in the mining camps. Because food and other supplies were scarce and demand was great, merchants could charge high prices. William McSwain complained that miners were paying one dollar for a pound of potatoes. In McSwain's home state of New York, potatoes cost only about one-half cent a pound. High prices and other challenges drove many to leave California. One miner declared "I have got enough of California and am coming home as fast as I can."

But others who came to California became successful selling supplies and services to the miners. Some entrepreneurs, such as **Luzena Stanley Wilson,** ran hotels and restaurants. Often these places were little more than shacks. "I bought two boards... (and) with my own hands I chopped stakes, drove them into the ground, and set up my (dining) table," Wilson reported. "Housekeeping was not difficult," she said, since there were "no windows to wash or carpets to take up." But the profits could be great. "Many a night have I shut my oven door on two milk pans filled high with bags of gold dust."

Shopkeeper **Levi Strauss,** an immigrant from Germany, moved to San Francisco in 1850. Strauss learned that miners wanted sturdy pants that would not easily fall apart. Together with a tailor, Strauss designed and made tough pants that were held together with rivets, or metal pins. At first the pants were made out of canvas, but later out of denim. Strauss's business prospered. Like many other newcomers to California, Strauss came to stay.

REVIEW Compare prices in California during the gold rush to those in New York. What accounts for the difference?

↻ **Compare and Contrast**

A Fast-Growing State

As a result of the gold rush, the population of California grew quickly. In 1845, about 15,000 people lived in Mexican-ruled California. In 1850, the year that California became a state, the United States census counted about 93,000 people there.

The new state's population was very varied. Tens of thousands were Native Americans—most not counted by the census. About 10,000 were Mexican Americans. They had become United States citizens after the Mexican War. Nearly one of every four Californians had immigrated from other countries.

Newcomers did find opportunities, but many also faced **discrimination,** or unfair treatment. In 1850, the state passed a law taxing immigrant miners $20 a month.

American-born miners did not have to pay the tax. Despite discrimination, however, many people continued to come to the "Golden State."

REVIEW Give details to support the main idea that California had a fast-growing population. **Main Idea and Details**

Summarize the Lesson

- **1848** Gold was discovered in California.
- **1849** Miners rushed to California from all over the world.
- **1850** Because of the gold rush, the population of California grew from 15,000 in 1845 to 93,000 in 1850, and became more varied.

LESSON 3 REVIEW

Check Facts and Main Idea

1. ↺ **Compare and Contrast** On a separate sheet of paper, fill in the box to describe what California was like before and after the discovery of gold.

Before 1848	After 1848

2. Who were the **forty-niners** and why were they called this name?

3. Describe three routes people from the eastern part of the United States used to travel to California.

4. Do you think the gold-mining life was what the miners expected it to be? Explain.

5. **Critical Thinking:** *Analyze Information* What might lead you to conclude that there was **discrimination** against immigrants in California in 1850?

Link to ⛓ Mathematics

Use a Chart Look at the chart on page 443. By how many people did San Francisco's population increase from 1847 to 1860?

Evaluate Advertisements

What? An advertisement tries to sell people goods, or services, or ideas. An advertisement, often called ad for short, may be printed, spoken, sung, or found on the Internet. The purpose is always the same—to interest people in what the advertiser is selling.

The advertiser may be selling any kind of goods, from toothbrushes, to clothing, to cars. Or the advertiser may be selling services, such as haircuts, cooking lessons, or a trip. Or the advertiser may even be selling an idea, such as urging people to vote for a person running for office.

The advertisement shown here was published in a newspaper in New York City during the early years of the gold rush.

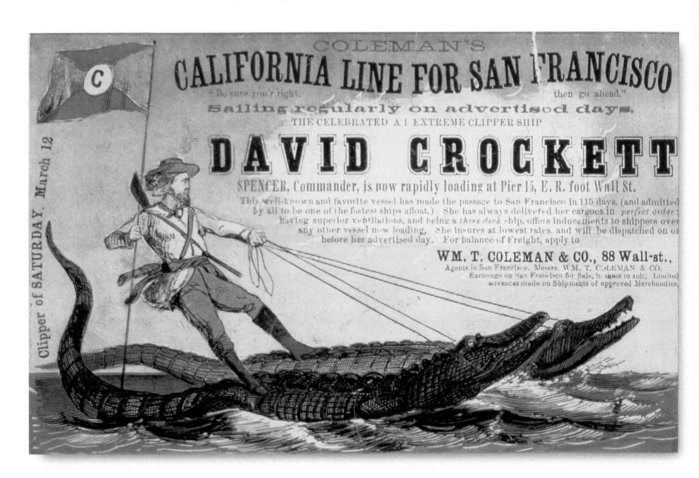

Orange juice is **GOOD** for you!

Drink **Orange Juice**

Get the vitamin C, fiber and potassium that you need!

Why? It is important to **evaluate,** or make judgments about, advertisements in order to make good decisions about what goods or services to buy or what ideas to accept.

Advertisements can give you helpful information, such as facts about what is being sold. Advertisements can also exaggerate. They might say or suggest things that cannot possibly be accurate. Something that is accurate is true or correct. Whether accurate or misleading, ads often use names or pictures intended to catch people's interest.

How? When you look at an advertisement, you need to ask some questions in order to evaluate its accuracy.

• What is the advertiser selling?
• Who are the people the advertiser is trying to reach?
• What facts can be found in the advertisement?
• What words or illustrations are used to encourage people to buy something or to support an idea?
• How accurate is the advertisement? Is there anything in the advertisement that cannot possibly be true?

Think and Apply

1. Look at the **advertisement** on page 446. What is it selling? Who might be interested in what is being sold?

2. What facts are given in the advertisement?

3. What does the picture show that cannot possibly be true?

1820   1830

1820s
United States settlers begin
moving to Texas and
continue settling the South

Chapter Summary

 Compare and Contrast

Use the diagram to compare and contrast the
reasons for population growth in Texas and
California during the first half of the 1800s.

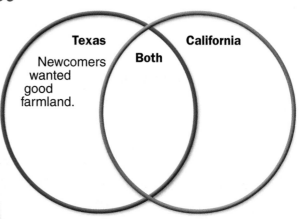

Texas | Both | California
Newcomers
wanted
good
farmland.

Vocabulary

Match each word with the correct definition or
description.

1 **annex** (p. 433)

2 **manifest destiny**
(p. 433)

3 **mountain men**
(p. 439)

4 **gold rush**
(p. 443)

5 **forty-niner**
(p. 443)

a. person who went to
California to look for
gold

b. fur trappers and
guides in the West

c. period when people
went to California in
search of riches

d. attach

e. belief that the
United States should
expand to the Pacific
Ocean

People and Places

Write a sentence explaining why each of the
following people or places was important in the
growing nation. You may use two or more in a
single sentence.

1 **Osceola**
(p. 431)

2 **Stephen F.
Austin** (p. 432)

3 **San Antonio**
(p. 432)

4 **Juan Seguín**
(p. 432)

5 **Oregon Trail**
(p. 439)

6 **Mormon Trail**
(p. 441)

7 **Brigham Young**
(p. 441)

8 **James Marshall**
(p. 443)

9 **San Francisco**
(p. 443)

10 **Luzena Stanley
Wilson** (p. 444)

1836
Republic of
Texas is formed

1840s
Families begin
moving west along
the Oregon Trail

1845
Texas and
Florida
became
states

1846
Mexican
War
begins

1848
United States wins
Mexican War

1849
Gold-seekers rush
to California from
all over the world

1850
California
becomes a state

Facts and Main Ideas

1 Name two events that led to war between the United States and Mexico.

2 In what ways did people profit from the gold rush?

3 **Time Line** How many years was Texas a republic before it became a state?

4 **Main Idea** How did the Texas Revolution and the Mexican War expand the territory of the United States?

5 **Main Idea** Why were people willing to face the hardships of the trails to the West?

6 **Main Idea** What changes took place in California as a result of the discovery of gold?

7 **Critical Thinking:** *Understand Viewpoints* Would you have been in favor of the war with Mexico in 1846? Why or why not?

Apply Skills

Evaluate Advertisements

Read the advertisement below. Then answer the questions.

1 What is this advertisement selling?

2 What does it show that cannot be true?

3 What words and phrases are used to suggest speed?

Write About History

1 **Write a news story** about the Battle of the Alamo.

2 **Write a letter to a friend** in the East about your travels along the Oregon Trail.

3 **Write an advertisement** for a product you are trying to sell to gold miners in 1849.

Internet Activity

To get help with vocabulary, people, and terms, select dictionary or encyclopedia from *Social Studies Library* at **www.sfsocialstudies.com**.

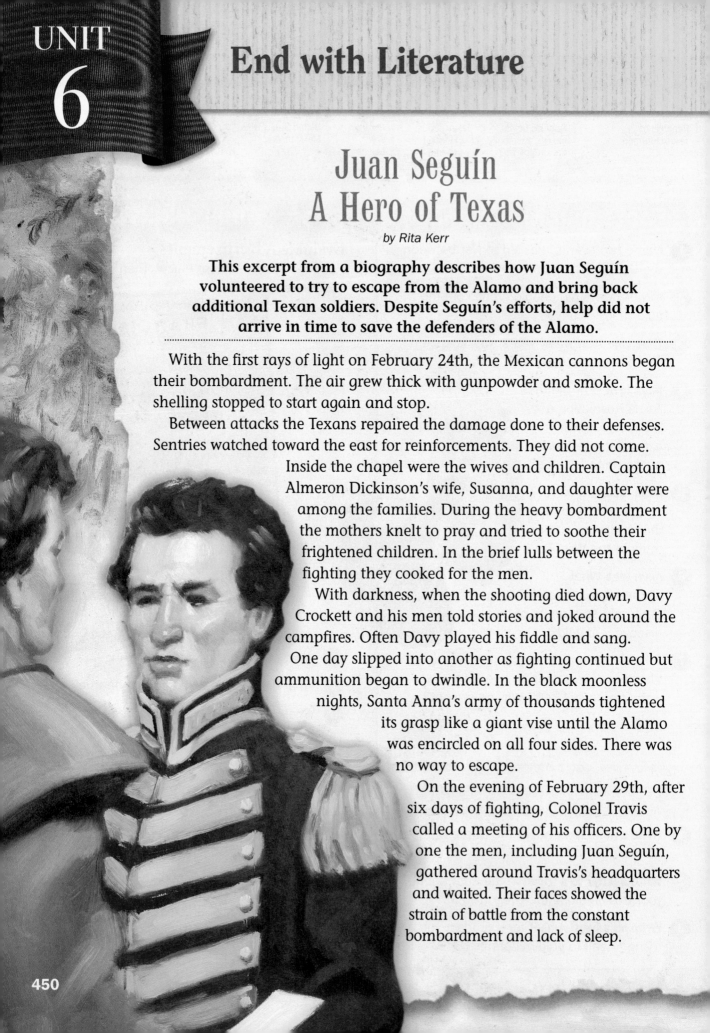

Juan Seguín
A Hero of Texas

by Rita Kerr

This excerpt from a biography describes how Juan Seguín volunteered to try to escape from the Alamo and bring back additional Texan soldiers. Despite Seguín's efforts, help did not arrive in time to save the defenders of the Alamo.

With the first rays of light on February 24th, the Mexican cannons began their bombardment. The air grew thick with gunpowder and smoke. The shelling stopped to start again and stop.

Between attacks the Texans repaired the damage done to their defenses. Sentries watched toward the east for reinforcements. They did not come.

Inside the chapel were the wives and children. Captain Almeron Dickinson's wife, Susanna, and daughter were among the families. During the heavy bombardment the mothers knelt to pray and tried to soothe their frightened children. In the brief lulls between the fighting they cooked for the men.

With darkness, when the shooting died down, Davy Crockett and his men told stories and joked around the campfires. Often Davy played his fiddle and sang.

One day slipped into another as fighting continued but ammunition began to dwindle. In the black moonless nights, Santa Anna's army of thousands tightened its grasp like a giant vise until the Alamo was encircled on all four sides. There was no way to escape.

On the evening of February 29th, after six days of fighting, Colonel Travis called a meeting of his officers. One by one the men, including Juan Seguín, gathered around Travis's headquarters and waited. Their faces showed the strain of battle from the constant bombardment and lack of sleep.

"Men," Travis said, looking from one to another. "We must get help and reinforcements. There has been no answer to the dispatches sent to Fannin. I have written another. The question is, who will go?" He paused. "You realize, of course, the danger of crossing the enemy lines. We are surrounded. Anyone want to volunteer?" He looked from Crockett to Dickinson on around the room.

No one spoke.

Captain Juan Seguín stepped forward. All eyes rested on him. "Sir, I will go!"

Travis protested, "But, Seguín, I need you."

"Sir, I think I am the only one who could get through those sentries. Being a Tejano, I could answer in Spanish if a soldier stopped me. I could pretend to be one of them." Travis shook his head. "I don't like it, but let's take a vote." The majority voted in favor of Juan Seguín being the messenger. Travis reluctantly agreed. "Besides, I'll be able to find my way in the dark, I know this country." "Colonel, I don't have a horse." Seguín paused to swallow the lump that formed in his throat with the thought of his Prince. "My horse was killed in one of their attacks. I'll ask Bowie if I can borrow his."

Travis nodded, rumpling his hair with his fingers. "Guess you are right, Seguín." He sighed. "Had hoped to use you if Santa Anna sent a message but this dispatch must get out of here. Better take one of your men with you." He handed Juan a paper from his desk. "Give this to Fannin. Tell him we must have help or—" He did not finish.

"Sir," Juan replied as he folded the message and put it in his pocket. "I'll take Antonio Oroche with me. But if we wait until it's dark and they've settled for the night, we'll have a better chance of getting through."

The Colonel sighed and agreed. "You're probably right. When you come back you'll hear a rifle shot every hour on the hour as a signal if we are still fighting. "Well," he paused, "good luck, Seguín. Our future rests on that message getting out so we can have reinforcements."

"I'll do my best, sir," Juan said and looked to his friends who shook his hand. "Good luck to you, amigos. Vaya usted con Dios." With a quick salute, Juan smashed his hat on his head and turned on his heels to walk out into the dusky evening. Drops of rain and a sharp north wind hit his face.

Main Ideas and Vocabulary

TEST PREP

Read the passage below and use it to answer the questions that follow.

After its fiftieth birthday in 1826, the United States grew in many ways. It gained land from Spain and Mexico and settled the Oregon border with Great Britain.

Canals, railroads, and better roads made travel faster. New routes such as the National Road and the Oregon Trail made it possible for people to move west.

During the Era of Good Feelings, a spirit of nationalism spread through the country. In the 1828 election of Andrew Jackson, more men voted than ever before. Jackson directed the forced removal of American Indians from the southeast to western lands.

Women began to work for suffrage and for other rights. People like Frederick Douglass and Sojourner Truth worked with others to try to end slavery.

Settlers from the United States moved to the new southern frontier and Texas. Mexico found it difficult to enforce its laws over the Texans, who fought the Texas Revolution to gain independence. The United States annexed Texas in 1845, setting off a war with Mexico. After winning the war, the United States bought new lands from Mexico in 1848.

People moved west to gain a better life in the Oregon Country. Many pioneers traveled in wagon trains. People poured into California after gold was discovered there in 1848.

1 According to the passage, what was one reason settlers moved west?
- **A** The government said they should move.
- **B** They went for a better life.
- **C** There was no longer enough space to live in the East.
- **D** They had to move because there were new forms of transportation.

2 In the passage, the word nationalism means—
- **A** attacking other nations
- **B** belief that the country had to grow
- **C** pulling together with pride in one's country
- **D** belief that all nations are equal

3 In the passage, the word suffrage means—
- **A** suffering for one's beliefs
- **B** the right to vote
- **C** ending slavery
- **D** property ownership

4 What is the main idea of the passage?
- **A** The United States was growing.
- **B** The United States was always at war.
- **C** People in the United States did not like the nation's policies.
- **D** California had a gold rush.

People and Terms

Match each person and event to its definition.

1 **Monroe Doctrine** (p. 403)

2 **Elizabeth Cady Stanton** (p. 419)

3 **Sam Houston** (p. 432)

4 **Narcissa Whitman** (p. 439)

5 **John Sutter** (p. 443)

6 **forty-niner** (p. 443)

a. owned land where gold was discovered

b. person who went to California to find gold

c. missionary to the Oregon Country

d. warned Europeans to stay out of Western Hemisphere

e. first president of Republic of Texas

f. fighter for women's rights

Write and Share

Present a Travel Talk Work in a group to present a talk about traveling to different parts of the country during the first half of the 1800s. Include different kinds of travel—railroads, roads, wagon trains, boats, combinations of travel—to different regions mentioned in this unit. Each student should write about his or her experiences and prepare maps or illustrations to show the routes taken. Each speaker should give a short talk and then answer questions about their reasons for travel and whether they found what they expected.

Read on Your Own

Look for books like these in the library.

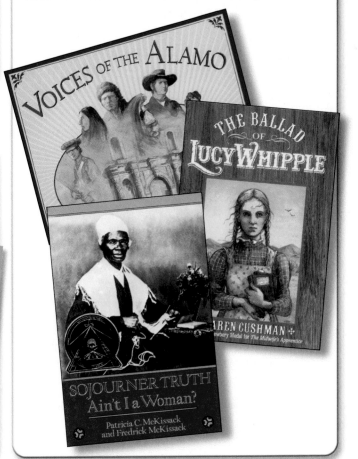

Apply Skills

Create Pioneer Advertisements Create advertisements to attract newcomers to places described in this unit, such as the Great Salt Lake, Oregon Country, or gold fields of California. Try to include some exaggeration, as the ads of the time did. Use the style of the ad on pages 446–447 as a model. Afterwards, share your ad with classmates so that they can evaluate its accuracy.

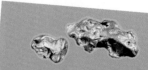

GOLD! GOLD! GOLD!

All the gold you ever want just waiting to be picked up.

Lure of the Land

Tell about a trail that the settlers may have taken as they traveled west.

1 **Form** groups to prepare a travel program about settlers moving west. Choose a trail they may have taken.

2 **Research** and write the reasons travelers journeyed to the West on this trail.

3 **Draw** a map that illustrates the route of the trail. You may also want to combine groups to create a poster or backdrop for your program.

4 **Present** your program to the class.

Internet Activity

Explore westward movement on the Internet. Go to **www.sfsocialstudies.com/activities** and select your grade and unit.

War Divides the Nation

What might cause a nation to break apart?

1820

1850

1860

1820
Congress passes
Missouri Compromise

1849
Harriet Tubman
escapes slavery on the
Underground Railroad

1860
Abraham Lincoln
is elected
President

April 1861
Southern forces
fire on Fort
Sumter,
beginning the
Civil War

January 1863
Emancipation
Proclamation
takes effect

> *"...that these dead shall not have died in vain— that this nation, under God, shall have a new birth of freedom..."*
>
> —Said by President Abraham Lincoln in the Gettysburg Address, November 19, 1863

This print by Currier and Ives shows the Fall of Richmond, Virginia, to Union forces in 1865.

1870

July 1863
Battle of Gettysburg is fought

April 1865
Confederacy surrenders, ending the Civil War

December 1865
The 13th Amendment ends slavery

March 1867
Congress passes Reconstruction Act

Meet the People

Henry Clay
1777–1852
Birthplace: Hanover County, Virginia
Lawyer, planter
- Nicknamed "The Great Compromiser"
- Helped create the Missouri Compromise in 1820
- Created the Compromise of 1850

Robert E. Lee
1807–1870
Birthplace: Stratford, Virginia
Army officer
- Fought in the Mexican War
- Turned down Lincoln's offer to command the Union army
- Became commander of the Confederate army

Jefferson Davis
1808–1889
Birthplace: present-day Todd County, Kentucky
Plantation owner
- Served as United States Senator from Mississippi
- President of the Confederacy during the Civil War
- Wrote a book about the Confederate government

Abraham Lincoln
1809–1865
Birthplace: Near Hodgenville, Kentucky
Lawyer
- Opposed the spread of slavery
- President of the United States from 1861–1865, during the Civil War
- Issued the Emancipation Proclamation

1770   1790   1810   1830

1777 • Henry Clay

1807 • Robert E. Lee

1808 • Jefferson Davis

1809 • Abraham Lincoln

about 1813 • Joseph Cinque

about 1820 • Harriet Tubman

1821• Clara Barton

1822 • Ulysses S. Grant

Joseph Cinque

about 1813–about 1879

Birthplace: present-day Sierra Leone, West Africa

Rice farmer, leader of slave ship rebellion

- African name was Sengbe Pieh, which was pronounced by the Spanish as "Cinque"
- Led African captives in a revolt aboard the slave ship *Amistad*
- Served as key witness during the *Amistad* trial

Harriet Tubman

about 1820–1913

Birthplace: Dorchester County, Maryland

Conductor on the Underground Railroad, abolitionist

- Escaped from slavery in 1849 and settled in Philadelphia
- Made 19 trips to the South on the Underground Railroad and helped free over 300 slaves
- Spoke out against slavery and for women's rights

Clara Barton

1821–1912

Birthplace: Oxford, Massachusetts

Teacher, nurse

- Volunteered as a nurse during the Civil War
- Nicknamed the "Angel of the Battlefield"
- Founded the American Red Cross

Ulysses S. Grant

1822–1885

Birthplace: Point Pleasant, Ohio

Army officer

- Won the first major Union victory of the Civil War at Fort Donelson
- Appointed to command the Union armies by President Lincoln
- Elected President of the United States in 1868

1850   1870   1890   1910

1852

1870

1889

1865

about 1879

1913

1912

1885

Reading Social Studies

War Divides the Nation

Main Idea and Details

Look at the diagram to see how details support a main idea.

A main idea is the most important idea of a paragraph.

Details are information related to the main idea.

Each detail helps to support the main idea.

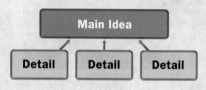

Read the following paragraph. The **main idea** and **details** have been highlighted.

In Chapter 13, you read about how the United States was growing and changing. The development of roads, waterways, and the railroad allowed people to move west. The nation's land was expanding. The way people lived was also changing. In some places, cities were growing and attracting factory workers. In other parts of the country, people were still living on farms but changing the way they harvested their crops.

Word Exercise

Use Context Clues Sometimes you can use clues from the text to help you figure out the meaning of an unfamiliar word. Read the third paragraph of the passage. Here is how to figure out the meaning of *victorious*:

1. Reread the sentence before the sentence with *victorious*: What are *victories*? (wins)

2. Now reread the sentence that *victorious* is in. What does *surrendered* mean? (gave up)

3. Using *victories* and *surrendered*, what is the meaning of *victorious*? (winning)

Main Ideas and Details of War Divides a Nation

Differences between the Northern and Southern states led to many problems for the United States. The rural South depended on farming and slavery. The North had more factories and larger cities than the South.

Trouble grew when Abraham Lincoln became President in 1861. South Carolina broke away from the Union. Before long, eleven states in the South had done the same and formed the Confederate States of America. The country was divided and went to war. This war was called the Civil War.

Each side won some battles. In late 1863, Northern victories increased. In 1865, the North was victorious and the South surrendered.

Lincoln hoped to reunite the nation, but he was killed shortly after the Civil War. President Andrew Johnson and Congress fought over Reconstruction, or the plans for rebuilding the South. Amendments to the Constitution ended slavery and gave the vote to all male citizens, black and white.

Federal troops and Reconstruction laws governed Southern states. The Freedmen's Bureau, a federal agency, provided aid and set up schools for African Americans.

When Reconstruction ended in 1877, some Southerners tried to keep freed slaves from voting. Groups like the Ku Klux Klan burned black schools and terrified black men who tried to vote. Southern states also passed Jim Crow laws, which said African Americans could only use designated non-white areas in restaurants, trains, buses, hotels, and other public places.

Use the reading strategy of main idea and details to answer questions 1 and 2. Then answer the vocabulary question.

1 What is the main idea of the first paragraph?

2 What details support that main idea?

3 What clues can help you figure out the meaning of the word *rural* in the first paragraph of the passage? When you think you know what *rural* means, check a dictionary to see if you are correct.

CHAPTER 14

A Divided Nation

1820
United States
About 1.5 million enslaved people live in the United States, most in the Southern states.

Lesson 1

1849
Philadelphia, Pennsylvania
Harriet Tubman escapes to freedom in Philadelphia on the Underground Railroad.

Lesson 2

March 1861
Washington D.C.
Abraham Lincoln is inaugurated as President.

Lesson 3

April 1861
Charleston, South Carolina
Southern troops fire on Fort Sumter.

Lesson 4

1

2

3

4

Why We Remember

"…one nation under God, indivisible, with liberty and justice for all."
These words are part of the Pledge of Allegiance, which Americans have said for many years. But there was a time when the words were not true for all Americans. In the middle 1800s, the United States was one nation divided into two parts, the North and the South. In the South, enslaved people grew crops such as cotton on plantations. In the North, where slavery was illegal, many people worked in factories and lived in cities. Differences between the North and the South sparked serious conflicts, which in 1861 set off a terrible war. By the end of the war, Americans began the long task of rebuilding the country—"with liberty and justice for all."

1840   1860

1846
Congress votes
to lower tariffs
on imports

1860
The number of enslaved African
Americans in the United States
reaches four million

PREVIEW

Focus on the Main Idea
Differences between North and
South led to growing tensions
between the two regions.

PEOPLE
David Walker

VOCABULARY
sectionalism

North and South Grow Apart

You Are There

The year is 1850, and you are a sailor on a ship that carries goods to and from ports on the East coast of the United States. Your ship glides into the port of Charleston, South Carolina, and ties up at a dock. You see hundreds of bundles of cotton waiting to be loaded onto your ship. The cotton has been grown on plantations across the South. You know that most of the work on those plantations is done by people who are enslaved.

You join the other sailors to unload your ship of its cargo of manufactured goods from Boston, Massachusetts. The cargo includes tools, machines, and cloth made by free workers in factories. You know that Charleston and Boston are part of the same country, the United States. Yet they are so different they might well be parts of different countries. Before long their differences will lead to war.

Main Idea and Details As you read, focus on how the North and South differed and how each of the differences pushed the two regions apart.

Two Regions

Many changes had taken place in the United States since the country was formed. The North and South had always been quite different geographically, but after the start of the Industrial Revolution, the differences between the two regions increased dramatically.

Southerners lived a mostly rural way of life. Most lived and worked on farms and in small towns. By the middle 1800s, few Southern cities had a population of over 15,000.

In contrast, many Northerners at that time lived an urban way of life. Although most Northerners still lived on farms, more and more people worked in factories and lived in large towns and cities. In 1860 nine of the ten largest cities in the United States were located in the North. The bar graph and circle graphs below show how the populations of the North and South differed in 1850.

Factory owners and factory workers in the North had different goals from those of planta- tion owners and farmers in the South. These different interests caused a strong disagree- ment in 1846. A law passed by Congress in that year caused the disagreement. The law lowered the tariffs the United States charged for goods imported from other countries. This made Northern factory owners angry.

The Northern states had wanted higher tar- iffs, or taxes on imported goods. Higher prices on imported goods would encourage Americans to buy manufactured goods from the North.

The Southern states, however, wanted lower tariffs. They preferred to buy the cheaper goods made in Great Britain.

The way of life of one section of the United States was threatening the way of life in the other section of the United States. These differences caused sectionalism in our country. **Sectionalism** is a loyalty to a section or part of the country rather than to the whole country.

REVIEW Explain how differences between the North and South led to conflict between them. ↻ **Main Idea and Details**

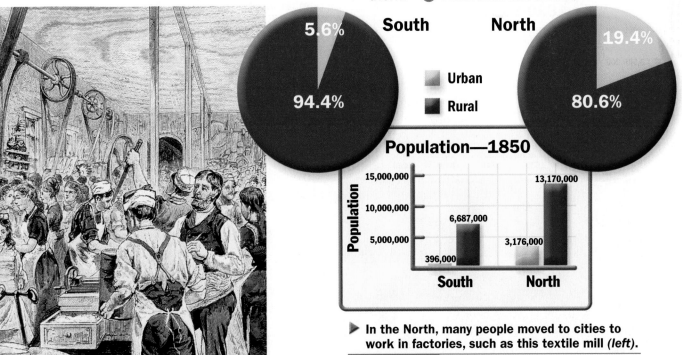

South — Urban 5.6% / Rural 94.4%

North — Urban 19.4% / Rural 80.6%

Urban / Rural

Population—1850

Population:
- 15,000,000
- 10,000,000
- 5,000,000

South: 396,000 / 6,687,000
North: 3,176,000 / 13,170,000

▶ In the North, many people moved to cities to work in factories, such as this textile mill *(left)*.

GRAPH SKILL *How many people lived in Northern cities in 1850?*

465

Slavery in the South

One very important difference between the North and the South was slavery. Slavery was allowed in the Southern states, where enslaved people grew such crops as cotton, tobacco, and rice. By 1850 most Northern states had outlawed slavery. Northern workers were free and were paid for their work. In many Northern factories, however, workers put in long hours, under difficult conditions, for low pay.

Slavery was profitable to the economy of the South. The goods an enslaved person produced brought in at least twice as much money as the cost of owning the slave. In 1850 about six out of every ten slaves in the South worked in the cotton fields. Cotton was usually grown on large plantations. However, many slaves lived on small farms. On these smaller farms, the owner often worked in the fields alongside a small group of slaves. But only about one-third of Southern farmers owned slaves.

By 1860 enslaved African Americans in the United States totaled almost four million people. In some states, they outnumbered the free whites. The line graph on this page shows how the number of enslaved people changed between 1820 and 1860. It also shows changes in the population of free African Americans during the same time. Most of the enslaved African Americans lived in the South, while most of the free African Americans lived in the North.

Even free African Americans did not always have the same voting rights as whites. In some states, only people who owned property could vote. However, in states where this requirement had been dropped for whites, such as in New York, blacks still had to own land before they could vote. Throughout the country African Americans suffered from discrimination. They did not have the rights of full citizenship.

REVIEW Identify the main reason why the South wanted to keep slavery.
⤵ **Main Idea and Details**

Free and Enslaved African Americans 1820-1860

Population

- 4,000,000
- 3,000,000
- 2,000,000
- 1,000,000

● Enslaved Population
○ Free Population

1820 1830 1840 1850 1860

▶ As Southern cotton plantations *(below)* grew, so did the number of enslaved African Americans.

GRAPH SKILL *About what was the population of free African Americans in 1840?*

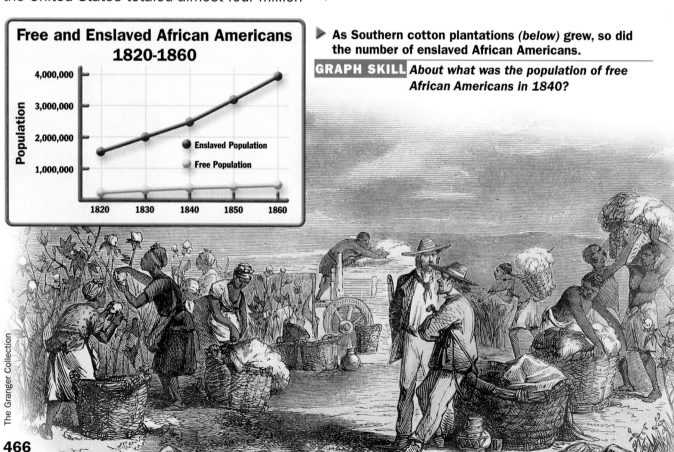

Different Views on Slavery

As you have read, abolitionists opposed the practice of slavery and fought to end slavery everywhere in the country. They insisted that slavery should be abolished because it was wrong for one human being to own another. One abolitionist, a free African American named David Walker, asked this about the Southern slave owners:

> *"How would they like us to make slaves of...them?"*

But Southern slave owners defended slavery. They pointed to the evils of factories in the North, where people worked long hours, in bad surroundings, for little pay.

Slave owners argued that slaves were better off than Northern factory workers.

Debate continued throughout the middle 1800s. But, as you will read, words were not the only weapons to be used against slavery.

REVIEW Identify one argument that supported the idea that slavery should be abolished. ⟳ **Main Idea and Details**

Summarize the Lesson

1846 Congress voted to lower the tariff on imports, which angered many Northerners.

1860 The number of enslaved African Americans in the United States reached almost four million.

LESSON 1   REVIEW

Check Facts and Main Ideas

1. ⟳ **Main Idea and Details** On a sheet of paper, complete the graphic organizer to show details supporting the main idea.

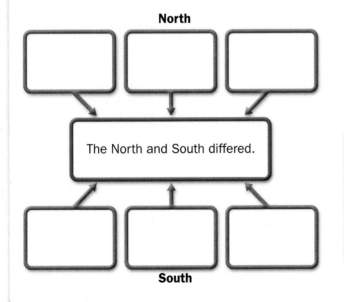

North

The North and South differed.

South

2. Describe how tariffs affected relations between North and South. Use the word **sectionalism** in your answer.

3. In 1860 were more African Americans enslaved or free? How do you know?

4. **Critical Thinking:** *Make Inferences* What conditions existed in the North that might lead to problems at a later date?

5. Describe the main argument of people opposed to slavery.

Link to ☐☐ Art

Create a Graph or Illustration Choose one topic from the lesson. Then show with a graph or a picture how the North and the South were growing apart.

Recognize Point of View

What? Point of view is the way a person looks at or thinks about a topic or situation. A person's point of view may be affected by his or her experiences and way of life. As you have read in Lesson 1, people had very different points of view about slavery.

In the selections on these pages, two writers expressed their points of view about slavery. The writers tried to support their points of view with descriptions and details.

Selection A was written by George Fitzhugh, a lawyer who was a supporter of slavery. His family had lived in the South for many years and had owned a 500-acre plantation.

Selection B was written by Frances Anne (Fanny) Kemble, a famous British actress married to Pierce Butler, an American. In 1836 Butler inherited two Southern plantations and became one of the largest slaveholders in the country. His wife became an opponent of slavery and moved back to Britain. Years later she wrote of her experiences in *Journal of a Residence on a Georgian Plantation*.

George Fitzhugh

Fanny Kemble

Why? As a reader, you need to be able to identify a writer's point of view so that you can understand the writer's choice of details. Writers may use their own feelings and beliefs when they decide what to include and how to tell their story.

How? To recognize a writer's point of view, you may follow these steps:

1 Identify the topic.

2 Determine which statements are fact and which are opinions.

3 Look for words or phrases that tell how a writer feels about the topic.

4 Consider the writer's experiences and way of life. How might these affect the writer's point of view?

5 Describe the writer's point of view.

Selection B

"I have sometimes been haunted [worried] with the idea that it was … [a] duty, knowing what I know, and having seen what I have seen, to do all that lies in my power to show the dangers and the evils of this frightful institution [slavery]…The handcuff, the lash—the tearing away of children from parents, of husbands from wives—the weary trudging [walking] …along the common highways, the labor of body, the despair of mind [hopelessness], the sickness of heart—these are the realities which belong to the system, and form the rule, rather than the exception, in the slave's experience."

—Fanny Kemble

Selection A

"The negro slaves of the South are the happiest, and in some sense, the freest people in the world. The children and the aged and infirm [sick or weak] work not at all, and yet have all the comforts and necessaries [needs] of life provided for them. They enjoy liberty, because they are oppressed [weighed down] neither by care nor labor. The women do little hard work, and are protected from … their husbands by their masters [slave owners]. The negro men and … boys work, on the average, in good weather, not more than nine hours a day. The balance of their time is spent in [relaxation]. Besides, they have their Sabbaths and holidays…. They can sleep at any hour…. We do not know whether free laborers [in the North] ever sleep."

—George Fitzhugh

Think and Apply

1. What is the subject of both of these writers?

2. What details does each writer use to support his or her point of view?

3. What are the points of view each writer reveals?

4. How might the experiences and way of life of each writer affect his or her point of view?

1830

1850

1831
Nat Turner leads a slave rebellion in Virginia

1841
The Supreme Court frees the prisoners from the slave ship *Amistad*

1849
Harriet Tubman escapes from slavery on the Underground Railroad

New Haven

Southampton County

PREVIEW

Focus on the Main Idea
Enslaved African Americans resisted slavery in many different ways.

PLACES
Southampton County, Virginia
New Haven, Connecticut

PEOPLE
Nat Turner
Joseph Cinque
Harriet Tubman
Levi Coffin
Catherine Coffin

VOCABULARY
slave codes
Underground Railroad

Resisting Slavery

You Are There September 11, 1853, in Richmond, Virginia. In a house in the city, J.H. Hill, an escaped slave, waits for a message.

Later Hill wrote, "Nine months I was trying to get away. I was secreted [hidden] a long time in a kitchen of a merchant." And then the long awaited message arrives. He is to meet a guide who will try to lead him to freedom in the North. Early next morning, Hill leaves his hiding place and carefully makes his way to the guide. "I felt composed [calm]," Hill reports, "for I had started…that morning for liberty or for death." Hill reached the North where, at last, he found liberty.

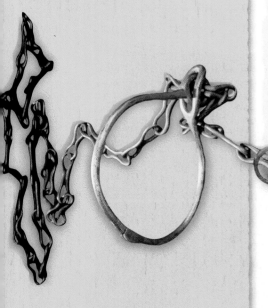

Main Idea and Details As you read, note the details that support the main idea that African Americans resisted slavery.

African Americans Resist Slavery

Some enslaved people, like J. H. Hill, resisted slavery by risking their lives in daring escapes. Other slaves found different ways to resist.

When enslaved people resisted slavery, they were fighting for their freedom. They were also fighting against a cruel system. They had no choices. They would be moved when they were sold, and they could not control who bought them. Many owners treated slaves well, but some beat or abused their slaves.

Another form of cruelty was the breaking up of families. Abream Scriven, a slave sold by his owner in 1858, was forced to leave his wife, father, and mother. He wrote these words to his wife:

> *"Give my love to my father and mother and tell them good bye for me, and if we shall not meet in this world I hope to meet in heaven."*

Slave owners had almost complete control over a slave's life. The owners told them when to start work and when to end work. Slaves could not leave the plantation without permission. Slave owners also decided whether slaves could marry and the age at which their children had to begin working.

Slave codes, or laws to control the behavior of slaves, also made life difficult for them. For example, most slave codes did not allow a slave to hit a white person, even in self-defense. Slaves were not allowed to own property, and few were allowed to buy and sell goods.

Resistance took many forms. Some slaves simply refused to obey the owner. Other slaves resisted by holding back the main thing they could control, their work. They worked more slowly, or pretended to be sick. Others broke the tools that were needed to do work.

Many enslaved people resisted by breaking rules that were meant to keep them ignorant. For example, slaves often were not allowed to learn to read or write. Some slaves learned in secret, risking punishment if they were found out.

REVIEW Describe some ways enslaved African Americans resisted slavery.
🔁 **Main Idea and Details**

▶ **Family members were often separated when slaves were sold.**

Slave Rebellions

To prevent enslaved people from planning rebellions, slave owners tried to keep slaves from gathering and meeting with one another. Still, rebellions did occur. One was planned and led by Nat Turner in Virginia.

In August 1831, Turner and his followers killed about 60 whites in Southampton County, Virginia. United States and Virginia troops were called in to stop them. The soldiers killed more than 100 African Americans before the rebellion was ended. Turner escaped but was later captured. He was hanged on November 11, 1831.

A later rebellion had a different ending. In 1839, a group of 53 captive Africans seized control of the Amistad, a Spanish slave ship carrying them from one port to another in Cuba. The Africans were led by a farmer from West Africa who became known as Joseph Cinque (SEEN kay). He told the Africans: "We may as well die in trying to be free."

After taking control of the ship, the Africans told a Spanish sailor to sail them back to Africa. But the Spaniard tricked them and instead sailed the Amistad north along the coast of the United States. The United States Navy captured the Amistad near Long Island, New York. The Africans were taken as prisoners to New Haven, Connecticut.

At first, the United States planned to return the ship and the Africans to the Spanish. Abolitionists and Northern newspapers printed articles against this plan and in support of the Africans. With their help, the Africans' fight for freedom eventually came before the Supreme Court. There, former President John Quincy Adams presented the Africans' case. He argued that the Africans were not property but human beings and should not be returned to Spain.

On March 9, 1841, the Supreme Court reached its decision. It agreed with Adams and freed the Africans. All 35 of the Africans who survived the rebellion sailed back to Africa later that year.

REVIEW Contrast the Nat Turner and Amistad rebellions. **Compare and Contrast**

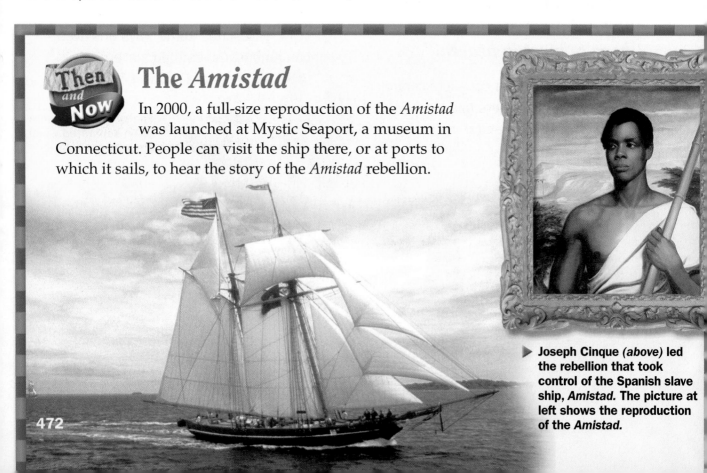

Then and Now

The *Amistad*

In 2000, a full-size reproduction of the *Amistad* was launched at Mystic Seaport, a museum in Connecticut. People can visit the ship there, or at ports to which it sails, to hear the story of the *Amistad* rebellion.

▶ Joseph Cinque *(above)* led the rebellion that took control of the Spanish slave ship, *Amistad*. The picture at left shows the reproduction of the *Amistad*.

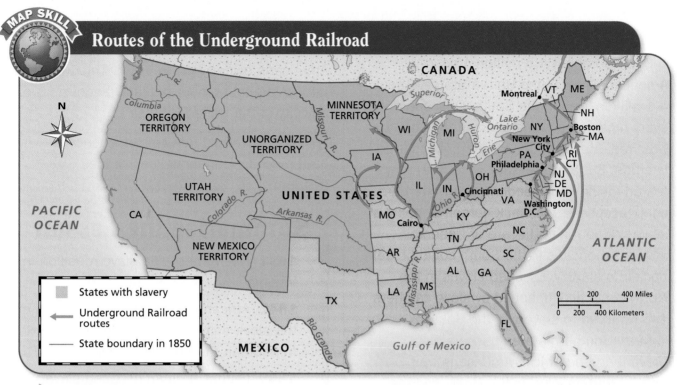

MAP SKILL
Routes of the Underground Railroad

▶ This map shows the routes traveled by people escaping from slavery on the Underground Railroad.

MAP SKILL Use Routes *To what other country did many slaves escape?*

Underground Railroad

Thousands of enslaved African Americans resisted slavery by trying to escape. The **Underground Railroad** was an organized, secret system set up to help enslaved people escape from the South to freedom in the North or Canada. The map on this page shows its routes.

The Underground Railroad probably got its name when railroads became popular. The guides, or people who helped those escaping, were called "conductors." The houses, barns, and other places where runaways hid along their journey were known as "stations."

To find their way north, escaping slaves were guided by the North Star. On cloudy nights they felt for moss on tree trunks, because moss tends to grow on the north side of a tree. All along the journey, they faced the risk of capture, a severe beating, or death.

Between 40,000 and 100,000 slaves escaped using the Underground Railroad. **Harriet Tubman** was the most famous "conductor." In about 1849, Tubman escaped from slavery herself and settled in Philadelphia. But before the Civil War she returned south 19 times to lead more than 300 people, including her mother and father, to freedom. Tubman later said, "On my underground railroad, I never ran my train off the track and I never lost a passenger." You can read more about Tubman in the Biography on page 475.

Not all "conductors" in the Underground Railroad were African Americans. **Levi Coffin** was a white teacher who had opened a school for slaves in North Carolina. After slave owners closed his school, Coffin moved to Indiana. There he became one of the leading "conductors" of the Underground Railroad. He and his wife **Catherine Coffin** helped more than 2,000 slaves escape to freedom.

REVIEW Write a brief summary of the way the Underground Railroad helped people escape slavery. **Summarize**

Free African Americans

By 1860 about 4.5 million African Americans lived in the United States. About 4.1 million lived in the South. Only one out of every nine African Americans in the country was free. Most free African Americans lived in cities. But although they were free, they feared losing their freedom. Any white person could accuse a free black person of being a slave. Without a certificate of freedom, African Americans in the South could be sent back into slavery. Escaped slaves in the North could be kidnapped by slave catchers and returned to slavery in the South.

Many Southern states passed laws preventing free African Americans from holding certain jobs. In the North and the South, finding work was made more difficult by threats and violence from white workers.

Still, thousands of free blacks found jobs and bought property. In New Orleans, 650 African Americans owned land in 1850. This was by far the largest number of black landowners of any city in the United States.

REVIEW Why did free African Americans have much to fear about keeping their freedom? ⟳ Main Idea and Details

Summarize the Lesson

1831 Nat Turner led a slave rebellion in Virginia.

1841 Africans who had seized control of the slave ship *Amistad* gained their freedom in the Supreme Court.

1849 Harriet Tubman escaped slavery and began leading people to freedom on the Underground Railroad.

LESSON 2 REVIEW

Check Facts and Main Ideas

1. ⟳ **Main Idea and Details** On a separate sheet of paper, complete the graphic organizer to show the details that support the main idea that enslaved African Americans resisted slavery.

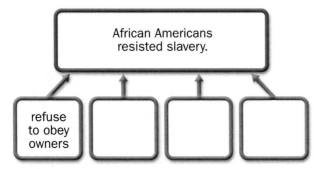

2. What was the purpose of the **slave codes**?

3. **Critical Thinking:** *Cause and Effect* Why would slave owners want to keep slaves from gathering or meeting one another?

4. Describe how enslaved African Americans escaped to freedom on the **Underground Railroad**.

5. What challenges were faced by free African Americans in the North and South?

Link to ⟷ Science

Locate the North Star Escaping African Americans used the North Star to help them find the direction north. Do research to locate the North Star. Then one evening, when it is dark enough, look for the star and determine north.

Harriet Tubman

1820(?)–1913

As a teenager in Maryland, Harriet Tubman had only known a life of slavery, yet she grew tougher by resisting or fighting back. She even survived a serious head injury that she suffered while helping another slave escape. As a result of the injury, for the rest of her life Harriet could not control falling asleep at odd times, suffered from bad headaches, and had a deep scar. Yet nothing could prevent her from seeking freedom.

When she was about 28 years old, Harriet Tubman escaped and made her way 90 miles on the Underground Railroad to Philadelphia. Although she was afraid, she later explained,

I had reasoned this out in my mind....I had a right to liberty or death; if I could not have one, I would have the other, for no man should take me alive.

Despite the dangers, before the Civil War Tubman returned again and again to the South to help lead other African Americans from slavery to freedom. No one in her care was ever caught.

BIOFACT

During the Civil War, Tubman served the United States army as a nurse and a scout, helping to free almost 800 slaves in one attempt.

Learn from Biographies

How do you think Harriet Tubman's scar and trouble with sleeping could have made her escape more dangerous? Why do you think that she returned to the South so many times despite all of the dangers?

For more information, go online to *Meet the People* at **www.sfsocialstudies.com.**

1820   1860

1820
Missouri
Compromise

1850
Fugitive
Slave Law

1857
Dred Scott
case

1860
Abraham Lincoln is
elected President

NEBRASKA
TERR.

KANSAS
TERR.

Harpers
Ferry

The Struggle over Slavery

PREVIEW

Focus on the Main Idea
Despite attempts to
compromise, the struggle over
slavery threatened to tear the
United States apart.

PLACES
Nebraska Territory
Kansas Territory
Harpers Ferry, Virginia

PEOPLE
John C. Calhoun
Henry Clay
Daniel Webster
Stephen Douglas
Harriet Beecher Stowe
Dred Scott
John Brown
Abraham Lincoln

VOCABULARY
free state
slave state
states' rights
Missouri Compromise
Fugitive Slave Law
Compromise of 1850
Kansas-Nebraska Act

You Are There Your old home in Ohio lies hundreds of miles behind you as you ride into the Kansas Territory. On this spring day in 1854, you meet a group of 650 settlers from New England. They tell you they have all pledged to keep Kansas free of slavery.

You have also met other people coming to Kansas who have different views. One group is from neighboring Missouri, a slave state. Their aim is to make the Kansas Territory a place where people can own slaves.

Wherever you go, you hear arguments about whether or not Kansas should allow slavery. You also hear stories of violence between people on both sides of this argument. The issue of slavery is splitting Kansas apart. Soon it will threaten to split apart the entire country.

Main Idea and Details As you read, look for details that support the main idea that slavery was threatening to split the country apart in the middle 1800s.

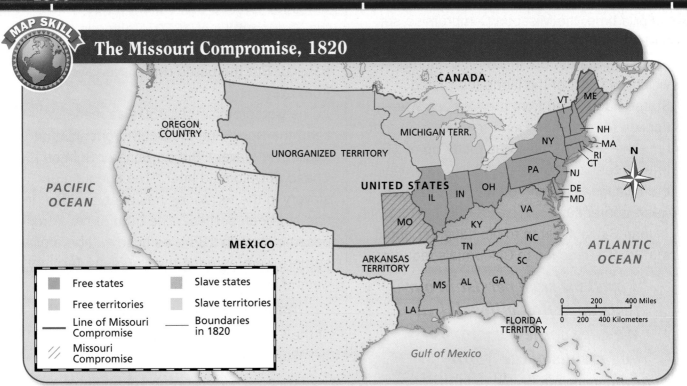

MAP SKILL

The Missouri Compromise, 1820

Map Key:
- Free states
- Slave states
- Free territories
- Slave territories
- Line of Missouri Compromise
- Boundaries in 1820
- Missouri Compromise

▶ **The Missouri Compromise kept the balance between free states and slave states.**

MAP SKILL Use a Map Key *Which two states were admitted as part of the Missouri Compromise?*

Missouri Compromise

In 1819, the United States was made up of 11 free states and 11 slave states. A **free state** was one in which slavery was not allowed. A **slave state** was one in which slavery was allowed. Since each state had two United States senators, the Senate was balanced evenly between senators that favored slavery and senators that opposed slavery.

In 1819 the people of Missouri asked for statehood as a slave state. Northern states did not want Missouri to be admitted as a slave state. Southern states took the opposite position.

John C. Calhoun from South Carolina was a leader of the Southerners in the Senate. Calhoun was a believer in **states' rights**—the idea that states have the right to make decisions about issues that concern them. According to Calhoun, slavery should be legal if a state's people wanted it to be.

Senator **Henry Clay** of Kentucky, who would become known as "The Great Compromiser," urged a solution called the **Missouri Compromise.** In 1820 Missouri was admitted as a slave state, and Maine was admitted as a free state. There were now 24 states, evenly balanced between free states and slave states.

What would happen when more new states were formed from land gained in the Louisiana Purchase? The Missouri Compromise tried to settle this question. Look at the map above and find the Missouri Compromise line. According to the Missouri Compromise, new states north of this line would be free states. New states south of this line could allow slavery.

REVIEW How did the Missouri Compromise affect the way future states would be admitted to the United States?
↻ **Main Idea and Details**

477

The Compromise of 1850

For a time, the Missouri Compromise settled the question about the balance of free and slave states. But in 1849, California—which was part of the lands the United States had gained from the Mexican War—applied for statehood as a free state. At that time the United States was made up of 15 free states and 15 slave states. Once again, the balance between free and slave states was threatened.

John Calhoun wrote to his daughter about the South's reaction to California's request:

"I trust we shall persist in our resistance [to California].... We have borne the wrongs and insults of the North long enough."

Calhoun hoped that the Southern members of Congress would force the North to turn down California's request to enter as a free state.

Henry Clay again suggested a compromise. Clay proposed that the South accept California as a free state. In return, the North should agree to pass the Fugitive Slave Law. This law said that escaped slaves had to be returned to their owners, even if they had reached Northern states where slavery was not allowed. Clay's compromise also suggested a way to accept other new states from the territories gained from Mexico. He proposed that slavery be allowed in these territories if the people living there voted for it.

Daniel Webster, a senator from Massachusetts, spoke in favor of the compromise. Webster was an opponent of slavery. Yet like Clay, he wanted to keep the country together. Webster said, "We must view things as they are. Slavery does exist in the United States."

With the support of Calhoun and Webster, Congress passed Clay's plan. It was called the Compromise of 1850. California became a free state, and the Fugitive Slave Law was passed. But the battle over slavery was far from over.

The Compromise of 1850 was made to keep the North and the South from splitting apart over slavery. But as Senator Salmon P. Chase of Ohio said later, "The question of slavery in the territories has been avoided. It has not been settled." The truth of his words became clear in 1854, as huge numbers of settlers were entering the Nebraska Territory west of the Missouri River.

REVIEW What were the main proposals of the Compromise of 1850?

Main Idea and Details

▶ Many newspapers printed opinions about the new Fugitive Slave Law.

Read and Ponder THE FUGITIVE SLAVE LAW!

Which disregards all the ordinary securities of PERSONAL LIBERTY, which tramples on the Constitution, by its denial of the sacred rights of Trial by Jury, *Habeas Corpus*, and Appeal, and which enacts, that the Cardinal Virtues of Christianity shall be considered, in the eye of the law, as CRIMES, punishable with the severest penalties,—*Fines and Imprisonment.*

Freemen of Massachusetts, REMEMBER, That Samuel A. Elliott of Boston, voted for this law, that Millard Filmore, our whig President *approved* it and the Whig Journals of Massachusetts sustain them in this iniquity.

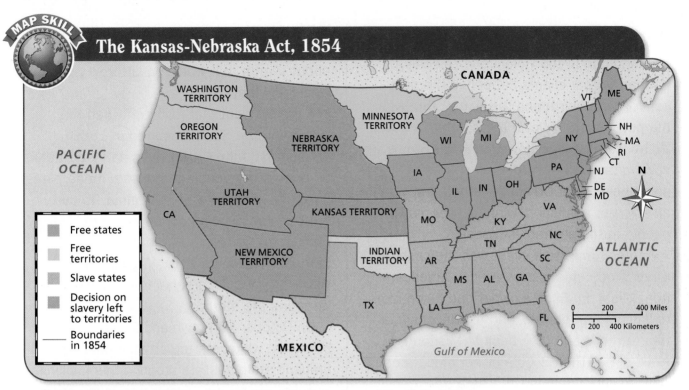

"Bleeding Kansas"

In 1854 Senator **Stephen Douglas** of Illinois proposed that Nebraska be split into two territories: the **Nebraska Territory** in the north and the **Kansas Territory** in the south. Because both territories were north of the Missouri Compromise line, both would be free territories. However, many Southerners insisted that slavery be allowed in both the Nebraska and the Kansas territories.

Congress again looked for a solution. Senator Douglas suggested a compromise: let the people of each territory decide whether it should be free or slave. Congress passed this law, which came to be known as the **Kansas-Nebraska Act.** Instead of solving the problem, the law created a new one in Kansas.

Because a majority vote would decide whether Kansas would be free or slave, people who favored one side or the other rushed to settle in Kansas. People against slavery came from the North. People for slavery came from the South, especially from neighboring Missouri, a slave state.

The people of Kansas voted for slavery. But many who voted were not Kansans at all. They had crossed the border from Missouri just to vote for slavery. Northerners claimed the vote was illegal. Southerners disagreed. Within Kansas, though most people just wanted to establish homes and live in peace, there were leaders on both sides of the slavery issue who were trying to cause a fight. Violence broke out in many parts of the Kansas Territory. Because of the many acts of violence, Kansas became known as "bleeding Kansas." These would not be the last drops of blood spilled between those who favored and opposed slavery.

REVIEW In what way did the Kansas-Nebraska Act change a part of the Missouri Compromise? **Compare and Contrast**

A Divided Country

In addition to the violence in "bleeding Kansas," other events deepened the split between the North and the South. One was the publication of *Uncle Tom's Cabin*, a novel by **Harriet Beecher Stowe,** in 1852 Stowe's novel described the cruelties of slavery. It sold about 300,000 copies in the first year after it was published, winning over many people to the abolitionist cause.

Another important event was the case of **Dred Scott,** an enslaved African American from Missouri. Scott's owner had taken him to Illinois, a free state, and to Wisconsin, a free territory, and then back to Missouri, a slave state. Then Scott's owner died. Scott went to court claiming he was a free man because he had lived in a free state.

Scott's case reached the United States Supreme Court. In 1857 the Court said that Scott "had no rights" because African Americans were not citizens of the United States. Many Americans were outraged by the Supreme Court's decision. Frederick Douglass said that the decision would bring about events that would "overthrow...the whole slave system."

Another event that further divided the North and the South occurred in 1859. Abolitionist **John Brown,** who had led attacks on pro-slavery people in Kansas, made plans to attack slave owners in Virginia. To carry out his plan, Brown needed weapons. He planned to steal them from the army's arsenal at **Harpers Ferry, Virginia** (now West Virginia). An arsenal is a place where weapons are stored.

On October 16 Brown and 21 other men, black and white, started on their raid. But federal and state soldiers stopped them, killing some of the raiders. Brown was taken prisoner and, after being found guilty, was sentenced to death. He was hanged. But his actions showed that the struggle over slavery was growing. Compromise was becoming harder to find.

REVIEW Contrast the goals of Dred Scott and John Brown. **Compare and Contrast**

Literature and Social Studies

In this excerpt from *Uncle Tom's Cabin*, Harriet Beecher Stowe describes the struggle of an enslaved mother named Eliza to keep her child from slave traders who wanted to take her child away from her.

"[Eliza's] room opened by a side door to the river. She caught her child, and sprang down the steps toward it. The [slave] trader caught a full glimpse of her, just as she was disappearing down the bank, and throwing himself from his horse...he was after her like a hound after a deer. In that dizzy moment her feet...[hardly] seemed to touch the ground, and a moment brought her to the water's edge....and, nerved with strength such as God gives only to the desperate, with one wild cry and flying leap, she vaulted sheer [jumped clear] over the ...current by the shore, on to the raft of ice beyond. It was a desperate leap,—impossible to anything but madness and despair."

The Granger Collection

▶ **Abraham Lincoln spoke out against the spread of slavery while running for the Senate against Stephen Douglas.**

A New Political Party

The issue of slavery led to the end of one political party and the beginning of another. The Whigs, split between a group against slavery and a group for it, ceased to exist. In 1854 some of its members who opposed slavery joined with other slavery opponents to form the Republican Party. Now, two major political parties, Republican and Democrat, battled over the issues of slavery and states' rights.

No election showed this conflict more clearly than the 1858 campaign for the United States Senate in Illinois. The Republicans chose **Abraham Lincoln** as their candidate. Lincoln was a lawyer from Springfield, Illinois.

Many people called him "The Rail Splitter," because when he was young he split logs with an axe to make the rails of fences. Lincoln was opposed to the spread of slavery and spoke of the "ultimate extinction," or final end, of slavery.

Lincoln's opponent was Democratic Senator Stephen Douglas. Douglas was known as the "Little Giant" because, although he was short, he was a giant when it came to making speeches that changed people's ideas. Douglas believed in states' rights. He said, "Each state...has a right to do as it pleases on...slavery."

The candidates made speeches and debated throughout Illinois about the spread of slavery. The Lincoln-Douglas debates became well known because both candidates were such good speakers. Lincoln said:

> *"If slavery is not wrong, then nothing is wrong....[But I] would not do anything to bring about a war between the free and slave states."*

Douglas stated:

> *"If each state will only agree to mind its own business... this republic can exist forever divided into free and slave states."*

Douglas won the election, but the debates made Lincoln the new leader of the Republican Party. Within two years, he would be the Republican candidate for President. You can read more about Lincoln in the Biography on page 483.

REVIEW Summarize the views on slavery held by Lincoln and Douglas. **Summarize**

Lincoln Is Elected President

In the election of 1860, the Democratic Party split. Northern Democrats chose Stephen Douglas to run for President. Southern Democrats chose John Breckinridge of Kentucky. The Republicans chose Abraham Lincoln.

Lincoln won the election, but without winning any Southern electoral votes. Southerners feared that Lincoln would attempt to end slavery not only in the western territories but in the Southern states as well. Southerners also worried that they would have no voice in the new government. Lincoln said to the South, "We must not be enemies." However, many on both sides viewed the other side as their enemy. In the North and South, the time of compromise had passed.

REVIEW Why do you think Lincoln said, "We must not be enemies" after he became President? **Draw Conclusions**

Summarize the Lesson

1820 Congress passed the Missouri Compromise.

1850 The Fugitive Slave Law was passed as part of the Compromise of 1850.

1857 In the Dred Scott case, the Supreme Court ruled that slaves were not citizens and had no rights, even in free states.

1860 Abraham Lincoln was elected President without any Southern support.

LESSON 3 REVIEW

Check Facts and Main Ideas

1. **Main Idea and Details** On a separate sheet of paper, complete the graphic organizer with details that support the main idea.

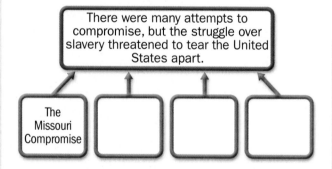

There were many attempts to compromise, but the struggle over slavery threatened to tear the United States apart.

The Missouri Compromise

2. How did the **Missouri Compromise** keep the balance of **free and slave states**?

3. How did the **Compromise of 1850** affect slavery in California and the territories gained from Mexico?

4. Who were Dred Scott and John Brown? How did their actions affect the split between the North and South?

5. **Critical Thinking: *Make Inferences*** What was more important to Abraham Lincoln, abolishing slavery or preserving the nation? Explain.

Link to Writing

Write a Conversation Write a conversation about the spread of slavery that might have occurred among Americans in the 1850s. You can base your conversation on the words of American leaders in this lesson, such as John C. Calhoun, Daniel Webster, Frederick Douglass, Harriet Beecher Stowe, Abraham Lincoln, and Stephen Douglas. Use the term **states' rights** in your conversation.

Abraham Lincoln *1809–1865*

Young Abraham Lincoln had to help his father on the family farm and only attended school for a total of about one year during his life. Yet Abe read anything he could get his hands on. He once said, "My best friend is the man who'll get me a book." So when a neighboring farmer, Josiah Crawford, offered to lend him a biography of George Washington, Abe was thrilled. Unfortunately, one rainy night, the book was left near the leaky cabin walls and got soaked. Abe told the truth, and Crawford was not angry. Abe paid him back by working in his fields.

The book on Washington became one of Abe's favorites, along with the autobiography of Benjamin Franklin. From these, Abe learned about the men who founded the United States and why the dream of a free country was so important to them.

BIOFACT

Lincoln grew his beard in response to a suggestion from 11-year-old Grace Bedell, who wrote him a letter.

Throughout his life, Lincoln educated himself through reading. When he decided to become a lawyer, he taught himself by studying law books. Even when he was the President, Lincoln read books to learn how to lead the war effort. After the election of 1860, President Lincoln made a speech sharing his deep belief in the future of the United States that he had read about since his childhood. With tension rising between the North and South, he said:

> *"If we do not make common cause to save the good old ship of the Union on this voyage, nobody will have a chance to pilot her on another voyage."*

Learn from Biographies

How do you think Lincoln's reading of how Washington met the challenges of the American Revolution helped Lincoln meet the challenges of the Civil War?

For more information, go online to *Meet the People* at **www.sfsocialstudies.com**.

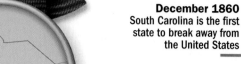

December 1860
South Carolina is the first state to break away from the United States

February 1861
Seven Southern states form the Confederate States of America

April 1861
Confederate forces fire on United States troops at Fort Sumter

Fort Sumter

PREVIEW

Focus on the Main Idea
Eventually 11 Southern states seceded from the United States, leading to the outbreak of the Civil War.

PLACES
Fort Sumter, South Carolina

PEOPLE
Jefferson Davis

VOCABULARY
secede
Confederacy
Union
border state
civil war

The First Shots Are Fired

You Are There

Dawn is about to break in Charleston, South Carolina. The date is April 12, 1861. Mary Boykin Chesnut, the wife of a Southern officer, is staying as a guest in a house near Charleston Harbor. Troops of the Southern states begin firing on Fort Sumter, a United States fort on an island in the harbor.

Chesnut describes the event in her diary:

"I do not pretend to go to sleep…How can I?" She is kept awake by the "heavy booming of a cannon." She springs out of bed and falls to her knees. "I prayed as I never prayed before." Chesnut then puts on her shawl and climbs to the top floor of the house to get a better view. "The shells were bursting." The roar of the cannons fills the air. "We watched up there, and everybody wondered that Fort Sumter did not fire a shot."

Sequence As you read, identify the events that led to the start of the Civil War.

Southern States Secede

Many Southerners believed that the South should **secede,** or break away, from the United States. In December 1860, almost two months after Abraham Lincoln was elected President, South Carolina decided to secede.

By February 1, 1861, six more states—Alabama, Florida, Mississippi, Georgia, Louisiana, and Texas—had seceded. Representatives from the seven seceding states met in Montgomery, Alabama. On February 8, they formed their own government. It was called the Confederate States of America, or the **Confederacy.**

The Confederacy adopted a constitution that supported states' rights and slavery. The Confederate constitution said that its congress could not pass laws that denied "the right of property in…slaves."

The Confederacy also elected **Jefferson Davis,** a former United States senator from Mississippi, as its President. Like Abraham Lincoln, Jefferson Davis was born in

Kentucky, in a log cabin. But Davis grew up in Mississippi on a plantation owned by his family. Later he developed his own plantation on land given to him by his oldest brother.

After becoming president of the Confederacy, Davis said the Southern states should "look forward to success, to peace, and to prosperity." But in a letter to his wife Varina, he wrote that the Southern states were "threatened by a powerful opposition." That opposition came from the United States and its newly elected President, Abraham Lincoln.

Lincoln was inaugurated on March 4, 1861. By then the Confederacy had taken control of most of the forts and military property of the United States in the South. The states that remained loyal to the United States government were called the **Union.** One of the forts still under Union control was **Fort Sumter,** in the harbor of Charleston, South Carolina.

REVIEW Summarize the events that occurred as the Confederacy was formed. Summarize

▶ **Jefferson Davis (below) was president of the Confederacy. The Confederate attack on Fort Sumter (left) was the start of the Civil War.**

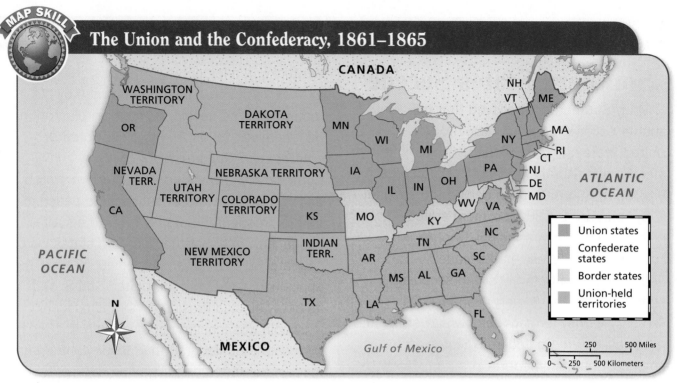

The Union and the Confederacy, 1861–1865

WASHINGTON TERRITORY

CANADA

OR

DAKOTA TERRITORY

MN

NH
VT
ME

WI
MI

NY

MA
RI
CT

NEVADA TERR.

NEBRASKA TERRITORY

IA

PA

NJ

UTAH TERRITORY

COLORADO TERRITORY

IL
IN
OH

DE
MD

ATLANTIC OCEAN

CA

KS

MO

WV
VA

PACIFIC OCEAN

KY

NEW MEXICO TERRITORY

INDIAN TERR.

AR

TN

NC

SC

N

MS
AL
GA

PACIFIC OCEAN

TX

LA

FL

MEXICO

Gulf of Mexico

Union states
Confederate states
Border states
Union-held territories

250   500 Miles

250   500 Kilometers

▶ This map shows the United States during the Civil War. Find West Virginia, which broke away from Virginia and voted to stay in the Union. West Virginia became a state in 1863.

MAP SKILL Place *Name the Confederate state that reached farthest to the west.*

The War Begins

On April 9, 1861, Jefferson Davis met with his advisers to discuss Fort Sumter. One adviser said that making the first strike against the Union would put the Confederacy "in the wrong." Davis disagreed and decided to send officers to ask for the surrender of the fort.

A Union officer, Robert Anderson, commanded Fort Sumter. He agreed to surrender if the Confederacy would wait three more days. But the Confederate commander, Pierre G.T. Beauregard (BOH ruh gard), had given orders to fire on Fort Sumter if Anderson did not surrender in one hour.

The Confederates began firing on Fort Sumter on Friday, April 12, at 4:30 A.M. The bombing continued into Saturday. With little food and water, Major Anderson was forced to surrender and left the fort on Sunday.

Lincoln responded to the attack on Fort Sumter and its surrender by asking Union states to supply 75,000 soldiers to put down the Confederate rebellion. Lincoln believed this could be done quickly, and said the soldiers would only be needed for 90 days.

Lincoln's call for troops so angered the states of Virginia, Arkansas, Tennessee, and North Carolina, that they seceded and joined the Confederacy. There were now 11 states in the Confederacy and 23 in the Union. Four of the Union states—Delaware, Maryland, Missouri, and Kentucky—were slave states that seemed unsure of whether to stay in the Union or join the Confederacy. These were called the **border states** because, as you see on the map above, they were located between the Union and Confederacy. Three of these states—Delaware, Missouri, and Kentucky—said they would not provide soldiers. Maryland said it would, but only to defend Washington, D.C.

Lincoln believed it was important to keep these border states in the Union, even though they were slave states. That is why in 1861 he continued to say that his aim was to hold the United States together, not to abolish slavery. You will soon learn that neither goal would be quickly or easily achieved.

The conflict between the states arose for a number of reasons. For Lincoln and his supporters, the main reason for fighting the war was to preserve, or keep together, the Union. However, other supporters of the North believed they were fighting to end slavery. Southerners fought the war to preserve states' rights and slavery. They also believed they were defending their homeland and their way of life.

The battle at Fort Sumter began the American Civil War. A **civil war** is a war between people of the same country. Some Northerners described the war as a rebellion and the Confederacy as a group of rebels. Many Southerners accepted the name *rebel* with pride. To them the conflict was known as the War for Southern Independence. They also called it the War of Northern Aggression. The title War Between the States is also commonly used. But no matter what it was called, the war would be longer and bloodier than anyone guessed in the spring of 1861.

REVIEW What were the main differences between the reasons the North and South fought the Civil War? Compare and Contrast

Summarize the Lesson

- **December 1860** South Carolina became the first state to secede from the United States.

- **February 1861** Seven Southern states formed the Confederate States of America.

- **April 1861** Confederate forces fired on United States troops at Fort Sumter, a battle that began the Civil War.

LESSON 4 REVIEW

Check Facts and Main Ideas

1. **Sequence** On a separate sheet of paper, complete the graphic organizer to show the events that led up to the start of the Civil War.

> The Civil War began
> on April 12, 1861

↓

↓

↓

2. Why did the southern states **secede?**

3. **Critical Thinking: *Draw Conclusions***
What might have been Jefferson Davis's reason for attacking Fort Sumter?

4. Describe Abraham Lincoln's main reason for fighting the Civil War.

5. Why, at the beginning of the Civil War, did Lincoln not say that he was fighting the war to end slavery?

Link to ∞ Writing

Write an Article Suppose you are part of the **Union** or **Confederacy** when the war began in 1861. Research the man who is your president and write a brief article explaining why he is qualified for his position.

1820   1830   1840

1820
Missouri
Compromise

1831
Nat Turner leads a slave
rebellion in Virginia

1846
Congress votes to lower
tariffs on imports

Chapter Summary

Main Idea and Details

On a separate sheet of paper, fill in the main compromises made in Congress before the Civil War.

▶ **Tattered flag from the battle at Fort Sumter**

> Congress made several compromises to keep the North and South from splitting apart.

> Missouri Compromise

> [ ]

> [ ]

Vocabulary

Match each word with the correct definition or description.

1 sectionalism (p. 465)

2 slave codes (p. 471)

3 free state (p. 477)

4 secede (p. 485)

5 Underground Railroad (p. 473)

a. state that does not permit slavery

b. loyalty to a part of a country, not to the whole country

c. secret system to help slaves escape to freedom

d. laws controlling behavior of slaves

e. break away

People and Terms

Write a sentence explaining why each of the following people or terms was important in the events that led to the start of the Civil War. You may use two or more in a single sentence.

1 David Walker (p. 467)

2 Nat Turner (p.472)

3 Confederacy (p. 485)

4 Harriet Tubman (p. 473)

5 John C. Calhoun (p. 477)

6 Fugitive Slave Law (p. 478)

7 Harriet Beecher Stowe (p. 480)

8 Dred Scott (p. 480)

9 Jefferson Davis (p. 485)

10 Union (p. 485)

1850 1860 1870 1880

1849
Harriet Tubman escapes slavery on the Underground Railroad

1857
Dred Scott case

1860
Abraham Lincoln is elected President

February 1861
Confederate States of America formed

April 1861
Southern forces fire on U.S. troops at Fort Sumter

Facts and Main Ideas

1. What kinds of control did slave owners have over the lives of slaves?

2. How did the issue of slavery lead to a new political party?

3. **Time Line** How many years were there between the Nat Turner revolt and the Dred Scott case?

4. **Main Idea** What were some differences between the North and South that increased tensions between the two regions?

5. **Main Idea** How did many slaves resist slavery?

6. **Main Idea** How did the differences over slavery threaten the existence of the United States?

7. **Main Idea** What effect did Lincoln's election have on the South?

8. **Critical Thinking:** *Draw Conclusions* Why did people work to keep a balance between the number of slave states and free states?

Write About History

1. **Write a journal entry** as a person who observed the battle at Fort Sumter.

2. **Write a poem** about a person mentioned in this chapter whom you admire.

3. **Write a short speech** you might have given as a senator for or against the Missouri Compromise.

Apply Skills

Recognize Point of View

Read the two sections below from the Lincoln-Douglas debates. Then answer the questions.

> *"If slavery is not wrong, then nothing is wrong…[But I] would not do anything to bring about a war between the free and slave states."*
>
> —Abraham Lincoln

> *"If each state will only agree to mind its own business…this republic can exist forever divided into free and slave states."*
>
> —Stephen Douglas

1. What is the subject of each section?

2. What is Lincoln's viewpoint about slavery?

3. What is Douglas's viewpoint about slavery?

Internet Activity

To get help with vocabulary, people, and terms, select dictionary or encyclopedia from *Social Studies Library* at **www.sfsocialstudies.com.**

CHAPTER 15

War and Reconstruction

1861

Manassas Junction, Virginia
Confederate troops win the first major battle of the Civil War.

Lesson 1

1

1863

Charleston, South Carolina
African American troops of the Union army attack Fort Wagner.

Lesson 2

2

1865

Appomattox Court House, Virginia
The South surrenders.

Lesson 3

3

1865

Washington, D.C.
President Lincoln is assassinated.

Lesson 4

4

Washington, D.C.

Manassas Junction (Bull Run)

Appomattox Court House

ATLANTIC OCEAN

Charleston

Why We Remember

"…that government of the people, by the people, for the people, shall not perish from the earth."

In 1863, in the middle of the Civil War, these words rang out over a scarred battlefield where many Union and Confederate soldiers had died a few months before. The battlefield was at Gettysburg, Pennsylvania. The speaker was President Abraham Lincoln. At the time, no one was sure who would win the war. But Lincoln was sure of his goal—to preserve the nation that had been born only 87 years earlier.

1861

April 1861
Union begins blockade
of Southern ports

July 1861
First Battle
of Bull Run

September 1862
Battle of Antietam

1863

The Early Stages of the War

PREVIEW

Focus on the Main Idea
In the early years of the Civil War, the North and South formed strategies in hopes of gaining a quick victory.

PLACES
Richmond, Virginia
Manassas Junction, Virginia

PEOPLE
Winfield Scott
Thomas "Stonewall" Jackson
Robert E. Lee

VOCABULARY
blockade
Anaconda Plan
First Battle of Bull Run
Battle of Antietam

▶ This canteen was carried by a Confederate soldier in the Civil War.

You Are There
It is the summer of 1861. Dawn breaks over your Kentucky farm. You hear a rooster crowing. Below your attic bedroom, your mother lets out a cry. You peer down from your room and see her holding a sheet of paper. It is a letter from your oldest brother Joshua. He left last night to join the Union Army.

Joshua and your second-oldest brother William had been arguing about the war since spring. "The Union forever!" Joshua would say. "Down with Northern tyranny!" William would shout. You just hope the war ends soon.

You read in the newspaper that the Confederates have just won a victory in Virginia. Expecting a short war, many Southern men are rushing to join the army before the war ends. You wonder if William will leave to join the Confederate forces. If he does, could he and Joshua end up fighting against each other, brother against brother?

Main Idea and Details As you read, note how the North and South prepared for war.

Target Skill

Advantages and Disadvantages

Many supporters of the North believed they were fighting to preserve the Union. However, most Southern supporters thought that they were fighting to preserve their way of life. Sometimes these different opinions divided families. Some of President Lincoln's own family sided with the South. Four brothers of his wife Mary fought for the Confederacy.

Besides strong feelings, each side thought that it had an advantage over the other. Southerners believed that their more rural way of life would better prepare soldiers for war. Many Southerners hunted and were familiar with weapons. The South also had a history of producing military leaders. A larger share of the Mexican War veterans came from the South.

But an army needed supplies. In 1860 the Northern states produced more than 90 percent of the country's weapons, cloth, shoes, and iron. They also produced more than half of the country's corn and 80 percent of the wheat.

Moving supplies was also important to an army. The Union had far more railroads, canals, and roads than the Confederacy. In addition, the Union was able to raise far more money. By the end of the war, the Union had spent more than $2.6 billion. The Confederacy had spent only $1 billion.

REVIEW Why did each side believe that it would win the war? **Summarize**

FACT FILE

Union and Confederacy, 1861

Look at the graphs below to compare resources each side had.

■ **Union**
▨ **Confederacy**

Union Flag

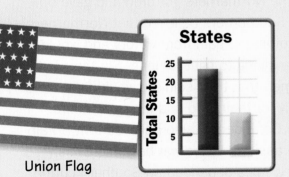

States

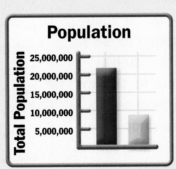

Population

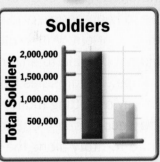

Soldiers

Factories

Farms

Railroads

Confederate Flag

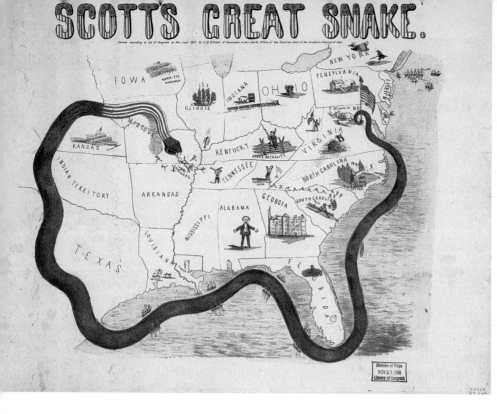

SCOTT'S GREAT SNAKE.

▶ This cartoon illustrated the Anaconda Plan by showing an anaconda snake surrounding the Confederacy.

Strategies

President Abraham Lincoln sought advice on how to win the war from General **Winfield Scott,** who had fought in the Mexican War. Scott planned a strategy with three parts. The first part was a blockade of the Atlantic and Gulf coasts of the Confederacy. A **blockade** is the shutting off of an area by troops or ships to keep people and supplies from moving in or out. With a blockade the South would not be able to ship its cotton for sale in Europe. Cotton sales were the South's main way of getting money to pay for the war.

The second stage of Scott's plan was to capture territory along the Mississippi River, the heart of the Confederacy. Gaining control of the Mississippi River would weaken the Confederacy by cutting the Southern states in two.

Third, the Union would attack the Confederacy from the east and west. Scott's strategy was called the **Anaconda Plan,** because he said that it would squeeze the Confederacy like an anaconda. An anaconda is a huge snake that kills prey by wrapping itself around an animal and suffocating it. Lincoln liked the plan. He ordered the blockade on April 19, one week after the fall of Fort Sumter.

The Confederate government had its own strategy for victory. First, it believed that the Confederacy only had to defend its territory until the Northerners got tired and gave up. Many Southerners believed that Northerners had nothing to gain from victory and would not be willing to fight for long. Southerners assumed that their soldiers would fight more fiercely for their land and their way of life.

The Confederacy also believed that Britain would assist it in the war because British clothing mills depended on Southern cotton. But Britain already had a surplus of cotton and was looking to India and Egypt for new sources of cotton. Britain allowed the South to build several warships in its shipyards, but it did not send any soldiers.

REVIEW How did Winfield Scott's Anaconda Plan attempt to weaken the Southern states?
🔁 **Main Idea and Details**

494

Early Battles

Early successes gave the Confederacy confidence. President Lincoln sent 35,000 troops to invade **Richmond, Virginia,** the capital of the Confederacy. On the way, on July 21, 1861, they met Confederate troops at a small stream called Bull Run near the town of **Manassas Junction, Virginia.**

The **First Battle of Bull Run** was a confusing event. Early on, the fighting went in the Union's favor. Some Confederate soldiers began to turn back, but one general from Virginia told his men to hold their place. Because the general and his men stood "like a stone wall," he became known as **Thomas "Stonewall" Jackson.**

More Confederates arrived, and soon the tide turned in their favor. The Union soldiers retreated. The casualties in the First Battle of Bull Run amounted to 3,000 for the Union and 2,000 for the Confederacy. Casualties include soldiers killed, wounded, captured, or missing.

Many battles took place across the South.

Union forces won some, but the Confederates seemed to be winning the war. In May 1862, "Stonewall" Jackson defeated the Union army in Virginia, and some feared that he could take over Washington, D.C.

On September 17, 1862, Union and Confederate forces met near the town of Sharpsburg, Maryland, in the **Battle of Antietam** (an TEET um). The battle involved one of the Confederacy's most capable generals, **Robert E. Lee.** He had been asked to fight for the Union, but refused. Lee decided to serve the Confederacy after Virginia, the state of his birth, joined the other Southern states. You will read more about Robert E. Lee in the Biography on page 497.

The battle was an important victory for the Union. After Antietam, Britain ended its support for the Southern states. The Confederacy would have to fight alone.

REVIEW What effect did winning the Battle of Antietam have on the Union? **Cause and Effect**

Lithograph by Kurz & Allison

▶ **With more than 23,000 casualties, the massive Battle of Antietam was the single bloodiest day of the entire Civil War.**

Technology and War

Recent technologies were used and new technologies were developed during the Civil War. Soldiers used rifles that could shoot farther and more accurately than guns used in previous wars. Railroads quickly moved troops and supplies to battlefronts. The Confederacy built several submarines—ships that could travel under the water's surface—to overcome the Union's blockade. Both sides used an early version of the hand grenade.

Another new weapon was the ironclad, or iron covered ship. The Confederates built an ironclad by taking an abandoned Union ship called the *Merrimack* and covering it with iron. They renamed it the *Virginia*. In March 1862, the *Virginia* easily sank several wooden Union ships. Union cannonballs simply bounced off the *Virginia's* iron sides. Then, on March 9, a Union ironclad named the *Monitor* arrived to battle the *Virginia*. The two ships fired at each other for hours. But neither ship was able to seriously damage the other.

These new technologies made the war more deadly, resulting in huge numbers of casualties. Unfortunately, medical knowledge had not advanced as much as other technologies. Many soldiers died from disease and infection.

REVIEW What were the advantages and disadvantages of new technology in the Civil War? **Compare and Contrast**

Summarize the Lesson

- **April 19, 1861** The Union began a blockade of Southern ports.
- **July 21, 1861** Confederate forces defeated Union troops in the First Battle of Bull Run in Manassas.
- **September 17, 1862** Union and Confederate troops fought a bloody battle at Antietam, an important Union victory.

LESSON 1   REVIEW

Check Facts and Main Ideas

1. 🔄 **Main Idea and Details** On a separate sheet of paper fill in the details of the **Anaconda Plan**.

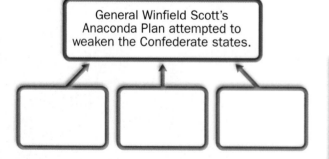

General Winfield Scott's Anaconda Plan attempted to weaken the Confederate states.

2. Compare advantages the Union had at the beginning of the war to those of the Confederacy.

3. How did the strategies of the North and South differ?

4. Summarize the events of the **First Battle of Bull Run**.

5. **Critical Thinking:** *Analyze Information* What effect did military technology have on Civil War soldiers?

Link to 🔗 Mathematics

Analyze Graphs Look again at the graphs on page 493. How many more people lived in the Northern states than in the Southern states? How many more miles of railroad did the North have compared to the South? Why would a larger population and more miles of railroad be an advantage?

Robert E. Lee 1807–1870

Robert E. Lee did not know his own father for a very long time. When Robert was six, his father, Harry Lee, visited a friend who published a newspaper that criticized the United States for going to war with Britain in 1812. Like his friend, Harry Lee opposed this war. A group of angry people attacked the newspaper offices while Harry Lee was inside, and he was badly beaten. Robert had to say goodbye as his father boarded a ship to Barbados, where he went to heal from his wounds. Harry Lee died before he could return home.

BIOFACT

Lee rode his beloved horse Traveller throughout the Civil War. Traveller outlived Lee, walked behind Lee's coffin at his funeral, and is buried near Lee's grave in Lexington, Virginia.

Many years later, at the beginning of the Civil War, Robert E. Lee was asked to make the most difficult decision of his life. Lee was a rising star in the United States Army. But Lee had been born and raised in Virginia, and, although he personally disapproved of slavery, he loved his home and his state. Perhaps he thought of his father, who had defended the things he loved at great cost to himself. Lee resigned from the United States Army, and wrote:

> *"I have not been able to make up my mind to raise my hand against my relatives, my children, my home."*

Lee hoped that Virginia would not take sides in the conflict, and he would not have to fight at all. But when Virginia seceded and joined the Confederacy, his path became clear to him. Lee accepted a position commanding Virginia's forces. Later, Lee's wife Mary remembered the night of his decision. She said that he had "wept tears of blood."

Learn from Biographies

Why was Lee's decision so difficult to make? What do you think his wife meant when she said that he "wept tears of blood"?

For more information, go online to *Meet the People* at **www.sfsocialstudies.com.**

Fort Wagner

1863

1864

January 1863
Emancipation Proclamation
takes effect

July 1863
African American troops
attack Fort Wagner

June 1864
Congress gives black and
white troops equal pay

PREVIEW

Focus on the Main Idea
As the Civil War continued,
people in the North and the
South suffered many
hardships, including the
growing loss of life.

PLACES
Fort Wagner, South Carolina

PEOPLE
Mathew Brady
William Carney
Belle Boyd
Clara Barton

VOCABULARY
draft
Emancipation Proclamation

Life During the War

You Are There These letters are from soldiers who fought in the Battle of Fredericksburg in Virginia on December 13, 1862. They were on opposing sides, but whether fighting for the Union or the Confederacy, soldiers were horrified by the loss of life.

December 16, 1862

Gone are the proud hopes, the high aspirations [goals] that swelled our bosoms [chests] a few days ago. Once more unsuccessful, and only a bloody record to show our men were brave.

Captain William T. Lusk, Union soldier

January 11, 1863

I can inform you that I have seen the Monkey Show [battle] at last, and I don't want to see it anymore. Martha I can't tell you how many dead I did see...one thing is sure, I don't want to see that sight anymore.

Private Thomas Warrick, Confederate soldier

Main Idea and Details As you read, note the difficulties during the Civil War for both soldiers and civilians.

Life for Soldiers

Families of soldiers like Captain Lusk and Private Warrick learned about the war from soldier's letters and newspaper articles. They could also see the horrors of war thanks to a new technology—photography. Civil War photographers like **Mathew Brady** took pictures of the countless dead on the battlefield. Photographs also showed soldiers warming themselves by the campfire or resting after a long day's march.

The soldiers Brady photographed were much like any young Americans of the mid 1800s. The average age of a Civil War soldier was about 25. However, drummer boys as young as twelve years old went to the battlefield.

A soldier's life was a hard one, even when he was not in battle. Soldiers might march as many as 25 miles a day while carrying about 50 pounds of supplies in knapsacks, or backpacks. They grew thirsty marching in summer's heat and shivered through winter's cold.

The marching was especially tough for Confederate soldiers. The Union blockade prevented many supplies from reaching Southern armies. Soldiers wore out their shoes, and often fought in bare feet until they could get another pair.

On both sides, soldiers were usually unhappy with the food. They were given beans, bacon, pickled beef, salt pork, and a tough flour-and-water biscuit called "hardtack." When they could, troops hunted for food in nearby forests, or even raided local farms.

As the war continued, volunteers for the war decreased. A volunteer is a person who chooses freely to join or do something. Both sides passed draft laws. A **draft** requires men of a certain age to serve in the military if they are called. However, Confederates who owned 20 or more slaves could pay substitutes to take their place. In the Union, men could pay $300 to avoid fighting in the war.

The draft was unpopular in the North and in the South, because it favored the wealthy. In July 1863, riots broke out in New York City to protest the draft. Many called the conflict "a rich man's war and a poor man's fight."

Losses on each side were terrible. A total of about one million Union and Confederate soldiers were killed or wounded. In comparison, only about 10,600 Patriots were killed in the Revolutionary War. Disease was the most common cause of death in the Civil War. Of the more than 360,000 soldiers that died in the Union army, only about 110,000 died in battle. In the Confederate army, 258,000 soldiers died, but only about 94,000 died in battle. As you read in Lesson 1, disease and infections killed many soldiers. This is because no one knew about germs yet, so doctors did not know how to keep wounds from getting infected.

REVIEW What were some of the challenges faced by Civil War soldiers?

⟳ **Main Idea and Details**

▶ **Life was difficult and dangerous for both Union soldiers (left) and Confederate soldiers (right).**

The Emancipation Proclamation

At first, the Civil War was not a war against slavery. Lincoln's goal was to preserve the Union, or keep the country together. By 1862, though, Lincoln began to believe that he could save the Union only by making the abolition of slavery a goal of the war.

Lincoln's advisers feared that ending slavery would hurt the war effort. Some said that it would unite the South and divide the North. But Lincoln explained, "Slavery must die that the nation might live."

On January 1, 1863, President Lincoln issued the **Emancipation Proclamation.** Emancipate means "to set free." A proclamation is a statement. The Emancipation Proclamation was a statement that freed all slaves in the Confederate states at war with the Union. Moments before signing the proclamation Lincoln said, "I never in my life felt more certain that I was doing right." The Proclamation said:

> "Slaves within any State. . . in rebellion against the United States, shall be then . . . and forever free."

The Emancipation Proclamation did not end slavery in the border states or in Confederate land that Union forces already controlled. It did declare an end to slavery in the rest of the Confederacy. But since Union forces did not control these areas, most African Americans remained enslaved.

Free African Americans like Frederick Douglass supported Lincoln's efforts. Douglass encouraged African Americans to assist the Union in the war. "Fly to arms," he wrote. Large numbers of African Americans responded by joining the Union army.

REVIEW What was a result of the Emancipation Proclamation?
Cause and Effect

HERE AND THERE Slaves and Serfs

At About the Same Time that President Lincoln was issuing the Emancipation Proclamation, people in other areas of the world were gaining liberty. In 1861 leaders in Russia began freeing people called serfs. Serfs worked on an owner's land in exchange for protection and housing. Like slaves, serfs could not marry, change their occupation, or leave the land without the owner's permission.

EUROPE RUSSIA ASIA

The African American soldiers of the 54th Regiment gained fame for their brave attack on Fort Wagner.

Library of Congress

The Granger Collection

African Americans in the War

In the beginning of the war, African Americans were not allowed to join the army. But they did serve as cooks, servants, and other workers. They were first allowed to join the Union army in 1862.

African American soldiers were not treated the same as whites. They received less pay than white soldiers. They had to buy their own uniforms, while white soldiers did not.

The situation improved for African Americans before the end of the war. One reason for this change was the role played by the Massachusetts 54th Colored Regiment. A regiment is a group of 600 to 1,000 soldiers. The 54th was one of the first groups of black troops to be organized for combat in the Union army.

On July 18, 1863, the 54th Regiment led an attack on **Fort Wagner** in South Carolina.

Confederate fire was heavy, but the men of the 54th charged the fort before being forced back. The group lost more than four out of every ten men.

A sergeant in the battle, **William Carney,** was seriously wounded. Yet he never dropped the regiment's flag. Carney later said that he had fought "to serve my country and my oppressed brothers." He was one of 16 African Americans to win the Congressional Medal of Honor during the war.

The Union did not win the battle at Fort Wagner. But the bravery of the 54th Regiment changed the minds of many Northerners who had doubted the abilities of black soldiers to fight. Nearly 200,000 black soldiers fought for the Union in the Civil War, and 37,000 lost their lives. In June 1864, Congress voted to give black and white troops equal pay.

REVIEW What conclusion can you draw about why African American troops fought in the Civil War? **Draw Conclusions**

Working for Lasting Peace

Many years after the terrible bloodshed of the Civil War, new kinds of weapons such as landmines pose a threat to the lives of innocent people.

When Jody Williams heard schoolchildren pick on her brother, Stephen, she got angry. "I couldn't understand why people would be mean to him because he was deaf," says Williams. From that early experience of cruelty in Poultney, Vermont, came Williams's fierce desire to "stop bullies [from] being mean to…people, just because they are weak."

Today defending innocent people against landmines is Jody Williams's life work. Landmines have been used since the late 1800s. They are hidden in the ground and are intended to harm enemy soldiers during war by exploding when people walk over them. When the wars end, however, many landmines remain. Today millions and millions of landmines are in the ground in about 70 countries—mainly poor ones like Angola, Afghanistan, and Cambodia. Williams says:

"The landmine cannot tell the difference between a soldier or a civilian [a person who is not soldier]….Once peace is declared, the landmine does not recognize that peace.

The landmine is eternally [always] prepared to take victims."

▶ **Jody Williams shared the 1997 Nobel Peace Prize with Tun Channareth, a victim of a landmine in Cambodia.**

BUILDING CITIZENSHIP

⭐ Caring

Respect
Responsibility
Fairness
Honesty
Courage

In the 1980s Jody Williams learned of the dangers of landmines while working for human rights in war-torn Central America. There she saw children who had lost legs or arms after stepping on buried landmines. She met families who could not farm land because there were so many landmines buried there.

In 1991 Jody Williams and others started the International Campaign to Ban Landmines (ICBL). Their goal is a landmine-free planet. Williams works tirelessly for a ban on landmines, visiting affected countries and sending e-mails and faxes to tell people around the world about the dangers of these buried killers.

In recognition of their efforts, Jody Williams and ICBL were awarded the Nobel Peace Prize in December 1997. At the end of 1997, leaders from 121 countries signed a treaty to outlaw landmine production and destroy existing landmines.

Caring in Action

Link to Current Events "When we began we were just three people sitting in a room," says Williams about ICBL's beginnings. "It's breathtaking what you can do when you set a goal and put all your energy into it." Get together with two other classmates. What caring action can you plan for your school or community? What are some steps your group could take to carry it out?

1863   1865

July 1863
The Union gains control of the Mississippi River

November 1863
President Lincoln delivers the Gettysburg Address

April 1865
The Confederacy surrenders to the Union

How the North Won

PREVIEW

Focus on the Main Idea
A series of Northern victories led to the end of the Civil War by 1865.

PLACES
Gettysburg, Pennsylvania
Vicksburg, Mississippi
Atlanta, Georgia
Savannah, Georgia
Appomattox Court House, Virginia

PEOPLE
Ulysses S. Grant
William Tecumseh Sherman

VOCABULARY
Battle of Gettysburg
Gettysburg Address
Battle of Vicksburg
total war

You Are There The date is November 19, 1863. About 15,000 people have gathered at Gettysburg, Pennsylvania. They are here for a ceremony to honor the soldiers who died in the Battle of Gettysburg just four months earlier. President Lincoln has been asked to speak.

The main speaker at the event is former Massachusetts governor, Edward Everett. He delivers a speech that lasts almost two hours. Finally President Lincoln rises and addresses the crowd for about three minutes. The speech is so short that no one realizes that Lincoln is finished. The crowd is silent for a moment. Then a few people begin to clap. Lincoln sits down before the photographer can take his picture.

One newspaper calls his speech "silly." Lincoln calls it "a flat failure." But his speech, the Gettysburg Address, will become known as one of the greatest speeches in United States history.

Main Idea and Details As you read, keep in mind the goals of the North as the war reached an end.

The Battle of Gettysburg

One of the most important battles of the Civil War was a three-day struggle fought in **Gettysburg, Pennsylvania.** This was the farthest north that Confederate forces had advanced into Union territory.

The **Battle of Gettysburg** began on July 1, 1863. The Confederates, led by Robert E. Lee, pushed the Union soldiers back, but missed an opportunity to pursue the Northerners and follow up their attack.

By the second day of fighting, more Union soldiers had arrived. The Confederates attacked again, but the Union troops held their ground. One Confederate from Texas remembered "the balls [bullets] were whizzing so thick that it looked like a man could hold out a hat and catch it full."

On July 3 more than 150 Confederate cannons fired at Union troops. The Northerners responded with their cannons. The noise was so loud, it was heard 140 miles away in Pittsburgh. Southern troops, including those commanded by General George Pickett, made an attack called "Pickett's Charge." Thousands of Confederates marched through open space toward the well-protected Union troops. The attack was a disaster. More than 5,000 Confederates were killed or wounded.

The Battle of Gettysburg was an important victory for the North. Lee's advance into the North was stopped, and he retreated back into Virginia. It was also a costly battle for both sides. There were more than 23,000 Union casualties. The South suffered more than 28,000 casualties.

REVIEW Describe the events of each day in the Battle of Gettysburg. **Sequence**

Map Adventure

Battle of Gettysburg, 1863

Suppose you are visiting the battle site where the fighting at Gettysburg took place. Today it is a national military park. Answer the questions about the battle site.

1. Describe the location of the Union and Confederate headquarters.

2. In which direction was Pickett's Charge made?

3. What advantage did the location of Little Round Top give the Union forces?

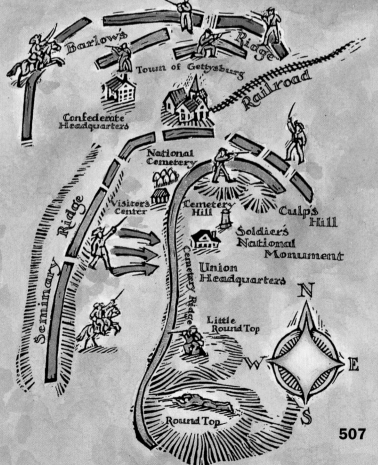

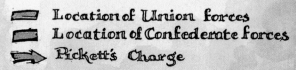

- Location of Union forces
- Location of Confederate forces
- Pickett's Charge

507

The Gettysburg Address

In November 1863, the Gettysburg battlefield was made into a national cemetery to honor the men who died there. As you have read, President Lincoln was one of the people asked to speak at the ceremony. Read his speech, known as the Gettysburg Address.

The Gettysburg Address inspired the Union to keep fighting. The speech made it clear that a united nation and the end of slavery were worth fighting for.

REVIEW How did President Lincoln express his admiration for the soldiers who had died at Gettysburg? Main Idea and Details

The Gettysburg Address

Four score [80] and seven years ago our fathers brought forth on this continent a new nation, conceived [formed] in Liberty, and dedicated [devoted] to the proposition [idea] that all men are created equal.

Now we are engaged in a great civil war, testing whether that nation, or any nation so conceived and so dedicated, can long endure. We are met on a great battlefield of that war. We have come to dedicate a portion of that field, as a final resting place for those who here gave their lives that that nation might live. It is altogether fitting and proper that we should do this.

But, in a larger sense, we cannot dedicate—we cannot consecrate [make worthy of respect]—we cannot hallow [make holy]—this ground. The brave men, living and dead, who struggled here, have consecrated it, far above our poor power to add or detract [take away]. The world will little note, nor long remember what we say here, but it can never forget what they did here. It is for us the living, rather, to be dedicated here to the unfinished work which they who fought here have thus far so nobly advanced. It is rather for us to be here dedicated to the great task remaining before us—that from these honored dead we take increased devotion to that cause for which they gave the last full measure of devotion—that we here highly resolve [are determined] that these dead shall not have died in vain—that this nation, under God, shall have a new birth of freedom—and that government of the people, by the people, for the people, shall not perish [die out] from the earth.

Painting by J. L. G. Ferris

508

The Tide Turns

The Battle of Gettysburg was one of a series of battles that turned the tide of the war in favor of the Union. As you read in Lesson 1, one part of the Anaconda Plan called for Union troops to gain control of the Mississippi River to weaken the Confederacy. Capturing **Vicksburg, Mississippi,** which lay on the east bank of the river, would achieve this goal.

General **Ulysses S. Grant,** who had served with General Robert E. Lee in the Mexican War, headed the Union forces in the **Battle of Vicksburg.** In May 1863, Union forces began a blockade of the city. They bombarded Vicksburg with cannon fire by land and sea for 48 days. Many people in the town dug caves in the hillside for protection.

Confederate civilians and soldiers in Vicksburg faced starvation under the Union blockade. Butcher shops sold rats, and soldiers received one biscuit and one piece of bacon a day.

Finally, on July 4, 1863, one day after the Battle of Gettysburg ended, the Southerners surrendered Vicksburg. The Confederacy was cut in two. Study the map below to see where Vicksburg and other major battles of the Civil War took place.

REVIEW Why do you think it took so long for the Confederates to surrender at Vicksburg? **Draw Conclusions**

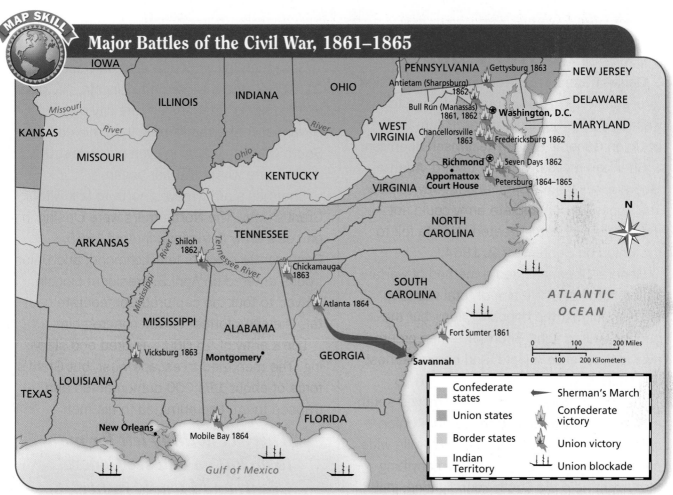

MAP SKILL

Major Battles of the Civil War, 1861–1865

▶ In July 1863, Union victories at Gettysburg and Vicksburg turned the tide of the war.

MAP SKILL Use a Map Scale *How many miles apart were the battles of Gettysburg and Vicksburg?*

General Ulysses S. Grant

General Robert E. Lee

North Winds Picture Archives

▶ After four years of fighting, General Lee agreed to surrender his army to General Grant.

The War Ends

General Grant was given control of all Union forces in March 1864. Grant continued to wear down the Confederate army with the help of Union General **William Tecumseh Sherman.**

Sherman moved his army toward **Atlanta, Georgia,** a vital industrial and railway center. The opposing Confederate army could not defend the city and retreated. Atlanta fell to the Union on September 2, 1864.

General Sherman used a method of warfare called **total war.** The aim of total war is to destroy not just the opposing army, but the people's will to fight. Sherman's men ordered everyone to leave Atlanta, and burned almost the entire city.

Starting in November, his army moved southeast toward **Savannah, Georgia.** The Union soldiers marched 300 miles in a 60-mile wide path. As they went, they destroyed anything that might help the South keep fighting, including houses, railroads, barns, and fields. Soldiers caused $100 million dollars worth of damage in Sherman's "March to the Sea."

Savannah fell without a fight on December 21, 1864. Sherman wrote to Lincoln, "I…present you as a Christmas gift the city of Savannah." Sherman's men then moved to South Carolina, causing even more destruction in the state where the war began.

Sherman's army moved north to link with Grant's army. The Northerners were closing in on Lee's army in Virginia. In April 1865, Confederate soldiers left Richmond, and Union troops entered on April 3. President Lincoln arrived to tour the captured Confederate capital. The city's former slaves cheered him.

Lee's army of 55,000 was tired and starving. The men tried to escape west, but Grant's force of about 113,000 outnumbered and trapped them. Lee admitted to his men,

"There is nothing left for me to do but go and see General Grant, and I would rather die a thousand deaths."

Generals Lee and Grant met in a farmhouse in **Appomattox Court House, Virginia,** on April 9, 1865 to discuss the terms of surrender. Grant allowed Lee's men to go free. The Southerners were allowed to keep their personal weapons and any horses they had. Grant also offered to give Lee's men food from Union supplies. Lee accepted. As Lee returned to his men, the Union soldiers began to cheer. Grant silenced them, explaining,

> *"The war is over; the rebels are our countrymen again."*

The Civil War was the most destructive war in United States history. About 620,000 soldiers died. Towns, farms, and industries—mostly in the South—were ruined. Families had been torn apart by the struggle.

Even so, Lincoln expressed sympathy for the South. After news of the Confederate surrender reached Washington, D.C., he appeared before a crowd and asked a band to play the song "Dixie," one of the battle songs of the Confederacy. "I have always thought 'Dixie' one of the best tunes I ever heard," he told the people.

Lincoln wanted the country to be rebuilt. He had a plan to heal the nation's deep divisions. But he would never see his plans carried out.

REVIEW What were the results of General Sherman's strategy of total war?
Cause and Effect

Summarize the Lesson

July 4, 1863 Union soldiers led by General Grant cut the Confederacy in two by capturing Vicksburg, Mississippi.

November 19, 1863 President Abraham Lincoln gave the Gettysburg Address honoring the men who died in battle there.

April 9, 1865 General Robert E. Lee surrendered to General Ulysses S. Grant at Appomattox Court House, Virginia, ending the Civil War.

LESSON 3 REVIEW

Check Facts and Main Ideas

1. **Main Idea and Details** On a separate sheet of paper, fill in the missing details to the main idea.

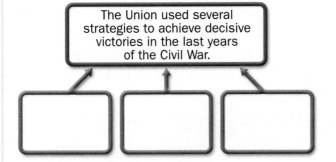

The Union used several strategies to achieve decisive victories in the last years of the Civil War.

2. What circumstances led the Union to victory on the third day in the **Battle of Gettysburg**?

3. What were Lincoln's goals as expressed in the **Gettysburg Address**?

4. **Critical Thinking:** *Interpret Maps* Look at the map on page 509. In what state did most of the major battles occur in the Civil War? Give a reason you think this would be so.

5. What was the purpose of **total war** and Sherman's "March to the Sea"?

Link to ∞ **Mathematics**

Analyze a Speech Reread President Lincoln's Gettysburg Address on page 508. What year was he referring to in the speech when he said "Four score and seven years ago"? Why would he have referred to that year?

Read a Road Map

What? A **road map** is a map that shows roads, cities, and places of interest. Different types of lines show large and small highways and even smaller roads. Symbols show if a road is a major **interstate highway,** a large road that connects cities in different states. Other symbols show state roads, and still others show smaller roads.

Different sizes of color areas and dots are used to show cities and towns of various sizes. Many road maps use special symbols to show places of interest. Some road maps also show distances from one place to another.

Why? People often have to drive to places they do not know. They may be traveling for business, vacation, or other reasons. Drivers use road maps to figure out how to get from one place to another.

Many people are interested in the history of the Civil War. Some visit Civil War sites. Our nation keeps many Civil War sites as parks or monuments. Tourists may go from one site to another during a vacation. Often they visit places they have never been before, and they find their way with road maps.

▶ **Today the Gettysburg battlefield is a national military park.**

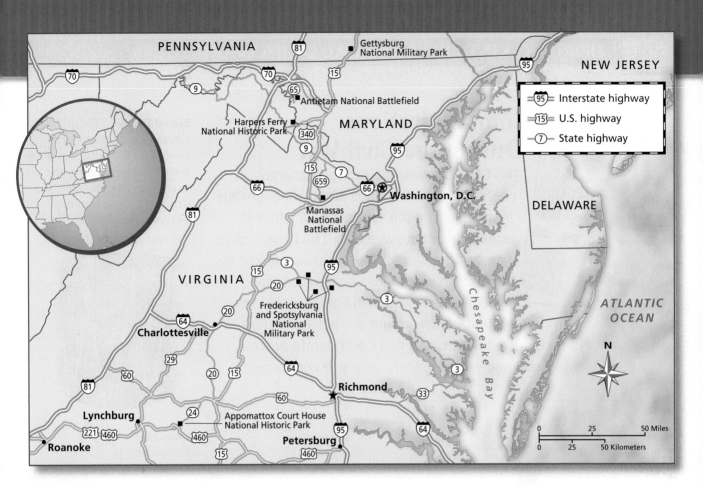

How?

To use a road map, you need to know where you are and where you want to go. Then you find these places on the map. You also have to understand what kinds of roads are shown and how they are marked on the map.

Say that you are starting at Richmond, Virginia, and want to get to Gettysburg, Pennsylvania. Look at the road map on this page, which shows many Civil War sites in Pennsylvania, Maryland, and Virginia. You notice that Gettysburg is about 180 miles north of Richmond. You see that Route 64 goes northwest from Richmond to Route 15. From there, Route 15 goes north all the way to Gettysburg.

Think and Apply

1. How would you travel from Gettysburg National Military Park to Manassas National Battlefield?

2. What interstate highway is part of the shortest route from Manassas National Battlefield Park to Washington, D.C.?

3. How would you travel from Washington, D.C. to the Fredericksburg and Spotsylvania National Military Park?

Internet Activity

For more information, go online to the *Atlas* at **www.sfsocialstudies.com**.

Communications During the Civil War

The Civil War was one of the first large conflicts in which armies could communicate instantly using the telegraph, which sent messages along wires. By 1861 every state east of the Mississippi River was linked by telegraph wires. That April, when the Confederacy attacked Fort Sumter in South Carolina, word went out immediately: "Fort Sumter is fired upon." Both Union and Confederate armies used Morse Code and secret military codes to communicate.

Signal Drum

Drums and bugles were played on the field, signaling instructions for firing and troop movements. This drum was found on the Gettysburg battlefield.

Animal hide drum head

Handpainted eagle and crest

Strapping to keep drum head taut

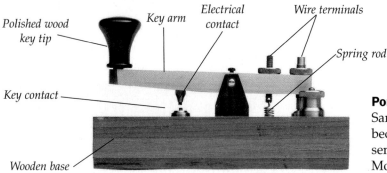

Polished wood key tip

Key arm

Electrical contact

Wire terminals

Spring rod

Key contact

Wooden base

Portable Telegraph Key

Samuel Morse, an American artist who became an inventor, developed a way to send telegraph messages using a code called Morse Code.

Rolled canvas window blind

Sending and receiving telegraphic terminals

One of two telegrapher's desks

Telegrapher

Signal officer

Army Field Telegrapher's Wagon

This portable telegrapher's office had sending and receiving sets.

Hanging Military Telegraph Wires

As armies moved, telegraph wires had to be strung to areas that might not have been wired yet. Army telegraph poles were often trees from which bark and limbs had been removed.

Insulated wire hook

Bamboo field poles for temporary hook-ups to existing heavy lines

Wire spool

Field telegrapher's wagon

Sending and receiving key and letter indicator

Brass wheel with stamped letters

Sending terminals

Receiving terminals

Beardslee Telegraph

Most soldiers could not read Morse Code, so the Union army adopted the Beardslee telegraph. Electric signals sent or received over the Beardslee system moved a metal arrow around a large brass wheel with the letters of the alphabet stamped on it. These letters spelled out messages in English or secret code. The Beardslee's range was limited to five miles.

Letter wheel gear mechanism

Wire wrapping

Service door

Carrying strap

Brass fittings

1865

April 1865
President Lincoln
is killed

December 1865
Thirteenth
Amendment
ends slavery

1867

March 1867
Congress
passes the first
Reconstruction Act

Washington,
D.C.

PREVIEW

Focus on the Main Idea
The country faced many
difficult challenges after the
Civil War ended, including
rebuilding the South and
protecting the rights of newly
freed African Americans.

PLACES
Washington, D.C.

PEOPLE
Andrew Johnson
Hiram R. Revels
Blanche K. Bruce

VOCABULARY
assassination
Reconstruction
Thirteenth Amendment
black codes
Freedmen's Bureau
Fourteenth Amendment
Fifteenth Amendment
impeachment
Jim Crow laws
segregation
sharecropping

The End of Slavery

You Are There
It is Friday, some time after 10:00
P.M. President Abraham Lincoln and
his wife, Mary, are enjoying a play.
The President and his guests are seated in a box above
the stage of Ford's Theater.

Suddenly, the audience hears something like an
explosion. Blue-colored smoke comes from the box
where the President is seated. Mary Lincoln screams.
President Lincoln has been shot.
The bullet has entered the back of
his head near his left ear. Lincoln is
still breathing, but is unconscious.

A young doctor comes forward
to aid the President. After checking
his wound, he says, "It is impossible for him to recover."

 Main Idea and Details
As you read, look for details
about rebuilding the nation
after the Civil War.

▶ **Poster for the play President Lincoln
was seeing when he was shot.**

A New President

After being shot, President Abraham Lincoln died in the early morning of April 15, 1865, in **Washington, D.C.** Until that time, no United States President had ever been assassinated. **Assassination** is the murder of a government or political leader.

Lincoln's killer was John Wilkes Booth, a 26-year-old actor who supported the Confederacy. Federal troops found Booth in a Virginia barn where he was shot and killed after he refused to surrender. Others who took part in the assassination plan were also caught and later hanged.

A funeral train carried President Lincoln's body to his hometown of Springfield, Illinois, where he was buried. People in New York City, Philadelphia, Cleveland, Chicago, and other cities paid their respects as the train passed through their communities.

▶ **People lined the streets when Lincoln's funeral train passed through New York City.**

Vice President **Andrew Johnson** became the new President. The former senator from Tennessee intended to carry out Lincoln's plan for **Reconstruction**—the rebuilding and healing of the country after the war.

One of the first steps toward reconstruction was ending slavery throughout the nation. The **Thirteenth Amendment,** which abolished slavery in the United States, took effect on December 18, 1865.

Johnson also had a plan to readmit the former Confederate states into the Union. Each state had to form a new state government. It had to pledge to obey all federal laws and deal fairly with newly freed African Americans. By the end of 1865, President Johnson believed that Reconstruction was complete.

Under Johnson's plan, though, Southern states were free to pass laws called **black codes.** These laws denied African American men the right to vote or act as jurors in a trial. Black people also could not own guns, take certain jobs, or own land. African Americans who were out of work might be fined or arrested. The laws had the effect of making an African American's life much the same as it had been under slavery.

Many in Congress were angered by the black codes. They thought Johnson's Reconstruction plan was too easy on the South. The Republicans, who had won a majority in both houses of Congress, did not trust Johnson, who was a Southerner and had been a Democrat before becoming Lincoln's Vice President. Members of Congress began developing a new plan of Reconstruction.

REVIEW What effect did black codes have on African Americans? *Cause and Effect*

Collection of the New York Historical Society

517

Reconstruction Under Congress

Congress passed the first Reconstruction Act in 1867. The former Confederate states were divided into five military districts, and about 20,000 federal troops were sent to the South. The troops, led by military governors, were responsible for maintaining order, supervising elections, and preventing discrimination against African Americans.

The Reconstruction Acts required Southern states to write new state constitutions giving African American men the right to vote. The Acts also prevented former Confederate leaders and military officers from voting or holding elected office.

The **Freedmen's Bureau** was established to help the 4 million freedmen, or former slaves, after the war. The Freedmen's Bureau built hospitals and schools for blacks in the South. The Bureau hired black and white teachers from the North and the South.

For the first time in United States history, African Americans became elected officials. In Mississippi, two African Americans were elected United States senators. In 1870 Republican **Hiram R. Revels,** a minister and teacher, was elected to the Senate seat that Jefferson Davis held before the Civil War. In 1874 **Blanche K. Bruce,** a former slave, was elected to the Senate. Twenty other African Americans from the South were also elected to the House of Representatives.

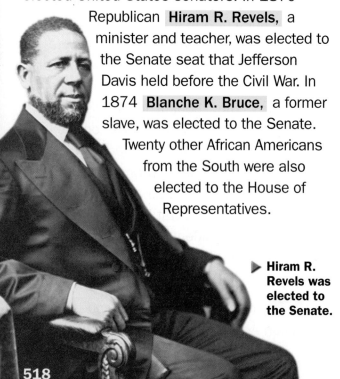

▶ Hiram R. Revels was elected to the Senate.

▶ **During Reconstruction, African American children studied at new schools in the South.**

Many white Southerners did not like the changes brought by Reconstruction. Some resented the new state governments, which they felt were forced on them by outsiders. Some were angered by Northerners who moved south to start businesses. These new arrivals were called carpetbaggers, because they often arrived carrying their belongings in suitcases made of carpet. Southerners who supported Reconstruction were called scalawags. Carpetbaggers and scalawags were accused of trying to profit from the hardships of the South.

New leaders raised taxes to help rebuild roads, construct railroads, and establish a free education system. Many Southerners had a hard time paying these taxes. They were trying to rebuild their own farms and businesses.

Some white Southerners also objected to the rights gained by African Americans. After the new state governments repealed black codes, a small group of white Southerners formed the Ku Klux Klan. The Klan's goal was to restore white control over the lives of African Americans. Members of the Klan burned African American schools and homes, and attacked blacks for trying to vote.

REVIEW What changes did Congress bring about in the South during Reconstruction?
🔄 Main Idea and Details

New Amendments

Before being readmitted into the Union, former Confederate states had to accept two new amendments. The **Fourteenth Amendment,** ratified in July 1868, gave African Americans citizenship and said that no state could deny the equal protection of the law to all citizens.

The **Fifteenth Amendment,** ratified in March 1870, gave all male citizens the right to vote. It stated,

> *"the right of citizens of the United States to vote shall not be denied...on account of race, color, or previous condition of servitude [slavery]."*

Sojourner Truth pointed out that a woman had "a right to have just as much as a man." But the Fifteenth Amendment did not give voting rights to women. This angered many women who had fought for abolition and thought women as well as African Americans should have the right to vote.

President Johnson opposed the Fourteenth Amendment and other Reconstruction laws. He believed that the Reconstruction Acts were unlawful because they were passed without the representation of Southern states in Congress. He tried to block the passage of several laws that granted further rights to African Americans.

Angry about Johnson's actions, the Republicans in Congress tried to remove him from office by **impeachment.** Impeachment is the bringing of charges of wrongdoing against an elected official by the House of Representatives. If found guilty in a Senate trial, an impeached President is removed from office. Johnson avoided being removed from office by one vote in May 1868, but his ability to lead the nation was weakened.

REVIEW Why did Congress want to impeach President Johnson? **Summarize**

▶ **After the Fifteenth Amendment became law, African American men were able to vote.**

CHART SKILL *Describe the rights provided by the Thirteenth, Fourteenth, and Fifteenth Amendments.*

Reconstruction Amendments, 1865–1870

Amendment	Ratified	Description
Thirteenth	December 1865	Declares slavery illegal
Fourteenth	July 1868	Declares former slaves to be citizens and guarantees equal protection of the law to all citizens
Fifteenth	February 1870	Prevents the denial of the right to vote based on race or previous condition of enslavement

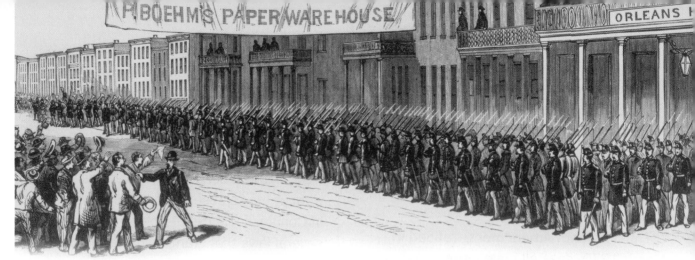
Library of Congress

▶ **Federal troops left the South in 1877, marking the end of Reconstruction.**

Reconstruction Ends

By 1870, all of the former Confederate states had met the requirements of Reconstruction and were readmitted to the Union. In 1877, the remaining federal troops were withdrawn from the South.

White Southern Democrats regained their power in state governments. Almost immediately, new laws were passed that again restricted the rights of African Americans. Whites tried to prevent blacks from voting in several ways. They set up voting booths far from African American communities, or changed the location of the booths without informing blacks. Some states required a poll tax, or a payment, in order to vote. Many African Americans could not afford the poll tax.

In some places blacks were forced to take a reading test before voting. Under slavery, many people had not been allowed to learn to read or write, and so they failed the test. A "grandfather clause" was added to some state constitutions. It said that men could only vote if their father or grandfather had voted before 1867. The "grandfather clause" kept most African Americans from voting because they had not gained the right to vote until 1870.

Jim Crow laws were also passed. These laws enforced **segregation,** or separation of blacks and whites. Under Jim Crow laws, blacks could not sit with whites on trains, or stay in certain hotels. They also could not eat in certain restaurants or attend certain theaters, schools, or parks.

During Reconstruction, Congressman Thaddeus Stevens said that every African American adult should be given "40 acres and a mule." His purpose was to help former slaves begin new lives. However, no land was ever distributed to former slaves.

Many African Americans were forced to return to the plantations where they had worked as slaves because they could not find jobs elsewhere. Many blacks as well as whites became trapped in a system called **sharecropping.** Sharecroppers rented land from landowners. They paid for their rent with a portion of their crop. Sharecroppers then used the rest of their crop to pay for food, clothing, and the equipment they needed to farm.

Usually, the costs of sharecropping were higher than the pay they received. Sharecropper John Mosley explained, "When our crop was gathered we would still be in debt."

REVIEW What conclusions can you draw about how life changed in the South after Reconstruction ended?
Draw Conclusions

After Reconstruction

Reconstruction had some successes in the South. A public school system was established and many industries were expanded. However, many of Reconstruction's goals failed to have a lasting impact.

After Reconstruction, the South remained the poorest section of the country. In addition, African Americans lost the political power they had gained during Reconstruction. Most blacks continued to perform the same labor they had done as slaves.

Many whites in the North lost interest in the problems faced by Southern blacks. The nation soon turned its attention to other issues. It would be many years before African Americans would gain the freedoms Reconstruction had hoped to guarantee.

REVIEW What were some of the successes and failures of Reconstruction?
Draw Conclusions

Summarize the Lesson

- **April 1865** President Abraham Lincoln was assassinated.
- **December 1865** The Thirteenth Amendment was adopted, abolishing slavery in the United States.
- **March 1867** Congress passed the Reconstruction Acts, sending military forces to the former Confederate states.

LESSON 4 REVIEW

Check Facts and Main Ideas

1. **Main Idea and Details** On a separate sheet of paper, fill in the details to the main idea.

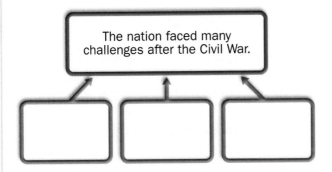

The nation faced many challenges after the Civil War.

2. Why did Republicans in Congress dislike Johnson's **Reconstruction** plan?

3. **Critical Thinking: Cause and Effect** How did the Reconstruction Acts affect the South?

4. Why were three amendments added to the Constitution during Reconstruction?

5. How were the lives of African Americans made more difficult after the end of Reconstruction? Use the word **segregation** in your answer.

Link to Writing

Research Biographies Many African Americans became government leaders for the first time during Reconstruction. Research Hiram R. Revels, Blanche K. Bruce, or another African American member of Congress elected during Reconstruction. Were they enslaved or free before the Civil War? How did they become involved in politics? How did the end of Reconstruction affect them? Write a summary of what you learn.

1861   1862   1863

April 1861
Union blockade of
Southern ports begins

January 1863
Emancipation Proclamation
takes effect

Chapter Summary

Target Skill

Main Idea and Details

On a separate sheet of paper, fill in other details that support the main idea. Find at least one detail for each lesson of the chapter.

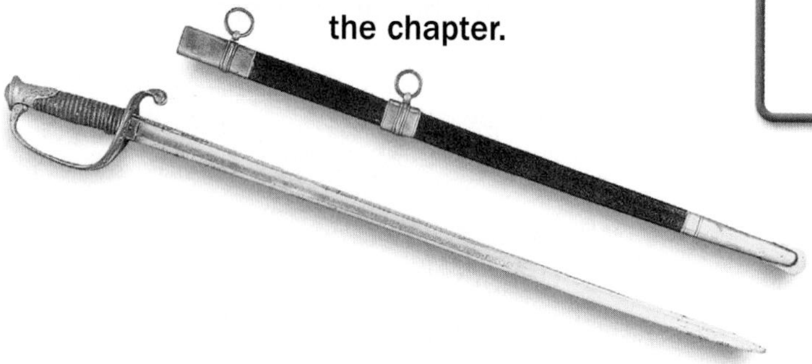

> The Civil War and Reconstruction had many effects on the nation.

Vocabulary

Match each word with the correct definition or description.

1. **blockade** (p. 494)

2. **draft** (p. 499)

3. **total war** (p. 510)

4. **black codes** (p. 517)

5. **impeachment** (p. 519)

a. preventing supplies from moving in or out

b. laws denying rights to African Americans

c. charging an official with unlawful action

d. destroying an enemy's will to fight

e. law requiring people to serve in the military

People and Terms

Write a sentence explaining why each of the following people or terms was important. You may use two or more in a single sentence.

1. **Anaconda Plan** (p. 494)

2. **Thomas "Stonewall" Jackson** (p. 495)

3. **Mathew Brady** (p. 499)

4. **Emancipation Proclamation** (p. 500)

5. **Clara Barton** (p. 502)

6. **Battle of Gettysburg** (p. 507)

7. **William Tecumseh Sherman** (p. 510)

8. **Freedmen's Bureau** (p. 518)

9. **Hiram R. Revels** (p. 518)

10. **Jim Crow laws** (p. 520)

1864   1865   1866   1867

July 1863
Battle of Gettysburg is a victory for Union forces

November 1863
President Lincoln delivers Gettysburg Address

April 1865
Confederacy surrenders President Lincoln is killed

December 1865
Thirteenth Amendment abolishes slavery

Facts and Main Ideas

1 What kinds of new technology were used during the Civil War?

2 Describe the significance of the attack on Fort Wagner.

3 **Time Line** How long did the Civil War last?

4 **Main Idea** What early strategies did each side plan for quick victories?

5 **Main Idea** What hardships did people on each side suffer during the Civil War?

6 **Main Idea** How did the Union army gain key victories in the final years of the war?

7 **Main Idea** What were the goals of Reconstruction?

8 **Critical Thinking:** *Compare and Contrast* Compare the lives of African Americans living in the South before the Civil War and after Reconstruction.

Write About History

1 **Write a newspaper story** about one of the battles discussed in your text.

2 **Write a journal entry** as a soldier describing General Robert E. Lee's surrender to General Grant.

3 **Write a letter** telling a friend about the *Monitor* or the *Virginia,* how these ironclads worked, and what they were like.

Apply Skills

Use Road Maps
Study the road map below. Then answer the questions.

1 Which three interstate highways lead into and out of Atlanta?

2 How would you travel from Atlanta to Savannah?

3 Andersonville National Historic Site is the location of a Civil War prisoner of war camp. How would you travel to Andersonville from Kennesaw Mountain National Battlefield?

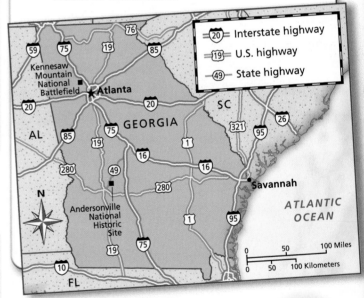

Internet Activity

To get help with vocabulary, people, and terms, select dictionary or encyclopedia from *Social Studies Library* at **www.sfsocialstudies.com.**

When Johnny Comes Marching Home

by Patrick S. Gilmore

The Civil War inspired many songs in the North and the South. Some songs became popular on both sides. One of these was "When Johnny Comes Marching Home," written in 1863 by Patrick Gilmore, a bandleader in the Union army. Who is "Johnny" in this song?

1. When John-ny comes march-ing home a-gain,
2. Let love _ and friend-ship on the day, Hur - rah! _ Hur - rah! _
3. Get read - y for the ju - bi - lee,

We'll give him a heart - y wel - come then,
Their choic - est trea - sure then dis - play, Hur - rah! _ Hur - rah! _
We'll give _ the he - ro three times three,

The _ men will cheer, _ the boys will shout, The _ la - dies they _ will all turn out,
And _ let each one _ per-form some part, To _ fill with joy _ the war-rior's heart,
The _ laur - el wreath _ is read - y now To place up - on _ his roy - al brow,

And we'll shout "Hur - rah" when John-ny comes march-ing home! _

Main Ideas and Vocabulary

Read the passage below and use it to answer the questions that follow.

The growing nation faced problems of sectionalism. Northerners and Southerners disagreed about whether slavery should be allowed in new states. Northern and Southern states also had different ways of life. Many Northerners and Southerners were loyal to their region of the country.

Abraham Lincoln joined the Republican Party, which opposed the spread of slavery. After he was elected President in 1860, South Carolina seceded from the Union. Other Southern states followed and formed the Confederacy. Confederate troops attacked Union-held Fort Sumter in April 1861, beginning the Civil War.

The Civil War dragged on for four years. New weapons of war left many soldiers dead or wounded. A lack of knowledge of disease killed many more. In the spring of 1865, the Confederacy surrendered. President Lincoln was killed shortly afterwards by a Confederate supporter.

Congress passed the Reconstruction Acts to rebuild the country and readmit the Southern states to the Union. Federal troops were sent to the South to maintain order and regulate elections. During this period, much of the damage from the war was repaired. African American men were granted the right to vote and some became members of Congress. The Freedmen's Bureau built hospitals and schools to help freed slaves.

When Reconstruction ended in 1877, many laws were passed to again restrict the rights of African Americans. Jim Crow laws segregated blacks and whites.

1. According to the passage, what was one difference between the North and South?
   A Northerners and Southerners had similar ways of life.
   B Northerners and Southerners disagreed about slavery in new states.
   C The South had more resources.
   D The North had more resources.

2. In the passage, the word sectionalism means—
   A wanting to divide the country in half
   B ending slavery in part of the country
   C loyalty to one's country
   D loyalty to one's region

3. In the passage, the word seceded means—
   A joined with others
   B broke away from a group
   C objected to something
   D formed a new government

4. What is the main idea of the passage?
   A The North won the Civil War.
   B The Civil War ended slavery.
   C Differences between North and South led to the Civil War.
   D War destroys people and places.

People and Terms

Match each person and term to its definition.

1. **Joseph Cinque** (p. 472)
2. **John Brown** (p. 480)
3. **border state** (p. 486)
4. **Catherine Coffin** (p. 473)
5. **Ulysses S. Grant** (p. 509)
6. **segregation** (p. 520)

a. abolitionist who attacked an arsenal at Harpers Ferry

b. separating people

c. helped slaves escape to freedom

d. leader of Union forces at the Battle of Vicksburg

e. leader of *Amistad* rebellion

f. allowed slavery but did not secede

Apply Skills

Prepare a scrapbook about different points of view on a current subject. First, choose the topic. Then clip articles that present opposing points of view about the topic. Paste the articles into a scrapbook. Under each article, write a sentence that summarizes the writer's point of view.

New Laws to Protect Endangered Species

The writer feels that the government is enacting laws to help save animals.

Hunting Season Helps Control Animal Overpopulation

The writer feels that hunting helps the animals by controlling overpopulation.

Write and Share

Create a Quiz Show Work with a group of students to create a quiz show about some of the main events and people in the period just before, during, and after the Civil War. Select a quiz show host and assistants to write the questions and answers. Then select contestants and develop a scoring system. Decide on a prize for the winner, and present the show to your class.

Read on Your Own

Look for these books in the library.

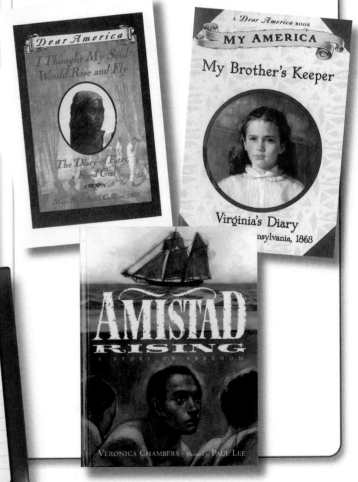

A *Dear America* BOOK
Dear America
I Thought My Soul Would Rise and Fly
The Diary of Patsy, a Freed Girl
Mars Bluff, South Carolina, 1865

A *Dear America* BOOK
MY AMERICA
My Brother's Keeper
Virginia's Diary
...nsylvania, 1863

AMISTAD RISING
A STORY OF FREEDOM
VERONICA CHAMBERS · *Illustrated by* PAUL LEE

History Speaks

Present the history of people from the time of the Civil War.

1 **Form** a group and choose a famous person who lived during the Civil War or Reconstruction.

2 **Write** a talk for the person to give to the class. Include details of what life was like during this time period.

3 **Choose** a person in your group to play the part of the famous person.

4 **Present** the talk to the class. You may want to include drawings of Civil War life to show to the class.

5 **Have** other students ask questions after the talk.

Internet Activity

Explore the Civil War.
Go to **www.sfsocialstudies.com/activities** and select your grade and unit.

Reference Guide

Table of Contents

Atlas
Map of the World: Political

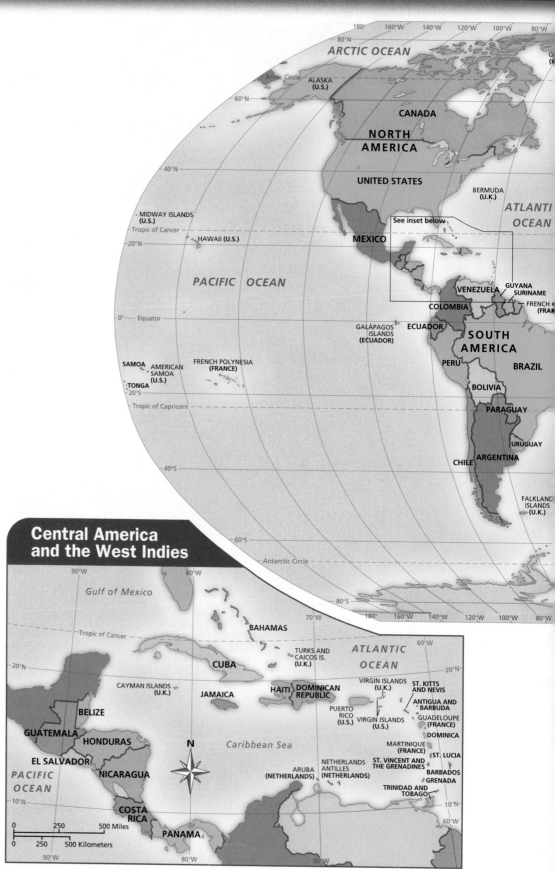

ARCTIC OCEAN

Arctic Circle

ALASKA (U.S.)

CANADA

NORTH AMERICA

UNITED STATES

BERMUDA (U.K.)

ATLANTIC OCEAN

See inset below

MEXICO

MIDWAY ISLANDS (U.S.)

Tropic of Cancer

HAWAII (U.S.)

PACIFIC OCEAN

VENEZUELA   GUYANA   SURINAME

COLOMBIA   FRENCH (FRA

Equator

GALÁPAGOS ISLANDS (ECUADOR)

ECUADOR

SOUTH AMERICA

PERU   BRAZIL

SAMOA   AMERICAN SAMOA (U.S.)

FRENCH POLYNESIA (FRANCE)

BOLIVIA

TONGA

Tropic of Capricorn

PARAGUAY

URUGUAY

CHILE   ARGENTINA

FALKLAND ISLANDS (U.K.)

Antarctic Circle

Central America and the West Indies

90°W   80°W

Gulf of Mexico

Tropic of Cancer

BAHAMAS

TURKS AND CAICOS IS. (U.K.)

ATLANTIC OCEAN

CUBA

CAYMAN ISLANDS (U.K.)

JAMAICA

HAITI   DOMINICAN REPUBLIC

VIRGIN ISLANDS (U.K.)

ST. KITTS AND NEVIS

ANTIGUA AND BARBUDA

PUERTO RICO (U.S.)   VIRGIN ISLANDS (U.S.)

GUADELOUPE (FRANCE)

DOMINICA

BELIZE

MARTINIQUE (FRANCE)

ST. LUCIA

GUATEMALA

HONDURAS

N

Caribbean Sea

ARUBA (NETHERLANDS)

NETHERLANDS ANTILLES (NETHERLANDS)

ST. VINCENT AND THE GRENADINES

BARBADOS

GRENADA

EL SALVADOR

PACIFIC OCEAN

NICARAGUA

TRINIDAD AND TOBAGO

COSTA RICA

0   250   500 Miles

0   250   500 Kilometers

PANAMA

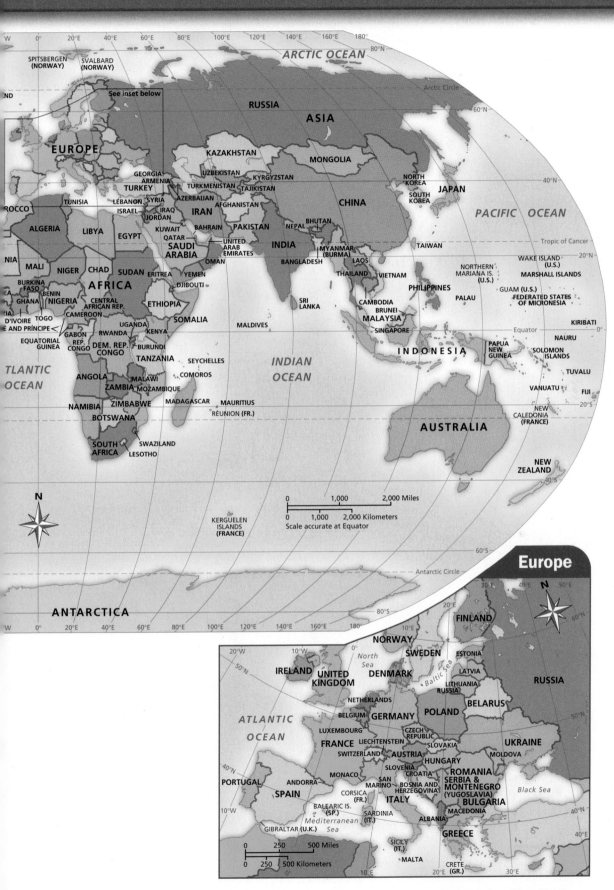

ARCTIC OCEAN

Arctic Circle

SPITSBERGEN
(NORWAY)
SVALBARD
(NORWAY)

See inset below

RUSSIA

ASIA

EUROPE

KAZAKHSTAN

MONGOLIA

NORTH
KOREA

JAPAN

PACIFIC OCEAN

GEORGIA
ARMENIA
TURKEY
UZBEKISTAN
KYRGYZSTAN
TURKMENISTAN
TAJIKISTAN
AZERBAIJAN
SOUTH
KOREA

TUNISIA

LEBANON
ISRAEL
SYRIA
IRAQ
JORDAN
IRAN
AFGHANISTAN
CHINA

MOROCCO

KUWAIT
QATAR
BAHRAIN
PAKISTAN
NEPAL
BHUTAN

Tropic of Cancer

ALGERIA
LIBYA
EGYPT
SAUDI
ARABIA
UNITED
ARAB
EMIRATES
INDIA
TAIWAN

WAKE ISLAND
(U.S.)

NIA
MALI
NIGER
CHAD
SUDAN
OMAN
BANGLADESH
MYANMAR
(BURMA)
LAOS
NORTHERN
MARIANA IS.
(U.S.)
MARSHALL ISLANDS

BURKINA
FASO
ERITREA
YEMEN
THAILAND
VIETNAM

GHANA
BENIN
NIGERIA
AFRICA
DJIBOUTI
GUAM (U.S.)

D'IVOIRE
TOGO
CENTRAL
AFRICAN REP.
CAMEROON
ETHIOPIA
PHILIPPINES
PALAU
FEDERATED STATES
OF MICRONESIA

E AND PRÍNCIPE
GABON
REP.
CONGO
UGANDA
SOMALIA
SRI
LANKA
CAMBODIA
BRUNEI
MALAYSIA
KIRIBATI

EQUATORIAL
GUINEA
RWANDA
KENYA
MALDIVES
Equator
0°

DEM. REP.
CONGO
BURUNDI
SINGAPORE
NAURU

TANZANIA
SEYCHELLES
INDONESIA
PAPUA
NEW
GUINEA
SOLOMON
ISLANDS

ATLANTIC
OCEAN
ANGOLA
MALAWI
COMOROS
INDIAN
OCEAN
TUVALU

ZAMBIA
MOZAMBIQUE
VANUATU
FIJI

NAMIBIA
ZIMBABWE
MADAGASCAR
MAURITIUS
NEW
CALEDONIA
(FRANCE)

BOTSWANA
RÉUNION (FR.)
AUSTRALIA

SOUTH
AFRICA
SWAZILAND
LESOTHO
NEW
ZEALAND

N

0   1,000   2,000 Miles
0   1,000   2,000 Kilometers
Scale accurate at Equator

KERGUELEN
ISLANDS
(FRANCE)

Antarctic Circle

ANTARCTICA

Europe

FINLAND

NORWAY
SWEDEN
ESTONIA

North
Sea

IRELAND
UNITED
KINGDOM
DENMARK
Baltic Sea
LATVIA
LITHUANIA
RUSSIA
RUSSIA

NETHERLANDS
BELARUS

ATLANTIC
OCEAN
BELGIUM
GERMANY
POLAND

LUXEMBOURG
CZECH
REPUBLIC
UKRAINE

FRANCE
LIECHTENSTEIN
SLOVAKIA
MOLDOVA

SWITZERLAND
AUSTRIA
HUNGARY

MONACO
SLOVENIA
CROATIA
ROMANIA

PORTUGAL
ANDORRA
SAN
MARINO
BOSNIA AND
HERZEGOVINA
SERBIA &
MONTENEGRO
(YUGOSLAVIA)
Black Sea

SPAIN
CORSICA
(FR.)
ITALY
BULGARIA
MACEDONIA

BALEARIC IS.
(SP.)
SARDINIA
(IT.)
ALBANIA

GIBRALTAR (U.K.)
Mediterranean
Sea
GREECE

SICILY
(IT.)

MALTA
CRETE
(GR.)

0   250   500 Miles
0   250   500 Kilometers

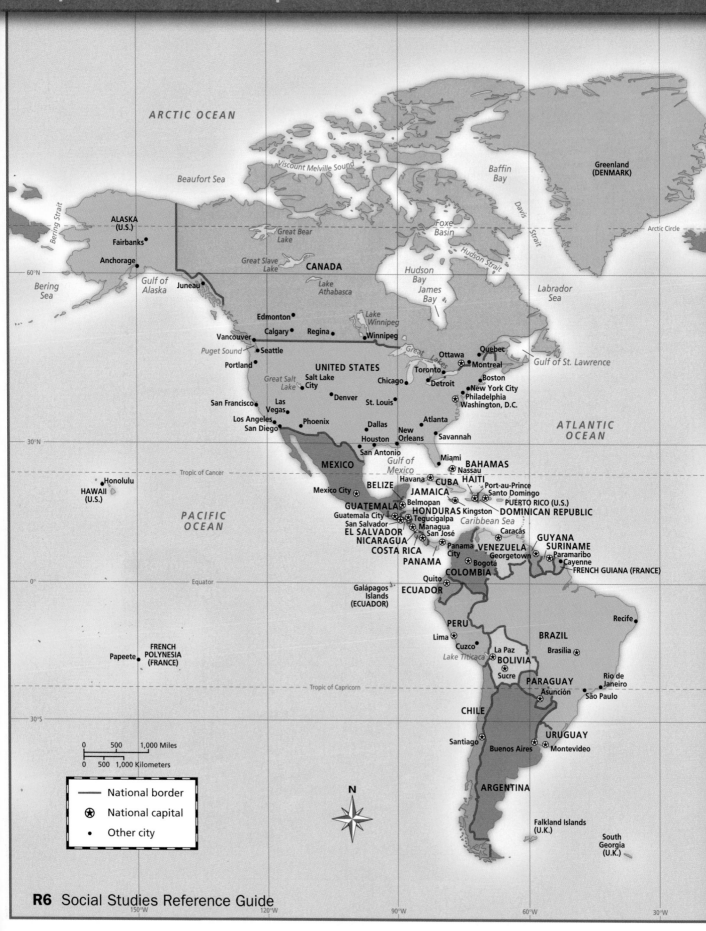

ARCTIC OCEAN

Beaufort Sea

Viscount Melville Sound

Baffin Bay

Greenland (DENMARK)

Great Bear Lake

Bering Strait

ALASKA (U.S.)

Fairbanks

Anchorage

Gulf of Alaska

Juneau

60°N

Bering Sea

Great Slave Lake

CANADA

Lake Athabasca

Davis Strait

Foxe Basin

Hudson Strait

Arctic Circle

Hudson Bay

James Bay

Labrador Sea

Edmonton

Vancouver

Calgary

Regina

Winnipeg

Lake Winnipeg

Puget Sound

Seattle

Portland

Great Salt Lake

UNITED STATES

Salt Lake City

Chicago

Great Lakes

Ottawa

Toronto

Detroit

Quebec

Montreal

Boston

New York City

Philadelphia

Washington, D.C.

Gulf of St. Lawrence

Denver

St. Louis

San Francisco

Las Vegas

Los Angeles

San Diego

Phoenix

Dallas

Houston

New Orleans

Atlanta

Savannah

ATLANTIC OCEAN

30°N

San Antonio

Miami

BAHAMAS

Nassau

Tropic of Cancer

Honolulu

HAWAII (U.S.)

PACIFIC OCEAN

MEXICO

Gulf of Mexico

Mexico City

BELIZE

GUATEMALA

Guatemala City

San Salvador

EL SALVADOR

Havana

CUBA

JAMAICA

Belmopan

Tegucigalpa

HONDURAS

Managua

NICARAGUA

San José

COSTA RICA

HAITI

Port-au-Prince

Santo Domingo

Kingston

DOMINICAN REPUBLIC

PUERTO RICO (U.S.)

Caribbean Sea

Caracás

Panama City

PANAMA

VENEZUELA

Bogotá

COLOMBIA

GUYANA

SURINAME

Georgetown

Paramaribo

Cayenne

FRENCH GUIANA (FRANCE)

Galápagos Islands (ECUADOR)

Quito

ECUADOR

0° Equator

PERU

Lima

Cuzco

La Paz

Lake Titicaca

BOLIVIA

Sucre

BRAZIL

Brasília

Recife

FRENCH POLYNESIA (FRANCE)

Papeete

Rio de Janeiro

São Paulo

PARAGUAY

Asunción

Tropic of Capricorn

CHILE

URUGUAY

30°S

Santiago

Buenos Aires

Montevideo

0 500 1,000 Miles

0 500 1,000 Kilometers

National border

National capital

Other city

N

ARGENTINA

Falkland Islands (U.K.)

South Georgia (U.K.)

150°W   120°W   90°W   60°W   30°W

ARCTIC OCEAN

North Magnetic Pole

Ellesmere Island

Queen Elizabeth Islands

Melville Island

Viscount Melville Sound

Devon Island

Banks Island

Baffin Bay

Greenland

Beaufort Sea

Point Barrow

Victoria Island

Foxe Basin

Baffin Island

Davis Strait

Bering Strait

Brooks Range

Yukon River

Great Bear Lake

Hudson Strait

Arctic Circle

Cape Farewell

Mt. McKinley 20,320 ft. (6,194 m)

Alaska Range

Yukon Plateau

Mackenzie Mts.

Mackenzie River

Hudson Bay

Labrador

Bering Sea

Gulf of Alaska

Mt. Logan 19,524 ft. (5,951 m)

Liard R.

Peace R.

Great Slave Lake

Athabasca R.

James Bay

Labrador Sea

CANADIAN

Alaska Peninsula

Kodiak Island

Queen Charlotte Islands

Coast Mountains

Lake Athabasca

Saskatchewan River

SHIELD

Newfoundland

Aleutian Islands

Vancouver Island

Puget Sound

Coast Ranges

ROCKY MOUNTAINS

GREAT PLAINS

Lake Winnipeg

NORTH AMERICA

Great Lakes

St. Lawrence R.

Gulf of St. Lawrence

Nova Scotia

Cascade Range

Black Hills

Missouri R.

Mississippi R.

Bay of Fundy

Cape Cod

Long Island

Sierra Nevada

Great Salt Lake

GREAT BASIN

Platte R.

Arkansas R.

Ohio R.

INTERIOR PLAINS

APPALACHIAN MTS.

ATLANTIC OCEAN

Mt. Whitney 14,495 ft. (4,418 m)

Colorado R.

Ozark Plateau

Death Valley (lowest point in N.A.) -282 ft. (-86 m)

Sonoran Desert

Rio Grande

COASTAL PLAIN

Cape Hatteras

Baja California

Sierra Madre Occidental

Sierra Madre Oriental

Gulf of Mexico

Bahamas

Hawaiian Islands

Tropic of Cancer

Cuba

Greater Antilles

Hispaniola

Puerto Rico

Citlaltépetl 18,701 ft. (5,700 m)

Yucatán Peninsula

Caribbean Sea

Lesser Antilles

PACIFIC OCEAN

Lake Nicaragua

Isthmus of Panama

Lake Maracaibo

Llanos

Orinoco R.

Guiana Highlands

Chimborazo 20,561 ft. (6,267 m)

Galápagos Islands

Rio Negro

Amazon R.

Cape São Roque

Line Islands

Equator

AMAZON BASIN

Tapajós R.

Xingu R.

Tocantins R.

São Francisco R.

Marquesas Islands

Huascarán 22,205 ft. (6,768 m)

Mato Grosso Plateau

Brazilian Highlands

Cook Islands

Tuamotu Archipelago

Lake Titicaca

Paraguay R.

SOUTH AMERICA

Society Islands

Altiplano

Atacama Desert

Gran Chaco

Paraná R.

Iguazú Falls

Tropic of Capricorn

Uruguay R.

Mt. Aconcagua 22,831 ft. (6,959 m)

Pampa

Patagonia

Valdés Peninsula (lowest point in S.A.) -131 ft. (-40 m)

Falkland Islands

South Georgia

Strait of Magellan

Tierra del Fuego

Cape Horn

0   500   1,000 Miles
0   500   1,000 Kilometers

N

▲ Mountain peak
— National border

150°W   120°W   90°W   60°W   30°W

Atlas
Map of North America: Political

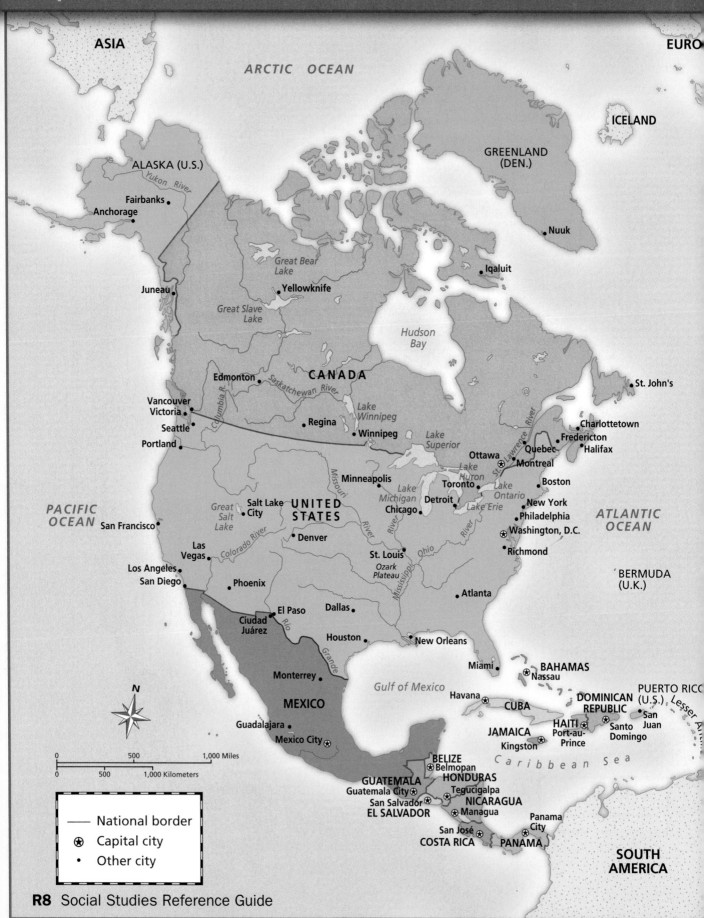

ASIA

EURO

ARCTIC OCEAN

ICELAND

GREENLAND (DEN.)

ALASKA (U.S.)

Yukon River

Fairbanks

Anchorage

Nuuk

Great Bear Lake

Iqaluit

Juneau

Yellowknife

Great Slave Lake

Hudson Bay

Edmonton

Saskatchewan River

CANADA

St. John's

Columbia R.

Vancouver
Victoria

Seattle

Portland

Regina

Lake Winnipeg

Winnipeg

Lake Superior

Charlottetown

Fredericton

Halifax

St. Lawrence River

Ottawa

Quebec

Montreal

Minneapolis

Lake Huron

Toronto

Lake Michigan

Detroit

Lake Ontario

Lake Erie

Boston

New York

Missouri River

Salt Lake City

UNITED STATES

Chicago

San Francisco

PACIFIC OCEAN

Great Salt Lake

Denver

Colorado River

Las Vegas

Los Angeles

San Diego

Phoenix

St. Louis

Ozark Plateau

Ohio River

Mississippi River

Philadelphia

Washington, D.C.

Richmond

ATLANTIC OCEAN

BERMUDA (U.K.)

El Paso

Ciudad Juárez

Dallas

Atlanta

Houston

Rio Grande

New Orleans

Monterrey

Miami

Gulf of Mexico

Havana

BAHAMAS

Nassau

PUERTO RICO (U.S.)

Lesser A...

MEXICO

CUBA

DOMINICAN REPUBLIC

San Juan

Guadalajara

Mexico City

JAMAICA

HAITI

Port-au-Prince

Santo Domingo

Kingston

Caribbean Sea

BELIZE

Belmopan

GUATEMALA

Guatemala City

HONDURAS

Tegucigalpa

San Salvador

EL SALVADOR

NICARAGUA

Managua

Panama City

San José

COSTA RICA

PANAMA

SOUTH AMERICA

N

0   500   1,000 Miles

0   500   1,000 Kilometers

—— National border

⊛ Capital city

• Other city

R8 Social Studies Reference Guide

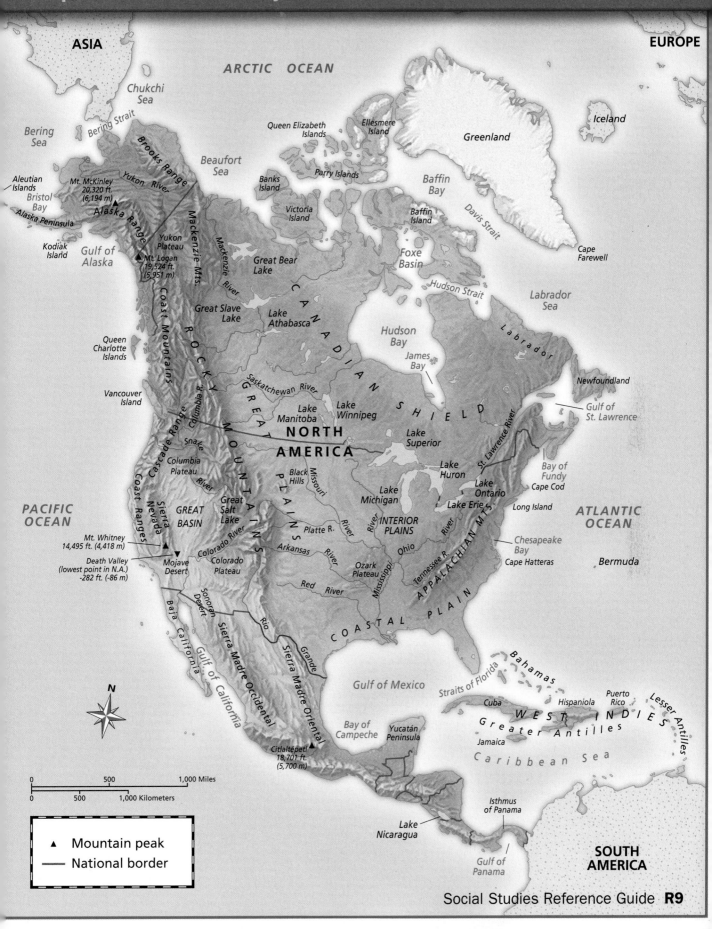

ASIA

EUROPE

ARCTIC OCEAN

Chukchi Sea

Bering Sea

Bering Strait

Brooks Range

Beaufort Sea

Queen Elizabeth Islands

Ellesmere Island

Greenland

Iceland

Aleutian Islands

Mt. McKinley 20,320 ft. (6,194 m)

Yukon River

Alaska Range

Banks Island

Parry Islands

Baffin Bay

Bristol Bay

Alaska Peninsula

Kodiak Island

Gulf of Alaska

Mt. Logan 19,524 ft. (5,951 m)

Yukon Plateau

Victoria Island

Baffin Island

Davis Strait

Cape Farewell

Mackenzie Mts.

Great Bear Lake

Foxe Basin

Mackenzie River

Coast Mountains

ROCKY

Great Slave Lake

Hudson Strait

Labrador Sea

Queen Charlotte Islands

Lake Athabasca

CANADIAN

Hudson Bay

Labrador

Vancouver Island

Saskatchewan River

SHIELD

James Bay

Newfoundland

GREAT

Lake Manitoba

Lake Winnipeg

NORTH AMERICA

Lake Superior

St. Lawrence River

Gulf of St. Lawrence

Columbia R.

Cascade Range

Snake

MOUNTAINS

PLAINS

Black Hills

Missouri

Lake Michigan

Lake Huron

Lake Ontario

Bay of Fundy

Cape Cod

Columbia Plateau

River

Lake Erie

Long Island

PACIFIC OCEAN

Sierra Nevada

GREAT BASIN

Great Salt Lake

Platte R.

River

River

INTERIOR PLAINS

River

APPALACHIAN MTS.

ATLANTIC OCEAN

Chesapeake Bay

Mt. Whitney 14,495 ft. (4,418 m)

Arkansas

River

Ohio

Cape Hatteras

Bermuda

Death Valley (lowest point in N.A.) -282 ft. (-86 m)

Mojave Desert

Colorado River

Colorado Plateau

Ozark Plateau

Tennessee R.

Mississippi

Red

River

Baja California

Sonoran Desert

Rio

COASTAL

PLAIN

Gulf of California

Sierra Madre Occidental

Grande

Sierra Madre Oriental

N

Bay of Campeche

Yucatán Peninsula

Gulf of Mexico

Straits of Florida

Bahamas

Cuba

Hispaniola

Puerto Rico

Lesser Antilles

WEST INDIES

Greater Antilles

Jamaica

Citlaltépetl 18,701 ft. (5,700 m)

Caribbean Sea

0   500   1,000 Miles

0   500   1,000 Kilometers

Lake Nicaragua

Isthmus of Panama

SOUTH AMERICA

Gulf of Panama

▲ Mountain peak

— National border

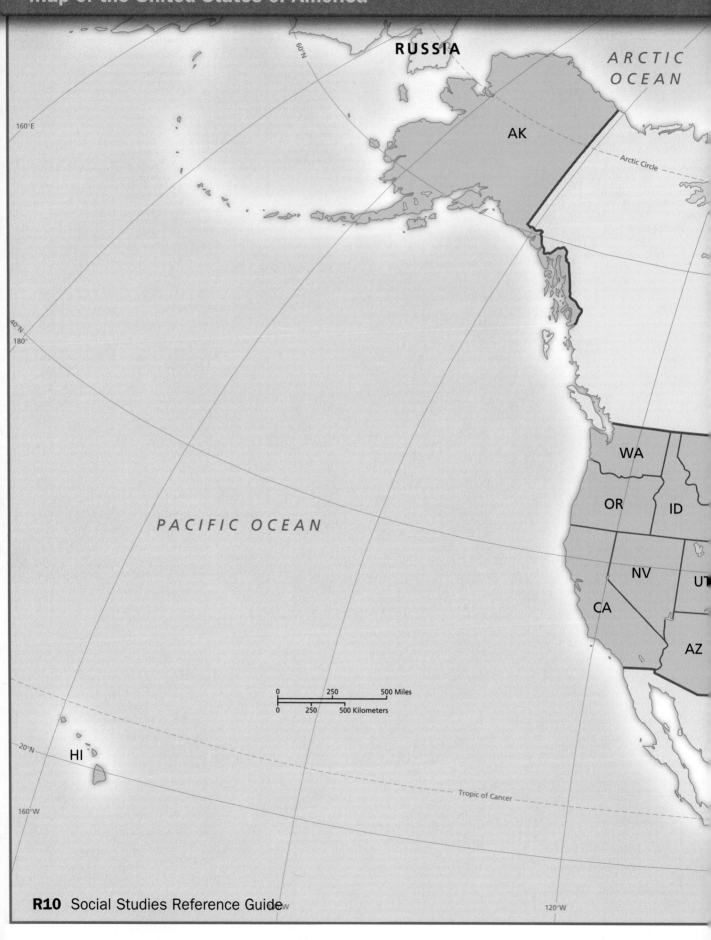

RUSSIA

ARCTIC OCEAN

AK

Arctic Circle

60°N

160°E

40°N
180°

PACIFIC OCEAN

WA

OR

ID

NV

UT

CA

AZ

0   250   500 Miles

0   250   500 Kilometers

20°N

HI

Tropic of Cancer

160°W

120°W

Greenland
(DENMARK)

CANADA

State or area	Abbreviation
Alabama	AL
Alaska	AK
Arizona	AZ
Arkansas	AR
California	CA
Colorado	CO
Connecticut	CT
Delaware	DE
District of Columbia	DC
Florida	FL
Georgia	GA
Hawaii	HI
Idaho	ID
Illinois	IL
Indiana	IN
Iowa	IA
Kansas	KS
Kentucky	KY
Louisiana	LA
Maine	ME
Maryland	MD
Massachusetts	MA
Michigan	MI
Minnesota	MN
Mississippi	MS
Missouri	MO
Montana	MT
Nebraska	NE
Nevada	NV
New Hampshire	NH
New Jersey	NJ
New Mexico	NM
New York	NY
North Carolina	NC
North Dakota	ND
Ohio	OH
Oklahoma	OK
Oregon	OR
Pennsylvania	PA
Rhode Island	RI
South Carolina	SC
South Dakota	SD
Tennessee	TN
Texas	TX
Utah	UT
Vermont	VT
Virginia	VA
Washington	WA
West Virginia	WV
Wisconsin	WI
Wyoming	WY

ND
MN
SD
WI
MI
ME
VT
NH
NY
MA
CT
RI
NE
IA
PA
NJ
IL
IN
OH
DE
MD
DC
KS
MO
WV
VA
KY
TN
NC
OK
AR
SC
MS
AL
GA
TX
LA
FL

ATLANTIC
OCEAN

Gulf of Mexico

N

MEXICO

BAHAMAS

CUBA

HAITI   DOM.
        REP.

JAMAICA

100°W

80°W

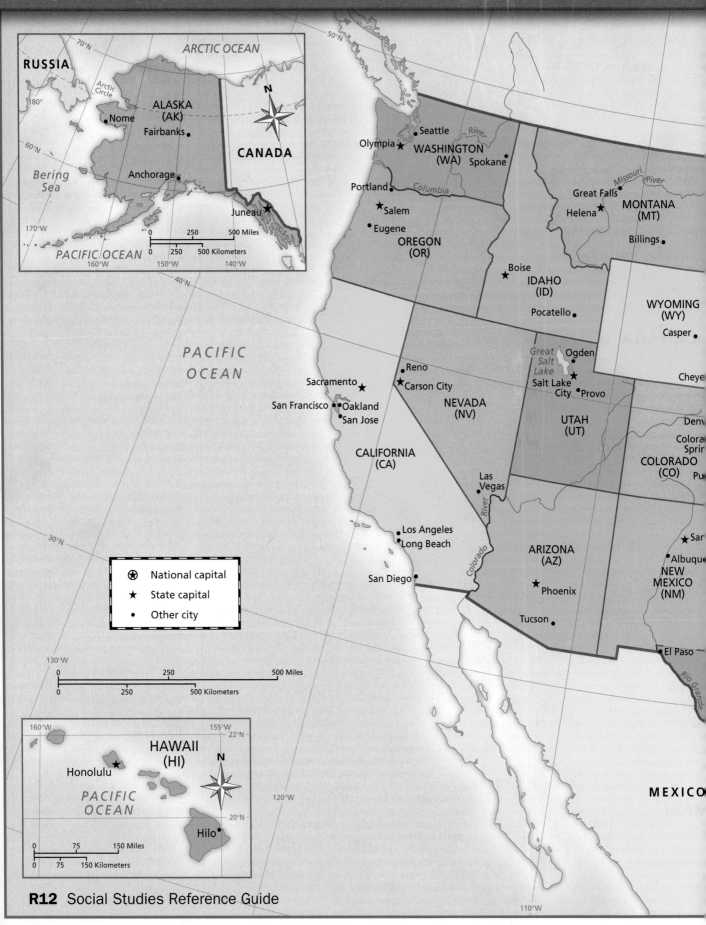

ARCTIC OCEAN

RUSSIA

Arctic Circle

180°

70°N

60°N

170°W

Bering Sea

160°W

PACIFIC OCEAN

150°W

140°W

ALASKA (AK)

• Nome

Fairbanks •

Anchorage •

Juneau ★

CANADA

N

0 250 500 Miles

0 250 500 Kilometers

50°N

40°N

30°N

PACIFIC OCEAN

• Seattle

Olympia ★

WASHINGTON (WA)

• Spokane

River

Portland •

Columbia

Salem •

• Eugene

OREGON (OR)

Boise •

IDAHO (ID)

Pocatello •

Great Falls •

Helena ★

MONTANA (MT)

Missouri River

Billings •

WYOMING (WY)

Casper •

Cheye

Reno •

Sacramento ★

Carson City ★

San Francisco •

Oakland •

San Jose •

NEVADA (NV)

Great Salt Lake

Ogden •

Salt Lake City

• Provo

UTAH (UT)

Denv

Colora Sprir

COLORADO (CO)

Pu

CALIFORNIA (CA)

Las Vegas •

River

Los Angeles •

Long Beach •

San Diego •

Colorado

ARIZONA (AZ)

Phoenix ★

Tucson •

Sar ★

Albuqu •

NEW MEXICO (NM)

El Paso •

Rio Grande

MEXICO

130°W

⊛ National capital

★ State capital

• Other city

0 250 500 Miles

0 250 500 Kilometers

160°W

155°W

22°N

HAWAII (HI)

Honolulu ★

N

PACIFIC OCEAN

20°N

120°W

0 75 150 Miles

0 75 150 Kilometers

Hilo •

110°W

CANADA

ORTH DAKOTA (ND)
★ Bismarck
Grand Forks
Fargo

UTH DAKOTA (SD)
★ Pierre
Sioux Falls

MINNESOTA (MN)
Duluth
Minneapolis
★ St. Paul

Lake Superior

Green Bay
WISCONSIN (WI)
Madison ★
Milwaukee

Lake Michigan

MICHIGAN (MI)
Grand Rapids
Lansing ★
Detroit

Lake Huron

Lake Ontario

NEW HAMPSHIRE (NH)
VERMONT (VT)
Burlington
Montpelier ★

MAINE (ME)
★ Augusta
Portland
★ Concord

Albany ★
NEW YORK (NY)
Buffalo

MASSACHUSETTS (MA)
Boston ★
★ Providence
Hartford ★

RHODE ISLAND (RI)
CONNECTICUT (CT)

NEBRASKA (NE)
Omaha
Lincoln ★

IOWA (IA)
Cedar Rapids
Rockford ●
Davenport
Des Moines ★

Chicago ●
Peoria ●
Springfield ★
ILLINOIS (IL)

Gary ●
Fort Wayne

INDIANA (IN)
Indianapolis ★

Toledo ●
Columbus ★
OHIO (OH)
Cleveland ●
Wheeling

PENNSYLVANIA (PA)
Harrisburg ★
Pittsburgh ●

Newark ●
★ New York
Trenton ★
Philadelphia ●

NEW JERSEY (NJ)

Baltimore ●
Dover ●
DELAWARE (DE)
⊗ Annapolis
Washington, D.C.
MARYLAND (MD)

KANSAS (KS)
Kansas City
Kansas City
Topeka ★
Wichita ●

MISSOURI (MO)
Jefferson City ★
St. Louis ●
Evansville

Cincinnati ●
Ohio River

WEST VIRGINIA (WV)
Charleston ★

Frankfort ★
Louisville
KENTUCKY (KY)

Richmond ★
VIRGINIA (VA)
Norfolk ●

OKLAHOMA (OK)
Tulsa ●
Oklahoma City ★

Fort Smith

ARKANSAS (AR)
Little Rock ★

Memphis ●

Nashville ★
TENNESSEE (TN)

Knoxville ●
Charlotte ●
Raleigh ●
NORTH CAROLINA (NC)

Columbia ●
SOUTH CAROLINA (SC)
★
Charleston ●

ATLANTIC OCEAN

Fort Worth ●
Dallas ●

Shreveport ●
LOUISIANA (LA)
Jackson ★

MISSISSIPPI (MS)

Birmingham ●
ALABAMA (AL)
Montgomery ★

★ Atlanta
GEORGIA (GA)
Columbus ●
Savannah ●

Jacksonville ●

TEXAS (TX)
Austin ★
San Antonio ●
Houston ●

Baton Rouge ★
New Orleans

Biloxi ●
Mobile ●

★ Tallahassee

FLORIDA (FL)
Tampa ●

Laredo ●
Corpus Christi ●

N

Gulf of Mexico

Miami ●

BAHAMAS

50°N
40°N
70°W
30°N
80°W
90°W

Vegetation Key
- Arid
- Evergreen forest
- Grassland
- Mixed forest
- Mountains
- Tundra

— National border
— State border
▲ Mountain peak
△ Highest point
▽ Lowest point

RUSSIA

ARCTIC OCEAN

BROOKS RANGE

AK

ALASKA RANGE

Mt. McKinley
20,320 ft.
(6,194 m)

Arctic Circle

N

CANADA

Bering Strait

Yukon River

Bering Sea

PACIFIC OCEAN

0 — 250 — 500 Miles
0 — 250 — 500 Kilometers

Mt. Rainier
14,410 ft.
(4,392 m)

WA

Mt. St. Helens
8,364 ft. (2,549 m)

RANGE

Columbia River

CASCADE

COAST RANGES

Mt. Hood
11,235 ft.
(3,427 m)

OR

COLUMBIA PLATEAU

Puget Sound

MT

ROCKY

ID

Snake River

Missouri River

Yellowstone River

TETON RANGE

WY

Cape Mendocino

COAST

Sacramento River

SIERRA NEVADA
CENTRAL VALLEY

San Francisco Bay

San Joaquin River

Lake Tahoe

GREAT

NV

BASIN

Great Salt Lake

GREAT SALT LAKE DESERT

UT

WASATCH

RANGE

MOUNTAINS

Mt. Elbert
14,433 ft.
(4,399 m)

Mt. Whitney
14,494 ft.
(4,418 m)

CA

RANGES

DEATH VALLEY
-282 ft. ▽
(-86 m)

MOJAVE DESERT

Lake Mead

Colorado River

COLORADO PLATEAU

AZ

Baldy Peak
11,403 ft.
(3,476 m)

NM

Salton Sea

SONORA DESERT

Gila River

Guadalupe Peak
8,749 ft.
(2,667 m)

PACIFIC OCEAN

130°W

160°W

Kauai

Oahu

HI

N

155°W

22°N

Maui

PACIFIC OCEAN

Hawaii

Mauna Kea
13,796 ft.
(4,205 m)

20°N

0 — 75 — 150 Miles
0 — 75 — 150 Kilometers

120°W

MEXICO

Rio

110°W

CANADA

Lake of
the Woods

Lake Superior

GREAT
LAKES

MESABI RANGE

St. Lawrence River

Mt. Katahdin
5,267 ft.
(1,605 m)
ME

ND

MN

Mt. Washington
6,288 ft.
(1,917 m)

WHITE MTS.

GREEN MTS.

VT

NH

SD

WI

Lake Michigan

MI

Lake Huron

ADIRONDACK
MTS.

Lake Ontario

NY

MA

Cape
Cod

CENTRAL   PLAINS

Hudson River

CT

RI

NE

IA

Lake Erie

PA

Long Island

40°N

Platte River

Missouri

IL

IN

OH

NJ

MD

DE

Delaware Bay

70°W

KS

MO

Wabash

River

WV

Ohio

River

Allegheny Mountains

APPALACHIAN

Potomac

MOUNTAINS

VA

River

Chesapeake Bay

Arkansas

INTERIOR   PLAINS

OZARK
PLATEAU

KY

Mt. Mitchell
6,684 ft.
(2,037 m)

PIEDMONT

NC

Cape
Hatteras

TN

River

Mississippi

OK

River

OUACHITA
MOUNTAINS

AR

Tennessee

SC

COASTAL   PLAIN

Cape
Fear

Red

Stone
Mountain

Savannah River

MS

AL

GA

Chattahoochee

ATLANTIC
OCEAN

30°N

TX

LA

Alabama
River

GULF   COASTAL   PLAIN

Brazos

River

Mobile Bay

Cape
Canaveral

Colorado River

Galveston
Bay

Mississippi
Delta

FL

Lake
Okeechobee

BAHAMAS

Tampa
Bay

Gulf of Mexico

Florida Keys

Straits of Florida

80°W

N

0   250   500 Miles

0   250   500 Kilometers

90°W

Social Studies Reference Guide   R15

Geography Terms

basin bowl-shaped area of land surrounded by higher land

bay narrower part of an ocean or lake that cuts into land

canal narrow waterway dug across land mainly for ship travel

canyon steep, narrow valley with high sides

cliff steep wall of rock or earth, sometimes called a bluff

coast land at the edge of a large body of water such as an ocean

coastal plain area of flat land along an ocean or sea

delta triangle-shaped area of land at the mouth of a river

desert very dry land

fall line area along which rivers form waterfalls or rapids as the rivers drop to lower land

floodplain flat land, near a river, that is formed by dirt left by floods

foothills hilly land at the bottom of a mountain

glacier giant sheet of ice that moves very slowly across la

gulf body of water, larger than most bays, with land aroun part of it

harbor sheltered body of water where ships safely tie up land

hill rounded land higher than the land around it

inlet narrow strip of water running from a large body of water either into land or between islands

island land with water all around it

lake large body of water with land all or nearly all around

mesa flat-topped hill, with steep sides

mountain a very tall hill; highest land on Earth

mountain pass narrow channel or path through a mountain range

mountain range long row of mountains

mountain range long row of mountains

mouth place where a river empties into another body of water

ocean any of the four largest bodies of water on Earth

peak pointed top of a mountain

peninsula land with water on three sides

plain very large area of flat land

plateau high, wide area of flat land, with steep sides

prairie large area of flat land, with few or no trees, similar to a plain

river large stream of water leading to a lake, other river, or ocean

riverbank land at a river's edge

sea large body of water somewhat smaller than an ocean

sea level an ocean's surface, compared to which land can be measured either above or below

source place where a river begins

swamp very shallow water covering low land filled with trees and other plants

tributary stream or river that runs into a larger river

valley low land between mountains or hills

volcano mountain with an opening at the top, formed by violent bursts of steam and hot rock

waterfall steep falling of water from a higher to a lower place

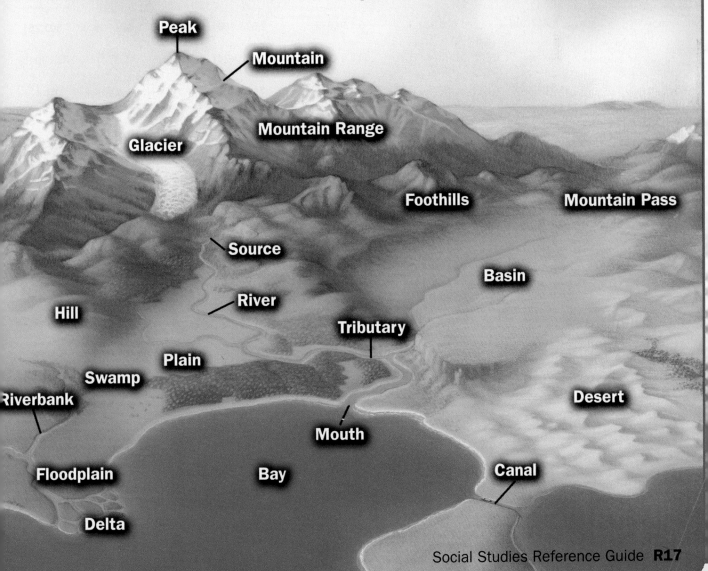

Facts About Our Fifty States

	Alabama	Alaska	Arizona	Arkansas	California	Colorado
Capital	Montgomery	Juneau	Phoenix	Little Rock	Sacramento	Denver
Date and order of statehood	1819 (22)	1959 (49)	1912 (48)	1836 (25)	1850 (31)	1876 (38)
Nickname	Heart of Dixie	The Last Frontier	Grand Canyon State	Land of Opportunity	Golden State	Centennial State
Population	4,447,100	626,932	5,130,632	2,673,400	33,871,648	4,301,261
Square miles and rank in area	50,750 (28)	570,374 (1)	113,642 (6)	52,075 (27)	155,973 (3)	103,730 (8)
Region	Southeast	West	Southwest	Southeast	West	West

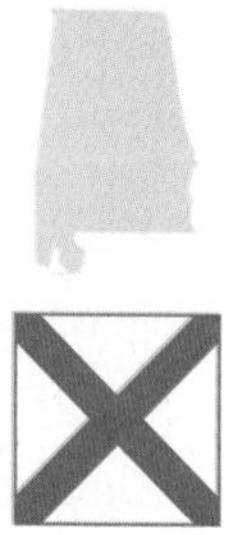

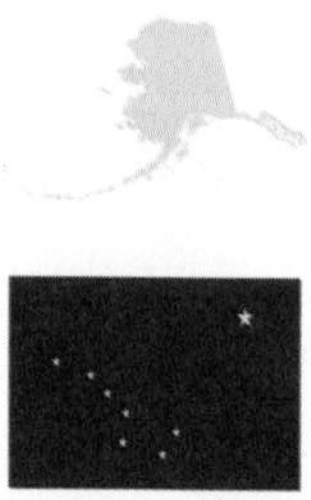

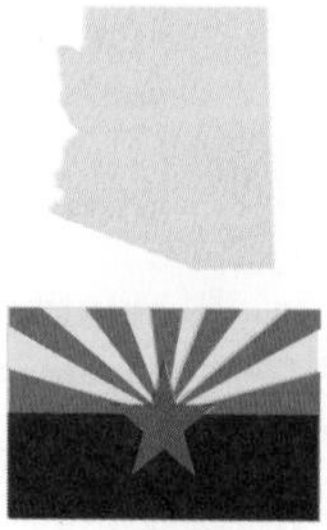

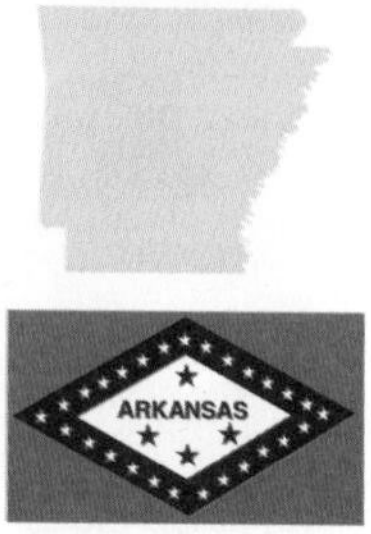

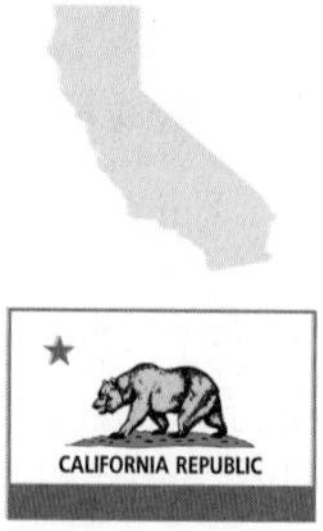

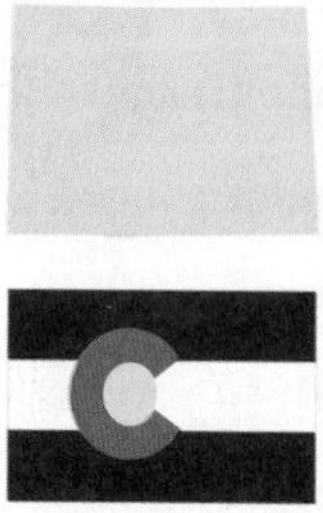

	Indiana	Iowa	Kansas	Kentucky	Louisiana	Maine
Capital	Indianapolis	Des Moines	Topeka	Frankfort	Baton Rouge	Augusta
Date and order of statehood	1816 (19)	1846 (29)	1861 (34)	1792 (15)	1812 (18)	1820 (23)
Nickname	Hoosier State	Hawkeye State	Sunflower State	Bluegrass State	Pelican State	Pine Tree State
Population	6,080,485	2,926,324	2,688,418	4,041,769	4,468,976	1,274,923
Square miles and rank in area	35,870 (38)	55,875 (23)	81,823 (13)	39,732 (36)	43,566 (33)	30,865 (39)
Region	Midwest	Midwest	Midwest	Southeast	Southeast	Northeast

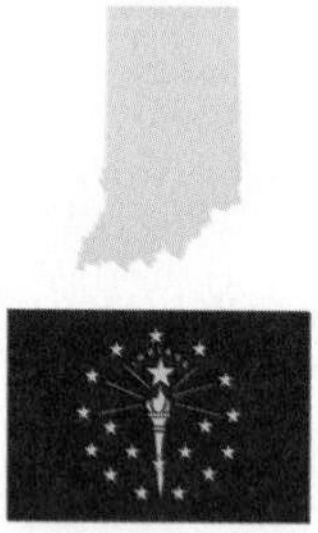

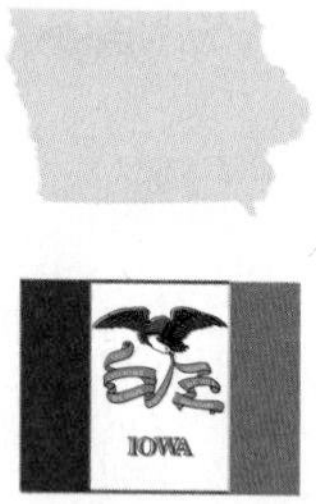

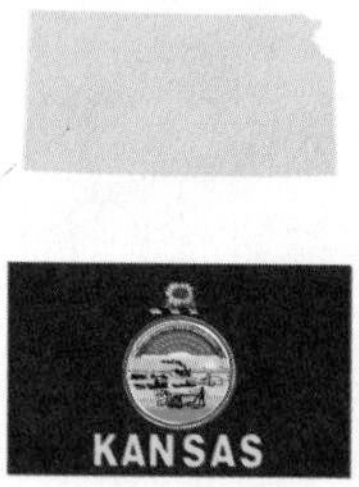

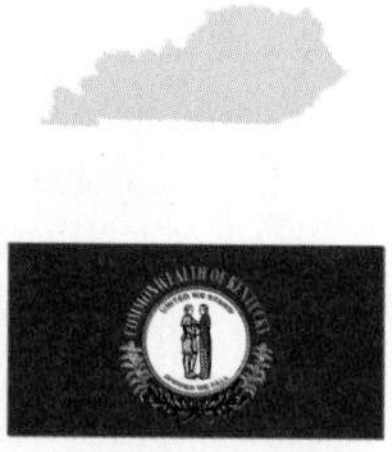

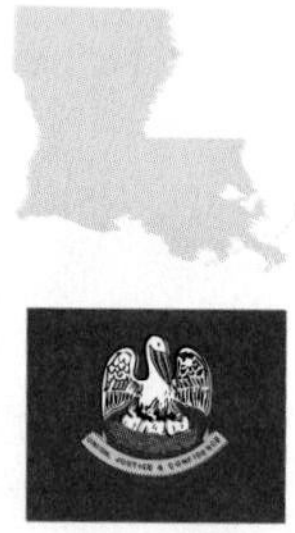

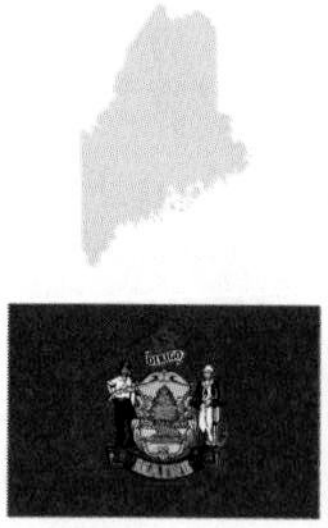

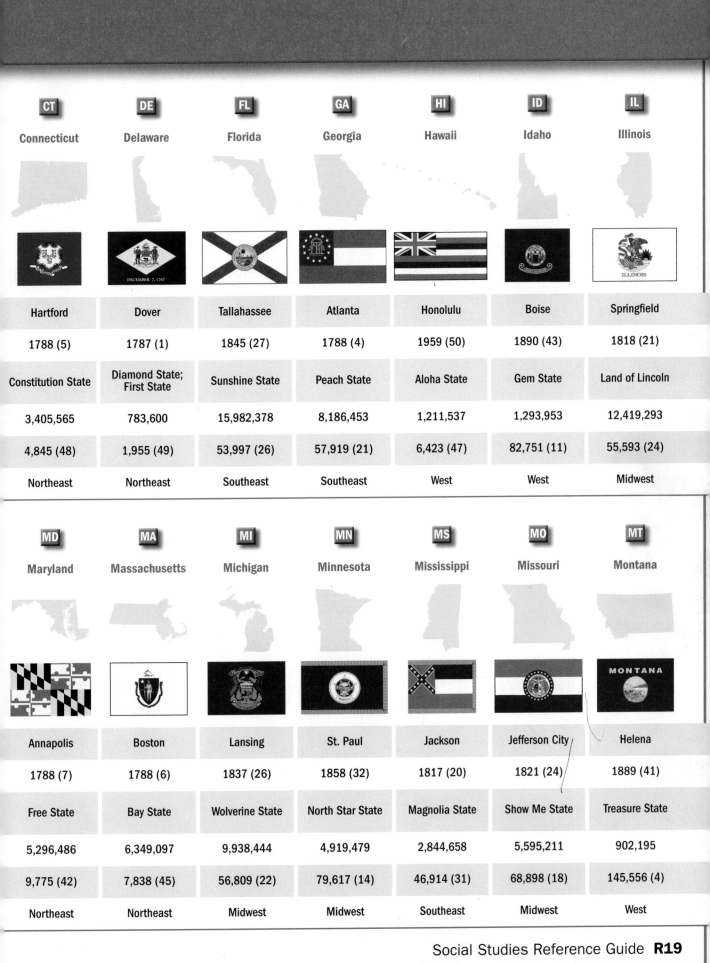

CT	DE	FL	GA	HI	ID	IL
Connecticut	**Delaware**	**Florida**	**Georgia**	**Hawaii**	**Idaho**	**Illinois**
Hartford	Dover	Tallahassee	Atlanta	Honolulu	Boise	Springfield
1788 (5)	1787 (1)	1845 (27)	1788 (4)	1959 (50)	1890 (43)	1818 (21)
Constitution State	Diamond State; First State	Sunshine State	Peach State	Aloha State	Gem State	Land of Lincoln
3,405,565	783,600	15,982,378	8,186,453	1,211,537	1,293,953	12,419,293
4,845 (48)	1,955 (49)	53,997 (26)	57,919 (21)	6,423 (47)	82,751 (11)	55,593 (24)
Northeast	Northeast	Southeast	Southeast	West	West	Midwest

MD	MA	MI	MN	MS	MO	MT
Maryland	**Massachusetts**	**Michigan**	**Minnesota**	**Mississippi**	**Missouri**	**Montana**
Annapolis	Boston	Lansing	St. Paul	Jackson	Jefferson City	Helena
1788 (7)	1788 (6)	1837 (26)	1858 (32)	1817 (20)	1821 (24)	1889 (41)
Free State	Bay State	Wolverine State	North Star State	Magnolia State	Show Me State	Treasure State
5,296,486	6,349,097	9,938,444	4,919,479	2,844,658	5,595,211	902,195
9,775 (42)	7,838 (45)	56,809 (22)	79,617 (14)	46,914 (31)	68,898 (18)	145,556 (4)
Northeast	Northeast	Midwest	Midwest	Southeast	Midwest	West

Facts About Our Fifty States

	NE Nebraska	NV Nevada	NH New Hampshire	NJ New Jersey	NM New Mexico	NY New York
Capital	Lincoln	Carson City	Concord	Trenton	Santa Fe	Albany
Date and order of statehood	1867 (37)	1864 (36)	1788 (9)	1787 (3)	1912 (47)	1788 (11)
Nickname	Cornhusker State	Silver State	Granite State	Garden State	Land of Enchantment	Empire State
Population	1,711,263	1,998,257	1,235,786	8,414,350	1,819,046	18,976,457
Square miles and rank in area	76,644 (15)	109,806 (7)	8,969 (44)	7,419 (46)	121,365 (5)	47,224 (30)
Region	Midwest	West	Northeast	Northeast	Southwest	Northeast

	SC South Carolina	SD South Dakota	TN Tennessee	TX Texas	UT Utah	VT Vermont
Capital	Columbia	Pierre	Nashville	Austin	Salt Lake City	Montpelier
Date and order of statehood	1788 (8)	1889 (40)	1796 (16)	1845 (28)	1896 (45)	1791 (14)
Nickname	Palmetto State	Mount Rushmore State	Volunteer State	Lone Star State	Beehive State	Green Mountain State
Population	4,012,012	754,844	5,689,283	20,851,820	2,233,169	608,827
Square miles and rank in area	30,111 (40)	75,898 (16)	41,220 (34)	261,914 (2)	82,168 (12)	9,249 (43)
Region	Southeast	Midwest	Southeast	Southwest	West	Northeast

North Carolina	North Dakota	Ohio	Oklahoma	Oregon	Pennsylvania	Rhode Island
NC	**ND**	**OH**	**OK**	**OR**	**PA**	**RI**
Raleigh	Bismarck	Columbus	Oklahoma City	Salem	Harrisburg	Providence
1789 (12)	1889 (39)	1803 (17)	1907 (46)	1859 (33)	1787 (2)	1790 (13)
Tar Heel State	Sioux State	Buckeye State	Sooner State	Beaver State	Keystone State	Ocean State
8,049,313	642,200	11,353,140	3,450,654	3,421,399	12,281,054	1,048,319
48,718 (29)	68,994 (17)	40,953 (35)	68,679 (19)	96,003 (10)	44,820 (32)	1,045 (50)
Southeast	Midwest	Midwest	Southwest	West	Northeast	Northeast

Virginia	Washington	West Virginia	Wisconsin	Wyoming
VA	**WA**	**WV**	**WI**	**WY**
Richmond	Olympia	Charleston	Madison	Cheyenne
1788 (10)	1889 (42)	1863 (35)	1848 (30)	1890 (44)
Old Dominion	Evergreen State	Mountain State	Badger State	Equality State
7,078,515	5,894,121	1,808,344	5,363,675	493,782
39,598 (37)	66,582 (20)	24,087 (41)	54,314 (25)	97,105 (9)
Southeast	West	Southeast	Midwest	West

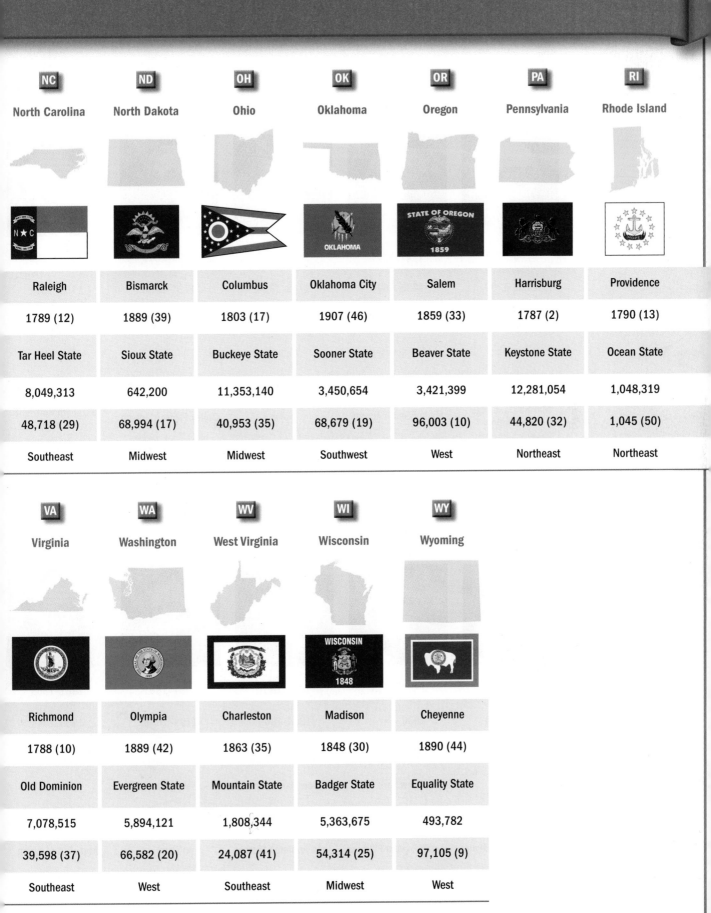

Facts About Our Presidents

	1 George Washington	**2** John Adams	**3** Thomas Jefferson	**4** James Madison	**5** James Monroe
Years in Office	1789–1797	1797–1801	1801–1809	1809–1817	1817–1825
Life Span	1732–1799	1735–1826	1743–1826	1751–1836	1758–1831
Birthplace	Westmoreland County, Virginia	Braintree County, Massachusetts	Albemarle County, Virginia	Port Conway, Virginia	Westmoreland County, Virginia
Home State	Virginia	Massachusetts	Virginia	Virginia	Virginia
Political Party	Federalist	Federalist	Democratic-Republican	Democratic-Republican	Democratic-Republican
First Lady	Martha Dandridge Washington	Abigail Smith Adams	None	Dolley Payne Madison	Elizabeth Kortright Monroe
Religion	Episcopalian	Unitarian	Deist	Episcopalian	Episcopalian

	12 Zachary Taylor	**13** Millard Fillmore	**14** Franklin Pierce	**15** James Buchanan	**16** Abraham Lincoln
Years in Office	1849–1850	1850–1853	1853–1857	1857–1861	1861–1865
Life Span	1784–1850	1800–1874	1804–1869	1791–1868	1809–1865
Birthplace	Orange County, Virginia	Cayuga County, New York	Hillsboro, New Hampshire	Mercersburg, Pennsylvania	Harden County, Kentucky
Home State	Virginia	New York	New Hampshire	Pennsylvania	Illinois
Political Party	Whig	Whig	Democratic	Democratic	Republican
First Lady	Margaret Smith Taylor	Abigail Powers Fillmore	Jane Appleton Pierce	None	Mary Todd Lincoln
Religion	Episcopalian	Unitarian	Episcopalian	Presbyterian	Attended Presbyterian services

6	7	8	9	10	11
John Quincy Adams	**Andrew Jackson**	**Martin Van Buren**	**William H. Harrison**	**John Tyler**	**James K. Polk**
1825–1829	1829–1837	1837–1841	1841	1841–1845	1845–1849
1767–1848	1767–1845	1782–1862	1773–1841	1790–1862	1795–1849
Braintree, Massachusetts	Waxhaw, South Carolina	Kinderhook, New York	Charles City County, Virginia	Charles City County, Virginia	Mecklenburg County, North Carolina
Massachusetts	Tennessee	New York	Ohio	Virginia	Tennessee
Democratic-Republican	Democratic	Democratic	Whig	Whig	Democratic
Louisa Johnson Adams	None	None	Anna Symmes Harrison	Letitia Christian Tyler; Julia Gardiner Tyler	Sarah Childress Polk
Unitarian	Presbyterian	Dutch Reformed	Episcopalian	Episcopalian	Presbyterian

17	18	19	20	21	22 24
Andrew Johnson	**Ulysses S. Grant**	**Rutherford B. Hayes**	**James A. Garfield**	**Chester A. Arthur**	**Grover Cleveland**
1865–1869	1869–1877	1877–1881	1881	1881–1885	1885–1889; 1893–1897
1808–1875	1822–1885	1822–1893	1831–1881	1829–1886	1837–1908
Raleigh, North Carolina	Point Pleasant, Ohio	Delaware, Ohio	Orange, Ohio	Fairfield, Vermont	Caldwell, New Jersey
Tennessee	Illinois	Ohio	Ohio	New York	New York
Democratic	Republican	Republican	Republican	Republican	Democratic
Eliza McCardle Johnson	Julia Dent Grant	Lucy Webb Hayes	Lucretia Rudolph Garfield	None	Frances Folsom Cleveland
No specific affiliation	Methodist	Methodist	Disciples of Christ	Episcopalian	Presbyterian

Facts About Our Presidents

	23 Benjamin Harrison	25 William McKinley	26 Theodore Roosevelt	27 William H. Taft	28 Woodrow Wilson
Years in Office	1889–1893	1897–1901	1901–1909	1909–1913	1913–1921
Life Span	1833–1901	1843–1901	1858–1919	1857–1930	1856–1924
Birthplace	North Bend, Ohio	Niles, Ohio	New York, New York	Cincinnati, Ohio	Staunton, Virginia
Home State	Indiana	Ohio	New York	Ohio	New Jersey
Political Party	Republican	Republican	Republican	Republican	Democratic
First Lady	Caroline Scott Harrison	Ida Saxton McKinley	Edith Carow Roosevelt	Helen Herron Taft	Ellen Axson Wilson; Edith Galt Wilson
Religion	Presbyterian	Methodist	Dutch Reformed	Unitarian	Presbyterian

	35 John F. Kennedy	36 Lyndon B. Johnson	37 Richard M. Nixon	38 Gerald R. Ford	39 James E. Carter
Years in Office	1961–1963	1963–1969	1969–1974	1974–1977	1977–1981
Life Span	1917–1963	1908–1973	1913–1994	1913–	1924–
Birthplace	Brookline, Massachusetts	Stonewall, Texas	Yorba Linda, California	Omaha, Nebraska	Plains, Georgia
Home State	Massachusetts	Texas	California	Michigan	Georgia
Political Party	Democratic	Democratic	Republican	Republican	Democratic
First Lady	Jacqueline Bouvier Kennedy	Claudia "Lady Bird" Taylor Johnson	Thelma "Pat" Ryan Nixon	Elizabeth (Betty) Warren Ford	Rosalynn Smith Carter
Religion	Roman Catholic	Disciples of Christ	Quaker	Episcopalian	Southern Baptist

29	30	31	32	33	34
Warren G. Harding	**Calvin Coolidge**	**Herbert Hoover**	**Franklin D. Roosevelt**	**Harry S. Truman**	**Dwight D. Eisenhower**
1921–1923	1923–1929	1929–1933	1933–1945	1945–1953	1953–1961
1865–1923	1872–1933	1874–1964	1882–1945	1884–1972	1890–1969
Morrow County, Ohio	Plymouth, Vermont	West Branch, Iowa	Hyde Park, New York	Lamar, Missouri	Denison, Texas
Ohio	Massachusetts	California	New York	Missouri	Kansas
Republican	Republican	Republican	Democratic	Democratic	Republican
Florence DeWolfe Harding	Grace Goodhue Coolidge	Lou Henry Hoover	Anna Eleanor Roosevelt	Bess Wallace Truman	Marie "Mamie" Doud Eisenhower
Baptist	Congregational	Quaker	Episcopalian	Baptist	Presbyterian

40	41	42	43
Ronald Reagan	**George H. W. Bush**	**William J. Clinton**	**George W. Bush**
1981–1989	1989–1993	1993–2001	2001–
1911–	1924–	1946–	1946–
Tampico, Illinois	Milton, Massachusetts	Hope, Arkansas	New Haven, Connecticut
California	Texas	Arkansas	Texas
Republican	Republican	Democratic	Republican
Anne "Nancy" Davis Reagan	Barbara Pierce Bush	Hillary Rodham Clinton	Laura Welch Bush
Disciples of Christ	Episcopalian	Baptist	Methodist

United States Documents
The Declaration of Independence

Sometimes in history it becomes necessary for a group of people to break political ties with the country that rules it. When this happens, it is proper to explain the reasons for the need to separate.

We believe that all men are created equal and given by their Creator certain rights that cannot be taken away. People have the right to live, be free, and seek happiness.

Governments are established to protect these rights. The government gets its power from the support of the people it governs. If any form of government tries to take away the basic rights, it is the right of the people to change or end the government and to establish a new government that seems most likely to result in their safety and happiness.

Wise judgment will require that long-existing governments should not be changed for unimportant or temporary reasons. History has shown that people are more willing to suffer under a bad government than to get rid of the government they are used to. But when there are so many abuses and misuses of power by the government, it is the right and duty of the people to throw off such government and form a new government to protect their basic rights.

The colonies have suffered patiently, and now it is necessary for them to change the government. The king of Great Britain has repeatedly abused his power over these states. To prove this, the following facts are given.

In Congress, July 4, 1776

When, in the course of human events, it becomes necessary for one people to dissolve the political bands which have connected them with another, and to assume, among the powers of the earth, the separate and equal station to which the laws of nature and nature's God entitle them, a decent respect to the opinions of mankind requires that they should declare the causes which impel them to the separation.

We hold these truths to be self-evident; that all men are created equal, that they are endowed by their Creator with certain unalienable rights, that among these are life, liberty, and the pursuit of happiness.

That to secure these rights, governments are instituted among men, deriving their just powers from the consent of the governed; that whenever any form of government becomes destructive of these ends, it is the right of the people to alter or to abolish it, and to institute new government, laying its foundation on such principles, and organizing its powers in such form, as to them shall seem most likely to effect their safety and happiness.

Prudence, indeed, will dictate that governments long established should not be changed for light and transient causes; and accordingly all experience hath shown that mankind are more disposed to suffer, while evils are sufferable, than to right themselves by abolishing the forms to which they are accustomed. But when a long train of abuses and usurpations, pursuing invariably the same object, evinces a design to reduce them under absolute despotism, it is their right, it is their duty, to throw off such government, and to provide new guards for their future security.

Such has been the patient sufferance of these colonies; and such is now the necessity which constrains them to alter their former systems of government. The history of the present king of Great Britain is a history of repeated injuries and usurpations, all having in direct object the establishment of an absolute tyranny over these states. To prove this, let facts be submitted to a candid world.

He has refused his assent to laws the most wholesome and necessary for the public good. He has forbidden his governors to pass laws of immediate and pressing importance, unless suspended in their operation till his assent should be obtained; and when so suspended, he has utterly neglected to attend to them.

He has refused to pass other laws for the accommodation of large districts of people, unless those people would relinquish the right of representation in the legislature, a right inestimable to them, and formidable to tyrants only.

He has called together legislative bodies at places unusual, uncomfortable, and distant from the depository of their public records, for the sole purpose of fatiguing them into compliance with his measures.

He has dissolved representative houses repeatedly, for opposing, with manly firmness, his invasions on the rights of the people.

He has refused, for a long time after such dissolutions, to cause others to be elected; whereby the legislative powers, incapable of annihilation, have returned to the people at large for their exercise; the state remaining, in the meantime, exposed to all the dangers of invasion from without and convulsions within.

He has endeavored to prevent the population of these states; for that purpose obstructing the laws for the naturalization of foreigners, refusing to pass others to encourage their migrations hither, and raising the conditions of new appropriations of lands.

He has obstructed the administration of justice, by refusing his assent to laws for establishing judiciary powers.

He has made judges dependent on his will alone for the tenure of their offices, and the amount and payment of their salaries.

He has erected a multitude of new offices, and sent hither swarms of officers to harass our people and eat out their substance.

He has kept among us, in times of peace, standing armies, without the consent of our legislatures.

He has affected to render the military independent of, and superior to, the civil power.

He has combined with others to subject us to a jurisdiction foreign to our constitution and unacknowledged by our laws, giving his assent to their acts of pretended legislation:

The king has not given his approval to needed laws. He has not allowed his governors to pass laws needed immediately. The king has made the governors delay laws until they can get his permission and then he has ignored the laws.

He has refused to pass other laws for the help of large districts of people, unless those people would give up the right of representation in the legislature, a right priceless to them, and threatening only to tyrants.

He has called together legislative bodies at unusual and uncomfortable places, distant from where they store their public records, and only for the purpose of tiring them into obeying his measures.

He has repeatedly done away with legislative groups that firmly opposed him for taking away the rights of the people.

After he has dissolved these representative meetings, he has refused to allow new elections. Because of this lack of legislative power, the people are exposed to the dangers of invasion from without and violence within.

He has tried to prevent people from immigrating to these states by blocking the process for foreigners to become citizens, refusing to pass laws to encourage people to travel to America, and making it harder to move to and own new lands.

He has interfered with the administration of justice, by refusing to approve laws for establishing courts.

He has made judges do what he wants by controlling how long they serve and how much they are paid.

He has created many new government offices, and sent many officials to torment our people and live off of our hard work.

In times of peace, he has kept soldiers among us, without the consent of our legislatures.

He has tried to make the military separate from, and superior to, the civil government.

He and others have made us live under laws that are different from our laws. He has given his approval to these unfair laws that parliament has adopted:

For forcing us to feed and house many British soldiers;

For using pretend trials to protect British soldiers from punishment for murdering people in America;

For cutting off our trade with the world;

For taxing us without our consent;

For taking away, in many cases, the benefits of trial by jury;

For taking us to Great Britain to be tried for made-up offenses;

For doing away with the free system of English laws in a neighboring province, and establishing a harsh government there, and enlarging its boundaries, as a way to introduce the same absolute rule into these colonies;

For taking away our governing documents, doing away with our most valuable laws, and changing our governments completely;

For setting aside our own legislatures, and declaring that Great Britain has power to make laws for us in all cases whatsoever.

He has deserted government here, by not protecting us and waging war against us.

He has robbed our ships on the seas, destroyed our coasts, burned our towns, and destroyed the lives of our people.

He is at this time sending large armies of foreign hired soldiers to complete the works of death, destruction, and injustice. These deeds are among the cruelest ever seen in history, and are totally unworthy of the head of a civilized nation.

He has forced our fellow citizens, who were captured on the high seas, to fight against America, to kill their friends and family, or to be killed themselves.

He has stirred up civil disorder among us, and has tried to cause the merciless killing of the people living on the frontiers by the Indians, whose rule of warfare includes the deliberate killing of people regardless of age, sex, or conditions.

In every stage of these mistreatments we have asked for a solution in the most humble terms; our repeated requests have been answered only by repeated injury. A leader who is so unfair and acts like a dictator is unfit to be the ruler of a free people.

For quartering large bodies of armed troops among us;

For protecting them, by a mock trial, from punishment for any murders which they should commit on the inhabitants of these states;

For cutting off our trade with all parts of the world;

For imposing taxes on us without our consent;

For depriving us, in many cases, of the benefits of trial by jury;

For transporting us beyond seas, to be tried for pretended offenses;

For abolishing the free system of English laws in a neighboring province, establishing therein an arbitrary government, and enlarging its boundaries, so as to render it at once an example and fit instrument for introducing the same absolute rule into these colonies;

For taking away our charters, abolishing our most valuable laws, and altering fundamentally the forms of our governments;

For suspending our own legislatures, and declaring themselves invested with power to legislate for us in all cases whatsoever.

He has abdicated government here, by declaring us out of his protection and waging war against us.

He has plundered our seas, ravaged our coasts, burned our towns, and destroyed the lives of our people.

He is at this time transporting large armies of foreign mercenaries to complete the works of death, desolation, and tyranny already begun with circumstances of cruelty and perfidy scarcely paralleled in the most barbarous ages, and totally unworthy the head of a civilized nation.

He has constrained our fellow citizens, taken captive on the high seas, to bear arms against their country, to become the executioners of their friends and brethren, or to fall themselves by their hands.

He has excited domestic insurrection among us, and has endeavored to bring on the inhabitants of our frontiers, the merciless Indian savages, whose known rule of warfare is an undistinguished destruction of all ages, sexes, and conditions.

In every stage of these oppressions we have petitioned for redress in the most humble terms; our repeated petitions have been answered only by repeated injury. A prince, whose character is thus marked by every act which may define a tyrant, is unfit to be the ruler of a free people.

Nor have we been wanting in attentions to our British brethren. We have warned them, from time to time, of attempts by their legislature to extend an unwarrantable jurisdiction over us. We have reminded them of the circumstances of our emigration and settlement here. We have appealed to their native justice and magnanimity; and we have conjured them, by the ties of our common kindred, to disavow these usurpations, which would inevitably interrupt our connections and correspondence. They, too, have been deaf to the voice of justice and consanguinity. We must, therefore, acquiesce in the necessity which denounces our separation, and hold them, as we hold the rest of mankind, enemies in war; in peace, friends.

We, therefore, the representatives of the United States of America, in General Congress assembled, appealing to the Supreme Judge of the world for the rectitude of our intentions, do, in the name and by the authority of the good people of these colonies, solemnly publish and declare that these United Colonies are, and of right ought to be, free and independent states; that they are absolved from all allegiance to the British crown, and that all political connection between them and the state of Great Britain is, and ought to be, totally dissolved; and that, as free and independent states, they have full power to levy war, conclude peace, contract alliances, establish commerce, and do all other acts and things which independent states may of right do. And, for the support of this declaration, with a firm reliance on the protection of Divine Providence, we mutually pledge to each other our lives, our fortunes, and our sacred honor.

We have also asked for help from the British people. We have warned them, from time to time, of attempts by their government to extend illegal power over us. We have reminded them of why we came to America. We have appealed to their sense of justice and generosity; and we have begged them, because of all we have in common, to give up these abuses of power. They, like the king, have not listened to the voice of justice and brotherhood. We must, therefore, declare our separation. In war the British are our enemies. In peace, they are our friends.

We, therefore, as the representatives of the people of the United States of America, in this General Congress assembled, appealing to God for the honesty of our purpose, do solemnly publish and declare that these United Colonies are, and rightly should be, free and independent states. The people of the United States are no longer subjects of the British crown. All political connections between the colonies and Great Britain are totally ended. These free and independent states have full power to declare war, make peace, make treaties with other countries, establish trade, and do all other acts and things which independent states have the right to do. To support this declaration, with a firm trust on the protection of Divine Providence, we pledge to each other our lives, our fortunes, and our sacred honor.

Button Gwinnett (GA)	Benjamin Harrison (VA)	Lewis Morris (NY)
Lyman Hall (GA)	Thomas Nelson, Jr. (VA)	Richard Stockton (NJ)
George Walton (GA)	Francis Lightfoot Lee (VA)	John Witherspoon (NJ)
William Hooper (NC)	Carter Braxton (VA)	Francis Hopkinson (NJ)
Joseph Hewes (NC)	Robert Morris (PA)	John Hart (NJ)
John Penn (NC)	Benjamin Rush (PA)	Abraham Clark (NJ)
Edward Rutledge (SC)	Benjamin Franklin (PA)	Josiah Bartlett (NH)
Thomas Heyward, Jr. (SC)	John Morton (PA)	William Whipple (NH)
Thomas Lynch, Jr. (SC)	George Clymer (PA)	Samuel Adams (MA)
Arthur Middleton (SC)	James Smith (PA)	John Adams (MA)
John Hancock (MA)	George Taylor (PA)	Robert Treat Paine (MA)
Samuel Chase (MD)	James Wilson (PA)	Elbridge Gerry (MA)
William Paca (MD)	George Ross (PA)	Stephen Hopkins (RI)
Thomas Stone (MD)	Caesar Rodney (DE)	William Ellery (RI)
Charles Carroll of Carrollton (MD)	George Read (DE)	Roger Sherman (CT)
George Wythe (VA)	Thomas McKean (DE)	Samuel Huntington (CT)
Richard Henry Lee (VA)	William Floyd (NY)	William Williams (CT)
Thomas Jefferson (VA)	Philip Livingston (NY)	Oliver Wolcott (CT)
	Francis Lewis (NY)	Matthew Thornton (NH)

"Among the natural rights of the Colonists are these: First, a right to life; Secondly, to liberty; Thirdly, to property; together with the right to support and defend them in the best manner they can."
Samuel Adams, The Report of the Committee of Correspondence to the Boston Town Meeting

"All, too, will bear in mind this sacred principle, that though the will of the majority is in all cases to prevail, that will to be rightful must be reasonable; that the minority possess their equal rights, which equal law must protect, and to violate would be oppression."
Thomas Jefferson, First Inaugural Address

We the people of the United States, in order to form a more perfect union, establish justice, insure peace in our nation, provide for our defense, promote the general welfare, and secure the blessings of liberty to ourselves and our descendants, do authorize and establish this Constitution for the United States of America.

ARTICLE 1
Legislative Branch

SECTION 1. Congress
Only the Congress of the United States has the power to make national laws. Congress is made up of a Senate and House of Representatives.

SECTION 2. House of Representatives
Members of the House of Representatives will be chosen every two years. People who are eligible to vote for state legislators are also eligible to vote for members of the House of Representatives.

To be a member of the House of Representatives, a person must be at least twenty-five years of age, and must have been a citizen of the United States for at least seven years, and live in the state the person is chosen to represent.

The number of representatives a state has is determined by the state's population. A census, or count, of the population must be taken every ten years. Each state shall have at least one representative.

W e the people of the United States, in order to form a more perfect union, establish justice, insure domestic tranquility, provide for the common defense, promote the general welfare, and secure the blessings of liberty to ourselves and our posterity, do ordain and establish this Constitution for the United States of America.

ARTICLE 1
Legislative Branch

SECTION 1. Congress
All legislative powers herein granted shall be vested in a Congress of the United States, which shall consist of a Senate and House of Representatives.

SECTION 2. House of Representatives
The House of Representatives shall be composed of members chosen every second year by the people of the several states, and the electors in each state shall have the qualifications requisite for electors of the most numerous branch of the State legislature.

No person shall be a representative who shall not have attained to the age of twenty-five years, and been seven years a citizen of the United States, and who shall not, when elected, be an inhabitant of that state in which he shall be chosen.

Representatives and direct taxes shall be apportioned among the several states which may be included within this Union, according to their respective numbers, which shall be determined by adding to the whole numbers of free persons, including those bound to service for a term of years, and excluding Indians not taxed, three fifths of all other persons.* The actual enumeration shall be made within three years after the first meeting of the Congress of the United States, and within every subsequent term of ten years, in such manner as they shall by law direct. The number of representatives shall not exceed one for every thirty thousand, but each State shall have at least one representative; and until such enumeration shall be made, the State of New Hampshire shall be entitled to choose three, Massachusetts eight, Rhode Island and Providence Plantations one, Connecticut five, New York six, New Jersey four, Pennsylvania eight, Delaware one, Maryland six, Virginia ten, North Carolina five, South Carolina five, and Georgia three.* (*Changed by the Fourteenth Amendment)

When vacancies happen in the representation from any state, the executive authority thereof shall issue writs of election to fill such vacancies.

The House of Representatives shall choose their speaker and other officers, and shall have the sole power of impeachment.

SECTION 3. Senate

The Senate of the United States shall be composed of two senators from each state, ~~chosen by the legislature thereof~~,* for six years; and each senator shall have one vote. (*Changed by the Seventeenth Amendment*)

Immediately after they shall be assembled in consequence of the first election, they shall be divided as equally as may be into three classes. The seats of the senators of the first class shall be vacated at the expiration of the second year, of the second class at the expiration of the fourth year, and of the third class at the expiration of the sixth year, so that one third may be chosen every second year; ~~and if vacancies happen by resignation, or otherwise, during the recess of the legislature of any State, the executive thereof may make temporary appointments until the next meeting of the legislature, which shall then fill such vacancies.~~*
(*Changed by the Seventeenth Amendment*)

No person shall be a senator who shall not have attained to the age of thirty years, and been nine years a citizen of the United States, and who shall not, when elected, be an inhabitant of that State for which he shall be chosen.

The Vice President of the United States shall be president of the Senate, but shall have no vote, unless they be equally divided.

The Senate shall choose their other officers, and also a president pro tempore, in the absence of the Vice President, or when he shall exercise the office of President of the United States.

The Senate shall have the sole power to try all impeachments. When sitting for that purpose, they shall be an oath or affirmation. When the President of the United States is tried, the Chief Justice shall preside: and no person shall be convicted without the concurrence of two thirds of the members present.

Judgment in cases of impeachment shall not extend further than to removal from office, and disqualification to hold any office of honor, trust or profit under the United States: but the party convicted shall nevertheless be liable and subject to indictment, trial, judgment and punishment, according to law.

When vacancies happen in the representation from any state, the governor of the state will call a special election to fill the empty seat.

The House of Representatives shall choose their speaker and other officers, and only the House of Representatives may impeach, or accuse, government officials of crimes in office.

SECTION 3. Senate

The Senate of the United States shall be made up of two senators from each state. Each senator serves for six years; and each senator shall have one vote.

(Until the Seventeenth Amendment, the senators were chosen by the legislature of the state they represented.)

Only one-third of the senators are up for election at one time.

(The remaining section was changed by the Seventeenth Amendment).

A senator must be at least thirty years old, a citizen of the United States for at least nine years, and live in the state the senator is chosen to represent.

The Vice President of the United States is also the president of the Senate, but has no vote, unless there is a tie.

The Senate chooses its own officers. The Senate also chooses a senator to be the president pro tempore who serves as the temporary president of the Senate in the absence of the Vice President, or when the Vice President acts as President of the United States.

Only the Senate has the power to try all impeachments. When meeting on an impeachment, the senators shall take an oath or affirmation. When the President of the United States is tried on impeachment charges, the Chief Justice shall be in charge: and no person shall be found guilty without the agreement of two-thirds of the members present.

Impeached officials who are convicted can be removed from office, and disqualified from holding any other government office. Other courts in the country may still try, judge, and punish the impeached official.

- establish punishments for counterfeiting, or making fake money, stocks, and bonds;
- establish post offices and roads for mail delivery;
- promote the progress of science and useful arts by protecting, for limited times, the writings and discoveries of authors and inventors by issuing copyrights and patents;
- create courts lower than the Supreme Court;
- define and punish crimes committed on the high seas, and crimes that break international laws;
- declare war and make rules about taking enemy property on land or sea;
- set up and supply armies. Congress cannot provide funding for the armies for more than two years at a time;
- set up and supply a navy;
- make rules for the armed forces;
- provide for calling the militia to action to carry out the laws of the country, put down revolts and riots and fight off invasions;
- provide for organizing, arming, and disciplining the militia, and for governing those employed in the armed service of the United States. The states have the right to appoint the officers, and the authority of training the militia according to the rules made by Congress;
- govern the nation's capital [Washington, D.C.] and military bases in the United States;
- make all laws needed to carry out the powers mentioned earlier in the Constitution, and all other powers placed by this Constitution in the government of the United States, or in any department or officer of the government.

SECTION 9. Powers Denied to Congress

Congress does not have the power to prevent enslaved people from being brought into the country until 1808, but a tax may be placed on each imported person.

(Congress passed a law in 1808 forbidding the slave trade.)

Congress may not do away with laws that protect an individual from being jailed unless the person goes to trial or unless specifie criminal charges are filed, unless the public safety requires it during a rebellion or invasion.

No law shall be passed that penalizes a person or group without the benefit of a trial or makes an action illegal after the action was taken.

To promote the progress of science and useful arts by securing for limited times to authors and inventors the exclusive right to their respective writings and discoveries;

To constitute tribunals inferior to the Supreme Court;

To define and punish piracies and felonies committed on the high seas, and offenses against the law of nations;

To declare war~~, grant letters of marque and reprisal, and make rules concerning captures on land and water~~;* (**These powers are no longer exercised by Congress.*)

To raise and support armies, but no appropriation of money to that use shall be for a longer term than two years;

To provide and maintain a navy;

To make rules for the government and regulation of the land and naval forces;

To provide for calling forth the militia to execute the laws of the Union, suppress insurrections and repel invasions;

To provide for organizing, arming, and disciplining the militia, and for governing such part of them as may be employed in the service of the United States, reserving to the States respectively the appointment of the officers, and the authority of training the militia according to the discipline prescribed by Congress;

To exercise exclusive legislation in all cases whatsoever, over such district (not exceeding ten miles square) as may, by cession of particular States and the acceptance of Congress, become the seat of the government of the United States, and to exercise like authority over all places purchased by the consent of the legislature of the State in which the same shall be, for the erection of forts, magazines, arsenals, dockyards, and other needful buildings; and

To make all laws which shall be necessary and proper for carrying into execution the foregoing powers, and all other powers vested by this Constitution in the government of the United States, or in any department or officer thereof.

SECTION 9. Powers Denied to Congress

~~The migration or importation of such persons as any of the States now existing shall think proper to admit shall not be prohibited by the Congress prior to the year one thousand eight hundred and eight, but a tax or duty may be imposed on such importation, not exceeding ten dollars for each person.~~

The privilege of the writ of habeas corpus shall not be suspended, unless when in cases of rebellion or invasion the public safety may require it.

No bill of attainder or ex post facto law shall be passed.

No capitation, or other direct,* tax shall be laid~~, unless in proportion to the census or enumeration herein before directed to be taken~~.* (*Changed by the Sixteenth Amendment)

No tax or duty shall be laid on articles exported from any State.

No preference shall be given by any regulation of commerce or revenue to the ports of one State over those of another; nor shall vessels bound to, or from, one State be obliged to enter, clear, or pay duties in another.

No money shall be drawn from the Treasury, but in consequence of appropriations made by law; and a regular statement and account of the receipts and expenditures of all public money shall be published from time to time.

No title of nobility shall be granted by the United States; and no person holding any office of profit or trust under them, shall, without the consent of the Congress, accept of any present, emolument, office, or title of any kind whatever, from any king, prince, or foreign State.

SECTION 10. Powers Denied to the States

No State shall enter into any treaty, alliance, or confederation; grant letters of marque and reprisal; coin money; emit bills of credit; make anything but gold and silver coin a tender in payment of debts; pass any bill of attainder, ex post facto law, or law impairing the obligation of contracts, or grant any title of nobility.

No State shall, without the consent of the Congress, lay any imposts, or duties on imports or exports, except what may be absolutely necessary for executing its inspection laws; and the net produce of all duties and imposts, laid by any State on imports or exports, shall be for the use of the Treasury of the United States; and all such laws shall be subject to the revision and control of the Congress.

No State shall, without the consent of Congress, lay any duty of tonnage, keep troops, or ships of war in time of peace, enter into any agreement or compact with another State, or with a foreign power, or engage in war, unless actually invaded, or in such imminent danger as will not admit of delay.

ARTICLE 2

The Executive Branch

SECTION 1. The President and Vice President

The executive power shall be vested in a President of the United States of America. He shall hold his office during the term of four years, and, together with the Vice President, chosen for the same term, be elected as follows:

No person in the United States may be taxed unless everyone is taxed the same. *(The Sixteenth Amendment allowed an income tax.)*

No tax shall be put on articles exported from any state.

No laws shall be passed that give special treatment to one state over those of another in trade. Ships shall not be required to pay a tax to enter another state.

No money shall be taken from the Treasury, without the Congress passing a law. A public record must be kept of money raised and money spent.

The United States shall not give any titles of nobility, such as king or queen. No person holding any government office shall accept any present, payment, office, or title of any kind from another country, without the consent of the Congress.

SECTION 10. Powers Denied to the States

No state can make treaties or alliances with other nations or issue official documents permitting private citizens to capture merchant ships or engage warships of another nation. No state can issue its own money or make anything, other than gold or silver, legal as currency. No state can pass laws that apply to actions done before the law was passed. No state may allow a person to be punished without a fair trial. No state can pass laws that excuse anyone from a contract. No state can give anyone a title of nobility.

Without approval from Congress, no state can collect taxes on goods coming in or going out of the state, except those small fees needed for customs inspections. Any taxes from trade become the property of the United States government.

Without approval from Congress, states are forbidden to tax ships or keep troops or warships in peacetime, unless endangered by actual invasion. States may not enter into an agreement with another state or foreign nation.

ARTICLE 2

The Executive Branch

SECTION 1. The President and Vice President

The President has the power to carry out the laws of Congress, and the President and Vice President serve a four-year term.

The legislature of each state determines the process for electing its representatives in the Electoral College, which officially elects the President and the Vice President. Each state's total number of electors is determined by the state's total number of members in Congress. No person holding any office in the federal government can become an elector.

(Until this was changed by the Twelfth Amendment, the person who received the most electoral votes became the President and the person with the next highest number became the Vice President. The Twelfth Amendment overruled this clause and changed the way the election process worked.)

Congress determines the date and time when each state's electors are to cast their votes for President and Vice President.

To become President a person must be born a citizen of the United States, be at least thirty-five years old, and have lived in the United States for at least fourteen years.

If a President dies, is disabled, or is removed from office, the Vice President becomes President.

(The Twenty-Fifth Amendment changed the method for filling these offices if they become vacant.)

Each State shall appoint, in such manner as the legislature thereof may direct, a number of electors, equal to the whole number of senators and representatives to which the State may be entitled in the Congress, but no senator or representative, or person holding an office of trust or profit under the United States, shall be appointed an elector.

~~The electors shall meet in their respective States, and vote by ballot for two persons, of whom one at least shall not be an inhabitant of the same State with themselves. And they shall make a list of all the persons voted for, and of the number of votes for each; which list they shall sign and certify, and transmit sealed to the seat of the government of the United States, directed to the president of the Senate. The president of the Senate shall, in the presence of the Senate and House of Representatives, open all the certificates, and the votes shall then be counted. The person having the greatest number of votes shall be the President, if such number be a majority of the whole number of electors appointed; and if there be more than one who have such majority, and have an equal number of votes, then the House of Representatives shall immediately choose by ballot one of them for President; and if no person have a majority, then from the five highest on the list the said House shall in like manner choose the President. But in choosing the President, the votes shall be taken by States, the representation from each State having one vote; a quorum for this purpose shall consist of a member or members from two thirds of the States, and a majority of all the States shall be necessary to a choice. In every case, after the choice of the President, the person having the greatest number of votes of the electors shall be the Vice President. But if there should remain two or more who have equal votes, the Senate shall choose from them by ballot the Vice President.~~* (*Changed by the Twelfth Amendment*)

The Congress may determine the time of choosing the electors, and the day on which they shall give their votes; which day shall be the same throughout the United States.

No person except a natural-born citizen, or a citizen of the United States, at the time of the adoption of this Constitution, shall be eligible to the office of President; neither shall any person be eligible to that office who shall not have attained to the age of thirty-five years, and been fourteen years a resident within the United States.

In case of the removal of the President from office, or of his death, resignation, or inability to discharge the powers and duties of the said office, the same shall devolve on the Vice President~~, and the Congress may by law provide for the case of removal, death, resignation, or inability, both of the President and Vice President, declaring what officer shall then act as President, and such officer shall act accordingly, until the disability be removed, or a President shall be elected.~~* (*Changed by the Twenty-Fifth Amendment*)

The President shall, at stated times, receive for his services a compensation, which shall neither be increased nor diminished during the period for which he shall have been elected, and he shall not receive within that period any other emolument from the United States, or any of them.

Before he enter on the execution of his office, he shall take the following oath or affirmation: — "I do solemnly swear (or affirm) that I will faithfully execute the office of President of the United States, and will to the best of my ability, preserve, protect and defend the Constitution of the United States."

SECTION 2. Powers of the President

The President shall be Commander in Chief of the Army and Navy of the United States, and of the militia of the several States, when called into the actual service of the United States; he may require the opinion, in writing, of the principal officer in each of the executive departments, upon any subject relating to the duties of their respective offices, and he shall have power to grant reprieves and pardons for offenses against the United States, except in cases of impeachment.

He shall have power, by and with the advice and consent of the Senate, to make treaties, provided two-thirds of the senators present concur; and he shall nominate, and by and with the advice and consent of the Senate, shall appoint ambassadors, other public ministers and consuls, judges of the Supreme Court, and all other officers of the United States, whose appointments are not herein otherwise provided for, and which shall be established by law; but the Congress may by law vest the appointment of such inferior officers, as they think proper, in the President alone, in the courts of law, or in the heads of departments.

The President shall have power to fill up all vacancies that may happen during the recess of the Senate, by granting commissions which shall expire at the end of their next session.

SECTION 3. Duties of the President

He shall from time to time give to the Congress information of the state of the Union, and recommend to their consideration such measures as he shall judge necessary and expedient; he may, on extraordinary occasions, convene both houses, or either of them, and in case of disagreement between them, with respect to the time of adjournment, he may adjourn them to such time as he shall think proper; he shall receive ambassadors and other public ministers; he shall take care that the laws be faithfully executed, and shall commission all the officers of the United States.

The President will receive a salary, but it cannot be increased or decreased during the term(s) of office. The President cannot have another occupation or receive outside compensation while in office.

Before assuming the duties of the office, the President must take the following oath or affirmation: "I do solemnly swear (or affirm) that I will faithfully execute the office of President of the United States, and will to the best of my ability, preserve, protect and defend the Constitution of the United States."

SECTION 2. Powers of the President

The President is the leader of the armed forces of the United States and of the state militias during times of war. The President may require the principal officer in each of the executive departments to write a report about any subject relating to their duties, and can grant delays of punishments or pardons for criminals, except in cases of impeachment.

With the advice and consent of two-thirds of the members of the Senate, the President can make treaties with foreign nations and can appoint ambassadors and other officials as necessary to handle our diplomatic affairs with other countries. The President can appoint federal judges and other key officers in the executive branch of government, with the consent of two-thirds of the Senate. Congress may give power to the President to appoint minor government officials and heads of departments.

When the Senate is not in session, the President can make temporary appointments to offices which require Senate approval. These appointments expire when the next session has ended.

SECTION 3. Duties of the President

The President must make a report to Congress on a regular basis, providing information concerning important national developments and goals. Law-making requests for Congress should be given as well. The President can call for special sessions of one or both houses of Congress for special reasons. If the houses of Congress cannot agree on a common date for adjournment, the President has the power to make that decision. The President is to officially receive foreign ambassadors and other public ministers. The President is to fully and faithfully carry out the laws of Congress and sign the documents required to give officers the rights to perform their duties.

SECTION 4. Removal from Office

The President, Vice President, and all civil officers can be removed from office if convicted on impeachment charges for treason, bribery, or other high crimes and misdemeanors.

ARTICLE 3
The Judicial Branch

SECTION 1. Federal Courts

The Supreme Court is the highest court in the land. Congress has the power to create all other federal courts. Federal judges may hold office for life as long as they act properly, and they shall receive a salary that cannot be lowered during the judge's time of service.

SECTION 2. Powers of Federal Courts

The power of the federal courts covers two types of cases: (1) those involving the interpretation of the Constitution, federal laws, treaties, and laws relating to ships on the high seas; and (2) those involving the United States government itself, foreign diplomats, two or more state governments, citizens of different states, and a state or its citizens versus foreign countries or their citizens.

Cases involving foreign diplomats and any state in the United States will be tried by the Supreme Court. Other cases tried by the Supreme Court are those appealed or brought forward from lower federal courts or from state courts. Congress can decide to make exceptions to these regulations.

Except for those trials involving impeachment, all persons accused of crimes are guaranteed a jury trial in the same state where the crime was committed. When a crime is committed outside of any state, such as on a ship at sea, Congress will decide where the trial will take place.

SECTION 3. Treason

Anyone who makes war against the United States or gives help to the nation's enemies, can be charged with treason. No one can be convicted of treason unless two witnesses support the charge or unless the person confesses to the charge in open court.

SECTION 4. Removal from Office

The President, Vice President, and all civil officers of the United States, shall be removed from office on impeachment for, and conviction of, treason, bribery, or other high crimes and misdemeanors.

ARTICLE 3
The Judicial Branch

SECTION 1. Federal Courts

The judicial power of the United States shall be vested in one Supreme Court, and in such inferior courts as the Congress may from time to time ordain and establish. The judges, both of the Supreme and inferior courts, shall hold their offices during good behavior, and shall, at stated times, receive for their services a compensation, which shall not be diminished during their continuance in office.

SECTION 2. Powers of Federal Courts

The judicial power shall extend to all cases, in law and equity, arising under this Constitution, the laws of the United States, and treaties made, or which shall be made, under their authority; — to all cases affecting ambassadors, other public ministers and consuls; — to all cases of admiralty and maritime jurisdiction; — to controversies to which the United States shall be a party; — to controversies between two or more States; — between a State and citizens of another State; —between citizens of different states — between citizens of the same State claiming lands under grants of different States, and between a State, or the citizens thereof, and foreign States, citizens or subjects.

In all cases affecting ambassadors, other public ministers and consuls, and those in which a State shall be party, the Supreme Court shall have original jurisdiction. In all the other cases before mentioned, the Supreme Court shall have appellate jurisdiction, both as to law and fact, with such exceptions, and under such regulations as the Congress shall make.

The trial of all crimes, except in cases of impeachment, shall be by jury; and such trial shall be held in the State where the said crimes shall have been committed; but when not committed within any State, the trial shall be at such place or places as the Congress may by law have directed.

SECTION 3. Treason

Treason against the United States shall consist only in levying war against them, or in adhering to their enemies, giving them aid and comfort. No person shall be convicted of treason unless on the testimony of two witnesses to the same overt act, or on confession in open court.

The Congress shall have power to declare the punishment of treason, but no attainder of treason shall work corruption of blood, or forfeiture except during the life of the person attainted.

ARTICLE 4
Relations Among the States

SECTION 1. Recognition by Each State
Full faith and credit shall be given in each State to the public acts, records, and judicial proceedings of every other State. And the Congress may by general laws prescribe the manner in which such acts, records, and proceedings shall be proved, and the effect thereof.

SECTION 2. Rights of Citizens in States
The citizens of each State shall be entitled to all privileges and immunities of citizens in the several States.

A person charged in any State with treason, felony, or other crime, who shall flee from justice, and be found in another State, shall on demand of the executive authority of the State from, which he fled, be delivered up to be removed to the State having jurisdiction of the crime.

~~No person held to service or labor in one State, under the laws thereof, escaping into another, shall, in consequence of any law or regulation therein, be discharged from such service or labor, but shall be delivered up on claim of the party to whom such service or labor may be due.~~ *
(*Changed by the Thirteenth Amendment)

SECTION 3. New States
New States may be admitted by the Congress into this Union; but no new State shall be formed or erected within the jurisdiction of any other State; nor any State be formed by the junction of two or more States, or parts of States, without the consent of the legislatures of the States concerned as well as of the Congress.

The Congress shall have power to dispose of and make all needful rules and regulations respecting the territory or other property belonging to the United States; and nothing in this Constitution shall be so construed as to prejudice any claims of the United States, or of any particular State.

SECTION 4. Guarantees to the States
The United States shall guarantee to every State in this Union a republican form of government, and shall protect each of them against invasion; and on application of the legislature, or of the executive (when the legislature cannot be convened), against domestic violence.

Congress has the power to decide punishments for acts of treason. The family of the traitor does not share in the guilt.

ARTICLE 4
Relations Among the States

SECTION 1. Recognition by Each State
Each state must recognize the laws, records, and legal decisions made by all the other states. Congress has the power to make laws to determine how these laws, records, and legal decisions can be proved.

SECTION 2. Rights of Citizens in States
States must give the same rights to citizens from other states that they give their own citizens.

If a person charged with a crime runs away to another state, the person must be returned to the original state for a trial.

No person who was a slave in one state may become free by escaping to a different state.

(This was changed by the Thirteenth Amendment, which made slavery illegal in all states.)

SECTION 3. New States
New states may become part of the United States with the permission of Congress. New states cannot be formed from land in an existing state, nor can two or more states or their parts join to create a new state without the consent of the states involved and of Congress.

Congress may sell or give away land or property belonging to the United States. Congress has the power to make all laws related to territories or other property owned by the United States and to make laws to govern federal territories and possessions.

SECTION 4. Guarantees to the States
The United States government is required to guarantee that each state has a republican form of government, a government that is responsible to the will of its people through their elected representatives. The federal government also must protect the states if they are invaded by foreign nations, and to do the same in case of riots, if requested by the governor or legislature of the state.

United States Documents
The Constitution of the United States of America

ARTICLE 5
Amending the Constitution

Amendments may be proposed by a two-thirds vote of each house of Congress or by a national convention called by Congress at the request of two-thirds of the states. To add an amendment to the Constitution, the legislatures or special conventions of three-fourths of the states must give approval or ratify it. However, no amendment can be added that keeps a state from having an equal vote in the United States Senate. No amendment may be added before 1808 that affects the slave trade or certain taxes. *(Congress passed a law in 1808 forbidding the slave trade protected under Article 1.)*

ARTICLE 6
Debts, Federal Supremacy, Oaths of Office

The federal government must pay all debts owed by the United States, including those debts which were taken on under the Articles of Confederation.

The Constitution and the laws of the United States are the supreme, or highest, laws of the land. All public officials in the federal government or within the states, regardless of other laws to the contrary, are bound by the Constitution and the national laws.

All officials in both federal and state governments must promise to obey and support the Constitution. No religious qualifications can be required as a condition for holding public office.

ARTICLE 7
Ratifying the Constitution

The Constitution will take effect when it is approved by at least nine of the thirteen states.

On September 17, 1787, all twelve state delegations present have given approval for adopting the Constitution. As proof, the delegates have each placed their signatures on the document.

ARTICLE 5
Amending the Constitution

The Congress, whenever two thirds of both houses shall deem it necessary, shall propose amendments to this Constitution, or, on the application of the legislatures of two thirds of the several States, shall call a convention for proposing amendments, which, in either case, shall be valid to all intents and purposes, as part of this Constitution, when ratified by the legislatures of three fourths of the several States, or by conventions in three fourths thereof, as the one or the other mode of ratification may be proposed by the Congress; provided ~~that no amendment which may be made prior to the year one thousand eight hundred and eight shall in any manner affect the first and fourth clauses in the ninth section of the first article and~~ that no State, without its consent, shall be deprived of its equal suffrage in the Senate.

ARTICLE 6
Debts, Federal Supremacy, Oaths of Office

All debts contracted and engagements entered into, before the adoption of this Constitution, shall be as valid against the United States under this Constitution, as under the Confederation.

This Constitution, and the laws of the United States which shall be made in pursuance thereof, and all treaties made, or which shall be made, under the authority of the United States, shall be the supreme law of the land; and the judges in every State shall be bound thereby, anything in the Constitution or laws of any State to the contrary notwithstanding.

The senators and representatives before mentioned, and the members of the several State legislatures, and all executive and judicial officers, both of the United States, and of the several States, shall be bound by oath or affirmation to support this Constitution; but no religious test shall ever be required as a qualification to any office or public trust under the United States.

ARTICLE 7
Ratifying the Constitution

The ratification of the conventions of nine States shall be sufficient for the establishment of this Constitution between the States so ratifying the same.

Done in Convention by the unanimous consent of the States present the seventeenth day of September in the year of our Lord one thousand seven hundred and eighty-seven and of the independence of the United States of America the twelfth. In witness whereof we have hereunto subscribed our names.

George Washington, *President* (Virginia)

Massachusetts
Nathaniel Gorham
Rufus King

New York
Alexander Hamilton

Georgia
William Few
Abraham Baldwin

Delaware
George Read
Gunning Bedford, Jr.
John Dickinson
Richard Bassett
Jacob Broom

Virginia
John Blair
James Madison, Jr.

Pennsylvania
Benjamin Franklin
Thomas Mifflin
Robert Morris
George Clymer
Thomas FitzSimons
Jared Ingersoll
James Wilson
Gouverneur Morris

New Hampshire
John Langdon
Nicholas Gilman

New Jersey
William Livingston
David Brearley
William Paterson
Jonathan Dayton

Connecticut
William Samuel Johnson
Roger Sherman

North Carolina
William Blount
Richard Dobbs Spaight
Hugh Williamson

South Carolina
John Rutledge
Charles Cotesworth Pinckney
Charles Pinckney
Pierce Butler

Maryland
James McHenry
Daniel of St. Thomas Jenifer
Daniel Carroll

"Let virtue, honor, and love of liberty and of science be and remain the soul of this constitution, and it will become the source of great and extensive happiness to this and future generations."

From Jay's charge to the Grand Jury of Ulster County. The Correspondence and Public Papers of John Jay, Henry P. Johnston, editor (New York: Burt Franklin, 1970), Vol. I, pp. 158-165, September 9, 1777.

"The power under the Constitution will always be in the people."

George Washington, The Writings of George Washington, Jared Sparks, editor (Boston: Russell, Odiorne and Metcalf, 1835), Vol. IX, p. 279, to Bushrod Washington on November 10, 1787.

FIRST AMENDMENT—1791
Freedom of Religion, Speech, Press, Assembly, and Petition

Congress shall not make any laws that set up an official national religion or that keeps people from worshiping according to their conscience. Congress may not limit the freedom of speech or the press, or the freedom to meet peaceably. People must have the right to ask the government to correct a problem.

SECOND AMENDMENT—1791
Right to Have Firearms

Because an organized militia is needed to protect the states, the right of people to keep and bear firearms shall not be violated.

THIRD AMENDMENT—1791
Right Not to House Soldiers

Soldiers may not be housed in private homes, without the consent of the owner, unless a law for that purpose is passed during a time of war.

FOURTH AMENDMENT—1791
Freedom from Unreasonable Search and Seizure

People and their property are to be protected from unreasonable search and seizure. Government authorities must have good cause and have a written order from a judge describing the place to be searched and the person or things to be seized.

FIFTH AMENDMENT—1791
Rights of People Accused of Crimes

A person may not be put on trial for a crime that is punishable by death or imprisonment without first being accused by a grand jury. [A grand jury is a group of citizens selected to decide whether there is enough evidence against a person to hold a trial.] However, during wartime or a time of public danger, people in military service may not have that right.

A person may not be put on trial twice for the same crime.

FIRST AMENDMENT—1791
Freedom of Religion, Speech, Press, Assembly, and Petition

Congress shall make no law respecting an establishment of religion, or prohibiting the free exercise thereof; or abridging the freedom of speech, or of the press; or the right of the people peaceably to assemble, and to petition the government for a redress of grievances.

SECOND AMENDMENT—1791
Right to Have Firearms

A well-regulated militia, being necessary to the security of a free state, the right of the people to keep and bear arms shall not be infringed.

THIRD AMENDMENT—1791
Right Not to House Soldiers

No soldier shall, in time of peace, be quartered in any house, without the consent of the owner, nor in time of war, but in a manner to be prescribed by law.

FOURTH AMENDMENT—1791
Freedom from Unreasonable Search and Seizure

The right of the people to be secure in their persons, houses, papers, and effects, against unreasonable searches and seizures, shall not be violated, and no warrants shall issue, but upon probable cause, supported by oath or affirmation, and particularly describing the place to be searched, and the persons or things to be seized.

FIFTH AMENDMENT—1791
Rights of People Accused of Crimes

No person shall be held to answer for a capital or otherwise infamous crime, unless on a presentment or indictment of a grand jury, except in cases arising in the land or naval forces, or in the militia, when in actual service in time of war or public danger; nor shall any person be subject for the same offense to be twice put in jeopardy of life or limb; nor shall be compelled in any criminal case to be a witness against himself, nor be deprived of life, liberty, or property, without due process of law; nor shall private property be taken for public use without just compensation.

SIXTH AMENDMENT—1791
Right to a Jury Trial in a Criminal Case

In all criminal prosecutions, the accused shall enjoy the right to a speedy and public trial, by an impartial jury of the state and district wherein the crime shall have been committed, which district shall have been previously ascertained by law, and to be informed of the nature and cause of the accusation; to be confronted with the witnesses against him; to have compulsory process for obtaining witnesses in his favor, and to have the assistance of counsel for his defense.

SEVENTH AMENDMENT—1791
Right to a Jury Trial in a Civil Case

In suits at common law, where the value in controversy shall exceed twenty dollars, the right of trial by jury shall be preserved, and no fact tried by a jury shall be otherwise reexamined in any court of the United States, than according to the rules of the common law.

EIGHTH AMENDMENT—1791
Protection from Unfair Bail and Punishment

Excessive bail shall not be required, nor excessive fines imposed, nor cruel and unusual punishments inflicted.

NINTH AMENDMENT—1791
Other Rights

The enumeration in the Constitution of certain rights shall not be construed to deny or disparage others retained by the people.

TENTH AMENDMENT—1791
Powers of the States and People

The powers not delegated to the United States by the Constitution, nor prohibited by it to the States, are reserved to the states respectively, or to the people.

People cannot be required to give evidence against themselves.

People may not have their lives, liberty, or property taken away without fair and equal treatment under the laws of the land.

People may not have their property taken for public use without receiving access to the lawful judicial processes.

SIXTH AMENDMENT—1791
Right to a Jury Trial in a Criminal Case

A person accused of a crime must have a speedy, public trial held before an open-minded jury made up of citizens living in the community where the crime occurred. The accused person must also be told about the nature of the charge of wrongdoing. Accused people are allowed to meet and question witnesses against them, to have witnesses testify in their favor, and to have the services of a lawyer.

SEVENTH AMENDMENT—1791
Right to a Jury Trial in a Civil Case

In civil cases, where the value of the property in question is over $20, the right of a jury trial is guaranteed. The decision of the jury is final and cannot be changed by a judge but only by a new trial.

EIGHTH AMENDMENT—1791
Protection from Unfair Bail and Punishment

Bails and fines must not be too large, and punishments may not be cruel and unusual.

NINTH AMENDMENT—1791
Other Rights

Fundamental rights not listed in the Constitution remain guaranteed to all citizens.

TENTH AMENDMENT—1791
Powers of the States and People

The states or the people keep all powers not granted to the federal government and not denied to the states by the Constitution.

ELEVENTH AMENDMENT—1795
Limits on Right to Sue States

A state government cannot be sued in a federal court by people from a different state or from a foreign country.

TWELFTH AMENDMENT—1804
Election of President and Vice President

In each state, members of the Electoral College vote on separate ballots for one person as President and another person as Vice President. At least one of these choices may not live in the same state as the electors. Each person, on the ballot, receiving votes in a given state must be listed by the total numbers of votes. Final counts of votes from each state must be signed and officially recognized as accurate and complete. These results must be delivered to the national capital to be opened and read aloud by the president of the Senate at a joint session of Congress.

If a person receives a majority of votes for President, that person shall be the President. If no person has a majority, then from the three who received the largest number of votes, the House of Representatives will immediately choose the President by ballot. But in choosing the President, the votes shall be taken by states, with each state having one vote. Two-thirds of the states must participate in this choice. (*Until changed by the Twentieth Amendment, if the House of Representatives failed to elect a President by March 4, the Vice President served as President.*)

If a person receives a majority of votes as Vice President, that person shall be the Vice President. If no person has a majority, then from the two highest numbers on the list, the Senate will choose the Vice President, provided that two-thirds of the senators are present to vote. A simple majority, with each senator voting individually, is necessary to make a final choice. A person who is not eligible to be President cannot be eligible for the office of Vice President.

ELEVENTH AMENDMENT—1795
Limits on Right to Sue States

The judicial power of the United States shall not be construed to extend to any suit in law or equity, commenced or prosecuted against one of the United States by citizens of another State, or by citizens or subjects of any foreign State.

TWELFTH AMENDMENT—1804
Election of President and Vice President

The electors shall meet in their respective States, and vote by ballot for President and Vice President, one of whom, at least, shall not be an inhabitant of the same State with themselves; they shall name in their ballots the person voted for as President, and in distinct ballots the person voted for as Vice President, and they shall make distinct lists of all persons voted for as President, and of all persons voted for as Vice President, and of the number of votes for each, which lists they shall sign and certify, and transmit sealed to the seat of the government of the United States, directed to the president of the Senate;—The president of the Senate shall, in the presence of the Senate and House of Representatives, open all the certificates and the votes shall then be counted;—The person having the greatest number of votes for President shall be the President, if such number be a majority of the whole number of electors appointed; and if no person have such majority, then from the persons having the highest numbers not exceeding three on the list of those voted for as President, the House of Representatives shall choose immediately, by ballot, the President. But in choosing the President, the votes shall be taken by States, the representation from each State having one vote; a quorum for this purpose shall consist of a member or members from two thirds of the States, and a majority of all the States shall be necessary to a choice. ~~And if the House of Representatives shall not choose a President whenever the right of choice shall devolve upon them, before the fourth day of March next following,~~* *then the Vice President shall act as President,* as in the case of the death or other constitutional disability of the President. The person having the greatest number of votes as Vice President shall be the Vice President, if such number be a majority of the whole number of electors appointed, and if no person have a majority, then from the two highest numbers on the list, the Senate shall choose the Vice President; a quorum for the purpose shall consist of two thirds of the whole number of senators, and a majority of the whole number shall be necessary to a choice. But no person constitutionally ineligible to the office of President shall be eligible to that of Vice President of the United States. (**Changed by the Twentieth Amendment*)

THIRTEENTH AMENDMENT—1865
Abolition of Slavery

SECTION 1. Slavery Outlawed
Neither slavery nor involuntary servitude, except as a punishment for crime whereof the party shall have been duly convicted, shall exist within the United States, or any place subject to their jurisdiction.

SECTION 2. Enforcement
Congress shall have power to enforce this article by appropriate legislation.

FOURTEENTH AMENDMENT—1868
Rights of Citizens

SECTION 1. Citizenship
All persons born or naturalized in the United States, and subject to the jurisdiction thereof, are citizens of the United States and of the State wherein they reside. No State shall make or enforce any law which shall abridge the privileges or immunities of citizens of the United States; nor shall any State deprive any person of life, liberty, or property, without due process of law; nor deny to any person within its jurisdiction the equal protection of the laws.

SECTION 2. Representation in Congress
Representatives shall be apportioned among the several States according to their respective numbers, counting the whole number of persons in each State, excluding Indians not taxed. But when the right to vote at any election for the choice of electors for President and Vice President of the United States, representatives in Congress, the executive and judicial officers of a State, or the members of the legislature thereof is denied to any of the male inhabitants of such State, being twenty-one years of age, and citizens of the United States, or in any way abridged, except for participation in rebellion, or other crime, the basis of representation therein shall be reduced in the proportion which the number of such male citizens shall bear to the whole number of male citizens twenty-one years of age in such State.* (*Restriction on race and ethnicity changed by the Fifteenth Amendment; restriction on gender changed by the Nineteenth Amendment; restriction regarding taxation changed by the Twenty-Fourth Amendment; restriction on age changed by the Twenty-Sixth Amendment)

THIRTEENTH AMENDMENT—1865
Abolition of Slavery

Slavery shall not exist anywhere in the United States or anyplace governed by the United States. Forced labor may only be required after a person has been fairly convicted of a crime.

Congress may make laws to enforce this article.

FOURTEENTH AMENDMENT—1868
Rights of Citizens

All persons born in the United States or granted citizenship are citizens of both the United States and of the states in which they live.
No state may pass laws which take away or limit the freedoms or privileges of any of its citizens. Citizens may not have their lives, liberties, or property taken away without access to a regular judicial process conducted according to the laws. All people must be protected equally by the laws.

A state's representation in Congress is determined by the state's population. A state which does not allow qualified voters to vote may have its representation in Congress reduced. (Other provisions of this section were changed by the Fifteenth, Nineteenth, Twenty-Fourth and Twenty-Sixth Amendments.)

No person may hold a civil or military office in the federal or a state government who had previously taken an oath to uphold the Constitution and then aided or helped the confederacy during the Civil War or other rebellions against the United States.

Congress may remove this provision by a two-thirds vote of both houses.

Any federal debts resulting from fighting to end a civil war or put down a rebellion must be paid in full. However, the federal or state government shall not pay debts made by those who participate in a rebellion against the United States.

Former owners of slaves shall not be paid for the financial losses caused by the freeing of slaves.

Congress has the power to pass laws to enforce the provisions of this article.

FIFTEENTH AMENDMENT—1870
Voting Rights

A citizen's right to vote in any election cannot be denied based on the person's race or color, or because they were once enslaved.

Congress has the power to pass laws to enforce the provisions of this article.

SIXTEENTH AMENDMENT—1913
Income Tax

Congress has the power to directly tax all individuals based on their personal incomes, without collecting taxes based on a division among the states or in consideration of a state's population.

SECTION 3. Penalties for Leaders of the Confederacy

No person shall be a senator or representative in Congress, or elector of President and Vice President, or hold any office, civil or military, under the United States, or under any State, who, having previously taken an oath, as a member of Congress, or as an officer of the United States, or as a member of any State legislature, or as an executive or judicial officer of any State, to support the Constitution of the United States, shall have engaged in insurrection or rebellion against the same, or given aid or comfort to the enemies thereof. But Congress may by a vote of two thirds of each house, remove such disability.

SECTION 4. Responsibility for the Public Debt

The validity of the public debt of the United States, authorized by law, including debts incurred for payment of pensions and bounties for services in suppressing insurrection or rebellion, shall not be questioned. But neither the United States nor any State shall assume or pay any debt or obligation incurred in aid of insurrection or rebellion against the United States, or any claim for the loss or emancipation of any slave; but all such debts, obligations and claims shall be held illegal and void.

SECTION 5. Enforcement

The Congress shall have power to enforce, by appropriate legislation, the provisions of this article.

FIFTEENTH AMENDMENT—1870
Voting Rights

SECTION 1. Suffrage for African Americans

The right of citizens of the United States to vote shall not be denied or abridged by the United States or by any State on account of race, color, or previous condition of servitude.

SECTION 2. Enforcement

The Congress shall have power to enforce this article by appropriate legislation.

SIXTEENTH AMENDMENT—1913
Income Tax

The Congress shall have power to lay and collect taxes on incomes, from whatever source derived, without apportionment among the several States, and without regard to any census or enumeration.

SEVENTEENTH AMENDMENT—1913
Direct Election of Senators

The Senate of the United States shall be composed of two senators from each State, elected by the people thereof, for six years; and each senator shall have one vote. The electors in each State shall have the qualifications requisite for electors of the most numerous branch of the State legislatures.

When vacancies happen in the representation of any State in the Senate, the executive authority of such State shall issue writs of election to fill such vacancies: Provided, that the legislature of any State may empower the executive thereof to make temporary appointments until the people fill the vacancies by election as the legislature may direct.

This amendment shall not be so construed as to affect the election or term of any Senator chosen before it becomes valid as part of the Constitution.

EIGHTEENTH AMENDMENT*—1919
Prohibition

SECTION 1. Liquor Banned
After one year from the ratification of this article, the manufacture, sale, or transportation of intoxicating liquors within, the importation thereof into, or the exportation thereof from the United States and all territory subject to the jurisdiction thereof for beverage purposes is hereby prohibited.*

SECTION 2. Enforcement
The Congress and the several States shall have concurrent power to enforce this article by appropriate legislation.*

SECTION 3. Time Limit for Ratification
This article shall be inoperative unless it shall have been ratified as an amendment to the Constitution by the legislatures of the several States, as provided in the Constitution, within seven years from the date of the submission hereof to the States by the Congress.* (*Repealed by the Twenty-First Amendment)

SEVENTEENTH AMENDMENT—1913
Direct Election of Senators

Two senators will represent each state in Congress, each elected for six-year terms and having one vote in the Senate. They will be elected directly by the qualified voters in the states (not by state legislatures, which was originally provided for in Article I, Section 3, Clause 1).

When vacancies occur in the Senate, the governor of the state will call for an election to fill the vacancy. In the meantime the state legislature will permit the governor to make a temporary appointment until the election occurs. The legislature organizes the election.

This amendment shall not affect the election or term of any Senator chosen before it becomes part of the Constitution.

EIGHTEENTH AMENDMENT*—1919
Prohibition

The making, selling, and transporting of alcoholic beverages anywhere in the United States and its territories is outlawed. This amendment takes effect one year after the amendment is passed.

Congress and the states will share lawmaking powers to enforce this article.

This amendment will become part of the Constitution only if it is ratified within seven years after Congress has sent it to the States.
(This amendment was repealed by the Twenty-First Amendment.)

NINETEENTH AMENDMENT—1920
Women's Right to Vote

A citizen's right to vote in any election cannot be denied based on the person's sex.

Congress shall have power to pass laws to enforce the provisions of this article.

TWENTIETH AMENDMENT—1933
Terms of Office

The terms of the President and Vice President end at noon on January 20th, and the terms of senators and representatives end at noon on January 3rd, following the federal elections held the previous November. The terms of their successors begin at that time.

Congress must meet at least once a year, and the session will begin at noon on January 3rd unless a law is passed to change the day.

If the President-elect dies before taking office, the Vice President-elect becomes President. If a President has not been chosen before January 20, or if the President-elect has not qualified, then the Vice President-elect acts as President until a President becomes qualified. If neither the President-elect or Vice President-elect is able to take office on the designated date, then Congress will decide who will act as President until a President or Vice President has been qualified.

If a candidate fails to win a majority in the Electoral College, and then dies while the election is being decided in the House of Representatives, Congress will have the power to pass laws to resolve the problem. Congress has similar power in the event that a candidate for Vice President dies while the election is in the Senate.

NINETEENTH AMENDMENT—1920
Women's Right to Vote

SECTION 1. Suffrage for Women
The right of citizens of the United States to vote shall not be denied or abridged by the United States or by any State on account of sex.

SECTION 2. Enforcement
Congress shall have power to enforce this article by appropriate legislation.

TWENTIETH AMENDMENT—1933
Terms of Office

SECTION 1. Start and End of Terms
The terms of the President and Vice President shall end at noon on the 20th day of January, and the terms of senators and representatives at noon on the third day of January, of the year in which such terms would have ended if this article had not been ratified; and the terms of their successors shall then begin.

SECTION 2. Congressional Meeting
The Congress shall assemble at least once in every year, and such meeting shall begin at noon on the third day of January, unless they shall by law appoint a different day.

SECTION 3. Successor for the President-Elect
If, at the time fixed for the beginning of the term of the President, the President-elect shall have died, the Vice President-elect shall become President. If a President shall not have been chosen before the time fixed for the beginning of his term, or if the President-elect shall have failed to qualify, then the Vice President-elect shall act as President until a President shall have qualified; and the Congress may by law provide for the case wherein neither a President-elect nor a Vice President-elect shall have qualified, declaring who shall then act as President, or the manner in which one who is to act shall be selected, and such persons shall act accordingly until a President or Vice President shall have qualified.

SECTION 4. Elections Decided by Congress
The Congress may by law provide for the case of the death of any of the persons from whom the House of Representatives may choose a President

whenever the right of choice shall have devolved upon them, and for the case of the death of any of the persons from whom the Senate may choose a Vice President whenever the right of choice shall have devolved upon them.

SECTION 5. Effective Date

Sections 1 and 2 shall take effect on the 15th day of October following the ratification of this article.

Sections 1 and 2 of this amendment shall take effect on October 15, after this amendment is ratified.

SECTION 6. Time Limit for Ratification

This article shall be inoperative unless it shall have been ratified as an amendment to the Constitution by the legislatures of three fourths of the several States within seven years from the date of its submission.

This amendment will become part of the Constitution only if it is ratified within seven years after Congress has sent it to the States.

TWENTY-FIRST AMENDMENT—1933
Repeal of Prohibition Amendment

TWENTY-FIRST AMENDMENT—1933
Repeal of Prohibition Amendment

SECTION 1. End of Prohibition

The eighteenth article of amendment to the Constitution of the United States is hereby repealed.

The Eighteenth Amendment, prohibiting the making, sale, and transportation of alcoholic beverages in the United States and its possessions, is repealed.

SECTION 2. Protection of State Prohibition Laws

The transportation or importation into any State, territory, or possession of the United States for delivery or use therein of intoxicating liquors, in violation of the laws thereof, is hereby prohibited.

Individual states may prohibit the transporting or importing of alcoholic beverages.

SECTION 3. Time Limit for Ratification

This article shall be inoperative unless it shall have been ratified as an amendment to the Constitution by conventions in the several States, as provided in the Constitution, within seven years from the date of submission hereof to the States by the Congress.

This amendment will become part of the Constitution only if it is ratified in seven years.

TWENTY-SECOND AMENDMENT—1951
Limit on Terms of the President

TWENTY-SECOND AMENDMENT—1951
Limit on Terms of the President

SECTION 1. Two-Term Limit

No person shall be elected to the office of the President more than twice, and no person who has held the office of President, or acted as President, for more than two years of a term to which some other person was elected President shall be elected to the office of the President more than once.

No person can be elected to the office of the President more than twice. If a President has served two or more years of a previous President's term, then the President may be re-elected for one additional term.

The current President in office at the time of this amendment's ratification process is not limited to term restrictions.

But this Article shall not apply to any person holding the office of President when this Article was proposed by the Congress, and shall not prevent any person who may be holding the office of President, or acting as President, during the term within which this Article becomes operative from holding the office of President or acting as President during the remainder of such term.

This amendment will become part of the Constitution only if it is ratified by three-fourths of the States within seven years after Congress has sent it to the States.

SECTION 2. Time Limit on Ratification

This article shall be inoperative unless it shall have been ratified as an amendment to the Constitution by the legislatures of three-fourths of the several States within seven years from the date of its submission to the States by the Congress.

TWENTY-THIRD AMENDMENT—1961
Presidential Elections for District of Columbia

Citizens living in the District of Columbia may elect members to the Electoral College to vote in federal elections for President and Vice President. The number of electors is limited to the number of votes of the least populated state. The voters must live in the district and follow all duties and procedures outlined in the Twelfth Amendment.

TWENTY-THIRD AMENDMENT—1961
Presidential Elections for District of Columbia

SECTION 1. Presidential Electors

The District constituting the seat of government of the United States shall appoint in such manner as the Congress may direct:

A number of electors of President and Vice President equal to the whole number of senators and representatives in Congress to which the District would be entitled if it were a State, but in no event more than the least populous state; they shall be in addition to those appointed by the States, but they shall be considered, for the purposes of the election of President and Vice President, to be electors appointed by a State; and they shall meet in the District and perform such duties as provided by the twelfth article of amendment.

SECTION 2. Enforcement

The Congress shall have power to enforce this article by appropriate legislation.

Congress has the power to make laws necessary to enforce this amendment.

TWENTY-FOURTH AMENDMENT—1964
Outlawing of Poll Tax

United States citizens may not have their voting rights restricted in federal elections by the establishment of a poll tax or other tax.

TWENTY-FOURTH AMENDMENT—1964
Outlawing of Poll Tax

SECTION 1. Ban on Poll Tax in Federal Elections

The right of citizens of the United States to vote in any primary or other election for President or Vice President, for electors for President or Vice President, or for senator or representative in Congress, shall not be denied or abridged by the United States or any State by reason of failure to pay any poll tax or other tax.

SECTION 2. Enforcement

The Congress shall have power to enforce this article by appropriate legislation.

Congress has the power to make laws necessary to enforce this amendment.

TWENTY-FIFTH AMENDMENT—1967
Presidential Succession

SECTION 1. Filling Vacant Office of President

In case of the removal of the President from office or his death or resignation, the Vice President shall become President.

TWENTY-FIFTH AMENDMENT—1967
Presidential Succession

If a President dies or is removed from office, then the Vice President will become President.

SECTION 2. Filling Vacant Office of Vice President

Whenever there is a vacancy in the office of the Vice President, the President shall nominate a Vice President who shall take the office upon confirmation by a majority vote of both houses of Congress.

If the office of Vice President becomes vacant, the President may nominate a new Vice President. The person nominated must be approved by a majority vote in both houses of Congress.

SECTION 3. Disability of the President

Whenever the President transmits to the president pro tempore of the Senate and the Speaker of the House of Representatives his written declaration that he is unable to discharge the powers and duties of his office, and until he transmits to them a written declaration to the contrary, such powers and duties shall be discharged by the Vice President as Acting President.

If the President sends a written notice to officers of both houses of Congress that the President is unable to perform the duties of the office, then the Vice President will become Acting President. The Vice President will act as the President until the President informs Congress that the President is again ready to take over the presidential responsibilities.

SECTION 4. When Congress Names an Acting President

Whenever the Vice President and a majority of either the principal officers of the executive departments or of such other body as Congress may by law provide, transmit to the president pro tempore of the Senate and the Speaker of the House of Representatives their written declaration that the President is unable to discharge the powers and duties of his office, the Vice President shall immediately assume the powers and duties of the office as Acting President.

Thereafter, when the President transmits to the president pro tempore of the Senate and the Speaker of the House of Representatives his written declaration that no inability exists, he shall resume the powers and duties of his office unless the Vice President and a majority of either the principal officers of the executive department or of such other body as Congress may by law provide, transmit within four days to the president pro tempore of the Senate and the Speaker of the House of Representatives their written declaration that the President is unable to discharge the powers and duties of his office. Thereupon Congress shall decide the issue, assembling within forty-eight hours for that purpose if not in session. If

If the President is unconscious or refuses to admit a disabling illness, the Vice President and a majority of the Cabinet have the right to inform Congress in writing that the President is unable to carry out the duties of being President. The Vice President then becomes Acting President until the President can return to work.

When the President informs the leaders of Congress in writing that the disability no longer exists, the President shall resume the office. But if there is a disagreement between the President and the Vice President and a majority of the Cabinet about the President's ability to carry out the duties of being President, the Vice President, or other appropriate authority, has four days to notify Congress, and Congress has the power to decide the issue. If not in session, both houses of Congress must meet within 48 hours for that purpose and will have 21 days to make a decision. A two-thirds vote in both houses of Congress is required to find the President unfit to perform the duties of the office.

the Congress, within twenty-one days after receipt of the latter written declaration, or, if Congress is not in session, within twenty-one days after Congress is required to assemble, determines by two-thirds vote of both houses that the President is unable to discharge the powers and duties of his office, the Vice President shall continue to discharge the same as Acting President; otherwise, the President shall resume the powers and duties of his office.

TWENTY-SIXTH AMENDMENT—1971
Voting Rights for Eighteen-Year-Olds

SECTION 1. New Voting Age

The right of citizens in the United States, who are eighteen years of age or older, to vote shall not be denied or abridged by the United States or by any State on account of age.

SECTION 2. Enforcement

The Congress shall have power to enforce this article by appropriate legislation.

TWENTY-SEVENTH AMENDMENT—1992
Limits on Congressional Salary Changes

No law varying the compensation for the services of the Senators and Representatives shall take effect, until an election of Representatives shall have intervened.

TWENTY-SIXTH AMENDMENT—1971
Voting Rights for Eighteen-Year-Olds

Citizens who are eighteen years of age or older have the right to vote in all elections.

Congress has the power to make laws necessary to enforce this amendment.

TWENTY-SEVENTH AMENDMENT—1992
Limits on Congressional Salary Changes

Salary changes for Congress cannot take effect until after the next federal election.

Gazetteer

This Gazetteer is a geographic dictionary that will help you locate and pronounce the names of the places in this book. Latitude and longitude are given for cities. The page numbers tell you where each place appears on a map (m) or in the text (t).

A

Africa (af′ rə kə) Second largest of Earth's seven continents. (m. R4–5, t. 107)

Alamo (al′ ə mō) Mission in San Antonio, Texas, which was used by Texans as a fort during the Texas Revolution. (t. 432)

American River (ə mer′ə kən riv′ər) River in California, where gold was discovered in 1848. (t. 443)

Antarctica (ant ärk′tə kə) One of Earth's seven continents, around the South Pole. (R4–5)

Antietam (an tē′təm) Creek near Sharpsburg, Maryland, site of a major Civil War battle in 1862. (t. 495)

Appalachian Mountains (ap′ə lā′chən moun′tənz) Chain of mountains in eastern North America, extending from Canada to Alabama. (m. 27)

Appomattox Court House (ap′ə mat′əks kôrt′hous) Town in central Virginia, site of Confederate General Lee's surrender to Union General Grant on April 9, 1865, ending the Civil War. (m. 506, 509; t. 511)

Arctic Ocean (ärk′tik ō′shən) Smallest of Earth's four oceans. (R4–5)

Asia (ā′zhə) Largest of Earth's seven continents. (m. R4–5, t. 103)

Atlanta (at lan′tə) Capital and largest city of Georgia, site of Union victory in a Civil War battle on September 2, 1864; 33°N, 84°W. (m. 506, 509; t. 510)

Atlantic Ocean (at lan′tik ō′shən) One of Earth's four oceans. (m. R4–5)

Australia (ȯ strā′lyə) Smallest of Earth's seven continents. (m. R4–5)

B

Bahama Islands (bə hä′mə ī′ləndz) Island group in the West Indies, southeast of Florida (m. 134, t. 135)

Baltimore (bȯl′tə môr) Seaport and largest city in Maryland; 39°N, 76°W. (m. 380, t. 383)

Bering Strait (bir′ing strāt) Narrow body of water that separates Asia from North America. (m. 54, 55; t. 55)

Pronunciation Key

a in hat	ō in open	sh in she
ā in age	ȯ in all	th in thin
â in care	ô in order	ŦH in then
ä in far	oi in oil	zh in measure
e in let	ou in out	ə = a in about
ē in equal	u in cup	ə = e in taken
ėr in term	u̇ in put	ə = i in pencil
i in it	ü in rule	ə = o in lemon
ī in ice	ch in child	ə = u in circus
o in hot	ng in long	

Gazetteer

Boston (bȯ′stən) Capital and largest city of Massachusetts; 42°N, 71°W. (m. 168, 216, 268, 276; t. 172, 217, 271, 277–280)

Bull Run (bu̇l run) Stream in northeastern Virginia, site of major Civil War battles in 1861 and 1862. (m. 491, t. 495)

C

Cahokia (kə hō′kē ə) Town in present-day Illinois, site of a 100-foot-high mound built by people called the Mound Builders; 39°N, 90°W. (m. 60, 62; t. 61)

California Trail (kal′ə fôr′nyə trāl) Trail from Independence, Missouri, to the Central Valley of California, used by gold seekers in 1849. (m. 440, 442; t. 443)

Canada (kan′ə də) Country in the northern part of North America, north of the United States. (m. R8, t. 241)

Canary Islands (kə när′ē ī′ləndz) Island group in the Atlantic Ocean off the northwest coast of Africa. (m. 141)

Cape of Good Hope (kāp əv gu̇d hōp) Southwestern tip of Africa. (m. 110, t. 114)

Caribbean Sea (kar′ə bē′ən sē) Part of the Atlantic Ocean, bordered by the West Indies and Central and South America. (m. 141)

Charleston (chärlz′tən) Port city in southeastern South Carolina; 32°N, 79°W. (m. 202, t. 206)

Charlestown (chärlz′ toun) Oldest part of Boston, near where the battle of Bunker Hill was fought in 1775. (m. 286, 290; t. 290)

Chesapeake Bay (ches′ ə pēk′ bā) Inlet of the Atlantic Ocean, surrounded by Maryland and Virginia. (m. 159)

Chicago (shə kȯ′gō) Largest city in Illinois, located on Lake Michigan; 41° N, 87°W. (t. 28)

China (chī′nə) Country in eastern Asia, with the world's largest population. (t. 28)

Coast Ranges (kōst rān′jəz) Mountains extending along the Pacific coast of North America. (m. R9, R14)

Colorado River (kol′ə rad′ō riv′ər) River in the southwestern United States, flowing from the Rocky Mountains to the Gulf of California. (m. 26)

Columbia River (kə lum′bē ə riv′ər) River in northwestern North America, which begins in Canada, forms part of the border between Washington and Oregon, and flows into the Pacific Ocean. (m. 26)

Concord (kong′kərd) Town in eastern Massachusetts, site of one of the first battles of the American Revolution, on April 19, 1775; 42°N, 71°W. (m. 286, t. 287)

Copán (kȯ pän′) Ancient city of the Maya, located in present-day Honduras; 15°N, 88°W. (m. 66, 68; t. 67)

Cumberland Gap (kum′bər lənd gap) Pass through the Appalachian Mountains, in northeastern Tennessee. (m. 370, t. 372)

Cuzco (küz′ kō) Capital of the Inca Empire, located in present-day Peru; 13°N, 72°W. (m. 66, 68; t. 69, 145)

D

Dallas (dal′əs) City in northeastern Texas; 33°N, 97°W. (m. R12–13)

Death Valley (deth val′ē) Lowest point in North America, located in the Mojave Desert in California. (m. R12–13)

Denver (den′vər) Capital and largest city in Colorado; 40°N, 105°W. (m. 26)

Detroit (di troit′) Largest city in Michigan; 42°N, 83°W. (m. 27)

E

Eastern Hemisphere (ē′stərn hem′ə sfir) Half of Earth east of the prime meridian, including the continents of Africa, Asia, Europe, and Australia. (m. H 10, t. H 10)

Eastern Woodlands cultural region (ē′stərn wu̇d′ləndz kul′chər əl rē′jən) Area in eastern North America that was home to many Native Americans such as the Iroquois. (m. 76, 77; t. 77)

Ellis Island (el′is ī′lənd) Island in New York Harbor, which was the entry point for immigrants from Europe from 1892 to 1954. (t. 10)

England (ing′ glənd) Part of the United Kingdom of Great Britain and Northern Ireland. England occupies the southern part of the island of Great Britain. (m. 206, t. 248)

Erie Canal (ir′ē kə nal′) Human-made waterway in New York State, connecting Lake Erie and the Hudson River. (m. 408, t. 411)

Europe (yu̇r′əp) One of Earth's seven continents. (m. R4–5, t. 103)

Everglades National Park (ev′ər glādz′ nash′ə nəl pärk) National park located in southern Florida. (m. 34, t. 37)

F

Florida (flôr′ə də) State located in the southeastern United States, settled by the Spanish in the middle 1500s. (m. 232, t. 233)

Fort Duquesne (fôrt dü kān′) Fort built by the French in 1754 in western Pennsylvania, site of present-day Pittsburgh. (m. 246, 248; t. 248)

Fort McHenry (fôrt mək hen′rē) Fort protecting the harbor of Baltimore, Maryland, site of a major battle in the War of 1812. (m. 380, t. 383)

Fort Necessity (fôrt nə ses′ə tē) Fort built by George Washington's soldiers in western Pennsylvania in 1754. (m. 246, t. 246–247)

Pronunciation Key		
a in hat	ō in open	sh in she
ā in age	ȯ in all	th in thin
â in care	ô in order	ᴛʜ in then
ä in far	oi in oil	zh in measure
e in let	ou in out	ə = a in about
ē in equal	u in cup	ə = e in taken
ėr in term	u̇ in put	ə = i in pencil
i in it	ü in rule	ə = o in lemon
ī in ice	ch in child	ə = u in circus
o in hot	ng in long	

Gazetteer

Fort Sumter (fôrt sump′tər) Fort in Charleston Harbor, South Carolina, site of the first battle of the Civil War in 1861. (m. 484, t. 485)

Fort Ticonderoga (fôrt tī′kon də rō′gə) Fort on Lake Champlain in northeastern New York, site of major battles in the American Revolution. (m. 302, t. 303)

Fort Vincennes (fôrt vin senz′) Fort on the site of present-day Vincennes, Indiana. (m. 314, 317; t. 316)

Fort Wagner (fôrt wag′ nər) Fort that protected the harbor of Charleston, South Carolina, attacked by the African American 54th Regiment in the Civil War in July, 1863. (m. 498, t. 501)

Four Corners (fôr kôr′ nərz) Place where four states—New Mexico, Arizona, Colorado, and Utah—come together; was the home of the Anasazi people. (m. 60, 62; t. 62)

France (frans) Country in Western Europe. (m. R4–5, t. 305)

 G

Gettysburg (get′ ēz bėrg′) Town in southern Pennsylvania, site of a major Union victory during the Civil War in 1863; 40°N, 77°W. (m. 506, t. 507)

Ghana (gä′ nə) Country in Africa, named for early kingdom in West Africa. (m. 106–107, t. 107)

Grand Canyon (grand kan′ yən) Large canyon on the Colorado River in northwestern Arizona. (m. 26, t. 26)

Great Lakes (grāt lāks) Group of five, large, freshwater lakes on the border between the United States and Canada. (m. 29, t. 27)

Great Plains (grāt plānz) Region in central North America, east of the Rocky Mountains and extending from Canada to Texas. (m. 26–27, t. 441)

Great Plains cultural region (grāt plānz kul′chər əl rē′jən) Area in central North America that was home to many Native Americans such as the Lakota and Cheyenne. (m. 82, 84; t. 83)

Great Salt Lake (grāt sȯlt lāk) Lake in northwestern Utah, largest salt lake in North America. (m. 440, R14–15; t. 441)

Greenland (grēn′ lənd) Island in the northern Atlantic Ocean, largest island on Earth. (m. 110–111, t. 111)

Gulf of California (gulf əv kal′ ə fôr′ nyə) Inlet of the Pacific Ocean, between Baja, California, and the western coast of Mexico. (m. 148)

Gulf of Mexico (gulf əv mek′sə kō) Inlet of the Atlantic Ocean, between the United States and Mexico. (m. 29)

 H

Harpers Ferry (här′pərz fer′ē) Town in northeastern West Virginia, site of federal arsenal raided by abolitionist John Brown in 1859; 39°N, 78°W. (m. 476, t. 480)

Hispaniola (his′ pə nyō′lə) Island in the Caribbean Sea, made up of Haiti and the Dominican Republic. (m. 146, 148; t. 150)

Hudson River (hud′ sən riv′ ər) River in eastern New York that flows into the Atlantic Ocean. (m. 164, 166; t. 165–166)

I

Indian Ocean (in′dē ən ō′shən) One of Earth's four oceans. (m. 114, t. 114)

Indian Territory (in′ dē ən tär′ ə tôr′ ē) Land set aside by the Indian Removal Act of 1830 for the Native Americans who were forced to move from the southeastern United States; now forms most of Oklahoma. (m. 402, t. 405)

Iroquois Trail (ir′ ə kwoi trāl) Trail that linked the lands of the Iroquois League, extended from present-day Albany to Buffalo. (m. 76–77, t. 77)

J

Jamaica (jə mā′ kə) Island country in the West Indies. (m. 687)

Jamestown (jāmz′ toun) First permanent English colony in North America, founded in 1607; located in eastern Virginia; 37°N, 77°W. (m. 156, t. 159)

K

Kansas Territory (kan′ zəs ter′ ə tôr′ē) Territory created in 1854 by the Kansas-Nebraska Act; became the state of Kansas. (m. 476, 479; t. 479)

L

Lake Champlain (lāk sham plān′) Lake between New York and Vermont. (m. 305, t. 305)

Lake Erie (lāk ir′ ē) Most southern of the Great Lakes, bordering the United States and Canada. (m. 29)

Lake Huron (lāk hyur′ ən) Second largest of the Great Lakes, bordering the United States and Canada. (m. 29)

Lake Michigan (lāk mish′ ə gən) Third largest of the Great Lakes, only one completely in the United States. (m. 27)

Lake Ontario (lāk on tär′ē ō) Smallest of the Great Lakes, bordering the United States and Canada. (m. 29)

Lake Superior (lāk sə pir′ ē ər) Largest of the Great Lakes, bordering the United States and Canada. (m. 29)

Lake Texcoco (lāk tes kō′ kō) Lake that was the site of the ancient Aztec city of Tenochtitlan in Mexico. (t. 68)

Pronunciation Key		
a in hat	ō in open	sh in she
ā in age	ȯ in all	th in thin
â in care	ô in order	ᴛʜ in then
ä in far	oi in oil	zh in measure
e in let	ou in out	ə = a in about
ē in equal	u in cup	ə = e in taken
ėr in term	u̇ in put	ə = i in pencil
i in it	ü in rule	ə = o in lemon
ī in ice	ch in child	ə = u in circus
o in hot	ng in long	

Gazetteer

Lame Deer (lām dir) City in Montana where an annual Northern Cheyenne Powwow is held; 46°N, 107°W. (m. 82, t. 85)

Lexington (lek′ sing tən) Town in eastern Massachusetts, site of the first battle of the American Revolution in 1775; 42°N, 71°W. (m. 286, t. 287)

Lima (lē′ mə) Capital of Peru, founded by Spanish conquistador Francisco Pizarro; 12°S, 77°W. (m. 142, t. 145)

Los Angeles (lòs an′jə ləs) Largest city in California, located in southern part of the state; 34°N, 118°W. (m. 26)

Louisiana (lů ē′ zē an′ ə) State in the southeastern United States, originally the name given to the entire Mississippi Valley. (m. 240–242, t. 242)

Louisiana Territory (lů ē′ zē an′ ə ter′ə tôr′ ē) The land included in the Louisiana Purchase in 1803 soon became called the Louisiana Territory. (m. 370, t. 374)

Lowell (lō′ əl) City in northeastern Massachusetts; 42°N, 71°W. (m. 408, t. 408–409)

★ **M** ★

Mali (mä′ lē) Kingdom in Africa in the early 1300s; present-day country in West Africa. (m. 106, t. 108)

Manassas Junction (mə nas′əs jungk′shən) Town in Virginia near a major Civil War battle in the 1860s; 39°N, 78°W. (m. 492, t. 495)

Maryland (mer′ ə lənd) Colony founded by Lord Baltimore, a Catholic, in 1632. Baltimore declared that his colony would be a safe place for Catholics. Maryland was also a proprietary colony, meaning that its land was controlled by landowners. (m. 177, t. 180)

Massachusetts Bay Colony (mas′ ə chü′ sits bā kol′ ə nē) Colony founded by the Puritans in New England in 1630. (m. 168, t. 172)

Mecca (mek′ə) City in Saudi Arabia, pilgrimage site for Muslims; 22°N, 40°E. (m. 106, t. 108)

Mesa Verde (mā′ sə ver′ dē) Anasazi community located in present-day Colorado; 37°N, 108°W. (m. 60, 62; t. 62)

Mexico (mek′sə kō) Country in North America, on the southern border of the United States. (m. 430, t. 432)

Mexico City (mek′ sə kō sit′ ē) Capital and largest city of Mexico, built as the capital of New Spain; 19°N, 99°W. (m. 142, t. 144)

Middle Colonies (mid′ l kol′ ə nēz) Region of the 13 Colonies, located between the New England and Southern Colonies. (m. 176, t. 179)

Middle West (mid′ l west) Region of the north-central United States. (m. 27, t. 27)

Mississippi River (mis′ ə sip′ ē riv′ ər) River in the central United States, flowing from Minnesota to the Gulf of Mexico. (m. 27, 240; t. 241)

Missouri (mə zùr′ē) The twenty-third state to join the United States, it was admitted in 1820. (m. 477, t. 477)

Missouri River (mə zùr′ē riv′ ər) Major tributary of the Mississippi River, flowing from Montana to Missouri. (m. 26, t. 374)

Montreal (mon′ trē òl′) Largest city in Canada; 46°N, 74°W. (m. 242)

Mormon Trail (môr′ mən trāl) Route west, named for the Mormons who traveled on it from Nauvoo, Illinois, to Salt Lake City, Utah, in the 1840s. (m. 438, 440; t. 441)

Mount Katahdin (mount kə täd′ən) Mountain in north central Maine. (m. 27, t. 25)

Mount McKinley (mount mə kin′ lē) Highest peak in North America, located in Alaska's Denali National Park. (m. 34, t. 37)

Mount St. Helens (mount sānt hel′ ənz) Active volcano in the Cascade Range in southwestern Washington. (m. 26, t. 25)

Mount Whitney (mount hwit′ nē) Highest mountain in the contiguous states, located in southeastern California. (m. R14–15)

 **N**

National Road (nash′ə nəl rōd) Road built in the early 1800s; extended from Cumberland, Maryland, to St. Louis, Missouri. (m. 412, t. 411)

Nebraska Territory (nə bras′ kə ter′ ə tôr′ē) Territory created in 1854 as a result of the Kansas-Nebraska Act. (m. 479, t. 479)

New Amsterdam (nü am′ stər dam) Settlement founded by the Dutch on Manhattan Island; became present-day New York City. (m. 164, 166; t. 165)

New England (nü ing′ glənd) Name given by John Smith to the northeastern region of North America; present-day name for part of the Northeast region of the United States. (m. 27, t. 27)

New England Colonies (nü ing′ glənd kol′ ə nēz) Region of the 13 Colonies that was located north of the Middle Colonies. (m. 176–177, t. 177–178)

New France (nü frans) Name given to the French colonies in North America, including large parts of present-day Canada and the United States. (m. 164, 166; t. 165)

New Haven (nü hā′ vən) City in southern Connecticut, site of the trial of Africans who took control of the Spanish slave ship *Amistad;* 41°N, 72°W. (m. 470, t. 472)

New Mexico (nü mek′ sə kō) State in the southwestern United States, originally the name given by the Spanish to what is now the entire Southwest region of the United States. (m. 234, t. 234)

Pronunciation Key

a in hat	ō in open	sh in she
ā in age	ò in all	th in thin
â in care	ô in order	ᴛʜ in then
ä in far	oi in oil	zh in measure
e in let	ou in out	ə = a in about
ē in equal	u in cup	ə = e in taken
ėr in term	ù in put	ə = i in pencil
i in it	ü in rule	ə = o in lemon
ī in ice	ch in child	ə = u in circus
o in hot	ng in long	

Gazetteer

New Netherland (nü neⱧ′ ər lənd) Dutch colony in North America, included parts of present-day New York, New Jersey, and Connecticut. (m. 164, 166; t. 165)

New Orleans (nü ôr′ lē ənz) Port city in Louisiana, largest city in the state; 29°N, 90°W. (m. 240, t. 243)

New Spain (nü spān) Colony established mostly in North America by Spain in 1535, included parts of what are today the United States, Mexico, Central America, and the West Indies. (m. 142, t. 144)

New Sweden (nü swēd′n) Swedish colony in North America, along the Delaware River. (m. 166)

New York City (nü yôrk sit′ ē) Largest city in the United States, located in southeastern New York; 40°N, 73°W. (m. 268, t. 270)

Newport (nü pôrt) City in southern Rhode Island; 41°N, 71°W. (m. 216, t. 218)

North America (nôrth ə mer′ ə kə) One of Earth's seven continents. (m. R8, R9, H8)

North Pole (nôrth pōl) Northernmost point on Earth; 90°N. (m. H9, t. H9)

Northeast (nôrth′ ēst′) Region in the northeastern United States. (m. 27, t. 27)

Northern Hemisphere (nôr′ ⱧHərn hem′ə sfir) Half the Earth north of the Equator. (m. H9)

Northwest Coast cultural region (nôrth′ west′ kōst kul′ chər əl rē′ jən) Area in northwestern North America that was home to many Native Americans such as the Kwakiutl, Tlingit, and Nootka. (m. 94–95, t. 95)

Northwest Territory (nôrth′ west′ ter′ ə tôr′ ē) Part of the lands that became part of the United States after the American Revolution. (m. 338, 342; t. 342)

Ohio River (ō hī′ ō riv′ ər) River in the east-central United States, which flows from Pittsburgh, Pennsylvania, to the Mississippi River at Cairo, Illinois. (m. 27, t. 248)

Ohio River Valley (ō hī′ ō riv′ ər val′ ē) Region of fertile land along the Ohio River. (m. 246, t. 247)

Oraibi (ôr ī′bē) Hopi village built about 1050, probably the oldest town in the United States; 36°N, 111°W. (m. 88, t. 91)

Oregon Country (ôr′ ə gən kun′ trē) Former region that makes up the present-day northwestern United States. (m. 438, t. 439)

Oregon Trail (ôr′ ə gən trāl) Route west used by the pioneers that extended from Independence, Missouri, to Oregon. (m. 438, t. 439)

Pacific Ocean (pə sif′ ik ō′ shən) Largest of Earth's four oceans. (m. R4–5)

Peru (pə rü′) Country in western South America; founded as a Spanish colony in the 1500s. (m. R6; t. 145)

Philadelphia (fil′ə del′ fē ə) City in southeastern Pennsylvania, was the capital of the United States from 1790 to 1800; 39°N, 75°W. (m. 210, t. 211)

Plymouth (plim′əth) Town in southeastern Massachusetts, founded by the Pilgrims in 1620; 42°N, 71°W. (m. 168, t. 170)

Portugal (pôr′chə gəl) Country in southwestern Europe. (m. 110, t. 113)

Providence (prov′ə dəns) Capital and largest city of Rhode Island; 41°N, 71°W. (m. R12–13, t. 178)

Quebec (kwi bek′) Capital of the Canadian province of Quebec, the first French colony in the Americas; 46°N, 71°W. (m. 164, t. 165)

Richmond (rich′mənd) Capital of Virginia, was capital of the Confederacy during the Civil War; 37°N, 77°W. (m. 492, t. 495)

Rio Grande (rē′ō grand′) River in southwestern North America, flowing from Colorado into the Gulf of Mexico; forms part of the border between the United States and Mexico. (m. 62)

Roanoke Island (rō′ə nōk ī′lənd) Island off the coast of North Carolina, site of England's first attempt at a permanent settlement in the Americas, known as the "Lost Colony." (m. 156, t. 157)

Rocky Mountains (rok′ē moun′tənz) High, rugged chain of mountains in western North America, extending from Alaska to Mexico. (m. 26)

Sahara (sə hâr′ə) Largest desert in the world, located in North Africa. (m. 106–107, t. 107)

Salt Lake City (sȯlt lāk sit′ē) Capital and largest city of Utah; 40°N, 111°W. (m. 438, 440; t. 441)

San Antonio (san an tō′nē ō) City in south central Texas, site of the Alamo; 29°N, 98°W. (m. 430, t. 432)

San Diego (san dē ā′gō) Port city in southern California; 32°N, 117°W. (m. R12–13)

San Francisco (san frən sis′kō) City in northern California; 37°N, 122°W. (m. 442, t. 443)

Santa Fe (san′tə fā) Capital of New Mexico; 35°N, 105°W. (m. 232, t. 234)

Pronunciation Key

a in hat	ō in open	sh in she
ā in age	ȯ in all	th in thin
â in care	ô in order	ᴛʜ in then
ä in far	oi in oil	zh in measure
e in let	ou in out	ə = a in about
ē in equal	u in cup	ə = e in taken
ėr in term	ù in put	ə = i in pencil
i in it	ü in rule	ə = o in lemon
ī in ice	ch in child	ə = u in circus
o in hot	ng in long	

Gazetteer

Saratoga (sär′ə tō′gə) Village in northeastern New York, site of a major Patriot victory in 1777 during the American Revolution; 43°N, 74°W. (m. 302, t. 305)

Savannah (sə van′ə) Port city on the coast of Georgia; 32°N, 81°W. (m. 314, t. 316)

Scandinavia (skan′də nā′vē ə) Region of northern Europe, includes the countries of Norway, Sweden, and Denmark. (t. 111)

Seneca Falls (sen′ə kə fôlz) Town in west central New York, site of the first women's rights convention in the United States, 1848; 43°N, 77°W. (m. 416, t. 419)

Shangdu (shang dü′) Town in China; 42°N, 114°E. (m. 102, t. 103)

Sierra Nevada (sē er′ə nə vad′ə) Mountain range in eastern California. (m. 33)

Silk Road (silk rōd) Network of overland trade routes between China and Europe. (m. 102–103, t. 103)

Songhai (song gī′) Kingdom in Africa that flourished from the middle 1300s through the 1500s. (m. 106, t. 108)

South America (south ə mer′ə kə) One of Earth's seven continents. (m. R4, t. 145)

South Pole (south pōl) Southernmost point on Earth; 90°S. (m. H 9, t. H 9)

Southampton County (south amp′tən koun′tē) County in southeastern Virginia, location of Nat Turner's slave revolt in 1831. (m. 470, t. 472)

Southeast (south′ ēst′) Region in the southeastern United States. (m. 27, t. 27)

Southern Colonies (suᴛн′ərn kol′ə nēz) Southernmost region of the 13 Colonies. (m. 176, t. 179–180)

Southern Hemisphere (suᴛн′ərn hem′ə sfir) Half the Earth south of the Equator. (m. H9, t. H9)

Southwest (south′west′) Region in the southwestern United States. (m. 26, t. 26)

Southwest Desert cultural region (south′west′ dez′ərt kul′chər əl rē′jən) Area in southwestern North America that was home to many Native Americans such as the Hopi, Zuni, and Pima. (m. 88–89, t. 89)

Spain (spān) Country in southwestern Europe. (m. 141, t. 135)

Springfield (spring′fēld) City in southwestern Massachusetts, site of Shays' Rebellion. (m. 338, t. 341)

St. Augustine (sānt ò′ gə stēn) City on the northeast coast of Florida, founded by the Spanish in 1565; was the first permanent European settlement in the United States; 29°N, 81°W. (m. 232, t. 233)

St. Lawrence River (sānt lôr′əns riv′ər) River in northeastern North America, forms part of the border between the United States and Canada. (m. 164, t. 165)

St. Louis (sānt lü′is) Port city in east central Missouri, was known as the "Gateway to the West"; 38°N, 90°W. (m. 370, t. 374)

Strait of Magellan (strāt əv mə jel′ən) Narrow waterway between the southern tip of South America and Tierra del Fuego, links the Atlantic and Pacific Oceans. (m. 137)

Tenochtitlan (tā nòch′tē tlän′) Capital of the Aztec Empire in the Valley of Mexico, on the site of present-day Mexico City; 19°N, 99°W. (m. 66, 68; t. 68)

Texas (tek′səs) State in the southwestern United States, part of Mexico until 1836. (m. 430, t. 431)

Timbuktu (tim′ buk tü′) Town in West African kingdom of Mali, was one of the important stops along the caravan routes; 17°N, 3°E. (m. 106, 107)

Trenton (trent′n) Capital of New Jersey, site of an important battle in the American Revolution in 1776; 40°N, 74°W. (m. 302, t. 304)

Valley Forge (val′ē fôrj) Site in southeastern Pennsylvania where George Washington and the Continental Army camped during the winter of 1777 to 1778; 40°N, 75°W. (m. 302, t. 308)

Valley of Mexico (val′ē əv mek′sə kō) Region in central Mexico, location of the Aztec city of Tenochtitlan. (t. 68)

Vancouver Island (van kü′vər ī′lənd) Island off the southwest coast of Canada. (m. 94, t. 95)

Venice (ven′is) Port city in northeastern Italy, built on 118 small islands in a lagoon in the Gulf of Venice; 45°N, 12°E. (m. 102–103, t. 103)

Vicksburg (viks′bərg) City in western Mississippi on the Mississippi River, site of a major Union victory during the Civil War in 1863; 32°N, 90°W. (m. 509, t. 509)

Vinland (vin′land) Name meaning "Land of Wine," given by Leif Ericsson to the present-day Canadian province of Newfoundland. (m. 110, t. 111)

Washington, D.C. (wäsh′ing tən dē cē) Capital of the United States; 38°N, 77°W. (m. 362, t. 365)

West (west) Region in the western United States. (m. 26, t. 26)

West Africa (west af′rə kə) Western region of Africa. (m. 202, 206; t. 206)

West Indies (west in′dēz) Islands between the Atlantic Ocean and the Caribbean Sea, extending from Florida in North America to Venezuela in South America. (m. 134, t. 135)

Pronunciation Key

a in hat	ō in open	sh in she
ā in age	ò in all	th in thin
â in care	ô in order	ᴛʜ in then
ä in far	oi in oil	zh in measure
e in let	ou in out	ə = a in about
ē in equal	u in cup	ə = e in taken
ėr in term	ù in put	ə = i in pencil
i in it	ü in rule	ə = o in lemon
ī in ice	ch in child	ə = u in circus
o in hot	ng in long	

Gazetteer

Western Hemisphere (west'ərn hem' ə sfir) Half of Earth west of the prime meridian; includes South America and North America. (m. H10, R6–R7; t. H10)

Wilderness Road (wil'dər nis rōd) Trail used by pioneers through the Appalachian Mountains from Virginia to Kentucky, established by Daniel Boone in 1775. (m. 370, t. 372)

Williamsburg (wil'yəmz bėrg) City in southeastern Virginia, capital of the colony of Virginia from 1699 to 1779; 37°N, 77°W. (m. 216, t. 217)

Yellowstone National Park (yel'ə stōn nash'ə nəl pärk) First national park in the United States, established in Wyoming in 1872. (m. 34, t. 37)

Yorktown (yôrk'toun) Town in southeastern Virginia near Chesapeake Bay, site of the last major battle of the American Revolution; 37°N, 76°W. (m. 317, t. 318)

Biographical Dictionary

This Biographical Dictionary tells you about the people in this book and how to pronounce their names. The page numbers tell you where the person first appears in the text.

A

Adams, Abigail (ad′əmz) 1744–1818 Writer and wife of President John Adams, she was the first First Lady to live in what later became known as the White House. (p. 366)

Adams, John (ad′əmz) 1735–1826 Patriot leader during the American Revolution and second President of the United States. (p. 277)

Adams, Samuel (ad′əmz) 1722–1803 Boston Patriot and organizer of the Sons of Liberty. (p. 270)

Allen, Ethan (al′ən) 1738–1789 Leader of the Green Mountain Boys, Vermont soldiers who captured Fort Ticonderoga in May, 1775. (p. 303)

Armistead, James (är′mə sted) 1759?–1830 African American Patriot who spied for the Americans during the American Revolution. (p. 306)

Arnold, Benedict (är′nəld) 1741–1801 Successful American general during the Revolution who turned traitor in 1780 and joined the British cause. (p. 305)

Atahualpa (ä′tə wäl′pə) 1502?–1533 Ruler of the Incas when the empire was invaded by the Spanish in 1531. (p. 145)

Attucks, Crispus (at′əks) 1723?–1770 African American Patriot and former slave who was killed in the Boston Massacre in 1770. (p. 277)

Austin, Stephen F. (ȯ′stən) 1793–1836 Pioneer who founded the first settlement for people from the United States in Texas in the 1820s. (p. 432)

B

Balboa, Vasco Núñez de (bal bō′ə, väs′kō nü′nyes dē) 1475?–1519 Spanish explorer who was the first European to reach the eastern shore of the Pacific Ocean. (p. 137)

Banneker, Benjamin (ban′ə kər) 1731–1806 Astronomer, inventor, mathematician, and son of a freed slave, he surveyed the land on which Washington, D.C., was built. (p. 365)

Barton, Clara (bärt′ən) 1821–1912 Civil War nurse and founder of the American Red Cross. (p. 502)

Boone, Daniel (bün) 1734–1820 American pioneer who led many early settlers to lands west of the Appalachian Mountains. (p. 372)

Boyd, Belle (boid) 1844–1900 Confederate spy during the Civil War. (p. 502)

Pronunciation Key

a in hat	ō in open	sh in she
ā in age	ȯ in all	th in thin
â in care	ô in order	ŦH in then
ä in far	oi in oil	zh in measure
e in let	ou in out	ə = a in about
ē in equal	u in cup	ə = e in taken
ėr in term	u̇ in put	ə = i in pencil
i in it	ü in rule	ə = o in lemon
ī in ice	ch in child	ə = u in circus
o in hot	ng in long	

Biographical Dictionary

Bradford, William (brad′fərd) 1590–1657 Leader of the Pilgrims who came to North America on the *Mayflower* and founded Plymouth colony in 1620. (p. 169)

Brady, Mathew (brā′dē) 1823?–1896 Civil War photographer. (p. 499)

Brown, John (broun) 1800–1859 Abolitionist who believed in the use of force to oppose slavery. He was hanged for leading a raid on Harpers Ferry, Virginia, in 1859. (p. 480)

Bruce, Blanche K. (brüs) 1841–1898 Former slave elected to United States Senate in 1874. (p. 518)

Burgoyne, John (bər goin′) 1722–1792 British general defeated by American forces at the Battle of Saratoga in 1777. (p. 305)

Bush, George H. (bùsh) 1924– Forty-first President of the United States, 1989–1993. (p. R25)

Bush, George W. (bùsh) 1946– Became forty-third President of the United States in 2001; son of President George H. Bush. (p. R25)

Cabeza de Vaca, Álvar Núñez (kä bā′sä de vä′kä) about 1490–1557 Spanish explorer who explored what is now Texas in 1528. (p. 147)

Calhoun, John C. (kal hün′) 1782–1850 United States senator from South Carolina who believed in states' rights. (p. 477)

Carney, William (kär′nē) 1840–1908 A hero of the Civil War battle at Fort Wagner in 1863; one of sixteen African Americans to win the Congressional Medal of Honor for heroism in the Civil War. (p. 501)

Carter, Jimmy (kär′tər) 1924– Thirty-ninth President of the United States, 1977–1981. (p. R24)

Carver, George Washington (kär′vər) 1861–1943 Scientist who discovered hundreds of new uses for peanuts, sweet potatoes, and other crops. (p. 28)

Champlain, Samuel de (sham plän′) 1567–1635 French explorer who founded Quebec, the first permanent French settlement in North America. (p. 165)

Cinque, Joseph (sin′kā) 1813?–1879? West African captive who led the 1839 slave revolt on the Spanish slave ship *Amistad*. (p. 472)

Clark, George Rogers (klärk) 1752–1818 Leader of a small Patriot force that captured British-controlled Fort Vincennes in the Ohio Valley in 1779. (p. 316)

Clark, William (klärk) 1770–1838 Shared command of the Lewis and Clark expedition with Meriwether Lewis. (p. 374)

Clay, Henry (klā) 1777–1852 United States senator who was nicknamed "The Great Compromiser" for helping to work out important compromises such as the Missouri Compromise in 1820 and the Compromise of 1850. (p. 382)

Clinton, Bill (klin′tən) 1946– Forty-second President of the United States, 1993–2001. (p. R25)

Coffin, Catherine (ko′fin) 1803–1881 Conductor on the Underground Railroad, she helped more than 2,000 people escape from slavery to freedom. (p. 473)

Coffin, Levi (ko′fin) 1798–1877 Conductor on the Underground Railroad; married to Catherine Coffin. (p. 473)

Columbus, Christopher (kə lum′bəs) 1451?–1506 Italian-born explorer who sailed to the Americas in 1492. He was the first European to establish lasting contact between Europe and the Americas. (p. 135)

Cooper, Peter (kü′pər) 1791–1883 Inventor of a steam-powered train, the *Tom Thumb,* in 1830. (p. 412)

Cornwallis, Charles (kôrn wä′lis) 1738–1805 Commanding general of the British forces that were defeated at Yorktown in 1781, ending the American Revolution. (p. 318)

Coronado, Francisco Vásquez de (kôr′ə nä′dō, frän sēs′kō väs′kes dä) 1510–1554 Spanish explorer of the American Southwest; searched for Cíbola, the legendary kingdom of gold. (p. 147)

Cortés, Hernando (kôr tez′) 1485–1547 Spanish conqueror of the Aztec empire. (p. 143)

Crockett, David (krok′it) 1786–1836 Frontiersman and member of Congress from Tennessee who died defending the Alamo. (p. 432)

da Gama, Vasco (də gä′mə, väs′kō) 1469?–1524 Portuguese explorer who sailed to India in 1497. (p. 114)

Davis, Jefferson (dā′vis) 1808–1889 President of the Confederacy during the Civil War and former United States senator from Mississippi. (p. 485)

Dawes, William (dȯz) 1744–1799 Patriot who rode with Paul Revere on the night of April 18, 1775, to warn colonists that British troops were coming. (p. 287)

Deere, John (dir) 1804–1886 Blacksmith who invented the steel plow. (p. 410)

Deganawidah (dā gän ə wē′də) 1500s Iroquois leader who told warring Iroquois groups to stop fighting. (p. 77)

De Soto, Hernando (di sō′tō) 1500?–1542 Spanish explorer who became the first European to reach the Mississippi River in 1541. (p. 147)

Dias, Bartolomeu (dē′əs) 1450?–1500 Portuguese explorer who sailed around the Cape of Good Hope, the southwestern tip of Africa. (p. 114)

Douglas, Marjory Stoneman (dug′ləs) 1890–1998 Writer who dedicated many years of her life to protecting the Everglades. (p. 37)

Douglas, Stephen (dug′ləs) 1813–1861 United States senator from Illinois who was defeated for the presidency by Abraham Lincoln in 1860. (p. 479)

Douglass, Frederick (dug′ləs) 1817–1895 Former slave who was a writer, editor, and leading abolitionist. (p. 418)

Pronunciation Key

a	in hat	ō	in open	sh	in she
ā	in age	ȯ	in all	th	in thin
â	in care	ô	in order	ᴛʜ	in then
ä	in far	oi	in oil	zh	in measure
e	in let	ou	in out	ə	= a in about
ē	in equal	u	in cup	ə	= e in taken
ėr	in term	u̇	in put	ə	= i in pencil
i	in it	ü	in rule	ə	= o in lemon
ī	in ice	ch	in child	ə	= u in circus
o	in hot	ng	in long		

Biographical Dictionary

Drake, Francis (drāk) 1540?–1596 First English sea captain to sail around the world in 1577. (p. 158)

Edison, Thomas (ed′ə sən) 1847–1931 Inventor whose many inventions included the light bulb and the phonograph. (p. 21)

Eisenhower, Dwight D. (ī′zn hou′ər) 1890–1969 Thirty-fourth President of the United States, 1953–1961. Commander of Allied forces in Europe during World War II. (p. R25)

Elizabeth I (i liz′ə bəth) 1533–1603 Queen of England during the English defeat of the Spanish Armada and the founding of Roanoke, England's first colony in the Americas. (p. 157)

Equiano, Olaudah (i kwē ä′nō) 1750–1797 African who was enslaved and brought to North America in 1756. He later wrote a book about the journey from West Africa to the colonies. (p. 227)

Eric the Red (âr′ik) 900s Viking explorer who sailed to Iceland in about 965 and Greenland in about 982. (p. 111)

Ericsson, Leif (âr′ik sən, lēf) late 900s–early 1000s Son of Eric the Red; sailed to North America in about 1000 and explored what is today known as Newfoundland. (p. 111)

Estéban (es te′bän) 1500s African sailor who traveled throughout the Southwest region of the United States. His stories led to the search for Cíbola. (p. 147)

Ferdinand (fėr′də nand) 1452–1516 King of Spain who agreed to finance Christopher Columbus's expedition to the Americas in 1492. (p. 135)

Ford, Gerald (fôrd) 1913– Thirty-eighth President of the United States, 1974–1977, took over as President when Richard Nixon resigned in 1974. (p. R24)

Franklin, Benjamin (frang′klən) 1706–1790 Writer, scientist, inventor, and diplomat. He helped write the Declaration of Independence and the Constitution. (pp. 211, 221)

Fulton, Robert (fŭlt′n) 1765–1815 Engineer who built the first successful steamboat, the *Clermont,* in 1807. (p. 411)

Gage, Thomas (gāj) 1721–1787 British general who controlled Boston following the Boston Tea Party. (p. 280)

Gálvez, Bernardo de (gal′vəz) 1746–1786 Governor of Spanish Louisiana and ally of the Patriots, he led Spanish troops against the British during the American Revolution. (p. 315)

Garrison, William Lloyd (gâr′ə sən) 1805–1879 Journalist and reformer, founder of the anti-slavery newspaper *The Liberator.* (p. 418)

George III (jôrj) 1738–1820 King of Britain during the time of the American Revolution. (p. 251)

Grant, Ulysses S. (grant) 1822–1885 Eighteenth President of the United States, 1869–1877. Commander of Union forces in the Civil War. (p. 509)

Greene, Nathanael (grēn) 1742–1786 Patriot general during the American Revolution. (p. 318)

Gutenberg, Johann (güt′n bėrg) 1395?–1468 German inventor of the printing press about 1450. (p. 112)

H

Hale, Nathan (hāl) 1755–1776 Patriot hanged as a spy by the British in 1776. (p. 304)

Hall, Prince (hȯl) 1745?–1807 Minister who fought in the Continental Army and became an early leader in the struggle to end slavery in the United States. (p. 306)

Hamilton, Alexander (ham′əl tən) 1755?–1804 Delegate to the Constitutional Convention and leader of the Federalists; first secretary of the treasury. (p. 345)

Hancock, John (han′kok) 1737–1793 Patriot leader and president of the Second Continental Congress; first person to sign the Declaration of Independence. (p. 287)

Hays, Mary Ludwig (hāz) 1744–1832 Patriot known for her brave service on the battlefield; nicknamed "Molly Pitcher." (p. 307)

Hendrick (hen′drik) 1680?–1755? Iroquois leader during the French and Indian War. (p. 249)

Henry, Patrick (hen′rē) 1736–1799 Virginia Patriot and lawyer known for his bold speeches in support of American independence. (p. 270)

Henry, Prince (hen′rē) 1394–1460 Prince of Portugal who established a school for sailors and navigators. (p. 113)

Hiawatha (hī′ə wäth′ə) 1500s Helped found the Iroquois League in the late 1500s. (p. 77)

Hooker, Thomas (hu̇k′ər) 1586–1647 Puritan minister who founded the colony of Connecticut in 1636. (p. 178)

Houston, Sam (hyü′stən) 1793–1863 Commander of victorious forces during the Texas Revolution; elected first president of the Republic of Texas in 1836. (p. 432)

Hudson, Henry (hud′sən) 1565–1611 English sea captain who explored North America in search of a Northwest Passage in the early 1600s. (p. 165)

Hutchinson, Anne (huch′ən sən) 1591–1643 Puritan leader banished from Massachusetts for her religious views. (p. 178)

I

Isabella (iz′ə bel′ə) 1451–1504 Queen of Spain who agreed to finance Christopher Columbus's expedition to the Americas in 1492. (p. 135)

Pronunciation Key

a in hat	ō in open	sh in she
ā in age	ȯ in all	th in thin
â in care	ô in order	ᴛʜ in then
ä in far	oi in oil	zh in measure
e in let	ou in out	ə = a in about
ē in equal	u in cup	ə = e in taken
ėr in term	u̇ in put	ə = i in pencil
i in it	ü in rule	ə = o in lemon
ī in ice	ch in child	ə = u in circus
o in hot	ng in long	

Biographical Dictionary

J

Jackson, Andrew (jak′sən) 1767–1845 Seventh President of the United States, 1829–1837. Army general who led American troops to victory at the Battle of New Orleans during the War of 1812. (p. 384)

Jackson, Thomas "Stonewall" (jak′sən) 1824–1863 Confederate general who helped the Confederates win several early victories in the Civil War. (p. 495)

James I (jāmz) 1566–1625 King of England who, in 1606, gave the Virginia Company of London a charter to set up a colony in Virginia. (p. 159)

Jefferson, Thomas (jef′ər sən) 1743–1826 Third President of the United States, 1801–1809. Member of the Continental Congress and main writer of the Declaration of Independence. (p. 298)

Johnson, Andrew (jon′sən) 1808–1875 Seventeenth President of the United States, 1865–1869. Took office following Abraham Lincoln's assassination. (p. 517)

Johnson, Lyndon B. (jon′sən) 1908–1973 Thirty-sixth President of the United States, 1963–1969. Took office after President John Kennedy was assassinated. (p. R24)

Jolliet, Louis (jō′lē et) 1645–1700 French fur trader and explorer who accompanied Jacques Marquette on an exploration of the Mississippi River in 1673. (p. 241)

Jones, John Paul (jōnz) 1747–1792 Patriot naval leader who commanded the American ship *Bonhomme Richard,* which defeated the British ship *Serapis* in 1779. (p. 316)

K

Kennedy, John F. (ken′ə dē) 1917–1963 Thirty-fifth President of the United States, 1961–1963; youngest person and first Catholic elected President. (p. 16)

Key, Francis Scott (kē) 1779–1843 Writer of the poem "The Star-Spangled Banner" during the War of 1812. This poem later became the national anthem of the United States. (p. 383)

Knox, Henry (noks) 1750–1806 Continental army leader who brought captured British cannons from Fort Ticonderoga to Boston in 1775. (p. 303)

Kosciusko, Thaddeus (kos ē üs′kō) 1746–1817 Polish engineer who served in the Continental Army; designed a fort near Saratoga, where Americans won a key victory. (p. 305)

Kublai Khan (kü′blī kän′) 1216–1294 Emperor of China who met with Marco Polo in the late 1200s. (p. 103)

L

Lafayette, Marquis de (lä fē et′, mar kē′ də) 1757–1834 French soldier who joined General Washington's staff and became a general in the Continental Army. (p. 315)

La Salle, Robert (lə sal′) 1643–1687 French explorer who explored the Mississippi River in 1681 and 1682. He claimed the entire Mississippi River valley for France, naming this territory Louisiana. (p. 242)

Las Casas, Bartolomé de (läs kä′säs) 1474–1566 Spanish priest who spoke out against the mistreatment of Indians in New Spain. (p. 149)

Lee, Richard Henry (lē) 1732–1794 Member of the Second Continental Congress who urged Congress to support independence; signer of the Declaration of Independence. (p. 298)

Lee, Robert E. (lē) 1807–1870 Commander of the Confederate forces in the Civil War. (p. 495)

L'Enfant, Pierre (län fän′) 1754–1825 French artist and engineer who designed Washington, D.C. (p. 365)

Lewis, Meriwether (lü′is) 1774–1809 Army captain appointed by Thomas Jefferson to lead the Lewis and Clark expedition to explore the lands gained in the Louisiana Purchase. (p. 374)

Lincoln, Abraham (ling′kən) 1809–1865 Sixteenth President of the United States, 1861–1865, who led the United States during the Civil War. (p. 16)

Lowell, Francis Cabot (lō′əl) 1775–1817 Boston merchant who built the first textile mill in the United States. (p. 409)

★ **M** ★

Madison, Dolley (mad′ə sən) 1768–1849 Wife of President James Madison, she rescued a famous portrait of George Washington from the White House when the British invaded Washington, D.C., during the War of 1812. (p. 383)

Madison, James (mad′ə sən) 1751–1839 Fourth President of United States, 1809–1817. One of the main authors of the Constitution. (p. 345)

Magellan, Ferdinand (mə jel′ən) 1480?–1521 Portuguese explorer who led the first expedition around the world. (p. 137)

Mansa Musa (män′sä mü′sä) 1312?–1337 King of the African kingdom of Mali in the early 1300s. (p. 108)

Marina, Doña (mə rē nə) 1501–1550 Aztec woman who became an interpreter for Hernando Cortés during his conquest of the Aztec empire. (p. 143)

Marion, Francis (mâr′ē ən) 1732–1795 South Carolina militia leader nicknamed the "Swamp Fox" for his hit-and-run attacks on the British during the American Revolution. (p. 316)

Marquette, Jacques (mär ket′, zhäk) 1637–1675 French missionary who explored the Mississippi River with Louis Jolliet in 1673. (p. 241)

Marshall, James (mär′shəl) 1810–1885 Discovered gold in California in 1848, leading to the Gold Rush. (p. 443)

Marshall, John (mär′shəl) 1755–1835 Chief Justice of the Supreme Court from 1831 to 1835. (p. 405)

Massasoit (mas′ə soit) 1580?–1661 Leader of the Wampanoag who signed a peace treaty with the Pilgrims at Plymouth. (p. 171)

Pronunciation Key

a	in hat	ō	in open	sh	in she
ā	in age	ȯ	in all	th	in thin
â	in care	ô	in order	ᴛʜ	in then
ä	in far	oi	in oil	zh	in measure
e	in let	ou	in out	ə	= a in about
ē	in equal	u	in cup	ə	= e in taken
ėr	in term	u̇	in put	ə	= i in pencil
i	in it	ü	in rule	ə	= o in lemon
ī	in ice	ch	in child	ə	= u in circus
o	in hot	ng	in long		

Biographical Dictionary

McCormick, Cyrus (mə kôr′mik) 1809–1884 Inventor of a mechanical reaper in 1831. (p. 410)

Menendez de Avilés, Pedro (me nen′dez dā ä vē′läs) 1519–1574 Commander of the Spanish fleet that defeated the French and took control of Florida, claiming it for New Spain in 1565. (p. 233)

Metacom (met ə käm′) 1640–1676 Massasoit chief called "King Philip" by the English. Led several Native American groups against the British during King Philip's War in the 1670s. (p. 247)

Moctezuma (mäk tə zü′mə) 1480–1520 Leader of the Aztecs when Hernando Cortés conquered the Aztec empire. (p. 143)

Monroe, James (mən rō′) 1758–1831 Fifth President of the United States, 1817–1825. (p. 373)

Mott, Lucretia (mot, lü krē′shə) 1793–1880 American abolitionist and supporter of women's rights. (p. 419)

Nampeyo (nam pā′yō) 1860?–1942 Pueblo woman who worked to re-create the Anasazi way of making pottery. (p. 65)

Nixon, Richard (nik′sən) 1913–1994 Thirty-seventh President of the United States, 1969–1974. First President to resign from office. (p. R24)

Oglethorpe, James (ō′gəl thôrp) 1696–1785 English leader who founded the colony of Georgia as a place where debtors from England could begin new lives. (p. 180)

Oñate, Don Juan de (ō nyä′te) 1550?–1630 Spanish leader who claimed the Southwest region of what is now the United States for the Spanish in 1598. (p. 234)

Osceola (os′ ē ō′ lə) 1803?–1838 Leader of the Seminole in Florida. (p. 431)

Paine, Thomas (pān) 1737–1809 Patriot and writer whose pamphlet *Common Sense,* published in 1776, convinced many Americans that it was time to declare independence from Britain. (p. 298)

Parker, John (pär′kər) 1729–1775 Captain of the Lexington minutemen; leader at the Battle of Lexington in April 1775, where the first shots of the American Revolution were fired. (p. 288)

Penn, William (pen) 1644–1718 Quaker who founded the colony of Pennsylvania in 1681. (p. 179)

Perry, Oliver Hazard (per′ē) 1785–1819 Commander of United States naval fleet that defeated the British in the Battle of Lake Erie during the War of 1812. (p. 382)

Pinckney, Eliza Lucas (pingk′nē) 1722–1793 South Carolina plantation owner who became the first person in the colonies to successfully raise a crop of indigo. (p. 213)

Pizarro, Francisco (pi zär′ō) 1478?–1541 Spanish conquistador who defeated the Inca empire in 1533. (p. 145)

Pocahontas (pō′ kə hon′təs) 1595?–1617 Daughter of Chief Powhatan, she helped establish a time of peace between the Powhatan and the English colonists in Jamestown. (p. 160)

Polk, James K. (pōk) 1795–1849 Eleventh President of the United States, 1845–1849. (p. 433)

Polo, Marco (pō′lō) 1254?–1324? Italian explorer who traveled through China in the late 1200s. (p. 103)

Ponce de Léon, Juan (pons′ də lē′ ən) 1460?–1521 Spanish explorer who reached the Florida peninsula in 1513. (p. 147)

Pontiac (pon′tē ak) 1720–1769 Ottawa leader who led Pontiac's Rebellion, a revolt against the British in 1763. (p. 251)

Popé (pō pā′) Pueblo leader who led the Pueblo Revolt against the Spanish in New Mexico in 1680. (p. 235)

Powhatan (pou′ ə tan′) 1550?–1618 Leader of the Powhatan people and father of Pocahontas. (p. 160)

Prescott, Samuel (pres′kot) 1751–1777 Doctor who helped William Dawes and Paul Revere warn Patriots about the arrival of the British on the night of April 18, 1775. (p. 287)

Prescott, William (pres′kot) 1726–1795 Patriot leader at the Battle of Bunker Hill in 1775. (p. 290)

Revere, Paul (ri vir′) 1735–1818 Patriot express rider and silversmith; rode from Boston to Lexington on the night of April 18, 1775, warning people that British soldiers were coming. (p. 278)

Rolfe, John (rälf) 1585–1622 Jamestown colony leader who showed that tobacco could be grown successfully in Virginia. (p. 161)

Roosevelt, Franklin D. (rō′zə velt) 1882–1945 Thirty-second President of the United States, 1933–1945. (p. R25)

Roosevelt, Theodore (rō′zə velt) 1858–1919 Twenty-sixth President of the United States, 1901–1909. Led the Rough Riders during the Spanish-American War in 1898. (p. 37)

Ross, John (rȯs) 1790–1866 Cherokee leader who argued that it was illegal for the United States to remove the Cherokee from their land. (p. 405)

Rush, Benjamin (rush) 1745?–1813 Patriot and doctor; signer of the Declaration of Independence and strong supporter of the Constitution. (p. 354)

Raleigh, Walter (rȯ′lē) 1552?–1618 English explorer and soldier who explored North America in the 1580s and founded the "Lost Colony" of Roanoke in 1587. (p. 157)

Reagan, Ronald (rā′gən) 1911–   Fortieth President of the United States, 1981–1989. (p. R25)

Revels, Hiram R. (rev′əlz) 1822–1901 First African American elected to the United States senate in 1870. (p. 518)

Pronunciation Key		
a in hat	ō in open	sh in she
ā in age	ȯ in all	th in thin
â in care	ô in order	ᴛʜ in then
ä in far	oi in oil	zh in measure
e in let	ou in out	ə = a in about
ē in equal	u in cup	ə = e in taken
ėr in term	u̇ in put	ə = i in pencil
i in it	ü in rule	ə = o in lemon
ī in ice	ch in child	ə = u in circus
o in hot	ng in long	

Biographical Dictionary

★ S ★

Sacagawea (sak′ ə jə wä′ ə) 1787?–1812 Shoshone woman who acted as guide and translator on the Lewis and Clark expedition. (p. 374)

Salem, Peter (sā′ləm) 1750?–1816 Patriot who fought at the Battle of Bunker Hill and the Battle of Saratoga. (p. 306)

Samoset (sam′ə set) 1590?–1655? Wampanoag man who helped the Pilgrims in 1620. (p. 170)

Sampson, Deborah (samp′sən) 1760–1827 Patriot who disguised herself as a man and served in the Continental Army. (p. 307)

Santa Anna, Antonio López de (sän′tä än′ä) 1795–1876 President of Mexico who led Mexican forces against Texas in the Texas Revolution of 1835–1836. (p. 432)

Scott, Dred (skot) 1795–1858 Enslaved African American who claimed he was free because he had lived in free states. His claim led to a key Supreme Court case. (p. 480)

Scott, Winfield (skot) 1771–1832 Hero of the Mexican War and leading Union general in the Civil War; architect of the Anaconda Plan. (p. 494)

Seguín, Juan (se gēn′) 1806–1889 Tejano leader who fought in the Texas Revolution. (p. 432)

Sequoyah (si kwoi′ə) 1770?–1843 Cherokee leader who developed a written alphabet for the Cherokee language. (p. 405)

Serra, Junípero (ser′rä) 1713–1784 Spanish missionary who founded the first Spanish missions in California. (pp. 236, 237)

Shays, Daniel (shāz) 1747–1825 Revolutionary War veteran and farmer who led Shays' Rebellion in 1786. (p. 341)

Sherman, William Tecumseh (shėr′mən) 1820–1891 Union general in the Civil War whose "March to the Sea" in 1864 helped defeat the Confederacy. (p. 510)

Slater, Samuel (slāt′ər) 1768–1835 Brought plans for cotton-spinning machine to the United States from Britain and started the first cottton-spinning factory in the United States in 1790. (p. 409)

Smith, John (smith) 1580–1631 Leader of the Jamestown Colony. (p. 159)

Smith, Joseph (smith) 1805–1844 Founder of the Mormons in 1830. (p. 441)

Smith, Venture (smith) 1729–1805 African enslaved in New England who purchased his freedom and wrote a book telling the story of his life. (p. 225)

Squanto (skwon′tō) 1590–1622 Pawtuxet Native American who helped English settlers at Plymouth by teaching them key survival skills, such as how to grow corn. (p. 171)

Stanton, Elizabeth Cady (stan′tən) 1815–1902 Women's suffrage leader who helped organize the first women's rights convention in 1848. (p. 419)

Steuben, Friedrich von (stü′bən) 1730–1794 Military officer from Germany who trained American soldiers during the American Revolution. (p. 315)

Stowe, Harriet Beecher (stō) 1811–1896 Author of *Uncle Tom's Cabin,* which exposed the cruelties of slavery to a wide audience before the Civil War. (p. 480)

Strauss, Levi (strous) 1829–1902 Immigrant to San Francisco who manufactured the first denim pants during the California Gold Rush. (p. 444)

Sutter, John (sut′er) 1803–1880 Pioneer on whose land gold was discovered in 1848, leading to the California Gold Rush. (p. 443)

Tecumseh (tə kum′sə) 1768?–1813 Shawnee leader who organized Native Americans in the Northwest Territory to resist pioneer settlement. (p. 381)

Tomochichi (tō mä chē′chē) 1650?–1739 Yamacraw chief who agreed to give James Oglethorpe land to found the new colony of Georgia. (p. 180)

Truman, Harry S. (trü′mən) 1884–1972 Thirty-third President of the United States, 1945–1953. (p. R25)

Truth, Sojourner (trüth) 1797?–1883 Abolitionist and women's rights leader who escaped from slavery in 1827. (p. 421)

Tubman, Harriet (tub′mən) 1820?–1913 Abolitionist who escaped from slavery in 1849 and became a conductor on the Underground Railroad. She led more than 300 slaves to freedom. (p. 473)

Turner, Nat (tėr′nər) 1800–1831 Leader of a slave rebellion in Southampton County, Virginia, in 1831. (p. 472)

Vespucci, Amerigo (ve spü′chē) 1454–1512 Italian navigator who sailed along the eastern coast of South America in 1501. (p. 137)

Walker, David (wȯ′kər) 1785–1830 Abolitionist who urged enslaved people to fight for their freedom. (p. 467)

Walker, Madam C. J. (wȯ′kər) 1867–1919 Entrepreneur who was the first African American woman to become a millionaire. (p. 21)

Warren, Mercy Otis (wôr′ən) 1728–1814 Patriot writer who wrote articles and plays in support of American independence. (p. 272)

Washington, George (wäsh′ing tən) 1732–1799 First President of the United States, 1789–1797. Commander-in-Chief of the Continental Army during the American Revolution and President of the Constitutional Convention. (p. 217)

Pronunciation Key

a in hat	ō in open	sh in she
ā in age	ȯ in all	th in thin
â in care	ô in order	ᴛʜ in then
ä in far	oi in oil	zh in measure
e in let	ou in out	ə = a in about
ē in equal	u in cup	ə = e in taken
ėr in term	u̇ in put	ə = i in pencil
i in it	ü in rule	ə = o in lemon
ī in ice	ch in child	ə = u in circus
o in hot	ng in long	

Biographical Dictionary

Washington, Martha (wäsh′ing tən) 1731–1802 Wife of President George Washington who assisted the Continental Army during the American Revolution. (p. 307)

Webster, Daniel (web′stər) 1782–1852 Senator from Massachusetts and opponent of slavery who supported the Compromise of 1850. (p. 478)

Wheatley, Phillis (hwēt′lē) 1753?–1784 Poet who was the first African American woman to have a book of poetry published. (p. 307)

White, John (hwīt) 1540?–1593 Leader of the English colony of Roanoke in 1587. (p. 157)

Whitefield, George (hwit′fēld) 1714–1770 Minister during the Great Awakening who traveled throughout the American colonies. (p. 218)

Whitman, Marcus (hwit′mən) 1802–1847 Missionary to Native Americans in the Oregon Territory beginning in 1836. (p. 439)

Whitman, Narcissa (hwit′mən) 1808–1847 Missionary to Native Americans in the Oregon Territory beginning in 1836. (p. 439)

Whitney, Eli (hwit′nē) 1765–1825 Inventor of the cotton gin in 1793. (p. 410)

Williams, Roger (wil′yəmz) 1604?–1683 Puritan minister who founded Rhode Island as a place of religious freedom in 1636. (p. 178)

Wilson, Luzena Stanley (wil′sən) 1821?–1890? Entrepreneur who ran hotels and restaurants during the California Gold Rush. (p. 444)

Wilson, Woodrow (wil′sən) 1856–1924 Twenty-eighth President of the United States, 1913–1921. (p. R24)

Winthrop, John (win′thrəp) 1588–1649 Puritan leader and first governor of the Massachusetts Bay Colony in 1630. (p. 172)

Wolfe, James (wŭlf) 1727–1759 British General who captured Quebec in 1759, helping Great Britain win the French and Indian War. (p. 250)

York (yôrk) 1770–1832? African American member of the Lewis and Clark expedition. (p. 374)

Young, Brigham (yung) 1801–1877 Mormon leader who founded Salt Lake City, Utah, and was first governor of the Utah Territory. (p. 441)

Zenger, John Peter (zeng′ər) 1697–1746 Printer who was arrested for libel in 1734. His trial helped establish the principle of freedom of the press. (p. 219)

Zheng He (zheng hu) 1371–1433 Chinese explorer who made seven major voyages to different parts of the world. (p. 104)

Glossary

This Glossary will help you understand the meanings and pronounce the vocabulary words in this book. The page number tells you where the word first appears.

 **A**

abolitionist (ab′ə lish′ə nist) Person who wants to abolish, or end, slavery. (p. 418)

advertisement (ad′vər tīz′mənt) Tries to sell people goods, services, or ideas. (p. 446)

agriculture (ag′rə kul ′chər) Business of growing crops and raising animals. (p. 28)

ally (al′ī) A friend who will help in a fight. (p. 143)

almanac (ôl′mə nak) Reference book with helpful facts and figures. (p. H6)

amendment (ə mend′mənt) A change, or addition, to the Constitution. (p. 354)

American Revolution (ə mer′ə kən rev′ə lü′shen) The war between the 13 Colonies and Great Britain from 1775 to 1783 in which the 13 Colonies won their independence and became the United States. (p. 289)

Anaconda Plan (an′ə kon′də plan) Union strategy for defeating the Confederacy. (p. 494)

annex (ə neks′) To add or attach. (p. 433)

Antifederalist (an′ti fed′ər ə list) Person opposed to the new U.S. Constitution and its emphasis on a strong national government. (p. 353)

apprentice (ə pren′tis) Young person who learns a skill from a more experienced worker. (p. 203)

archaeologist (är kē ol′ə jist) Scientist who studies the artifacts of people who lived long ago and draws conclusions from them. (p. 56)

Articles of Confederation (är′tə kəlz əv kən fed′ə rā′shən) First plan of government for the United States, in effect from 1781 to 1789. It gave more power to the states than to the central government. (p. 339)

artifact (är′tə fakt) Object made by people in the past. (p. 56)

artisan (är′tə zən) Skilled worker who makes things by hand. (p. 203)

assassination (ə sas ə nā′shən) The killing of a high-ranking official or leader. (p. 517)

astrolabe (as′trə lāb) Navigational tool that helped sailors use the sun and stars to find their way. (p. 109)

atlas (at′ləs) Book of maps. (p. R2)

Pronunciation Key

a in hat	ō in open	sh in she
ā in age	ȯ in all	th in thin
â in care	ô in order	ᴛʜ in then
ä in far	oi in oil	zh in measure
e in let	ou in out	ə = a in about
ē in equal	u in cup	ə = e in taken
ėr in term	u̇ in put	ə = i in pencil
i in it	ü in rule	ə = o in lemon
ī in ice	ch in child	ə = u in circus
o in hot	ng in long	

Glossary

back country (bak kun′trē) In the 13 Colonies the rugged stretch of land near the Appalachian Mountains. (p. 247)

Battle of Antietam (bat′l əv an tē′təm) Union victory over Confederate forces in the Civil War in 1862 that was fought near Sharpsburg, Maryland. (p. 495)

Battle of Bunker Hill (bat′l əv bung′kər hil) Costly victory for British troops over the Patriots in Charlestown, Massachusetts, in the American Revolution on June 17, 1775. (p. 291)

Battle of Gettysburg (bat′l əv get′ēz bėrg) Union victory over Confederate forces in 1863 near Gettysburg, Pennsylvania, that marked a turning point of the Civil War. (p. 507)

Battle of New Orleans (bat′l əv nü ôr′lē ənz) Victory of United States forces commanded by Andrew Jackson over the British in the War of 1812. (p. 384)

Battle of Saratoga (bat′l əv sâr′ə tō′gə) American victory over British troops in 1777 that was a turning point in the American Revolution. (p. 305)

Battle of Tippecanoe (bat′l əv tip ē kə nü′) Battle between United States soldiers and the Shawnee in 1811 that neither side won. (p. 381)

Battle of Vicksburg (bat′l əv viks′bėrg) Union victory over Confederate forces in 1863 at Vicksburg, Mississippi, that split the Confederacy in two. (p. 509)

Bear Flag Revolt (bâr flag ri vōlt′) Rebellion of California settlers against Mexican rule in 1846. (p. 434)

Bill of Rights (bil əv rīts) First ten amendments to the Constitution, ratified in 1791. (p. 354)

black codes (blak kōdz) Laws passed by Southern state governments after the Civil War that denied African Americans many civil rights. (p. 517)

blockade (blo kād′) Shutting off an area by troops or ships to keep people and supplies from moving in or out. (p. 494)

border state (bôr′dər stāt) During the Civil War, a state between the Union and the Confederacy that allowed slavery but remained in the Union. (p. 486)

Boston Massacre (bô′stən mas′ə kər) Event in 1770 in Boston in which British soldiers killed five colonists who were part of an angry group that had surrounded them. (p. 277)

Boston Tea Party (bô′stən tē pär′tē) Protest against British taxes in which the Sons of Liberty boarded British ships and dumped tea into Boston Harbor in 1773. (p. 279)

boycott (boi′kot) Organized refusal to buy goods. (p. 272)

Cabinet (kab′ə nit) Officials appointed by the President as advisers and to head the departments in the executive branch. (p. 363)

canal (kə nal′) Human-made waterway. (p. 411)

caravan (kar′ə van) Group of traders traveling together, especially in the desert. (p. 107)

cardinal direction (kärd′n əl də rek′shən) One of the four main directions on Earth: north, south, east, and west. (p. H17)

caring (kâr′ing) Being interested in the needs of others. (p. H2)

cash crop (kash krop) Crop grown to be sold for profit. (p. 161)

cause (kôz) Action that makes something happen. (p. 264)

census (sen′səs) Count of the population. (p. 8)

ceremony (ser′ə mō′ nē) Activity done for a special purpose. (p. 61)

charter (chär′tər) Official document giving a person or group permission to do something. (p. 159)

checks and balances (cheks and bal′ən səz) System set up by the Constitution that gives each branch of government the power to check, or limit, the power of the other branches. (p. 348)

citizen (sit′ə zən) Member of a country. (p. 16)

civil war (siv′əl wôr) War between people of the same country. (p. 487)

civilization (siv′ ə lə zā′shən) Culture with organized systems of government, religion, and learning. (p. 67)

climate (klī′mit) Weather in an area over a long period of time. (p. 29)

climograph (klī′mə graf) Graph that shows the average temperature and average precipitation for a place over time. (p. 58)

colonist (kol′ə nist) Person who lives in a colony. (p. 144)

colony (kol′ə nē) Settlement far from the country that rules it. (p. 136)

Columbian Exchange (kə lum′bē ən eks chānj′) Movement of people, animals, plants, diseases, and ways of life between the Eastern Hemisphere and Western Hemisphere following the voyages of Columbus. (p. 136)

Committees of Correspondence (kə mit′ēz əv kôr ə spon′dəns) Groups of colonists formed in the 1770s to spread news quickly about protests against the British. (p. 278)

compass rose (kum′pəs rōz) Pointer that shows directions on a map. (p. H17)

compromise (kom′prə mīz) Settlement of a disagreement in which each side agrees to give up part of its demands. (p. 347)

Compromise of 1850 (kom′prə mīz əv) Law passed by Congress under which California was admitted to the Union as a free state and the Fugitive Slave Law was passed. (p. 478)

conclusion (kən klü′ zhən) Opinion that is formed based on facts. (p. 334)

Confederacy (kən fed′ər ə sē) Confederate States of America formed by the 11 Southern states that seceded from the Union. (p. 485)

Pronunciation Key

a in hat	ō in open	sh in she
ā in age	ȯ in all	th in thin
â in care	ô in order	ᴛʜ in then
ä in far	oi in oil	zh in measure
e in let	ou in out	ə = a in about
ē in equal	u in cup	ə = e in taken
ėr in term	u̇ in put	ə = i in pencil
i in it	ü in rule	ə = o in lemon
ī in ice	ch in child	ə = u in circus
o in hot	ng in long	

Glossary

conquest (kon′kwest) Capture or taking of something by force. (p. 144)

conquistador (kon kē′stə dôr) Spanish word for conquerors who came to the Americas in the 1500s. (p. 143)

conservation (kon′ sər vā′shən) Protection and careful use of natural resources. (p. 36)

constitution (kon′ stə tü′shən) Written plan of government. The United States Constitution, adopted in 1789, is the plan for the national government. (p. 15)

Constitutional Convention (kon′stə tü′shə nəl kən ven′shən) Meeting of delegates who met in Philadelphia, Pennsylvania, in 1787 and replaced the Articles of Confederation with the Constitution. (p. 345)

consumer (kən sü′mər) Person who buys or uses goods and services. (p. 21)

Continental Army (kon′ tə nen′ tl är′mē) Army formed in 1775 by the Second Continental Congress and led by General George Washington. (p. 297)

convert (kən vėrt′) To change from one belief to another. (p. 144)

cotton gin (kot′n jin) Machine invented by Eli Whitney that cleaned the seeds from cotton. (p. 410)

courage (kėr′ij) Doing what is right even when it is frightening or dangerous. (p. H2)

cross-section diagram (krȯs sek′shən dī′ə gram) Drawing that shows a view of something as if you could slice through it. (p. 414)

cultural region (kul′chər əl rē′jən) Area in which people with similar cultures live. (p. 77)

culture (kul′chər) Way of life of a group of people. (p. 7)

dateline (dāt′lin) Line at the beginning of a newspaper article that tells where and when the story was written. (p. 209)

Daughters of Liberty (dȯ′tərz əv lib′ər tē) Groups of American women Patriots who wove cloth to replace boycotted British goods. (p. 272)

debtor (det′ər) Person who owes money. (p. 180)

Declaration of Independence (dek′lə rā′shən əv in′di pen′dəns) Document declaring the 13 American colonies independent of Great Britain, written mainly by Thomas Jefferson and adopted on July 4, 1776, by the Second Continental Congress. (p. 298)

degree (di grē′) Unit of measuring, used in latitude and longitude. (p. H5)

delegate (del′ə git) Person chosen to represent others. (p. 345)

demand (di mand′) Amount of a product that people are willing to buy. (p. 19)

democracy (di mok′rə sē) Government that is run by the people. (p. 15)

dictionary (dik′shə ner′ē) Alphabetical collection of words that includes the meaning and pronunciation of each word. (p. H6)

discrimination (dis krim′ə nā′shən) Unfair treatment of a group or individual. (p. 445)

dissenter (di sent′ər) Person whose views differ from those of his or her leaders. (p. 178)

distribution maps (dis′ trə byü′shən maps) Maps that show how people or resources are spread out over an area. (p. 378)

draft (draft) Law that requires men of a certain age to serve in the military, if called. (p. 499)

drought (drout) Long period without rain. (p. 63)

★ E ★

economy (i kon′ə mē) System for producing and distributing goods and services. (p. 19)

effect (ə fekt′) What happens as a result of an action. (p. 264)

El Camino Real (el kä mē′nō rē′əl) Spanish for "the royal road," a route that linked Spain's colonies in the American Southwest with Mexico. (p. 234)

electoral college (i lek′tər əl kol′ij) Group of people chosen by the people of each state who vote for President. (p. 363)

elevation (el′ ə vā′shən) Height of the land above sea level. (p. H21)

elevation map (el′ ə vā′ shən map) Physical map that uses color to show elevation. (pp. H21, H32)

Emancipation Proclamation (i man′ sə pā′shən prok′lə mā′shən) Statement issued by President Abraham Lincoln on January 1, 1863, freeing all slaves in Confederate states still at war with the Union. (p. 500)

emperor (em′pər ər) Ruler of an empire. (p. 103)

empire (em′pīr) Large group of lands and peoples ruled by one leader. (p. 68)

encomienda (en kō mē en′də) Grant given by the King of Spain to wealthy settlers in New Spain. Gave settlers control of all the Native Americans living on an area of land. (p. 148)

encyclopedia (en sī′ klə pē′dē ə) Book or set of books with articles, alphabetically listed, on various topics. (p. H6)

entrepreneur (än′ trə prə nėr′) Person who starts a new business, hoping to make a profit. (p. 21)

environment (en vī′ rən mənt) All things that surround us, such as land, water, air, and trees. (p. 36)

equator (i kwā′tər) Imaginary line around the middle of Earth, halfway between the North Pole and the South Pole; 0° latitude. (p. H12)

Era of Good Feelings (ir′ə əv gu̇d fē′lingz) Name given to the period after the War of 1812 marked by optimism, a geographically expanding country, and a growing economy. (p. 403)

ethnic group (eth′nik grüp) Group of people who share the same customs and language. (p. 8)

evaluate (i val′yü āt) To make judgments about. (p. 447)

Pronunciation Key

a in hat	ō in open	sh in she
ā in age	ò in all	th in thin
â in care	ô in order	тн in then
ä in far	oi in oil	zh in measure
e in let	ou in out	ə = a in about
ē in equal	u in cup	ə = e in taken
ėr in term	u̇ in put	ə = i in pencil
i in it	ü in rule	ə = o in lemon
ī in ice	ch in child	ə = u in circus
o in hot	ng in long	

Glossary

executive branch (eg zek′yə tiv branch) Part of the government, headed by the President, that carries out the laws. (p. 339)

expedition (ek′ spə dish′ən) Journey made for a special purpose. (p. 135)

export (ek′spôrt) Good that one country sells to another country. (p. 20)

fact (fakt) Statement that can be proven to be true. (p. 174)

fairness (fer′ness) Not favoring one more than others. (p. H2)

feature article (fē′chər är′tə kəl) Newspaper article about people, places, or events. (p. 208)

federal (fed′ər əl) Refers to the national government. (p. 353)

Federalist (fed′ər ə list) Supporter of a strong national government and in favor of adopting of the Constitution. (p. 353)

Federalist, The (fed′ər ə list) Series of essays in 1787 and 1788 by James Madison, Alexander Hamilton, and John Jay that urged support of the new Constitution. (p. 353)

Fifteenth Amendment (fif′tēnth′ ə mend′mənt) Amendment to the Constitution, ratified in 1870, that gave the right to vote to male citizens of all races. (p. 519)

First Battle of Bull Run (fėrst bat′l əv bùl run) First major battle of the Civil War, on July 21, 1861. (p. 495)

First Continental Congress (fėrst kon′ tə nen′tl kong′gris) Meeting of representatives from every colony except Georgia held in Philadelphia in 1774 to discuss actions to take in response to the Intolerable Acts. (p. 281)

forty-niner (fôr′tē nī′ nər) Nickname for a person who arrived in California in 1849 to look for gold. (p. 443)

fossil fuel (fos′əl fyü′əl) Fuel, such as coal, oil, or natural gas, that is formed from the remains of plants and animals that lived thousands of years ago. (p. 35)

Fourteenth Amendment (fôr′tēnth′ ə mend′mənt) Amendment to the Constitution, ratified in 1868, that said that no state could deny any citizen the equal protection of the law. (p. 519)

free enterprise (frē en′tər prīz) Economic system in which people are free to start their own businesses and own their own property. (p. 19)

free state (frē stāt) State that did not allow slavery. (p. 477)

Freedmen's Bureau (frēd′mənz byùr′ō) Federal agency set up in 1865 to provide food, schools, and medical care to freed slaves in the South. (p. 518)

French and Indian War (french and in′dē ən wôr) War fought by the British against the French and their Native American allies in North America, which was won by the British in 1763. (p. 249)

frontier (frun tir′) Outer edge of a settled area. (p. 372)

Fugitive Slave Law (fyü′jə tiv slāv lô) Law passed by Congress in 1850 that said escaped slaves had to be returned to their owners. (p. 478)

G

generalization (jen′ ər ə lə zā′shən) Broad statement or idea about a subject. (p. 320)

geography (jē og′rə fē) Study of Earth and how people use it. (p. 25)

Gettysburg Address (get′ēz bėrg′ ə dres′) Famous Civil War speech given by President Lincoln in 1863 at the site of the Battle of Gettysburg. (p. 508)

glacier (glā′shər) Thick sheets of ice that covered Earth's surface during the Ice Age. (p. 55)

globe (glōb) Round model of Earth. (p. H12)

gold rush (gōld rush) Sudden movement of many people to an area where gold has been found. (p. 443)

Great Awakening (grāt ə wā′kə ning) Important religious movement among Christians that began in the colonies in the 1730s. This movement revived many colonists' interest in religion. (p. 218)

Great Compromise (grāt kom′prə mīz) Agreement at the Constitutional Convention to create a Congress with two houses. First proposed by Roger Sherman of Connecticut. (p. 347)

Green Mountain Boys (grēn moun′tən boiz) Group of Vermont soldiers who captured Fort Ticonderoga in 1775. (p. 303)

grid (grid) Pattern of criss-crossing lines that can help you find locations on a map. (p. 140)

H

haciendas (hä′sē en′dəz) Large estates built by wealthy Spanish ranchers in North America. (p. 234)

headline (hed′lin) Words printed in large type at the head, or beginning, of an article. Often includes the main idea of the article. (p. 209)

hemisphere (hem′ə sfir) Half of a sphere or globe. Earth can be divided into hemispheres. (p. H13)

honesty (on′ə stē) Truthfulness. (p. H2)

House of Burgesses (hous əv bėr′jis ez) Law-making assembly in colonial Virginia. (p. 162)

I

Ice Age (īs āj) Period during which low temperatures caused large areas of Earth's water to freeze. (p. 55)

ideals (ī dē′əlz) Important beliefs. (p. 7)

immigrants (im′ə grənts) People who leave one country to go live in another country. (p. 10)

Pronunciation Key

a in hat	ō in open	sh in she
ā in age	ȯ in all	th in thin
â in care	ô in order	ᴛʜ in then
ä in far	oi in oil	zh in measure
e in let	ou in out	ə = a in about
ē in equal	u in cup	ə = e in taken
ėr in term	ù in put	ə = i in pencil
i in it	ü in rule	ə = o in lemon
ī in ice	ch in child	ə = u in circus
o in hot	ng in long	

Glossary

impeachment (im pēch′mənt) Bringing of charges of wrongdoing against an elected official. (p. 519)

import (im′pôrt) Good that one country buys from another country. (p. 20)

inauguration (in ȯ′gyə rā′shən) Ceremony in which a newly-elected President takes office. (p. 363)

indentured servant (in den′chərd sėr′vənt) Person who agreed to work for someone for a certain amount of time in exchange for the cost of the voyage to North America. (p. 161)

Indian Removal Act (in′dē ən ri mü′vəl akt) Law passed in 1830 forcing American Indians living in the Southeast to be moved west of the Mississippi. (p. 405)

Industrial Revolution (in dus′trē əl rev′ ə lü′shən) Period of important change from making goods by hand to making goods by machine in factories. (p. 409)

inflation (in flā′shən) Economic condition in which prices rise very quickly. (p. 340)

inset map (in′ set′ map) Small map within a larger map. Shows areas outside of or in greater detail than the larger map. (p. H18)

interdependent (in′tər di pen′dənt) Needing each other. (p. 30)

intermediate direction (in′ tər mē′dē it də rek′shən) Pointers halfway between the main directions: northeast, northwest, southeast, southwest. (p. H17)

Internet (in′tər net′) Worldwide network of computers; became popular in the 1990s. (p. 86)

interstate highway (in′tər stāt hī′wā′) Road that connects cities in different states. (p. 512)

Intolerable Acts (in tol′ər ə bəl akts) Laws passed by British Parliament to punish the people of Boston following the Boston Tea Party. (p. 280)

irrigation (ir ə gā′shən) Method of bringing water to dry land. (p. 28)

Jim Crow laws (jim′ krō lôz) Laws passed in the South after Reconstruction establishing segregation of whites and blacks. (p. 520)

judicial branch (jü dish′əl branch) Part of the government that decides the meaning of laws. (p. 339)

Kansas-Nebraska Act (kan′zəs nə bras′kə akt) Law passed in 1854 allowing these two territories to decide for themselves whether or not to allow slavery. (p. 479)

key (kē) Box explaining the symbols on a map. It is also known as a legend. (p. H16)

King Philip's War (king fil′əps wôr) War in 1670s between Native Americans and English settlers living in New England. (p. 247)

large-scale map (lärj′ skāl map) Map showing a small area in detail. (p. 244)

latitude (lat′ə tüd) Distance north or south of the equator, measured in degrees. (p. H15)

league (lēg) Union of people or groups. (p. 77)

legislative branch (lej′ə slā′ tiv branch) Part of the government that passes laws. (p. 339)

locator (lō′kāt′ər) Small map that appears with a larger map. A locator shows where the subject area of the larger map is located on Earth. (p. H16)

lodge (loj) Large, round hut built by Plains Indians. (p. 83)

longhouse (lông′ hous′) Building used for shelter by Iroquois. (p. 78)

longitude (lon′jə tüd) Distance east or west of the prime meridian, measured in degrees. (p. H15)

Louisiana Purchase (lü ē′ zē an′ ə pèr′ chəs) Territory purchased by the United States from France in 1803, extending from the Mississippi River to the Rocky Mountains and from the Gulf of Mexico to Canada. (p. 373)

Loyalists (loi′ə lists) Colonists who remained loyal to the British during the American Revolution. (p. 280)

─────────── ⭐ **M** ⭐ ───────────

magnetic compass (mag net′ik kum′pəs) Chinese invention that aided navigation by showing which direction was north. (p. 104)

manifest destiny (man′ə fest des′tə nē) Belief that the United States should expand west to the Pacific Ocean. (p. 433)

manufacture (man′yə fak′chər) To make goods from raw materials. (p. 409)

Mayflower Compact (mā′flou′ ər kom′pakt) Plan of government written by the Pilgrims who sailed on the *Mayflower.* (p. 170)

mechanical reaper (mə kan′ə kəl rē′pər) Machine invented by Cyrus McCormick that could harvest wheat quickly. (p. 410)

mercenaries (mèr′sə ner′ ēz) Soldiers from one country who are paid to fight for another country. (p. 303)

meridian (mə rid′ē ən) Imaginary line extending from the North Pole to the South Pole, also called longitude line. (p. H15)

mesa (mā′sə) High, flat landform that rises steeply from the land around it. (p. 62)

Mexican War (mek′sə kən wôr) War lasting from 1846 to 1848 in which the United States defeated Mexico and gained Mexican territory. (p. 434)

Middle Passage (mid′l pas′ij) Name given to the second leg of the triangular trade routes; extended from West Africa to the West Indies. (p. 206)

migrate (mī′grāt) To move from one area to another. (p. 55)

militias (mə lish′əz) Volunteer armies. (p. 281)

mineral (min′ər əl) Substance such as gold, copper, or salt that is found in the earth and is not a plant or animal. (p. 35)

Pronunciation Key

a in hat	ō in open	sh in she
ā in age	ò in all	th in thin
â in care	ô in order	ᴛʜ in then
ä in far	oi in oil	zh in measure
e in let	ou in out	ə = a in about
ē in equal	u in cup	ə = e in taken
ėr in term	ú in put	ə = i in pencil
i in it	ü in rule	ə = o in lemon
ī in ice	ch in child	ə = u in circus
o in hot	ng in long	

Glossary

minutemen (min′it men′) Colonial militia groups that could be ready to fight at a minute's notice. (p. 281)

mission (mish′ən) Religious settlement where missionaries live and work. (p. 149)

missionary (mish′ə ner′ē) Person who teaches his or her religion to others who have different beliefs. (p. 149)

Missouri Compromise (mə zùr′ē kom′prə mīz) Law passed in 1820 dividing the Louisiana Territory into areas prohibiting slavery and areas allowing slavery. (p. 477)

Monroe Doctrine (mən rō′ dok′trən) Policy declared by President James Monroe warning European nations not to interfere in the Western Hemisphere. (p. 403)

mountain men (moun′tən men) Fur trappers who helped explore and settle the Oregon Country. (p. 439)

national anthem (nash′ə nəl an′thəm) Official song of a country. "The Star-Spangled Banner" is the national anthem of the United States. (p. 383)

nationalism (nash′ə nə liz′ əm) Strong feeling of pride in one's country. (p. 403)

natural resource (nach′ər əl ri sôrs′) Something found in nature that people can use. (p. 35)

navigation (nav′ ə gā′shən) Science used by sailors to plot their course and determine their location. (p. 113)

neutral (nü′trəl) Not taking sides. (p. 381)

New Jersey Plan (nü jėr′zē plan) Proposal during the Constitutional Convention that each state should have the same number of representatives in Congress. (p. 346)

news article (nüz är′tə kəl) News story based on facts about recent events. (p. 208)

nonfiction book (non fik′shən bùk) Book that is based on fact. (p. H6)

nonrenewable resource (non′ ri nü′ə bəl ri sôrs′) Resource that cannot be easily replaced, such as a fossil fuel. (p. 36)

Northwest Ordinance of 1787 (nôrth′ west′ ôrd′n əns əv) Federal order that divided the Northwest Territory into smaller territories and created a plan for how the territories could become states. (p. 342)

Northwest Passage (nôrth′ west′ pas′ij) Water route that explorers hoped would flow through North America, connecting the Atlantic and Pacific oceans. (p. 165)

Olive Branch Petition (ol′iv branch pə tish′ən) Letter sent by the Second Continental Congress to King George III in 1775 in an attempt to avoid war. (p. 297)

opinion (ə pin′yən) Personal view about an issue. (p. 174)

parallel time lines (par′ə lel tīm līnz) Two or more time lines grouped together. (p. 116)

Parliament (pär′lə mənt) Britain's law-making assembly. (p. 269)

Patriots (pā′trē əts) American colonists who opposed British rule. (p. 280)

periodical (pir′ ē od′ə kəl) Newspaper or magazine that is published on a regular basis. (p. H6)

persecution (pėr′sə kyü′ shən) Unjust treatment because of one's beliefs. (p. 169)

physical map (fiz′ ə kəl map) Map showing geographic features such as mountains and rivers. (p. H17)

pilgrim (pil′grəm) Person who travels to a new place for religious reasons. (p. 169)

pilgrimage (pil′grə mij) Journey taken for religious reasons. (p. 108)

pioneer (pī′ə nir′) Early settler of a region. (p. 372)

plantation (plan tā′shən) Large farm with many workers who live on the land they work. (p. 148)

point of view (point əv vyü) A person's own opinion of an issue or event. (p. 468)

political map (pə lit′ə kəl map) Map that shows borders between states or countries. (p. H16)

political party (pə lit′ə kəl pär′tē) Organized group of people who share similar views of what government should do. (p. 364)

pollution (pə lü′shən) Something that dirties the water, air, or soil. (p. 38)

Pontiac's Rebellion (pon′tē aks ri bel′yən) Native American rebellion led by the Ottawa leader Pontiac in 1763. (p. 251)

population density map (pop′ yə lā′shən den′sə tē map) Map that shows the number of people living in a certain amount of space, such as a square mile. (p. 378)

potlatch (pot′ lach′) Native American celebration in which the hosts give gifts to their guests. (p. 95)

powwow (pou′wou) Native American ceremony that often includes traditional dancing and games. (p. 85)

Preamble (prē′am′ bəl) Introduction to the Constitution, beginning, "We the People of the United States . . ." (p. 348)

precipitation (pri sip′ ə tā′ shən) Moisture that falls to Earth in the form of rain, snow, or sleet. (p. 29)

presidio (pri sid′ē ō) Military fort built by the Spanish. (p. 234)

primary source (prī′mer′ ē sôrs) Eyewitness account of an historical event. (p. H6)

prime meridian (prīm mə rid′ē ən) Line of longitude marked 0 degrees. Other lines of longitude are measured in degrees east or west of the prime meridian. (p. H12)

private property (prī′ vit prop′ər tē) Something owned by individual people. (p. 19)

Proclamation of 1763 (prok′lə mā′shən əv) Law issued by King George III stating that colonists were no longer allowed to settle on land west of the Appalachian Mountains. (p. 251)

profit (prof′it) Money a business has left over after it has paid all its costs. (p. 19)

proprietor (prə prī′ə tər) Owner. (p. 180)

pueblo (pweb′lō) Spanish word for "village." (p. 89)

Pronunciation Key

a in hat	ō in open	sh in she
ā in age	ȯ in all	th in thin
â in care	ô in order	ᵺ in then
ä in far	oi in oil	zh in measure
e in let	ou in out	ə = a in about
ē in equal	u in cup	ə = e in taken
ėr in term	ú in put	ə = i in pencil
i in it	ü in rule	ə = o in lemon
ī in ice	ch in child	ə = u in circus
o in hot	ng in long	

Glossary

Pueblo Revolt (pweb′lō ri vōlt′) Native American revolt in the late 1600s in which the Pueblo temporarily drove the Spanish out of New Mexico. (p. 235)

Puritans (pyùr′ə tənz) Group of people who wanted to "purify" the Church of England. They established the Massachusetts Bay Colony in 1630. (p. 172)

pyramid (pir′ə mid) Building with three or more sides shaped like triangles that slant toward a point at the top. (p. 67)

ratify (rat′ə fī) To officially approve (p. 339)

Reconstruction (rē′ kən struk′shən) Period of rebuilding after the Civil War during which the Southern states rejoined the Union. (p. 517)

reform (ri fôrm′) Change. (p. 417)

region (rē′jən) Large area that has common features that set it apart from other areas. (p. 25)

Renaissance (ren′ ə säns′) Period in Europe beginning in about 1350 during which there was a new desire to learn more about the arts, sciences, and other parts of the world. (p. 112)

renewable resource (ri nü′ə bəl ri sôrs′) Resource that can be renewed or replaced, such as a tree. (p. 36)

repeal (ri pēl′) To cancel. (p. 270)

republic (ri pub′ lik) Form of government in which the people elect representatives to make laws and run the government. (p. 15)

reservation (rez′ ər vā′shən) Land set aside by the United States government for Native Americans. (p. 80)

reserved powers (ri zėrvd′ pou′ərz) Powers in the Constitution that are left to the individual states. (p. 348)

respect (ri spekt′) Consideration for others. (p. H2)

responsibility (ri spon′ sə bil′ə tē) Doing what you are supposed to do. (p. H2)

revival (ri vī′vəl) Act of awakening or strengthening people's religious feelings. (p. 419)

road map (rōd map) Map showing roads; can be used to plan driving trips to cities or other places of interest. (p. H22)

saga (sä′gə) Long, spoken tale repeated from one generation to the next. (p. 111)

scale (skāl) Tool that helps you measure distances on a map. (p. H18)

sea level (sē lev′əl) An ocean's surface, compared to which the height of land is measured either above or below. (p. 32)

search engine (sėrch en′jən) Computer site that searches for information from numerous Internet Web sites. (p. H7)

secede (si sēd′) To break away from a group, as the Southern states broke away from the United States in 1861. (p. 485)

Second Continental Congress (sek′ənd kon′ tə nen′tl kong′gris) Congress of American leaders that first met in 1775, declared independence in 1776, and helped lead the United States during the Revolution. (p. 297)

secondary source (sek′ən der′ ē sôrs) Description of events written by people who did not witness the event. (p. H15)

sectionalism (sek′shə nə liz′ əm) Loyalty to one section of a country rather than to the whole country. (p. 465)

segregation (seg′ rə gā′shən) Separation of people of different races. (p. 520)

self-sufficient (self′ sə fish′ənt) Ability to rely on oneself for most of what one needs. (p. 212)

Seneca Falls Convention (sen′ə kə fôlz kən ven′shən) First national convention on women's rights, organized in 1848 by Lucretia Mott and Elizabeth Cady Stanton. (p. 419)

separation of powers (sep′ ə rā′shən əv pou′ərz) Division of power among the three branches of the federal government under the Constitution. (p. 348)

Separatists (sep′ər ə tists) Group of people from England who wanted to separate themselves from the Church of England. Some traveled to North America in search of religious freedom. (p. 169)

shaman (shä′mən) Native American doctor or healer. (p. 96)

sharecropping (shâr′krop′ ing) System of farming in which farmers rented land and paid the landowner with a share of the crops they raised. (p. 520)

Shays' Rebellion (shāz ri bel′yən) Revolt of Massachusetts farmers against high state taxes, led by Daniel Shays. (p. 341)

slave codes (slāv kōdz) Laws designed to control the behavior of slaves. (p. 471)

slave state (slāv stāt) State in which slavery was legally allowed. (p. 477)

slave trade (slāv trād) Buying and selling of human beings. (p. 113)

slavery (slā′vər ē) Practice of owning people and forcing them to work. (p. 68)

small-scale map (smôl skāl map) Map showing a large area of land but not much detail. (p. 244)

society (sə sī′ə tē) Group of people forming a community. (p. 148)

Sons of Liberty (sunz ov lib′ər tē) Groups of Patriots who worked to oppose British rule before the American Revolution. (p. 271)

specialize (spesh′ə līz) Focus on one particular product, activity, or job. (p. 67)

Stamp Act (stamp akt) Law passed by Parliament in 1765 that taxed printed materials in the 13 Colonies. (p. 269)

states' rights (stāts rīts) Idea that states have the right to make decisions about issues that concern them. (p. 477)

stock (stok) Share in a company. (p. 159)

Stono Rebellion (stō′nō ri bel′yən) Slave rebellion in South Carolina in 1739. (p. 227)

suffrage (suf′rij) Right to vote. (p. 404)

supply (sə plī′) Amount of a product that is available. (p. 19)

Pronunciation Key

a in hat	ō in open	sh in she
ā in age	ȯ in all	th in thin
â in care	ô in order	ŦH in then
ä in far	oi in oil	zh in measure
e in let	ou in out	ə = a in about
ē in equal	u in cup	ə = e in taken
ėr in term	u̇ in put	ə = i in pencil
i in it	ü in rule	ə = o in lemon
ī in ice	ch in child	ə = u in circus
o in hot	ng in long	

Glossary

surplus (sėr′pləs) More than is needed. (p. 67)

symbol (sim′bəl) Something that stands for something else. (p. H16)

tariff (tar′if) Tax on imported goods. (p. 272)

tax (taks) Money or goods people pay to a government. (p. 107)

Tea Act (tē akt) Law passed by Parliament in the early 1770s stating that only the East India Company, a British business, could sell tea to the 13 Colonies. (p. 279)

technology (tek nol′ə jē) Use of scientific knowledge or new tools to make or do something. (p. 409)

telegraph (tel′ə graf) Machine used to send messages along wires using electricity. (p. 514)

temperance (tem′pər əns) Moderation, usually in drinking of alcohol. (p. 417)

tepee (tē′pē) Dwelling built by Plains Native Americans, made of poles arranged in a circle covered by buffalo hides. (p. 83)

Texas Revolution (tek′səs rev′ ə lü′shən) War between Texas settlers and Mexico from 1835 to 1836 resulting in the formation of the Republic of Texas. (p. 432)

theory (thē′ər ē) One possible explanation for something. (p. 55)

Thirteenth Amendment (thėr′ tēnth′ ə mend′mənt) Amendment to the Constitution in 1865 that ended slavery. (p. 517)

Three-Fifths Compromise (thrē′ fifths′ kom′prə mīz) Agreement made at the Constitutional Convention that only three-fifths of the slaves in a state would be counted for representation and tax purposes. (p. 347)

time zone (tīm zōn) Region in which one standard time is used. There are total of 24 around the world. (p. H20)

time zone map (tīm zōn map) Map showing the world's or any country's time zones. (p. H20)

title (tī′təl) Name of something, such as a book or map. (p. H16)

total war (tō′tl wôr) Method of warfare used by Union General William Sherman in which both the opposing army and an enemy's civilian population are targets. (p. 510)

totem pole (tō′təm pōl) Wooden post carved with animals or other images; often made by Native Americans of the Pacific Northwest to honor ancestors or special events. (p. 95)

town common (toun kom′ən) Open space in the center of many New England and Middle Colony towns where cattle and sheep could graze. (p. 212)

Townshend Acts (toun′zend akts) Laws passed by Parliament in 1767 that taxed goods imported by the 13 Colonies from Britain. (p. 272)

trading post (trād′ing pōst) Place in colonial North America where settlers and Native Americans met to trade goods. (p. 241)

Trail of Tears (trāl əv tirz) Forced march of 15,000 Cherokee from the southeastern United States to Indian Territory in present-day Oklahoma in 1838. (p. 406)

traitor (trā′tər) Person who works against his or her country. (p. 300)

travois (trə voi′) Sled made of poles tied together; used by Native Americans to transport goods across the plains. (p. 83)

Treaty of Guadalupe Hidalgo (trē′tē əv gwä′ də lü′ pā hi däl′gō) Treaty ending the Mexican War in 1848. Mexico gave up most of its northern territory to the United States in return for $15 million. (p. 435)

Treaty of Paris (trē′tē əv par′is) Treaty signed in 1783 that officially ended the American Revolution. Great Britain recognized the United States as an independent country. (p. 319)

triangular trade route (trī ang′gyə lər trād rout) Three-sided trade route between the 13 Colonies, the West Indies, and Africa; included the slave trade. (p. 206)

tribe (trīb) Group of families bound together under a single leadership. (p. 77)

tributary (trib′yə ter′ē) Stream or river that flows into a larger river. (p. 242)

tribute (trib′yüt) Payment a ruler demands from people he or she rules. (p. 68)

Underground Railroad (un′ dər ground′ rāl′rōd) System of secret routes used by escaping slaves that led from the South to the North or Canada. (p. 473)

Union (yü′nyən) United States of America. (p. 485)

veto (vē′tō) Power of the President to reject a bill passed by Congress. (p. 348)

Virginia Plan (vər jin′yə plan) Proposal during the Constitutional Convention that Congress be given greater power over the states and that large state have more representatives in Congress than small states. (p. 346)

wagon train (wag′ən trān) Common method of transportation to the West, in which wagons traveled in groups for safety. (p. 439)

wampum (wäm′pəm) Belts or strings of polished seashells that were used for trading and gift-giving by Iroquois and other Native Americans. (p. 79)

War Hawks (wôr hôkz) Members of Congress who supported war with Britain in 1812. (p. 382)

War of 1812 (wôr əv) Conflict between the United States and Britain that lasted from 1812 to 1815. (p. 382)

Web site (web sīt) Place on the World Wide Web where information can be found. (p. 86)

Pronunciation Key

a	in hat	ō	in open	sh	in she
ā	in age	ȯ	in all	th	in thin
â	in care	ô	in order	ᴛʜ	in then
ä	in far	oi	in oil	zh	in measure
e	in let	ou	in out	ə	= a in about
ē	in equal	u	in cup	ə	= e in taken
ėr	in term	u̇	in put	ə	= i in pencil
i	in it	ü	in rule	ə	= o in lemon
ī	in ice	ch	in child	ə	= u in circus
o	in hot	ng	in long		

Index

This Index lists the pages on which topics appear in this book.
Page numbers after an *m* refer to a map. Page numbers after a *p* refer
to a photograph. Page numbers after a *c* refer to a chart or graph.

Britain. *See* England, Great Britain

Brown, John, 480

Bruce, Blanche K., 518

Bruchac, Joseph, 120–121

Buchanan, James, R22

Buddhists, 63

buffalo, 83–84, 377

Bunker Hill, Battle of, 290–291, 306, 310, *m290, p306*

Burgoyne, John, 305

Bush, George H.W., 15, R24

Bush, George W., R25

Cabinet, 335, 363–364

Cabot, John, 166

Cahokia, 61, *p61*

Calhoun, John C., 477–478

California, 399, 442–445, 478, R18, *p434*

California Trail, 443, *m440*

Canada, 241

canal, 411, *c414– 415*

Cape of Good Hope, 114

caravan, 107

cardinal directions, H17

careers, 22

Caribbean region, countries of, *mR8*

Carney, William, 501

Carter, James E., 15, R24

Cartier, Jacques, 166

Carver, George Washington, 28, 31, *p31*

cash crop, 161

Castro, Fidel, 640

Catholics. *See* Roman Catholic Church, Roman Catholics

cause and effect, 85, 167, 251, 264–265, 273, 282, 291, 292, 300, 322, 384

census, 8–9

Champlain, Samuel de, 128, 165–166, *p128*

character traits,
caring, H2, 504–505
courage, H2, 92–93
fairness, H2, 422–423
honesty, H2, 274–275
respect, H2, 184–185
responsibility, H2, 40–41

Charles I, King of England, 180

Charles II, King of England, 179

Charleston, South Carolina, 206, 464, 484–485

Charlestown, Massachusetts, 290

charter, 159

checks and balances, 349, *c349*

Cherokee, 405–406, *m77, m405, p406*

Chestnut, Mary Boykin, 484

Cheyenne, 84–85, *m84, p84, p85*

Chicago, Illinois, 28

Chickasaw, 405, *m405*

China, 63, 102–105

Choctaw, 405, *m405*

Christianity, 136, 148, 218, 234, 238, 417. *See also* Great Awakening, missionary, Pilgrims, Protestants, Puritans, Quakers, Roman Catholics, Second Great Awakening

Church of England, 169, 172

Church of Jesus Christ of Latter-day Saints, 441

Cíbola, 147

Cinque, Joseph, 459, 472, *p459*

circle graphs, reading, 12–13, *c13*

cities, colonial, 211, *c211*

Cities of Gold, 147, 238

citizen, 16

citizenship
caring, H2, 504–505
courage, H2, 92–93
decision-making, H3
fairness, H2, 422–423
honesty, H2, 274–275
problem-solving, H3
respect, H2, 184–185

responsibility, H2, 40–41

Civil War
African Americans and, 501, *p501*
attack on Fort Sumter, 484, 486
battles of, 495, 507, 509, *m509*
communications during, 514–515, *p514, 515*
definition of, 487
life during, 498–503
secession of Southern states, 485
slavery and, 10
strategies of, 494
technology, 496
women and, 502

civilization, 67

Clark, George Rogers, 316, *p316*

Clark, William, 36, 374–375, 377, *p374*

Clay, Henry, 382, 458, 477–478, *p458*

Cleveland, Grover, R23

climate, 19, *m29*

Clinton, William J., R25

Code Talkers, 92–93, *p92*

Coffin, Catherine, 473

Coffin, Levi, 473

Colombia, 403, 688, *m403, 689*

colonial America
cities of, 211, *c211*
economies of, 205, *m205*
families in, 214

Index

Eastern Hemisphere, H14

Eastern Woodlands cultural region, 77, *m77*

economic freedoms, 19

economy, 19. *See also* colonial America, economies of

Edison, Thomas, 21, 23, *p21*

education
colonial, 216–217
public, 342, 420, 518, 521
Puritans and, 173
during Reconstruction, 518

Eisenhower, Dwight D., R25

El Camino Real, 234, *m234*

electoral college, 363

elevation, 32

elevation maps, reading, H21, 32–33, *m33*

Elfreth's Alley, Philadelphia, 211, *p211*

Elizabeth I, Queen of England, 157, *p157*

Ellis Island, 10

Emancipation Proclamation, 500

emperor, 103

empire, 68

encomienda, 148–151

encyclopedia, H17

England. *See also* Great Britain
colonies of, 168–173, 176–182, *m177, c181*
exploration and, 138, 166
Pilgrims and, 169
Spain and, 157–158

entrepreneur, 21

environment, 36, 38

E Pluribus Unum, 7

equator, H12, H13, H15

Equiano, Olaudah, 197, 206, 227, *p197*

Era of Good Feelings, 403

Eric the Red, 110–111

Ericsson, Leif, 48, 111, *p48*

Erie Canal, 411, 414–415, *c414–415, p414*

Estéban, 147

ethnic group, 8, *c8*

Everglades, 39

Everglades National Park, 37

executive branch, 339, 346, 348, *c349*

expedition, 135

export, 20, 161, *c20, 161*

express riders, 278, *m278*

fact and opinion, 174–175

fair trial, right to, 16

families
colonial American, 214
slave, 471, *p471*

feature article, 208

federal, 353

Federalist, The, 351, 353, *p353*

Federalists, 353–354

Federalists (political party), 364, 368

Ferdinand, King of Spain, 135

Fifteenth Amendment, 519, *c519*

Fillmore, Millard, R22

First Amendment, 351

First Battle of Bull Run, 495, *m509*

First Continental Congress, 265, 281, 297

"First Flute, The," 120–121

Fitzhugh, George, 468–469, *p468*

Florida, 180, 232–233, 399, 403, 431, R19

Ford, Gerald, R24

Fort Duquesne, 248–249

Fort McHenry, 383

Fort Necessity, 246–247, 249

Fort Sumter, 484–486

Fort Ticonderoga, 302–303

Fort Vincennes, 316

Fort Wagner, 501

Forty-niners, 443–444

fossil fuels, 35

Four Corners, 62–63, 89

Fourteenth Amendment, 519, *c519*

Fourth of July, 295

France
American Revolution and, 305, 315
exploration and, 240–243
French and Indian War and, 249–250
Louisiana Purchase and, 373
revolution in, 341, *p341*
settlements of, 165, 243

Franklin, Benjamin, 6, 196, 210–211, 218–219, 298, 305, 344, 350, 355, *p6,196, 299, 349*

free enterprise, 18–19, 21–22

free states, 477, *m479*

Freedman's Bureau, 461, 518

freedom, economic, 19

freedom, political. *See* specific freedoms

French and Indian War, 199, 246, 249–250, *m250*

French Revolution, 341, *p341*

Index

frontier, 372

Fugitive Slave Act, 478, *p478*

Fulton, Robert, 411

Fur Trade, 165

Gadsden Purchase, 435, *m435*

Gage, Thomas, 280, 287

Gálvez, Bernardo de, 263, 315, *p263, 315*

Gandhi, Mohandas, 311, *p311*

Garfield, James A., R23

Garrison, William Lloyd, 418

generalizations, make, 320–321

geography

definition of, 25

of United States, 24–30

themes of, H10–H11. *See also* specific themes

George III, King of England, 251, 269–270, 272, 274–275, 279, 282, 297, 303, 316, *p269*

Georgia, 180–181, R19, *c181*

Gettysburg Address, 457, 491, 506, 508

Gettysburg, Battle of, 507, 509, *m507*

Gettysburg, Pennsylvania, 491, 506–508, *p512*

Ghana, 107, *m107*

Gilmore, Patrick S., 524

glacier, 55

globe, H8

gold rush, 443–445

Gordimer, Nadine, 223

Grant, Ulysses S., 459, 509–511, R23, *p459, 510*

graphs, reading

circle, 12–13, *c13*

line, 12–13, *c12*

Great Awakening, 218. *See also* Second Great Awakening

Great Britain. *See also* England

American Revolution and, 295, 303, 305, 315, 319

Civil War and, 494

colonists and, 268–273, 280, 282, 298

French and Indian War and, 249–250

Industrial Revolution and, 409

Oregon Country and, 439

War of 1812 and, 382–384

Great Compromise, 347

Great Plains, 28, 441, *m26–27, p27*

Great Plains cultural region, 83, *m84*

Great Salt Lake, 441

Great Seal of the United States, 6–7, *p7*

Great Serpent Mound, 60–61, *p60*

Green Mountain Boys, 303

Greene, Nathanael, 318

Greenland, 111

Grenville, George, 268–269, *p268*

grid, 140

Guatemala, *mR4, R8*

Gutenberg, Johann, 112

haciendas, 234, 238, *p239*

Haiti, *mR4, R8*

Hale, Nathan, 304

Hall, Prince, 306, 310, *p310*

Hamilton, Alexander, 333, 345, 353, 363–364, 368, *p333, 353, 364, 369*

Hancock, John, 287, 297, 300, 353, *p297*

Harding, Warren G., R25

Harpers Ferry, Virginia, 480

Harris, Mike, 40–41, *p40*

Harrison, Benjamin, R24

Harrison, William H., R23

Harvard University, 217, *p217*

Hawaii, *mR6–7, R19*

Hayes, Rutherford, R23

Hays, Mary Ludwig, 307, *p307*

headline, 209

hemisphere, H13–H14

Hendrick, 249

Henry, Patrick, 270, 274–275, 282, 353, *p274*

Henry, Prince of Portugal, 49, 113, *p49, 113*

Henry VIII, King of England, 169

Hessians, 304

Hiawatha, 49, 76–77, *p49, 76*

Hispanics, 8, *c8*

Hispaniola, 150

Hooker, Thomas, 178, *c181*

Hoover, Herbert, R25

Hopi, 63, 88–89, *p90, 91*

House of Burgesses, 162, 270, 274

House of Representatives, U.S., 347. *See also* Congress

Houston, Sam, 432–433, *p432*

Houston, Texas, 28

Hudson, Henry, 165–166, *p165*

Hudson River, 165

human-environment interaction (as geographical theme), H6–H7, 62

Hutchinson, Anne, 129, 178, 184–185, *p129, 185*

Ice Age, 55, 57

Idaho, R19

ideals, 7, 11, 17

Illinois, 376, R19

immigrants
African, 10
Asian, 10, *p10*
European, 10, *p10*
Latin American, 10

impeachment, 519

import, 20, *c20*

inauguration, 363

Inca, 69, 70, 145, *m68*

indentured servant, 161

India, 114

Indian Removal Act, 405

Indian Territory, 405

Indiana, 376, R18

Indians. *See* Native Americans

indigo, 205, 213, 215

Industrial Revolution, 401, 409

inflation, 340

information, gathering and reporting, 356–357

inset map, H18

interdependence, 30

intermediate directions, H17

Internet, H7, 86–87

interstate highway, 512

interview, H8

Intolerable Acts, 280

Inuit, 64

inventions. 21, 23, 31, 410 *See also* technology

Iowa, R18

Iroquois, 77–80, 249–250

Iroquois League, 77, 80, 249

Iroquois Trail, 77

irrigation, 28, *p28*

Isabella, Queen of Spain, 135

Islam, 107

Iwo Jima, 92

Jackson, Andrew, 384, 396, 403–405, 407, 433, 431, R23, *p396, 404, 407*

Jackson, Thomas "Stonewall," 495

James I, King of England, 159, 161

Jamestown, Virginia, 131, 159–161, 163, *m159, p161*

Jay, John, 353

Jefferson, Thomas, 6, 263, 298–299, 301, 351, 353, 363–364, 368–376, 381, 402, R22, *p263, 299, 301, 364, 369*

Jews, 218, *c8*

Jim Crow laws, 461, 520

Jingsheng, Wei, 223

Joan of Arc, 311, *p311*

Johnson, Andrew, 461, 517, 519, R23

Johnson, Lyndon B., R24

Jolliet, Louis, 241, *p241*

Jones, John Paul, 316, *p316*

judicial branch, 339, 346, 348, *c349*

Kachina, 90, *p90*

Kansas, 479, R18

Kansas-Nebraska Act, 479, *m479*

Kansas Territory, 476, 479

Kennedy, John F., 16, R24, *p16*

Kentucky, 376, R18

Key, Francis Scott, 361, 383, 388, *p388*

key, map, H16

Kimble, Frances Anne, 468–469, *p468*

King Philip's War, 247

Knox, Henry, 303–304, *p303*

Kosciusko, Thaddeus, 305

Ku Klux Klan, 461, 518

Kublai Khan, 103

Kwakiutl, 94–97, *p97*

Lafayette, Marquis de, 315, 341, *p315*

Lakota, 83, 120–121

Lamar, Mirabeau, 432

Lame Deer, Montana, 85

landforms, 28

landmines, 504–505

L'anse aux Meadows, 111, *p111*

large-scale map, 244–245, *m245*

La Salle, Robert, 196, 242, 248, *p196, 242*

Las Casas, Bartolomé de, 149–151, *p128, 151*

Latinos, 8

latitude, H15, H19, 140–141, *m140, 141*

league, 77

Lee, Richard Henry, 298

Index

Index

Index

Credits

TEXT:

Dorling Kindersley (DK) is an international publishing company specializing in the creation of high quality reference content for books, CD-ROMs, online and video. The hallmark of DK content is its unique combination of educational value and strong visual style. This combination allows DK to deliver appealing, accessible and engaging educational content that delights children, parents and teachers around the world. Scott Foresman is delighted to have been able to use selected extracts of DK content within this Social Studies program.

70–71 from Eyewitness: Aztec, Inca & Maya by Elizabeth Baquedano. Copyright ©2000 by Dorling Kindersley Limited.

139 from Eyewitness: Explorer by Rupert Matthews. Copyright ©2000 by Dorling Kindersley Limited.

238–239 from Eyewitness: Wild West by Stuart Murray. Copyright ©2001 by Dorling Kindersley Limited.

312–313 from The Visual Dictionary of Military Uniforms. Copyright ©1992 by Dorling Kindersley Limited.

377 from Eyewitness: Explorer by Rupert Mattews. Copyright ©2000 by Dorling Kindersley Limited.

514–515 from The Visual Dictionary of the Civil War by John Stanchak. Copyright ©2000 by Dorling Kindersley Limited.

Excerpts from *Juan Seguín –A Hero of Texas by Rita Kerr.* Copyright © 1985 by Rita Kerr. Used by permission of Eakin Press. 432

Excerpt from *The Log of Christopher Columbus,* translated by Robert H. Fuson. Copyright © 1987 by Robert H. Fuson. Reprinted by permission. 135

Excerpt from *Friends of the Everglades—Marjory Stoneman Douglas* by Tricia Andryszewski. Reprinted by permission of The Millbrook Press. 37

Excerpts from ballad in *The English Literature of America 1500-1800* edited by Myra Jehlen and Michael Warner. Copyright © 1997 by Routledge. Reprinted by permission. 188–189

"I, Too" from *The Collected Poems of Langston Hughes* by Langston Hughes, copyright © 1994 by the Estate of Langston Hughes. Used by permission of Alfred A. Knopf, a division of Random House, Inc. 618

Excerpt from "I Have a Dream" speech by Martin Luther King, Jr. Reprinted by permission. 646

Song "Let There Be Peace on Earth" words and music by Sy Miller and Jill Jackson. Used by permission of Jan-Lee Music.

Excerpt from *When China Rules the Seas, The Treasure Fleet of The Dragon Throne 1405-1433* by Louise Levathes. Copyright © 1994 by Louise E. Levathes. Reprinted by permission. 105

Excerpts from *Native American Animal Stories* told by Joseph Bruchac. Copyright © 1992 by Joseph Bruchac. Used by permission of Fulcrum Publishing. 120–121

"Did people work hard in colonial days?" from *If You Lived in Colonial Times . . .* by Ann McGovern. Copyright © 1964 by Ann McGovern. Reprinted by permission of the author. 254–255

Excerpt from Island. *Poetry and History of Chinese Immigrants on Angel Island* by Him M. Lai, Genny Lim and Judy Yung. Reprinted by permission. 569

Fair Use

From *The March on Washington Address* by Martin Luther King, Jr. Reprinted by arrangement with the Estate of Martin Luther King, Jr. c/o Writers House as agent for the proprietor. Copyright Martin Luther King 1963, copyright renewed 1991 Coretta Scott King.

From "George Percy's Relation." Copyright © 1997, 2000 by The Association for the Preservation of Virginia Antiquities. Found on http://www.apva.org/findingpercy.html.

From *Smithsonian Visual Timeline of Inventions* by Richard Platt. New York, New York: Dorling Kindersley, 1994.

From *The Annals of America, Vol. 1, Encyclopedia Britannica,* pages 97, 98, 115, and 329.

From *In Defense of the Indians,* translated and edited by Stafford Poole, C.M. Dekalb Illinois: Northern Illinois University Press.

From *History of the Indies,* translated and edited by Andree Collard. New York, New York: Harper & Row, 1971.

From *Witnessing America,* compiled and edited by Noel Rae. New York, New York: First published in 1996 by Penguin Reference, an imprint of Penguin Books, USA.

From *Edison His Life and Inventions,* by Frank Lewis Dyer, et al. New York, New York: Harper Brothers, 1929.

From *The English Literatures of America,* by Frank Lewis Dyer and Thomas Commerford Martin. New York, New York: Routledge, 1997

From George Washington Carver. Tuskegee Institute National Historical Site, http://www.nps.vov/bowa/tuskin.html.

From *Madam C.J. Walker* by A'Lelia Perry Bundles. Pittsburgh, Pennsylvania: Chelsea House Publishers, a division of Main Line Book Co., 1991.

From *A History of English Speaking Peoples,* Volume 2, The New World. New York, New York: Dodd, Mead & Company, Inc.

From *In Their Own Words THE COLONIZERS,* collected and edited by T.J. Stiles, pages 68 & 91. New York, New York, The Berkley Publishing Group, a member of Penguin Putnam, Inc.

From *Settlements to Society,* 1607-1763, edited by Jack P. Greene. New York, New York: W.W. Norton & Company, Inc.

From *Modern History Sourcebook: William Bradford: from History of Plymouth Plantation, c1650.* http://www.fordham.edu/halsall/mod/1650bradford.html.

From *The Alleged Gov. Bradford First Thanksgiving Proclamation, Who Attended the 1621 "First Thanksgiving,"* http://www.plimoth.org/library/Thanksgiving/thnksref.html.

From *Of Plymouth PLANTATION 1620-1647,* pages 85, 87 and 88, by William Bradford. New York, New York: Random House, Inc. 1981.

From *William Penn* by Rebecca Stefoff. Pittsburgh, Pennsylvania: Chelsea House Publishers, a division of Main Line Book Co., 1998.

From *Women's Rights on Trial* by Elizabeth Frost-Knappman and Kathryn Cullen-DuPont. Detroit, MI: Gale Research, 1997.

From *Time-Life Books 1930-1940,* Volume IV by the editors of Time-Life Books. Alexandria, VA: Time Life, Inc., 1969.

From *Time-Life Books 1940-1950,* Volume V by the editors of Time-Life Books, Alexandria, VA: Time Life, Inc., 1969.

From *The Report from the Dachau Liberation,* 1st Lt. William Cowling. Found on http://remember.org/witness/cowling.html.

From *Stride Toward Freedom, The Montgomery Story* by Martin Luther King, Jr. New York, New York: Harper&Row Publishers.

From *The Autobiography of Malcolm X* with the assistance of Alex Haley, introduction by M.S. Handler, epilogue by Alex Haley. New York, New York: Grove Press, Inc.

From *American Women of Achievement: Sandra Day O'Connor* by Peter Huber. New York, New York: Chelsea House Publishers, 1990.

From *Dolores Huerta Biography.* Found on http://www.ufw.org/ufw/dh.htm.

From *CNN Cold War, Interviews: George Bush.* Found on http://cnn.net/SPECIALS/cold.war/episodes/23/interviews/bush.

From *The Autobiography of Martin Luther King, Jr.,* edited by Clayborne Carson. New York, New York: Warner Books, 1998.

From *Life in a Japan American Internment Camp* by Diane Yancey. San Diego, CA: Lucent Books, 1998.

From *The Quotable Woman: Volume One* compiled and edited by Elaine Partnow. Los Angeles, CA: Pinnacle Books, Inc., 1980.

From *"Back to Hell"* by Samuel Cranston Benson. Chicago, IL: A.C. McClurg & Company, 1918.

From *Out of the Sweatshop: The Struggle for Industrial Democracy.* New York, New York: Quadrangle/New Times Book Company, 1977.

From *The Globe and Mail,* Friday, March 7, 1997. Found on http://www.freethe children.org/info/mediacanada08.htm.

From *Florence Kelley Speaks Out on Child Labor and Woman Suffrage,* Philadelphia, PA, July 22, 1905 found on http://www.pbs.org/greatspeeches/timeline/f_kelley_s.html.

From *The West: An Illustrated History* by Geoffrey C. Ward. The West Book Project, 1996.

From *Bury My Heart at Wounded Knee: An Indian History of the American West* by Dee Brown. New York, New York: Holt, Rinehart & Winston, 1971

From *The Importance of Alexander Graham Bell* by Robyn M. Weaver. San Diego, CA: Lucent Books, 2000.

From *The Promised Land* by Mary Antin, 1881-1949. New York, New York: Arno Press, A New York Times Co., 1980.

From *Northland Stories* by Jack London. New York, New York: Penguin Books, 1997.

From *The Spirit of Seventy-Six: The Story of the American Revolution* as told by the Participants edited by Henry Steele Commager and Richard B. Norris. New York, New York: Da Capo Press, 1995.

From *PATRIOTS The Men Who Started the American Revolution* by A.J. Langguth. New York, New York: Simon & Schuster, 1989.

From *Voyages of Marquette in The Jesuit Relations,* 59 by Jacques Marquette. University Microfilms, Inc., 1966.

From *The Life and Times of Fray Junípero Serra, O.F.M. or The Man Who Never Turned Back (1713-1784),* a biography by Maynard J. Geiger, O.F.M., Ph.D. VOLUME 1. Washington, DC: Academy of American Franciscan History, 1959.

Quote by Mohandas Gandhi, January 4, 1932 from *Messages to the United States* found on http://www.mkgandhi.org/letters/index.htm.

Quote by Nelson Mandela, March 27, 1993 from *Keynote Address by Nelson Mandela, President of the African National Congress,* to the conference of the broad patriotic front found on http://www.anc.org.za/ancdocs/history/mandela/1993/sp930327.html.

Quote by Joan of Arc, 1429, found on http://dc/smu.edu/ijasdelteil.html.

Quote by Venture Smith from Venture Smith's Narrative found on http://www.pbs.org/wgbh/aia/part2/2h5t.html.

From *The Courage to Stand Alone, Letters from Prison and Other Writings* by Wei Jingsheng. New York, New York: Viking Penguin, a division of Penguin Books USA Inc., 1997

From *A Brief Narrative of the Cage and Trial of John Peter Zenger* by James Alexander. Cambridge, Massachusetts: Harvard University Press, 1972.

From *Equiano's Travels, The Interesting Narrative of The Life of Olaudah Equiano or Gustavus Vassa the African* abridged and edited by Paul Edwards. New York, New York: Frederick A. Prager, Inc., 1966.

From *The Encyclopedia of Native America* by Trudy Griffin-Pierce.

Quote by Nadine Gordimer from *"Censorship and its Aftermath,"* address, 1990, found on http://informatics.buffalo.edu/faculty/ellison/quotes/ifquotesg.html

"Thomas Jefferson Survives": Susan Boylston Adams Clark to Abigail Louisa Smith Adams Johnson, July 9, 1826, A.B. Johnson Papers, MHS.

From *Cherokee Legends and the Trail of Tears* adapted by Thomas Bryan Underwood. Cherokee, NC: Cherokee Publications.

From *The Shaping of America* by Richard O. Curry, John G. Sproat, Kenyon C. Cramer. New York, New York: Holt, Rinehart and Winston.

From *Frederick Douglass, Selected Speeches and Writings* edited by Philip S. Foner, abridged and adapted by Yuval Taylor. Chicago, IL: Laurence Hill Books, 1999.

From *Narrative of the Life of Frederick Douglass, An American Slave,* written by Himself edited with an introduction by David W. Blight. Boston, MA: Bedford Books of St. Martin's Press, 1993.

From TEXAS *From the Frontier to Spindletop* by James L. Haley. New York, NY: St. Martin's Press, 1985.

From *STEPHEN F. AUSTIN, Empresario of Texas* by Gregg Cantrell. New Haven, CT: Yale University Press.

From *STEPHEN F. AUSTIN, Founder of Texas, 1793-1836* by Eugene C. Barker. Dallas, TX: Cokesbury Press, 1925.

From *The Gold Rush* by Liza Ketchum. The West Project, Inc., 1996.

From *Harriet Tubman, Conductor on the Underground Railroad* by Ann Petry. New York, NY: HarperCollins Publisher, Inc, 1996.

From *The Oxford History of the American People, Volume Two, 1789 Through Reconstruction* by Samuel Eliot Morison. New York, NY: Meridian, an imprint of Dutton Signet, a division of Penguin Books USA Inc., 1994.

From *The Civil War, A Narrative* by Shelby Foote. New York, NY: Random House, 1994.

Quote by Jody Williams from *Jody Williams: The woman who waged war on land minds* found on http://www.cnn.com/SPECIALS/1997/nobel.prize/stories/williams.profile/.

From *Uncle Tom's Cabin or Life Among the Lowly* by Harriet Beecher Stowe. New York, NY: Signet Classic , an imprint of New American Library, a division of Penguin Putnam, Inc., 1998.

From *Nobel Lecture* by Jody Williams found on www.icbl.org/resources/jodynobel.html.

From *The Negro People in the United States* edited by Herbert Aptheker. New York, NY: Citadel Press, Inc., 1969.

From *Cannibals All!, or Slaves Without Masters* by George Fitzhugh found on http://docsouth.unc.edu/fitzhughcan/fitcan.html.

From *The Underground Railroad* by William Still. Chicago, IL: Johnson Publishing Company, Inc., 1970.

MAPS:

MapQuest.com, Inc.

ILLUSTRATIONS:

114 Mike Reagan, 120 Marcela Cabrera, 136 Albert Lorenz, 159 John Sandford, 163, 188, 189, 310, 311 Troy Howell, 184, 185 Gregory M. Dearth, 212 Robert LoGrippo, 230 Guy Porfirio, 274, 275 Stephen Snider, 278 Barbara Emmons, 365 John Sandford, 367, 548 Troy Howell, 388 Domenick D'Andrea, 412 Kate Thomssen, 417 Robert Van Nutt, 450 Edward Martinez, 507 Barbara Emmons, 577 David Cunningham, 588, 589 Shelly Hehenberger, 606 Tom Herzberg

PHOTOGRAPHS:

Every effort has been made to secure permission and provide appropriate credit for photographic material. The publisher deeply regrets any omission and pledges to correct errors called to their attention in subsequent editions.

Unless otherwise acknowledged, all photographs are the property of Scott Foresman, a division of Pearson Education.

Photo locators are denoted as follows: Top (T), Center (C), Bottom (B), Left (L), RIght (R), Background (Bkgd).

Cover: ©Mitchell Funk/Getty Images, Steve Allen
Endsheets: (R) ©Mitchell Funk/Getty Images, (L) Steve Allen
Front Matter:
E2-E3 Colonial Williamsburg Foundation E3 ©Richard T. Nowitz/Corbis, (BR) Getty Images E4 (BL) Getty Images, Hemera Technologies, (TR) ©Gary Hush/Getty Images E5 (TC) ©Marvin E. Newman/Getty Images, (L) ©Mark E. Gibson Stock Photography, (TL) ©Connie Coleman/Getty Images, (C) Getty Images, (BR) ©David Bishop/FoodPix E6 (BL, TR) Getty Images, (C) SuperStock, (B) ©John Springer Collection/Corbis E7 (TL) ©Davies & Starr/Getty Images, (CR) ©Schenectady Museum, Hall of Electrical History Foundation/Corbis, (C, TC) Corbis, (B) ©Michael Freeman/Corbis E8 (TR) ©Pete Saloutos/Panoramic Images, (CL) ©Gerd Ludwig/NGS Image Collection, ©Peter Essick/Aurora & Quanta Productions, Getty Images E9 (CL) ©Brian Sytnyk/Masterfile Corporation, (C) ©Peter Griffith/Masterfile Corporation E9 (BC) Getty Images, (BR) Hemera Technologies E10 Getty Images, (TR) ©Grant Faint/Getty Images E11 (C) ©Chris Simpson/Getty Images, (Bkgd) Getty Images, (BR) Corbis E12 (BL) Thinkstock, (BC) ©Michael Newman/PhotoEdit, (Bkgd) ©Donovan Reese/Getty Images E13 ©Jeff Greenberg/Photo Researchers, Inc. E14 (BL) ©Joseph Sohm, Visions of America/Corbis, (BL) ©Squared Studios/Getty Images, (C) ©Kelly Harriger/Corbis, (C) Corbis E15 (L) ©Bob Krist/Corbis, (C) Corbis, (BC) ©Lester Lefkowitz/Corbis E16 ©F. Damm/Zefa/Masterfile Corporation, ©Richard Sisk/NGSImages.com/Panoramic Images, ©Aaron Haupt/Photo Researchers, Inc., (Bkgd) Hemera Technologies iii Superstock iv David David Gallery, Philadelphia/Superstock v ©Bettmann/Corbis vi The Granger Collection vii Photo from the collection of the Lexington, Massachusetts Historical Society viii The Granger Collection ix The Granger Collection x The Granger Collection xi From the Original painting by Mort Künstler, "First View of the Lady" ©1986 Mort Künstler, Inc. xii Identikal/Artville H4-H5 Colonial Williamsburg Foundation H6 (BR), (BC) ©Dave Bartruff/Corbis, (Bkgd) Joel Sartore/Grant Heilman Photography H7 (BR) ©Phil Schermeister/Corbis, (L) Joel Sartore/Grant Heilman Photography H8 Earth Imaging/Getty Images H15 Michael Newman/PhotoEdit H19 PhotoDisc
Overview:
1, 2, 3 SuperStock 5 PhotoDisc 6 Historical Society of Pennsylvania 8 (TL) ©Joseph Sohm; ChromoSohm Inc/Corbis 9 PhotoDisc 10 (R) Brown Brothers, (L) Courtesy National Archives of the United States (from The National Archives of the United States by Herman J. Viola, ©1984 Harry N. Abrams, Inc. New York) 13 Ramey/PhotoEdit 15 (B) ©Dennis Degnan/Corbis 16 (B) Bob Daemmrich Photography, (T) ©Bettmann/Corbis 19 New York Public Library Picture Collection 21 (BL) The Granger Collection,

Credits